SEEKING THE
FABLED
CITY

ALSO BY ALLAN LEVINE

NON-FICTION

The Exchange: 100 Years of Trading Grain in Winnipeg

*Your Worship: The Lives of Eight of Canada's Most Unforgettable Mayors
    (editor)*

Scrum Wars: The Prime Ministers and the Media

*Fugitives of the Forest: The Heroic Story of Jewish Resistance and Survival
    During the Second World War*

Scattered Among the Peoples: The Jewish Diaspora in Ten Portraits

The Devil in Babylon: Fear of Progress and the Birth of Modern Life

Coming of Age: A History of the Jewish People of Manitoba

King: William Lyon Mackenzie King: A Life Guided by the Hand of Destiny

Miracle at the Forks: The Museum That Dares Make a Difference (co-author)

Toronto: Biography of a City

FICTION

The Blood Libel

Sins of the Suffragette

The Bolshevik's Revenge

Evil of the Age

The Bootlegger's Confession

SEEKING
THE
FABLED
CITY

THE CANADIAN JEWISH EXPERIENCE

ALLAN LEVINE

McClelland & Stewart

Library and Archives Canada Cataloguing in Publication data is available upon request

ISBN: 978-0-7710-4805-0
ebook ISBN: 978-0-7710-4806-7

Library of Congress Control Number is available upon request

Jacket image: William James Topley / Library and Archives Canada / PA-010400
Jacket design by Leah Springate

Typeset in Jenson by M&S, Toronto
Printed and bound in the USA

McClelland & Stewart,
a division of Penguin Random House Canada Limited,
a Penguin Random House Company
www.penguinrandomhouse.ca

1   2   3   4   5   22   21   20   19   18

Penguin
Random House
McCLELLAND & STEWART

To my darling granddaughter Ana,
so that you will always remember your heritage and history
—With much love, Zaida.

A people's memory is history; and as a man without a memory, so a people without a history cannot grow wiser, better.

ISAAC LEIB PERETZ, 1890

Jews are reflective people. We do have a deep sense of both memory and history. Part of it is we want to make sure because we are a small group we are not forgotten. It is important to us that we have a record. There is a deep desire to memorialize oneself and be remembered. That's who we are.

RABBI BARUCH FRYDMAN-KOHL, 2016

CONTENTS

Acknowledgements xi

Introduction: The Quintessence of a Minority 1

PART ONE: IN A CHRISTIAN LAND

Chapter One: They Came First 15

Chapter Two: La Famille Hart 23

Chapter Three: A British Subject (and Israelite) I Was Born 39

Chapter Four: Synagogue Politics 48

Chapter Five: From Coast to Coast 57

Chapter Six: In Search of the Golden Land 67

PART TWO: JEWISH CANADIANS

Chapter Seven: It's a Living 83

Chapter Eight: Out of Ghetto Streets 96

Chapter Nine: Intellectuals and Radicals 109

Chapter Ten: Class Struggle 117

Chapter Eleven: For King and Country 124

Chapter Twelve: Dreaming of Zion 130

Chapter Thirteen: Gentiles Only 139

Chapter Fourteen: The Jewish Problem 157

Chapter Fifteen: We Demand Work 180

PART THREE: CANADIAN JEWS

    Chapter Sixteen: A Duty to the Jewish People the World Over   197

    Chapter Seventeen: Prejudice Exists   214

    Chapter Eighteen: Devoted Zionists and Loyal Canadians   229

    Chapter Nineteen: An Admirable Element of the Community   242

    Chapter Twenty: Living Together   253

PART FOUR: THE MAKING OF TOLERANT CANADA

    Chapter Twenty-One: A Lot of Jews   269

    Chapter Twenty-Two: Israel is Everybody's Business   280

    Chapter Twenty-Three: Marching for Refuseniks   291

    Chapter Twenty-Four: Nationalistic Impulses   302

    Chapter Twenty-Five: Confronting the Deniers and Israel-Haters   312

    Chapter Twenty-Six: The Hadassah Ladies Rise Up   323

    Chapter Twenty-Seven: Checks and Balances   338

Conclusion: The Never-Dying Canadians   352

Appendix   365

Notes   367

Selected Bibliography   441

List of Interviews   457

Permissions   458

Image Credits   459

Index   461

Acknowledgements

The idea for this book originated with Scott Sellers, Vice President, Associate Publisher, and Director of Marketing Strategy for Penguin Random House Canada and my editor, Doug Pepper, the publisher of Signal at Penguin Random House Canada. I thank both of them for involving me in this project, and Doug, especially, for his advice in helping me shape and improve the manuscript. I am beholden as well to their wonderful team of talented individuals: Elizabeth Burns; Leah Springate, for the cover design; Shannon Parr; Joe Lee; Gemma Wain; and Kimberlee Hesas, McClelland & Stewart's tireless and excellent managing editor.

I owe my usual debt of gratitude to my literary agent and friend, Hilary McMahon, for always "watching my back." Thanks also to the many individuals who have provided advice, research information and agreed to be interviewed (a complete list can be found in the Bibliography).

In particular, I would like to acknowledge the assistance of the following: Ellin Bessner, a professor of journalism at Toronto's Centennial College; writer Bill Gladstone, an expert on Toronto Jewish history; Faye Blum, Assistant Archivist, Ontario Jewish Archives; Ester Reiter, professor emerita at York University; Saundra Lipton at the University of Calgary; Michael Schwartz, Coordinator of Programs and Development at the Jewish Museum and Archives of British Columbia; Professors Irving Abella and Harold Troper; Yoni Goldstein, the editor of the *Canadian Jewish News* as well as the newspaper's reporter Ron Csillag and its Montreal correspondent, Janice Arnold; Elaine Goldstine, the CEO of the Jewish Federation of Winnipeg and Shelley Faintuch, the Jewish Federation of Winnipeg's former

Community Relations Director (and a long-time friend); Naomi Rosenfield, executive director of the Atlantic Jewish Council; Dr. Michael Rasminsky; Israeli dance teacher Teme Kernerman; Ryla Braemer and Yacov Fruchter, who I have known for many years, for agreeing to participate in this project; Josh Goldberg, an enthusiastic and knowledgeable guide for the Jewish Museum of Montreal, for a fascinating tour around St. Lawrence Boulevard; Franklin Bialystock of the University of Toronto for his review comments on current Jewish organizational issues; Rabbi Michal Shekel, Executive Director, Toronto Board of Rabbis; and finally, Ira Robinson, Chair in Canadian Jewish Studies and Director of the Institute for Canadian Jewish Studies at Concordia University Montreal for reviewing an earlier draft of the manuscript. Thanks as well to Dr. Michael Rasminsky, Richard Lowy, Teme Kernerman, Trudy Harowitz, Kim Garzon, Brooke Cromar, Ryla Braemer and Justice Rosalie Abella who kindly provided photographs.

I also appreciate the following publishers permitting me to use material from several of my books: McClelland & Stewart for *Scattered Among the Peoples: The Jewish Diaspora in Ten Portraits* and *The Devil in Babylon: Fear of Progress and the Birth of Modern Life*; Douglas & McIntyre for *King: William Lyon Mackenzie King: A Life Guided by the Hand of Destiny* and *Toronto: Biography of a City*; and the Jewish Heritage Centre of Western Canada for *Coming of Age: A History of the Jewish People of Manitoba*.

I am grateful, of course, to Angie, who over the course of thirty-six years has learned to live with the ups and downs of book writing (generally with a smile); and our ever-expanding family: Alexander and Shannon, and Mia and Geoff. Most importantly of all, I dedicate this book to our precious granddaughter, Ana (Alexander and Shannon's daughter), who gives special meaning to our lives.

It goes without saying that all omissions, misinterpretations, and errors of fact and judgment are solely my own.

Allan Levine
Winnipeg, February 2018

The Quintessence of a Minority

One evening, early in February 1970, the *"machers"* or community "big shots"—predominately men in those days, accompanied by their wives—were out in full force at a black-tie gala at Montreal's Hotel Bonaventure. This was definitely an event for the city's "uptown" rather than "downtown" Jews—which would have likely described many of the parents and grandparents of those in attendance. Most partygoers were the sons and daughters of Russian and Eastern European immigrants who had resided in and around the mythical St. Lawrence Boulevard, or "The Main," as it has been fondly feted by A.M. Klein, Mordecai Richler, and many other members of Montreal's historic Jewish literati. The gala's guest of honour was Liberal prime minister Pierre Trudeau, then two years into his mandate. In between the cocktails, hors d'oeuvres, and incessant schmoozing, he graciously accepted the Anti-Defamation League of B'nai Brith's Canadian Family of Man Award. Intellectual and slightly aloof, yet charming and charismatic, he was Ottawa's most talked-about political celebrity—and the guests eagerly awaited their turn to greet him.

Trudeau anointed multiculturalism as a major policy promoted by his government, which, in theory at least, significantly altered Canadian values to the betterment of Jews and other ethnic groups. He also appointed Jews to his cabinet, the judiciary, and the civil service in record numbers. But, not all that surprisingly, the Family of Man Award loomed larger for the community than for Trudeau and his officials. As confidential discussions about the award ceremony show, it was perceived by officials at the Prime Minister's Office (PMO) as a politically opportune time for the prime minister to address the

Jewish community in a formal setting; merely one more speaking engagement and event in a very long list that was discussed and coordinated by the PMO.

Nonetheless, on this night Trudeau was lauded for his "contribution and record of achievement in expanding the scope of human freedom," among other notable accomplishments. Accepting the award, Trudeau remarked that "the Canadian brotherhood within which the Jews form a community . . . is truly remarkable for its origins and for the quality of its contribution to the Canadian way of life . . . So outstanding is the Jewish contribution that it is difficult to imagine our society without it." Jews, he added, "are destined to remain a minority amongst the peoples of the world. They are in fact the quintessence of a minority."

It was pretty heady stuff. Doubtless a majority of the guests—high achievers in business, academia, government, medicine, and law—returned to their fashionable homes in Westmount and Hampstead feeling that Jews had finally been given the respect they deserved by a sitting prime minister. They knew they had made it, but they took some satisfaction in knowing that Trudeau did, too.

Trudeau was indeed correct: Jews are and always have been the "quintessence of a minority," in a saga of survival that dates back more than two thousand years. Given the intense prejudice and discrimination Jews have endured over several millennia, their continued existence is rather amazing. All things considered, Jews should have vanished long ago, to be studied only as anthropological museum exhibits. So how have they done it? Perseverance—though that word does not quite do justice to it—has been one reason for their survival. But so has their uncanny ability to tolerate abuse, and to adapt, assimilate, and positively contribute to the non-Jewish societies they have found themselves in. The real miracle is that Jews have achieved this without completely sacrificing their religion, culture, and way of life.

Canada is one of those countries in which Jews have a past, present, and future, despite serious and legitimate concerns about intermarriage and low birth rates. (Jews are famous for being pessimistic, a consequence of centuries of persecution and dispersion, as the classic Jewish telegram sums up: "Begin worrying. Details to follow." As does the Jewish proverb, "A pessimist, confronted with two bad choices, chooses both.") In 2011, the Jewish population of Canada was approximately 392,000, which was the fourth largest in the world, behind Israel, the United States, and France. Of that Canadian total, 189,000 (now more than 200,000)—or about 48 per cent—lived in the Greater Toronto Area (GTA), and another 90,000—or 23 per cent—were located in Greater Montreal. Thus, as of 2011 (and the numbers have slightly increased in the past seven years), an estimated 71 per cent of all Canadian Jews made their homes in two major urban centres. Toronto, in particular, is unique in Canada, with a large number of synagogues and parochial schools in operation, which address the spiritual and educational needs of Jews of every conceivable religious ideology on the spectrum—from ultra-Orthodox and Conservative, to Reform and Humanistic Judaism. No other city in Canada (though Montreal is a close second) offers such a variety of religious and secular programming. There are lectures, cultural festivals—the city's Ashkenaz Festival, a biennial celebration of klezmer and Yiddish music and Eastern European Jewish culture attracts more than 60,000 people—fundraising events, more than a dozen local and Israeli institutions such as the UJA Federation of Greater Toronto and the Jewish National Fund, musical concerts, holiday and Shabbat (Sabbath) gatherings, Israeli dancing classes, and sports competitions. The list is seemingly endless. It is like this, to different degrees, in Montreal, Ottawa, Winnipeg, Calgary, Edmonton, and Vancouver. In fact, there are so many activities that Jewish organizations compete against each other for participants, and for the dollars available to support these often-expensive events. From pricy private (or parochial) school tuition to synagogue dues, kosher food, summer camps, life cycle events, and frequent requests for institutional contributions, the cost of being Jewish is fairly high, and is challenging for many middle-class families to sustain.

Whereas some urban Jewish communities in Canada have difficulties supporting one Jewish Community Centre (JCC), the GTA now has three—one downtown and two in the north part of the city in and around Bathurst Street, a thirty kilometre corridor that stretches from south of Eglinton Avenue all the way to Richmond Hill. In short, Jews are everywhere in this concentrated geographic area. As Rabbi Yael Splansky of the Holy Blossom Temple, the largest Reform congregation in Canada, remarks, "Living in Toronto, my children don't know that Jews are a minority."

There is in the vicinity of Bathurst a large contingent of "Orthodox Jewish suburbanites," as historian Etan Diamond calls them—religious Jews who want to live within walking distance of synagogues and kosher shops, just as impoverished immigrants did decades earlier. Except these Jews are more affluent: they own homes worth $1 million or more and participate in the secular and consumer culture that surrounds them on their own terms.

Jews in Canada represent only 1.2 per cent of the country's total population, but there is likely no field of endeavour, no profession or pursuit, in which a Jewish presence has not and does not continue to be evident. This exceptional achievement did not happen overnight.

More than a century ago, Jewish immigrants from Russia and Eastern Europe arrived in Canada in large numbers, seeking the "fabled city," to borrow that phrase from the revered Montreal Jewish writer A.M. Klein's 1942 poem "Autobiographical." They wanted a home and country in which they could not only survive and prosper, but one in which they could leave a positive legacy for their children, grandchildren, and the generations that followed.

They did indeed find the fabled city they were searching for in Canada, yet their acceptance and integration into the larger society was not always wanted or welcome, and the struggles they faced caused much inner turmoil and hardship. "There are only two characteristics which most Jews have in common," a Jewish lawyer explains in Gwethalyn Graham's award-winning 1944 novel *Earth and High Heaven*, one of the first works of fiction published in Canada to address antisemitism[*], "one of them is a determination to survive, if possible, and the other is a basic sense of insecurity."

Jews—or "Hebrews," as they were more commonly referred to in the late nineteenth and the first half of the twentieth centuries by English Canadians—might have been beneficial for trade and business, but they were

---

[*] Throughout this book, other than in direct quotations, the term "antisemitism" is used rather than the more common "anti-Semitism," because as scholars—such as the late Emil Fackenheim, a Holocaust survivor who taught for many years at the University of Toronto—have argued, "the spelling ought to be antisemitism without the hyphen, dispelling the notion that there is an entity 'Semitism' which 'anti-Semitism' opposes."

also a (supposed) "race" of people to be wary of. When a member of the majority thought about or met a Jew, they made little distinction about who this person was and what he or she believed in. Did this Jew attend synagogue regularly or at all? Did he or she keep kosher? Was being Jewish, however that was defined at any particular time and place, a significant component of this individual's identity as a human being? It's a safe bet that there was little appreciation back then of the great and enduring conundrum: "Who is a Jew?" Are Jews a religion, ethnic group, culture, or all three?

Today, when so much of being Jewish in Canada and elsewhere is wrapped up with being a supportive Zionist, can you be a "good Jew" and still be critical of Israel? Some Jews don't think so. What of the children of inter-marriages? Jewish law stipulates a matrilineal descent, that a person is only Jewish if their mother is also Jewish, a rule firmly adhered to by the Orthodox and Conservative branches of Judaism (derived from wanting to "conserve" Jewish traditions), yet not by Reform Jews, at least in the United States, who since 1983 have also accepted patrilineal descent. Finally, what if an individual—and several make appearances in this book—disavows being Jewish? Do they still count as a Jew in the larger historical perspective?

From the standpoint of the non-Jewish world, the old law tends to hold true: a Jew is a Jew is a Jew. In tabulating Jewish population figures for Canada, demographers have used what is known as the "Jewish Standard Definition." According to this criterion, a Jew was defined as "anyone who specified he or she was: Jewish by religion and ethnicity; Jewish by religion and having another ethnicity; or having no religious affiliation and Jewish by ethnicity."

The reality is complicated. For apart from strong religious differences, Jews more in the past than the present, have also been divided internally—often bitterly so—by ideology, politics, and class. There were Zionists who fought for a Jewish homeland in Palestine; socialists who battled for the rights of the workers; and liberals who advocated Jewish assimilation into western society. Each segment—and some, like the socialists and Zionists, were divided further still—had their own associations, mutual aid societies, schools, synagogues, and political clubs. So a Jewish identity is anything but as straightforward as non-Jews perceived it. As Kurt Lewin, a noted Jewish German-American psychologist put it in 1948, "There are, I think, few chores more bewildering than that of determining positively the character of the Jewish group."

Interestingly, Jews themselves don't usually have the same problem, and can innately tell who is Jewish and who is not—sometimes even which neighbourhoods they live in. "I can be with a person and within five minutes of social exchange I can almost tell you [in which area of the city] they live," asserts the Montreal-based *National Post* columnist Barbara Kay, "and within thirty seconds whether they live in Westmount."

With this diversity of opinion and the intellectual ferment that has characterized Canadian Jewish history, there also arose schisms, bickering, and personality clashes of colossal proportions. At any moment in the annals of Jewish Canada, you can always count on the fact that whenever a Jewish leader or organization, after long hours of closed-door deliberations, arrived at a solution to deal with a specific problem and then presented it to the larger community, it was (and continues to be) greeted with some approval, but generally with much criticism. "Why wasn't this, that, and the other done?" community members have demanded to know. This is usually accompanied with the cry of "I could've done it better." Whether it is about synagogue prayers, kosher rules, Zionist policy, Jewish school curricula, community governance, politics, or support for Israel, one aspect of Jewish life in Canada has been (and is) a definite certainty: there always has been plenty of arguing. Or, as the great Yiddish writer Sholem Aleichem observed, "Two Jews have three opinions. When one says this, the other says yes, but not like that." Elaine Goldstine, the current CEO of the Jewish Federation of Winnipeg, puts a more positive spin on this incessant kvetching. "The members wouldn't complain so much," she says, "if they didn't care."

True enough. But this has resulted in thousands of stormy meetings so everyone around the table—no matter how much money they make or what their contribution to the synagogue is—can be heard. A strong sense of justice and fairness, values deeply held by the members of Jewish communities in Canada and elsewhere, demand it. It is only when there is the perception that justice and fairness are absent—as it was for some with the establishment of the Centre for Israel and Jewish Affairs (CIJA), and the contentious decision to abolish the Canadian Jewish Congress (CJC) in 2011 as the chief advocate for Canadian Jews—that tempers are sharp, memories are long, and anger takes a long time to subside.

The one powerful bond that all Jews share, regardless of their religious or ideological convictions, is that they have been disdained and hated as the outsider, the unwanted. Antisemites rarely distinguish between the varieties of Jews: they detest them all equally. In modern times, the worst antisemitic viciousness has occurred in Europe, but such hatred has not been absent in Canada. The multicultural tolerance that Canadians currently are so proud of dates only from the late sixties and early seventies. Hence, for at least 210 (if not more) of the 270 or so years chronicled in this narrative—from about 1750 to 1960—Jews faced all forms and varieties of prejudice and discrimination. Moreover, during the period from the early 1880s to the early 1960s, antisemitism was ingrained in the fabric of Canadian society, imposed and practised openly, usually without hesitation, qualifications, or shame. Shopping at a Jewish-owned store or using the services of a Jewish tailor was tolerable for most Gentile Canadians. But it was not acceptable to have Jewish work colleagues, Jewish neighbours, or worst of all, Jewish members at private sports and social clubs. That was just the way it was.

"To my parents' generation," says Barbara Kay, who grew up in Montreal in the forties and fifties, "anti-Semitism was an eternal fact of life, virtually encoded in the DNA of non-Jews." The fact is that few Jews in Canada have not experienced some type of antisemitism, whether it was being denied a job in the past, or more recently being sworn at, bullied, or made the target of vandalism or violence. Sometimes it was merely being the victim of ignorant prejudice.

Bernie Farber, who worked for the CJC for close to three decades, rising up the ranks to be its chief executive officer from 2005 to 2011, was born in 1951 and raised in Ottawa. His father, Max, was a Holocaust survivor, and his mother Gertrude came to Canada as a child in the years before the Second World War. Farber attended a local Ottawa high school in a nice downtown neighbourhood. He was, however, one of only a handful of Jewish students in the school, and the only one in his grade ten class. Being called a "fucking

Jew" was the norm, he recalls. In one English class, the teacher, who Farber says "was not a bad guy," announced that the students would be studying Shakespeare's *Merchant of Venice*, a play with antisemitic themes and overtones. The teacher started assigning parts to each student, and when he got to Farber he said, "Bernie, since you're the Jew, you'll play Shylock." Farber remembers that he was devastated. That night he told his father about what had happened. His father, who before the war had acted in the Yiddish theatre, offered to assist him so that he would be the best Shylock ever. Farber agreed and diligently rehearsed. When it came time to act out the play, Farber was brilliant. "That was very good, Bernie," the teacher told him, "but next time put on the Yiddish accent like your father." More than fifty years later, Farber still shakes his head at the memory of that comment by a teacher who had no idea he was offending his only Jewish student.

Farber's story is only one of thousands of such examples; many more are related in the pages that follow. Whether Canadians want to admit it or not, at the heart of the Jewish history of Canada, or at least hovering over it, is a frequently unrelenting antisemitism that has impacted the lives of generations of Canadian Jews. Still, it does not define them.

The ultimate goal of Jews is to survive as a people. And survival, the most powerful human purpose of all, impelled Jews to ignore the antisemitism as much as was possible and to establish their own communities, brick by brick. Apart from finding shelter and work, the earliest immigrants were mainly motivated by economic necessities and religious precepts. So in nearly every community in Canada in which Jews settled, a similar pattern of development was more or less followed. The first requirement was almost always the establishment of a *chevra kadisha* or "holy society," which ensured that a Jewish cemetery was available and that the bodies of the deceased were prepared for burial according to Jewish custom. The community also required a synagogue to worship in, whether makeshift or an independent structure; a *shochet* or ritual slaughterer, who might also double as a butcher so kosher meat and chicken could be distributed; a rabbi, or someone knowledgeable enough to lead the prayer services; Jewish teachers and a school to educate the young, especially young men who had to prepare for their bar mitzvahs at the age of thirteen with the transition to adulthood; and self-help organizations to assist fellow Jews in need. In later years would come sports clubs, Young Men's Hebrew Associations, Yiddish theatre, community newspapers, and cultural activities of every conceivable type and variety.

Money was crucial, of course. Building a community infrastructure was not inexpensive, and it still isn't. There is—and has been for a long time—an army of dedicated professionals and volunteers who devote their careers to sustaining Jewish institutions. A sizable bureaucracy exists across Canada connected to the Jewish Federations of Canada-UIA (United Israel Appeal), whose main purpose is to raise sufficient annual funds to support local needs and contribute to Israel. There are expectations, even if unsaid, that it is the duty of every Jew to give something to community development and to assist the State of Israel. Income and ideological differences can dictate the size of a donation, or if one is made at all. Beyond the millions donated each year, however, is the reality that among members of various Jewish communities there is at the end of the day only a finite amount of funds to divvy up between the local and national organizations and Israel. Not every organization sees eye to eye with one another—an understatement, if there ever was one. And so discussions and arguing ensue.

There is and always has been a truism in the history of Jewish communities: money talks, and it always has in most Jewish organizations, too. It carries influence, and certainly has from the moment Jewish immigrants arrived in this country. Good or bad, that is a fact of life, and it could be no other way. Because if the wealthy and professional men—as for much of nearly three centuries of Canadian Jewish history, it was men—did not offer their money and time to building communities, none would have been built. It's as simple as that. Evidence of the critical importance of this largesse is indicated in Halifax, Saint John, Moncton, and the few other smaller-populated Jewish communities in the Maritimes, where the required funds to establish and support institutions are lacking, and fostering a Jewish communal structure and identity has been problematic.

In the larger cities, in contrast, raising sufficient money generally has not been a problem; it's the decision-making process that has caused all the fuss. There were (and are) many community advocates across the country, who devoted (and still do) thousands of hours of their time to community work. This mixture of genuine altruism with wealth, ego, and what might be called the *macher* gene—the overwhelming desire to exercise power and influence and to be recognized as someone truly important—has proven volatile. The men in charge did not want to be told what to do—and certainly not by their wives or any other women. Though there were exceptions, such as Ida Siegel in Toronto and Lillian Freiman in Ottawa in the first part of the twentieth century, women were generally relegated to the Jewish ladies' groups, such as Hadassah and Pioneer Women, and raised money for children, hospitals, the poor, and Palestine (Israel after 1948). Meanwhile, a select group of men made the most important decisions.

For the most part, the Jewish communities in Montreal, Toronto, Winnipeg, and elsewhere were governed by a "political tradition of aristo-cratic republicanism"—to use McGill University political scientist Harold Waller's apt term—in which "leadership was based on scholarship, wealth, or social class." In other words, the old boys' club prevailed.

Beyond the noisy boardrooms, there has long been a notion that Jews in the United States are more patriotic than Jews in Canada. As the late Toronto rabbi Gunther Plaut said in a 2002 interview, "One of the great differences between Jews in Canada and the U.S. was that when asked to describe their identity, Jews in the U.S. would say American. In Canada they would say Jew . . . It took a long time in Canada to say Canadian. It took Jews in the U.S. no time at all."

The late Gerald Tulchinsky, the dean of Canadian Jewish historians who passed away in December 2017, argued that "while American Jewry yearned for integration into the mainstream of the great republic, Canadians strove to express their Jewishness in a country that had no coherent self-definition—except perhaps the solitudes of duality, isolation, northernness, and borrowed glory." Though this theory sounds plausible, Plaut, Tulchinsky, and the others who subscribe to it may be overstating the case. As this book relates, even before Confederation the Jews in Canada were very much "Canadian" in mind and spirit, though that did not mean they surrendered their identity as Jews— far from it. At least two generations of Jews from the 1880s to the 1950s saw the world through a narrow Jewish lens, judging each issue with the proverbial question: "Is it good for the Jews?"

In 1919, when discussion was underway about the establishment of a national Canadian Jewish organization, there was a heated debate—naturally—about what to call this new body. Suggestions included the Canadian Jewish Committee, the Jewish Canadian Congress, and the Congress of Canadian Jews. Ultimately, delegates to the inaugural convention decided to go with the "Canadian Jewish Congress," because that moniker (like "Canadian Jewish Committee") captured the essence of what this organization was to symbolize: Jews in Canada who put "Canada" ahead of being Jewish. The CJC epitomized their desire to fit in—to be citizens who would do everything in their power to enhance the country they called home. "In Canada, the Jews are, and always will be, a small minority group of persons individually integrated into the social, economic and political life of the country while as a group they strive to retain their religious and cultural identity in a democracy which permits them to worship and to live their lives in accordance with their traditions and religious principles," wrote the CJC's board chairman, the Montreal whisky magnate Samuel Bronfman, in a 1966 magazine article (Bronfman had been president of the CJC from 1939 to 1962). "Our survival as Jews necessitates the maintenance of our cultural and religious identity as a group in an active and vital form."

This is the story of how that dynamic process of adaptation, integration, and controlled assimilation (especially by Orthodox Jews) has played out over close to three hundred years, warts and all: from the decades preceding the conquest of New France in 1759, when small numbers of Sephardi Jews of Spanish and Portuguese descent (or Sephardim) arrived in British North America; through the great wave of Russian and Eastern European Jewish immigration at the turn of the twentieth century; to the present time, in which Canada's Jewish community, no longer hindered by the antisemitism of the past, is free to flourish. And yet as Rabbi Baruch Frydman-Kohl, the senior rabbi at Toronto's Conservative Beth Tzedec congregation, one of the largest synagogues in North America, argues, "Yes, Jews are assimilated today, but they also remain outsiders. On the one hand, Jews are political, financial, intellectual leaders, and at the same time . . . Jews are singled out [and not always positively] more than other groups in society and are identified as such." Making sense of this alleged contradiction is what is in part examined in the following pages.

This is not, it must be stressed, an academic study or an encyclopedia of Canadian Jewish history—of every city, town, and village that Jews have inhabited; every religious institution and organization they have established; every accomplished Jewish man and woman in the annals of Canada's past, though the life stories of many are told. It is, rather, the chronicle of a people and their experience written for the general reader. This story is a drama with a cast of thousands that takes place in dozens of locales across the country—mainly in the large cities, but also in West Coast and Maritime towns and tiny prairie villages. It unfolds in countless synagogues, school classrooms, kosher butcher shops, impoverished urban neighbourhoods, rural general stores, university lecture halls, law and medical offices, garment factories; and at innumerable union gatherings, social and sports clubs, musical presentations and Yiddish stage productions, and businesses of every type. At its core are the Jewish immigrants and their children, grandchildren, and great-grandchildren—some more prominent than others—who were not only shaped by the British and French society and culture they lived in, but in turn shaped its development and progress.

They came seeking A.M. Klein's "fabled city" and they found it. As the last lines of "Autobiographical" go:

> It stands in space's vapours and Time's haze;
> Thence comes my sadness in remembered joy
> Constrictive of the throat;
> Thence do I hear, as heard by a Jewboy
> The Hebrew violins,
> Delighting in the sobbed oriental note.

PART ONE

IN A
CHRISTIAN
LAND

They Came First

Who was the first Jew?

That simple question, loaded with symbolism, echoes through the ages in all of its manifestations. Who was the first Canadian Jew to make it in politics, business, medicine, teaching, the civil service, and a thousand other pursuits? Try as they might, historians of the community (including me) cannot ignore such inquiries, for each new achievement—the first Jewish judge, senator, cabinet minister, university president—marks an important sign of change and acceptance. In chronicling Canadian Jewish history, these accomplishments, many of which demonstrate a new enlightened attitude among white Anglo and French Canadians, are impossible to ignore. It's akin to a board game played over the decades, in which the contestants mark each new triumph with an asterisk that exhibits a special religious and ethnic pride—what could be described in Yiddish as a collective *shepping nachas*.

Let's start with the granddaddy of the "firsts." Who was the first Jew to settle in Canada, or more properly the land colonized initially by the French and then the British that would become the Dominion of Canada in 1867?

As early as the 1560s, there were likely Portuguese Jewish navigators and fishermen on ships off the Grand Banks of Newfoundland. In 1677, Joseph de la Penha, a young Sephardi Jewish merchant, shipowner, and financier of privateers from Rotterdam, landed on the coast of Labrador and claimed the territory for the Stadtholder William of Orange. Some years later, so one version of this story goes, La Penha saved William—now King William III of England—from drowning during a stormy sea voyage. Another version has it that one of La Penha's ships protected the English coast from attack by the French in 1696. In any event, to show his gratitude, William bequeathed La Penha all of Labrador. This generous gift was confirmed in an official document from 1697 signed at Het Loo Palace, the Dutch vacation home of William and his wife Mary.

Two hundred and thirty years later, when the Judicial Committee of the Privy Council in London ruled that Labrador belonged to the then colony of Newfoundland in 1927, Isaac de la Penha, the cantor at Montreal's Spanish and Portuguese synagogue and one of Joseph's direct descendants, filed a lawsuit claiming Labrador for the family. The case stalled, but was restarted in 1950 by a group of de la Penha's descendants in Europe and Israel. Nothing came of that either. Then, in 1983, Daniel de la Penha, a retired physician in South Carolina and another descendant of Joseph, launched a third claim for part of Labrador in the Newfoundland courts. After losing his first challenge, he appealed to the province's Supreme Court. Alas, Newfoundland Chief Justice Alex Hickman ruled that de la Penha did not have sufficient proof "that he was entitled to a piece of Labrador." De la Penha appealed his case to the Supreme Court of Canada, but the court refused to consider it.

Catholic and autocratic pre-revolutionary France absolutely forbade non-Catholics—Huguenots (or French Protestants), dissenters, and Jews—from settling in New France and most other overseas colonies. This order was given further credence in Louis XIV's *Code Noir* (Black Code) of 1685, which stipulated that "we enjoin all of our officers to chase from our islands all the Jews who have established residence there. As with all declared enemies of Christianity, we command them to be gone within three months of the day of issuance of the present [order], at the risk of confiscation of their persons and their goods."

The most well-known story of a Jew attempting to settle in New France is the tale of twenty-year-old Esther Brandeau, who tried to elude the authorities disguised as a young man named Jacques La Fargue. Born in about 1718 to a Sephardi family residing in Saint-Esprit (a suburb of Bayonne in southwest France), Brandeau was sent by her parents to live with a brother and aunt in Amsterdam. The ship she was travelling on was wrecked soon after it left port. Rescued by the crew, she was taken to Biarritz, where she decided to take on a Christian male persona, likely because she believed as a young Jewish woman she would be in danger.

It is not known why Esther did not immediately return to her parents, or why she disguised herself for about five years. Possibly she contemplated passing herself off as a Christian to escape the arduous life of a Jew in France. Using various male aliases, she made money in a series of menial jobs. She worked for a tailor in Rennes; as a servant of the Recollects; a mendicant Catholic order; a helper for a baker in Saint-Malo; and eventually posed as a labourer named Jacques La Fargue on a ship headed to New France.

Once she arrived in Quebec in 1738, she decided that continuing her charade was not practical and revealed her true identity as a Jewish woman. At first, she declared her intention to convert to Catholicism, yet within a few months she had second thoughts, aggravating the intendant (the colony's chief administrator), Gilles Hocquart. "She is so flighty that she has been unable to adapt herself, either in the Hôpital Général or in several other houses," he reported. "Her conduct has not been precisely bad, but she is so fickle, that at different times she has been as much receptive as hostile to the instructions that zealous ecclesiastics have attempted to give her; I have no alternative but to send her away." By the fall of 1739, Hocquart, annoyed by her "frivolity" and "stubbornness," carried through with his threat and deported her back to France, where she vanished from the historical record.

Determining who was truly the first Jew to call Canada home is a toss-up between two entrepreneurial traders—or "Jew traders," as they were casually referred to by their Christian associates, though not generally with malice— Samuel Jacobs, a resourceful merchant and accomplished fiddle player, and Aaron Hart, the patriarch of the celebrated Hart (originally Hertz) family, whose illustrious members appear so prominently in the annals of Quebec.

Like many of their Jewish contemporaries in British North America, both men were born in Central Europe, probably in the early 1720s: Jacobs in Alsace and Hart in Bavaria (or possibly England). And as young

Dorfjuden—village Jews of Ashkenazi ancestry who spoke German, Yiddish, and English—both were in search of economic opportunities, adventure, and the relative freedom that was offered to Jews in the British colonies.

During the late fifteenth and sixteenth centuries, in a world governed by religious dogma and conflict, Sephardi Jews found refuge in the Ottoman Empire, where the sultans appreciated their skills as craftsmen and merchants, and in Holland, where after the Thirty Years' War (1618–48) the Dutch Calvinist leaders understood the economic value of a strong Jewish merchant class. Though not everyone embraced the *Portuguese de nação*—the "Portuguese of the [Hebrew] Nation"—Amsterdam became known as the "Dutch Jerusalem." But by the 1650s, the British gradually challenged and then replaced the Dutch as the dominant commercial empire-builders, and London soon eclipsed Amsterdam as the centre of global business.

Jews had been expelled from London in 1290, though a tiny community of about a hundred people, harassed from time to time, remained. No law was passed to prevent Jews from coming to England, and slowly Sephardi Jews from Holland and elsewhere migrated to London beginning in the mid-1650s—along with thousands of less affluent, Ashkenazi Jews from Poland, German states, and Holland. The Sephardim in particular were assimilated, and lived and behaved much like their Christian neighbours.

But the civil and political rights of Jews were vague and frequently at the whim of judicial and municipal officials. Jews in Britain "could not hold civil office, become freemen of the City of London, attend the ancient universities, or enter certain professions," historian Todd Endelman points out, "since doing so required the taking of an oath 'upon the true faith of a Christian'"—an issue that was to be significant to the political rights of Jews in British North America as well.

However, British politicians recognized the value of Jewish mercantile expertise in expanding colonial trade. So, while they refused to extend Jewish rights in Britain, they adopted a more liberal approach in British North America and the British West Indies. By virtue of the Plantation Act of 1740, Jews were allowed to become naturalized citizens once they had lived in a colony for seven years. This did not remove political and civil disabilities for

Jewish settlers, but the Plantation Act was "by far the most important law of the eighteenth century relating to the rights of Jews and foreign Protestants," in the words of Canadian Jewish history scholars Sheldon and Judith Godfrey.

Jacobs had journeyed to Halifax, Nova Scotia in 1749 and later for a brief time found work as a purveyor to the British Army during the Seven Years' War (1756–63), in the years before the British conquest of New France in 1759–60. Supplying the armies of Europe—whether Catholic or Protestant; or British, French, or German—was a profitable enterprise that attracted numerous Jewish merchants during this era. Despite the rights the Plantation Act afforded them, Jacobs and other Jewish merchants who wound up in Nova Scotia and Quebec after 1760 had to make their way in a Christian world—a world not devoid of prejudice, discrimination, and innumerable obstacles.

Jacobs, like other Jewish merchants, was assimilated and not overtly religious, though he had a rudimentary understanding of the Hebrew language and often signed his name as "Shemuel." (It goes without saying that truly observant Jews would have stayed in Europe, with the continent's established Jewish communities, synagogues, and access to kosher food.) As was common among traders, he married a French-Canadian (Catholic) woman, Marie-Josette Audet dit Lapointe, and thus his descendants were not Jewish.

Apart from Jacobs, among Halifax's earliest Jewish inhabitants were a number of other merchants who had journeyed north from Boston and New York in the mid-1740s. They would be joined in the next few years by another twenty-five Jewish men, women, and children, mostly from Newport, Rhode Island.

There was also interest from Jews in London connected to the Bevis Marks synagogue (the oldest synagogue in the United Kingdom), who imagined Nova Scotia as a potential haven for impoverished Jewish families looking for a new start. So desperate was Colonel Edward Cornwallis, the governor of Nova Scotia, to increase the colony's population that he seriously considered the request from the synagogue's representative for a group of Jews to settle in the future Canadian province. Nothing came of this proposal mainly due to bureaucratic disagreements, but soon after, British and German Jews from the Thirteen Colonies were welcomed—a definite "first." This seemingly enlightened attitude was born of economic and demographic realities rather than a sudden embrace of Jews by Cornwallis and other British officials. Nonetheless, the change in policy enabled Jacobs to receive a land grant, in August 1749, something that would not have happened in Britain or anywhere else in the British Empire, where the Plantation Act was not always applied to the letter. Merchants Isaac Levy and Nathan Nathans, who had come to Halifax from Newport, were permitted to open a sales shop without the usual myriad political and citizenship restrictions they would have faced in many of the Thirteen Colonies. More remarkably, members of the tiny Halifax Jewish community were invited to serve on juries.

Jacobs and others kept the Sabbath and holy days, and members of this pioneer community of Jews gathered for daily prayers in a house large enough to accommodate at least the ten men required for a *minyan*—the quorum necessary to conduct a service. No synagogue was built in the early 1750s though there were plans for a Jewish cemetery. It is unknown if they had their own *shochet* for kosher meat, but as the handful of merchants were nearly all married to Jewish women, when any of the women gave birth to a son and the services of a *mohel* for a ritual circumcision were required, the community sent for one from Newport or New York.

But the changing geopolitical situation impacted on Jewish fortunes. Soon after the French and Indian War began in 1754—the first phase of the Seven Years' War—the nascent Halifax Jewish community dwindled to only few souls; it would take several more decades before another group of Loyalists and immigrants from Britain and Europe rejuvenated it.

By 1758, Samuel Jacobs had moved on to Fort Cumberland (close to Sackville, N.B.), where he sold liquor. During the war, he was a partner in a distillery on Cape Breton Island. His non-Jewish partners in the enterprise, merchants Alexander Mackenzie and William Buttar, were not troubled by the fact that he was Jewish. He also supplied goods to the British during the months leading up to the decisive Battle of the Plains of Abraham in mid-September 1759, and the British conquest of Quebec that would be formalized by the Treaty of Paris in 1763. By late 1760, Jacobs, who spoke French, was in Quebec. He received a land grant and smartly took advantage of the commercial opportunities now open in light of the regime change. Jacobs's network of fellow Jewish merchants included Aaron Hart, who was soon established in Trois-Rivières, and forty-four-year-old Eleazar Levy, a New Yorker who became part of the small but growing Jewish community in Montreal. In 1766, Levy would be appointed a notary, the first Jew in North America given such a responsibility. To make this honour possible, British authorities decided to remove all references to "Christ" in his appointment.

In 1763, Jacobs finally settled in Saint-Denis, along the Richelieu River and northeast of Montreal, where he prospered as a merchant and landowner. His account books from 1770 show, for instance, that he owned land valued at £2,700 and had debts owed to him from 183 customers totalling £5,270. He also had interest in another distillery in Quebec with merchant John Hay and Benjamin Price, who was associated with James Murray, the British governor of Quebec from 1763 to 1768. During the American Revolutionary War and the siege and the Battle of Quebec in 1775, Jacobs supplied the rebel General Benedict Arnold with oats and other food for his troops. While many of his neighbours cheered "Congress and Liberty," Jacobs feigned his support of the Americans. He kept a record of the occupation of Quebec that he wrote in an indecipherable Hebrew script.

Jacobs and his wife, Marie-Josette—they were only officially married in 1784—had several children, though none were Jewish. Two of his daughters were sent to a convent school run by the Ursuline nuns of Quebec, though more because he wanted them to have a proper education than a Catholic one. One of his daughters, Marie-Geneviève, wanted to marry a Captain Stanislas Vigneau. But for a reason not known Jacobs did not approve of her choice and told her in no uncertain terms that she would receive no inheritance if she disobeyed him. In 1786, only months before Jacobs died, Marie-Geneviève wrote to her father begging him to change his mind: "Let me with the greatest sincerity assure [you], it is not [from] ingratitude, nor for want of love for you that I marry. Be persuaded that it is the sincere love I have for him."

Jacobs and Marie-Josette's son Samuel Jr. was also a concern. When the boy was sixteen, he was sent to Quebec to study at a private school operated by Dr. John Reid, and lived in the city with Elias Solomon, an elderly Jewish merchant who Jacobs knew well. Jacobs and Solomon, however, argued about Solomon's bill for boarding his son, and so Samuel Jr. was sent to live with Reid. In December 1781, Reid wrote to tell Jacobs that his son had broken into Solomon's home and stolen a watch. According to merchant Charles Grant, another of Jacobs's associates, young Samuel had "contracted a set of acquaintances here which soon must prove his ruin, if not immediately removed out of the place." Disheartened, Jacobs asked Grant to "manage" the "unhappy boy" as he saw fit. In a postscript to this letter of February 1782, Jacobs added a note to young Samuel, explaining the choices he had before him: "Mr. Sam: I was your father and did my duty. Your conduct has made it void and null. If your future behaviour merits every good man's esteem and pity, [and] your past folly [and] repentance opens your eyes, I then with joy and tenderness will own you again as my child. Till then I am only your well-wisher." Young Samuel apparently got the message; he returned to his family at the end of the year "very sorrowful" for his past behaviour. Within three years, he left his parents for Jamaica, where he hoped to emulate his father's accomplishments as a merchant. Whether he succeeded or not remains unknown.

Samuel Jacobs Sr. did not belong to a synagogue, nor did he ever make a donation to the synagogue in Montreal. He married a Catholic woman and raised his children as Christians. Yet he never stopped thinking of himself as a Jew. "I was disputing all last night with a German officer about religion," he wrote to a non-Jewish friend in 1778. "[Though] I am not a wandering Jew, yet I am a stirring one."

La Famille Hart

At the end of the Seven Years' War, in 1763, Aaron Hart had been living in Trois-Rivières for about a year. Located at the junction of the Saint-Maurice and Saint Lawrence rivers (its name derives from the three channels the rivers form), the village would remain under military occupation until the summer of 1764. Hart had a reputation as a diligent and loyal merchant and had served and supplied the British Army. With his powdered wig, fine coat, and white cravat he looked the part of a pioneer aristocrat. The Harts' motto was the German "*Schnellfüssig und Frey,*" or "Rapid, Light, and Free," embodied by the stag on the run portrayed on the family's coat of arms. It was a phrase that accurately described Aaron's approach to the world, too.

In August 1763, Frederick Haldimand, the military governor of Trois-Rivières—a village with a predominately French-Canadian population of approximately four hundred people—had to appoint an English-speaking postmaster. He thus did not have a lot of options. The choice came down to a selection between what he described as "a Jew, a [British] sergeant and an Irish soldier on half pay." He selected the Jew, Aaron Hart—or "my Jew," as he referred to him. Since Hart was short of stature, Haldimand's secretary Hector Cramahé, a Huguenot, called him the *petit juif*, or "little Jew." The appointment meant that Hart was in all probability the first Jew to hold a public office in Quebec.

Another significant appointment, which occurred in 1768, was the selection of John Franks—who like Samuel Jacobs had briefly lived in Halifax before he settled in Quebec in 1761—as the "Overseer of the Chimnies [sic] for the Town of Quebec." Not only was the duty he was entrusted with of preventing fires crucial for the town's inhabitants, but more significantly Guy Carleton, who had replaced James Murray as governor, permitted Franks to swear an oath "upon the true faith of a Jew," rather than "upon the true faith of a Christian," as the oath of abjuration stipulated. It was an extraordinary decision that went against prescribed British legislation passed in 1766, but Carleton, ruler of a province with 60,000 French Catholics and only a small number of Protestants and Jews, felt compelled to enlist the services of Jews such as Franks, who he rightly regarded as loyal to the Crown. This was, as Sheldon Godfrey points out, "the first recorded instance of an appointment by commission from the colonial government of a Jew in Canada."

Back in Trois-Rivières, Aaron Hart, who was always on the lookout for commercial opportunities, tapped into the fur trade network that had been established by the French. In 1765, he dispatched a group of experienced voyageurs to travel inland and trade directly on his behalf with aboriginals, most likely with the Algonquin. They brought the furs back to Trois-Rivières and Hart sold them to British dealers, making a lucrative profit.

But Hart was not the only Jew to engage in the fur trade. In the early 1760s, a small band of self-styled Jewish voyageurs had gone one step further than Hart: rather than hiring men to conduct business in their name, they boldly ventured west to trade with aboriginals themselves, though not always with positive results. This consortium consisted of Ezekiel Solomons, who had relocated from Albany to Quebec in 1760, his cousin Levy Solomons, Chapman Abraham, Benjamin Lyon, and Gershon Levy, the titular head of Gershon Levy and Company under which the traders operated. The firm's chief investors were Samuel Jacobs and his business partner in the distillery, Alexander Mackenzie. With outposts in Niagara, Detroit, and Fort Michilimackinac (Mackinaw City, Michigan), Gershon Levy and Company captured a sizable percentage of the fur trade business around the Great Lakes.

The firm encountered trouble in 1763 during the bloody three-year uprising led by the aboriginal leader Pontiac, an ally of the French—a last stand against the British conquest of much of North America. Caught in the midst of the attacks, Ezekiel and Levy Solomons, Chapman Abraham, and Gershon

Levy barely escaped with their lives. Abraham, forty years old, who had emigrated from Holland via England to New York, was nearly burned alive at the stake and only survived after pretending he was mad.

Reverend John Heckewelder, an American missionary and chronicler of early white-aboriginal interactions, heard from Abraham himself the details of this ordeal. "Tied to the stake and the fire burning by his side, his thirst, from the great heat, became intolerable, and [Abraham] begged that some drink might be given to him," Heckewelder wrote. When his captors gave Abraham a hot bowl of broth, he threw it back at them in a fit of rage. They believed him mad and, as per their custom, released him.

Though Abraham and the others managed to avoid being killed, their cargo of furs and supplies was seized, leaving them with debts estimated at £18,000 and a lot of unhappy creditors. They remained in business, but spent the next five years or more trying to settle their hefty losses.

During this period Aaron Hart was acquiring as much land as he could, which included a large tract of the seigneury of Bécancour, located across the Saint Lawrence River. As early as 1858, this ever-expanding land-holding generated for the family an annual income in rent of nearly $4,100. He also had slaves to work his land—slavery was not banned in the British Empire until 1833–34—ostensibly to enhance his profits. He owned a black slave, a young boy named Pompée he bought in New England in 1774 for approximately £50. Later in 1779, he owned a young woman, Phoebe, who he acquired for £45 in Montreal. Hart was not troubled about owning slaves, and likely perceived it as enhancing his social status in the community.

Establishing a family was also important for Hart. More than a decade earlier, he had returned to England during the summer of 1767, with the specific intention of finding a Jewish wife. There, he met and soon married his young cousin Dorothea Judah, who was twenty years his junior and the sister of Uriah and Samuel Judah, British Jewish merchants who had moved from London to Montreal in the late 1760s. She was a handsome woman, if a portrait of her painted when she was much older is a fair representation.

The newlyweds soon travelled back to Quebec to start a family, and over the course of their marriage Dorothea would give birth to four sons and

four daughters, several of whom—most notably their second son, Ezekiel—
followed in the footsteps of their illustrious father and contributed in a
meaningful way to Canadian Jewish history.

From the start of their marriage, Aaron and Dorothea intended to live as
Jews, as much as that was possible in Trois-Rivières. Their sons were circumcised by *mohalim* brought in from New York and Montreal, and they
attempted to keep kosher. This meant ensuring they only ate meat that had
been slaughtered by a *shochet* according to Jewish law. It is unclear whether
Hart arranged for a New York–based ritual slaughterer to visit him from time
to time (*mohalim* who were good with a knife sometimes did double duty as
shochetim), or found someone in Quebec who could perform this duty. (Jacob
Raphael Cohen, noted below—who was in Montreal for a few years—could
perform both tasks and did visit Hart.) The Hart family house in Trois-
Rivières even had two kitchens, one presumably used for meat and the other
for milk products, a dietary custom that some wealthy observant Jews would
have followed (having separate dishes and utensils for meat and milk products is more the norm).

Hart also made a point of ensuring his young sons had a Jewish education
by sending them to schools in New York and Philadelphia. But his eldest boy,
Moses, was impetuous and enjoyed his access to his father's wealth. He also
was less enamoured with Judaism than his other siblings. In 1790, Hart wrote
to Moses, then twenty-one years of age, firmly advising that he return home
in time for Passover. Much to Aaron's annoyance, Moses skipped the Hart
family Passover Seder in Trois-Rivières and instead caught a few New York
plays and bestowed "lavish tips to hotel barmen," as he recorded in his diary.

Despite his adherence to Jewish custom and law, however, Aaron had
opted not to be involved as a founder of or financial contributor to Canada's
first synagogue, the Shearith Israel ("The Remnant of Israel"), which was
founded in Montreal in late December 1768.

Aaron Hart died on December 28, 1800 at the age of about seventy-six. He
left his wife Dorothea and children—mainly his sons, as was the custom of
the day—the bulk of his estate and properties. His four daughters each

received £1,000, provided they abided by certain conditions. There was much family squabbling about who got what, and even a series of lawsuits that pitted Dorothea against two of her sons, Moses and Ezekiel.

Among Aaron and Dorothea's children, the antics of Moses made them the most anxious. Denis Vaugeois, the family's biographer, calls him the "black sheep" of the Hart clan. That was putting it mildly. "Moses was born temperamental, undisciplined," historian Raymond Douville wrote of him. "He lived unrepentant and did not greatly lament it. If he had curbed his passions more, he might have left a more enduring testimony. But he was one of those who are bent on pleasures that pass away. He has passed away with them."

As the first-born male, Moses was supposed to succeed in life—and from his father's point of view, maintain the family's Jewish traditions. It did not quite work out that way. When he was in his early twenties, Moses tried to emulate Aaron's business accomplishments. With backing from his father, he opened his own general store in Nicolet, a small town on the south side of the Saint Lawrence River, across from Trois-Rivières. When that failed to generate sufficient cash flow, he tried again further west in the town of William Henry (later Sorel), with better results. Over time, his commercial interests and holdings expanded into finance, shipping, and a sizable amount of property. He also owned an enslaved black woman named Jane and her six-month-old daughter Mary, whom he had purchased in Albany.

In 1796, Moses announced that he was running for a seat in the Assembly of Lower Canada for William Henry. (In response to the influx of Loyalists from the former Thirteen Colonies, British authorities in 1791 enacted the Constitutional Act, which divided the old province of Quebec into Upper and Lower Canada. In 1867, these territories became the provinces of Ontario and Quebec respectively.) Aaron Hart was not happy about his son's decision. "What I do not like is that you will be opposed as a Jew," he warned him. In this instance, Moses listened to his father—not something he always did—and withdrew his candidacy before the vote was taken.

Moses somewhat naively believed that being Jewish in the late eighteenth and early nineteenth centuries was not a barrier to his aspirations. He was mistaken, but resolute. In 1798, when he applied for a dozen or so land grants among more than two hundred being auctioned off by the Crown in Upper Canada, he ran up against the bias of John Elmsley, Upper Canada's chief justice, who ruled—incorrectly, as it turned out—that "Jews cannot hold Land in this Province." Unwilling to accept Elmsley's interpretation of the law, Moses appealed and was eventually approved for two grants.

He was also unwilling to give up on his dream of serving as a politician. He ran in another three elections over the years, but lost on each occasion. His last failed bid for a seat in the assembly was in 1844, when he was seventy-five years old. He campaigned as well for appointments to both the Executive and Legislative Councils (akin to the cabinet and the Senate in today's federal government), yet those efforts did not pan out either—perhaps because he was Jewish, but more likely owing to his reputation as a serial philanderer.

Pressured to start a family of his own, he married his first cousin Sarah Judah in the summer of 1799. Sarah's father (and Moses's uncle) Uriah was not thrilled with the marriage—and for good reason. Moses was a poor husband, prone to outbursts of violence. During one civil court proceeding, a servant described how Moses had thrown a bowl of sugar and bottle of milk at Sarah and would have followed that with a kettle of boiling water if the servant had not intervened to stop him. In 1807, the couple separated, then reconciled before legally separating for good in 1816. While Sarah might have found solace in her affair with Moses's younger brother Alexander, her husband had many affairs with many women with whom he had many children. If Vaugeois's calculations are correct, in addition to the three children he had with Sarah, Moses fathered eighteen children with twelve women, all non-Jewish (that's a lot of descendants from just one Hart). As Sarah summed up Moses's behaviour in an affidavit of 1814: "For seven or eight years, the defendant [Moses], forgetting his duties as a husband, abandoned himself to debauchery with women of poor reputation and kept them at his home . . . to the shame of the complainant and the scandal of her family."

Increasingly eccentric as he got older, Moses—influenced by the French Revolution and an assortment of philosophers—advanced the crazy idea of starting a new religion, in around 1815. He outlined it in a pamphlet he published entitled *Modern Religion,* his treatise on God, the existence of man, and his personal interpretations of the Old and New Testaments. Few people in the Canadas, Jewish or otherwise, took him seriously.

Aaron and Dorothea Hart's second son, Ezekiel, was more grounded than his older brother and inherited his father's shortness and restrained ambition. Ezekiel Hart was also the central figure in the early Canadian Jewish struggle for equality, and has been remembered somewhat inaccurately as a victim of antisemitism, decades before the term—which was first used in 1860 by the Austrian Jewish scholar Moritz Steinschneider—was popularized by the German journalist and political propagandist Wilhelm Marr.

After attending school in New York, Ezekiel joined his father in the family business. In late 1796, he and his brothers Moses and Benjamin established a brewery; Ezekiel eventually sold his interest in this enterprise to Moses. Three years earlier, during a lengthy stay in New York City, the twenty-three-year-old Ezekiel met a young woman about his age, Frances Lazarus. Within about six months, Ezekiel and Frances were married. They soon returned to Trois-Rivières and Frances began having children—thirteen in all, seven of whom survived to adulthood. Their son Aaron Ezekiel Hart, born in 1803, would in 1824 become the first Jewish lawyer called to the bar in Lower or Upper Canada, at the age of twenty-one.

Ezekiel shared Moses's passion for politics, though he waited until his father had died before seeking a seat in the Assembly of Lower Canada. When he attempted to do so the first time in 1804, he lost. Three years later, on April 11, 1807, he tried running as a candidate in a by-election for one of Trois-Rivières' two seats. He was successful, defeating three opponents and taking 59 of the 116 votes cast.

In winning, he triggered, through no fault of his own, what has become known as *L'affaire Hart.* In the 1940s to 1970s, early chroniclers of Canadian Jewish history were quick to label what transpired in the Lower Canadian assembly during 1808 and 1809 as a clear case of antisemitism. Over the years, however, Hart's experience has been reconsidered. Anti-Jewish feelings did play a part; as a Jew, Ezekiel was an easy target. Yet Hart was also caught up in the political power struggle that had gradually erupted between the English and French members of the assembly.

The Constitutional Act of 1791 had provided a representative assembly in that the British permitted elected representatives, but purposely not one that was "responsible." In a system of responsible government, the members of the executive—the prime minister and the cabinet—are responsible to the elected representatives of the people and can only remain in office provided they maintain the confidence of the assembly or House of Commons. Such a system would become a reality in Canada in the late 1840s. Until then, power in colonial Canada was in the hands of the British-appointed governor and his appointed Executive and Legislative Councils, which had veto power over the elected assemblies and control of patronage.

In 1808, the governor in Lower Canada was James Craig, a stiff, no-nonsense military leader who had coincidentally befriended Aaron Hart during the American Revolutionary War. Opposing Craig and his chief sup-porters, the English-speaking group of "Tories"—Lower Canada's so-called aristocracy—were French-Canadian members of the assembly, a liberal elite of sorts who were increasingly angry with the status quo and imbued with the sense of nationalism that has been a core component of Quebec history. In 1806 they had formed themselves into an influential organized faction within the assembly known as the *Parti canadien* or *Parti patriote*, and were led by Pierre-Stanislas Bédard, a quiet though determined lawyer and politician. That same year he was also one of the founders of the weekly newspaper *Le Canadien*, a journal established specifically to challenge British rule and to counter the pro-British propaganda of the Tories' newspaper, the *Mercury*. With the motto "*Nos institutions, notre langue et nos droits*" ("Our institutions, our language, our rights"), *Le Canadien* became the organ of the *Parti canadien*—until 1810, when the autocratic Craig shut it down and arrested Bédard and several of his associates. It was in this increasingly hostile confrontation between English and French that Ezekiel Hart's attempt to take his seat as the first Jew elected to an assembly in Canada became unwittingly entangled.

Many of the English and French-Canadian voters in Trois-Rivières had no problems electing Hart, even if there was an immediate backlash in the pages of *Le Canadien* that portrayed Hart, not entirely incorrectly, as a Tory—and worse, a Jew. Pointing out in an editorial of April 18, 1807 that it was a "religious duty" of Jews to maintain a separateness from the societies in which they lived, the newspaper wondered: "How can a Jew who thinks of no one but himself and his sect be charged with representing the interests of all the people, and how can one expect such a man to work for the general good of all."

But nasty newspaper commentary was the least of Hart's problems. The real challenge was that, once he was in Quebec City, he had to swear an oath in order to take his seat. The accepted tradition among members of the assembly was to swear the state oath of abjuration, which included the phrase "upon the true faith of a Christian." Clearly, this oath was problematic for Hart, as it would be for any semi-observant Jew. He could have eliminated this problem the way a Halifax Jewish Loyalist called Samuel Hart (no relation) had in 1793—by converting to Christianity. But Ezekiel had no intention of abandoning Judaism. After seeking legal opinions from a few trusted advisors, he arrived in Quebec City in January 1808 in time for the beginning of the next session. At the gathering convened for the swearing-in of new members, Hart adhered to Jewish custom: he covered his head, placed his right hand on the Old Testament, but swore a secular oath of office, which was technically his right under colonial statute. Hence, he pledged allegiance to King George III, but instead of ending with the traditional words "upon the true faith of a Christian," Hart declared "so help me God."

That should have been the end of this matter and Hart should have been able to take his seat in the assembly as one of the members for Trois-Rivières. But the oath issue and how it was applied to Jews and dissenters was complicated and open to various (and incorrect) legal interpretations. Rightly or wrongly, the majority of the Christian members of the assembly, English and French—as well as other British officials who weighed in on this matter— maintained that the state oath of abjuration was the required oath, and no substitutions were acceptable. Once it was known what Hart had done, a motion was passed making it impossible for him to take his seat. In the ensuing debate about Hart's actions, the focus was on the fact that he was Jewish and therefore disqualified as a member of the assembly. Or, as the motion of

February 17 put it, "That Ezekiel Hart, Esquire, professing the Jewish Religion, cannot take a seat, nor sit, nor vote, in this House."

From the point of view of Bédard and the French-Canadian majority in the assembly, Hart's status as a Jew was mostly a convenient excuse. (While the Parti *canadien* had a majority in the assembly, the real power remained in the hands of British Tories appointed to the Executive and Legislative councils by the governor.) Their endgame was preventing the Tories and supporters of Governor Craig from gaining another member. On the other hand, several English members, such as the principled attorney general Jonathan Sewell, a former Loyalist, also voiced their disapproval of Hart, who would have likely sided with them in future votes—as the *Parti canadien* feared. Though it is impossible to determine precisely what motivated the anti-Hart Tories, their opposition was probably based on a firm desire to maintain the Christian integrity and purity of the assembly—as in the British Parliament, which did not allow Jews to serve as MPs in the House of Commons, and would not until 1858.

In hindsight, Hart was fighting a losing battle. Still, he eloquently spoke in his own defence. "I profess the religion of my father; a religion tolerated by my King and Country and not forbidden by the Constitutional Act," he stated. "Mr. Speaker, I think I have a right to take my seat in this Honourable House, and I am now ready to do my duty therein." The majority of the members disagreed with him and voted to expel him. The anti-Hart voters included all of the French-Canadians. In one last attempt, Hart, with the support of a petition signed by several Lower Canadian Jews—perhaps the first, but definitely not the last time a Jewish community in Canada (no matter how small) would stand beside one of their own—appealed to Governor Craig for help, but he opted not to interfere. Locked in a dispute with the *Parti canadien*–dominated assembly, Craig did dissolve the house and set a date for an election: May 17, 1808.

Hart remained determined. He once again stood for election in Trois-Rivières and once again won a seat with the second-most votes in a four-man contest. During the month-long campaign, Hart's oath problems as a Jew were not raised. The new session of the assembly did not start until mid-April 1809. In the interim, a decision rendered by Judge Edward Bowen stipulated that all members in the assembly were required to take the "Oath in the Customary manner upon the Holy Evangelists (New Testament), and not otherwise." Left with no choice but to comply and compromise his principles, Hart took the same oath as the Christian members, with his head uncovered and his hand on the New Testament. At the end of the ceremony, in a display of reverence, he leaned down and kissed the book. But this concessionary act still did not satisfy Hart's detractors. Now they argued that as a Jew, Hart could not be bound by the oath sworn by Christian members since "he has profaned the religion of the oath." He still had no right to take his seat in the assembly. Following a couple of weeks of debate on the issue of Hart's eligibility, another vote was taken in early May 1809. Ezekiel Hart was formally expelled for a second time, and his seat declared vacant.

Governor Craig—who remained locked in a battle with the *Parti canadien*—and his Executive Council were of the opinion that Hart's expulsion was unjustified. Craig did dissolve the assembly a few weeks later, but not because of the treatment of Hart. The governor was angry about the expulsion of a French-Canadian magistrate who the members deemed also could not sit in the assembly. Craig might have felt privately that Hart had been wronged, yet he was not about to champion Jewish rights. But going after the right of magistrates to serve in the assembly was something else entirely.

Craig asked Lord Castlereagh, the colonial secretary, for advice on what had transpired with Hart and with the magistrate. He received a reply from London in early September 1809. "With regard to the endeavours to expel Mr. Hart for being a Jew," Castlereagh wrote, "it was obvious that a real Jew could not take the oath upon the Gospels." Had Hart converted to Christianity, then he could have rightfully claimed his seat. But as a Jew it was impossible, at least according to Castlereagh—who, as it turned out, was wrong. You would have thought that, as colonial secretary, Castlereagh would have had a sound grasp of the legislation dealing with Britain's colonies, such as the Plantation and Constitutional Acts. This was clearly not the case, as Hart had been the victim of a concerted effort to thwart the intent of these acts as they applied to Jewish rights. It is important to note, however, that the animosity toward Hart sitting as a member in the assembly did not result in a campaign to prevent Jews in Lower Canada from voting. The attitude of Bédard and the *Parti canadien* was a "reflection of the selective liberalism characteristic of these early nationalists," suggests historian Richard Menkis.

Ezekiel Hart chose not to run in the 1809 election, and never stood for public office again. Instead, he focused on his family and his business. As a loyal Lower Canadian, he also served as a lieutenant in the 8th Battalion of Trois-Rivières militia and fought in the War of 1812—as did many other Jews, including his own sons, despite the resistance to the appointment of Jewish officers. When Ezekiel Hart died in 1843, all of Trois-Rivières paid their respects to him. By then, he had lived to see a victory for Jewish civil rights in the Lower Canadian assembly in the late 1820s and early 1820s thanks to a fight in which several of his sons played a significant role.

Through the 1820s and 1830s, the number of Jews in British North America remained small—an estimated 107 in 1831, and about 154 a decade later. A trickle of German and Polish Ashkenazi Jews made their way to Montreal, some via stops in the United States; there were a few Jewish merchants and peddlers in Halifax and Saint John; and there might have been a few Jews in Toronto—known as York from 1793 to 1834—as early as 1817, though the evidence is scant.

The first Jew known to settle in York was fittingly a Hart: Arthur Wellington Hart. Arthur (his full given name was Samuel Arthur Wellington) was one of the eight (surviving) children of Benjamin and Harriot Hart and a grandson of Aaron Hart. Born in Trois-Rivières in 1813, he was only nineteen years old when he arrived in muddy York in 1832—a town of 4,500 people, a population that doubled when York was incorporated as the City of Toronto two years later. Young Arthur was probably sent west by his father to boost Benjamin's up-and-down commission business, an enterprise which dealt in everything "from sherry to shovels." Once in York, Arthur also became an agent for the Eagle Life Assurance Company of London and rented a shop on King Street, the city's main commercial avenue. By 1840, a small number of Jews with British and German roots had joined him—Judah Joseph from Cincinnati, Henry Joseph from Sorel in Lower Canada, and from England,

Alfred Braham and Samuel Casper. All were involved as merchants, selling jewellery, clothes, and similar products.

But it was in Montreal and Quebec City where the fight for equality continued. Attitudes about Jewish rights had changed among the French-Canadian nationalists who controlled the Lower Canadian assembly. Led by the eloquent and charismatic lawyer Louis-Joseph Papineau, the assembly's former speaker (from 1815 to 1822), the *Parti patriote*—as they now called their faction—saw themselves as the guardians of freedom for all minorities at the mercy of the "Château Clique," the Anglican ruling group of merchants who served on the Executive and Legislative Councils and had the ear of the governor. Papineau and the *patriotes*, who were ever frustrated by the perceived injustice of the Anglo oligarchy thwarting their democratic and nationalist interests, and felt stymied by the British refusal to address their legitimate concerns, took up arms in 1837. Before the eruption of violence, however, Papineau ensured that Jewish civil and political rights were nearly solidified (an event celebrated in Historica Canada's *Heritage Minute*, "Hart & Papineau"). He also had a good relationship with the Hart family and socialized with them on his visits to Trois-Rivières, which on at least one occasion in February 1835 included imbibing excellent Bordeaux and Madeira wines.

Jewish civil and political rights in Lower Canada were advanced in two stages. First, in 1828, the *patriote*-dominated assembly supported a petition from "certain Israelites of the District of Montreal" for the right to register births, marriages, and deaths on the public registers and to hold title to the synagogue's cemetery land, rights that were previously denied persons "professing the Jewish faith." The bill incorporating the community's demands was passed in the assembly and ratified by the Legislative Council, but the governor requested approval from British authorities, who refused to support it. Reintroduced in the assembly in the spring of 1830, the bill on this second try succeeded in winning assent from the governor on January 18, 1831.

Next was a petition of February 7, 1831 from Samuel Becancour Hart, Ezekiel's eldest son—with assistance from his uncle Benjamin and his brother Aaron Ezekiel, a lawyer—for the assembly to address the long-standing injustice that "persons professing the Jewish religion are excluded from office in a manner very public and mortifying." The Harts wanted this matter rectified in the Jewish community's favour. With minimal discussion, a bill was passed unanimously in the assembly and approved by the Legislative Council a few weeks later. The newly appointed governor of Lower Canada, Lord Aylmer, another military man with limited political experience, passed off the decision to the British. Though Jews in Britain had yet to be granted this right—and would not be for more than two decades—the Brits signed off on the Lower Canadian legislation and the bill received royal assent on April 12, 1832. Henceforth "all persons professing the Jewish Religion being natural born British subjects inhabiting and residing in this Province, are entitled . . . to the full rights and privileges of the other subjects of his Majesty." On the 150th anniversary of the act in 1982, René Lévesque, then the premier of Quebec and the leader of the separatist Parti Québécois, did not miss the opportunity to highlight the fact that Jewish rights in the province had been expanded due to the support of the French-Canadian nationalists led by Papineau, who in the midst of a valiant struggle had not forsaken minority rights.

Upper Canada followed in 1833 with a more comprehensive act eliminating state oaths for Jews and dissenters. As historian Irving Abella has pointed out, after Jamaica, "Canada became the first colony in the British Empire to emancipate Jews." As true as this statement is, there were some hiccups. Even after 1832, Jews in Lower Canada were still required to swear the oath of abjuration with the phrase "upon the true faith of a Christian." In the spring of 1833, Samuel Becancour Hart, Benjamin Hart, and Moses Judah Hayes, an innovative community leader in Montreal who served as the city's police chief from 1854 to 1861, were included on a list of candidates to be justices of the peace. Lawyer Aaron Philip Hart (Benjamin's son) advised the trio to refuse the honour because of the enforcement of the state oaths. Benjamin and Moses heeded Aaron Phillip's counsel, but Samuel did not. Instead he maneuvered around the regulations and the assembly, after yet another inquiry into this matter reaffirmed the right of Jews to amend the wording of the oath of abjuration.

Benjamin Hart finally became a Justice of the Peace in the spring of 1837, about six months before the conflict between the *patriotes* and the British was to turn violent. The Harts and other Jews supported Papineau's demands for real political power. Yet when the *patriotes* took up arms against British soldiers and English-speaking Lower Canadian volunteers, the family, like nearly every Jew in Quebec, sided with the British, who to them represented law and order and the future of the country. Perhaps for that reason, after the rebellion in Lower Canada failed, the French-Canadian radical Hunters' Lodges (*Frères chasseurs*) plotted another attack that "called for the strangling of all Jews and the confiscation of their property."

So what did it mean to be Jewish in pre-Confederation Canada? You lived your life as a member of a tiny minority in a British world, dressed and acted as your Christian neighbours did, and participated in the significant political events of the day. Not all occupations and professions were open to you, but you took advantages of the commercial opportunities which presented themselves. That usually meant a career in business, as a merchant, agent, or trader. In short, you tried to fit in. But differences nevertheless remained, and your otherwise friendly Gentile neighbours rarely let you forget that, like your ancestors, you still wore a yellow badge that marked you as a Jew—except your yellow badge was invisible.

To counter this underlying prejudice, you called yourself an "Israelite" rather than a Jew—or officially a person "who professed the Jewish religion," always stressing that Judaism was not a nation but a religion, a theme emphasized at the time by many Western European writers and politicians. Only when left with no alternative, did you emerge from the shadows to fight boldly for Jewish civil and political rights. This was a battle for equality and also one for greater assimilation. You didn't necessarily want your children to marry non-Jews, but you didn't oppose it all that stringently either.

Hence, the last thing you would have wanted were Jewish immigrants in your midst—"foreigners" who did not speak English or French very well, if at all, and who clearly appeared and behaved "too Jewish" for your liking. The tense interaction between Jews who had already integrated themselves into Canadian society and newly arrived immigrants, especially those who came from Russia and Eastern Europe, was to play out many times from 1800 to the 1950s, a clash arising from perceived Jewish concerns about acceptance and fears of an antisemitic backlash.

Nearing seventy years old, Benjamin Hart was set in his ways. Hart, a key member of the Shearith Israel congregation and one of its proprietors, was incensed that a small number of German and Polish newcomers were, in his opinion, threatening the Sephardi traditions of the synagogue—customs that Hart had enshrined in the synagogue's by-laws more than a decade ear-lier. The illusion that the members of Shearith Israel were full-blooded Sephardim—when in fact, nearly all of them (like the vast majority of Jews living in British North America before the 1880s) had German and Polish roots, rather than Spanish, Portuguese, or British—persisted for decades.

Hart needn't have been overly upset about it. The German and Polish Jews he objected to had already decided that the Shearith Israel was not for them. Unhappy with the Portuguese Sephardi traditions they encountered in Montreal in 1846, the newcomers organized their own services in a rented room on St. James Street so that they could pray in the Asheknazi style they were accustomed to. They were soon legally recognized by the government as the English, German, and Polish Congregation, and were given the same rights as Shearith Israel. But this initial effort to establish a second congrega-tion in Montreal was not entirely successful, and it took a while and new leadership before an enduring congregation and synagogue became a reality. By 1859, the English, German, and Polish Congregation could afford its own synagogue, which in 1886 officially changed its name to Shaar Hashomayim (the "Gate of Heaven").

Though the first generation of Quebec Jews like Benjamin Hart and his family—descendants of Aaron Hart—did not fully grasp it at the time, Jewish Canada was about to be dominated by the Ashkenazim—who, like in the larger Jewish world, would supplant the Sephardim in positions of power and influence.

A British Subject (and Israelite) I Was Born

By around 1890, Montreal's Shearith Israel was more commonly known as the Spanish and Portuguese synagogue, and still is in the present day. The synagogue took its name and lead from the Sephardi synagogue in New York established in 1654, as well as Bevis Marks in London—despite the fact that nearly all of its founders were Ashkenazi Jews. This group included the fur traders Chapman Abraham, Benjamin Lyon, and Ezekiel and Levy Solomons, all of whom spent some of each year in Montreal.

In the midst of the American Revolutionary War, and still reeling from the rebel occupation of Montreal from November 1775 to May 1776, almost all the original synagogue members were Loyalists devoted to upholding the British Crown. Their decision to model their synagogue after the one in New York City was likely therefore not a political statement. Rather, it was based on their familiarity with the Sephardi-style prayer services many of them had experienced when living in the Thirteen Colonies, and the fact that Sephardi congregations in New York, London, and elsewhere at that time had funds available for co-religionists.

What is more interesting is that many of the founders of the Montreal congregation were not married to Jewish women. Among them was Ezekiel Solomons, who had married a Christian woman, Louise Dubois, in a ceremony held at an Anglican church. Their children were all baptized. (In the summer of 2003, sixty of Solomons's descendants gathered for a family reunion at Fort Michilimackinac, Michigan, close to where Ezekiel and Louise had lived when the area was still part of Quebec. None of them were Jewish.) Solomons was, nevertheless, chosen as Shearith Israel's treasurer. And when one of his young sons died, the synagogue board permitted Ezekiel to inter the boy at the synagogue's cemetery, on land acquired at St. Janvier Street, though the child was not recognized as being Jewish.

By 1778, Shearith Israel had its first synagogue, a small stone building on Little St. James Street, east of Place d'Armes. It was built on land owned by young David David, son of the trader Lazarus David and the first Jew born in Quebec (in 1764). Lazarus had acquired a lot of property in Montreal, and following his death in 1776 (he was the first person interned at the synagogue's cemetery), the family donated the Little St. James site for the synagogue as well as funds to buy land for the cemetery.

Like all congregations, Shearith Israel's first order of business was setting rules and appropriate punishments for members who misbehaved. Disrupting meetings, refusing to serve as an officer, and not performing a *mitzvah* or duty when required were deemed "offences" for which fines could be levied—all at the discretion of the dictatorial founding members, who formed a junta. In addition, rule 13—enacted on December 22, 1778—stipulated that any new "Israelites" who settled in Montreal and who did not join the congregation within three weeks were essentially blacklisted. Jews outside the city were given six months to make up their minds. Though the synagogue fashioned itself as traditional (what would today be called Orthodox), its members were not all observant Jews, as this was next to impossible in eighteenth-century Montreal. Shearith Israel had High Holiday services and, depending on the occasion, had prayers if a *minyan* of ten men was available.

In 1778, Haym Myers, a merchant who had recently returned to London from Montreal, arranged for Reverend Jacob Raphael Cohen to travel to Montreal (Jewish minister-preachers in Britain who were not ordained used the title "Reverend"). Multi-talented, Cohen was offered a three-year contract (worth £50 per year) to serve as Shearith Israel's *mohel*, *shochet*, and *hazan* (in Sephardi congregations, this was the title for a non-ordained synagogue leader and prayer reader). Cohen brought three Torah scrolls with him for the synagogue (one was paid for; two were gifts).

Soon after his arrival in Quebec, Cohen, accompanied by Aaron Hart, travelled to Trois-Rivières for the circumcision of his son Benjamin, born in

August 1779; and again after his son Alexander's birth three years later. Cohen adequately fulfilled his contract with Shearith Israel and served the various needs of the small community, though in the months before he left he became embroiled in a nasty dispute about money he said was owed to him by the synagogue board, primarily Levy Solomons, the synagogue's president or *parnas*. (The synagogue's executive was dominated by men, and it took 244 years—until 2012—for a woman, Danielle Benchimol Mashaal, to be elected the synagogue's president.) On his way back to London, Cohen's ship was diverted to New York by the British, who were preparing to relinquish control of the city. He remained in the United States serving synagogues in New York and then Philadelphia, where he died in 1811.

In 1846, Shearith Israel's trustees—with assistance from the Spanish and Portuguese synagogues in New York and London—embarked on a search for the ideal candidate to lead the Montreal congregation. The successful prospect had to be able to deliver sermons in English. From a list of three possible candidates, the trustees chose twenty-one-year-old Abraham de Sola, who was not an ordained rabbi and used the title "Reverend." He accepted the offer and never looked back. With the "bearing of [an] ancient high priest," De Sola was Canada's first true Jewish religious leader. He influenced all those who crossed his path, and rightly commanded respect from Jews and Christians alike as a "gentleman of high intellectual powers."

De Sola was born in London in 1825. His family's Sephardic origins went back to fifteenth-century Spain and Portugal; his great-great-great grandfather David de Sola was tortured in the Portuguese Inquisition, and David's son Aaron (Abraham's great-great grandfather) fled Portugal for the safety of London in the 1740s. Both Abraham's maternal grandfather, Dr. Raphael Meldola, and his father, David Aaron de Sola, were rabbinical scholars associated with the Sephardi Bevis Marks synagogue—Meldola as chief rabbi and de Sola as a non-ordained *hazan*. Both, too, wrote influential religious commentaries. David Aaron de Sola was especially prolific, translating the Hebrew Scriptures into English and authoring books on Sephardi history and culture. Abraham was tutored by his father as well as by Dr. Louis Loewe, a German

Jewish academic and "Oriental" (Middle Eastern and Asian) language expert. The intellectual drive, work ethic, and religious philosophies of his grand-father, father, and teacher had a powerful impact on young Abraham. So, too, did the liberal education he received at the City of London School. By the time he was a teenager, Abraham was a model anglicized Orthodox Jew.

After accepting the post at Shearith Israel, de Sola journeyed to New York and then Montreal the following January, a trip that took forty-three days. Montreal in 1847 was no longer the mere town it had been in 1800. Now it was the largest city in British North America, and the key urban centre of the United Province of Canada—in 1840, the British had passed the Act of Union, uniting Upper and Lower Canada (now designated Canada West and Canada East respectively)—with a population that had more than quadrupled in four and half decades to about 50,000. It was a thriving city dominated by the English, Scottish, Irish, and French, and home to less than 250 Jews. Culturally, Montreal in the pre-Confederation period was definitely a British city. "The English language was everywhere," the city's historian Paul-André Linteau notes. "Protestant churches, schools, and associations multiplied. The city's architecture was transformed as it began to draw on British inspiration."

Following his father's approach, de Sola freely used English in his sermons and writings, but disdained any attempts to "Protestantize" Judaism—with organ music, for example, or bar mitzvahs that resembled confirmations—as the growing Reform movement advocated. His view was more moderate on the religious debate that ultimately laid the foundations for the Conservative branch of Judaism. In this enduring and contentious dispute, de Sola was a follower of the German Ashkenazi rabbi Samson Raphael Hirsch (1808–88), who melded Orthodox Judaism with the modern world.

Unlike the pious Hasidim who deliberately isolated themselves, Hirsch maintained it was possible to be a devout Jew and also receive a secular educa-tion, attend theatre, and read German literature. His motto was, in Hebrew, "Torah im derekh eretz"—that Torah, or Jewish law, should accommodate to derekh eretz, the general norms of the non-Jewish world—a precept that de Sola preached and practised throughout his life. "I too am a reformer as far as endeavours which I believe to be consistent and legal in the manner of Synagogue worship are concerned," he later wrote to his friend and mentor Isaac Leeser, the lay leader of the Congregation Mikveh Israel in Philadelphia. "I don't think the cause of orthodoxy would suffer much did conservative synagogues introduce quiet and respectability in their services ... Orthodoxy by nature and by character is respectable. Absurd and inconsistent novelty in the Synagogue is disreputable in its very essence."

Within five years of arriving in Montreal, de Sola had married Esther Joseph, the youngest daughter of the successful fur and tobacco merchant Henry (Harry) Joseph of Berthier-en-Haut (Berthierville), a nephew of Aaron Hart and the son-in-law of Levy Solomons. According to educator Dr. Susan Landau-Chark, Esther could be considered Montreal's first *rebbetzin* (a title for a rabbi's wife). She and Abraham were provided with a house next to the synagogue and in time would have seven children—among them Meldola, who followed his father as the religious leader at Shearith Israel, and Clarence, a wealthy businessman and early Zionist leader.

One of Abraham de Sola's responsibilities was to promote and foster Judaism among families in which intermarriage was frequent. Indeed, he tackled his new position with the zealousness of a workaholic, emulating his father's drive and scholarship. And when not leading regular services at the synagogue and diplomatically dealing with the various contentious religious and member-related issues that the role entailed, he kept himself busy with other tasks and initiatives. Within a few months of his appointment he had started a synagogue Sunday Hebrew school for children, and then in 1874 he was the driving force behind opening the first Jewish private day and boarding school in Canada. The Spanish and Portuguese free school offered religious instruction in Hebrew as well as classes in English. Most unusual of all, especially given Shearith Israel's poor finances, the school was free and open to Jewish children regardless of whether their parents were members of the congregation or not. The school—and subsequent attempts to establish other Jewish schools in Montreal—was not without its problems, though, due to the bickering within the community and the challenges of navigating through the minefield of Quebec's dual Catholic and Protestant school system.

Like his father, Abraham De Sola was a prolific scholar. He wrote articles and books on Jewish law, the plight of Jews in Persia (Iran), chronicles of Jews in Poland and France, and explored scientific and medical aspects of the Scriptures—among other diverse subjects that drew his interest. Ahead of his time, he argued that providing women with painkilling medication during childbirth was not, as was believed, contrary to the Scriptures. He regularly contributed to Jewish newsletters like the *Occident*, the first English-language Jewish journal in the United States, established by his friend Isaac Leeser in 1843. And he lectured on Hebrew, rabbinic, and Middle Eastern literature at McGill University, after he was recruited by William Dawson, McGill's esteemed principal. None of these pursuits—including his synagogue position—paid him much money, and he perpetually struggled to support his family financially. On more than one occasion, he contemplated job offers from synagogues in the United States, yet each time the Shearith Israel trustees convinced him to stay and raised sufficient funds to keep him happy, if temporarily.

McGill, like many Canadian universities and colleges, was later tainted with antisemitism, but not in the mid-nineteenth century, when the number of Jews in Montreal was insignificant in comparison to the period after the First World War. De Sola told Leeser that Dawson "has a claim on Jews. He respects Hebrew learning and the Hebrew language . . . He is a man of depth, and he is out on our side." He wasn't exaggerating. In 1858, McGill awarded de Sola with an honorary Doctor of Laws—another Jewish first in England and North America—proof to him, as he told Alexander Levy, the president of Shearith Israel, of "the cheering fact that in Montreal at least there is no bar, unless our want of self-respect erect it, to prevent the Israelite from reaching the goal which all right thinking men aspire to attain." He was further assured of the correctness of his opinion when in the spring of 1864 he was asked to impart his wisdom in the convocation address. And then, in 1872, in a singular distinction and an indication of his respected reputation outside Montreal, he was invited—possibly by U.S. President Ulysses Grant, hoping to ease tensions with Britain arising from the Civil War years—to offer a prayer for the opening session of Congress. He was not the first Jew asked to do this, but he was the first British subject and foreigner to be accorded such an honour.

Abraham de Sola's energy was high and his interests were varied. He participated in Montreal's Mercantile Library, Literary Club, Mechanics Institute, and Natural History Society, which elected him president in 1867–68. As small groups of German and Polish Jews, many who were impoverished, arrived in the city—some via the United States—they increased Montreal's Jewish (or "Israelite") population to approximately 950 by 1881 (the number had decreased in the 1870s and then rebounded). In response, de Sola established the Hebrew Philanthropic Society, with assistance from community leaders such as Moses Hays, to raise money for the newcomers. Still, he was a Sephardi snob on the subject of "backward" Polish Jews, who he referred to as "Pollacks." In 1859, he had refused to attend the ceremony for the official laying of the cornerstone for the new English, German, and Polish congregation synagogue on St. Constant Street (now Rue de Bullion), though this was likely less a disagreement about religious customs and owed more to the fact that de Sola had got caught up in a financial dispute between members of his board and the board of the Ashkenazi synagogue. (Rabbinical disagreements aside, the members of the two synagogues did work together on the Young Men's Hebrew Benevolent Society, which was founded in 1863 and was the community's first major Jewish charitable organization.) He had similar attitudes toward French Canadians, noting in 1861 with typical Anglo superiority that the Canadian *habitants* were "doubtless a worthy, happy, contented [people] so far as creature comforts, and, perhaps, business transactions, are concerned . . . yet few would charge them with too much intellectuality, enterprise, or with a too free spirit of inquiry either in matters spiritual or secular."

In 1874, the philanthropic society, which subscribed to the principal "Union is Strength," divvied up $542 between forty-two immigrant families. The Ladies' Hebrew Benevolent Society, which de Sola also helped organize, did its part, too. As his reputation grew beyond the city, de Sola, who corresponded regularly with Isaac Leeser as well as Sir Moses Montefiore, the British financier and philanthropist, linked Montreal with the worldwide Jewish community. Still, ignorance about Canada's relatively small Jewish populationand its key leaders persisted. In an 1886 feature article about established Anglo Jewish families in the *Jewish Chronicle* of London, the most widely read English-language Jewish newspaper of the era, de Sola, who had died four years earlier on trip to New York, barely got a mention.

In Montreal, Abraham de Sola's life, career, and death—he was only fifty-six years old when he passed away in June 1882—was news among the city's Jews and the larger Anglo community. His eldest son Meldola assumed his father's position as the rabbi at the Shearith Israel (the Spanish and Portuguese synagogue, as it was then known), where he led the congregation until his own death in 1918, cementing the de Sola dynasty for seventy-one years.

Meldola, who with his neatly trimmed hair and beard was the epitome of a modern man, was seemingly easy-going, yet that was merely a facade. Underneath that veneer, he was a "born meddler" (as historian Michael Brown labels him) and a fierce opponent of the Reform movement, which in the latter part of the nineteenth century had gradually migrated to Canada from the United States and Western Europe. In numerous mainly anonymous letters to newspapers and journals, Meldola derided all attempts to reform or Protestantize Judaism. To him, such Reform practices as mixed seating (in Orthodox synagogues, men and women sit separately), prayer services conducted almost entirely in English, integration of music and choirs, the playing of church-like organs, and in later years optional use of prayer shawls and *kippot* (skull caps), were anathema. In 1888, he even publicly castigated the members of his own congregation who he charged were "indifferent . . . to the religious education of their children" and more concerned with "music, painting, drawing, and dancing . . . [than] Hebrew and religious knowledge." At the dedication ceremony for the new Shearith Israel on Stanley Street (the synagogue's third home) two years later, Meldola, as reported in the *Montreal Herald*, delivered a sermon "admonishing the congregation to uphold Orthodox Judaism and to remain faithful to its teachings." In line with modern Orthodox thinking (as opposed to ultra-conservative and insular Hasidism), he was also a supporter of the early Zionist movement—he was later involved with the Canadian Zionist Society—and a Jewish homeland in Palestine, years before Theodor Herzl became Zionism's most well-known advocate.

Meldola was close to his younger brother Clarence, a successful business-man, contractor, philanthropist, and committed Zionist leader. Owing to Clarence's connection to a Belgian steel company, he was appointed Belgium's consul to Montreal in 1905. Clarence, an avid sportsman when he was younger, enjoyed social activities with his many non-Jewish friends. And in 1901, on the occasion of the visit of the Duke and Duchess of Cornwall and York (later King George v and Queen Mary) to Montreal, Meldola and his wife Katie were proudly among those invited to meet with the royal couple.

The de Sola brothers thus had one foot in the Anglo world and the other firmly in the Orthodox Jewish world of their father. Both brothers kept kosher (as did their other siblings), and kept the Sabbath and the other Jewish holidays. Yet they were no less proud of being British subjects than Canada's first prime minister, John A. Macdonald, who famously proclaimed during his last election campaign in 1891, "A British subject I was born—a British subject I will die." The de Solas and their friends were British subjects who merely happened to be Israelites.

Synagogue Politics

There were only about 120 Jews living in Toronto in the 1850s. The majority were immigrants from England and Central Europe who had come to the city from the U.S. or Montreal. Most of the men were shopkeepers who sold jewellery, clothing, and tobacco. At a time when the city was dealing with the impact of thousands of impoverished Irish Catholic immigrants—by 1851, one in four Torontonians (7,940) was Catholic and nearly all of those were Irish—the hundred or so Jews in the city were a secondary consideration.

The Rossin brothers, Marcus and Samuel, arrived in Toronto from Germany in 1842. They established a store on King Street, close to the main shopping area, specializing in "Jewellery, Watches, and Fancy Goods," according to an 1846 advertisement. The Rossins were astute businessmen. In 1855, the brothers purchased an empty plot of farmland on the southeast corner of King and York streets and erected Rossin House, five storeys high with white pressed brick. The total cost was about $250,000. When it opened two years later, it was Toronto's finest hotel. The Rossin House Hotel was able to accommodate more than five hundred guests, and it was the establishment of choice for visiting dignitaries and celebrities. This included Albert Edward, the eighteen-year-old Prince of Wales (the future King Edward VII), who stayed at the hotel in September 1860 during the tour of Canada and the United States he undertook at the behest of his mother, Queen Victoria.

But the Rossins soon ran into bad luck. In mid-November 1862, the hotel was destroyed in a raging fire in which several guests died. The property damage was $200,000 and the brothers did not carry enough insurance to rebuild it. The brothers carried on with their jewellery store and also opened a wholesale tobacco shop. Dissatisfied with their future prospects, Samuel soon departed Toronto for the United States, and Marcus went back to Germany in 1864.

Lewis Samuel, an Orthodox British Jew—"stout" and "hearty" according to his son, the noted Toronto business tycoon and arts patron Sigmund Samuel—was instrumental in organizing one of Toronto's first synagogue congregations in 1856, almost as soon as he had arrived in the city. In 1843, when he was sixteen years old, Samuel had left his religious Jewish family in London for the United States. He lived in New York and Syracuse before moving briefly to Montreal in 1855 (where his brother Mark worked as a fur trader), with his wife Kate Seckelman and their young children. Unhappy with Montreal, and following the death of two of their children from cholera, Lewis and Kate opted for Toronto. Lewis's brother soon joined him and they opened a wholesale hardware trade company; they decided on a wholesale business mainly because working on the Sabbath was not required, unlike for a retail shop. This marked the beginning of Lewis Samuel's successful business career, in which he was involved in a range of commercial enterprises, among them pioneering the manufacturing of barbed wire that his company supplied to the Canadian Pacific Railway (CPR).

In early September 1856, Samuel, who had arranged for a New York *shochet* who could also lead prayer services to come to Toronto, organized a meeting for other members of the city's budding Jewish community. Sufficient funds were pledged for the establishment of the Toronto Hebrew congregation, which held prayers in a rented room over Neil Love's drug store on Yonge Street near Richmond. With Torah scrolls borrowed from the Spanish and Portuguese synagogue in Montreal, the inaugural High Holiday services were held there at the end of the month. In attendance were about a hundred men and women, including Jews from nearby towns and villages.

The Toronto Hebrew congregation was to endure as the Holy Blossom synagogue. The name change originated in 1857 from the gift of a Torah scroll and silver pointer (used in reading the Torah) by Gottschalk Ascher of

Montreal, whose son Albert was a synagogue member. Inscribed on the pointer in Hebrew was: "The Holy Congregation, Blossoms of Holiness [in Hebrew, *Pirchei Kodesh*], in the city of Toronto." The use of the term "Blossoms of Holiness" (or Holy Blossoms) was a bit of a mystery and may have been based on a Talmudic reference. Whatever the reason, it resonated with the membership and its adoption as the synagogue's name was eventually made official in July 1871, at first as the Toronto Holy Blossoms congregation, until "Blossoms" was altered to "Blossom." The controversial transition from Orthodox to Reform would not occur officially until 1920. However, there was a tug of war for many years between traditionalists like Lewis Samuel and the increasing number of liberals who preferred a more modern prayer service with English, mixed seating, and instrumental and vocal music.

As Toronto's Jewish population increased, reaching 350 in 1875, the rented room above the drug store proved inadequate. Samuel, then the synagogue president, led a fundraising campaign to purchase land on the south side of Richmond Street, east of Victoria, and build the Holy Blossom's first home for a cost of $12,000. Jewish as well as non-Jewish donors from Toronto, Montreal, New York, and Boston contributed to the new synagogue that could seat four hundred people. Reverend Meldola de Sola, visiting from Montreal, officiated over the dedication service in late January 1876, in which a ladies' choir sang, a sign of encroaching liberalism in the view of some members of the congregation. The festivities ended with a ball and a dinner that evening at Albert Hall, where about sixty couples "seemed to thoroughly enjoy themselves," as the *Globe* reported. "Dancing was kept up to an early hour of the morning."

An early, though not lasting, supporter of the synagogue was Newman Leopold Steiner, an immigrant from Bavaria who had come to Toronto at the age of twenty-three in 1852. He opened N.L. Steiner Marble Works, a successful enterprise which provided marble for the construction of many of the city's buildings. In 1870, Steiner was appointed a Justice of the Peace, and a decade later was elected an alderman for St. James' Ward, the beginning of a career as a civic politician that stretched into the 1890s. Though he is remembered as the first Jew in Toronto's history to serve at City Hall, the truth was that by the time of his first electoral victory, he had already distanced himself from the Holy Blossom and the Jewish community. Later, members of his family, though not him, joined the Unitarian Church. When he died in 1903, he was buried in his family's non-denominational plot in Mount Pleasant Cemetery.

The Holy Blossom's main problem was the same one experienced by nearly every other early Canadian synagogue: finding religious officials to lead the services and perform Jewish rituals. It took until 1880 for the Holy Blossom to hire a properly trained cantor, and it was another decade before it found an ordained minister, Reverend Barnett Elzas, who was married to Annie Samuels, the sister of Katie de Sola, Mendola's wife. But the fact that Elzas and Mendola de Sola were brothers-in-law did not stop Mendola from publicly criticizing Elzas's embrace of Reform Judaism.

Elzas's key ally was the leader of the liberal faction at Holy Blossom, Edmund Scheuer, a diehard proponent of Reform. Born in 1847 in a Prussian village southwest of Koblenz, Germany, Scheuer had immigrated to Canada at the age of twenty-four to join a relative who had established a jewellery business in Hamilton, Ontario. There were less than fifty Jews living in Hamilton at the time and only one congregation—Temple Anshe Sholom, Canada's first Reform synagogue. Within two years, Scheuer became president of Anshe Sholom's board, a position he held until he relocated to Toronto in 1886 to open a wholesale jewellery company. In Hamilton, he had founded and taught at the Anshe Sholom's religious school and advanced Reform-style customs. As a member of the Holy Blossom board, which he served on for more than five decades, Scheuer campaigned relentlessly for a radical reinvention of the prayer services—a battle he ultimately won. When he died in July 1943 in a collision with a streetcar, he was rightly hailed as the "Father of Reform Judaism in Canada."

Until Elzas and his family left for the United States in 1892, where he became an important figure in the American Reform movement, he was embroiled in the Orthodox-Reform feud at the Holy Blossom over contentious issues like the use of an organ during Sabbath prayers, which was contrary to Orthodox Jewish law. He tried to appease the Orthodox faction, but intellectually and spiritually he was a Reform Jew. Eventually, in a religious dispute repeated in numerous Canadian Jewish communities, many of the Orthodox members abandoned Holy Blossom and joined the more tradi-tional Goel Tzedec congregation (later Beth Tzedec).

In Toronto, Lithuanian and other Eastern European Jews, who had arrived in the city beginning in the early 1880s (discussed in further detail in Chapter Six) and who were not happy with the increasingly Reform-style prayer services at the Holy Blossom, established Goel Tzedec ("Righteous Redeemer") in 1883. Services were first held in a rented room at the corner of Richmond and York Streets. A year later, the congregation relocated to a former Methodist church at University Avenue and Elm Street.

Despite the hardships of their lives, the Eastern Europeans were insistent on praying in synagogues which were in accord with their old-world tradi-tions. The result was a plethora of new and small synagogue congregations in Montreal, Toronto, and Winnipeg, most established by *landsmen*, immigrants who came from the same old-country geographic area, village, or *shtetl*. Thus in 1886, when the English, German, and Polish congregation vacated their building on St. Constant Street in Montreal, the B'nai Jacob ("Sons of Jacob") congregation—organized by Russian Jews—purchased the property. Like-wise, a group of Romanian Jews established Beth David ("House of David") and moved into Shearith Israel's former home on Chenneville Street. And Beth Yehuda ("House of Judah") was started by Orthodox Jews from Russia, who worshipped initially at a rabbi's home before purchasing a former theatre in the 1890s; while Chevra Kadisha ("Holy Society") was organized in 1893, initially as a benevolent burial society in a former factory on the lower part of St. Urbain Street.

In 1887, in a common occurrence, old-country differences over synagogue customs and rituals surfaced, and a group of Russians and Galician Jews (from southeastern Poland and northwestern Ukraine) left Toronto's Goel Tzedec to establish their own congregation, Beth Hamidrash Hagadol Chevra Tehillim ("The Great House of Prayer of the Congregation of Psalms"). Their first services were held above a blacksmith's shop, also near Richmond and York, and by 1905 the congregation had its own synagogue on McCaul Street, beyond the border of the Ward and closer to the Spadina–Kensington Market area, which Toronto Jews dominated in the years before and after the First World War. Though the two synagogues reunited in the 1950s to establish the current Beth Tzedec on Bathurst Street, south of Eglinton Avenue, in the early years the Goel Tzedec members regarded the Chevra Tehillim with a snobbish disdain, referring to the breakaway congregation as the *Kosatzke shul* or the "synagogue of the Cossacks."

By 1914, there were close to two dozen different synagogues and mutual aid societies or *landsmanshaftn* in Toronto. Russian Jews had the Shaarei Tzedec, established in 1902 and Romanians the Congregation Adath Israel of Toronto, which was organized in 1902. There was the "Kiever" synagogue, started in 1912 by immigrants from Kiev, which ran out of a rented house in the Ward for more than a decade until sufficient money was raised for a real sanctuary on Bellevue Avenue near Spadina. Also in 1912, Jews from Minsk established the Beth Israel Anshei Minsk congregation, or the "Minsker," which was also in the Kensington Market area—and remains there to this day, though in another building across the street from its original location. Today, the Anshei Minsk is the lone downtown synagogue still to hold daily services, while the Kiever offers Sabbath and High Holiday services.

In 1890, a group of Galician Jews had established Shomrai Shabbos Anshei Estreich Minhag Sefard ("Guardians of the Sabbath, Men of Austria who pray according to Sephardi custom"), which used rented rooms on Richmond Street before moving to a building on Chestnut Street in 1899 (today the Orthodox synagogue is known as Shomrai Shabbos-Chevrah Mishnayos and is located north of Eglinton on Glengrove Avenue West, where it has been for nearly five decades). Seven years later, the synagogue welcomed newly arrived Galician immigrants as members of the congregation—members who had their own ideas about certain religious customs. (Galicia, which borders Poland and the Ukraine, was under the control of the Austro-Hungarian Empire until after the First World War.) A bitter feud soon erupted between the two sides about the synagogue's practices and future direction.

In April 1906, at the prayer services held on the eve of Passover, the newcomers and older members became embroiled in a heated dispute over the synagogue's finances and operations. The disagreement turned into a physical altercation, and the police had to be called to break up the riot, which spilled out onto Chestnut Street. The sordid details—much to the embarrassment of the entire Toronto Jewish community—were reported in the next day's newspapers. Most of the disgruntled members soon left the Shomrai Shabbos and joined with another smaller Galician congregation to form a new synagogue on Terauley Street (Bay Street), which they gave the name Machzikei Hadath ("Upholders of Tradition"). There was no hiding their feelings of anger and defiance.

Ottawa's tiny Jewish community—numbering only forty-six people in 1891—had a very different dilemma. In 1892, the Adath Jeshurun ("Congregation of Israel") was the first congregation in the city, and as of 1895 it was located in a small wooden structure in Lowertown, where the immigrant Jews resided. The problem was that next to the synagogue, on Murray Street in the ByWard Market, was a food processing plant that used lots of pork. And hence the smell of cooking pork constantly wafted through the synagogue.

The story in Winnipeg was similar to that in Montreal and Toronto. The Orthodox Russian Jews organized their own traditional congregations almost immediately, yet as in other cities they remained divided by old-country or work connections. There was Anshay Roosia ("People of Russia") above the Royal Crown Soap factory on Henry Avenue and close by on Higgins Avenue was the small Milchige ("Milk") synagogue, so called because everyone, from the president of the synagogue on down, was a milkman. Yet another was the Shtall Shulach or "Little Stable synagogue," which was located beside a livery barn.

The English and German settlers, along with some of the more prominent Russian newcomers, established the Shaarey Zedek synagogue in 1889 at the corner of King Street and Henry Avenue, south of the CPR tracks. In this congregation, the use of the English language was deemed acceptable. Thereafter, the Shaarey Zedek—which relocated to a larger building on Dagmar Street in 1907, and then to its current home in the south end of the city on Wellington Crescent and Academy Road in 1949—was the synagogue of the establishment, and remains so in the present day.

The peace between the modernists and the traditionalists, the majority of whom were Russian, did not last long at the Shaarey Zedek, however, and by 1890 a splinter group had left to form their own synagogue, the Beth Israel on Martha Street. A fire later destroyed the Beth Israel, and the congregation decided to purchase a property across the street in order to build a new wooden synagogue called the Rosh Pina ("Head of the Cornerstone," and also the name of a town founded in then northern Palestine in 1882).

One of Rosh Pina's first members was Ekiel Bronfman, who had come to Canada in 1891 from Bessarabia (now the Republic of Moldova) with his wife Mindel and their children, Abe, Harry, Laura, and Sam, the youngest. Though Sam was likely born on the ship during the journey, the legendary business tycoon later claimed he was born in Manitoba. For about a year, Ekiel had attempted farming with Jews at an agricultural colony near Wapella (now in Saskatchewan) and living in a sod hut, but like many others he could not make a go of it. By the spring of 1892, Bronfman was peddling wood in Brandon, Manitoba, and moved his entire family there. As Brandon did not yet have a proper synagogue, the Bronfmans travelled into Winnipeg for the High Holidays, and thus Ekiel's link with the Rosh Pina congregation was established.

During the winter months, the Rosh Pina frequently had difficulty assembling the requisite ten men for a *minyan* for daily prayer services. On one occasion, Moishe Elitzer, the synagogue's sexton, ran out onto Martha Street in search of Jewish men for that day's *minyan*. As Isaac Portigal, a long-time member of the Rosh Pina, later told the story: Elitzer saw three bearded men in black suits and hats. "*Kumen arein tzu a minyan*" ("Come in for a *minyan*"), he said to them. The men hesitated, but followed Elitzer into the synagogue. The service proceeded, and when the prayers were completed, the other congregants offered their hands to the three newcomers. It was only then that everyone realized the three men were not Jewish at all, but Mennonite farmers.

Despite the continual bitter disputes over customs and rituals, the leaders of the small Winnipeg Jewish community—which numbered only 1,200 by 1901—forged ahead, despite being isolated on the Prairies. They established synagogue-based schools, Jewish cemeteries, and supported kosher butchers

and a *shochet*. In 1895, the Young Hebrew Social Assembly Club was organized, which was renamed the Young Men's Hebrew Association four years
later. That same year, Jewish Winnipeggers enjoyed a performance of the
visiting Hebrew Operatic and Dramatic Society of New York—in a show
that the *Manitoba Free Press* called "a novelty in the West." It marked the
beginning of the community's vibrant culture of Yiddish and Hebrew music
and drama that was to develop more fully in the years ahead.

From Coast to Coast

As the story goes, the 1879 Yom Kippur prayer service in Saint John, New Brunswick, almost didn't happen, because the men gathered for a *minyan* could not find the required tenth adult male. Why one of the other ten to fifteen Jewish men (of the city's total Jewish population of approximately forty-eight people) would not participate is unclear. Desperate, the leader of the *minyan* spotted a Jewish traveller in a hotel about to head back to his home in Boston, and convinced him to remain long enough for the Day of Atonement prayers to be recited.

Like those who lived elsewhere in Canada, the Jews who found their way to Saint John were largely engaged in small business. And most, such as Nathan Green and his brother-in-law Solomon Hart, were tobacco merchants. Green was born in Amsterdam in 1828, lived for a time in London, and then moved to New York City in the early 1850s. In 1859, Green and his wife Jane Hart joined her brother Solomon and his wife Alice in Saint John, where they had settled a year earlier.

The city, then the third-largest in British North America, was for a brief moment, or so it seemed later, a thriving port and the focus of the timber trade and shipbuilding industry. That prosperity was to decline within a decade, as steam and iron replaced "wood, wind and sail" (as the *Canadian Encyclopedia* puts it). Thereafter, Saint John's economy stagnated and its population decreased. Green and Hart nonetheless had faith in the city's future. They built up their tobacco enterprises and laid the foundations of the city's Jewish community and its institutions. In 1882, Green's eldest son Louis married his first cousin Elizabeth Hart, Solomon's daughter, in the first Jewish wedding celebrated in the Maritimes. A rabbi from Boston officiated. Their son Solomon Hart Green, born in 1885, became a lawyer and moved to Winnipeg in 1907. At the age of twenty-four, he was to become the first Jew elected to the Manitoba legislature.

The Saint John Jewish community reached a population of 848 in 1921, its highest total. Since then, the number of the Jews in the city has steadily dropped. As of 2013, there were less than two hundred, and only one synagogue was still in operation, the Shaarei Zedek ("Gates of Righteousness").

Since Confederation, the Jewish population of the Maritimes has remained tiny: in 1881, there were only about eighty-seven Jews living in Nova Scotia, New Brunswick, and Prince Edward Island; a decade later, there were just over a hundred. About thirty Jews, most of whom came from the Thirteen Colonies, had settled in Halifax as early as the 1750s, but a century later little trace of them or their families remained. Most of the Maritime Jews worked as merchants, yet they frequently did not live as Jews, either by choice or because of the isolated communities they resided in. It would take some years before enduring (though still relatively small) Jewish communities—mainly the result of the post-1880 immigration from Eastern Europe—would take shape in Halifax, Saint John, and a few other cities in the region. In 1931, for example, Halifax's Jewish population was 582, which more than doubled by 1991 and reached 2,120 in 2011. By the early 1990s, there were two synagogues: the Baron de Hirsch Hebrew Benevolent Society, an Orthodox synagogue that had been established in 1890, which eventually became known as the Beth Israel synagogue; and a Conservative splinter, Shaar Shalom, that was founded in 1953 by Baron de Hirsch families who desired mixed seating. In Prince Edward Island, it was not until 1975 that a High Holiday service took place—using a Torah scroll borrowed from a synagogue in Halifax.

Across the vast expanse of the continent, in Victoria, a far different Jewish story was unfolding during the mid-nineteenth century. As of 1849, the town was the frontier hub of the British Crown Colony of Vancouver Island, which in 1866 was merged with the mainland Crown Colony of British Columbia, a territory that would become the province of British Columbia in 1871.

Victoria had been founded in 1843 as a Hudson's Bay Company (HBC) out-post to trade with the area's First Nations. The discovery of gold on the main-land along the banks of the Fraser River, and then further north in the remote Cariboo region, transformed Victoria, as the only ocean port along the Island coast, into a distribution centre and entrance point for the long journey to the gold fields. Among the throngs flocking north to Fort Victoria from San Francisco and nearby towns—but looking to cash in on new economic opportunities as suppliers, rather than as gold miners—were dozens of Jews of British, German, and Polish origin, who had originally ventured to California when gold was discovered there. In Jackson, about two hundred kilometres east of San Francisco, John Levinsky—an observant Prussian-Jewish merchant, who with his two brothers, Louis and Mark, had opened a store and helped established a synagogue in 1857—decided to try his luck in B.C. But after a brief stay, Levinsky returned to the United States. Many more Jews such as Selim and Lumley Franklin, Henry Nathan Jr., and David Oppenheimer remained in the province. All four were destined to be elected to public office, and played key roles in the development of Victoria and Vancouver. But it was Victoria, a bustling tent city that almost overnight became a viable commercial centre, that was their first stop.

By 1862, the newly incorporated city had some eighty Jewish families numbering approximately 220 people, about four per cent of Victoria's total population. A decade later, once the gold rush had ended, only ninety-three remained. At the height of gold fever, Jews in Victoria operated a total of seventy shops and businesses—grocery, tobacco, clothing, and jewellery stores, as well as a few hotels and restaurants, and five auction houses.

In the fall of 1858, High Holiday services were held at a private residence. The next year, a group purchased land for a cemetery and organized the "Victoria Hebrew Benevolent Society." That in turn led to a successful fund-raising campaign, and by 1863 to the construction of the Temple Emanu-El, the oldest synagogue in Western Canada. Congregation Emanu-El, as it is known today, is still serving Victoria's Jewish community. The congregation only had fifty members when the cornerstone was laid, but in a spirit of optimism it was built to seat 350 people. Much of Victoria attended the synagogue's festive opening ceremonies, which included a marching band and a parade of notables. In the *British Colonist's* coverage of the celebrations there was nothing but praise for the "Hebrews" of Victoria. In the years that followed, the annual ball of the Hebrew Ladies of Victoria was a key event in the social calendar. There was, however, conflict within the community. The Victoria congregation experienced the emotional and divisive Orthodox and Reform dispute that characterized other early Canadian synagogues, with the Reform side ultimately prevailing.

The Franklin brothers were among the earliest Jewish settlers in the city. Selim Franklin had left the family's home in Liverpool in 1849 during the California gold rush and settled in San Francisco, where he opened a general store. By 1857, his older brother Lumley had joined him. By then, Selim was an auctioneer and land agent. With news of gold in British Columbia, Selim, ever the adventurer, journeyed to Victoria; again, his older brother Lumley soon followed him. The brothers went into business together under the name Selim Franklin & Company, Auctioneers and Land Agents.

The Franklins wisely befriended the governor of British Columbia and Vancouver Island, James Douglas. He appointed Selim, dubbed "silver tongued Franklin" in the press, as the colonies' official auctioneer. The Franklins made a lot of money in commissions, selling land in Victoria and at the future site of New Westminster on the mainland. Selim's wealth did not go unnoticed; he was accused of being a dishonest "land shark and specu-lator," a charge that likely had some validity. Still, Selim and Lumley, who did not broadcast the fact they were Jewish, were active in local affairs in Victoria, a town far more concerned about Aboriginals—and American and Chinese immigrants—than Jews.

In 1860, Selim was elected to the legislative assembly for the colony of Vancouver Island. He briefly became embroiled in an Ezekiel Hart–like controversy after he took the oath of office but omitted the phrase "on the true faith of a Christian." Two years earlier, the British Parliament had seem-ingly settled this issue when it passed the Jewish Disabilities Bill, which finally permitted Jews elected to the House of Commons (such as Lionel de Rothschild) to take their seats without first swearing the Christian oath.

Moreover, Governor Douglas had sought to eliminate any problems faced by Jews and Quakers with a new Oaths Act. Nonetheless, a few obstinate members of the Vancouver Island assembly were not as certain about the legislative changes. A heated debate ensued for a few weeks before the matter was resolved in Franklin's favour. He served in the assembly for several terms, resigning in 1866. The editor of the *Victoria Gazette*, no doubt echoing the sentiments of many people in the town, criticized the few assembly members who had raised the issue for their intolerance. "It is utterly absurd," he wrote, "to object to any man's religious opinions unless they interfere with his civil duties—and it cannot be asserted that a Jew's do. It is more probable that a Roman Catholic's might, yet he is admitted without hesitation."

Lumley Franklin did not face such problems in becoming the second mayor of Victoria in 1865 (and thus the first Jewish mayor of a Canadian city). In early November 1865, the *Daily Colonist* (formerly the *British Colonist*) published an open letter submitted by sixty of Franklin's friends urging him to run for the position of mayor. There were Jewish names on this list, but mainly it was Gentile business associates who were supporting his candidacy. In reply, Franklin wrote that he had not contemplated being the mayor of Victoria, but he was prepared to accept the "very flattering invitation" to let his name stand. He narrowly won the contest, defeating his opponent by five votes, and served with distinction. The fact that he was Jewish does not appear to have been a factor, nor as far as can be determined was it commented upon in the press during his term.

Henry Nathan Jr. had a similar experience. In 1871, he was elected a Member of Parliament (MP) for the constituency of Victoria in the new province of British Columbia and thus was the first Jew to have a seat in the House of Commons. (In 1856, George Benjamin, a newspaper owner from Belleville, east of Toronto—who eschewed his Jewish background—had been elected to the Province of Canada's legislative assembly, thus making him "the first Jew to be elected to the Canadian parliament," as his biographers Sheldon and Judith Godfrey assert.) Being Jewish played no part, one way or the other, in his short political career. Born in London, England, in 1842, Nathan had arrived in Victoria with his father, Henry Nathan Sr., when he was twenty years old. The two opened a wholesale importing business on Wharf Street, offering for sale everything from blankets, suits, and hats to fine brandy, sardines, and assorted twine.

He was first elected to the Legislative Assembly of British Columbia after the 1866 merger of Vancouver Island and the mainland. A staunch advocate for British Columbia to join Canada, he won a seat in 1871 in the House of Commons as a Liberal—first by acclamation in a November 1871 by-election, and again in the general election held in the fall of 1872. In Ottawa, the thirty-year-old Nathan was regarded "as a young gentleman of much promise as a public speaker." Despite being a Liberal Party MP, he was friendly with Conservative prime minister John A. Macdonald. During his two and half years in Parliament, Nathan wholeheartedly supported Macdonald's plans for the construction of a transcontinental railway—one of the incentives offered to B.C. to join Confederation—and he was later a member of the CPR's board of directors.

David Oppenheimer, who served as Vancouver's second mayor from 1888 to 1891—to date, the city's only Jewish mayor—experienced an even greater degree of tolerance; though it is also true that he was, like many of the Jews in British Columbia in this period, highly assimilated. With his distinguished black and silver van Dyke beard and his pince-nez eyeglasses, Oppenheimer had the regal bearing of a Prussian prince. He was born in 1834 in the picturesque town of Blieskastel in Bavaria, into a large Jewish family. In 1848, like thousands of other Jews who left Germany for America between 1815 and 1860, David and at least four of his brothers—Meyer, Charles, Godfrey, and Isaac—departed, leaving behind their parents and the economic hardships and political problems of their homeland. In search of new business ventures, they went first to New Orleans, before being lured to California by the commercial opportunities connected to gold mining.

With the onset of the Fraser gold rush, Oppenheimer and his brothers Charles and Isaac moved to Victoria and initially established a grocery business. They smartly followed the miners into the Interior, opening a wholesale supply firm with headquarters in a brick warehouse as well as a general store in Yale—with outlets at Lytton and Barkerville, among other mainland locales northeast of Vancouver. Their company, Oppenheimer Brothers, had its economic ups and downs, and the brothers temporarily lost control of the business for a few years, but it was reclaimed by Charles, David, and Isaac in 1871.

Venturing into the B.C. Interior at that time was fraught with danger. There were hostile aboriginals who were angry about the gold prospectors' invasion of their territory, and ruthless outlaws on the hunt for miners and merchants transporting lucrative gold through the treacherous frontier. Morris Price, who had immigrated to Victoria from Berlin in 1859, also followed the miners and established a general store at Cayoosh Flat (now Lillooet), 148 kilometres north of Yale, where the Oppenheimers' business was located. Late on February 1, 1861, two Aboriginal men entered Price's store, and robbed and murdered him. He was found the next morning "lying on his back with his throat cut from ear to ear," according to one local newspaper report. The perpetrators of the crime were eventually captured, tried before Judge Matthew Begbie, and hanged. Price was the first person to be interred in the Victoria Jewish Cemetery.

When the gold rush fever died down, David and Isaac Oppenheimer—who now controlled the Oppeheimer Brothers company—returned to Victoria and set up an import wholesale business on Wharf Street. With the CPR's decision to build its western terminus in the town of Granville—incorporated as the City of Vancouver in 1886—the Oppenheimers astutely moved again to the mainland, where David had already acquired a considerable amount of property, in 1885 or 1886. Thereafter, David emerged as one of the city's major boosters. He was instrumental in organizing the Vancouver Board of Trade, and his move into civic politics—first as an alderman in 1886 and then as mayor in December 1887—was a natural progression of his enthusiasm for all things Vancouver. Though not without his critics—who charged that he was "blinded by vanity and [an] overwhelming sense of his own importance," as the *Vancouver Daily News-Advertiser* put it—during his four terms as mayor, he supported the publicly owned Vancouver Waterworks Company and the expansion of electricity and streetcars, in which he was an active investor. When he died in December 1897, even the *Daily News-Advertiser* declared him as "the best friend Vancouver ever had."

Twenty years after he had left office, and fourteen years after his death, he was hailed as "Vancouver's greatest mayor" and was honoured by B.C.'s premier Richard McBride, Vancouver mayor Louis Taylor, and the rest of the city's WASP political establishment with a statute at the Beach Avenue entrance of Stanley Park, which Oppenheimer had officially opened as mayor in 1888.

Further east, a small Jewish community had also been established on the Prairies in Winnipeg, which was incorporated as a city in 1873. Winnipeg in this era was essentially a backwater village, with a few saloons and muddy streets so thick with gumbo that horse-pulled carts were regularly bogged down. Nevertheless, the mainly Ontario businessmen and traders who ventured west to populate the city were wildly optimistic about its future prospects. At some point during the mid-1870s, this optimistic fervour attracted the attention of the three Coblentz brothers—Adolphe, Edmond, and Aachel—who had emigrated from France to the United States in 1872. The brothers found their way to Bethlehem, Pennsylvania—a farming area founded by German-speaking Moravians, a Protestant sect from Saxony. Quite possibly, the Coblentzes heard about Manitoba from their Moravian and Mennonite business clients.

The eldest brother, Edmond, arrived in Winnipeg in 1877, and his wife Sarah and their two children followed a year later, along with Aachel and Adolphe. They were Winnipeg's first permanent Jewish residents. Edmond worked in a dry goods store before opening his own shop in a French-speaking village east of the city. Aachel also found employment in a dry goods store, and eventually went into business with Philip Brown (or Braun), another early Jewish settler. Adolphe and Sarah and their family remained in Winnipeg for several years. Sarah gave birth to a second son, William, in January 1879, the first Jewish child born in Manitoba. Eventually Adolphe and Sarah moved south, near Emerson, where Adolphe owned a small inn. In one classic photograph, the three brothers are impeccably dressed in fine black suits, and white shirts accented with wing-tipped collars and ascot ties. They sport fashionable thick moustaches, and gold watch chains dangle from their vest pockets. In every sense they were assimilated Europeans who also happened to be Jewish—or, more accurately, Israelites. They followed Jewish religious law as much as was possible in a nineteenth-century Western Canadian prairie town, but most of Adolphe and Sarah's children abandoned Judaism as adults. Only their daughter, Gabriella, married a Jew—Edgar Frankfurter, the son of George and Fanny Frankfurter, early Jewish immigrants to Winnipeg.

In 1881, a short-lived but utterly frantic land boom was triggered in Winnipeg by the news that the CPR was to build its main line through the city, rather than via Selkirk twenty-five kilometres to the north, where it had been originally proposed. Speculation was rampant, and profits on real estate skyrocketed to unheard-of levels, attracting more newcomers wanting a piece of the action. By the fall of 1881, when the boom was at its height, there were thirty-three Jewish families living in the city—about a hundred people in all. There were tailors, such as Philip Brown and Hiram Rosenthal, while Louis Wertheim owned a tobacco shop, and Hyman Miller was a partner in a hardware store.

George Frankfurter, who was born in a village near Hamburg, had left Germany in 1867 when he was twenty-five years old to make his way to New York City. After he met and married Fanny Saunders, they lived in Detroit, Omaha, and Iowa, and he became involved in the cigar business. George and Fanny decided to move to Winnipeg in 1880. Within four years, George had amassed enough money to open a dry goods store on Main Street. Two decades later, he transformed his retail business into G. Frankfurter & Sons, a large wholesaler.

There were also the Ripstein brothers—David, aged twenty-six, and Simon, twenty-one in 1877—who sold groceries, liquor, and cigars. Like Frankfurter, the Ripsteins came to Winnipeg via the United States, though they hailed from Kovno (Kaunas) in Lithuania. In the early 1870s, they had accompanied their parents to New York City, where the brothers learned to be merchants. David also worked in Denver and Montreal before he and his brother arrived in Winnipeg. Both, along with their brother Isaac, who was born in New York, became prominent leaders in the community. On July 29, 1882, in Manitoba's first Jewish wedding, David married twenty-three-year-old Annie Feinberg. The ceremony was performed by Reverend Abraham Benjamin, who had recently arrived in Winnipeg from New Orleans. Yet David and

Annie's marriage was to be short; three years later, in August 1885, Annie died of unknown causes. David was soon remarried to Mary Shapiro, a woman fifteen years his junior.

In 1882, there was still no synagogue in Winnipeg, though the issue of establishing one was under discussion. Prayer services were held in rented halls. Kosher meat was available—there was a part-time *shochet*—but Reverend Benjamin was the only Jewish clergyman in the city. For the most part, these early pioneers—like the Jews in Victoria, Toronto, Montreal, and other towns—were content with their status. While they maintained their religious traditions, they preferred to blend into the large communities in which they resided. They generally spurned public attention to their Jewish heritage. Such interest was tolerated with a shrug. In 1882, the migration of thousands of impoverished Yiddish-speaking Russian and Eastern European Jews to North America, many of whom landed in Canada, was to profoundly impact their lives and add a new dimension that was culturally enriching, as well as problematic and challenging.

In Search of the Golden Land

All through the latter half of 1881, and continuing into 1882, stories dispatched by European correspondents appeared regularly in Canadian newspapers, documenting the horrific treatment of Russian Jews, who were the victims of violent pogroms. The murder, rape, torture, beatings, and pillaging they were subjected to had been triggered by the assassination of Czar Alexander II on March 13, 1881, though that was merely a convenient excuse for the onslaught. Only one young Jewish woman, Gesia Gelfman, was thought to have been connected to the revolutionaries of the Narodnaya Volya ("The People's Will"), the perpetrators who bombed the czar's carriage in St. Petersburg. Nonetheless, in the weeks following the assassination there was a series of seemingly spontaneous, ruthless assaults on Jews in the southwest region of the Russian Empire. The bloody attacks were not planned by conspiratorial government officials, as was popularly believed at the time and afterward. In fact, the newly anointed Alexander III, who had inherited his father's throne, was shocked and unsettled by the violence. Still, the police in most instances did little to stop the carnage or protect the victims.

For instance, in mid-June 1881, as chronicled in the Toronto *Globe*, a witness near Kiev in Ukraine saw "a Jew attacked and barbarously maltreated in the street in the presence of the mounted police." Another Jew's house, "which was situated exactly opposite the police station," was wrecked. "Valuable furniture and other costly articles were hurled into the street and destroyed." In subsequent *Globe* articles there were also references to "indescribable misery," and the "horrible cruelties" inflicted on the Russian Jews.

The pogroms persisted for about sixteen months. The catalyst for the violence might well have been the murder of the czar, yet in the background was excessive poverty, high taxes, and the antisemitic laws of the empire, which "marked the Jews as distinctly inferior by discriminating against them even more than against the peasants themselves," in the words of historian Michael Aronson. Since the time of Catherine the Great in the late eighteenth century, Russian Jews had been compelled to live in the crowded western area of the mighty Russian Empire, in what was designated as the Pale of Settlement, the largest ghetto in the world. (The term "pale" originated from the Latin word *palus*, meaning a stake, or an area enclosed by a fence or boundary.)

By the 1850s, the Pale's fifteen provinces, which stretched north incorporating present-day Lithuania and southeast to the Black Sea—a vast area, as big as France and the United Kingdom combined—were home to nearly three million Jews, the majority of whom were of Polish descent. In time, many of these Jews would leave the Pale's small villages—the *shtetl* immortalized in the writings of the popular Yiddish and Hebrew writer Sholem Aleichem, whose stories about Tevye the Dairyman were transformed into the Broadway musical, *Fiddler on the Roof*—and migrate to the urban centres of the region: Vilna, Minsk, Kiev, and Bialystok. From there, around two million Jews from would leave the empire (as well as Romania) between 1882 and 1914. They journeyed to Western Europe and across the ocean to the United States—the *goldeneh medina*, or "golden land"—and Canada. In New York's Lower East Side, Montreal's "The Main," Toronto's St. John's Ward, and Winnipeg's North End, they established their unmistakable presence and a vibrant Yiddish culture that resonated for much of the twentieth century.

Canada was a clear second choice to the U.S., yet that did not stop close to 10,000 Russian and Eastern European Jews from coming to the country between 1880 and 1900—and close to 100,000 between 1901 and 1914. In 1881, Canada's total Jewish population was 2,473; by 1921 it was 125,197—about 1.42 per cent of the total Canadian population. Much of this increase was due to immigration from Russia and Central and Eastern Europe, a mass movement of people that was far from smooth.

———

In the aftermath of the 1881 pogroms, thousands of Jewish refuges made their way to Brody, a small city in Austro-Hungarian territory that was soon overwhelmed. Much like refugees from Syria in recent years, many Jews starved from lack of food, water, and shelter. Organizations like the Paris-based Alliance Israélite Universelle offered as much aid as they could, but there was also concern expressed about newcomers' quality. "The emigrants must be checked, otherwise we shall receive here all the beggars of the empire," Charles Netter, an official of the Alliance who visited Brody, told his superiors in Paris.

Meanwhile, established Jews in the United States as well as Canada— though moved by the terrible human rights situation—also wondered how their small charities would cope with so many destitute newcomers, regarded by some as "half-barbarians," in the view of Der Zeitgeist, a German Jewish journal published in Chicago and "wild Asiatics," according to the American Hebrew, a New York weekly. Worse, by association they would lower the estimation of the public toward all Jews in North America, "bringing them into contempt," declared Hyman Miller, a travelling salesman, who had arrived in Winnipeg from England in 1879.

Not everyone felt that way, and groups of Jews and Christians began meeting and organizing assistance efforts. In Montreal in January 1882, the Citizens' Committee Jewish Relief Fund was formed with much support from the Montreal Gazette, whose editors continually pressed the federal government to bring some of the refugees to Canada. Within several months, owing to the efforts of the Anglican bishop of Montreal, William Bennett Bond, the committee raised nearly $5,000. The city's Jewish men's and ladies' benevolent societies, along with the Anglo-Jewish Association of Montreal, also created an umbrella group, the Jewish Emigration Aid Society (JEAS)— similar to the Hebrew Immigrant Aid Society established in New York City in 1881—to prepare for the arrival of the refugees.

In London, the stories of Russian Jewish suffering had an impact on Christian leaders. On February 1, 1882, a public meeting was arranged at Mansion House, the residence of London's mayor, Sir John Whitaker Ellis, to discuss the issue. In attendance were Cardinal Henry Manning, the archbishop of Westminster; scientists Charles Darwin and John Tyndall;

representatives of the Baron Edmond de Rothschild of Paris; and from Canada, Alexander T. Galt, a father of Confederation and the country's first high commissioner to the United Kingdom. One result of this gathering was the creation of a fund to aid Jews who wanted to emigrate. Within a short time, this esteemed group had raised £100,000, and almost immediately Russian Jews began arriving in London at a rate of about a hundred per week, most telling lurid stories of misery.

Alexander Galt, astute and self-confident but with a penchant to be stubborn, moody, and "unstable as water," as Prime Minister John A. Macdonald called him, was motivated to assist the Jews by both his strong sense of humanitarianism and the economic benefits he anticipated for Canada—not least of which was attracting investment from the Rothschilds for a potential colonization company and possibly even the financially strapped CPR, then still under construction. In his opinion, the Russian Jews were "a superior class of people," as he told Macdonald. The key was controlling the flow. "We might have a lot of them thrown up on our shores unprovided for. By being on the Committee I can prevent this," Galt assured the prime minister. Thus the plans were set in motion for Canada's first post-Confederation experience with refugees.

Like many Canadians at the time, Macdonald was wary of admitting a large number of impoverished Jews into the country. But he agreed with Galt that a small group—"a Jew colony," as he described it—might in the long run prove useful. If they were not successful as farmers, the Jews would probably take up peddling and trade in second-hand clothing and other goods. "The 'Old Clo' [clothing] move is a good one," Macdonald wrote to Galt at the end of February 1882. "A sprinkling of Jews in the North West would do good. They would at once go in for peddling and politics and be of much use in the New Country as Cheap Jacks [hucksters] and Chapmen [peddlers]."

With official government approval, Galt worked out the arrangements with the Mansion House committee to transport a group of Russian Jewish refugees to Canada. In mid-May 1882, the first contingent of 260 arrived in Montreal, and over the next month a few hundred more came to settle in Ontario and Manitoba. According to the *Gazette*, the newcomers were "not particularly distinguished for cleanliness." A warehouse near Montreal's waterfront was converted into a dormitory, while some also boarded with the city's existing Jewish families. With funds from Mansion House, about 180 found housing and menial jobs and remained in Montreal. Their hopes high, the members of JEAS set up the Jewish Colonization Association, with the plan to settle some of the Russian Jews in Canada's northwest.

In the 1880s, the northwest was a massive area that incorporated a region that extended west from Manitoba to the Alberta-British Columbia border and north to the Arctic. Macdonald's first and biased thought had been that the Russian Jews would take up the traditional and oft-maligned Jewish vocation of peddling. However, the optimistic leaders of JEAS, as well as the idealistic members of the Am Olam ("Eternal People") socialist movement in Russia—of which a tiny minority of the refugees belonged—dreamed of becoming farmers in the New World, and transforming the Jews' long-standing and frequently detested economic role as middlemen.

About seventy of the newly-arrived Russian refugees moved on to Toronto, where they briefly resided in the basement of the Holy Blossom synagogue on Richmond Street. While the *Globe* urged Torontonians to offer the refugees assistance, only a few dozen of the Russian Jews ultimately stayed. Some preferred to try other cities and towns further west; others left Canada for the United States. More did arrive in the decades that followed, adding to the Eastern European and Yiddish flavour of Toronto's Jewish population.

By early June 1882, about 350 refugees finally reached Winnipeg after a difficult journey. They had little or no money and could not speak a word of English. There were tailors, blacksmiths, and cabinetmakers among them, in addition to many who were intent on life as pioneer settlers.

With hardware merchant Victor Victorson, who lived in Winnipeg, acting as their translator, the refugees spent their initial days on the prairies in the rickety wooden federal government immigrant sheds (located today near the Forks) living under military supervision. Funds and supplies to help them were raised, with donations coming from the mayor of Winnipeg, Alexander Logan, and Robert Machray, the bishop of Rupert's Land. Several of the

Jewish men jumped at the opportunity provided by a local businessman to earn a few dollars working half the night unloading two rafts of lumber. Other such menial jobs would be offered to them in the days and months ahead.

On their first Saturday in Winnipeg, the Russians held a Sabbath service in the sheds and tents, which elicited a few comments in the press. "The Jewish immigrants, who recently arrived, held divine service in the immigrant sheds this morning, presided over by one of the old Jewish rabbits [sic]," observed the *Winnipeg Daily Times*. It was left to the *Free Press* to correct its competitor, pointing out that "rabbis" rather than "rabbits" led Jewish prayers.

As many of the refugees waited patiently for the federal government to provide them with farmland, others took on back-breaking work with the CPR—splitting rails, laying track, and digging ditches. It was less than desirable employment, and made some of them tired and disillusioned. Early reports from the federal immigration agent and local employers were not especially encouraging, mainly because of language difficulties and the fact that they would not work on Saturdays. W.L. Bruce, who ran an employment agency, told the *Daily Times* that the newcomers were "very lazy." They refused to take on piecework, would only consent to contracts by the day, and then had the impudence to "ask the very highest wages." During a four-month period, the men earned about $250 each. But then they were swindled out of that money by, of all people, a CPR foreman named Kaufman, who was Jewish. He convinced them to invest in a land development which turned out to be worthless property.

There were also several incidents of antisemitic violence. In early July, at one work site at Whitemouth, Manitoba, northeast of Winnipeg, a group of Russian Jews who had been hired to work on the rail line faced undue harassment from the foreman. Then, as they were bedding down for the night in makeshift huts, a kind of Manitoba pogrom erupted. A mob of at least seventy men attacked them, beat them, and stole their kosher food (which the railway had graciously provided). Terrified, they fled, and with the aid of a Swedish machinist found refuge for the night at a country hotel, whose owner grudgingly let them hide in his barn. The next day, most of them returned to the city, but a brave bunch continued working for the railway.

But the most notorious episode of the time was an unprovoked attack on Kieva Barsky. He was laying tracks at Rosser station, northwest of Winnipeg, and by all accounts not troubling anyone. Suddenly, without warning, one of the non-Jewish workers, Charles Wicks, struck Barsky with an iron bar, injuring him. Once he recovered, Barsky reported the assault to the police, who arrested Wicks. The case against Wicks for attempted murder went to trial before Manitoba chief justice Edmund Burke Wood in mid-August. An interpreter was required for the proceedings, since Barsky and the other Jews who testified on his behalf could not speak English. After hearing conflicting testimony from a variety of witnesses, Judge Wood determined that there was not sufficient evidence to convict Wicks on the attempted murder charge. Instead, he found him guilty of assault and sentenced him to one month's imprisonment.

What made this case so noteworthy was not the attack on Barsky, though it indicated that the attitude toward the Russian Jews among some segments of the population was hardly welcoming; rather it was the passionate and liberal speech Judge Wood delivered when he sentenced Wicks. As the chief justice explained:

The complainant is of the race of the Jews ... The senseless and unmeaning persecution of that people by Christian communities—the once chosen people of God—driven from the home of their fathers by fire and sword into every land under heaven, now for upwards of 1800 years, appeals strongly to our sympathy, and makes us blush for our common Christianity. This man [Barsky] with others, by Russian Christianity, has been lately driven to our borders as an asylum from persecution of the laws aside from all other considerations; but in the case of the Hebrews, whenever they appear, they excite the warmest sympathy.

Jews like Barsky now understood that in Canada the law did not discriminate against them—in theory, at least. Because in practice Jews faced discrimination in and outside of the courtroom for many decades to come. Nevertheless, in hindsight it was a key moment in the country's Jewish history.

———

There was no doubting the genuine concern for the welfare of the Russian Jewish refugees by the larger Canadian Gentile community. Yet their strangeness, as both foreigners and Jews—the language problems, bizarre customs, dietary restrictions, and, like the victims of the Great Irish Famine forty years earlier, discernible poverty—produced a mixture of xenophobia and antisemitism of varying levels that persisted well into the twentieth century. In short, not every Canadian was as enlightened as Chief Justice Wood. In the view of Yosef Bernstein, one of the Jewish newcomers living in Montreal, the country had its share of "Haman-like people." And just as Haman—the villain from the Book of Esther, the tale recited during the holiday of Purim— wanted to annihilate Persian Jews, antisemites in Canada, Bernstein wrote in the Russian Jewish weekly *Ha-Melitz* in 1884, "impatiently await the day when they can demonstrate their anger . . . against the Jews."

The "angriest" and the "greatest of the antisemites," in Bernstein's view, was Goldwin Smith, revered in Toronto as the "sage of the Grange." Smith is usually remembered as a renowned liberal intellectual, which he was—except, that is, on the subject of Jews. Historian Gerald Tulchinsky concurs with Bernstein's assessment, designating Smith as "Canada's best known Jewhater." Smith was not sure what to do with the European Jews, yet he argued in 1878 that their disappearance from the continent would eliminate a "danger from Western civilization."

Canadians in the late nineteenth century did not spend a lot of their time thinking about Jews. But if they did, they were probably influenced by Smith, as was young William Lyon Mackenzie King, who in the early 1890s was a student at the University of Toronto and revered Smith. Decades later, when King had been prime minister for many years, he remembered what his old mentor Goldwin Smith had once said to him about Jews: "that they were poison in the veins of a community." His legendary diary has numerous references to Jews, and most of them are not positive.

Before coming to Canada in 1871, Smith taught modern history at Oxford and later at Cornell University in Ithaca, New York. In 1875, he smartly married Harriet (Dixon) Boulton, the wealthy widow of William Henry Boulton, a lawyer and member of Toronto's elite. She had her own family money and inherited the Boulton property, the Grange (now part of the Art Gallery of Ontario). Smith made the mansion his own, and its drawing room became the salon where he wrote and pontificated on the various issues of the day: democracy, imperialism, Canada–U.S. relations, women's suffrage, trade unions, Darwinism, urbanization, immigration, and, above all, Jews. He wrote for many magazines and newspapers, including his own review of current affairs, the *Bystander*, which was published intermittently between 1878 and 1891.

Smith was governed by one overarching conviction: his fervid belief in the superiority of the white Anglo-Saxon race. Any obstacle or threat to the white race's God-given right to dominate the Earth was to be dealt with and expunged. Consequently, Jewish enterprise—he detested the fact that a select number of Jews in Western Europe owned newspapers—and immigration to North America were troublesome, and even to be feared.

In Smith's view, Jewish determination to maintain a separate religious identity and not embrace the "civilized" Christian world was part of the problem. In his editorial articles, which were frequently reprinted in Canadian newspapers, he regularly promoted the classic negative stereotypes of Jews as deceitful and conspiratorial. The idea of Jews becoming farmers in the northwest was castigated.

As vitriolic as Smith was, he merely wrote and publicized negative views about Jews that were widely shared in North America during the late nineteenth and early twentieth centuries—especially about the downtrodden immigrants. Over the summer and into the fall of 1882, the initial sympathy and fascination with the Russian Jews waned. An editorial in the *Globe* in mid-July, pointing to the traditional role of Jews as middlemen, concluded that "while we cannot refuse hospitality and a fair chance to all who may come relying upon their own energies to make their way, the Jews are by no means the class of persons whose immigration should be aided by public funds."

In Winnipeg, the *Daily Times* was far nastier. Was there a "more helpless and useless lot of creatures [that ever] crossed the Atlantic," it asked its readers. Jews were "communistic," and "do not seem to know cleanliness." Meanwhile, the *Edmonton Bulletin* declared that, owing to the Dominion government's lax immigration policies, the country was being invaded by "Jews and heathens, paupers and criminals." The *Manitoba Free Press* was kinder, arguing that the future of the Jews in Canada was not "hopeless," as its competitors argued. Still, its editors conceded that "it is not denied that [the Jews] came here only half-civilized; indeed, after having been as a people, for ages ground down by their oppressors, they could hardly be otherwise." Ever optimistic, the newspaper offered a degree of hope that—despite their lack of English-language skills, their poverty and clannishness—the Russian Jews might well become worthy citizens one day. That optimism, however, gradually faded. By January 1883, the *Free Press* conceded that refugees "are not likely to be of any great value to the country, it being one of the characteristics of this people that they avoid productive labour, and are always found in occupations where they can gratify their propensity for trade and barter, and the accumulation of money."

That the indigence and alien aspect of the Jewish immigrants provoked much of the prejudice against them was clear—even from the so-called establishment Jews. In September 1897 Toronto's Holy Blossom synagogue relocated from Richmond Street to a much more majestic and Moorish-style building on Bond Street (it is now the St. George's Greek Orthodox Church), where the congregation remained until it moved in the late 1930s to its current home on Bathurst Street near Eglinton Avenue. Though the Bond Street synagogue was designed as Orthodox in the placement of the ark (where the Torah scrolls are kept) and the separate gallery for women, the prayer services soon featured more English and music, among other Reform practices. At the official opening, the Holy Blossom's young rabbi-preacher, Reverend Abraham Lazarus, who had come to Toronto from London in 1893, urged Eastern European Jewish newcomers in particular to give up their "oriental" customs and remember that Jews in Toronto were "a homemade article and not a foreign production."

Most of the esteemed Gentile guests who attended the ceremony—and several had contributed funds to the building campaign—would have concurred with such an assimilationist sentiment, even if many harboured serious reservations about the suitability of the Eastern European Jews as full-fledged

Canadians. The Christian luminaries included Toronto mayor John Shaw; Timothy Eaton, the department store merchant; members of the Massey family, who owned an agricultural implement enterprise and the city's largest factory; and, most curiously of all, Goldwin Smith. Perhaps he thought it was his duty as a Toronto patriarch to make an appearance at this auspicious occasion—or maybe he was merely being polite. Yet it was also the case that he tempered his anti-Jewish views when it came to Jews who looked and acted much like him and his peers, as many of the members of the Holy Blossom congregation did.

An even more interesting example of the respect granted to assimilated Jews was the respect and support given to Montreal's Louis Rubenstein, an avid sportsman and the country's best figure skater from 1878 to 1892, who won Canadian and U.S. championships. He was president of the Montreal Young Men's Hebrew Association (YMHA), curled at the decidedly non-Jewish St. Andrews Curling Club, and was a superb cyclist and bowler, later recognized as the "Father of Bowling in Canada," according to the *Montreal Star*. In the 1880s, at a time when Jews were prevented from joining athletic or golf clubs in Canada, Louis—with his distinguished moustache and bowler hat—emerged as "one of Canada's finest all-round athletes," as the *Canadian Encyclopedia* dubs him. He was also a Montreal city alderman from 1914 until his death in 1931.

Politicians from all three levels of government attended his funeral—certainly a rarity for a Jewish community leader in those days—and those giving the eulogies included Montreal's mayor, Camillien Houde. The *Montreal Star* wrote an editorial extolling his virtues and mourning the fact that the city's working class had lost a true champion. A water fountain memorial was erected in his honour six years later near the old YMHA at the foot of Mount Royal. It was likely the first public monument in Quebec to honour a Jew.

Like many acculturated English and German Jews, Louis Rubenstein lived in a world that was somewhat removed from the Russian and Eastern European immigrants. Needless to say, figure skating and sports were not their priorities; survival was. In Montreal, Toronto, Winnipeg, and elsewhere, that meant finding somewhere to live and obtaining a job—no easy task. Jewish as well as Christian charities offered much-needed assistance—in addition to $2,000 sent to Winnipeg by London's Mansion House in early January 1883, a local skating rink asked skaters for a twenty-five-cent contribution for "the suffering Jews," among other contributions—but it is fair to say that the immigrants were largely on their own.

The Yiddish-speaking newcomers were not prepared to forsake the strongly held Orthodox religious customs that had strictly governed their lives in the old country. Hence, their requirement for kosher meat as well as a job that did not compel them to work on the Sabbath—as the late Stephen Speisman, the historian of the Toronto Jewish community put it, in those years "one did not seek employment by Gentiles except as a last resort"—and demand for synagogues that offered traditional prayer services with the degree of piety they were accustomed to. There was, admittedly, a difference between custom and religion, and not all of the Eastern Europeans were excessively religious in the truest sense of the term. Still, their diet, rituals, and world view were shaped by their old-country *shtetl* experiences, and would define them for the rest of their lives.

This was a point not lost on German and English Jews such as Alfred Benjamin, a scion of the Holy Blossom congregation, who saw it as his duty to "anglicize" and "Canadianize" the newcomers. It was also one of the reasons why in 1897 a small group of Montreal Jewish community leaders—including Lyon Cohen, the grandfather of singer and poet Leonard Cohen, and Sam Jacobs, who was elected to the House of Commons in the federal election of 1917 and served as an MP for twenty-one years—established the English-language weekly newspaper, the *Jewish Times*. Apart from drawing attention to international Jewish issues, in its column "As Others See Us" the paper offered a tutorial on how decent and appreciative Canadian Jews should conduct themselves. Even when confronting blatant antisemitism, proper manners were essential, the newspaper's editor advised. Similarly, in Toronto, that city's branch of the National Council of Jewish Women of Canada took a keen interest in Eastern European immigrant girls and offered programs that socialized them on "the best of Canadian life."

This paternalistic attitude was based in part on a profound faith in the supremacy of British and Canadian institutions, and partly on self-preservation:

Benjamin and other established Jews abhorred the idea of being lumped together with the backward Eastern Europeans. As it was, Canadian newspapers of this era almost always identified a Jew, especially in stories dealing with the law or courts. In October 1882, for example, merchant David Ripstein was angry with the *Manitoba Free Press* for identifying him in news story about a "Jew by the name of Ripstein" who "was summoned on a charge of selling liquor to Indians." He wrote a letter to the editor to voice his outrage: "I want to know why you should refer to my religion, any more than to that of any other man . . . As for the charge itself, I am innocent of it as will be shown." In reply, the *Free Press* editor justified the reporting by pointing out that "in nine cases out of ten the term 'Jew' is used without the slightest intention of offending, and more to indicate race than religion . . . But we agree with our correspondent that in this country we should regard no distinctions whatever of race or religion." Slightly more than a week later, another story in the *Free Press* referred to a store "kept by a Jew named Rosenthal."

The differences between the old and new Jewish communities and their perceptions of what constituted an assimilated Jewish Canadian perpetuated a class division between them for many years, and eventually among the immigrants themselves. It was a distinction based on employment and what neighbourhood you lived in, but primarily on wealth. "Making it" as a Jew in Canada—having the reputation as a *macher* deserving of respect—long has been synonymous with being rich. Yet achieving this dream was much easier said than done.

PART TWO

JEWISH CANADIANS

It's a Living

The economic challenges the Jewish newcomers faced were daunting. With limited financial resources, the immigrants could only afford to rent generally inadequate housing, shacks, and cottages in the poorest areas of the cities. Work and religious demands, plus a desire to live among other Jews who spoke Yiddish, resulted in the establishment of crowded, *shtetl*-like Jewish Eastern European enclaves in Montreal, Toronto, and Winnipeg. In each city, Jewish immigrants shared their destitute neighbourhoods with a diverse group of other newcomers—Italian, Polish, Ukrainian, and other Europeans. This was especially the case after Clifford Sifton, the federal minister of the interior in charge of immigration in Wilfrid Laurier's government from 1896 to 1905, purposely opened Canada's door to "stalwart peasants in sheepskin coats," as he later described them. Sifton's practical policy aimed for the hardworking immigrants to farm the prairies, which many did. But many others (including Jews) found their way to the country's major cities, where they transformed the urban environment and experienced the good and bad of late-nineteenth and early-twentieth-century industrialization, and all the attendant social and economic problems it gave rise to.

In Montreal, the immigrants congregated initially in the lower part of St. Lawrence Boulevard near where it intersects with St. Catherine Street; in Toronto it was in the "Ward," the north and central part of St. John's Ward, in a rectangle bounded by Queen Street to the south, University Avenue to the west, College Street to the north, and Yonge Street to the east; and in Winnipeg, they made their homes initially in a neighbourhood off Main Street north of the CPR tracks that divided the North End from the downtown, in a dilapidated area which became known as the foreign quarter, New Jerusalem, and more disparagingly as Jew Town. The Russian Jews who lived in the shacks on muddy dirt roads caustically referred to this Winnipeg neighbourhood as *Mitzrayim* ("Egypt"), since for many it seemed like a place of biblical bondage.

In all three cities, derelict slum conditions were the norm for decades. Access to water was limited and outdoor privies dominated the landscape, even after the cities had banned them. Tiny, dingy flats and homes with enough room for three or four people often had twice or three times as many residents. The conditions were appalling, a fact which gravely concerned a small army of religious leaders, public health officials, and urban reformers whose sacred duty it was to improve this dreadful situation and save the immigrants from themselves.

In time, the Jews eked out livings serving the needs of the community as kosher butchers, bakers, grocery store owners, and underpaid rabbis, *shochetim* and teachers. In September 1897, young William Lyon Mackenzie King—a few years before he embarked on a career in the federal labour department and then in politics—wrote a series of articles about Toronto poverty and immigration issues for the *Mail and Empire*. He found that Jews monopolized the city's second-hand clothing stores and small number of junk shops. "The number of [Polish and Russian] Jewish peddlers who go about the city and out among the farmers in the country is fairly large," he wrote, "and the quantities of old rubbish they collect and utilize is something amazing. Almost the entire rag and scrap iron trade is carried on by Jews, and of the eight pawn shops in Toronto they are the owners of four."

King's assessment was fairly accurate: many Eastern European Jews indeed toiled as peddlers. It was a gruelling, thankless, low-paying job. Owning a pushcart, which some peddlers used, required a minimal investment. For those peddlers who opted to obtain a horse and wagon the cost was much higher, approximately $550 in Toronto during the 1890s—about what a labourer earned in an entire year. On top of this there were also civic licensing fees of twenty to thirty dollars annually. Jewish peddlers sought out loans from relatives and friends, mutual aid societies, charities, and wholesalers and merchants who extended them credit. Only the independence of being self-employed made the rag-and-bottle trade slightly tolerable. The *Manitoba Free Press* claimed in August 1893 that "Canadians never heard of peddling until the Jews came." That was not true, yet Jews and peddling became intrinsically linked in the public's imagination—and not in a good way.

Gentile mothers invoked the figure of the Jewish peddler, the *Jewish Times* noted in 1913, as a "bogeyman" to hush their children. A newspaper in rural Manitoba recommended that its readers "give pedlars [sic] the cold shake . . . [because] they had no business reputation to sustain . . . [and were] more likely to skin you than not." Even the revered novelist Lucy Maud Montgomery in her 1908 classic, *Anne of Green Gables*, had a German Jewish peddler trick her lovable protagonist Anne Shirley into buying the dye that turns her hair green rather than the "beautiful raven black" he had promised her it would. In a real sense, the entire Jewish community was tarnished by the negative stereotyping of peddlers as dishonest and shady. This was so much so that in the 1890s, Winnipeg newspapers—like other newspapers in North America—used the verb "to jew" as a synonym for "to cheat," leading to bizarre reports like the one that appeared in the *Winnipeg Tribune* on May 11, 1894: "Detective Leach arrested a young man yesterday afternoon named Fred Morrison going round among the Jews in the north end with several forged cheques . . . He managed to jew three of the Hebrew merchants to the extent of about $3.50 each."

Jewish peddlers were frequently dragged from their wagons by gangs of ruffians, or had garbage and stones hurled at them. "Any rags, any rubbers, any bottles today, Ikey, Ikey," children shouted at any passing peddler. Stories of Jewish peddlers getting into trouble were always entertaining copy for the press. Other than appealing for help to the police, who were fairly disinterested in the plight of the Hebrew junk dealers, there was little the peddlers could do to stop this daily harassment.

In Montreal, for a brief time in the early 1880s, the Young Men's Hebrew Benevolent Society—which later became the Baron de Hirsch Institute, after a generous donation from the $100-million estate of the German Jewish financier, Baron Maurice de Hirsch—provided Jewish peddlers with financial assistance. Yet for the most part, the peddlers in Montreal and elsewhere had to depend on the kindness of Jewish merchants or their own ingenuity to acquire their goods—an assortment of food, old clothes, furs, tobacco, hairbrushes, razors, rags, and bottles. Like any small business, success or failure was dependent on hard work, ingenuity, and a bit of *mazel* (luck)—often in short supply.

One of those struggling to eke out an existence in this way was Alton (Alter in Yiddish) Goldbloom's father, Samuel, who immigrated to Montreal from Lithuania in 1880 (or slightly earlier) at the age of seventeen. He was married within a few years, and a decade later, Alton—who would become a noted pediatrician—was born; Alton's mother, Belle, had already lost three children by then.

Samuel barely made a living as peddler. The family lived in a small flat on St. Antoine Street, close to the Saint Lawrence River, with only cold water, kerosene for light, and a latrine in the backyard. "There were flies, manure and dirt," as Goldbloom later recalled. The rent was six dollars a month and his father did not always make enough money to cover that expense. In search of business, his father went on the road, heading west to Winnipeg and also locales in the northwest, where he peddled watches and diamonds he had acquired on consignment from Montreal jewellers. Goldbloom remembered his father as "a nomad . . . an almost legendary figure who came home two or three times a year for a stay of six weeks, bringing with him tales of adventure from western Canada." He was fairly successful as a travelling salesman, but he also lost a lot of money gambling and on speculating in wheat futures on the Winnipeg Grain Exchange.

More stable and upwardly mobile were the male members of the extended Greisman family, who lived in the Ward in Toronto. All of them worked as peddlers at one time or another in the 1890s. Joseph Greisman, thirty-one years old at the start of the decade, was a peddler for two years before he opened his own grocery store in 1893. He temporarily returned to peddling seven years later. By 1905 or so, he had been hired by Eaton's as a garment operator in the company's factory, and then eventually opened a tailor shop. Likewise, his brother Henry, seven years younger, peddled for several years and made enough money to buy a handful of properties on Chestnut Street in the Ward. In later years, he owned two warehouses, operated the King Suspender & Neckwear Company, and lived in an upscale home in the fashionable Annex neighbourhood, west of Spadina Road.

In the 1880s and early 1890s, Jews in Montreal had another employment option: working in a garment factory or doing piecework from their homes. Industry in Montreal was boosted tremendously by the imposition of protective tariffs, a key plank of the National Policy John A. Macdonald put into action in 1879 (the other two complementary parts of the policy were building the CPR and settling the west). As the clothing industry expanded there was high demand for inexpensive labour, and Jewish immigrants, some of whom had old-country experience as tailors and seamstresses, were hired as labourers. The work of sewing coats, jackets, dresses, and hats was long, arduous, and woefully underpaid. From about the mid-1880s on, the battle for trade unions was an arduous one in Canada, and the fight for workers' rights was bitterly contested by managements that thought nothing of compelling their employees to toil ten and eleven hours a day, six days a week, for subsistence wages.

Under the circumstances, non-British or non-Western European immigrants—skilled or not—were largely on their own. Jewish garment-factory owners like Solomon Levinson, a Russian immigrant who had come to Canada in 1869 at the age of seventeen and had opened a clothing store in Montreal before expanding into the wholesale manufacturing of men's clothing, were more sympathetic to the plight of Eastern European Jews. But business was business.

In general, the booming demand for clothing was both a blessing and a curse. To keep up with orders, manufacturers were forced to farm work out to contractors. The contractors then hired subcontractors, who in turn recruited cheap immigrant labour—including many Eastern European Jews who lived around St. Lawrence Boulevard—to sew buttons, make button-holes, and finish garments. "Many families," geographers Sherry Olson and Patricia Thornton wrote in their history of Montreal, "were living in flats that accommodated at once sleeping, cooking, child minding, the stoves and irons of the pressers, and the tailors cross-legged on their benches, all investing in the long hours of 'sweated labour.'"

Testifying in 1889 before the Royal Commission on the Relations of Labor and Capital in Canada, one of several inquiries convened to investigate labour conditions in the country, Isaac Gold, a thirty-year-old Jewish immigrant tailor, stated that he worked at home and employed six women and two men to assist him in the piecework he did for a subcontractor. In an era when twenty-five to thirty dollars a week was considered a decent salary, the women Gold hired were paid only three dollars a week, and the men up to six dollars for at least fifty to fifty-five hours. Many other witnesses told similar stories. Jacob Rosen, also a young Montreal tailor, related to the commissioners that he obtained piecework for overcoats and buttonholes. He employed his father and two girls. He was paid a dollar to a dollar and seventy-five cents for each coat, and he paid the two girls three dollars a week.

Little had changed by 1896, when another royal commission on the "sweating system" was undertaken, nor a year after that when Mackenzie King ventured into the Ward to investigate Toronto's growing garment trade. He was escorted on tours through sweatshops in the Ward by Benjamin Gurofsky, who King thought "a very decent jew[sic]," as he noted in his diary. They visited with a Polish Jewish family, spoke with Italian workers, examined slum housing, and witnessed first-hand the grinding poverty and hardship that took such a brutal toll on the lives of so many. "What a story of Hell," King concluded. "My mind all ablaze."

The immigrants he visited made on average four dollars and fifty cents a week, for fifty to sixty hours of labour—not sufficient for rent and food in late-nineteenth-century Toronto. In one small shop in the Ward, King found a husband and wife, their two children, and a Polish Jewish woman who boarded with the family. All of them spent long hours making buttonholes for cloaks and overcoats, and received a dollar or less per hundred completed. King concluded his series with a call for labour reforms that increased the remuneration paid to the immigrant workers, "who are toiling from dawn till sundown." He was to support such reforms as prime minster later in his life, too, but it took many years before his wishful idealism became a reality.

Beyond Canada's major cities, Russian and Eastern European Jews like Ekiel Bronfman in Manitoba jumped at the opportunity to prove that Jews could be farmers, no different than German Mennonite, Icelandic, and Scandinavian immigrants. For Jews, working the land was a way to escape the squalor of the cities and live the noble and virtuous life associated with being a farmer.

The task of supplying the immigrants with land and supplies to fulfil their aspirations belonged to the Jewish Colonization Association (JCA), which owed its existence to financing provided by Baron Maurice de Hirsch. His objective, as he put it, was "to make the Jew a farmer and keep the Jew a farmer." The wealthy German businessman had little patience for what he regarded as the "fantasy" of a Jewish state in Palestine, and thus he was amenable when Herman Landau, a Jewish entrepreneur in London with ties to the CPR, encouraged him to support the idea of setting up Jewish agricultural colonies in North and South America. Baron de Hirsch and his wife Clara, who as the daughter of the banker Jonathan-Raphaël Bischoffsheim was wealthy in her own right, had lost their only child in 1887—their son, Lucien, who died at the age of thirty. The baron was naturally heartbroken and searched for a philanthropic project that would give his life meaning. The colonization plan accomplished that.

During the late 1890s and early 1900s, the JCA used the funds from de Hirsch, about $36 million in all, to purchase tracts of land mainly in the U.S., Canada, and Argentina. As part of its Canadian operations, the association, subsequently established several farm settlements in Western Canada. The colonies of Hirsch, Edenbridge, and Sonnenfeld—all located in Saskatchewan—were among the best known. But skepticism about the ability of Jews to succeed as farmers was constant. "A false impression has become prevalent . . . that there is no such thing as a Jewish farmer," wrote Louis Rosenberg, an educator who taught briefly at the Jewish farm settlement in Lipton, Saskatchewan, before becoming the JCA official in Regina in 1919. "So much is this belief widespread among Jews and non-Jews alike, that when a

Jew declares himself to be a farmer, doubts are expressed as to the possibility of his being a Jew, and if he declares himself to be a Jew it is taken for granted that he is no farmer."

Even before the JCA became involved, a group of Russian Jews, with assistance from the Mansion House funds secured by Alexander Galt, had attempted to farm on land granted to them in and around Moosomin in the District of Assiniboia (now in southern Saskatchewan), about 350 kilometres west of Winnipeg. They were given a few hundred dollars for farm implements, brought with them a Torah, and ensured kosher meat was available. But though there were high hopes for this "New Jerusalem," as the community of twenty-seven families called their primitive settlement, this experiment failed, a fact that angered Galt. The flimsy shanties the pioneers built were no match for the bitterly cold prairie winter—the colony's rabbi suffered from such a bad case of frostbite that he had to have his feet amputated—and an early frost ruined their crop in August 1885. In the previous two decades, Scottish and Mennonite farmers had faced similar adversity.

Despite the failure of Moosomin, by 1886 another group of Jews had settled close by, near Wapella. This attempt at farming was more successful, and in the next two decades as more families arrived, the settlement's population exceeded two hundred people. Wapella's "spiritual" leader was Edel Brotman, who officiated at weddings and bar mitzvahs before he moved to Winnipeg to open a liquor store. Still, the land around Wapella was poor, the mosquitoes terrible in the summer, and the settlers were threatened by wolves. Some, like Ekiel Bronfman, tolerated this crude lifestyle only for a brief time. To supplement his low farming income, Bronfman hauled and sold wood all year long, even when the weather in the winter reached minus thirty-five degrees Celsius. Eventually, he decided that relocating to Brandon made more sense. His eldest son, Abe, soon moved to Winnipeg to apprentice as a cigar maker, while Ekiel and his sons Harry and later Sam investigated the possibility of purchasing a hotel and saloon.

Funds from the JCA were used in 1892 to establish the colony appropriately called Hirsch, thirty kilometres east of Estevan. The settlement had the blessing of Conservative prime minister John C. Abbott, who assumed the office after the death of John A. Macdonald in June 1891. In May of the following year, about 150 immigrants who had recently arrived in Canada from the Pale made their way west to Hirsch. None could speak English or had ever used a plough. "God help the poor Jews," an Ontario newspaper declared.

The novice Jewish farmers did need the Lord's assistance, as well cash infusions from the JCA. And somehow, they survived the first few years generally unscathed. Rabbi Marcus Berner, an English immigrant, accepted a position as spiritual leader in 1891, and stayed for the next three decades. His presence was pivotal in keeping the settlement going. In time, a lot of the settlers moved to Winnipeg or other cities, though Jews lived and farmed at Hirsch into the 1950s.

As more Jewish immigrants arrived in Canada, the JCA arranged for many to settle in two new agricultural colonies in Saskatchewan: Sonnenfeld, and the cleverly named Edenbridge—the word derived from the wooden *Yidden Bridge* (or "Jews' Bridge") that was built by the Jewish colonists across the Carrot River.

Israel Hoffer and his wife Clara were among Sonnenfeld's young settlers. Before leaving Galicia in Eastern Europe, Hoffer had received agricultural training at a Baron de Hirsch school, which had been established through a foundation the Baron had created specifically to help Jews in Galicia. Still, this education did not adequately prepare him for his harsh and arduous experience in southwestern Saskatchewan (Sonnenfeld was located about seventy-five kilometres west of Estevan). Israel and Clara—and, for a time, Israel's father Reb Moshe, who had accompanied them—lived in a "simple box-like" home, as Clara later described it, with no electricity or indoor plumbing. Their drinking water derived from a well the settlers had to dig, and they subsisted on a steady diet of potatoes. Reb Moshe, a "pious Jew," continually questioned how he had allowed his son to talk him into moving halfway across the world to this "wild sprawling prairie wilderness." Exasperated that there were not enough Jews for a daily *minyan*, the elder Hoffer decried this decision as "the height of madness," according to Clara's account. But the Hoffers and the other colonists were, if anything, stubborn. They constructed a small synagogue, and hired a Hebrew teacher for their children and a *shochet* so they had a supply of kosher meat. By 1925, the colony had a population of ninety-nine people and a total of 9,600 acres of farmland.

Among the new arrivals the following year were brothers Kiva and Moses Kives (or Keives) and their families—Romanian Jews who had come to Canada from Turkey, where Kiva and Moses had resided since the late 1890s. With assistance from the JCA, they had settled on land near the ancient city of Eskişehir, 250 kilometres southeast of Constantinople (Istanbul). But in the economic and political turmoil that followed the First World War, and as hostilities against Jews in Turkey intensified, the JCA helped move them again to the distant Canadian Prairies. Arriving in Saskatchewan in November 1926, when the weather was already cold, Moses's nine-year-old daughter Edith—wearing only a light dress—wanted to return to the warm weather of Turkey.

Kiva, who was a more adept farmer than Moses, worked the land the JCA provided him, together with his wife Laya (she was also called Laika or Lily) and their two young children, Sophie and George. In 1929, in the nearby hamlet of Oungre (named for the JCA general manger Dr. Louis Oungre), Laya gave birth to their second son, Philip. By the time he was in his early thirties (Kives passed away in April 2016), he launched K-tel, the Winnipeg-based international gadget and music company that would eventually earn him the distinction of being named in 2003 by the *Globe and Mail's Report on Business* magazine as Canada's "best salesman."

The Edenbridge colony, 113 kilometres east of Prince Albert, also had its own unique story. The settlement was the most economically successful of the Jewish agricultural colonies, yet for decades its members were embroiled in a bitter dispute which pitted the Orthodox traditionalists against a group of socialist freethinkers. A JCA agent who visited the colony in 1914 was appalled by the feuding he found. "Socially, the farmers of the Edenbridge settlement are the worst people I came across," he reported. "Their acrimoniousness towards each other [has] exceeded all bounds."

Representative of the traditionalists were the Vickar brothers—Sam, David, and Louis—Lithuanian Jews who had first emigrated to South Africa in 1898 before deciding to make the long trek to Canada four years later. (The family's surname was actually Ibedas. According to folklore, a zealous South African immigration agent gave them the name Vickar, after learning that several of them had served as sextons at their synagogue.) Their first few months at Edenbridge were fraught with the same problems faced by most inexperienced Jewish colonists: primitive living conditions and poor farm-land. And Louis and his wife Rachel, who had two young children, Ada and Charles, had suffered a tragedy soon after they arrived in Winnipeg, when two-year-old Ada became ill with measles and diphtheria, and died. Unhappy with life in Edenbridge and grieving the death of their daughter, in 1907 Louis and Rachel took Charles and left Edenbridge for New York, where Rachel's parents lived. Some years later, they returned to Edenbridge briefly with Charles and their daughter Sarah, who had been born in New York, and then settled permanently in Winnipeg, where Louis became the associate editor of the Winnipeg Jewish newspaper, the *Israelite Press*.

The other two Vickar brothers stayed put and prospered. Sam and David met their Jewish wives in Winnipeg—the Gelman sisters, Gertrude (or Gella) and Sophie—and they became leaders of Edenbridge, supporting the community's small Beth Israel synagogue and school. Rabbi Max Shallit came to Edenbridge in 1908, and for the next six decades served as the colo-ny's chief religious official, *shochet*, and Hebrew teacher.

The traditionalists were challenged by a group of Russian and Eastern European Jews who had come to Saskatchewan from the East End of London, where they had endured long hours in the garment and fur-cutting sweat-shops in Whitechapel. A revamped economic system based on the principles of socialism, they believed, offered them salvation from this misery. Their dedicated leader was Mike Usiskin (known as "Uncle Mike"), who together with his brother David wanted to give his fellow Jews power over their down-trodden lives. Becoming a "pioneer of the soil," as Mike termed it, was the solution he was seeking.

Once the Usiskins and their followers arrived in Edenbridge in 1910 and 1911, they eschewed the colony's religious institutions and demanded their own schools and community centre, which were eventually built. The Vickars and their supporters became known as the "Afrikaners," and the Usiskin-led group, the "Londoners" or the "Townshippers," since they resided near the township line. But although political and religious ideology may have divided them, the realities of life in a prairie wilderness did not. After days spent clearing trees and building roads, Mike Usiskin conceded that he was no more prepared for surviving in Edenbridge than the Vickars had been. "Unfortunately, my grandfather was not a woodcutter," he later wrote in his Yiddish memoir, *Oxen un Motoren* ("From Oxen to Tractors"), written in 1945 (and in 1983 translated into English as *Uncle Mike's Edenbridge* by his niece Marcia Usiskin Basman).

Though the Edenbridge farmers organized a diverse number of cultural activities—from a literary and dramatic club to debates about the Russian Revolution and Zionism—the bickering between the two groups took its toll. On the occasion of the colony's twenty-fifth anniversary in 1931, the festivities were disrupted by the enduring feud between the Afrikaners and the Londoners. It took the intervention of Louis Rosenberg of the JCA to keep the peace. Rosenberg was upset by two decades of confrontation between the two sides, yet reported that Edenbridge was thriving nonetheless, even at the outset of the Great Depression. "The spirit and attitudes of the Jewish farmers of this colony . . . augur well for the continued success and emancipation of the Jewish farmers of the neighbourhood," he asserted.

The agricultural settlements loom large—admittedly too large—in the history of Jews in Western Canada. They epitomized the pioneer spirit and persistence that characterized the first and second waves of immigrants. Yet no more than 2,500 Jews—or 2 per cent of the total Canadian Jewish population—engaged in agriculture from the 1880s to the 1920s, and the majority of them were located in Saskatchewan and Manitoba (there was also a small Jewish farming colony near Krugerdorf, Ontario, northeast of Sudbury). The Jewish settlers' rate of success was not markedly different from that of other European ethnic groups who attempted to farm on the prairies. Hungarians and Icelanders struggled as well.

As the late Abraham Arnold, who devoted many years to researching and writing about Canadian Jewish history, noted, the Jews who stayed on the land were "among the first independent entrepreneurs in Western Canada. Yet Jewish entrepreneurs were not regarded as preferred immigrants." Cut off from Jews in the cities, these families found it difficult to keep kosher, provide a Jewish education, and live culturally as Jews. Truth be told, in the so-called Promised Land, the future was not promising. And that was the reason why so many were compelled to abandon the settlements. "Experience has shown no matter how successful a Jewish farmer may be from agricultural and financial standpoints," Louis Rosenberg concluded in 1950, "if he is isolated and cut off from a Jewish environment he will ultimately leave the farm if he wants his family to remain Jewish."

In nearly all cases, the Jewish farmers chose to relocate to urban locales such as Winnipeg, Regina, Calgary, and Edmonton, where dynamic communities were taking shape in the first decades of the twentieth century. And no one could dispute that the settlers were industrious and that their presence was evident from the moment they arrived in their new homes and neighbourhoods.

Out of Ghetto Streets

braham Moses Klein was an infant when his father Kalman (or Koifman) and mother Yetta journeyed to Montreal in 1910 from the town of Ratnoin the Volhynia region (in present-day north-western Ukraine). Both Kalman, who was in his mid-thirties, and Yetta, who was about twenty-eight, had lost their first spouses at relatively young ages. Soon after they were married in 1897, Yetta gave birth to two daughters, and then in 1909 to Abraham and a twin boy. Tragically, Abraham's twin brother became ill and died on the ocean crossing to Canada. A gentle man and a pious Jew, Kalman Klein could only take solace that his baby son's passing was the will of God, an act to be mourned but not questioned. Deciding that Abraham would have more opportunities if he was a native-born Canadian rather than an immigrant, his parents later declared in official documents that he was born in Quebec.

In Montreal, the Kleins found a small apartment close to the Main (St Lawrence Boulevard), the heart of the city's vibrant Jewish neighbourhood, "sandwiched between the numerically dominant working-class Franco-Catholic majority to the east and the economically dominant Anglo-Protestant elite to the west," as Yiddish-language chronicler Rebecca Margolis describes it. (Since 1905, the street has been officially known as Boulevard Saint-Laurent or simply "Saint-Laurent." During the period before the mid-sixties, and even to this day, Montreal's Jews and most other Anglos called it by the English version, St. Lawrence Boulevard, or its nickname, "the Main.") With its narrow alleyways and the area's daily hubbub and distinctive Yiddish culture—a teeming *shtetl*-like bazaar of bartering, bickering, and gossip; the home of Jewish organizations, Yiddish theatre, a bookstore, library, the Yiddish newspaper the *Keneder Adler* ("Canadian Eagle"), and shops of every kind and variety—the Main made an indelible impression on young Abraham. Even the Chinese laundryman in the neighbourhood spoke impeccable Yiddish. In Abraham's opinion, there was nothing better than munching on Hyman (Chaim) Seligman's tasty bagels, or feasting on a smoked meat sandwich at Ben and Fanny Kravitz's sweet shop.

Decades later, the only remnants of the old Jewish quarter are the quaint headquarters of the Museum of Jewish Montreal (which offers informative guided tours of the neighbourhood), Moishes Steakhouse, and Schwartz's Deli, founded in 1928 by Romanian Jewish immigrant Reuben Schwartz in another shop not far from its current location at 3895 St. Lawrence Boulevard, where long lines still twist down the block most lunch hours, with locals and tourists waiting patiently to savour smoked meat sandwiches. Otherwise, the synagogues, schools, garment factories, and shops have been either demolished or long since sold and transformed into tacky apartment blocks, high-priced gentrified tenements, and more modern stores. Only faint Stars of David on the once proud and active synagogues are still visible.

Abraham, who grew up to become the celebrated poet A.M. Klein, dissected the St. Lawrence neighbourhood's many moving parts and ruminated on its multi-faceted character, as well as the ideological and religious conflicts and development that occurred as Jews attempted to assert themselves in a city with a wide gulf between the English and the French. As Klein portrayed it in his 1942 poem "Autobiographical":

> *Out of the ghetto streets where a Jewboy*
> *Dreamed pavement into pleasant bible-land,*
> *Out of the Yiddish slums where childhood met*
> *The friendly beard, the loutish Sabbath-goy,*
> *Or followed, proud, the Torah-escorting band*
> *Out of the jargoning city I regret*
> *Rise memories, like sparrows rising from*
> *The gutter-scattered oats,*

Like sadness sweet of synagogal hum,
Like Hebrew violins
Sobbing delight upon their eastern notes.

Other Montreal-based Jewish writers, journalists, and politicians born between 1908 and 1935—including Irving Layton, Mordecai Richler, and Klein's good friend David Lewis, who became the leader of the New Democratic Party in 1971—were also to probe the city's Jewish life and wrestle with how it shaped them and influenced the contours of Canadian Jewish history. The soulful Leonard Cohen, on the other hand, who was born in 1934, grew up above the Main in a solidly middle-class Jewish home in Westmount, where he attended Westmount High School—a school which was more Gentile than Jewish.

Like thousands of other Jewish newcomers, Kalman Klein got a job as a presser in a garment factory, working long hours in conditions that had barely improved since the 1880s, and otherwise devoted himself to his family and his religious duties and studies. He had little time or patience for the socialist dogma preached by the increasing number of Jewish immigrants who inexplicably believed more in the teachings of Karl Marx than they did the Talmud. Many of these left-wing zealots, as Kalman saw them, had departed the Pale of Settlement following the failed 1905 Russian Revolution or after the Bolshevik Revolution of 1917.

Among the latter group was Moishe Losz (the family name was changed to Lewis in Canada), who with his wife Rose and their three children— Charlie, Doris, and David, the future politician—emigrated from the Polish town of Świsłocz (now in Belarus) to Montreal in 1921. Jews like Moishe brought with them as part of their "cultural baggage" the spirit of the Bund, the Jewish workers' political and labour movement established in Russia in 1897. Their ardent faith in Marxist and socialist principles, their love for Yiddish language and culture, and a secular rather than religious emphasis on Judaism redefined for many adherents what it meant to be Jewish. They were the first and only generation of a true Jewish "proletariat" in Canada, and were prepared to stand up for themselves in the factory, whether their bosses were Jewish or not. Some were dedicated radicals; others embraced the socialist principles of their leaders only because it provided them with the hope that their miserable lives would improve. Moishe Lewis was a fervent Bundist. He found a job in the city's garment industry, and quickly became an active member of the local union of the Amalgamated Clothing Workers of America at a time when the relationship between management and labour was tense and confrontational.

Abraham Klein, an avid reader at a young age who had an intellectual bent like his father, attended a Protestant elementary school, as was the norm for Jewish youngsters in Quebec's dual Catholic and Protestant school system. Within the Protestant school system, however, Jewish students and parents were subjected to legalized discrimination.

In 1901, Jacob Pinsler, a Canadian-born Jewish student who also attended a Protestant school, was entitled to a scholarship based on the high grades he had achieved, yet he was deliberately excluded from selection on the grounds that he was a Jew. Pinsler's parents took the matter to court but got nowhere. In the months that followed the court ruling, the Legislative Assembly of Quebec passed an act in which Jews were for educational purposes classified as "honorary Protestants."

Neither Protestant school officials nor members of Quebec's Jewish community were especially happy with this enactment. Since Jews in Montreal lived in such a concentrated area, schools around St. Lawrence Boulevard were overwhelmingly Jewish, a demographic that Protestant officials found troubling. By 1914, Jewish students made up more than 40 per cent of all students enrolled at Montreal's Protestant schools. Exacerbating this issue further was the fact that most Jews were not directly paying property taxes to the schools, because so many of them rented rather than owned their place of residence. Protestant school officials thus felt overwhelmed by the large number of Jewish students they had to educate, an arduous responsibility for which in their view they did not receive adequate public funding. The Jewish students were also perceived to be a threat to the schools'—and in the larger perspective, Canada's—Christian character. To this end, Jewish parents were denied the right to serve on Protestant school boards until

1965, and only a token number of Jewish teachers were hired to work at Protestant schools for decades.

Jews were in control of their own community schools, at least, and Abraham Klein cherished his Sunday and late-afternoon Hebrew and Talmudic classes at the Talmud Torah—the Kerem Israel Hebrew Free School on St. Dominique. By the time he was a teenager, his immersion in Jewish education had fostered his strong support of Zionism and the dream of establishing a Jewish homeland in Palestine. He shared these dreams for the future with many of his friends at Baron Byng High School on St. Urbain Street, where the vast majority of students were Jewish. Klein also wandered the so-called ghetto's streets and hung out at Dufferin Square, the "Jewish park" that was the best spot to catch up on the latest old-country and Canadian news. In later years, as the editor of the *Canadian Jewish Chronicle* from 1938 to 1955, he wrote eloquently about all facets of Jewish life.

The Kleins were part of a distinctive Jewish growth spurt in Canada. During the first two decades of the twentieth century, the country's total Jewish population increased from 16,401 in 1901 to 125,197 in 1921, which represented 1.42 per cent of the country's total population. (In the same period, an estimated 41,000 Jews, many newly arrived immigrants, left Canada for the United States.) Still, whether they settled in Montreal, Toronto, or Winnipeg, whose Jewish populations increased dramatically from 1900 to 1920, or Saint John, Saskatoon, and Edmonton—each with a Jewish population of less than one thousand people in 1921—they shared a common story, making their way in cities, towns, and villages that did not especially welcome them with open arms. In mid-1899, a ship transporting Russian and Polish Jews on their way to Halifax and points west stopped in the harbour in St. John's Newfoundland, and attracted hundreds of curious spectators anxious to see these "peculiar people," as the *Evening Herald* labelled them. They "are but poor specimen of the genus homo," the newspaper concluded, "some few being classed as superior, but most are the lowest order . . . They are a quiet people, religious in a way but, the officers say, great thieves . . . They are a hardy race and will live on almost anything in their effort to make money."

The not-so-subtle antisemitism aside, this genuine quest to "make money" was merely about survival. The majority of the immigrants were initially unable to speak English (or French) and many were compelled to compromise their religious principles in order to earn a living. Others slogged as peddlers or garment factory workers for paltry wages. Yet the journey did transform them; if they could afford it, one of the first things they did soon after they came to Canada was have their picture taken so they could send the photograph back home to show their relatives how "Americanized" they had become in such a short time.

Whether they lived in Montreal with a Jewish population of 45,803 in 1921, Ottawa with 3,041, Saskatoon with 599, or Brandon with 222, Jews were all generically classified as "Hebrews" by the non-Jewish world, which did not appreciate or even understand the religious and ideological distinctions within the larger Jewish community, or its ancient disputes. Canada was and remained primarily white, Anglo-Saxon, and Protestant. In 1912 and 1913 the country received 776,626 immigrants, of which 39 per cent were British. And by 1921, English, Scottish, and Irish (many Roman Catholic) Canadians accounted for approximately 53 per cent of the country's total population. Add in the French, Germans, and Scandinavians, and Canada was overwhelmingly Northern European. Nevertheless, Jews, Italians, Ukrainians, and other Eastern Europeans attracted a lot of attention—and little of it positive.

The ever-increasing number of Jews in Toronto, for example, was disturbing for the white Protestant majority. In 1921, the city's Jewish population was 34,770, which was only 6.6 per cent of the total; yet it was 30,000 more than there had been two decades earlier. They were a highly visible group, segregated as they were in the Spadina–Kensington Market area. The *Globe's* editors raised an alarm about "a Jewish invasion of the public schools." And the *Toronto Telegram* expressed grave concerns about the opening of the new and impressive Beth Jacob synagogue on Henry Street in 1922. Two years later, the same issue was addressed even more virulently by the *Telegram*. "An influx of Jews puts a worm next the kernel of every fair city where they get a hold," an editorial stated. "These people have no national tradition . . . They are not the material out of which to shape a people holding a national spirit ... Not on the frontiers among the pioneers of the plough and axe are they found, but in the cities where their low standards of life cheapen all about them."

In the minds of politicians, public health officials, church leaders, teachers, journalists, and members of the business community, the Jewish, Southern and Eastern European, and Asian newcomers were members of objectionable "races," who dressed in peculiar garb, ate food with garlic and other Byzantine spices, and spoke strange languages. It was the conventional wisdom of the day that these immigrants contributed to the growing poverty and congestion in downtrodden urban neighbourhoods where drunkenness, crime, and prostitution flourished.

There was some truth to these charges. Around St. Lawrence Boulevard in Montreal, the Ward in Toronto, and the North End of Winnipeg, many Jewish immigrants indeed lived in abject poverty in slum housing (often rented from Jewish landlords) where disease was rampant. In 1906, a group of ladies from the Winnipeg Ministerial Association visited a North End Jewish home and reported on the appalling living conditions they discovered. "Forty-five families inhabited a very small space, living in a manner that was to say the least disgraceful," the ladies wrote. "Diseases of all kinds were common ... It was just the spot for a plague to begin and sweep over the city, and it was providence that such had not occurred." In Montreal in 1908, Jewish cemeteries did not have room for the large number of Jewish paupers who required free burial.

There may not have been many Jewish brothel owners or pimps, but small-scale bootlegging was definitely popular among Jewish immigrants as a way to make a few dollars. The long list of Jewish bootleggers included Getel (Gertrude) Shumacher (the grandmother of Toronto civic politician Howard Moscoe) who followed in the footsteps of her brother Shmuel, who was also a bootlegger, and sold shots of whiskey out of the self-styled "grocery store" located in her house in Toronto's Ward neighbourhood to supplement the family income; the parents and grandmother of Toronto Jewish boxing champion Sammy Luftspring, who offered their clientele twenty-five-cent glasses of rye; and Abraham Bellow in Montreal. By 1923, Abraham, then forty-two—and the father of eight-year-old Saul, destined to become one

of the great American writers of the twentieth century—was up to his neck
in debt. He had already failed as a baker, dry goods salesmen, junk dealer,
marriage broker, and insurance agent, among other pursuits. Bootlegging was
a last resort and a poor choice: he and his partner were beaten and robbed
while driving to the Quebec–New York border with a truckload of whiskey.

Offering some relief to the immigrants were mutual aid societies, orphanages, and private clinics set up in several key cities. These included Montreal's
Herzl Dispensary and the Hebrew Maternity Hospital—the brainchild of
the "greene *rebbetzin*," Taube Kaplan (the Russian immigrant wife of Rabbi
Jacob Kaplan), who spent several years single-handedly raising enough money
to open it in 1916; the Jewish Dispensary in Toronto, which evolved in 1923
into the Hebrew Maternity and Convalescent Hospital and eventually
became Mount Sinai Hospital; and the Mount Carmel Clinic in Winnipeg.
These clinics had doctors and staff who could speak Yiddish and charged fees
of only fifty cents (or less), half of what it cost to see a private physician.

Across the country, Jewish communities—large, medium, and small—
quickly learned that no one was responsible for the welfare of their members
except the communities themselves. The success of these various endeavours
owed mainly to the philanthropic efforts of selfless individuals, among them
two remarkable women, Ida (Lewis) Siegel and Lillian (Bilsky) Freiman,
both born in 1885.

Siegel was from Pittsburgh, but as a young girl came to Toronto with her
mother to reunite with her father, who had found work in the city. She was
(like her older brother Samuel Lewis) a committed Zionist, and in 1906, at
the age of twenty-one, she was instrumental in organizing a group to assist
young Jewish immigrant women and mothers—only the first in a long list
of her volunteer achievements. She actively promoted education for girls,
sports for Jewish children, and was one of the founders of Hadassah, the
most notable Zionist women's group in Canada.

Lillian Freiman and her husband Archie were also committed Zionists.
Thirty years old when the First World War broke out in 1914, Lillian spear-
headed numerous charitable activities. She supported the Red Cross, raised
money for orphanages and refugee efforts—in Ottawa, she was later known

as the "Poppy Lady" for her pioneering work promoting the poppy campaign for veterans—and became president of the Dominion Hadassah women's organization. Siegel and Freiman set the standard for others to follow. And, as a response to the many needs of the Eastern European immigrants, ladies' Hebrew benevolent societies were organized in nearly every Canadian Jewish community across the country.

Still, there were grumblings about Jewish self-segregation and the impact of the newcomers from established Jews such as Montreal lawyer Maxwell Goldstein, who in 1917 became the first president of the Federation of Jewish Philanthropies, which evolved into the Combined Jewish Appeal. In a 1909 interview with *London's Jewish Chronicle*, he bemoaned that the cause of many of the community's problems was "the vast influx of foreign Jews into the Dominion." These immigrants, he added, "form ghettos among themselves and create a great deal of prejudice." The great irony of this classic catch-22 situation would have been lost on Goldstein. Jews could not win, no matter what they did. If they remained poor and ghettoized, they were disdained as a cancer on Canadian society. On the other hand—at least until the 1960s—the more acculturated Jews became, the more they were resented by the Christian majority for being too pushy and for threatening the status quo.

Compassion and understanding for this deplorable situation only went so far among large segments of the WASP majority. There was, in fact, a backlash against undesirable minorities, the result of a deep-seated xenophobia that was to remain a part of un-multicultural Canadian society at least until the 1960s. Expressing a widely shared view, Frederick Barlow Cumberland, a British-born Ontario writer and sportsman, declared to the members of Toronto's Empire Club in 1904 that "we are the trustees for the British race ... We hold this land in allegiance." French-Canadian nationalists were of the same mind: in 1911, while addressing an Anglo-Canadian meeting, journalist Olivar Asselin complained about the "exotic babbling" Jews in Montreal, who in his view had degraded the city's character. (Asselin later reconsidered his attitude toward Jews, and condemned French-Canadian antisemitism.)

In an age when the eugenics movement, with its theories about the alleged link between biology and morality, was popular, Canada—or so it seemed— was under siege from unwanted "foreigners" and "aliens" who could never assimilate to "Canadian" values and standards. In J.S. Woodsworth's book *Strangers Within Our Gates*, published in 1909, the saintly and compassionate Social Gospel advocate—who in the face of the severe urban problems of the early twentieth century preached an activist Christian charity to improve the lives of the poor and destitute—and politician outlined his belief (shared by many others) that British, Scandinavian, German, and French immigrants would make much better Canadians than "Hebrews," Slavs, and "Orientals" (Chinese, Japanese, and Hindus). The prospects for "Negroes" and "Indians" (Indigenous Canadians) were even more dismal.

Public school teachers ultimately tasked with "Canadianizing" the immigrant children were likewise skeptical. Teachers encouraged their foreign students to learn English by any means possible—and, more significantly, imparted to their young charges the "correct" moral values. This meant teaching them respect for law and order and having them embrace "thrift, punctuality, and hygiene." As one Toronto public school teacher put it, Canadians are "tidy, neat and sincere—foreigners are not." The conservative *Winnipeg Telegram* summed up such fears even more concisely. "Better by far to keep our land for children, and children's children of Canadians," its editors argued in mid-May 1901, "than to fill up the country with the scum of Europe."

It was such thinking that was behind the zealous campaign to pass the federal Lord's Day Act in 1906 as a way to ensure Canada remained a Christian country and to preserve the sanctity of Sunday as a day in which religious activities were paramount as well as to battle the evils of foreigners, prostitutes, and liquor abuse. Predictably, the proposed law was unpopular in the Jewish community, since it meant that religious Jews, who refrained from working on Saturdays, would now be penalized from earning a living on Sundays. In a rather bold move for the time, the "establishment" leaders of the Baron de Hirsch Institute in Montreal aggressively lobbied the federal government to include an amendment that would exempt Jews who kept Saturday as their day of rest. How such an exemption might be enforced was never really answered. It hardly mattered, because among Ottawa politicians the firmly held view was that making a special exception for Jews was bad politics. Jews—it was argued by many MPs, as well as the members of the Protestant Lord's Day Alliance—should abide by the Christian character of Canada in all of its forms.

The irrational fear of a Jewish presence in Canadian society was constant, though the antisemitism varied. In 1905, Jacques-Édouard Plamondon, a Quebec City lawyer and author, became one of the founders of the Quebec weekly *La Libre Parole*, a nationalist organ with a definite anti-Jewish slant. Plamondon modelled himself after the French journalist Édouard Drumont, who had also established a newspaper called *La Libre Parole*, and in 1886 had published the vile antisemitic tract *La France juive*. An instant bestseller that was eventually translated into six languages, Drumont's book linked the medieval variety of antisemitism with its more modern, social Darwinist, racial variety. Hence, Jews were ugly with hooked noses, and were also spies, traitors, and carriers of disease who could not be trusted.

At the end of March 1910, Plamondon spoke at a gathering in Quebec City organized by the Association Catholique de la Jeunesse Canadienne-Française, which had already been receptive to antisemitic ideas. Using Drumont's writings as his inspiration, Plamondon delivered an inflammatory diatribe, which was published in his newspaper two weeks later and then distributed as a pamphlet. In it, he painted Jews as dangerous and the Talmud as promoting a grand conspiracy, echoing the claims of a notorious piece of Russian antisemitic propaganda, *The Protocols of the Elders of Zion* (1903). "The Jew," Plamondon declared, "by his beliefs and by his acts, is the enemy of our faith, our lives, our honour, and our property."

His widely publicized remarks immediately stirred up trouble. Jews were roughed up on the streets of Quebec City and the local synagogue was vandalized. Two prominent members of the community—Louis Lazarovitz and Benjamin Ortenberg, whose shop was also targeted—launched a libel suit against Plamondon (and the printer of the pamphlet, René Leduc). One of the lawyers representing Ortenberg was Samuel Jacobs of Montreal, whose role in this case as a champion of Canadian Jews boosted his political aspirations (which were to be realized in the federal election of 1917). The trial took place in mid-May 1913, and pitted Catholic priests, who supported Plamondon's distorted views of the Talmud, against Rabbi Herman Abramowitz of the Shaar Hashomayim synagogue in Montreal—who offered a passionate and vigorous defence of Jewish law—and Frederick G. Scott, an Anglican priest (and poet) from Quebec City.

Plamondon escaped fairly unscathed from the legal proceedings. The Quebec Superior Court judge ruled that his remarks had been about the community, rather than a specific individual, and that therefore he could not be found guilty of libel. Ortenberg and Lazarovitz appealed that decision, and the higher court decided the judge was mistaken—"that members of a community were entitled to sue for libel or slander when that collectivity was small, since individuals in such a group might suffer." But they were not prepared to punish the defendants all that harshly. In late 1914, Plamondon was forced to pay a fine of fifty dollars, and Leduc, twenty-five dollars. The Plamondon Affair, as it became known, served as a warning to others who would besmirch Jews in Canada. The message, if somewhat muted by the appeal court's leniency, was clear: Jews would not tolerate such malicious prejudice.

There were numerous other examples of Jews forced to defend their religious principles and to battle antisemitic stereotypes and insults from ignorant bullies in the street who taunted Jewish children on their way to school; as well as from educated and influential individuals who espoused the prejudice and discrimination of the era. In what was to be an ongoing problem for Jews in Canada for decades, university officials at various institutions spent an exorbitant amount of time figuring out ways to limit the number of Jewish students they had to accept. In 1919, Queen's University principal Reverend R. Bruce Taylor patted himself on the back "that there were only five Jews at Queen's," adding that "the presence of many Jews tended to lower the tone of Canadian Universities." Taylor said it was "best" to keep the number of Jews as low as possible.

But as routine as antisemitism was in Canadian society in this period, there were a number of Jewish success stories. In 1904, thirty-two-year-old

Moses Finkelstein, who had come to Winnipeg as a young boy in 1882, was working at his own enterprise, the North West Hide and Fur Company. He was involved with the local YMHA and the Winnipeg Zionist Society. He had also been made a Justice of the Peace in 1900, which gave him a slightly higher profile than most members of the Jewish community. And, according to his grandson Paul Silverstone, Moses spoke English without an accent, a distinct advantage for any early-twentieth-century Jewish politician. In late 1904, a group of community leaders convinced him to run as an alderman in the civic election for Ward 5, which encompassed nearly all of the Jewish streets of the North End. He reluctantly agreed to do so and won, becoming the first Jew to hold elected office in Manitoba. Still, during this era there was no so-called Jewish vote that was guaranteed to a Jewish candidate.

Ten years later, Victoria-born Samuel Schultz, an accomplished Vancouver lawyer, was appointed a Vancouver county court judge at the age of forty-nine, making him the first Jewish judge in Canada. Throughout his career, he was pro-Zionist, a staunch defender of Jewish rights, and was a founding president of the Samuel Lodge of the Independent Order of B'nai B'rith.

And in 1918, in the small town of Alexandria, Ontario, about a hundred kilometres east of Ottawa, twenty-eight-year-old George Simon—born in Brantford and owner of the Alexandria's general store—was elected mayor in 1918 for a five-year term. He then served again decades later, from 1952 until his death in 1964. Like other Jewish storekeepers, he was a popular member of the town, and the fact that he was Jewish was not an issue in the elections he contested. In all of these cases, individual personalities and reputations in the community often trumped blatant prejudice. Thus, there was some hope for the future.

Intellectuals and Radicals

Antisemitism may have united Jews for a common cause, yet they remained divided on most other aspects of their lives. As it had been in the 1880s and 1890s when the first wave of Russian and Eastern European Jews arrived, religious and synagogue rituals continued to drive a wedge in most communities. From the perspective of newcomers, the Orthodox prayer rituals and customs of the old country were not something to be tinkered with or revamped. They could not accept—initially, at least—synagogue services with English, music, and choirs. And proper decorum was another matter. Unhappy with the older community members' more liberal approach to Judaism, Eastern Europeans quickly established their own congregations, despite the expense of doing so.

In Saint John, the split, which lasted for more than a decade, had a twist. The Ahavith Achim ("Brotherly Love") synagogue on Carleton Street had been built in 1899, when the city's Jewish population was less than two hundred. Its key members were members of the Hart, Green, and Isaacs families, who had settled in New Brunswick before 1880. With the arrival of a few hundred (mainly Lithuanian) Yiddish-speaking Jews, or "Litvaks," the Ahavith Achim's English approach—which insisted on "Presbyterian-like" conduct—became a matter of contention. The "uptown" and "downtown" economic, social, and psychological split that divided Jewish communities in Montreal, Toronto, and Winnipeg now divided Saint John, too. Bitter disagreements erupted between the two sides, especially about proper conduct during prayer services. "The incessant squabbling of the Litvaks," according to New Brunswick writer Craig Chouinard, "combined with the class snobbery and condescension of the English-speakers, served to make matters unbearable: They could not agree on anything."

In this case, the newcomers did not depart and organize their own congregation. Instead, the conflict subsided when the existing community members opted to leave Ahavith Achim to the Lithuanians and build a new and more modern synagogue on Hazen Avenue. The arguing stopped, though not the condescension. Teenagers from the Hazen Avenue synagogue enjoyed sneaking into the Ahavith Achim, where they revelled in the organized chaos and watched the Litvaks "yell" at each other. But demographics and economic realities—plus the acculturation of the Eastern Europeans, which lessened the divisions between the two groups—led to a reunification in 1919. Sustaining two synagogues had become impossible for a community of 850, and the obvious answer was to merge into a new congregation. Shaarei Zedek, a Conservative synagogue, opened in a former Presbyterian church, and served the small number of Jews in Saint John until the building was sold in 2008. Since then, Shaarei Zedek has operated out of a building on Leinster Street close to the downtown area, which also houses the Saint John Jewish Historical Museum.

With guidance from such wise rabbis as Jacob Gordon in Toronto, who served the Goel Tzedec as well as several other Orthodox congregations, and Israel Isaac Kahanovitch of Winnipeg's Beth Jacob synagogue—who also was given the honorary title "Chief Rabbi of Western Canada"—traditionalists attempted to foster Jewish religious precepts among the members of their communities.

Born in a town near Vilnius, Lithuania, Gordon was in his mid-twenties when he settled in Toronto in early 1905 with his wife and daughter. He quickly became the most significant rabbinical leader in the city, and was involved in everything from enforcing acceptable kosher regulations to forging links with Jewish garment workers. Gordon was very much an old-country rabbi: he refused to deliver sermons in English, preferring to speak to his congregants in Yiddish, and he staunchly opposed the decision of Jewish socialists to establish their own secular Yiddish-language afternoon school. He was especially incensed in 1912 when the National Radical School convened a picnic on the Sabbath.

Rabbi Kahanovitch, who was about eight years older than Gordon, was also a Lithuanian-born *shtetl*-style rabbi. He was the focus of much activity from the moment he arrived in Winnipeg in 1906 from Scranton, Pennsylvania, where he had served a small congregation for a year. From his small house on Flora Avenue in the North End, Kahanovitch greeted a never-ending number of visitors seeking his counsel with a hearty "*shalom aleichem*," meaning "peace be upon you." (He also spoke Yiddish to the five nanny goats he kept in his backyard, and they understood him.) Like Gordon, Kahanovitch immersed himself in synagogue politics, kosher disputes, charity work, and efforts to combat antisemitism. But he was also decidedly inflexible when it came to Orthodox religious customs, and on one memorable occasion he berated the young members of the Winnipeg Jewish orphanage's small congregation because girls had been permitted to sing in the synagogue's choir.

Both rabbis were instrumental in the establishment of Talmud Torahs in their respective cities, which initially offered afternoon and Sunday-morning Hebrew classes to children to educate them in Jewish history, Zionism, and the Hebrew language. (Following the pedagogical work of New York City Jewish educator Samson Benderly, the Talmud Torahs in Canada later adopted what was called *Ivrit b'Ivrit*, "Hebrew in Hebrew" instruction.) In Toronto, the Simcoe Street Talmud Torah (otherwise known as the Hebrew Religious School) was opened in 1907 in a beat-up old building and soon had about hundred students. Though it had its competitors and detractors—mainly secular socialists and radicals who organized their own school—as well as economic challenges, this school eventually developed in the early 1920s into a larger and more popular Talmud Torah on Brunswick Avenue.

In Winnipeg, with Rabbi Kahanovitch's leadership, sufficient money was raised to purchase a lot and build a Talmud Torah—the Winnipeg Hebrew Free School, which opened in 1913. The teaching may not always have been first-rate, and following a full day of regular school the children were not always as enthusiastic as they might have been; yet the Winnipeg Talmud Torah, like other Talmud Torahs in Canada and the United States, was ultimately successful in strengthening the Jewish identity of the local young people—an identity that was admittedly frequently in a constant state of flux.

The rooms, auditorium, and library were also used by numerous Jewish organizations and clubs.

The Yiddish radicals, themselves divided, saw the world somewhat differently. They were influenced by the writings of three literary masters: Isaac Leib Peretz, who encouraged Eastern European Jews to take charge of their often pathetic lives; Sholem Abramovich, who was known as Mendele Mocher Sforim ("Mendele the Bookseller"), a wicked satirist; and the indomitable Solomon Rabinovich, or Sholem Aleichem, whose witty and learned stories and novels probed the Jewish soul. Despite any reservations Eastern European Jewish intellectuals had about the crudeness of Yiddish, they came to understand that in the struggle against capitalism and autocratic government, it was the only language they could use to reach the masses.

The statistics bear out that truth. While Hebrew at this time was primarily the language of synagogue prayers (it was more widely used after the establishment of the State of Israel in 1948), Yiddish was the language of everyday life used by many Jews in the country. According to the 1921 census, 91 percent of Canadian Jews declared Yiddish as their mother tongue. By then, Yiddish had come to denote the culture, politics, and passion of thousands of immigrants. Nowhere was that more the case than in Montreal, where in late 1914 the city council decided it was a good idea to publicize announcements about civic affairs in Yiddish as well as English and French. As Abraham Klein had experienced on St. Lawrence Boulevard, Yiddish was the language of business, culture, and the garment factories where so many Jews worked long hours, often six days a week. And Yiddish was central to the popularity of the secular schools the socialists, radicals, and anarchists established—a clear statement of defiance against the traditionalists and businessmen who perceived themselves as the true leaders of the communities in Montreal and elsewhere.

Labour Zionists, Socialist-Territorialists, anarchists, communists, and members of the Arbeiter Ring (Workmen's Circle) initially worked together to open National Radical Schools—renamed I.L. Peretz Schools following the writer's death in 1915—in Montreal, Toronto, and Winnipeg so that their children could be inculcated with the principles of Jewish left-wing secularism. By the 1930s, there were Peretz Schools in Edmonton and Vancouver as well. Winnipeg's Peretz School went one step further than other Jewish schools in Canada: in 1902, it offered daytime lessons for the grade one class, making it one of the first Jewish day schools in North America, and within two decades it was operating a parochial day school for children from grades one to seven. But these popular secular schools were also the focus of much community controversy, and denounced by rabbis in Montreal, Toronto, and Winnipeg as "godless" institutions.

At the same time, internal ideological differences hindered the secularists as much, or even more so, than the traditionalists, and this infighting led to the organization of rival secular schools. In Montreal, for example, the break-away Jewish People's School, which offered its students more extensive Hebrew instruction than other similar schools, was established in 1914 in a split that lasted for the next fifty years—and only ended in 1971, when financial issues and the retirement of two long-serving administrators led to a merger. In Toronto, there was also a Jewish Folks' Shule, which had a more left-wing Zionist and Hebrew curriculum; and in Winnipeg, philosophical disputes led to the opening of the Arbiter Ring School and the Jewish Folk School, organized in 1929 by disenchanted parents who wanted more Hebrew instruction in the curriculum than was then offered by the Peretz School (the Jewish Folk School and the Peretz School reunited in 1944).

This bickering aside, the shared essence of the secular schools was their idealism, faith in social justice, equality—students referred to their instructors as "chaver" or "comrade"; though most Jewish socialist men were as traditional about the role of women as their Orthodox counterparts—and the radical view that Jewish learning could go beyond the Old Testament and Talmud studied in synagogues and religious schools. This was a distinction not immediately understood by many of the children. "We felt, but did not understand, our difference [from other Jewish children in the neighbourhood], when, after a day's study in English school, we did not study with a Rabbi at home or in a cheder [traditional school] but rather went to a secular Jewish school," remembered Esther Zuker, who attended Montreal's Peretz School. She added:

Over time we became so immersed in [school] activities that our closest friends became other [school] children, who came from different neighbourhoods in the Jewish "Downtown," from homes similar to our home. Only in our later childhood years did we begin to see that our parents were not non-believers but rather possessed a new belief: the belief in a new, secular Yiddishkayt that attached to everyday life a conscious sense of belonging to the folk, a closeness to Jewish culture, studying in a National Radical School, celebrating our holidays in a unique manner with Hasidic melodies and Jewish folksongs.

This same folk spirit also explains the popularity—for several decades, at least—of the Yiddish theatre, which was considered another "irreligious" pastime by the Orthodox, especially since the theatres offered Saturday matinee performances. The theatre captured the drama of immigrant life in a way that appealed to the audience's most basic instincts. New York's Lower East Side gave rise to North American Yiddish theatre and was home for many of its celebrities, like actors Jacob Adler and Madame Keni Liptzin, and playwright Jacob Gordin, whose melodramas such as *The Jewish King Lear* and *Mirele Efros* made enthusiastic audiences at Montreal's Monument Theatre, Toronto's Lyric Theatre and later the Standard, and Winnipeg's Queen's Theatre laugh and cry.

Gordin's plays were morality lessons about the joys and hardships of immigrant life, bringing Jewish audiences a sense of satisfaction and comfort that they were not alone. Montreal journalist Israel Medres recalled that during performances of *Mirele Efros*—a heart-wrenching play that reaffirms Jewish survival in the Diaspora and celebrated Jewish motherhood—women (and men) in the audience would routinely cry.

The comings and goings of the Yiddish enclaves were covered in minute detail by the Yiddish press: *Der Yidisher Zhurnal* ("The Jewish Journal"), founded in Toronto in 1913; *Der Kanader Yid* ("The Canadian Israelite"), established in 1910 and by 1913 known as *Dos Yiddishe Vort* ("the *Israelite Press*"); and, in particular, Montreal's "downtown" newspaper, the *Keneder*

Adler ("Canadian Eagle"), launched in 1907 and arguably the most influential Yiddish paper in the country.

The *Adler* was the brainchild of thirty-year-old Hirsch Wolofsky, a struggling businessman whose first venture, a fruit store on St. Lawrence Boulevard, had been ruined in a fire. Wolofsky was born in a small town in Poland to a Hasidic family. Orphaned as a teenager, he lived for a time in Łódź before emigrating to Canada with his wife, Sarah. He had family members in Montreal, and he and Sarah arrived in the city in 1900. With insurance money he received after his fruit store burned down, he and several investors started the *Adler*.

By October 1908, the paper was a daily, yet in its early days it was constantly on the brink financially. More than once Wolofsky contemplated giving up, but then the newspaper became more economically sound. While the *Adler* was slanted toward a Labour Zionist perspective, Wolofsky envisioned it as an organ which would represent all Jewish interests, and its news and cultural stories, editorials, and reviews generally reflected that balanced approach. During heated labour disputes in the garment industry that rocked Montreal's Jewish community, the paper did its best to steer a middle course, slightly veering to the left. It did not support striking workers unreservedly, but rather counselled compromise. This was probably because Wolofsky and his editors could not afford to alienate so-called "establishment" Jews who generally opposed labour action and who also were the *Adler*'s chief advertisers.

In 1914, Wolofsky acquired the English-language *Canadian Jewish Times* and turned it into the more influential *Canadian Jewish Chronicle*, hiring editors such as the brilliant, eloquent, and multilingual Ida Seigler to edit the weekly from 1917 to 1925 (Seigler was the first Jewish female newspaper editor in Canada). Wolofsky also played a key role in organizing Montreal's Vaad Ha'ir (Jewish Community Council), the centralized agency for more than sixty Jewish groups. In 2005, fifty-six years after Wolofsky died in 1949, the city of Montreal honoured him by dedicating a small park in his name on Avenue Coloniale, close to where the *Adler* was once located.

Above all, the *Adler*'s offices became the home for Montreal's "emerging Yiddish intelligentsia," as Rebecca Margolis puts it. Their other favourite haunts were Horn's Cafeteria, on the ground floor of the same building on St. Lawrence and Duluth; anarchist Hersh (Harry) Hershman's Jewish bookstore and reading room; and by 1914, the Yidishe Folks Biblyotek or Jewish Public Library, otherwise known as "the People's Library."

The library loomed large in the imagination of Jewish Montreal. As David Rome, the Canadian Jewish Congress archivist who served as the library's director for many years, said in a 1983 interview, "From day one the Jewish Public Library considered itself and was considered by others as one of the great institutions of the world, regardless of how small it was." Among those who enhanced the quality of the *Adler* and frequented the library were writers and Yiddishists such as J.I. Segal, a young poet; Israel Medres, who was connected to the newspaper for close to five decades and was a prolific commentator on Montreal Jewish life; and A. Almi (Eli Almi), a Jewish poet, essayist, and the author of twenty-six books.

Wolofsky also recruited Reuben Brainin, an internationally recognized Hebrew writer and critic who was living in the United States and had first visited Montreal in 1909 while he was on a speaking tour. An intense and soulful man with deep, penetrating eyes, a full salt-and-pepper beard, and an aristocratic bearing, Brainin worked at the *Adler* from 1912 to 1915. He immersed himself in Yiddish literature and actively promoted the Jewish Public Library during his brief stay in the city. One of his successors was Hershl Hirsch, a university-educated immigrant from a town near Kiev, who helped establish the *Zhurnal* in Toronto before relocating to Montreal a year later, in 1914. Hirsch, a playwright and the author of several Yiddish books, edited the *Adler* from 1918 to 1923.

By all accounts, readers appreciated the *Adler's* articles and insightful commentaries on various aspects of Jewish life, but working-class Jews equally faced hardships and labour difficulties that could not be wholly rectified by the erudite wisdom offered by the newspaper's editors. Genuine action was required and genuine action was what was taken.

Class Struggle

B eyond intellectual and cultural pursuits, the true hardships of Jewish immigrant life played out with all the melodrama of a Yiddish theatre production in the garment factories of Montreal, Toronto, and Winnipeg, where an intense and frequently bitter power struggle took place, a class conflict between owners and their underpaid and overworked employees. Many of the owners—all in Montreal—were Jewish. But for these entrepreneurs, business considerations almost always trumped any feelings of kinship they had for their workers. If that meant using strike-breakers— "scabs" in the eyes of the workers—during a labour stoppage, then so be it.

This confrontation was part of a larger and decisive showdown occurring throughout the Western world, between capital and labour; a clash between the unregulated world of the nineteenth century, in which labour was a commodity to be exploited, and the more modern and complex world of the early twentieth century, when workers not only questioned their place in society, but also demanded change. Despite any accusations to the contrary about communist plots and revolutions, the battles and ensuing strikes in the garment industry—as in other sectors—came down to a fight over union recognition, collective bargaining, higher wages, shorter hours (a sixty-hour work week was typical), and better working conditions.

In a 1912 *Maclean's* magazine feature article, John McAree estimated that "probably 75 percent of the Canadian Jews who have a trade are garment makers, furriers or cap makers." That high figure was the result of two related factors. The first was that setting up a small garment operation was inexpensive; in the early 1900s, one hundred dollars was all that was needed to acquire a sewing machine or two, a second-hand cutting knife, and an empty loft or garage for a "factory." And on the other side of the labour equation, many (though certainly not all) Jews arrived in Canada with the skills that they had gained in the factories and sweatshops of Europe and England. Their fame as skilled tailors was well known. "At a machine," McAree suggested, "two Jews are worth, at the lowest calculation, three Gentiles. One manufacturer told me the other day that one Jew is worth four Gentiles."

Many of these prodigious tailors were, in fact, Jewish seamstresses, who accounted for more than 60 per cent of all needleworkers in Canada. Their labour was plentiful and cheap. Tellingly, one of the first English-language phrases an immigrant garment worker learned in a Montreal factory was "Hurry up," because you could never work fast enough to satisfy the ill-tempered and impatient foremen.

In the early years of the twentieth century, the most active so-called Jewish unions were the United Garment Workers of America (UGWA) and the International Ladies' Garment Workers' Union (ILGWU), both with their main headquarters in New York City. Attempts to organize locals in Canada had to be done quietly, lest the owners find out what was afoot.

"Unyielding and adamant" would hardly describe the position of the owners, who subscribed to a position articulated by the operator of a Winnipeg metal factory, L.R. Barrett. "God gave me this plant," Barrett once declared, "and by God I'll run it the way I want to!" Hence, strikes over shorter hours by garment workers in Montreal and Winnipeg in 1907 and 1908 met with fierce management resistance. Another of the affected Jewish owners, Alan J. Hart (of the Hart clan and a member of the Spanish and Portuguese synagogue), called for the "foreign [Jewish] agitators" involved in the strike at his factory to be deported.

The more obdurate the owners, the angrier and more militant the unions became. The situation boiled over in 1912, with lengthy and acrimonious strikes that nearly tore apart Jewish communities in Montreal and Toronto. In Montreal, the garment factory owners had exasperated union officials and workers by banding together as the Montreal Clothing Manufacturers' Association. All the key Jewish owners—Solomon Levinson, Lyon Cohen,

Harris Keller, Noah Friedman, Harris Vineberg, and Jacob Elkin—were members. Cohen, the son of Polish Jewish immigrants who at the time of the strikes was living with his wife and children in a large brick house in Westmount, was their acknowledged leader. In his lifetime, he was a revered community stalwart, philanthropist, and Zionist. He famously welcomed Jewish immigrants to the city and genuinely cared about their welfare— provided that any newcomers who worked in his garment factory did not impede its smooth operation or compromise profit margins with what he and his fellow owners regarded as unacceptable demands about union rights.

Fed up by management's intransigence, the UGWA called a strike, which according to the *Adler* soon affected "every third person in Montreal." One of the leaders of the strike was Hananiah Meir Caiserman, a bright thirty-one-year-old accountant with strong socialist convictions. From the moment he arrived in Montreal in 1911 from Romania, he had immersed himself in labour issues and Yiddish culture. He and his wife Sarah were both committed Labour Zionists and they hosted numerous literary events in their home. In later years, he moderated his views sufficiently to serve as the general secretary of the Canadian Jewish Congress.

Another key personality on the side of labour was a skilful and engaging lawyer named Peter Bercovitch. He was born in Montreal in 1879 soon after his parents immigrated to Canada from Romania. A graduate of McGill and Laval, Bercovitch was called to the bar in 1901 and was appointed a King's Counsel a decade later; at the time he was the youngest lawyer to receive this honour in Quebec. In 1916, with much support from members of the city's Jewish community (as well as non-Jewish voters), he was elected to the Legislative Assembly of Quebec as a Liberal—unlike Ezekiel Hart in the early 1800s, Bercovitch was the first Jew allowed to take his seat in the assembly—and served for the next two decades. Then, in a 1938 federal by-election, he became an MP and represented the riding of Cartier until his death in 1942 at the age of sixty-three. Throughout his political career, he was a staunch defender of Canadian Jewish interests, refusing to back down from any perceived prejudicial or discriminatory attacks. And during the strikes of 1912, he assisted Jewish workers on the picket line who had been harassed by the police, and gained a well-deserved reputation as an "uptown" Jew who could be trusted.

The garment factory owners were firm in their resolve that local union leaders, denounced by them as "professional agitators" and "demagogues," had to be thwarted. They initially refused to negotiate and instead recruited burly private detectives to assault the strikers. That tactic merely had the opposite effect, and the workers grew more determined than ever to stand their ground. After nearly two months of animosity, a truce was agreed to at the end of July. The workers won reduced weekly hours, from fifty-five to forty-nine, but had to capitulate, at least for the moment, on the larger issues of shop unionization and collective bargaining.

In Toronto, many Jewish garment workers toiled at the T. Eaton Company's clothing factories. The head of the company, John Craig Eaton, was quite proud that he ran a non-union shop.

In February 1912, Eaton's management precipitated a confrontation when sixty-five tailors were given the time-consuming task of sewing in coat-linings but were not compensated for this extra work, which previously had been done by female seamstresses and finishers. The men said no. "We will not take the morsel of bread from the mouths of our sisters," they declared in Yiddish. Unwilling to tolerate such disobedience, the managers had the police march the tailors out of the factory and then locked them out. Within days, 1,200 workers—members of the ILGWU—were on a sympathy strike, yet John Craig Eaton and his managers remained resolute, declaring that unions had no legal right to interfere in the affairs of the company. Eaton also stated that he would shut down the factory before he acceded to union demands.

The Jewish community rallied to support the strikers with food and charity, and the ILGWU doled out meagre strike pay. Jewish women attempted to raise money for the strikers on the streets, until city officials ordered them to stop. A huge pro-labour rally was convened at Massey Hall on March 20, with three thousand vocal Yiddish and English unionists in the audience. Later that day, thousands joined in a parade of solidarity through the streets of the downtown, marching past the Eaton's factories and down to the Labor

Lyceum on the corner of Spadina Avenue and St. Andrew Street, the head-quarters of the city's Jewish garment unions. Many of those in attendance urged those attending the gathering to boycott Eaton's department store, though nothing came of that.

The key problem for the strikers was that their battle with Eaton's was per-ceived by non-Jewish workers to be strictly a Jewish labour matter, and they were not anxious to join in the fight. As had been the case in Montreal, wealth-ier, middle-class Jewish merchants and businessmen opposed the strike action and eschewed the negative attention about the community it garnered in the press. Many of them were members of the Holy Blossom congregation, includ-ing Sigmund Lubelsky, a senior Eaton's manager. The synagogue's rabbi, Solomon Jacobs—who asserted that "Jews must not rebel" if they hoped to fit into Canadian society—tried to mediate a settlement, together with Jacob Cohen, the first Jewish magistrate in Toronto and a former president of Holy Blossom. Yet Eaton's management refused to negotiate with the strikers, and ran ads in England and Wales for strike-breakers. By mid-April, with strike pay dwindling, the union more or less surrendered. A handful of the tailors were rehired by the company, though the majority were forced to find employment elsewhere. In the years that followed, Eaton's did not moderate its anti-union position, and for a time even stopped hiring Jewish workers.

The outbreak of the First World War in September 1914 was a boon for the country's garment industry, as government demand sustained factories with orders for military uniforms and other clothing. To keep the peace in the factories, owners acquiesced slightly and paid their workers enough to keep them happy—at least for a short period. In 1914, an internal struggle among UGWA officials and members in the U.S. led to the establishment of a more radical, Jewish-dominated splinter group, the Amalgamated Clothing Workers of America (ACWA), which soon attracted support among tailors and seamstresses in Montreal, Toronto, and Hamilton. This new union was not reticent about taking on management, and in several brief strikes in Montreal in 1916 it won recognition for collective bargaining at a few factories and higher wages for its members.

Most owners, however, had not changed their anti-unionization stance. This included Lyon Cohen, now the president of the Montreal Clothing Manufacturers' Association. It was the association's position that their workers, led astray by "alien agitators," were well paid and well treated but that the majority were "idle," which they argued was unpatriotic during a war. As further accusations were made that the Jewish members of the ACWA were in reality German agents—a charge repudiated by, among others, Peter Bercovitch in the Quebec Assembly—a volatile strike in one factory spread to others. Cohen was the catalyst for another lengthy and bitter confrontation— "eight savage weeks," as ACWA officials later described it—when at the end of December 1916, he fired one of his employees who was associated with the ACWA. By mid-February 1917, an estimated 4,500 garment workers were on the picket line against more than sixty garment businesses, and the Montreal menswear industry was essentially shut down. So unpopular was Cohen that when he tried to speak at the opening of the new Adath Jeshurun synagogue on St. Urbain Street, he was jeered loudly. While the *Adler* had mostly backed the strikers up to this point, the newspaper's publisher, Hirsch Wolofsky— who was in attendance—lectured the labour agitators that it was "not fitting for Jewish workers to disturb a religious ceremony."

Cohen's friend Sam Jacobs, who by the end of the year would be a Member of Parliament, offered to mediate the strike. But Cohen and the other owners, as they had initially done during the 1912 fight, remained determined to break the union and refused to negotiate. Not surprisingly, the owners' decision to bring in strike-breakers led to violent clashes that required intervention from the police.

The law was somewhat blind and prejudiced when it came to the rights of the union members, particularly because they were Jews. During one court proceeding, for instance, a judge noted that he had a hard time believing the testimony of the three Jewish defendants. They gave, he suggested, "evidence directly contrary to that of five constables, who from their many years of experience know what it is to perjure themselves and are, at least, Christians." Following a protest march by the strikers, *Le Devoir*'s editors equally felt it important to point out to their readers that "a very large part of the demonstrators, especially the women, were by their appearance Israelites."

The Jewish garment workers were disappointed by what they felt was the lukewarm support given to their struggle by the *Adler*, as well as the near silence about their battle from religious leaders. No doubt several of the more influential rabbis were too timid to publicly criticize the owners, many of whom were prominent members of the "uptown" Spanish and Portuguese and Shaar Hashomayim synagogues. Most, too, regarded the left-wing strikers—secular Jews and socialists—as "ungodly."

By March, several smaller independent factories had agreed to settlements, and the members of the manufacturers' association had softened their stand and were finally prepared to talk. Three months later, a negotiated compromise was reached, giving the workers a forty-six-hour week (down from the fifty hours they'd had to work prior to the strike), a two-dollar-a-week raise for all workers, and most importantly of all, recognition of the union. Other confrontations involving the ACWA were also settled in Toronto and Hamilton.

The 1917 strike was not the end of labour strife for Jewish workers in Montreal—or elsewhere. While the garment unions, like other unions in Canada (several with U.S. affiliations), gradually won more rights and greater influence on the factory floor, many of the strikes that followed over the next several decades were marked by violence, police abuse, and bitterness. And in the major Canadian cities, this perpetual class struggle continued to strain relations within Jewish communities.

For King and Country

The advent of the First World War in August 1914 produced a range of reactions among Canada's Jews. Community rallies were organized to raise funds for Jews caught in the European conflict, particularly those in the eastern part of the continent and in Russia. Many young Jewish men immediately volunteered for military service but were conflicted about fighting on the same side as Britain's ally, Czarist Russia, who had oppressed their family members. Others took steps to hide their ethnicity, like twenty-one-year-old Samuel Waskey, a printer from Winnipeg who was a private in the 44th Battalion and was killed at the Battle of the Somme in October 1916. He had changed his surname to Waskey from Warshawsky so that he would not be identified as a Jew. Others, according to Louis Rosenberg, "in order to avoid unpleasant experiences," took a more drastic step and changed their religious affiliation and registered as Protestants. By the end of the war, four bloody years later, approximately 2,700 Jewish men (though likely more) had served in the Canadian Expeditionary Force (CEF), with about 1,200 seeing action in Europe. Of those, an estimated 123 died in battle—and memorials with the names of fallen heroes were soon put up at numerous synagogues and cemeteries. At least seventy-five Canadian Jewish soldiers were honoured with various medals for bravery and distinguished service.

Most of the men had enlisted voluntarily, like twenty-five-year-old Samuel Hackman of Calgary, a Russian immigrant who quit his job at the Royal Crown Soap Works and became an infantryman in the CEF. A year later, he was killed in the Battle of the Somme, the first Jewish soldier from Calgary to die in the war. One month earlier, he had written home to his mother,

Pearl: "Don't worry much about me. I'm alright and I believe that I'll see you yet and we will be together. It is the opinion here of the men and officers that the war won't last very long the way our troops are pressing the enemy from all sides. I'm not downhearted and I'm still very courageous."

Another young man who made the ultimate sacrifice was twenty-year-old Edward Joseph Seidelman of Vancouver. His family called him Joe or Joseph. His father, William, was a Hungarian Jewish immigrant who, after living in Kansas and Seattle, had settled in Vancouver in the 1890s. There he met Esther Pearlman from Winnipeg. The two were married in 1896 and Joseph was born a year later. A daughter, Rachel, followed in 1898; Harry in 1900; Benjamin in 1902; and William Jr. in 1907, who was born a few months after his father died at the age of fifty-three. William and Esther were observant Jews. At their home on 2nd Avenue, they kept a chicken coop, and William slaughtered the chickens himself as skilfully as any *shochet* would. The Seidelmans owned a general store on Powell Street, but William's death led to several years of economic hardship for the family.

In 1916, Joseph had been a student at the University of British Columbia. Nearly six decades later, his sister Rachel remembered him as "a very able and very bright young man." He felt compelled to do his patriotic duty and at the beginning of May he enlisted in the 196th (Western Universities) Battalion, which was made up of more than 150 students from universities in Manitoba, Saskatchewan, Alberta, and B.C. Following a few months of training in Vancouver and at Camp Hughes in Manitoba, Seidelman was in England by November. Early in 1917, he was sent to northern France and found himself in the mucky trenches of the Western Front, where the shelling was constant and death was a daily occurrence. Even more ominously, he had been transferred to the 46th Battalion, which had the unfortunate reputation of being known as the "Suicide Battalion," since so many of its men were killed or wounded.

In the first week of April 1917, Seidelman wrote to Rachel about the lousy European weather. He also hoped that the war might end soon, though he was not optimistic. The "chances of peace do not ... look as rosy as I thought," he added, "but the Huns will be defeated ultimately." In the dozens of letters Joseph sent to Rachel, he never once commented on any antisemitic incidents he experienced or witnessed—or indeed any issue related to him being a Jewish soldier.

Shortly after writing that letter in April, Seidelman was one of thousands of Canadian soldiers who fought and won the Battle for Vimy Ridge, which is remembered as the country's defining moment of the war. The victory was costly: more than 3,500 Canadian soldiers perished during the four-day battle. Joseph Seidelman, however, survived. At the end of the month, possibly at the Battle of Arleux, he was wounded in his right leg during an attempt to capture German trenches, and sustained what he told his sister was "two very small pieces of shrapnel." He assured her that there was "absolutely nothing whatsoever for you to worry about." Nevertheless, the injury kept him convalescing in an army hospital for next five weeks.

Seidelman returned to the front in mid-June with a piece of shrapnel still lodged in his leg and the guns of "the Hun"—as he always referred to the Germans in his letters—"thundering" in the distance. During the ensuing fighting, he bravely rescued an officer who had been wounded near a barbed-wire entanglement. With the help of a stretcher-bearer, he carried the officer back to the trenches, where the wounded man received medical care.

The summer passed without much incident. Then, on October 10, he wrote to Rachel that he was caught in days of unrelenting rain "on the march to another town" in France. He and the other members of the 46th Battalion were, in fact, headed further north, toward Ypres in Belgium and then east to Passchendaele. The rain had turned the ground into a muddy bog, making any military manoeuvres next to impossible. That hardly made a difference to the British Army commander, Field Marshal Douglas Haig, as inflexible a military leader as there was during the war. He had decided that capturing the village of Passchendaele was the key to victory—bad weather and terrible land conditions or not. After several weeks of fighting and numerous casualties, Haig—who had also been responsible for the carnage of the Somme in 1916—convinced Canada's General Arthur Currie to undertake the assault. The Canadian Corps fought courageously, and during a three-week offensive achieved its objectives by capturing the ridge beyond the village, yet lost 15,654 men doing so. Young Joseph Seidelman did not live to see the victory, as pyrrhic as it turned out to be. He died on October 26, the first day of the battle, making him the first Jewish Canadian soldier from Vancouver to be killed in the war.

Twenty-three-year-old Lieutenant Myer Tutzer Cohen, from Toronto, also perished at Passchendaele. A member of the famed 42nd Battalion (Royal Highlanders of Canada), Cohen must have been one of the few Jewish soldiers in the war who felt comfortable enough to wear a kilt. The other men in the battalion affectionately called him "MacCohen." In October 1917, he led raids on German trenches during fighting in northern France and captured six enemy soldiers. For these actions, he was awarded the Military Cross. A month later, however, his luck ran out. On November 3, 1917, during the intense fighting near Passchendaele, Cohen and some of his men were caught in a German counterattack and all of them were killed. Later, when the Black Watch erected a stained-glass window in the Church of St. Andrew and St. Paul in Montreal, a Star of David was included as part of the design, to remember and honour Cohen.

In 1916, the same year Joseph Seidelman enlisted, an attempt was made to organize a separate Jewish regiment. The idea had been debated in Montreal almost from the day the war began. The *Adler*'s editor Reuben Brainin, among others, opposed the plan, regarding it as an unnecessary form of segregation. But during the summer of 1916 there was sufficient political and financial support to proceed, with the help of a generous contribution from the Montreal tobacco magnate and Jewish community philanthropist Sir Mortimer Davis. And so Sam Hughes, the minister of defence, permitted Captain Isidore Freedman, a thirty-six-year-old Glasgow-born diamond merchant, to recruit a Jewish Reinforcement Draft Company. Soon there were publicity posters in English and Yiddish proclaiming that "Britain expects every son of Israel to do his duty." The patriotic appeal worked. Freedman succeeded in attracting four hundred men, who were dispatched to England in 1917. However, military bureaucracy killed the dream: they never fought as a single unit and were divided among other Canadian battalions.

Jewish socialists and labourites held a different view of the war than Freedman and the Jewish volunteers for military service. They advocated neutrality and opposed the repressive aspects of the Canadian government's War Measures Act. Such attitudes were widely regarded as disloyal—especially if the immigrants in question had originated from one of the enemy countries—Germany or Austria-Hungary—or from post-Revolution Russia, which withdrew from the conflict following the signing of an armistice with Germany and its allies in December 1917. Thereafter, Jews and Bolshevism were intrinsically linked in the public's imagination by the press, and the authorities kept a close eye on a number of Jewish organizations.

After the war ended in November 1918, the situation worsened—especially in Winnipeg, which was the scene of the greatest labour strike in Canadian history in the spring of 1919 and was a city on the edge. Many returning soldiers were angry about the lack of jobs and were quick to blame "foreigners." In one incident, a group of veterans stormed the dry cleaning business of Jewish socialist Sam Blumenberg and forced his wife to kiss the British flag. They also attacked other Jewish businesses on Selkirk Avenue, the North End's main commercial centre.

Like most other strikes in Canada during this era, the Winnipeg General Strike was about union recognition, collective bargaining, and improved working conditions. Yet, partly due to the strike leaders' ill-conceived strategy, local and national authorities and the Winnipeg business community and mainstream press perceived the massive labour stoppage as the first step toward a Soviet-style revolution, all masterminded by foreign agitators. A report sent to officials in Ottawa from a Royal North West Mounted Police officer about the situation in Winnipeg suggested quite absurdly that "rich Jews" were meeting as part of a plot to overthrow the state. "The object of these secret meetings . . . [is to support] the strikers financially," the Mountie noted. "The Jews [are] fulfilling a mission for the higher up Bolsheviks."

In reality, the strike was mainly managed by British-born working-class men such as Robert Russell, Reverend William Ivens, and Frederick Dixon. The most prominent Jewish member of the strike committee was Abraham Heaps, a thirty-four-year-old English Jew whose parents had emigrated from Russia to Britain. Heaps, an upholsterer by training, had come to Winnipeg in 1911 and become involved with the city's Trades and Labour Council. On

June 17, the week before the strike officially ended, Heaps was arrested with the other strike leaders and charged with seditious conspiracy. At his trial, he skilfully defended himself and was acquitted.

In the 1925 federal election, as a candidate for the Independent Labour Party, he successfully ran for a seat in the House of Commons in the riding encompassing the immigrant North End. As an MP for the next fifteen years, Heaps—who later represented the Co-operative Commonwealth Federation (CCF)—worked with his fellow labourite from Winnipeg, J.S. Woodsworth, advocating for old age pensions and unemployment insurance.

Dreaming of Zion

The First World War and the redrawing of the global map at the signing of the Treaty of Versailles in 1919 also advanced the aspirations of the Zionist movement. For at least two generations of Jews, the idea of a Jewish homeland in Palestine, the biblical Holy Land, seemed like a remote, if improbable, possibility. Yet the dreamers, visionaries, and early pioneers—the *chalutzim* from Russia and Eastern Europe who had settled in Ottoman-controlled Palestine in the 1880s and 1890s—never gave up hope. They had, in their view, no choice.

The dream became more serious with the emergence of the modern Zionist movement at a congress held in Basel, Switzerland, in August 1897, and with the election of the Austro-Hungarian Jewish journalist Theodor Herzl as the Zionist Organization's first president. A mythical figure in modern Jewish history, Herzl—only forty-four when he died in July 1904—had articulated his conviction about the enormous need for a Jewish homeland in his pamphlet *Der Judenstaat* ("The Jewish State"), published in 1896. As in Russia, the persistence of antisemitism in Europe—including witnessing the degradation of the French army captain Alfred Dreyfus who in January 1895 was falsely convicted of treason in what would become an intense political and judicial scandal—had convinced him that assimilation was both unattainable and detrimental to the future of the Jewish nation.

In the years after the Basel congress, Zionism attracted a lot of support in Canada, despite it being problematic. About the last thing established Jews wanted was to be accused of disloyalty to the country that had so generously taken them in. Was it possible to raise funds and actively campaign for a

Jewish homeland in Palestine and still be a devoted Canadian? For the vast majority of Canadian Jews, who had absolutely no desire to relocate halfway across the world to the primitiveness of Jerusalem, the answer was a resounding yes. The splintering of the movement into a half-dozen factions, from the general to the religious Mizrachi, to Labour Zionism and the Socialist-Territorialists (who were prepared to accept a temporary homeland such as Uganda, which for a few years was hotly debated) weakened its overall appeal.

Still, mainstream Zionist groups for men and women were organized in Montreal, Toronto, and Winnipeg, as well as in cities with smaller Jewish populations such as Kingston, Hamilton, and Ottawa. By November 1899, these various groups became part of a national Federation of Zionist Societies of Canada (FZSC)—the first such national Jewish organization in Canada—with nearly one thousand members (approximately 20 per cent of the total Jewish population), and more kept joining each year. In 1907 in Calgary and Edmonton—with their tiny Jewish populations of less than six hundred in Calgary and less than two hundred in Edmonton—Zionist societies were also established. Blue and white Jewish National Fund coin boxes were soon mandatory in many Jewish homes and offices, and at bar mitzvahs and weddings. Lectures by visiting Zionist dignitaries like Dr. Nahum Sokolow and David Ben-Gurion, the future prime minister of Israel, attracted large Jewish and non-Jewish crowds. When Sokolow came to Toronto in 1913, for instance, the mayor of the city, Horatio Hocken, arranged that he be given a personal tour and even hosted a kosher lunch for him at a downtown hotel.

The mainstream movement's key personality in its early years was Clarence de Sola—forty-two years old in 1900 and a member of Montreal's most famous rabbinical family. An observant Jew, de Sola was a successful commission agent and businessman (and, as previously noted, was appointed Belgium's consul to Montreal in 1905). He was also a generous philanthropist and deeply committed to sustaining the city's Jewish community—as he envisioned it. In 1899, he had been elected the FZSC's first president, and immediately became the face and voice of the cause throughout the country. He was indeed a devoted champion of Zionism, but he also did not like being questioned and was used to having his own way.

The Zionist movement in Canada, like nearly every other Jewish institution and organization, was built on a passionate volunteerism that persists to the present day. Over time, the Zionist cause attracted a small army of loyal devotees. It was true (also like other Jewish organizations) that money bought prestige and influence among local Zionist groups: the more you gave, the more everyone around the table was prepared to listen to your opinion—no matter how much they might disagree with it.

The movement greatly benefited, too, from the dedication and hard work of thousands of Jewish women across the country—members of Canadian Hadassah chapters, successors to the smaller Daughters of Zion groups and modelled after the American Hadassah organization established by teacher and social activist Henrietta Szold in New York in 1912. Among the founders of the Canadian organization were Torontonians Anna Selick, Rose Dunkelman, and Rebecca Brickner, the wife of Rabbi Barnett Brickner of Holy Blossom, who also organized the synagogue's active sisterhood. Together with Labour Zionism's Pioneer Women, the ladies of Hadassah were the Zionist "shock troops," as Gerald Tulchinsky describes them. Hadassah, in particular, "soon became the most continuously active arm of Zionism in Canada, infusing the movement with a sense of immediate and pressing concern."

The Hadassah spirit was epitomized by Lillian Freiman of Ottawa, Hadassah's first national president. In their day, she and her husband Archie were the most steadfast and dynamic Zionist duo in the country. Archie, who was born in Lithuania in 1880 as Aharon Yaacov Freiman, had come with his parents to Canada in 1893, settling in Hamilton. He eventually moved to Ottawa and ran a successful furniture department store on Rideau Street. Archie and Lillian, who had been born in 1885 in the lumber town of Mattawa, three hundred kilometres northwest of Ottawa, were married in 1903.

Lillian's father was the colourful Moses Bilsky, an immigrant from Lithuania who is recognized as one of the first Jews to settle in Ottawa (in 1856 or 1857). He was also instrumental in the founding of the city's first synagogue in 1892, Adath Jeshurun, as well as the burial society and a Zionist group, and taught his children the importance of giving back to the community, a lesson that Lillian learned well.

By their wedding day, Archie was already an active community volunteer and a member of Ottawa's Zionist society. The year he got married, he was elected the president of the Adath Jeshurun synagogue—which soon relocated a few blocks from its aging building on Murray Street to a new and distinguished synagogue on King Edward Street (hence it was popularly known as the "King Edward shul")—a position he held for the next two-and-a-half decades. At the end of the First World War, Lillian visited Jewish communities from Halifax to Vancouver and single-handedly raised close to $200,000 in cash and supplies for Palestine reconstruction—a significant amount of money from a total Canadian Jewish population of about 120,000. A year later, she became president of the national Hadassah organization, a position she held until her death in 1940.

In their quest to collect funds for schools, hospitals, and impoverished children in Jerusalem and elsewhere in Palestine, the women of Hadassah held bazaars, raffles, and other such events. In later years, they also organized Zionist study groups, offered courses in Jewish history, and financially supported Jewish libraries. They were "frantically active," as one delegate to the 1924 Zionist Societies' annual meeting described it. The Hadassah philosophy was that "to be a good Zionist is to be a good Canadian," and that motto epitomized the positive contributions of chapters across the country. While working-class Jews sometimes used the term "Hadassah ladies" to describe wealthy Jewish women with too much time on their hands, the truth was that these women accomplished a great deal. They made a difference in their own right, asserting themselves as legitimate leaders in the Jewish community—not an easy task in a male-dominated world. As one Labour Zionist from Toronto so succinctly remarked about the Pioneer Women: "The women wanted to break away from the men because the men didn't think that the women had any brains."

Clarence de Sola focused his energies on raising funds, which he maintained was the most effective way Canadian Jews could assist the cause, rather than actually emigrating to Palestine. Some Zionists outside of North America later considered this enduring Canadian—and American—approach hypocritical. "A Canadian Zionist," caustically remarked the Palestinian-born

Aron Horowitz, who worked in Winnipeg as a Zionist official in the late thirties, "is a person who obtains a donation from a second person to send a non-Canadian or a non-American Jew to Palestine."

In the spring of 1917, de Sola met with the British foreign secretary, Arthur Balfour, who advised him about a positive shift in British policy toward Jews and Palestine. In the midst of the war, the British were most keen to secure the support of the "international power of the Jews," as the British Conservative MP Robert Cecil termed this imaginary influence—a misconception opportunistically fostered by Chaim Weizmann (the first president of Israel) and other Zionists in an attempt to convince the British government that a strong Jewish presence in Palestine was in Britain's best geopolitical interests.

Months later, de Sola was as delighted as other Canadian Jews with the so-called Balfour Declaration. In a letter of November 2, 1917—published in the press in a brief article a week later—from Balfour to Walter Rothschild (the 2nd Baron Rothschild), a leading British Zionist, Balfour indicated that "His Majesty's Government view with favour the establishment in Palestine of a national home for the Jewish people." The wording, which had been suggested by British Zionists and then revised by Prime Minister David Lloyd George and members of his inner war cabinet, was deliberately ambiguous. And as subsequent events over the next two decades were to show, British commitment in the face of Arab hostility wavered to the point where the declaration became almost meaningless. In truth, as historian Jonathan Schneer concludes in his study of the making of the Balfour Declaration, the British were duplicitous with every party involved in the question of Palestine: the Jews, Arabs, French, and Turks. But in 1917, a Jewish homeland in Palestine seemed imminent. For years after, the declaration was celebrated like a regular Jewish holiday in Canada, as "Balfour Day," with parades, mass meetings, and receptions. As Winnipeg lawyer Mark Shinbane put it, after the Balfour Declaration was announced, "everybody became a Zionist."

With absolute faith in the British government, de Sola argued that much of his work was completed and that the British should be allowed to advance the cause. Many Zionist leaders in Canada strongly disagreed, believing that their lobbying of the British and fundraising must continue, and a power struggle ensued. In 1919, at a Zionist gathering in Toronto, de Sola resigned as president and the more amenable Archie Freiman—who adopted a more egalitarian approach—was soon elected by a committee to replace him.

Some of the opposition to de Sola had come from younger members. The dream of a Jewish homeland in Palestine had attracted much support from idealistic and eager young adults—none more so than Bernard Joseph of Montreal. In 1910, the precocious Joseph, then only eleven years old, organized the first Young Judaea club in Canada. When he was a McGill student in 1917, he played a key role in establishing the Young Judaea National League of Canada. Less than a decade later, there were seventy-five affiliated clubs across the country. The majority of those who joined were keen to study Jewish history, promote Hebrew language and literature, and march in support of "Jewish national regeneration." Joseph, more zealous than most Canadian Zionists, took this one step further. In the spring of 1918, together with a few hundred other young Canadian men, he joined the British-organized Jewish Legion (made up mostly of American volunteers) to help liberate Palestine from Ottoman control.

He later continued his studies in Montreal and London. By the early 1930s, he had changed his name to Dov Yoseph and made *aliyah* (literally, "to go up")—i.e., immigrated to Palestine. He settled in Jerusalem, worked as lawyer, and became a high-ranking Zionist official and later a prominent Israeli politician. During the 1948 War of Independence, Joseph was appointed the military governor of Jerusalem. He was the second person to hold that position since Pontius Pilate had served as the Roman prefect of Judaea from AD 26 to 36.

Though Zionism had united Canadian Jews in a common cause, there were demands from community leaders in Montreal, Toronto, and Winnipeg for a broader and more democratically elected Jewish parliament, which it was believed could more effectively coordinate fundraising efforts and address a wide range of issues affecting Jews in Canada and across the world. Paramount was the plight of Jews in Russia and Eastern Europe in the years after the Russian Revolution. The civil war, poverty, and antisemitism of the new regime had led to the death of an estimated hundred thousand, and left as many as sixty thousand children as orphans. Jews in Canada felt helpless to do anything about this tragedy.

The view was that if Canadian Jews could overcome the various divisions within the larger community—and that remained to be seen—the establishment of a central Jewish organization was a smart idea, at least in theory. Still, if the backers of this congress, who genuinely desired to take positive action, had been honest with themselves, they would have admitted that in 1919 true Jewish power and influence in Canada was extremely limited. They forged ahead regardless.

As a first step, Labour Zionists and representatives of other Jewish organizations in Montreal met early in 1915 to discuss ways to aid Jews in Europe impacted by the war. At this gathering, it was decided to create the Canadian Jewish Alliance, with representatives of about a dozen other Montreal Jewish organizations, which within four years became the Canadian Jewish Congress (CJC). Reuben Brainin, who was still the editor of the *Adler* in 1915—and was chosen as the Alliance's first president—was especially supportive of the plan to establish a Canada-wide Congress, and wrote many editorials extolling its importance, as did the Yiddish press in Toronto and Winnipeg. Modelled after the American Jewish Congress established at a convention in Philadelphia in 1918, the CJC's mandate was to support the British promise of a Jewish homeland in Palestine; to campaign for equal rights for Jews and end antisemitic practices; and to aid Jews in Europe with relief and an open Canadian immigration policy. None of these goals would be easily or quickly achieved.

Every adult Jewish man or woman, for a nominal payment of ten cents, was eligible to vote or run for one of the 209 Congress delegate positions; these were determined through a division of the country into Jewish population districts. In the hundreds of cities and towns wherever Jews could be found, an array of community activists, religious leaders, organizers, businessmen, and labourers from every walk of life and representative of nearly every political viewpoint and organization took up the challenge and stood as candidates. This show of democracy and the participation of so many Eastern European immigrants and their children signalled a power shift among Canada's Jews. The days when Jewish life was dictated by a select group of Anglo and German "uptowners" in Montreal and Toronto had seemingly ended.

In early March 1919, twenty-five thousand voters (about 20 per cent of the total Canadian Jewish population) cast ballots in community offices and synagogues. But of those elected to the inaugural Congress, the vast majority were men. This included the Congress's first president, Lyon Cohen—the Montreal garment factory owner—and Yiddish and labour advocate Hananiah Caiserman, its general secretary, who had played a pivotal role in making the Congress a reality. Only six women were elected—three from Montreal and three from Toronto, including twenty-seven-year-old Betty Goldstick, who was active in the Toronto Zionist movement.

There was a tremendous sense of anticipation at the opening of Congress's first plenary session, convened at Montreal's Monument-National theatre from March 16 to 19, 1919. The delegates, who hailed "from St. John's to Vancouver," and more than 2,500 visitors truly heeded the words of the *Canadian Jewish Chronicle*, which had declared that at this historic gathering "the destiny of our people is being shaped." Schoolchildren performed and sang in Yiddish and Hebrew. And then, accompanied by an orchestra, everyone in attendance sang "Hatikvah," the Zionist anthem, with great enthusiasm. On their feet, the delegates, as was later recorded, "waved flags and drowned the final notes in a thunder of applause lasting several minutes." Then Lyon Cohen's stirring inaugural presidential address urged them to be prudent in their deliberations and respectful of each other's ideas.

The delegates took Cohen's words seriously. But though they debated many issues, one of the few actual decisions reached was to support the formation of the Jewish Immigrant Aid Society (JIAS), "to urge the liberalization of Canada's immigration laws and to co-ordinate Jewish war relief activities across Canada." The Congress's chief advocate and the chair of its immigration committee was Sam Jacobs, who had been elected as a Liberal in the Montreal riding of George-Étienne Cartier—which incorporated the St. Lawrence Boulevard neighbourhood—in the federal election of December 1917 that had bitterly divided the country over the issue of conscription. He was at the time and for some years the only Jewish MP in the House of Commons—in

fact he was the first Jewish MP since Henry Nathan of Victoria in 1871–72—
and so was expected to represent Jewish interests.

Jacobs's victory cemented a strong tie between the leaders of the Jewish
community, especially in Montreal and Toronto, with the federal Liberal
Party. For decades after, and despite less than preferential treatment for
Jewish immigrants, Jewish businessmen raised money and voted for the
Liberals rather than the Conservatives. Still, after his victory, the *Adler* had
reminded Jacobs that he was "not elected by wealthy 'Uptown' Jews but [by]
the common masses of the 'Downtown'" who were counting on him. He took
those words and this responsibility to heart.

The Congress's first meetings concluded with optimism about the future.
Summing up that spirit of cooperation in an editorial, the *Canadian Jewish
Chronicle* put it like this: "We are a peculiar people, all the more peculiar in
that each one of us is an individualist in thought and action but we can meet
on common ground and that ground is the welfare of the Jew."

This was true for a vital issue such as immigration. Yet two years of local
self-interest, geographic distances, political diversity, and plain narrow-
mindedness all crippled the Congress's advancement. Cohen did not provide
adequate leadership, money dried up, and the Congress became dormant for
the next thirteen years—until the rising threat of antisemitism in Europe
spurred Jewish community leaders to revive it.

[13]

Gentiles Only

I n its early years, the Jewish Immigrant Aid Society was not the national
organization the Congress envisioned, nor did it have sufficient financial
support. But that did not stop its devoted volunteers from doing all they
could to assist Russian and Eastern European Jews devastated by the horrific
civil war that followed the Bolsheviks' seizure of power in late 1917. In all,
more than a million people were displaced by the conflict. Though the
International Red Cross and later the nascent League of Nations did help
many refugees, they did not have the necessary resources to adequately deal
with a human rights disaster on such a grand and tragic scale.

In Montreal and Ottawa, Jewish leaders turned to Lillian Freiman to coordinate relief efforts. The initial plan was ambitious—to raise sufficient funds
and find foster homes for one thousand Jewish orphans. Freiman was up to
the challenge. She recruited to the cause Sir Mortimer Davis's wife, Henriette,
as well as two high-profile, non-Jewish honorary patrons: Isabel Meighen, the
wife of Arthur Meighen, the newly installed prime minister; and Laura
Borden, the wife of Meighen's immediate predecessor, Sir Robert Borden.
Travelling across the country, she and the women who assisted her raised
close to $100,000 and obtained applications from 1,500 potential foster fam-
ilies, mostly from Western Canadian cities and towns. In the meantime, "on
humanitarian grounds" the federal government's immigration branch had
capped the number of children permitted into the country at two hundred,
provided they met certain health standards. By the spring of 1921, it was
decided that only 146 children should be sent to Canada; the reality was that,
of the 1,500 initial expressions of interest, only 149 of the foster family

applications were properly completed and approved. Freiman journeyed to Antwerp in Belgium to meet the first group of about a hundred, who she brought with her to Quebec. The rest of the children arrived weeks later. The orphans affectionately called her "Mama Freiman."

That Freiman and her supporters succeeded in bringing any Jewish orphans to Canada at all was surprising. In the wake of the Russian Revolution, political turmoil in Europe, rising fear of communism and foreigners, and the serious economic dislocation caused by the First World War, Canadian immigration had become more restrictive—at least when it came to such groups as Jews, who faced numerous obstacles, and Chinese immigrants, who were banned entirely.

During the twenties and thirties, Jews were frequently portrayed in the English- and French-language press, and by politicians, church leaders, and businessmen, as dangerous Bolshevik sympathizers; urbanites, rather than famers, who threatened the virtuous rural ideal imagined for Canada; and, above all, as a "race" that could never truly assimilate into a Christian nation. It hardly mattered that the country's 126,000 Jews in 1921 represented only 1.4 per cent of the total population, and that they wielded no real political or economic power. The popular mainstream view was that there were too many Jews in the country and that Canada definitely did not need any more. Regardless, Jewish newcomers kept arriving during the 1920s. (According to Louis Rosenberg's figures, even with the stringent federal government rules, 44,897 Jewish immigrants entered Canada from 1919 to 1931, compared to 69,897 from 1903 to 1915.)

Antisemitism became an entrenched and acceptable aspect of Canadian society. Summer resorts, beaches, and golf clubs and hotels from Halifax to Victoria barred Jews, with signs proclaiming "Gentiles Only." St. Andrews Golf Club was opened in 1925 (it is no longer in operation) on property in North York (north of Toronto). Though several Jews had been investors, that still did not stop the board of the club from erecting the sign: "This course is restricted to Gentiles only. Please do not question this policy." Left with no alternative, some of the wealthier members of the Jewish community opened their own club, the Oakdale Golf Club on Jane Street and Sheppard Avenue West, which still has a large Jewish clientele to this day. In 1923, Westdale, a new suburb in the western area of Hamilton, "marketed itself as a WASP only zone," explains labour historian Craig Heron. The developers' advertisement declared that "None of the lands described . . . shall be used, occupied by or let or sold to Negroes, Asiatics, Bulgarians, Austrians, Russians, Serbs, Romanians, Turks, Armenians, whether British subjects or not, or foreign-born Italians, Greeks, or Jews."

Jews who had experienced antisemitism in Europe were not surprised by this treatment: it was the way it had always been. Others tried to explain it as the product of discrimination. If Jews were indeed radicals as they were accused of being, the editor of the *Canadian Jewish Chronicle* reasoned, then the antisemitism was a backlash to the persecution and prejudice they had been subjected to. "[The] Gentile environment has created the modern Jew," the paper concluded in a November 1920 editorial, "yet he himself is being credited or debited, as the case may be, with all its results . . . the Gentiles, of course, rarely stop to think that perhaps they themselves are responsible, and the Jew is consequently made the scapegoat for all the crimes that have to be expiated."

Insisting that it was possible to improve the situation (which it wasn't), the editors of Toronto's *Canadian Jewish Review* advised readers to take the high road, to refrain from complaining or writing letters to the editor about anti-semitic incidents. "Jews are expected to be better than Gentiles when there are Gentiles about," the journal suggested. "Each one knows that he can bring the race into unpleasant prominence with little effort and so is always of good character." The *Review* urged Jews to be more patient and to ignore the slights if at all possible.

Neither understanding the root cause of antisemitism nor transforming all Jews into model Canadian citizens would have made one iota of difference, however. Prejudice and discrimination against Jews was endemic during the twenties, and only became worse in the decade of the Great Depression that followed. The more Jews tried to move out of the garment factories and into middle-class professional pursuits, into the non-Jewish world, the more resistance they faced. Jewish doctors and medical students had an impossible time finding hospitals which would offer them clinical appointments or intern-ships. The 351 Jewish lawyers in Canada in 1931 (of a total of 8,058 lawyers in Canada), including two Jewish women practising in Ontario, were only hired by Jewish law firms. Qualified Jewish teachers were overlooked for teaching positions; and department stores including Eaton's and Ogilvy's refused to employ Jewish clerks for many years. As Winnipeg's *Jewish Post* noted in an editorial of January 1928, if during a job interview prospective employees identified themselves as Jewish, the odds were that the position was "already filled." "It is often harder for a Jew to get a job, everything else being equal, simply because he is a Jew," the newspaper observed.

Starting in 1926, McGill University officials who were unhappy with so many Jewish students—25 per cent of the students in the 1924–25 first-year class were Jewish—came up with creative and discriminatory ways to cut the "Hebrew" enrolment, so that by 1935 the number of Jews attending the univer-sity had declined by half. Other universities followed suit, implementing formal and informal quota systems against Jews that became more pronounced in the 1930s. Ira Mackay, McGill's dean of the faculty of arts—a professor of inter-national and constitutional law who was hailed at the time of his death in 1934 for his "brilliant scholastic ability and recognized keen perspective"—expressed what must be the clearest statement of academia's attitudes toward Jews. "The simple obvious truth is that the Jewish people are of no use to us in this country," he told Arthur Currie, McGill's principal (and the commander of the Canadian Corps in the First World War) in a letter of April 1926. "Almost all of them adopt one of the four following occupations, namely merchandising, money lending, medicine and law, and we have already far too many of our own people engaged in these occupations and professions at the present ... [While I have] the highest regard for the better class of Jews ... as a race of men their traditions and practices do not fit in with a high civilization in a very new country."

Owing to Quebec's dual Protestant and Catholic school system, Montreal's Jews had their own particular problems to confront. In 1924, the city's Protestant School Board had had enough of overseeing and supporting the education of thousands of Jewish children, as had been its responsibility for more than two decades. Officials griped about the lack of tax money allocated to finance this education—using financial figures that were debatable, according to the *Canadian Jewish Chronicle's* calculations—and continued to rebuff lobbying by the Jewish community to appoint a Jewish board member. Reluctantly, the board had hired some Jewish teachers in schools where there were high numbers of Jewish students, yet board members stood firm, as they had for many years, that appointing even one Jew to the Protestant board was contradictory to the "Christian character" of the school system.

The issue split the city's Jewish community more or less along the uptown-downtown divide: most "uptowners" opposed segregation and believed it was more sensible to maintain the status quo, but with Jewish representation on the board; while the "downtowners" felt humiliated by what they perceived as the Protestant board's treatment of them as second-class, and demanded a separate, publicly funded Jewish school system with Jewish teachers and board members.

The school question was investigated by a provincial royal commission, considered by the courts, and endlessly debated and commented on in the press for six years before a compromise deal favouring the uptown position was agreed to in 1930. Still, it was not much of a compromise: Jewish students were to remain the responsibility of the Protestant board, yet were to be penalized for missing classes during Jewish holidays, and the board was to continue to employ Jewish teachers at its discretion.

During the commission's hearings, Protestant animosity toward the Jews on both sides was evident. The message was clear: rather than complaining, Jews should be grateful for the education they received and had no right to demand anything. As the editors of *Le Soleil* in Quebec City pointed out in February 1926, as "immigrants and sons of immigrants, [Jews] have no special rights." Later that same week, in another editorial, the paper offered this observation: "We owe nothing to Jews . . . We are a Christian country, a Christian nation and not a neutral, unbelieving and materialistic one."

Le Soleil's blunt view that religious differences made it impossible for Jews to fully assimilate, forever branding them as outsiders and a legitimate threat to Canada's Christian identity, became a frequent topic—if not an obsession—for French Catholic and nationalist advocates and journalists during the interwar years. More extreme in their opinions than Protestant English-Canadians, and more insecure about their place in Canada, many French Catholic writers—but by no means all—demonized Jews "as a parasite, the bearer of a germ spreading an insidious disease that was undermining the national health," in the words of historian Irving Abella. Typical was the anti-Jewish invectives of Abbé Édouard-Valmore Lavergne of Notre-Dame-de-Grâce in Quebec City. A prolific writer, in an editorial of September 1921 entitled "Haine aux Juifs" ("Hate the Jews") and published in *L'Action Catholique*, the influential church organ whose pages frequently condemned Jews, he wrote, "The Jews, as a race are our born enemies. Their goal is the destruction of Christianity. In order to achieve this goal, it was necessary to shed rivers of blood."

One solution to Quebec's Jewish problem that was launched in the early twenties was the *Achat chez nous* ("Buy From Us") movement. Ostensibly it was started to promote French-Canadian merchants and businesses, but in reality it was a campaign to boycott Jewish commercial interests—to "free" French Catholics "from Jews and usurers," as Abbé Philibert Grondin (who believed as early as 1910 that Jews were taking over the province's finances) explained. The logic of the boycott was simple. "If we do not buy from them," *L'Action Catholique* declared, "then they will leave."

"They" never did leave, however, and the boycott movement—like today's Boycotts, Divestment, and Sanctions (BDS) campaign against Israel—had limited impact. In a lucid moment in 1933, Abbé Lionel Groulx, the revered priest, historian, and nationalist who inspired a generation of Quebec intellectuals, came to regard antisemitism as "a negative and silly solution," though he still endorsed the anti-Jewish boycott, wrote about race purity, and blamed Jews for corrupting Quebec's morals and values.

Groulx's view that Jews were responsible for the "moral decay" of society was an old charge that dated back to the early nineteenth century. There was also the widely held perception that Jews monopolized the liquor business, reaping huge profits from bootlegging during the Prohibition era in Canada—from about 1915 (it varied according to province) to 1922—and the United States, from 1919 to 1933. And it was true: selling liquor to American bootleggers like Chicago gangster Al Capone made such Jews as Charlie Burns (originally Bernstein) of London, Ontario, very rich. By the early thirties, however, he had lost his fortune in the stock market crash.

There were also the Bronfmans (fittingly, in Yiddish, Bronfman means "whiskey man"), especially brothers Harry and Sam. "Mr. Sam," as he was affectionately called, who became head of the family business, was a mercurial personality. He lived his life, as he liked to put it, "at the head table."

The Bronfman family's meteoric rise started with their purchase of a few hotels in Manitoba and Saskatchewan, which also brought them into the liquor trade. In 1912, Sam was only twenty-three years old when he was running the Bell Hotel on Main Street in Winnipeg and by his account making about $30,000 a year, a lot of money for the time. Gossip over the years had it that the Bell, as well as the family's hotels in Yorkton, Saskatchewan, were being used as brothels. All Sam, who enjoyed a witty retort, would say when he was asked about this story was, "if they were, they were the best [brothels] in the West."

Though provincial governments started passing Prohibition legislation in 1915 and 1916, so that by 1917 every province except Quebec was technically "dry," the demand for liquor did not suddenly vanish, as it hadn't in the U.S. after 1919. Since the provinces could only control the sale of liquor within their own boundaries, the Bronfmans and other liquor dealers remained in business, shipping booze from one province to thirsty customers in another until the federal government tried to stop this interprovincial trade with national Prohibition legislation in 1918. Even then, there were enough loopholes to drive a large truck through, and buying booze via physicians and pharmacists was fairly easy. Sam later estimated that during the two-year period from 1916 to 1918, the family booze business made a very respectable $400,000 after accounting for expenses—the equivalent of approximately $6 million in Canadian dollars in 2018.

With the introduction of Prohibition in the United States, those profits skyrocketed. Even if U.S. officials had allocated proper funds to do so—which they hadn't—enforcing the ban on alcohol or bootlegging was nearly impossible, especially along the isolated American border with Manitoba and Saskatchewan. The U.S. "noble experiment" and the continuing demand for booze in speakeasies and private saloons was too good an opportunity for gangsters such as Arnold Rothstein, Meyer Lansky, and Al Capone to pass up. That meant that the Bronfmans were dealing indirectly with some nefarious criminals. The business was lucrative but dangerous, and never more so than in 1922.

Late on the night of October 4, Paul Matoff, a thirty-five-year-old Russian Jewish immigrant who was the husband of Sam's sister Jean—and the father of two young daughters—was murdered in the tiny town of Bienfait, Saskatchewan, sixteen kilometres north of the U.S. border. A flamboyant character, Matoff was the manager of the Bronfmans' "boozorium," a liquor warehouse they had set up to take advantage of the sales opportunities offered by American Prohibition. That night, Matoff was sitting in the town's railway station telegraph office with $6,000 he had collected from a North Dakota bootlegger named Lee Dillege (or Dellage) when, according to Colin Rawcliffe, the station's telegrapher, the only witness to the crime who was in the ticket office, someone poked a twelve-gauge shotgun through the station's bay window and shot him dead. By the time Rawcliffe came to Matoff's aid, Dillege was sitting beside Matoff cradling his head. The money as well as Matoff's ring and diamond tie pin were later found to be missing and it is unknown when they were taken or by whom. The police eventually charged Dillege, the most likely suspect, and a local driver named Jimmy Lacoste, who worked with him, with the murder and robbery. Yet there was insufficient evidence to convict them—the crime may, in fact, have been perpetrated by other bootleggers Matoff had dealings with—and the case was never solved.

Matoff's death was a tragedy that scandalized the Bronfman family and their business, adding more credence to the distorted view that only Jews were shipping liquor to the U.S. It was not illegal to do so, but in the eyes of many, selling whisky was a "moral abomination". Few of these critics, however, were bothered that the biggest producers of liquor in Canada—the Hudson's

Bay Company, Gooderham and Worts, and Hiram Walker—made their millions exactly the same way as the Bronfmans: by taking advantage of loopholes in weak Canadian and American Prohibition laws.

When Sam and his wife Saidye relocated to Montreal from Winnipeg in 1924, they were "downtown" Jews, though not for long. By 1930, two years after the Bronfmans acquired the Seagram distillery company, he and Saidye and their three children—Minda, Phyllis, and Edgar (Charles was born in 1931)—had definitely become "uptown" Jews, and were ensconced in "Oaklands," their Westmount mansion on Belvedere Road. Suffice it to say that few immigrants from the villages of the Pale owned homes that were anointed with a name.

Active in the Jewish community and president of the revamped Canadian Jewish Congress from 1939 to 1962, Sam Bronfman was the proverbial outsider always trying to force his way in. He transformed himself into an "Anglophile," according to his son Edgar, and craved being part of the non-Jewish establishment. He and Saidye sent Edgar and Charles to a non-Jewish private school, Selwyn House, as Anglo an institution as there was in Montreal in the thirties and forties. For years, all Sam wanted was a respectable Senate appointment, but he never got it, mainly because of his links to liquor and the fact he was a Jew, and a rich one at that. (The first Jew appointed to the Senate was David Croll in 1955. He was a former mayor of Windsor and member of the Ontario provincial cabinet from 1934 to 1937, another Jewish first.)

Sam Bronfman's wealth and impressive success as a businessman owed to his clever, astute, and legal marketing of booze—though his many detractors saw it differently. The double standard in judging the Bronfmans' legacy comes down, at least partly, to the fact that they were Jewish. As a young man, Edgar found this confusing. "Despite their immense wealth, my parents did not escape [the] pain [of antisemitism]," he wrote in his autobiography, published three years after his death in 2013. "On the one hand they were clearly Jews, but on the other they were empire builders who longed to be bona fide members of the non-Jewish power elite, the majority of whom were not welcoming Jews. Though they never said so, my guess is that if others had allowed them to do so, they might have cast off their Jewish identity at the first opportunity." Yet, when that proved impossible, Sam Bronfman did the next best thing: through his position on the Canadian Jewish Congress, he became the most important Jew in Canada.

While antisemitism definitely impeded Jewish professional and work oppor-tunities and social acceptance, it by no means defined Jewish life in Canada during the 1920s. If anything, the prejudice and discrimination reinforced the will to fight back and adapt. Cowering from hatred and unfair treatment was rarely an option. In 1918, when the YMCA in Toronto instituted a policy seg-regating Jewish members into separate clubs, Toronto Jews soon organized their own athletic and social organization, known as the Hebrew Association of Young Men's and Young Women's Clubs. By the late twenties, "Young Women" was dropped from its name and it became known as the Young Men's Hebrew Association or the YMHA, which operated for many years out of the basement of the Brunswick Avenue Talmud Torah.

At Baron Byng High School in Montreal, Harbord Collegiate in Toronto, and St. John's Technical High School in Winnipeg, three schools located in predominately Jewish neighbourhoods—which in turn meant large Jewish student populations—Jewish teenagers thrived in and out of the classroom, leading rich, full, and fun lives. Their Anglo teachers worked hard at "Canadianizing" them, a process that did encourage greater assimi-lation and caused concern among rabbis and community leaders. Yet, each school had a distinctive Jewish character, whether the principals and teach-ers liked it or not.

It was during the inaugural meeting of Baron Byng's Sholem Aleichem Club—the only club at a Montreal Protestant high school to be named for a Yiddish writer—that A.M. Klein became fast friends with future politi-cian David Lewis. Abe Klein was a Zionist and Lewis a social democrat and they argued about everything, though remained companions. It was through Lewis that Klein met his wife Bessie Kozlov. In 1926, the couple were co-valedictorians for that year's graduating class. Lewis also introduced Klein to another up-and-coming Jewish poet, Irving Layton (born Israel

Lazarovitch in Romania in 1912), who had been expelled from Baron Byng because of his perceived radicalism. Klein tutored Layton in Latin so he could write his junior matriculation exams and attend McGill University.

Among other Baron Byng Jewish luminaries over the next decade and half were author Mordecai Richler; his close friend, entrepreneur Jack Rabinovitch, who established the Giller Prize for outstanding Canadian fiction; actor William Shatner of *Star Trek* fame; and Supreme Court judge Morris Fish. In a 1961 essay for the American Jewish magazine *Commentary*, Richler recalled the uniqueness of his Baron Byng homeroom, classroom 41, which was "one of the few to boast a true Gentile . . . His name was Whelan—and he certainly was a curiosity." (Classroom 41 also was Duddy Kravitz's homeroom in Richler's breakthrough novel published in 1959, *The Apprenticeship of Duddy Kravitz*.)

St. John's High in Winnipeg's North End catered to the children of Jewish, Ukrainian, and Polish immigrants. Though there were occasional scraps in the schoolyard between Jews and other students, caused mainly by festering old-country racist ideas which had been nourished in Canada, the Jewish students, for the most part, shined as scholars and athletes.

Toronto's Harbord Collegiate was located west of the Spadina–Kensington Market area, and an estimated 85 per cent of its student body was Jewish during the twenties and thirties. The list of Harbord's Jewish graduates from this period who later went on to succeed in their chosen professions is an impressive one—the result of hard work and excessive encouragement from loving immigrant parents who put a premium on education and high achievement. Among the stars at Harbord were Louis Rasminsky, the class valedictorian in 1925 and the first Jewish governor of the Bank of Canada; Sam "The Record Man" Sniderman; Sam Shopsowitz, of Shopsy's deli; clothing retailer Harry Rosen; pollster Martin Goldfarb (his immigrant mother called the school "Harbord Collision"); journalist Morley Safer of the CBS television news show *60 Minutes* (also a Clinton Street Public School graduate); Philip Givens, who was mayor of Toronto from 1963 to 1966; and comedians Frank Shuster and Louis Weingarten (a.k.a. Johnny Wayne). It was in history teacher Charles Girdler's after-school Oola Boola Club that Frank and Lou—soon to be immortalized as the celebrated duo Wayne and Shuster—first experimented with the amusing sketches that were to propel them to international fame.

At Harbord, there was also Fanny "Bobbie" Rosenfeld. Though her immigrant parents had named her Fanny, she was dubbed "Bobbie" after she "bobbed" her hair as a young woman—more out of practicality for sports purposes than as a fashion statement—and that was how she was thereafter known.

Antisemitism certainly did not stop Rosenfeld from becoming one of the great female athletes in Canadian history. Her success in sports trumped prejudice and discrimination, as it had for star figure skater Louis Rubenstein in the 1880s and 1890s. Rosenfeld was invited to join the Toronto Ladies' Athletic Club in 1923, an organization founded at the time by young white Anglo women. Almost overnight, she was one of the club's best performers, winning track meets and setting records.

A woman with a mind of her own, Rosenfeld refused to wear the ladylike skirts that were the custom of the day, and opted for her brother's baggy shorts and a T-shirt or jersey—or her father's bathing trunks on one occasion. Between 1923 and 1927, Rosenfeld, who possessed a sharp wit, became one of the most famous sports figures in Toronto. Her skill and success convinced the country's curmudgeonly sports aficionados to accept women as legitimate athletes.

In 1925, Bobbie set a new world record for the 100-yard dash and her fame spread. Her most celebrated achievement was at the 1928 Summer Olympics in Amsterdam, as one of the "Matchless Six," the six Canadian women who were competing for the first time in track and field events (it was the first year that women's athletics had been included in the Games). She won a gold medal as a member of the 400-metre relay team, a silver medal for the "disputed" 100-metre sprint (which she likely won but technically lost due to judges' error), and placed fifth in the 800-metre race, the result of allowing an injured teammate to finish ahead of her in what was considered at the time a magnanimous act of sportsmanship. A *Globe* sports reporter called her "Toronto's fleet-footed Jewish maiden."

Fiercely competitive, Rosenfeld rarely backed down from a sports challenge. But one obstacle she could not overcome was arthritis, which she began suffering from in 1929, when she was only twenty-five years old. Ultimately forced to retire as an athlete in 1933, she reinvented herself as a sports columnist for the *Globe and Mail*. In her writing, she rarely missed an opportunity to advocate for women and minorities in amateur and professional sports. In 1950, in one of the greatest honours for a Jewish woman up to that point, she was named Canada's outstanding female athlete of the first half of the twentieth century. And in 1991—twenty-two years after she died at the age of sixty-four—Bobbie Rosenfeld Park was established by the city of Toronto in an area between Rogers Centre and the CN Tower.

Whatever obstacles Jews faced, they remained resolute that support of local community institutions—synagogues, schools, hospitals, orphanages, old folks' homes, libraries, and athletic clubs—was paramount. Admittedly, this was partially a response to antisemitism: if social clubs were restricted, then Jews would create their own. But it was much more about responding to the needs of Jewish community members, young and old, and about leaving an institutional legacy for future generations—no easy task.

In communities such as Ottawa, Hamilton, Saskatoon, Edmonton, and Calgary, with Jewish populations in 1931 ranging from 3,482 in Ottawa to 691 in Saskatoon, compromise and cooperation were essential. Not that arguing ceased entirely, but a unified effort was required—for instance in Ottawa, to raise the $23,000 needed for the purchase of a former public school in 1919, which would reopen five years later as the city's Talmud Torah. The new school functioned as a community centre, where large gatherings were convened and various clubs and organizations met.

The fostering of Jewish religious and cultural values in small rural towns was even more challenging. Along with a church, school, grain elevator, and a Chinese café, the odds were fairly good in most prairie towns that there was also a lone Jewish general store merchant and his family. In his history *The Jews in Manitoba* (1961), Rabbi Arthur Chiel estimated that during the twenties, "Jewish community merchants could be found in at least one hundred and eighteen towns and villages in Manitoba."

The decision by young Jewish men and women to leave Winnipeg and venture into the countryside was dependent on several factors. Jewish-owned grocery and dry goods wholesale companies—in addition to several friendly non-Jewish companies—were prepared to provide the rural merchants with goods on credit. There was also start-up capital available from open-minded bankers and successful Jewish store merchants who had been in the business for a while. These budding entrepreneurs were interested in making smart investments in a network of country stores, and also desired to help out the newcomers.

In the case of Sam Kliman (my maternal grandfather), who arrived in Canada from Mezirich, Russia (now the Ukraine), in 1921 at the age of nineteen—along with his brother Meyer, who later established a general store in the western Manitoba town of McCreary, and several other family members—the required financing was arranged with Max and Jacob Rabkin of Portage la Prairie, who were successful immigrant merchants.

Decent and compassionate men, the Rabkin brothers decided to help out immigrants such as Max Kirshner, who worked in their store, and his cousins, Sam and Meyer Kliman. In the mid-twenties, purchasing and setting up a general store cost approximately $10,000, an amount that would have been impossible for any Jewish immigrant to secure even from a friendly banker. Instead, the Rabkins kindly provided these young entrepreneurs with sufficient funds to open general stores in various rural locales. Everyone prospered in this arrangement. By the early 1940s, both Kliman brothers—Sam and his family in the southwestern Manitoba town of Holland, and Meyer in nearby McCreary—had made enough money to pay back what they owed the Rabkins.

Rural towns were not devoid of antisemitism by any means. Occasionally, Jewish merchants were accused of selling faulty goods at inflated prices, and their children were harassed. Sam Kliman had married Sarah Rosen, a girl from Portage la Prairie, in 1928. Almost immediately after the wedding, they opened their first store in the village of Brookdale, Manitoba, yet were forced to sell it after a year because they encountered anti-Jewish attitudes. They moved to Holland soon after. Rural communities, however, needed the services of the Jewish merchants, and racist animosities were mostly kept in check.

Though it was not easy being the only Jewish family in the town, families such as the Klimans managed. Kosher food was brought in from Winnipeg, and on the High Holidays and Passover families would visit relatives in larger cities or towns with synagogues. Tutors were hired to prepare young boys for their bar mitzvahs. Jewish parents living in the country shared one great fear—that their children would not marry within the faith. Friendships were acceptable, and the Jewish children who grew up in rural towns have many fond memories of skating, curling, and going to hockey and baseball games with their schoolfriends. Actual dating, however, was out of the question. In time, most of the families sent their children into Winnipeg or other nearby cities to complete their schooling and find a Jewish spouse.

In larger urban centres, there were different concerns and problems. By the early twenties, community leaders deemed that centralization was the key to undertaking the fundraising required to support and sustain all of the various Jewish schools and organizations in a city—irrespective of any antisemitism that Jews faced. Establishing the Federation of Jewish Philanthropies in Montreal and Toronto in 1917, the Winnipeg Jewish Charities Endorsation Bureau in 1927, and similar associations in Hamilton and Ottawa, however, was fraught with competing interests and personalities. In each city, local organizations that had existed for decades were not happy about relinquishing control to a central body that was largely in the hands of what could be described as the Jewish volunteer establishment. Nor did women's groups appreciate the male domination of the federations. On the executive committee of Montreal's federation in 1917 there were seventeen members, four of whom were women. In Toronto, Ida Siegel, who was largely responsible for getting the federation going, was the lone woman on the federation for many years. She faced an uphill battle and was denied real power by men who would not take orders from a woman.

Attempts to establish rabbinical councils—or Vaad Ha'ir—to supervise and ensure that proper kosher rules were being followed caused even greater discord. This legendary feuding was the result of the combustible mixture of strongly held religious convictions, the raging egos of many of the rabbis involved, and ritual slaughterers and butchers who were seeking to increase their profit margins. In Montreal, there was a "kosher war," as its been remembered, from 1923 to 1925—a showdown between two main rivals for control of the council: Rabbi Zui Hirsch Cohen, who represented the Lithuanian faction and who many in the community regarded as Montreal's Chief Rabbi, and Rabbi Yudel Rosenberg, who advocated for the Orthodox Polish side. They differed in their Talmudic interpretations of Jewish law—an enduring clash of religious principles that had erupted during the first half of the eighteenth century in Eastern Europe between the supporters of the mystical Rabbi Yisrael ben Eliezer, the founder of Hasidism who was also known as the Baal Shem Tov ("Master of the Good Name"), and their rivals, the Mitnagdim ("Opponents"), devoted followers of the sage Rabbi Eliyahu, the Vilna Gaon. Personality differences and stubbornness also contributed to the bitter fighting. Before a peace agreement was negotiated in late 1925, Rabbi Rosenberg was attacked in the street and there was a boycott of an alleged "butcher trust" whose members were accused of price gouging.

Similarly, in Toronto in the twenties there was a fierce battle over the control of a proposed *kehillah* (an official communal organization). On one side of this fight were Rabbis Jacob Gordon and Joseph Weinreb, who represented the influential Lithuanian, Galician, and Russian members of the community; and on the other, Rabbi Yehuda Leib Graubart, who had arrived in Toronto in 1920 and become the spiritual leader of the city's Polish Jews and the head of a competing kosher council. Each faction attempted to control as many *shochtim*, butchers, and wholesalers as they could.

Matters took a turn for the worse—an embarrassing one, according to some Toronto Jews—when in 1925 a local butcher, Jacob Cohen, who had been under the supervision of Gordon and Weinreb, switched his allegiance to Graubart. Cohen determined that he could obtain his meat at a lower price from a wholesaler regulated by Graubart. Though other butchers had also done this, Gordon and Weinreb and their rabbinical allies publicly denounced the forty-year-old Cohen in a series of advertisements in the Yiddish newspapers for selling "meat unfit according to law," because it was reported to them that he had been seen riding a streetcar on a Saturday, breaking Sabbath rules. In reality, the attack was aimed at Rabbi Graubart for challenging Gordon and Weinreb's authority and for asserting that he had set up a separate *kehillah*.

So irate was Cohen that he took Gordon and Weinreb and two others to court for libelling him and trying to ruin his business. But the focus of the case was Cohen's connection to Graubart, and Graubart's right to designate kosher meat. Uncertain how to handle this curious matter, Justice William H. Wright of the Supreme Court of Ontario took the unprecedented route of convening a rabbinical tribunal to determine the legitimacy of Graubart's *kehillah*. The Toronto press was not sure what to make of the case either, nor the three American rabbis invited to the city to render a decision. The *Star* found them "venerable figures" in black skull caps and black robes, yet also "jolly men" whose eyes "twinkle[d]." In their ruling, the visiting rabbis vindicated Gordon and Weinreb and compelled Graubart to compromise and join their *kehillah*, the only one Toronto could have according to Jewish law; they deemed all others were forbidden. Rabbi Graubart reluctantly merged his group with Gordon's, though the animosity continued and Graubart refused to attend meetings if Gordon was present. Until further disputes arose in the 1930s challenging the *kehillah*'s power, Toronto Jews had one body of rabbis supervising and determining kosher regulations.

The importance given to ensuring *kashrut* or the adherence of proper kosher rules in the post–First World War period reflected the religious dietary requirements of a majority of Canadian Jews who maintained kosher homes, though certainly not all. Secularization and changing beliefs about adherence to Jewish ritual were already evident. As the editors of the *Canadian Jewish Review* pointed out in the summer of 1926 after the Toronto kosher dispute was finally settled, younger Jews were indifferent to the biblical struggle. "They were conducting their business affairs," the paper noted, "following their professions, playing their golf and pinnacle as if the loom of history were not working overtime right in their own midst. The quarrels, the recriminations, the jealousies, the coming and going of the rabbis—all these in the name of an old and cherished religion—did not concern them. There seemed to be a wide gulf between the two generations, definitely separating them."

That gulf was to grow wider still during the ensuing decades, as a larger number of Jews in Canada sought to identify themselves less through religion and more via cultural institutions and Zionism.

The Jewish Problem

The federal election of July 28, 1930, was fought over one key issue: Conservative Party leader R.B. Bennett's charge that his Liberal Party opponent, Prime Minister William Lyon Mackenzie King had no clue about dealing with the worsening economic crisis. It was a successful strategy. Bennett, who declared that he would use tariffs "to blast a way into the closed markets of the world," swept King and the Liberals from office. On the night of the election, however, many Jews who had voted for the Liberals in Toronto still had reason to celebrate.

For decades, Toronto had been solid Tory, and it was expected that Conservative candidates would win in all nine Toronto-area ridings. That prediction came to pass, except in the riding of Toronto West Centre, which incorporated the Spadina–Kensington Market neighbourhood. Rather miraculously, Samuel Factor, a thirty-seven-year-old Jewish lawyer who had served as a member of the Toronto school board and as a city alderman, defeated the popular former Toronto mayor Tommy Church, who had been an MP since 1921. Factor won by 564 votes over Church and received 49 per cent of the votes. He was Ontario's first Jewish MP.

The city's Jewish population was about 45,000 in 1930, and many of those who lived in the Toronto West Centre riding no doubt voted for Factor. He was one of them. He spoke Yiddish and had grown up in a working-class family. Factor had come to Toronto with his parents from Czarist Russia in 1902, when he was ten years old. He grew up in the Ward and graduated high school from Jarvis Collegiate Institute. He then studied law at Osgoode Hall as a scholarship student, and began working as a lawyer in 1915. Two years later, in the midst of the First World War, he left his law practice and enrolled in an officer training program, becoming a lieutenant. He also later served in the Royal Canadian Air Force during the Second World War.

His career as a politician began in 1923 with his election as a Toronto Board of Education school trustee. Three years after that he won a seat on the city council for Ward 4, the Kensington Market neighbourhood; he served alongside Nathan Phillips, who was to become the city's first Jewish mayor in the civic election of 1954.

Factor's victory celebration in July 1930 carried on into the wee hours of the morning around College Street and Spadina Avenue. He stopped in at Rubin's restaurant and Wexler's Café and was greeted by adoring fans. Church was surprised but gracious in defeat (he won a by-election in 1934 and remained in Parliament until the 1950s). If he was upset about being beaten by a Jew, he did not say so, and neither did his supporters. Though that did not mean there were no snide comments made about Factor's win.

Five months later, it was the same somewhat surprising story in nearby Windsor, Ontario. Thirty-year-old David Croll, a Russian Jewish immigrant, was elected mayor of the small city directly across the river from Detroit. A lawyer, labour advocate, and dedicated Zionist, Croll defeated his closest rival (among the four he faced) by more than one thousand votes. The editors of the *Border Cities Star* in Windsor were impressed. "The *Star* regards the result as a commendable example of the fact that racial and religious tolerance abounds in Windsor," an editorial pointed out the day following the election. "Mr. Croll was attacked in some quarters, we regret to say, on the grounds that he happens to be a member of the Jewish faith, also that he was born in Moscow, Russia. The result of the vote shows what the people of Windsor think of 'antics' of that kind." In late 1932, he won a second term by an even greater margin (more than seven thousand votes over his nearest opponent) despite facing a "campaign of innuendo and sly whispers," which the *Star* noted did not amount to much and merely appealed to "race prejudice."

In 1934, at the behest of the mercurial Ontario provincial Liberal leader, Mitch Hepburn, Croll ran for a seat in the Ontario legislature and was victorious, as was Hepburn and the party. Hepburn appointed him the minister of municipal affairs and minister of labour and he thus became the first Jew in a federal or provincial cabinet. Three years later, he resigned from the Hepburn cabinet following a nasty split with the premier over the treatment of striking automobile workers in Oshawa.

In 1938, he ran a third time for the office of mayor in Windsor and defeated the incumbent, despite the publication of a letter from Hepburn denouncing him as "undeserving" of support. After serving in the Canadian forces during the Second World War, Croll ran in Samuel Factor's federal Toronto–Spadina riding and won in the 1945 election as a Liberal. Neither Mackenzie King nor his successor Louis St. Laurent asked Croll to join their respective cabinets. But in 1955 St. Laurent appointed Croll as the country's first Jewish senator.

Despite the electoral successes of Factor and Croll, among other Jewish Canadians, and the admirably progressive attitude of the *Border Cities Star* editors, genteel antisemitism was nonetheless prevalent. Few non-Jews were troubled by this. Quotas, resort and club "Gentile only" policies, and employment discrimination were the norm and more or less acceptable to the country's majority. Toronto Maple Leafs owner Conn Smythe, for example, refused to hire Jewish boys to sell programs or refreshments at games. Jews were stereotyped as greedy capitalists or evil Bolsheviks, and restrictive immigration policies which made it next to impossible for German Jewish refugees fleeing Nazism to escape to Canada were more or less acceptable to the country's majority. Where many non-Jews drew the line in the 1930s was at the ugly portrayal and occasional violent treatment of Jews by a small, though vocal, group of fascists, whose attitudes and actions were curiously regarded as "un-Canadian." Nearly nine decades later, this distinction is absurd. Yet during the Great Depression, despite the fact that racism and antisemitism increased as economic conditions worsened, a majority of Canadians thought of themselves as being moderate in their views about race. Yes, they did not want more Jews in the country but in their minds, that was quite different than advocating the extreme notions about racial purity, eugenics, and a Jew-free world advanced by Adolf Hitler and his fanatical followers. And, to a degree they were right. Yet from today's perspective that still did not absolve them from holding prejudicial views, nor make them into the liberal champions they perceived themselves to be. Antisemitism even if its mild is still antisemitism.

In March 1935, the editors of the *Ottawa Journal* were aghast at the Nazi-like propaganda distributed by the Quebec right-wing extremist Adrien Arcand's Parti National Social Chrétien (National Social Christian Party or PNSC). They were optimistic that such a bigoted appeal would "do little harm because racial prejudice is foreign to the Canadian tradition and abhorrent to all instincts of fairness and decency."

Antisemitism during the thirties did become more extreme and public, however. Arcand and his Blue Shirts in Quebec were the worst of it, along with small fascist groups in other provinces. Though their total numbers were never that large, these right-wing cranks increased the anxiety levels of Jewish community leaders, who sprang to action to counter the campaign of hate. Nonetheless, the intellectual backflips of most newspaper editors, who were blind to the blatant prejudice and discrimination in their midst, was astonishing. Antisemitism, in short, remained acceptable as long as it was done with discretion—as it was at several Canadian universities, where the quotas against Jewish students implemented during the twenties became more restrictive.

That the perceived "Jewish problem" was more pronounced in Montreal, Toronto, and Winnipeg, where the majority of Canadian Jews resided, was not surprising. Jewish students did graduate in medicine, law, architecture, arts, and sciences throughout the 1930s at universities in these cities. (In 1931, there were ninety-seven Jewish doctors in Montreal, seventy-three Jewish lawyers, and forty-seven Jewish dentists.) Universities did not as official policy ban Jews from fraternities or clubs but most refused to accept them as members forcing Jewish students to organize their own fraternities. A survey conducted in 1933 among non-Jewish students at the University of Toronto, for example, indicated that 80 per cent preferred that their clubs remain Jew-free.

A token number of Jewish faculty members were hired as instructors; among them was Jacob Finkelman, who in 1930 was the first Jew appointed a lecturer at the University of Toronto Faculty of Law. Four years later, in another first for Jews at U of T, Finkelman was offered a full-time assistant professorship. He would end up teaching at the university for the next three and a half decades.

One of Finkelman's students and friends was Bora Laskin; Laskin was the oldest son of Russian Jewish immigrants, who had lived in Winnipeg for a few years before settling at Fort William, where he was born in 1912. His given name was Raphale, but his mother was a fan of American Senator William E. Borah, "a defender of the Jewish people" so she called her son Bora and it stuck. Laskin was a star student at the University of Toronto, obtaining a BA in 1933, an MA two years later, and a law degree in 1936 from Osgoode Hall Law School.

As a Jewish articling student, however, he had difficulty finding a lawyer who would mentor him until W.C. Davidson, a King's Counsel who specialized in commercial law, finally agreed to do so. In 1936–37, Laskin spent the year at Harvard and obtained his Master of Laws degree. Yet when he returned to Toronto, no established firm would hire him, which was entirely due to the antisemitic climate of the times. Eventually he tried to obtain an academic posting, but again that was not easy. Cecil "Caesar" Wright, Osgoode's dean, recommended to his friend Sidney Smith, the former dean of Dalhousie's law school who had been appointed the president of the University of Manitoba in 1934, that he hire Laskin. "Unfortunately, he is a Jew," Wright told Smith in a letter of May 1939. "This may be fatal regarding his chances with you. I do not know. His race is, of course, proving a difficulty for him in Toronto so far as obtaining a good office is concerned . . . Laskin is not one of those flashy Jews, and the highest recommendation which I could give him is to say that." Smith passed on Laskin; the University of Manitoba did not hire a full-time Jewish professor until 1965, though Samuel Freedman did teach part-time starting in 1941. It took another year before Laskin was hired by the University of Toronto law school's dean W.P.M. Kennedy, one of his early supporters. This was the beginning of a distinguished career as a teacher and legal scholar that earned him an appointment to the Ontario Court of Appeal in 1965. (When Laskin's wife, Peggy, told her mother about the appointment, she remarked, "That's very nice, dear, but I always said he should have been a rabbi.")

Laskin was not the first Jewish judge on the Ontario Court of Appeal. That distinction goes to Abraham "Abe" Lieff, a well-respected Ottawa lawyer who lived to the age of 103, passing away in 2007. Leiff was appointed to the court by Lester Pearson in 1963, who thought (as he explained to Liberal Party member Robert Winters) that "it was decided that there should be a judge of the Jewish race appointed." Laskin's Jewish "first" occurred in 1970 with his appointment as a justice on the Supreme Court of Canada in 1970. Then, three years later, Prime Minister Pierre Trudeau named him Chief Justice.

Most university administrators were not as open-minded as Wright and Kennedy, however. Obstacles based on "race" existed, and university officials, some of whom denied quotas against Jews existed, worked diligently behind the scenes to keep them firmly in place. When challenged about these restrictions, their strategy was rationalizations steeped in fantasy. Asked in 1938 about the few spaces given to Jews at the McGill Faculty of Medicine, the associate dean, Dr. J.C. Simpson, declared that the quota permitting only eight Jewish students (out of 160 students admitted) had been set following consultations with Jewish students, graduates, and "several prominent Jewish citizens of Montreal." The consensus, according to Simpson, was that the quota was reasonable given "the difficulty that Jews have in securing hospital internships."

Dean Simpson might have had in mind the infamous intern strike at Montreal's Catholic Notre-Dame Hospital. In mid-June 1934, thirty-one of thirty-two French-Canadian interns went on strike to protest the hospital's decision to offer a one-year senior intern position to the "Hebrew" Samuel Rabinovitch, a top graduate of the University of Montreal who had completed twelve months as a junior student intern. The strike soon spread to four other nearby Catholic hospitals. Demanding that the hospital rescind the offer made to Rabinovitch four months earlier, the striking interns agreed that Jews should not be permitted to work in a Catholic hospital, because, as they explained to the respected nationalist journalist Olivar Asselin, "Catholic patients found it repugnant to be treated by a Jewish doctor."

While the interns did have support from such extreme nationalist organizations as the Société Saint-Jean-Baptiste as well as Catholic clergy, even Le Devoir, whose editors spent much of the decade demonizing Jews for all sorts of alleged sins, criticized the young doctors at Notre-Dame and the other hospitals for abandoning their patients—as did the Montreal Gazette.

Apologists for the students then and later claimed their actions during the Depression were motivated by fear of future competition from other Jewish physicians, though that was merely a convenient justification for an anti-semitic overreaction. After interviewing several of the strikers, Asselin, for one, found their refusal to admit that "racial hatred was at the basis of their actions" highly disingenuous. Meanwhile, the administrators of Notre-Dame Hospital refused to be bullied by the strikers, and enlisted other physicians on staff to cover their duties in the emergency department—an example that antisemitism was not consistent.

The strike lasted four days. Unwilling to be responsible for hospital patients not receiving proper care, twenty-five-year-old Sam Rabinovitch resigned his position. Almost immediately, the striking interns were back at work, and though hospital officials contemplated firing all of them, in the end they did not.

The interns' abysmal treatment of Rabinovitch gave even more signifi-cance to the opening of Montreal's Jewish General Hospital four months later—an institution in which the religion and ethnic background of patients and physicians were not a consideration. At the same time, Notre-Dame administrators did arrange for Rabinovitch to undertake his internship at a hospital in St. Louis. He returned to Montreal in 1940 as an internal medi-cine specialist and had a long and distinguished career as a physician, working into his nineties. He died in Montreal in November 2010 at the age of 101. On the seventieth anniversary of the strike in 2004, he reflected on his ordeal. "I bear no ill will toward anybody," he said. "The hospital administration was wonderful to me—it was just a few instigators that stirred up all the trouble, and for them it was just the case that I was Jewish and they were Catholics. I just did not belong. I suppose in the end that is the frightening thing about hatred . . . it is just that simple."

It was not only in Quebec where Jewish doctors and medical students were discriminated against, or at least allegedly so. In February 1934, medical administrators of the Regina General Hospital refused to consider two Jewish radiologists, Dr. M.D. Teitelbaum from Chicago and Dr. J. Freidman of Montreal, for a position they had advertised, because it was felt that hiring them would be "unacceptable" to the staff and the public. Representatives of the Canadian Jewish Congress in Regina wrote a letter to the hospital "taking exception" to the statements that were made about the Jewish physicians as reported in the Regina *Leader-Post*. On the defensive, the hospital's board of governors replied to the CJC that its officials had been "misinformed" as to the facts of the case and the hospital's policy was that "race or creed [were] not considered in the application of any position in the hospital where the applicant has the necessary ability and qualification." The CJC accepted this explanation, though it is not clear why neither Teitlebaum, whose salary request of $3,600 per year was the lowest of any candidate, nor Freidman were hired, since they both had the necessary qualifications. Contrary to the board's assertion, the fact that both were Jewish likely did disqualify them in the eyes of the hiring committee.

While there was no quota against Jews at the University of Toronto Faculty of Medicine—in 1932, 27 per cent of the students in the first-year class were Jewish—the Toronto General Hospital accepted only one Jewish intern a year.

The worst case of a medical school quota system aimed at restricting Jews and other immigrant groups occurred at the University of Manitoba. Admittance to the university's Faculty of Medicine was based on academic grades and the "moral, social and physical qualities" of the applicant. During the twenties, approximately sixty-four new students (on average) were admitted each year into the faculty. Of these, eighteen (or about 28 per cent) were Jewish—a fair number by any estimation. With the appointment of Dr. Alvin T. Mathers, a pioneer in the emerging field of psychiatry, as dean of the faculty in 1932, the system changed for the worse.

Starting that year—and continuing for the next twelve—strict quotas were set which severely regulated the number of Jews, Ukrainians, Poles, and an assortment of other ethnic groups who could be admitted. Women were doubly discriminated against, making it next to impossible for a Jewish woman to be admitted. (Mindel Cherniak, the daughter of Yiddish socialist advocate Joseph Alter Cherniack, was an exception. She later worked with Tommy Douglas and the Co-operative Commonwealth Federation [CCF] in

Saskatchewan and was involved in planning the province's pioneering medicare program.) In 1933, Mathers told Rabbi Solomon Frank and other members of the Shaarey Zedek congregation that if Jewish students did not apply in huge numbers, he would admit ten Jews each year. The rabbi agreed, though it was not as if he had much choice in the matter. He likely felt that drawing attention to this encounter in the press would have made the situation worse. Moreover, it is unclear how exactly Frank figured he could stop Jewish students from applying to the faculty, since he did not even control the actions of his own congregation, let alone the actions of every potential Jewish medical student in the city.

In any event, Mathers broke his word, and less than ten Jewish students were admitted per year from 1934 onward (the average from 1936 to 1943 was just over 4 per cent). The members of the faculty administration and its professors were aware of the change in admittance practices, though it was not publicized. High grades or other qualifications made little difference—indeed, Jewish students with averages above 80 per cent were often turned down. The only criterion that ultimately mattered was "race."

Each applicant had to designate his or her "racial origin" on the entrance application form. The faculty then made its selection from "preferred" and "non-preferred" lists, with only about fourteen spots of the sixty-four annually offered set aside for students on the latter list. This practice frequently led to some absurd situations. In 1943, for instance, the faculty turned down Jewish and other ethnic students with exceptionally high marks and accepted five "preferred" students who had not passed their university examinations. The university permitted these select few to make up the courses they had failed in a special summer school.

As far as can be determined, the logic of the quota system was based on Dean Mathers's thinking, similar to that of Ira Mackay's at McGill, that given current attitudes it made sense to train only a small number of Jewish and immigrant doctors since ethnic physicians would find it difficult, if not impossible, to practise and serve the medical needs of the larger community.

It took the diligent work of the Avukah Zionist Society, a small Jewish university group, to expose the quota system. Significantly, this occurred without the support of Winnipeg leaders of the cJC or B'nai Brith, who according to one of the members of Avukah, Shlomo Ben Adam (formerly Shlomo Mitchell), did not want to create a fuss or tarnish the reputation of the university. But Avukah was not to be deterred. In 1943, after hearing from many Jewish students with high marks who were denied entry, the society's members tracked down hundreds of students who had applied for medical school between 1926 and 1943, identifying on index cards all relevant biographical information. A friendly secretary in the dean's office provided them with valuable student data. The whole operation took about five months.

Before they could act, Morris Gray, a Jewish community leader who had been elected to the Legislative Assembly of Manitoba for the CCF and had no qualms about going after the university, was informed about Avukah's investigation. He publicly accused the Manitoba Minister of Education of discrimination at the Faculty of Medicine. The minister denied the allegations and Gray was ordered to produce evidence or withdraw his accusation. The Avukah Society assisted Gray, and their findings cataloguing this blatant discrimination were presented to a legislative committee. Still, officials from the university including Mathers denied that the quota system existed, but Judge A.K. Dysart, chairman of the university's board of governors, agreed to a request to investigate further and report back to the legislative committee. Five months later, Dysart was forced to admit that Avukah's findings had been proven: the faculty was guilty as charged of practising discrimination for the past twelve years. On threat by the provincial government of changing the University of Manitoba Act, the board of governors agreed to halt the practice immediately and insert into its regulations that henceforth "the selection [of the Faculty of Medicine's candidates] shall be made without regard to the racial origin or religion of the applicant." This was an important and symbolic victory, though the fear of producing too many Jewish physicians in the province did not end.

Quebecers, whether they were English or French, were not necessarily more racist than other Canadians. It was only that the antisemitism in Quebec during the 1930s was more pronounced, received more prominent attention in newspapers like *Le Devoir*, and was more volatile than elsewhere in the country. This was the result of French-Canadian nationalist insecurities, compounded by the severe worldwide economic crisis and the influence of Nazi and fascist ideology from Germany and Italy, linked to the rise of Hitler and Mussolini.

The contentious debate in the early part of the decade over whether to establish a separate Jewish school system in Quebec triggered a variety of negative reactions from the Catholic establishment, and was a key factor in launching Adrien Arcand's role as a virulent antisemitic propagandist.

Catholic and nationalist journals and newspapers regularly denounced "the Jew" symbolically as a foreign invader and an immoral threat, and as personally introducing impurities into the Canadian gene pool. Jews—wrote the lawyer Anatole Vanier in *L'Action nationale*, the journal of Ligue d'Action nationale, in September 1933—were "one of the worst viruses to attack our religious and national traditions."

Georges Pelletier would have agreed with that statement. In 1932 he succeeded Henri Bourassa as editor of *Le Devoir*, the influential, though financially strapped, nationalist organ. Pelletier kept the paper going, but also enhanced its anti-Jewish slant. So highly regarded is *Le Devoir* that accusations about its rabid antisemitism during the thirties—as well as that of the still-revered Abbé Lionel Groulx—by historian Esther Delisle in her controversial 1993 book, *The Traitor and the Jew*, reverberated throughout Quebec for several years—and still do. According to Delisle's content analysis of the paper, Jews were referred to in *Le Devoir* in the 1930s as "aliens, circumcised, criminals, mentally ill, trash of nations, Tartars, infected with Semitism, malodorous—they smell of garlic, live in lice-ridden ghettos, have greasy hair and pot bellies, big crooked noses, and they are dirty." Needless to say, Pelletier opposed permitting German Jewish refugees into the country, asserting in December 1938 that Canada could not accept "more or less unassimilable people, unaccustomed to working the land anywhere in the world."

Such notions were shared to different degrees by a generation of prominent Quebec leaders. Among them was journalist and activist André Laurendeau, a future editor of *Le Devoir*. As a member of the right-wing nationalist group Jeune-Canada, he contributed articles to *Le Devoir*, many of which were laced with anti-Jewish comments and stereotypes (decades later he deeply regretted this bigotry). Even a young Pierre Trudeau wrote a "satirical comedy" in the late thirties entitled *Dupés* ("We've been duped!"), which incorporated antisemitic stereotypes.

Adrien Arcand, the editor of several money-losing newspapers and the leader of the fascist PNSC, was far worse. Apart from emulating Hitler and Mussolini and mimicking the Judeophobia of Nazi Julius Streicher's propaganda sheet *Der Stürmer*, Arcand was also influenced by Oswald Mosley, the founder of the British Union of Fascists. He had as his ultimate goal a "British imperial fascist" empire of which Canada would be a key member. But it all started with ridding the country of Jews; for Arcand, antisemitism was "almost a religion." In an eerily prophetic diatribe, he mused that as Jews were "like cockroaches and bugs," it was "too bad we cannot exterminate them with insecticide."

Promoting himself as the "Canadian Führer," he remained an extremist on the fringe of society and never came close to recruiting the 100,000 members he claimed he had by 1937 (according to his biographer, Jean-François Nadeau, Arcand's group had less than 2,000 members). Three years later, federal justice officials interned him for the remainder of the Second World War. Still, his anti-Jewish rantings, as well as those of right-wing nationalists— who generally did not support Arcand's fascism or his fascination with British imperialism—did have a significant impact inside Quebec and beyond. In Ottawa and Winnipeg, two of Arcand's disciples—Jean Tissot, a Belgian-born police detective, and William Whittaker, a veteran English soldier— attracted a small number of supporters through their fiery rhetoric and propaganda.

In Quebec and Ontario, Jewish politicians Peter Bercovitch, a Liberal Party member of the Quebec Legislative Assembly, and John J. Glass, a Liberal member of the Ontario government of Mitch Hepburn both independently sought to have pioneering human rights legislation enacted to allow for prosecution of group libel and hate of the kind Arcand and others were spreading. Yet for a variety of reasons—the *Globe and Mail* dismissed

Glass's efforts to curtail the distribution of antisemitic propaganda and posting of signs as an attack on freedom of speech and as "mischievous, undemocratic and anti-British"—both were unsuccessful.

Marcus Hyman, an Independent Labour Party member of the Legislative Assembly of Manitoba, had more luck. In March 1934, he introduced an amendment to the province's libel act. It passed unanimously. The first such law of its kind in the country, it was known as the Manitoba Defamation Act, or the "Hyman Act," and allowed "any individual or group maligned or defamed because of race or religion" to take appropriate legal action. This included an injunction to halt publication of material which the group or person in question believed contributed to the "hatred, contempt, or ridicule" of the offended party.

Soon after the act was ratified, William Whittaker published an article in his tabloid the *Canadian Nationalist*, alleging that Jews were guilty of ritual murder—the blood libel that had been levelled against Jews for almost a millennium and which accused them of using the blood of Christian children in the making of matzoh for Passover. Utilizing the new law, First World War veteran and lawyer William "Billy" Tobias launched a defamation action against Whittaker, as well as the printer of the newspaper. He was victorious—Whittaker was forced to halt distribution of his paper in Manitoba and pay Tobias's court costs of $300. This was only a partial victory for the city's Jewish community, however, since Whittaker circumvented Manitoba's new libel law by transferring the printing and distribution of his newspaper to Ontario. He also continued to organize rallies.

Members of youth wing of the Anti-Fascist League of Winnipeg, organized by left-wing Jews and non-Jews to combat antisemitism and right-wing activity in the city, also took on Whittaker and his Brown Shirts. They were not prepared to keep quiet and look the other way when confronted by blatant racism, as their grandparents' and parents' generations generally had. In early June 1934, the league's members heard that Whittaker and his Canadian Nationalists were planning a large parade. On the day of the march, dozens of fascists and many more anti-fascists clashed in a bloody riot at Market Square. It was the worst violence in the city since the General Strike of 1919.

That day, the anti-fascists taught Whittaker and his men a lesson; the Brown Shirts did not try to march in Winnipeg again.

A year earlier, a similar, though better known, confrontation between anti-semites and young Jews had occurred in Toronto. In the Beaches area off Queen Street East, a small Jewish enclave had developed. The residents generally coexisted with the larger Anglo population in the neighbourhood. During July and August, however, many more Jews from the Spadina area were travelling by streetcar to spend an enjoyable afternoon picnicking by the lake, a situation which annoyed and angered some Anglos. "Do you think it would be possible to place a few picnic tables under the trees in Kew Beach Park ... and also to place a sign upon the trees—The area for Gentiles only," one unnamed resident asked the Parks Department in a letter of June 1933. "At the present time it is quite impossible to get a table in the Park, at all on Sunday: for the Jewish people seem to get every table in the Park and even if there were room for others to sit at the same table, one would hardly like to share the same table with them as our ways are so entirely different."

That year, these unwanted and "obnoxious" visitors became the target of the pro-Nazi Balmy Beach Swastika Club, whose members were Anglo-Canadian young men and boys. As relations between the two groups deteriorated, altercations between Jewish youth—who, like young Jews in Winnipeg, refused to be bullied—and the local toughs were inevitable. When the members of the club held a dance in early August and put up large swastikas on the side of their headquarters, they were confronted by about fifty Jewish boys. The police—who were known to be unfriendly to Jews in general, if not outright antisemitic, and had been up to this point reluctant to intervene in this ongoing dispute—arrived in time to ensure that no serious fighting broke out.

In response to the problems at the Beaches, a group of young Jews organized the League for the Defense of Jewish Rights. The simmering animosity finally exploded on the evening of August 16, 1933, at the baseball diamond at Christie Pits (originally Willowvale Park) on Christie Street, north of Bloor Street. Two nights earlier—during a softball game played between a team from the Catholic St. Peter's Church and Harbord Playground, a predominately Jewish team—two spectators had displayed a large swastika. Once the game was over, the spectators—joined by several of their friends, who were members of the neighbourhood Willowvale Swastika Club—ran onto the field shouting "Heil Hitler" at the Jewish players. But no fighting broke out. Sometime later that night, the troublemakers painted a large (and misspelled) "Hail Hitler" on the side of the Willowvale Park clubhouse.

This set the scene for the riot on August 16, when another game was being played between St. Peter's and Harbord Playground in front of a crowd of about 10,000, more than 1,000 of whom were Jewish. During the second inning, members of the local Pits Gang, all from Anglo working-class families who resided near the park, started chanting "Heil Hitler." A nearby group of Jews charged at their antagonists armed with lead pipes and batons and a brief fight erupted. The police arrived to keep the peace and the game continued. Once the game ended, however, a few Pits Gang members unfurled a white blanket with a black swastika sewn on it. That impudent act triggered a bloody six-hour riot, as more gangs of Gentiles and Jews went at each other with baseball bats, broom handles, and lead pipes. The handful of policemen present were unable to do much to stop the fighting. Nearby Jewish shops were vandalized. No one was killed in the melee, though many youths on both sides sustained serious injuries. There were two arrests and only one man was charged—he had been apprehended as he was about to strike a person on the ground with a club, and was sentenced to two months in jail or a fifty-dollar fine.

The riot at Christie Pits naturally received a great deal of newspaper coverage and attention from Toronto politicians. The mayor immediately banned further displaying of the swastika. The *Toronto Telegram* placed the blame on "Jewish toughs" and "Communists," an accusation shared by several other papers. Only the liberal-minded *Star* was more judicious, describing the riot as an isolated incident and in its view certainly not representative of a wave of antisemitism engulfing Toronto—a fair assessment. The Jewish community's newspaper, *Der Yiddisher Zhurnal*, compared the fight to a Russian pogrom, an exaggeration to be sure.

Stories about the riot were told and retold for many years afterward. In the Jewish community, the battle has been steeped in mythology as a courageous moment when Jews refused to be pushed around—as Cyril Levitt and William Shaffir showed in their detailed account of the conflict, *The Riot at Christie Pits* (1987). Most recently, on the eightieth anniversary of the confrontation in August 2013, Joe Black, who was seven years old in 1933, shared his recollections in press interviews, and the United Jewish Appeal Federation of Greater Toronto hosted a baseball game to commemorate the occasion.

Like Arcand and Whittaker, members of the Pits Gang and the Beaches Swastika Club were hardly sophisticated in their intense dislike for the city's Jews. The events of August 16 were indeed a crude outburst of the xenophobia that had been exacerbated by the rise of the Nazis in Germany.

Somewhat more organized was the anti-Jewish campaign in Alberta propagated by members of the newly created Social Credit Party, a political response to the Great Depression. There were only 3,722 Jews in the province in 1931, and the odds were good that a majority of the Social Crediters had never met anyone Jewish. That hardly dissuaded many of them from believing that Jews and communism were intrinsically linked and that "International Jewry" was behind the financial crisis.

Social Credit in Alberta began as a movement initiated by William Aberhart, a Sunday school preacher who in the late 1920s discovered the tremendous power of the radio in spreading his fundamentalist gospel message. At the height of his career as a radio priest, an estimated 350,000 listeners on the Canadian Prairies and in the northwestern U.S. tuned in to hear his Sunday-afternoon sermons. As the economy worsened, Aberhart embraced the quirky Social Credit monetary theories of Scottish engineer Major Clifford H. Douglas (which stipulated that the disparity of wages could be solved by the government issuing social dividends and giving consumers more money). Using the radio to spread his message of hope and his promise to get money back into the hands of those who earned it, he soon transformed the Alberta Social Credit organization from a lobby group into a political party. In August 1935, the Social Credit Party swept to power and Aberhart became the province's premier.

While Aberhart, who had at least one Jewish friend, was not openly anti-semitic, Douglas certainly was, and he influenced members of Aberhart's government and caucus. In September 1938, after Douglas denounced Jews as "parasites" for their alleged control of trade and banking, Aberhart repudiated him and reasserted that Social Credit in Alberta was not antisemitic. In other statements and letters, however, Aberhart insisted that he did not have anything against Jews, only Jewish financiers, who controlled the financial system and were in cahoots with "sinister" Anglo-Saxons.

Unlike the brash and bold approach of some young Jews when confronting antisemitic bullies, the country's Jewish community leaders were generally reticent to draw attention to prejudice and discrimination. Nothing could be gained, it was argued, by publicizing the "Jewish problem" or protesting the treatment of Jews in Nazi Germany. Even if this publicity produced a sympathetic reaction, it was firmly believed that it would impair "the relationship with non-Jews at home," as suggested by William Zukerman, a Jewish American journalist reporting from Europe in 1938. The fact was that—contrary to the conspiracy-like theories advanced by Major Douglas, automobile magnate Henry Ford, and others—Jewish influence in Canada (and the United States) during this troubled decade was minimal in shaping the country's economic, financial, or political policies.

As the situation in Germany worsened, however, Jewish leaders, including those who would have preferred to remain silent, felt that they had to do something even if unobtrusively. Antisemitic incidents in Canada and events in Germany demanded a response. "The most frightening development in Canada during the 1930s," Hananiah Caiserman, the first general secretary of the Canadian Jewish Congress, later reflected, "was the transition from sporadic and unorganized types of anti-Semitism to organized activities sponsored by national organizations directed by professional agents of Nazi Germany." This alarming situation was enough to rejuvenate the dormant CJC.

In May 1933, Jewish organizations in Winnipeg took the initiative and formed a Western CJC committee. At a subsequent meeting, delegates were unanimous in their support of revitalizing the CJC to combat racism and antisemitic propaganda distributed in the country. Further discussions and a larger gathering in Toronto in 1934 led to the formal rebirth of the CJC, with Montreal MP Sam Jacobs as the new president, a position he served until his death in August 1938. (At a convention held in Toronto in January 1939, Samuel Bronfman was elected the CJC's next president.) Operating as three semi-independent divisions in Montreal, Toronto, and Winnipeg, Congress members focused their energies on assisting German Jewish refugees and combating antisemitic propaganda. But old divisions between "uptown" and "downtown" Jews remained, hampering the Congress's effectiveness. Given the dire economic situation, the CJC also experienced financial problems, since communities were slow to raise the funds the organization desperately required. Jacobs was busy in Ottawa and so it fell to Caiserman to keep the Congress's day-to-day operations going.

One early lobbying effort, which in the end was not successful, was a campaign for Canada to boycott the 1936 Winter and Summer Olympics, which were scheduled to be held in Nazi Germany. The call for a boycott became paramount with the Nazis' imposition of the discriminatory Nuremberg Laws in September 1935, which deprived German Jews of their citizenship and established the racial definition of who was a Jew. Caiserman, who was back in his role as the CJC's general secretary, and others appealed to newspapers' sports editors to support the boycott, though most were either cool or apathetic about the idea. And so under the auspices of a nonpartisan organization they created—the Unity and Goodwill Association—they tried to sell the boycott as a non-Jewish issue. That poorly disguised charade fooled no one, however. In November 1935, the Canadian Olympic Committee voted to participate in the Winter Olympics in Bavaria and the Summer Olympics in Berlin.

The handful of Canadian Jewish athletes who wanted to compete at the Olympics were especially conflicted. The popular Toronto boxer Sammy Luftspring was one of them. Born in 1916, he had grown up in the city's Ward before his family moved west to the Jewish and Italian area around College and Spadina. His father was shoemaker, but his parents, immigrants from Poland, also made money (with assistance from his grandmother) selling home-brewed rye whiskey for twenty-five cents a shot. He learned to box as a teenager at the

Hebrew Association of Young Men's and Young Women's Clubs (later the YMHA), then located in the basement of the Brunswick Avenue Talmud Torah. Famous for displaying a Star of David on his trunks, Luftspring—who won 100 out of 105 bouts between 1932 and 1936—took tremendous pride in being a Jew who did not back down from a fight. He also revelled in the newspaper attention he received, and had no problem with *Toronto Star* sports columnist Lou Marsh referring to him as an "aggressive little Jew boy."

At first, Luftspring and his fellow Jewish boxer Norman "Baby" Yack (born Benjamin Norman Yakubowitz), who both made Canada's Olympic boxing team, declared that they were going to go to Berlin. Luftspring's parents and family were against his decision, and CJC officials in Toronto did everything they could to change his mind. Otto Roger of the CJC Central (Ontario) Division offered to fund Luftspring and Yack's trip to the alternative protest games in Barcelona, the People's Olympiad, if they agreed to cancel their plans to box in Germany. This incentive did not sit well with many Jewish community leaders, who believed that the Jewish athletes had a "moral" obligation not to participate. Finally, on July 7, less than a month before the Berlin Olympics were to start, Luftspring and Yack in a public letter stated that they were not competing in Berlin. "As Canadian boys, we would be personally safe," they wrote. But they added that "all true Canadian sportsmen will appreciate that we would have been very low to hurt the feelings of our fellow Jews by going to a land that would exterminate them if they could."

Within a short time Luftspring and Yack—accompanied by Harry Sniderman, a star baseball pitcher in Toronto, who as their manager had made the arrangements and secured the financing—were on their way to Barcelona with other Canadian athletes. They never competed, however. By the time they reached Toulouse in southwestern France, the outbreak of the Spanish Civil War had led to the cancellation of the People's Olympiad. The only Canadian Jewish athlete who did go to Berlin was Irving "Toots" Meretsky from Windsor, a member of the Canadian basketball team. He had no qualms about participating. Years later, he remembered a walk he took through a Berlin Jewish neighbourhood. "It was obvious they were all scared," he said.

———

The CJC as well as the few federal Jewish politicians also failed at arguably the most significant lobbying effort they undertook during the thirties: convincing Mackenzie King's Liberal government to admit German Jewish refugees fleeing Nazi Germany. As we know now from Irving Abella and Harold Troper's groundbreaking 1982 book, *None Is Too Many: Canada and the Jews of Europe, 1933–1948*, they never really had a chance. Fearing an even greater antisemitic backlash, the CJC and Zionist organizations insisted that "discreet diplomacy"—notably the persistent, though ineffective, efforts of Jewish MPs Samuel Jacobs, Samuel Factor, and Abraham Heaps—rather than mass protests would alter the government's inflexible position against permitting the refugees into the country.

Three main obstacles that were beyond the community leaders' control proved insurmountable. The first was the fact that King followed the advice of Frederick Blair, the veteran Immigration Branch bureaucrat and its director from 1936 to 1943. His antisemitic intransigence is now legendary, and he wielded enormous power over the fate of the Jewish refugees. Classically, as Abella and Troper note, he did not consider himself to be antisemitic, merely "realistic about Canada's immigration needs and about the unsuitability of the Jew to those needs." The country did not have an official refugee policy at the time, so the German Jews had to be considered under the restrictive immigration regulations of the day—and Jews were not "preferred" immigrants under any circumstance.

In June 1939, when 907 German Jewish refugees on board the S.S. *St. Louis* were refused entry into Cuba, whose government officials would not accept their landing certificates or transit visas, no country wanted them, including Canada. Jewish groups and an assortment of Canadian writers and academics—among them, historian George Wrong; B.K. Sandwell, the editor of *Saturday Night*; and Robert Falconer, the former president of the University of Toronto—beseeched King to show "true Christian charity of the people of this most fortunate and blessed country," but neither the prime minister nor Blair could be persuaded. As Blair told Oscar D. Skelton, the under-secretary of state for external affairs, no country could "open its doors wide enough to take in the hundreds of thousands of Jewish people who want to leave Europe: the line must be drawn somewhere."

King's relationship with Ernest Lapointe—the justice minister and King's influential French-Canadian lieutenant—and Lapointe's perception of anti-Jewish attitudes in Quebec was a second factor. King and Lapointe had a close twenty-five-year friendship based in part on Lapointe ensuring that the Liberals captured nearly all of Quebec's then sixty-five seats, election after election. King trusted Lapointe's political judgement on all things to do with the province. And Lapointe kept close tabs on anti-Jewish attitudes in Quebec, especially among ardent nationalists.

On the subject of Jews, not much escaped his notice. Samuel Jacobs, who had a friendly relationship with King—in 1925, the prime minister had nominated Jacobs for membership of the Rideau Club, the only Jew to be accepted and the lone exception until 1964—had been denied a cabinet appointment because Lapointe and other French-Canadian MPs objected to selecting a Jew. (Likewise, in 1940, French-Canadian Liberals vetoed the appointment of Samuel Factor to the cabinet.) In 1937, Jacobs was keen to attend the coronation of King George VI and Queen Elizabeth being held in London that May. King likely would not have objected to Jacobs going, except Lapointe and Pierre-François Casgrain, the Liberal speaker of the House of Commons, intervened; they did not want Quebec to be "represented by a Jew." Well aware of the hostility in Quebec toward Jewish immigration, whether immigrants were refugees or not, Lapointe's opposition remained "implacable," in the words of his biographer, Lita-Rose Betcherman. There was absolutely nothing the CJC and other Jewish leaders could have done to change Lapointe's mind on this subject. Throughout the late thirties, as the German Jewish refugee question was debated by the cabinet, Lapointe led a majority of French- and English-speaking minsters who refused to yield and allow the refugees in.

Mackenzie King himself was the crucial third factor. King frequently expressed his sympathy for the German Jews, yet also maintained his belief—really nothing more than a convenient excuse—that allowing in more Jews would increase antisemitism in Canada. A guarantee made to him by Jacobs, Factor, and Heaps in May 1938 that if Canada was to admit five thousand refugees over a period of four years, the Jewish community as a whole would be financially responsible for them, fell on deaf ears when it was debated by a cabinet committee of which Lapointe was a key member. Events in Europe did tug at King's conscience and a powerful sense of Christian charity—but most of the time not enough to overcome his political opportunism. He was deeply troubled by the news of *Kristallnacht*, the "Night of Broken Glass" in Germany, when Jewish shops were destroyed and countless synagogues burned. "The sorrows which the Jews have to bear at this time are almost beyond comprehension . . . Something will have to be done by our country," he wrote in his diary on November 12, 1938.

In the end, however, his cold-hearted pragmatic side won out. Neither a series of peaceful demonstrations by Canadian Jews, held across the country in mid-November 1938 with much non-Jewish support, nor further promises from Jewish community leaders of financial commitments for the immigrants, convinced him or most members of his cabinet to bend. He did waver on at least one occasion, however. At a cabinet meeting in late November 1938, King astutely urged his colleagues to "view the refugee problem from the way in which this nation will judged in years to come, if we do not play our part, along with other democracies, in helping to meet one of humanity's . . . needs." This plea fell on deaf ears, as did the declaration a week later of Thomas Crerar—the minister responsible for immigration, who was more sympathetic—that he was prepared to admit ten thousand refugees. (Australia had announced its intention to accept fifteen thousand German Jews.) Various excuses were given—the provinces had to be consulted and antisemitism might rise—but the bottom line was that most members of the government just did not want to let any more Jews into the country. "We don't want to take too many Jews," observed Norman Robertson, who worked in the external affairs department, "but, in the present circumstances particularly, we don't want to say so." This was in line with recommendations being forwarded to the cabinet by Blair, which King strictly abided by.

Like U.S. President Franklin Roosevelt and the other Western leaders who refused to admit some desperate Jewish immigrants, King could not have predicted the tragic fate that awaited millions of European Jews in the ghettos and at Auschwitz and the other Nazi death camps. Yet, given the news reports of violence against German Jews and synagogue burnings, King could have shown leadership on this issue if he had wanted to, even if the Depression was not over and unemployment remained a factor in any debate about immigration. It was one of his worst and weakest moments as prime minister, as he allowed political expediency to override his humanitarian concerns when his own conscience told him to follow a more empathetic path.

The consequence of this intractability: between 1933 and 1945, Canada allowed approximately 5,000 Jewish refugees (perhaps a few thousand more) into the country, compared to 200,000 permitted into the United States, 70,000 into Britain, and 25,000 into China. Even Bolivia and Chile made room for 14,000 each. In 1938, the *Toronto Telegram*, which had opposed Jewish immigration, summed up the situation in a statement that the government and a majority of Canadians agreed with: "It cannot be denied that Jewish people as a class are not popular in Canada."

We Demand Work

W hile average Jewish Canadians heeded the dire news from Europe, during the worst years of the Depression—from about 1931 to 1937—most were just trying to survive, like the millions of other Canadians who were unemployed and struggled to put food on the table. Within four years of the stock market crash of October 1929, more than two million people were unemployed and in need of government relief—as humiliating an experience as there was at the time.

Everyone pitched in. At the age of eleven, in 1934, future Toronto business-man and boxing promoter Irving Ungerman found a job as a delivery boy for a drugstore. He worked six days a week for $2.50 and gave nearly all of it to his parents. Max Bregman and two partners, Alex Newman and Max Robinowitz, opened the Russian Bagel Bakery (later the Canadian Bagel Bakery, because by 1939 the federal government would not permit them to use the word "Russian") on Kensington Avenue in 1936. All three of the men's families lived above the store in a small apartment with one bathroom, and their eleven children helped run the business. Following Max's death in 1954, his son Louis opened his own shop (initially partnering with Max Robinowitz for a few years) and eventually became Toronto's most famous seller of bagels.

In Montreal in 1931, the year author Mordecai Richler was born, his parents, Moses and Lily, barely managed to feed Mordecai and his older brother Avrum. For a brief time before the stock market crash, Moses had owned his own auto parts shop, but it soon failed. He was forced to toil in a junkyard and drive a delivery truck for long hours, while Lily and the children hid from bill collectors.

The one constant around St. Lawrence Boulevard was unemployment, as many of the area's garment factories laid off workers or farmed out piecework and paid as little as possible for it. Earning ten dollars a week would have been considered good. People ate subsistence diets of day-old bread, potatoes, and eggs, and went cold during the winter because they could not afford to buy coal to heat their apartments and homes.

The memory of those hard days remained vivid for poet Irving Layton, who turned twenty years old in 1932. "Misery and heartbreak were apparent in all the familiar streets of my neighbourhood . . . You walk down St. Lawrence or one of the streets just east of it and you feel the terrible Depression in your bones and marrow. You feel the hopelessness and pain, the bewilderment and panic."

Community organizations, themselves low in cash, tried to help. The *Keneder Adler* staff in Montreal initiated an "Emergency Fund" for the "newly impoverished," and arranged it so handouts were doled out discreetly. Labour Zionists and the Arbeiter Ring set up a soup kitchen, the "People's Kitchen," which could not keep up with demand. In 1931, the People's Kitchen served 10,000 meals, and during the first part of 1932, another 30,000. Miss A. Schwartz of the "Employers of Jewish Help" associated with Montreal's Jewish Federation of Philanthropies placed an ad in the *Jewish Chronicle* in late January 1931 asking "employers of Jewish help and labour" to contact her, as she had a large list of unemployed individuals searching for work. "These men and women are not asking for charity," the advertisement made clear, "but [seeking] employment, whether temporary or permanent."

An ad was placed, too, in the *Jewish Post* in Winnipeg in early April 1932— by the community's United Hebrew Relief organization, who pleaded with those who could help to do so: "Passover is fast approaching. Over five hundred Jewish families, through no fault of their own and against their will, have become destitute and in need of direct help from us—from you. They need your help and our help." Author Adele Wiseman, who grew up in Winnipeg during the thirties, figured that her family "must be the poorest people in the world, but their poverty was to be kept a secret." She and her siblings always had enough to eat, but only because, she later realized, her parents went hungry. Like other Canadians, many Jews absolutely refused to accept handouts and worked eighteen-hour days for little pay, doing what they could to survive.

The Depression hit the Canadian garment industry especially hard. No one group was impacted worse by this downturn than Jewish workers and owners—of which there were approximately 1,200. By 1931, Jews made up roughly 35 per cent (and as high as 46 per cent in Toronto) of the garment workforce in the county. After the crash, orders dried up, wages were severely cut, workers were laid off, and firms went bankrupt. Only the Second World War was to revive the trade. "How's business?" one dressmaker manufacturer was supposed to have asked another. "How's business?" his friend replied. "Business is so bad that even the customers who don't intend to pay aren't buying." That was the simple truth. In the major garment centres of Montreal, Toronto, and Winnipeg, the problems in the garment factories had a domino effect: clothing merchants went bankrupt and employees lost their jobs.

As was revealed in witness testimony at the Royal Commission on Price Spreads, convened in 1934, women—"industrial slaves," in the view of one left-wing union organizer—were at the bottom of an ever-dwindling pay scale, and in many cases were barely surviving on less than ten dollars a week for upward of fifty hours of work. Conditions in many factories were as terrible as they had always been. They were dark and damp with poor ventilation, which contributed to a high rate of tuberculosis among garment and fur workers. During each shift, workers were pushed to the limit to meet production quotas. Failure to do so, or complaining about it, could result in firing. Any griping or talk of unions was met with the harshest of consequences.

There had been dozens of garment industry strikes, most brief and ineffective, during the twenties. The bosses had for the most part (though not in all cases) held firm to their position: they did not negotiate with unions. The real trouble began in the summer of 1928, with the establishment of the Industrial Union of Needle Trades Workers of Canada (IUNTW). Its organizers and leadership, many of whom were Jewish, were members of the Workers' Unity League, a front for the Communist Party. In the womenswear factories, the IUNTW was a direct challenge to the supremacy of the International

Ladies' Garment Workers' Union (ILGWU), which in turn adopted a more radical position as the Depression worsened.

Perceiving themselves as the underdogs in a mighty class struggle for economic fairness and social justice against their greedy bosses, symbolic of the evils of the capitalist system which enslaved them, Jewish workers gravitated to the IUNTW. Predictably, the owners—Jewish and non-Jewish—detested and feared the new union, and this set the stage for the bitter conflicts which followed.

An effective tactic employed by owners was to ferment discord between allegedly radical Jewish workers and non-Jewish workers, who were more conservative and harboured resentment toward Jewish-controlled unions. This acrimony existed across the industry, and in 1927 it had led to the establishment of the National Clothing Workers of Canada (NCWC), affiliated with the All-Canadian Congress of Labour and promoted by the union and management in Toronto as a "Gentile-only" union.

In 1933, for instance, the garment factory owner of Ontario Boys' Wear was upset by a strike engineered by the Jewish-dominated Amalgamated Clothing Workers of America for union recognition. He made a deal for the NCWC to step in, and the owner and the NCWC's officials made much of the fact that Ontario Boys' Wear aimed to be a "non-Hebrew shop." Similarly, a year earlier, with tensions high among Toronto locals of the International Fur Workers' Union, the owners succeeded in dividing the Jewish and non-Jewish workers. When a large-scale strike began, the Jews joined the picket line, while the non-Jews remained in the factories.

Jewish owners, too, "did not hesitate to try to discredit the Jewish unions through appeals to anti-Semitism," as Ruth Frager explains in her study of the Toronto garment industry. Back in 1925—during a strike of cloak-making workers in Toronto in which the ILGWU was involved—J.M. Leiderman, a Jewish owner and a spokesman for fourteen other manufacturers, had been castigated by many in the community for commenting in interviews with the press that he and the other owners were willing to employ "Jewish operatives," but only if they were not "controlled by Jewish radicals." Gentile workers, he suggested, were a lot less trouble. This prompted Mary McNab of the ILGWU to tell the *Telegram* that "it was rather laughable to have a Jew manufacturer claim defence of Gentile girls." By 1934, Jewish garment owners in Montreal were relocating their factories to small towns far enough away from the city that they did not have to hire any troublemaking Jewish tailors and seamstresses. One such move in December 1936 left 270 Jewish workers in Montreal unemployed, when their boss fired them and opened a new factory in Sherbrooke in the Eastern Townships, 156 kilometres away.

The Jewish owners' treatment of Jewish workers who fought for union recognition, improved factory conditions, and higher wages deeply troubled Rabbi Harry Stern of Temple Emanu-El, Montreal's Reform congregation, who pointed out the supreme irony of the situation. "Are there not many [owners] even today despite minimum wage laws who keep the pay of their employees down to the lowest notch?" he asked in a *Canadian Jewish Review* column of early January 1937. "And are not these often the persons who head [Jewish] charity lists?" In other words, the owners bizarrely separated their often abysmal attitude to and treatment of their Jewish employees from their desire to be recognized for their philanthropic work and generosity in providing funds for the community—including struggling garment workers!

During the height of the Depression, wages fell 30 to 50 per cent, while hours increased to often sixty hours a week. Piecework fees were slashed: Prior to the Depression Eaton's in Toronto had on average paid about $3.60 for a dozen voile dresses; after 1933, the company paid only $1.75 for the same number of garments. There was frustration and desperation on the factory floors and at labour halls across the country. Workers had zero patience for the intransigence of owners, no matter what their religion or ethnic background. It is hardly surprising that the Communist Party, which was the most vocal about the exploitation of the masses, appealed to a lot more Jews than it ever had. During the 1932 May Day parade in Winnipeg, Labour Zionists marched with their old foes, the Communists, under a banner which declared, in Yiddish and English, "*Mir Fodern Arbeit*, We Demand Work."

From about 1931 to 1937, garment workers and owners clashed like never before. Strikes, walkouts, and violence on the picket lines crippled factories and caused economic chaos for months at a time. The urgent contest between the IUNTW and the ILGWU for recognition as the premier garment union in womenswear propelled the labour confrontations. By one count, in the three-year period from 1931 to 1934, the IUNTW led about two hundred strikes involving more than four thousand workers in Montreal, Toronto, and Winnipeg. Many of the workers were Jewish, though in Montreal the ILGWU also fought for the rights of thousands of French-Canadian women—the so-called *midinettes*, young Catholic girls (the name was according to the Museum of Jewish Montreal "a French contraction of midi and dinette [and] referred to their 'short lunch' and the phenomenon of thousands of girls appearing suddenly on Ste. Catherine and Bleury Streets at noon-time.")

The Montreal labour battle eventually pitted two young and unyielding Jewish unionists against each other: Bernard Shane of the ILGWU and Joshua "Joe" Gershman of the IUNTW. Shane was from New Jersey, and had spent time organizing cloakmakers in Toronto from 1929 to 1931 before being dispatched to Montreal in 1934, where he was told by union officials he would be spending no more than three weeks. He never left, and during the next four decades he left his mark on the Canadian labour movement. Early on, Shane won concessions for coat makers, pressers, and cutters. He was intensely anti-communist, so much so that he tried to sabotage a IUNTW-led Montreal garment strike in August 1934, in which four thousand dressmakers from 125 shops and factories demanded shorter hours and higher wages.

In the middle of that strike was thirty-two-year-old Gershman, by then a committed communist and an experienced union organizer. He had immigrated to Canada from a small town in the Ukraine in 1921 and settled in Winnipeg, where his father had moved eight years earlier. The First World War and then the Russian Revolution had prevented Gershman and the members of his family from joining him. By the time Gershman made it to Winnipeg, his father had died. He found a job in a fur-making factory and immersed himself in the city's left-wing Yiddish culture. Within two years, he had joined the Communist Party and become a leading unionist. He later recalled that during one protracted strike he was arrested fourteen times and feared he might be deported. In 1926, he moved to Toronto, where he came into contact with Tim Buck, soon to be the country's most infamous Commie, and was involved in the formation of the IUNTW. Later, he became the uncompromising editor of two Toronto-based Yiddish-language Communist organs: *Der Kamf* ("The Struggle"), which had been started in Montreal in 1934 but was moved to Toronto two years later; and in 1940, *Vochenblatt*, or the *Keneder yiddische vochenblat*, the less-threatening sounding "Canadian Jewish Weekly," in which he regularly castigated community leaders like Ben Kayfetz of the CJC and fur union organizer Max Federman for actions he did not agree with. (As Kayfetz later recalled, the only person "lower" than Federman in Gershman's opinion was him.)

During the 1934 strike in Montreal, workers who walked off the job clashed several times with strike-breakers attempting to enter the factories. They were in turn attacked with "bludgeons, lead pipes and rubber hoses filled with sand," wielded by "American goons," as the *Montreal Herald* dubbed them, who had been brought in by the owners. This was a similar tactic to that employed by the manufacturers when dressmakers in the city had gone on strike a year earlier. Gershman remembered that Montreal Jewish owners had hired gangsters "to beat up workers on [the] picket line." Many of the gangsters, he added, were "Jewish boys." Gershman knew some of them, and when they confronted him, he made a deal with them. He bandaged himself up and pretended to have been attacked so that the men, who desperately needed money—which was the reason they had accepted the nasty job in the first place—would get paid by the manufacturers. Gershman and his alleged attackers celebrated with a dinner at the LaSalle Hotel.

The 1934 strike dragged on into September, and almost all of the owners refused to negotiate with communists, despite the Quebec government's efforts to mediate a settlement. By the time the strike officially ended in early October, some of the owners had conceded to slightly higher wages and less hours of work, but few of them would recognize the IUNTW.

Ironically, Shane, much to his chagrin, was later accused by Catholic Church spokesmen of being a "foreign" agitator and a communist during the contentious 1937 dressmakers' strike. With the help of the talented New York unionist Rose Pesotta and others, Shane had an estimated five thousand workers on the street marching for recognition of the ILGWU, rather than the conservative Catholic unions (connected to the NCWC) that were also negotiating with the owners. At one point, Premier Maurice Duplessis, who had recently passed the notorious Padlock Law aimed at clamping down on communists, issued an arrest warrant for Shane and Raoul Trépanier of the Montreal Trades and Labour Council (and head of the strike committee) for conspiracy against the public order. Neither was ever apprehended or charged, and three weeks after the strike began Shane and his ILGWU team had what seemed like a victory: a 10 per cent salary increase for the workers, a forty-four-hour week, a grievance process, acceptable piecework rates, and most significantly, "total recognition of the union" and collective bargaining. Yet, after the strikers returned to the shops, the owners did not abide by the agreement, and the workers, Shane conceded many years later, became "apathetic"— a situation he claimed was made worse by communist influences.

Jewish garment trade workers (and owners) in Toronto and Winnipeg experienced similar turmoil to that in Montreal. In the summer of 1934, at the Eaton's factories in Toronto, management introduced a new and more complicated dress pattern, yet refused to compensate its workers accordingly. Upset by what they perceived to be an unfair demand, a group of thirty-eight women requested that they be allowed to consult with their union representatives. Eaton's managers consented, but then locked the women out and the dressmakers declared themselves on strike. The company used strike-breakers and private detectives to intimidate and hassle the workers on the picket line, and the strike ultimately failed. Later, when charged at the Royal Commission on Price Spreads hearing by several witnesses of treating their workers harshly, the company's spokesmen vigorously defended themselves, insisting that Eaton's did not "hound" its workers.

Divisive, as well, was a strike that same year by predominately Jewish workers against the Superior Cloak Company. Established by Abraham Posluns in 1916, Superior was run in the 1930s by his sons, Sam and Louis, pillars of the Toronto Jewish community. (Louis's son Wilfred—along with Winnipeg entrepreneur Jimmy Kay—later established the clothing giant

Dylex.) So hostile were the Posluns toward the ILGWU and its members that they locked out two hundred workers, hired strike-breakers, and then temporarily moved the company's plant to Guelph.

Strikers from Toronto travelled to Guelph to confront their replacements, which led to trouble. Over the course of several days, there were violent clashes with the local police, who were assisted by firemen and reinforcement police officers from Kitchener. During one altercation, Samuel Posluns shot a gun close enough to a striker that he was later charged with discharging a revolver with intent to injure. Sam Kraisman, an ILGWU organizer, claimed he was roughed up by the Posluns' thugs. And two Jewish picketers, Joe Zlotnick and Gael Goldenberg—labelled "foreigners" by the *Telegram*—were arrested and charged with disturbing the peace and ordered by a magistrate to "get out of town immediately and stay out." The strike lasted through the summer, until the Posluns eventually agreed to mediate the dispute.

In Winnipeg, bitter strikes in 1933 and 1934 targeting fur manufacturers resulted in police harassment and violent confrontations. A young agitator named Freda Coodin led a group of strikers to the front steps of furrier Abraham Hurtig's North End house and was arrested. Then, she allegedly threatened several female workers—"scabs," in her view—who dared to cross the picket line, and was arrested again. "If she goes to work, they'll break every bone in her body," Coodin was supposed to have told the mother of one of the workers. "And she'll be carried home on a stretcher." Her fellow workers disputed this version of what had transpired, and Coodin claimed that a burly male strike-breaker had assaulted her. A petite girl, less than five feet tall, Coodin had the spunk of a prizefighter and was as committed to communist doctrines as Lenin was. Following a brief trial, in which the judge dismissed Coodin's testimony that she had been attacked, she was found guilty of assault, unlawful assembly, and a seldom-invoked section of the Criminal Code (501) which essentially made it illegal to "watch" the house of someone and prevent them from leaving it or doing any other lawful act. She was sentenced to one year in the provincial jail for women at Portage la Prairie.

Coodin may have been already ill with tuberculosis before her incarceration, or she contracted it in prison. Shortly before her release, her health worsened and she was hospitalized. She died at the King Edward Hospital on April 6, 1935, at the age of twenty-three (though the provincial death certificate and gravestone listed her age as twenty-seven). Her comrades hailed her as a martyr. A large funeral was held for her at the Liberty Temple, and Winnipeg alderman Joe Forkin, a communist, delivered a moving eulogy. On her headstone at the Shaarey Zedek Cemetery was engraved: "A Victim of the Hurtig Furrier Strike August 1933." That epitaph remained intact for exactly one night. The name "Hurtig" was then scratched out by one of her capitalist antagonists.

A few months after Coodin's death, a Jewish labour organizer from the ILGWU who was to have a lasting impact on the industry arrived in Winnipeg. His name was Sam Herbst—which he pronounced "Oiybst" in his thick Russian-Yiddish Brooklyn accent. As part of the ILGWU's strategic plan to be the number-one garment union, David Dubinsky, the New York–based president of the ILGWU, sought to take advantage of the IUNTW's failure to make any real headway in Winnipeg and so dispatched Herbst to Manitoba.

Herbst later recalled that in Winnipeg (or "Veenepeg," as he said it) he discovered that conditions in the garment factories were "astounding" and "unbelievable." Wages were low and workers had little protection against management exploitation. Like most ILGWU members, he did not trust the Communist Party members of the IUNTW, but cleverly he did not ignore them either. He talked to them about a possible merger between the two unions, though nothing came of that unorthodox idea. Herbst then negotiated a deal with the owners of Jacob and Crowley, one of the largest garment operations in the city, convincing them that unions and labour peace would increase their profit margins. The new contract was, despite the grumbling of some radicals, a landmark achievement in the city's history of the Manitoba labour movement, and forever altered the lives of the Jewish working class. The work week was set at forty-four hours, and every employee in Jacob and Crowley's factory—now deemed a "closed shop" in which all workers had to be a member of the ILGWU —received a raise of one dollar per week. Several other garment owners soon signed on.

Other bitter strikes between Jewish owners and fur workers did erupt in the city in the years before the Second World War, yet by the late forties Winnipeg's garment trade had expanded into a $50 million enterprise employing more than six thousand workers. By then, like in Montreal and Toronto, this generation of Jewish working-class radicals was nearing retirement, and their children had become entrepreneurs and professionals rather than garment workers and furriers. The Jewish garment trade owners, however, remained powerful and influential in all three cities. And more often than not, they used some of the enormous wealth they generated—from a radical perspective, wealth generated on the backs of their workers—for the benefit of the Jewish community at large.

Beyond the factories, some Jews sought more creative ways to make a dollar. Good Jewish boys, these were not. Harry Ship and his friends raked in cash from illegal gambling operations during the late 1930s and 1940s. Such Montreal nightclubs as Tic Toc, the Gayety, the Hawaiian Lounge, and Ruby Foo's had links to illegal gambling run by Eastern European Jews. Canada never quite had the Jewish gangster problem of the U.S., where infamous mobsters like Meyer Lansky and Benjamin "Bugsy" Siegel made millions of dollars from gambling and selling liquor during the Prohibition era, and racketeer Louis "Lepke" Buchalter organized a contract-killing hit squad, later known as Murder, Inc. (and by its members as "The Combination"). This notorious Jewish and Italian gang—including the ever-feared killer-for-hire Samuel "Red" Levine (absolutely no relation to the author), who was an observant Jew who wore a kippah and avoided murder jobs on the Sabbath, if he could help it—was likely responsible for more than five hundred murders. But though there may not have been any activity on that scale in Canada, several Montreal Jewish immigrants were heavily involved in trafficking opium, morphine, and heroin—and paid the ultimate price.

Harry Davis, born Chaskel Lazarovitch in Romania in 1898, arrived in Canada at the age of ten. He grew up dirt poor, and never forgot that. Before he was twenty-five years old, Davis, who loved fine and expensive suits, was making big money from gambling, prostitution, fencing stolen property, and dealing in drugs. For a time, he conducted his operations from a shop on St. Urbain Street. The Royal Canadian Mounted Police (RCMP) came after Davis and his chief partner, former featherweight boxer Eddie "Kid" Baker, a Russian Jewish immigrant and professional gambler who later had a financial interest in the Gayety Theatre. During the late twenties, both were convicted of conspiracy to traffic in drugs, though only served short prison sentences.

By the time the Depression crippled the Canadian economy, Davis had teamed up with two other Jewish toughs: Pincus "Pinky" Brecher from New Jersey, and "Fat" Charlie Feigenbaum. Like an early version of *The French Connection*, they planned to smuggle in cocaine and heroin worth more than $200,000 (over $4 million today) from Paris into the Port of Montreal.

One of Feigenbaum's responsibilities was looking after three hundred slot machines in resort hotels in the Laurentians. He also made money illegally bringing in silk, which at the time was subject to high government tariffs. Bribing custom officials was a piece of cake for Fat Charlie. Nonetheless, late in 1930 the law caught up with him. Convicted of silk smuggling, he was sentenced to five and half years in prison—and was miserable about it.

Meanwhile, in April 1933, having become aware of the Davis gang's drug operations, the RCMP swooped in and arrested Davis, Brecher, and six others. All of them were charged with drug smuggling. Feigenbaum was tired of rotting in prison. He had intimate knowledge of how Davis and Brecher worked, and offered to testify against his former partners—he became a "stool pigeon," as the press later put it—in exchange for a reduced sentence. In a brief trial held in October 1933, and owing to Feigenbaum's detailed descriptions of the gang's drug business, Davis was sentenced to ten strokes of the lash, a $10,000 fine, and fourteen years in Laval's Saint-Vincent-de-Paul Penitentiary. Brecher's trial was not scheduled for another year.

Feigenbaum, forty-eight years old, was back on the streets of Montreal by the summer of 1934. Despite being an informer, he was foolish enough to believe that he could resume life with his wife and children and get back into smuggling and illegal gambling. He was wrong. Late in the afternoon on August 21, 1934, he walked out of his brother's house on Esplanade Avenue, a few blocks from the Main, accompanied by his eighteen-year-old son Jackie.

There was a black Hudson sedan parked across the street. The man in the passenger seat got out, moved closer to Feigenbaum, and shot him six times in the chest and head. He then calmly returned to the car, which sped off. Other residents on the street witnessed the murder, but the killer and the driver—who might have been a local Jewish hood named Louis Bercovitch—were never apprehended. (The murder was famous in Montreal police history because it was the first time radio-equipped cars were summoned to the scene of a crime.)

Many members of the Montreal Jewish community were shocked at the killing and embarrassed by the Jewish connection to gambling and crime commented on in the French and English newspapers. True, the murder occurred "in the heart of the Jewish quarter," the *Adler* noted in an editorial a few days after Feigenbaum's death, and the victim was Jewish. But the paper stressed "it is clear that this has nothing to do with the Jewish community as a whole . . . For the well-being of the Jewish community it would be much better if the Jews were to be clean of such men and of such damaging spectacles." Clearly not everyone around St. Lawrence Boulevard felt that way—an estimated three thousand people, presumably many of them Jews, attended Feigenbaum's funeral. A month later, and despite the absence of Feigenbaum as a star witness, Brecher was also convicted of drug trafficking. Before he could be sentenced, however, he managed to break free from the guards watching him and leap over an open passageway. He fell thirty-five feet onto the hard asphalt below and died.

Having endured five lashes when he arrived at the penitentiary and five before he was released, Harry Davis was a free man again in 1945, and immediately got back into illegal gambling. With the death of Eddie Baker, Davis became the "edge man": he collected money from his fellow bookies and gamblers and regularly paid off the police to look the other way.

In the spring of 1946, Louis Bercovitch, the alleged driver of the car at the Feigenbaum murder who used the alias "Joe Miller," wanted to open his own gambling operation. Davis, who had the final word about such activities, told him no. Bercovitch was angry about this and soon heard a rumour that Davis had put out a contract on his life. On the afternoon of July 25, 1946, Bercovitch met with Davis at his office on Stanley Street, half a block from Ste. Catherine, supposedly to smooth things out. The discussion immediately became heated. According to Bercovitch, Davis threatened him. "What we did to Feigenbaum, the same could happen to you," he was alleged to have said. A few minutes later, and again according to Bercovitch, Davis reached for a gun and so did Bercovitch, who fired first. Davis was killed instantly and Bercovitch fled the scene. Realizing that too many people had seen him enter Davis's office, a few hours after the shooting Bercovitch contacted a reporter at the *Montreal Herald*, told him his version of the altercation, and then turned himself in to the police. At his trial three months later, the jury more or less believed him that he had shot Davis in self-defence—though it was common knowledge that Davis did not normally carry a revolver—and found him guilty of manslaughter. He still received a life sentence, and appealed. He was not released until January 1958, having served eleven years.

The funeral of Harry Davis on July 28, 1946 was another big occasion in the city's Jewish quarter. It was like a "midway side show," the *Globe and Mail* reported, with a crowd of about five thousand people gathering outside the funeral home on St. Urbain Street. Newspaper photographers tried to take pictures of the two hundred or so mobsters attending the service, and were threatened with physical harm. A long motorcade followed the hearse carrying his casket to the Saint Laurent Jewish cemetery.

The *Adler* was once more on the defensive, and scrambled to explain the violent death of another Jewish gangster, supposedly a "victim of circumstances." This time, they blamed police corruption, which was likely not far from the truth. "If the police were not corrupt and had not taken bribes," an editorial of July 30, 1946 pointed out, "gambling houses would not be able to operate and the Harry Davis's of the world would perhaps be forced to earn their living in the usual manner."

With the death of Davis, the ever-flamboyant Harry Ship, now in his early thirties, was soon anointed the "King" of the Jewish bookies and gamblers in the city. Ship, who had studied business at Queen's University in Kingston for a few years, was already heavily involved in gambling, and at one point was bringing in $1,500 a day (and likely more). He was also later celebrated for being the model for Mordecai Richler's fictional character Jerry Dingleman, the "Boy Wonder," in *The Apprenticeship of Duddy Kravitz*. Besides operating the popular nightclub Chez Parée and a swanky illegal gambling club in Côte Saint-Luc—politicians, lawyers, and judges were patrons, and guests were served whisky and filet mignon on the house—Ship was a stellar self-promoter. He distributed thousands of pencils with bookies' phone numbers on them so that his many customers could more easily place their bets.

His reign was not without its headaches, however. Montreal's crime-fighting lawyer, Pacifique "Pax" Plante, the deputy director of the city's police department, made it his mission to shut down organized crime and gambling and clean up police corruption. He quickly targeted Ship, who was arrested and convicted on three counts of keeping a common betting house. Evidence presented by Plante showed that Ship's cigar store on Ste. Catherine Street East took in $1.2 million in 1945 and 1946. He was sentenced to three six-month terms to be served concurrently, a sentence that Ship appealed. The case wound its way through the court system, and it was not until March 1949 that Ship finally lost his bid to quash the original conviction. He was forced to serve his sentence and post a $20,000 bond to keep the peace for two years. Once out of prison, he ran cabarets during the fifties, and told and retold the tales of his storied career until the day he died from lung cancer at age eighty-two in late 1998.

PART ONE

(clockwise from top left)

1. As the religious head of Montreal's Spanish and Portuguese synagogue from 1847 until his death in 1882, Abraham de Sola was Canada's first true Jewish religious leader.

2. Aaron Hart, one of the first permanent Jewish settlers in Quebec and the patriarch of the celebrated Hart family.

3. Ezekiel Hart, a son of Aaron Hart and a central figure in the early Canadian Jewish struggle for equality.

4. "New Jerusalem," Winnipeg's impoverished immigrant quarter north of the downtown area, in the 1880s. The North End was home to the first wave of Jewish settlers in the city.

5. In 1871, Henry Nathan Jr. became a member of Parliament for the new province of British Columbia, and the first Jew to have a seat in the House of Commons after Confederation.

PART TWO

6. *(above, left)* Clarence de Sola, the son of Abraham de Sola and a modern and assimilated Jew, was one of Canada's first Zionist leaders in the early twentieth century.

7. *(above, right)* Edward Joseph ("Joe") Seidelman from Vancouver, who served in the Canadian Expeditionary Force during the First World War. He died in action at the age of twenty, at the Battle of Passchendaele in October 1917.

8. The great Yiddish writer Sholem Aleichem (second row, fourth from right) on a visit to Montreal in June 1915 with journalist Reuben Brainin (second row, third from right).

9. Teachers and students at the Arbeiter Ring (Workmen's Circle) School in Winnipeg in 1927, where a Jewish socialist curriculum was taught. Supporters of the Arbeiter Ring had ardent faith in Marxist and socialist principles, a love for Yiddish language and culture, and a secular rather than religious emphasis on Judaism. Note the Communist hammer and sickle symbols on the back wall under the word "Socialism," and the photographs of Yiddish writer I.L. Peretz (bottom), Karl Marx (right), and the nineteenth-century Russian anarchist, Mikhail Bakunin (left).

10. The dashing Montreal Jewish figure skating champion Louis Rubenstein in 1893. He was also a Montreal city alderman from 1914 until his death in 1931.

11. *(above, left)* Israel Hoffer and his wife Clara were among the hard-working settlers in the Jewish agricultural colony at Sonnenfeld in Saskatchewan in the early 1920s. The Jewish farmers epitomized the pioneer spirit and persistence that characterized the first and second waves of immigrants to Canada.

12. *(above, right)* Rabbi Israel Kahanovitch, Chief Rabbi of Winnipeg and Western Canada, with the Kashruth Council of Canada in Winnipeg in 1906. For decades, Kahanovitch was the most significant rabbinical leader in the city and was involved in everything from enforcing acceptable kosher regulations to forging links with Jewish garment workers.

13. The indomitable Samuel Bronfman, "Mr. Sam," who built a multi-million-dollar whisky empire and was the head of the Canadian Jewish Congress from 1939 to 1962.

14. The Polish passport of immigrant and storekeeper Sam Kliman (the author's maternal grandfather), who came to Canada in 1921 at the age of nineteen. Following his marriage to Sarah Rosen of Portage la Prairie in 1928, the couple ran a general store in Holland, Manitoba, and raised their four children. They were the town's only Jewish family.

15. Montreal writer A.M. Klein in the mid-1940s. His poignant poems like "Autobiographical," penned in 1942, captured the essence of Jewish immigrant life in Canada.

16. (*above*) Fanny "Bobbie" Rosenfeld at the 1928 Summer Olympics in Amsterdam (second from left, no. 677). She won a gold medal as a member of Canada's 400-metre relay team and a silver medal for the "disputed" 100-metre sprint, which she likely won. In 1950, she was named Canada's outstanding female athlete of the first half of the twentieth century.

17. (*left*) Ottawa's Lillian Freiman, shown here in 1908, and her husband, Archie, were significant Zionist and social welfare leaders for many years.

(clockwise from top left)

18. Louis Rosenberg at Lipton, Saskatchewan, in 1916. Rosenberg was one of the key organizers of the Jewish agricultural colonies, and was a demographer of Canadian Jewish society in his role as the research director of the Canadian Jewish Congress.

19. Russian Jewish immigrants arriving in Canada in 1911. Fleeing economic hardship and persecution in the Russian Empire's Pale of Settlement, immigrants like this family sought new opportunities in North America.

20. Antisemitism in the form of property covenants and club restrictions was prevalent in Canada up until at least the 1950s. This is a typical "Gentiles Only" sign, posted at Forest Hill Lodge at Burleigh Falls, Ontario, in 1940.

21. (*above, left*) In an age when men overwhelmingly dominated the leadership of Jewish community organizations, Ida Siegel of Toronto was a notable exception. Here she stands beside Edmund Scheuer, a staunch advocate of Reform Judaism, at the Canadian Jewish Farm School in Georgetown, Ontario, in 1927.

22. (*above, right*) Famous for displaying a Star of David on his trunks, Toronto Jewish boxing champion Sammy Luftspring—shown here in a 1930 promotional picture—won 100 of 105 bouts between 1932 and 1936. He took tremendous pride in being a Jew who did not back down from a fight.

23. The lot of the peddler, like this one pictured in 1911 making his way through the streets of Toronto's St. John's Ward immigrant quarter, was a difficult one. Gentile mothers invoked the figure of the Jewish peddler as a bogeyman, to hush their children.

24. The establishment of the Canadian Jewish Congress as a "Jewish Parliament" in 1919 was a proud moment for the community. Delegates (above) from St. John's to Vancouver convened in Montreal for the CJC's first plenary session, which the *Canadian Jewish Chronicle* hailed as a historic gathering where "the destiny of our people is being shaped."

25. Jewish gangsters based in Montreal made money during the Great Depression from gambling, prostitution, fencing stolen property, and dealing in drugs. As this story from the *Montreal Daily Star* on August 22, 1934 relates—and much to the embarrassment and horror of the city's Jewish community leaders—"Fat" Charlie Feigenbaum, who had provided damaging testimony against several of his former partners, was assassinated on a residential street.

26. Canadian Jews marched in solidarity to protest the harsh treatment of Jews in the Soviet Union and the Soviet government's refusal to permit many Jews to immigrate to Israel or North America. In February 1977, a group of Jewish women in Winnipeg protested the arrest of Amner Zavurov, who received a three-year prison sentence for not having proper internal papers, and Dr. Naum Salansky, who was charged with "anti-Soviet slander."

PART THREE

27. Canadian Jews like this happy group gathered in front of Histadrut House, the Labour Zionist Alliance's headquarters in Montreal, rejoiced at the establishment of the State of Israel in 1948.

28. Toronto lawyer Bora Laskin in 1935. Laskin was a brilliant University of Toronto constitutional law professor. He was appointed to the Ontario Court of Appeal in 1965 and then to the Supreme Court of Canada in 1970, the first Jew to be so honoured. Three years later, in another Jewish first, Prime Minister Pierre Trudeau named Laskin the Supreme Court's Chief Justice.

29. In such novels as *The Apprenticeship of Duddy Kravitz*, Mordecai Richler—one of Canada's most well-known and controversial authors—profiled the good and the bad of Jewish life around Montreal's St. Lawrence Boulevard, where he grew up. He was also not shy about denouncing the antisemitic history of Quebec and elsewhere, nor about replying to his many critics, who were as outspoken as he was.

30. As a fighter pilot with 404 Squadron RCAF, based in Scotland in 1942, Flight Lieutenant Sydney Shulemson—shown here standing beside a Fleet Finch II aircraft—and his mates attacked enemy ships near the coastlines of Norway and the Netherlands. For his bravery throughout the war, he was awarded a Distinguished Service Order in 1944.

31. Joseph B. Salsberg came to Toronto with his family from Poland in 1913, when he was eleven years old. He embraced socialism, and became a union organizer and a member of the Communist Party. He was elected as an alderman in the Toronto civic election of 1938, and then ran for the Labour-Progressive Party in the Ontario provincial election of 1943. He won a seat and served for the next twelve years. This Yiddish poster from his campaign states:

For happiness [or peace/freedom] – Against further arming of Germany

For jobs – and economic improvement for the masses

Your beloved incumbent representative

J.B. Salsberg, Progressive-Labour Party candidate

32. Louis Rasminsky, the first Jewish Governor of the Bank of Canada, and his wife Lyla, c.1965. Rasminsky's career at the bank and his appointment as governor in 1961 by Prime Minister John Diefenbaker was a sign that prejudice and discrimination in Canada were gradually declining.

33. Future Supreme Court of Canada justice Rosalie Abella as a baby in the Stuttgart camp for displaced persons, after the Second World War. Holding her is Zysla Krongold, her maternal grandmother, standing between Rosalie's parents, Jacob and Fanny Silberman. The couple's firstborn son, Julius, had died during the Holocaust.

34. Twins Leo and Miriam Lowy, Holocaust survivors, in Europe—before they immigrated to Vancouver to rebuild their lives.

35. The ladies of Hadassah-WIZO in Toronto (pictured here c.1950s) and across the country worked tirelessly for Zionist and Jewish community causes. Hadassah was established in Canada during the First World War. As one historian puts it, they were the Zionist "shock troops," becoming "the most continuously active arm of Zionism in Canada, infusing the movement with a sense of immediate and pressing concern."

36. In the 1960s and 1970s, Canadian Jews held rallies for Jewish causes—like this group in Montreal in 1971. In countless marches and demonstrations, they lobbied the federal government to come to the aid of persecuted Jews in the Soviet Union, who were denied the exit visas they needed to leave the country for Israel or North America.

37. (*above, left*) With the establishment of the State of Israel in 1948, Israeli dancing groups like Winnipeg's famed Sarah Sommer Chai Folk Ensemble (pictured here in a 1970s performance) provided a strong Jewish and Zionist bond for young people.

38. (*above, right*) One of the breakers of the Jewish community's glass ceiling was Dorothy "Dodo" Heppner, who in 1983 became the first female president of Allied Jewish Community Services in Montreal.

CONCLUSION

39. Being Jewish in Canada comes down to family, and the desire of parents to pass on the traditions of the past. One such Jewish Canadian family are Yacov Fruchter and Ryla Braemer of Toronto, and their two daughters, Sheelo and Lev.

PART THREE

CANADIAN
JEWS

A Duty to the Jewish People the World Over

When Canada officially declared war on Germany on September 10, 1939, twenty-three-year-old Syd Shulemson was working at his uncle's print shop. Like almost all other Montreal Jewish kids who grew up within walking distance of St. Lawrence Boulevard, Shulemson was a graduate of Baron Byng High School. His life plan was to become an aeronautical engineer. Syd was smart, had high marks, and was able to enroll in McGill University, despite its quota for Jewish students. A friendly professor steered him toward an aeronautical program in Detroit, but in the midst of the Great Depression the tuition and living expenses were too much of a burden for his parents to bear. For a time, he worked in the advertising business in New York City, before returning to Montreal and a job at the print shop.

On September 10, together with other young men, Shulemson queued up in front of the Royal Canadian Air Force's offices in Westmount. His intention was to enlist and become a pilot. After a three-hour wait, the corporal supervising the sign-up ignored his question about becoming a pilot and instead asked him if he could cook. "Outside, outside," the corporal barked. "We need cooks." Determined to fly a fighter plane, Shulemson endured a bureaucratic gauntlet for about two years until finally, in September 1941, he attended flight school at Aylmer, Ontario. Like the other nearly 17,000 Jewish men and women (16,441 men and approximately 279 women, though the number of women was likely higher according to Saundra Lipton of the University of Calgary) who served in the Canadian Forces during the Second World War (many of the women were part of the Canadian Women's Army

Corp or CWAC, and the RCAF Women's Division), Shulemson wanted to enlist for his country as well as his people. "I knew that Hitler and the Nazis were extremely anti-Semitic and I was very motivated to fight for that reason," he would recall more than six decades later.

As a fighter pilot with No. 404 Squadron of the RCAF—based in 1942 in Wick, at the northeast tip of Scotland—Flight Lieutenant Shulemson and his mates attacked enemy ships near the coastlines of Norway and the Netherlands. On his first mission, he and his navigator, Al Glasgow, destroyed a large German Seedrache (Sea Dragon) flying boat. This and other successes confirmed Shulemson's reputation as a skilled "anti-shipping expert."

Antisemitism was by no means rampant in the forces and, as in Canada generally, it depended on individual personalities and attitudes. Some Jewish men experienced it; others such as Shulemson claimed they did not. "I ran into very little anti-Semitism in the RCAF," he later recalled. "The guys on my squadron would follow me into hell and back, they had a lot of faith in what I could do."

Shulemson learned quickly to fly at low altitudes to avoid German radar units and anti-aircraft batteries. This required tricky and skilful operation of the Bristol Beaufighter bombers he piloted. On one occasion, he engaged a Messerschmitt Bf 109 in a ten-minute dogfight low over the water. After taking a lot of fire that put bullet holes in his plane, he outmanoeuvred his enemy with "a series of flick rolls in the opposite direction at wave-top height." Another time, flying over the Bay of Biscay close to the western coast of France, he and his navigator destroyed a German convoy. Heading back to base, a member of his team came under heavy fire from an enemy plane. Shulemson immediately joined the battle, and following a bitter air fight forced the German plane to withdraw.

For his bravery, he was awarded a Distinguished Service Order in 1943. Yet his greatest achievement was as a strategist. Working with his 404 Squadron Leader from the Royal Air Force (RAF), Ken Gatward, Shulemson figured out the precise speed and angle to launch rockets from RAF planes so that enemy targets were hit nearly every time. He began training pilots and was recruited to oversee proper rocket installation and procedures by RAF Captain

J.W. Max Aitken, the son of Max Aitken, Lord Beaverbrook, the Canadian-born Fleet Street press baron. So valuable was Shulemson that, before the war ended, he was grounded lest he be put in any further danger. His work with rockets earned him a second medal, the Distinguished Flying Cross, making him "the most decorated Jewish Canadian serviceman in World War Two," according to Montreal Jewish historian and journalist Joe King.

When the war was over, Shulemson returned to his job at his uncle's print shop but he remained a military man. He knew that the new state of Israel would never survive without proper air defence. He played a key role in the establishment of Israel's nascent air force during the 1948 War of Independence and was instrumental in recruiting pilots. He secured two hundred surplus British de Havilland Mosquito fighter-bombers that were in the possession of China, and arranged for the planes to be shipped to Israel. A bachelor until he married in 1989 at the age of seventy-four, he died in January 2007 still shunning the notion that he was a hero.

Syd Shulemson was lucky; he lived through the war and returned to his family. Among Canadian Jewish servicemen, the ultimate sacrifice was made by close to 450 (at least one servicewoman also died). Most of those who died during the war were members of the RCAF, which offered more opportunities to young Jewish men for officer training than the Canadian army and navy. Still, RCAF interview records reveal that recruiters regularly kept tabs on whether a candidate was "Jewish" or "a Hebrew." "One of the best Jewish lads I have ever met," a report of May 1940 put it. Or, "Hebrew descent but good type," added another. Meanwhile RCAF instructors in Regina stereotypically commented that Mark Abramson of Ottawa was a "noisy, talkative type."

In battle or under fire, of course, it did not matter if you were Jewish or not. George Meltz of Toronto was the youngest of Nathan and Rachel Meltz's ten children. In the years before the war, he was employed by a wallpaper company as a salesman and installer. Early in September 1940, Meltz, then twenty-one years old, enlisted in the Canadian Armed Forces and joined the 3rd Anti-Tank Regiment of the Royal Canadian Artillery (RCA). While training in London in the fall of 1941, he met and then married Trudy Lewis. He took part in D-Day on June 6, 1944, as part of the massive assault on Normandy, France. A month later, on July 8, he was killed by a German sniper and was buried at the Canadian War Cemetery at Reviers, south of Juno Beach at Courseulles-sur-Mer, close to where he had landed.

Winnipegger Sam Sheps, the son of Winnipeg community leader Ben Sheps, had received a Bachelor of Arts degree from the University of Manitoba in 1934 and then enrolled in the university's law school, graduating in 1938. Tall, dark, and charming, Sheps was also known for his acting abilities with the University of Manitoba Dramatic Society and enjoyed doing radio plays in English and Yiddish. In the late thirties, he married Phyllis Cohen and they had one daughter, Roberta. Sheps enlisted in September 1939 and was trained as an artillery gunner. He rose to the rank of captain with the RCA, travelled to England in the spring of 1941, and saw combat in Italy beginning in November 1943. Less than a year later, on September 16, 1944, he was killed in a battle near Rimini in northeastern Italy. Letters sent to his wife after his death revealed Sheps's strong leadership skills as well as his popularity with Jewish and non-Jewish soldiers alike. "Being the padre from another faith," wrote Captain H.G. Meiklejohn, the Protestant chaplain for the 5th Canadian Medical Regiment, "I found no barrier between Sam and myself. We often talked freely of Hebrew scripture and language and of common interests of our men and people."

Albert "Sherry" Margolis was one of ten Jewish servicemen from Calgary who died during the war. He was with the RCAF in Burma (Myanmar) battling the Japanese. Margolis had operated a delicatessen before the war, and was a member of the B'nai Brith. He enlisted in 1940, became a flight sergeant and trained as an observer. Seconded to the RAF after the attack on Pearl Harbor, he flew on missions in India and the Pacific theatre. He was twenty-eight years old when he was reported missing and presumed shot down on September 9, 1942.

You did not have to leave Canada to die in the war. Rose Goodman was born in 1920 in New Glasgow, Nova Scotia, where her father Sol ran a department store. Like about eighty other Jewish women in Canada, she had joined the RCAF Women's Division in 1941; its motto was "We Serve That Men May Fly."

Following training in Toronto, she graduated as a sergeant instructor in physical training and was stationed in New Brunswick. Within a short time, she was promoted to adjutant and transferred to the RCAF Service Flying Training School at Claresholm, Alberta (near Calgary). On January 26, 1943, she was a passenger in a twin-engine aircraft on its way from Lethbridge to Claresholm. She and the pilot, Flight Lieutenant Stephen Strauss, hit bad weather and Strauss was forced to make a crash landing. He survived but Goodman, twenty-three years old, did not. Her body was transported back to Montreal for burial in the cemetery of the Spanish and Portuguese synagogue.

Other Jewish women in uniform, all who survived the war (less than 15 per cent of the women wound up overseas, and a majority of those were stationed in England), served as clerks, nurses, hospital assistants, drivers, and (as Goodman had) instructors. As Saundra Lipton found, several women were also assigned to special projects: Ruth Offstein was in a "top secret military location" doing office work; Esther Raber of Medicine Hat was posted to the RCAF Defence Headquarters "working on a top secret project involving radar"; and Sergeant Mollie Mickelson from Alberta "was involved with secret confidential material in her 1942–43 role as secretary to Roy Foss, Commanding Officer of the No. 9 Bombing and Gunnery School in Mont-Joli, Quebec."

There were internal and external pressures on young Jewish men and women to enlist. After nearly a decade of disturbing news about the terrible abuse of German Jews, which culminated in the violence and destruction of *Kristallnacht* in 1938, few Canadian Jews could ignore the Nazi threat to Jews everywhere—a threat that over the next five years was to escalate in unimaginable ways. The question was how to respond. Though Syd Shulemson and many others like him felt strongly that it was their moral duty as Jews and Canadians to fight, not every military-aged Jewish man or woman felt that way. Participating in war, no matter how urgent the circumstances, was not a decision to be made lightly or easily.

Percy Jacobson, a Canadian-born "uptown" Jewish businessman and dramatist who lived in Westmount in Montreal, resigned himself to the fact that his twenty-one-year-old son Joe had enlisted in the RCAF. "I know he can't keep out," Jacobson wrote in his diary on September 13, 1939. Joe was likely as assimilated a young Jew as there was in Canada in 1939. A McGill University graduate with a Bachelor of Commerce who excelled at football, he was eager to fight. He regarded it as an imperative duty to his country and his people.

Joe "was Jewish through his community, by association and habit rather than conviction," the Jacobson family's biographer, Peter J. Usher, writes. The younger Jacobson did not have a lot of patience for immigrant Jews, and in his travels he was annoyed and embarrassed when someone Jewish he encountered acted in a stereotypical manner. (He even detested the taste of gefilte fish that was served to him in 1940 by a Jewish family in Preston, Ontario, and which he misspelled in a letter to his parents as "Kafilta fish.") Nonetheless, by the fall of 1939 he also understood that the Nazis had to be stopped. His father, who was not shy about writing a letter to the editor of the *Gazette* about the "disease" of antisemitism, was right to be worried: on January 28, 1942, newly promoted Flight Sergeant Joe Jacobson, an observer, was in the air on his twenty-fourth bombing mission over enemy territory in northwestern Europe when he and his team were shot down. His death was confirmed to his parents two days later.

There is no evidence that Joe Jacobson was the target of antisemitic abuse, but he was astute enough to grasp that the prejudice he had grown up with put Canadian Jewish volunteers under a microscope. About 49 per cent of Jewish men between the ages of eighteen and forty-five enlisted or were drafted as conscripts (3,479 in total) for home defence under the National Resources Mobilization Act of 1940 —until the last year of the war when the federal government changed the policy, forcing 2,463 of the home defence conscripts to join units overseas—compared to 41 per cent of all Canadian men of that cohort. Nonetheless, there was an unfair and enduring perception that Jews were not sufficiently doing their part and were instead profiting from the war. "What is the Jews' favourite song?" a popular joke went. The answer: "Onward Christian Soldiers." It was "a lie," a *Winnipeg Free Press* editorial of early September 1940 asserted about the unsubstantiated charges, that "the Jews won't join up," yet the finger-pointing persisted.

The Joint Public Relations Committee (JPRC)—which was formed in 1938 to combat antisemitism, and united the CJC and the Anti-Defamation League of B'nai B'rith—tried to counter these false charges as best it could. Sam Bronfman, who became the Congress president in 1939, publicly declared the loyalty of Canadian Jews to the country and Britain time and again. This was despite the fact that the Mackenzie King government admitted only a tiny number of German Jewish refugees into Canada (and did so reluctantly) before and during the war.

Among the new committees Bronfman established was the War Efforts Committee to promote Jewish enlistment. He had a lot of guidance and help from lawyer Saul Hayes, the CJC's astute and well-connected new executive director, who took over many of Hananiah Caiserman's administrative responsibilities. Hayes, who had an air of confidence about him, was one of the few people Bronfman would listen to—at least most of the time. The committee opened offices in Montreal and Toronto, published promotional material in English and Yiddish about Canadian Jewish soldiers—including a comic book about the heroic exploits of Syd Shulemson and others—and pushed and prodded young Jewish men to enlist.

The War Efforts Committee had some success—and following the Nazi attack on the Soviet Union in June 1941 they gained the support of the Jewish left—though not quite enough to silence the naysayers still claiming that Jews in Canada were not doing enough. Public displays of loyalty were always important and encouraged.

Canada's military was willing to accept Jewish volunteers, but was hardly more open or enlightened than any other institution in the country. Ben Dunkelman, the son of Tip Top Tailors founder David Dunkelman, was a strapping young man who grew up amid wealth on a ninety-acre estate called Sunnybrook Farm, then on the outskirts of city (today it is the Sunnybrook Health Sciences Centre on Bayview, north of Eglinton Avenue) and far from the Spadina Jewish enclave, both geographically and mentally. His mother, Rose, was active in Hadassah and a committed Zionist, as were Ben and his siblings. Ben and his brother Joe attended Upper Canada College, the only Jewish students in the school at the time. Probably because of their size, the Dunkelman brothers did not experience any overt antisemitism. Ben was also a star football player, and "stopping Dunkelman" was a tough assignment for opposing teams.

In the fall of 1939, Ben tried to enlist in the Royal Canadian Navy. He was told that he was "over qualified" to be an ordinary seaman and that "their quotas were full" for officer training. As Dunkelman subsequently discovered, the navy was not eager to accept Jewish officers. (According to Toronto journalist Ellin Bessner, who has extensively researched Canadian Jewish involvement in the Second World War, only about 550 Jewish men enlisted in the navy and a "few," she says, became officers.) He next tried the army, and was able to enlist in the 2nd Battalion of the Queen's Own Rifles. The Canadian army was more liberal; he was able to take an officer course, become a lieutenant, and eventually was given command of a mortar platoon which he courageously led during the D-Day invasion.

Fear of antisemitism in the service as well as possible capture by the Nazis was a reason for some young Jewish men to be hesitant. But many enlisted regardless of the prejudice they anticipated facing or the danger of becoming a Nazi prisoner. When Ernest Sirluck, a graduate student in English at the University of Toronto, first enlisted, he purposely wrote "none" when asked to give his religion on the army application form. He reasoned that if he "should fall into German hands alive it wouldn't be pleasant to have 'Jew' on my name-tag." The officer in charge, however, suggested he write down "C of E," which he did. "How many other Jews were registered in the Canadian armed forces as 'Church of England' or the less specific 'Protestant,'" he later wondered.

A ruthless enemy and the camaraderie of military experience united most Canadians in the service. There were exceptions, however. Toronto lawyer Eddie Goodman, an officer in the Fort Garry Horse, recalled that a Jewish soldier from Winnipeg did not take kindly to a sergeant calling him a "fucking Jew." The soldier beat up the sergeant and received a month in confinement as punishment. But for the most part, antisemitism—as Canadian military historian David Bercuson argues—was "subtle." In the RCAF, for instance, there were many more Jewish air observers than pilots, mainly because the air force clung to racial stereotypes that categorized Jews as having the "mental skills" to be observers but not the "physical skills, hand-eye coordination and courage" required to be pilots. Those qualities were considered Anglo-Saxon rather than Jewish.

Most Jewish men likely did not hide their religious and ethnic identity. They also enthusiastically attended High Holiday services led by Jewish chaplains, of which there were ten for the Canadian Armed Forces—including the first one appointed (in 1941), Rabbi Gershon Levi, the educational director of Montreal's Shaar Hashomayim synagogue. Levi's appointment had been delayed for more than a year by a dispute between Jewish politicians and CJC leaders about who should be selected for the position—as well as by red tape until the military was convinced there were at least a thousand soldiers the rabbi could minister to.

It was a challenging job. Levi had to define his role as a chaplain, seek out his "congregation," and deal with the fact that he was a "Jew among Gentiles," as he put it. "As a wandering Jew, I walked into more than one officers' mess only to find the buzz of conversation suddenly fall silent—more from embarrassment, I think, than for any other reason. Many Canadians, especially those from outside the larger centres of population, had never met a Jew."

After D-Day, Levi, who was in London from 1942 to 1944, organized Sabbath synagogue services in a "broken-down shack" in Normandy, France. "It was a dramatic and solemn event," he remembered, "its poignancy heightened by the presence of an elderly Jewish woman from Paris who had been in hiding for years to escape the Nazis. That night she lit candles in the traditional Jewish manner. To the assembled Canadian soldiers, she was a symbol of Jewish suffering and martyrdom—the first Jewish person they liberated in Europe."

Many Canadian Jews fought bravely for their country and people, and 196 of them were honoured with medals and decorations by the Canadian, British, American, Dutch, and Czechoslovak governments. Nearly seventy-five years later, the question about whether or not there were sufficient numbers of young Jewish men and women hardly seems important in light of the enormous tragedy the war inflicted on European Jews.

Captain Maurice Victor, a physician—the son of Dr. Ben Victor of Winnipeg, a dedicated Yiddishist and committed socialist—enlisted into the Royal

Canadian Army Medical Corps in 1942, a year before he was scheduled to graduate from the Manitoba Medical College (he had been accepted to the college during the period when the quota was being enforced). He served in Holland and was made a Knight Officer of the Order of Orange-Nassau with Swords by the Dutch government. He received the decoration from Queen Wilhelmina on December 25, 1945, at a ceremony at the royal palace in The Hague. After the war, Victor moved to Cleveland, Ohio, where he became a renowned neurologist.

In November 1944, Victor sent a letter to his parents about the persecution of Jews he had met in Antwerp, Belgium. It was reprinted in the Yiddish *Vochenblatt.* "The large mass [of Antwerp's 65,000 Jews] suffered the fate of which we have been reading for the past ten years, 27,000 have been sent to concentration camps in Poland alone," he wrote. "The fortunate ones hid out in cellars for four years . . . Not a single leaf in Hitler's book of sadism and brutality remained unturned in his efforts to exterminate this helpless group. It was a painful experience listening to their recital of unbelievable horrors . . . Certainly nothing that we have read of Nazi bestiality has been exaggerated."

In an interview decades later, he also recalled the experience of driving into the Bergen-Belsen concentration camp with a British division. "The stench of the dead and dying was just overwhelming, cadaverous people were literally stacked up like cords of wood in rows, some of them still squirming," he said. "It had to be seen, it had to be smelled, for anyone to grasp what the camps meant. My driver knew now, for the first time, what the war was really all about . . . For both of us, what we were doing here, far from home, had finally crystallized."

If an eyewitness to the brutality and carnage of the Holocaust such as Victor recoiled in disbelief, this was doubly the case back in Canada. Incredulity greeted each new horrible revelation that was reported periodically in newspapers as the war progressed. Early in the conflict, Yiddish newspapers (as well as several Polish ones) carried regular reports on the persecution of European Jews. These news articles were "from a variety of American as well as European sources, including underground reports from the Soviet Union and firsthand accounts from Jews across Europe who had managed to evade death," notes University of Ottawa professor Rebecca

Margolis. In the summer of 1944, the *Adler* in Montreal, for instance, ran a story by journalist Raymond Davies about the liberation of the Majdanek death camp near Lublin, and the full extent of the atrocities was revealed. "I saw with my own eyes," Davies wrote, "pile[s] of shoes numbering at least eight hundred thousand, whole boxes [of] eyeglasses, whole shelves [of] . . . prayer books."

Mainstream papers, on the other hand, were slow to cover the story. And even when they did, there was skepticism—perhaps understandable, but a reflection, too, of the negative attitudes toward Jews in Canada. By September 1943, the mass killings had been reported in more detail—and officially acknowledged by the British and American governments on behalf of the Allied Powers in a widely-publicized joint declaration of December 17, 1942—yet Louis Robillard of *Le Devoir* prefaced his comments about the terrible slaughter by wondering "if the Jews aren't exaggerating these number in some Middle Eastern or Talmudic manner." Across the country in Alberta, the Social Credit Party, convinced that all Jews were communists and liars, as Janine Stingel, who has studied the relationship between Jews and the Social Credit Party sums up, postulated that Jews "were behind Germany's war against the Allies; that they themselves were to blame for the Holocaust; and that the Holocaust was, in fact, a Jewish fabrication." (It was not only members of Social Credit who distrusted Jews: in 1940, when Bora Laskin was hired as a lecturer by the University of Toronto Faculty of Law, he was compelled to declare in front of witnesses that he had no ties to communism.)

Of the major Canadian English-language newspapers, the *Toronto Star* (as Ontario historian Ulrich Frisse's content analyses of the paper's wartime coverage show) paid the closest attention to the unfolding Jewish tragedy; though even that was lacking until mid-1942, with the publication of a news article on April 1 noting that "the Nazis are pursuing a policy of systematized extermination in Poland, Czechoslovakia Serbia and elsewhere . . . The first victims usually are Jews." Throughout the rest of the year and for the duration of the war, the *Star* continued to highlight the herding of Jews into ghettos, and the killings that were by this time referred to as "systematic murder on a mass scale."

On June 24, 1943, Scott Young of the Canadian Press—in a news story carried in the *Star* as well as other newspapers—reported from London that Jews in occupied Poland were being "steamed to death" by the Nazis. The article was based on information supplied by the Polish underground, with details about "major [Nazi-run] extermination camps in eastern Poland." Young's story was incorrect about the gruesome method of death—millions of Jews were being killed by lethal Zyklon B gas rather than steam. Five months later, in a report that also appeared in Canadian newspapers, the *New York Times* published an account given by the Kiev Atrocity Commission of the mass killing at Babi Yar (outside of Kiev) in September 1941, in which 33,771 Jewish men, women, and children were murdered over a two-day period. (Though the commission had incorrectly provided a figure of between 50,000 to 80,000 people killed, and the *Times'* correspondent William Lawrence admitted that he was not able "to judge the truth or falsity of the story told to us," since he did not hear from any eyewitnesses.)

The following year, major magazines such as *Maclean's* and *Liberty* carried more accurate stories of this incomprehensible slaughter, complete with photographs of the crematoriums, Zyklon B canisters, and vast piles of the victims' shoes. Editorial comment, however, was curiously missing. By then, the federal government had also received accurate and shocking reports of the genocide, and accounts of Auschwitz and the other camps in the press brought the Holocaust into most Canadian homes. Still, in the months ahead—as victory was proclaimed in Europe in May 1945, and in Japan three months later—most Canadians were much more concerned about the post-war economy and ensuring the country was not flooded by unwanted European refugees, especially Jewish Holocaust survivors.

Canadian Jewish Congress officials were not immune to doubt about the news from Europe themselves. "The reports were so unbelievable," Saul Hayes recalled, "that the responsible Jewish authorities which received them hardly dared make them public and the allied governments were slow to accept them." Nonetheless, in mid-October 1942 to draw attention to the Nazi atrocities, the cjc's national executive did organize mass protest meetings in Montreal, Toronto, and Winnipeg which was noted in several Canadian newspapers. From 1938 onward, Bronfman, Hayes, and other CJC representatives had worked diligently lobbying for European Jewish refugees to come to Canada. On a number of occasions, they met in private with Liberal cabinet ministers, but it was to no avail. Prime Minister Mackenzie King, who operated from the premise that there was nothing to gain politically by admitting more Jews—but much to lose in the way of support from Quebec—continued to abide by the antisemitic dictates of Frederick Blair, the director of the immigration branch.

The CJC also lobbied to free German Jews who had fled to Britain, been interned there, and then wholly unjustly transported to an internment camp in Canada as enemy aliens. One of the internees was Erwin Schild, who after the war became the rabbi of Toronto's Adath Israel congregation. In 1938, the eighteen-year-old Schild had managed to escape from Germany to England only to be treated as an enemy. In 1940, he was sent to Canada with other German and Austrian Jews, and spent two traumatic years incarcerated in camps in Quebec and New Brunswick.

At the end of October 1945, five months after the war in Europe had ended, many of these individuals were granted Canadian citizenship. This modest achievement was in the view of historian Paula Draper, who extensively researched this episode, the "only major wartime success of the CJC." Saul Hayes, she adds, "walked a fine line—never able to completely satisfy the refugees, [Frederick] Blair . . . or the Canadian Jewish community which he served."

Not surprisingly, Jewish newspaper editors were critical of the CJC's "business as usual" efforts, as the *Jewish Chronicle's* editor A.M. Klein caustically described them. In his view, it was too little too late. "Where is the thunderbolt of invective which these events call forth?" Klein asked as early as July 1942. "Where are the keepers of the world's consciousness, its intellectual leaders?" Three years later, the *Jewish Post's* Hy Sokolov bemoaned from Winnipeg that "too long have we stood in abject fear of our own shadow."

They were right to be indignant, but neither rescuing large numbers of Jews trapped in Nazi-occupied Europe, which we now know was next to impossible, nor altering the dogmatic policies of Mackenzie King and his Liberal government was realistic. When the next federal election was held in 1945, politics again took precedence over humanitarianism, and Holocaust survivors found that Canada's postwar refugee policy was not much more accommodating than it had been before the conflict.

In December 1945, as part of the CJC's relief efforts, Saul Hayes arranged for Hananiah Caiserman and Sam Lipshitz to visit war-torn Poland. Lipshitz was a Polish-born journalist who had immigrated to Montreal with his parents when he was a boy. He had worked for the *Adler* and the Jewish Public Library, and became a loyal and ardent communist. After he moved to Toronto, he teamed up with his left-wing rival, Joe Gershman of *Der Kamf* (as well as *Vochenblatt*, which Lipshitz edited from 1943 to 1954). During the thirties, an estimated 30 per cent of Communist Party members were Jewish, and the number was much higher according to some sources. When the party was outlawed in 1940, Lipshitz was instrumental in reorganizing it as the Labour-Progressive Party in 1943. (Devout Jewish Communist Fred Rose, who had been born in Lublin, Poland in 1907, represented the party as an MP from the Montreal riding of Cartier from 1943 until he was expelled in January 1947 after being found guilty of espionage as a Soviet spy.) Lipshitz also played a key role in the founding of the United Jewish People's Order (UJPO), the Jewish communist-socialist organization established in Toronto in 1945.

Conceived as an independent Jewish left-wing group, the UJPO, with approximately 2,700 members by 1947 (including six hundred women), was strongly connected to the Communist Party—though according to its historians Ester Reiter and Roz Usiskin, it also "provided mutual fraternal assistance, medical help and financial aid to [its] Jewish working-class members." Many of its members regarded themselves as "progressives": champions for "equality, social justice, socialism and the new world order," as Usiskin, a long-time Winnipeg member, has put it. Like members of other Jewish organizations in the country, members of the UJPO were eligible to be elected delegates to Canadian Jewish Congress plenary sessions. But then global politics intervened.

In the immediate aftermath of the war, the UJPO opposed the rearmament of West Germany by the United States, a position that would be supported by the federal Liberal government as part of the Cold War campaign to stop the spread of communism in Europe. The CJC, rightly or wrongly, felt it had been tarred by its association with the UJPO, and in 1951 broke all ties, which angered the UJPO's leaders. "In the Cold War atmosphere," Reiter and Usiskin have argued, the "UJPO became the scapegoat, the 'enemy,' and had to be excommunicated to strengthen the inner solidarity of Congress." The group was not reinstated to the CJC until 1995, by which time its popularity among middle-class Jews had seriously waned. Nothing symbolizes the decline of the Jewish left more than the fact that, in June 2016, the UJPO's publication, *Outlook: Canada's Progressive Jewish Magazine*, was forced to cease operations. Roz Usiskin lamented the end of the magazine as "a loss for Canadian Jewry" and the loss of "an alternate voice."

Sam Lipshitz would become disillusioned with the UJPO following a trip to the Soviet Union in 1956 with his wife Manya and a four-member Communist Party delegation. The group included Joseph B. Salsberg, a dedicated union organizer and former Toronto city alderman, who had served as a Labour-Progressive member of the Ontario Legislature from 1943 to 1955. Lipshitz and Salsberg felt they could not ignore the ruthless Soviet anti-semitism they had seen under Joseph Stalin and which remained under his successor, Nikita Khrushchev. Both men soon broke with the Communists and eventually with the UJPO. An internal and acrimonious debate over the UJPO's support of the Soviet Union raged for several years among its members.

Arriving in Warsaw early in 1946, Caiserman and Lipshitz came face to face with the destruction five years of war had wrought. As they eventually learned, of the 3.3 million Jews in Poland before 1939, only an estimated 380,000—or about 12 per cent—survived the Holocaust. "The impression was shattering," Caiserman reported. A stop at Auschwitz-Birkenau was worse. The death complex, he added, was "the greatest inhumanity in the imagination of human beings. There are no words to describe it."

Desperate to help the survivors—and to support the work of the United Nations Relief and Rehabilitation Administration (UNRRA), the American Jewish Joint Distribution Committee, and the United Jewish Relief Agencies of Canada—in late 1945 and the first part of 1946 the CJC set about trying to raise $1.5 million, or about nine dollars for every Jewish man, woman, and child in Canada. That amount only translated into about five dollars for every survivor, however. It was a start, but hardly adequate. As the prolific and caustic Archie Bennett, who had been involved with the CJC in Toronto for many years, pointed out in his column in the *Chronicle* in early April 1946: "Canadian Jewry has not made its weight felt. Individuals and small units are indicating their aliveness to the challenge. It is, indeed, pathetic to see the way the numerous hometown associations are blindly threshing about in a desperate striving to do something . . . They are calling meetings, they are collecting money, and they are running around in circles . . . They are almost ludicrous in their confused futility." He dismissed the $1.5 million campaign as "Very penetrating. Very profound. Very noble."

The even greater challenge—and a better example of "confused futility"—was in trying to convince the King government to admit some of the estimated 250,000 dispossessed and homeless Jews relegated to displaced persons (DP) camps in Germany, Austria, Italy, and other countries being cared for by UNRRA. Telegrams and face-to-face meetings with ministers and bureaucrats produced minimal results. King was moved by stories of the tragedy and sorrow experienced by Jewish survivors, but his position remained firm: he understood that from a political perspective welcoming thousands of Jewish refugees to the country remained a losing proposition, and said so in May 1947. In a major speech on the federal Liberal government's postwar immigration policy, the prime minister—one year away from retirement—made it clear that Canada would open its doors to more newcomers, yet would also exercise control over which immigrants it permitted into the country so as not "to change the fundamental composition of the Canadian population." King assured Canadians that he was not being discriminatory.

Though the full magnitude of the Holocaust was not yet understood and would not be for several more years, King, his government, and a majority of Canadians had a fairly good notion of the annihilation of millions of Jews. Nonetheless, in the late forties Canadians initially greeted the idea of permitting "non-assimilable racial groups"—as the government classified them—into the country with almost outright hostility.

In October 1946, a Gallup poll showed that in the opinion of a majority of Canadians, the two least-desirable immigrant groups were the Japanese followed by the Jews. At the Canadian High Commission office in London, there was little sympathy for the survivors' plight. One official who visited the DP camps in Germany, Percival T. Molson (related to the Molson beer family), had reported about the "black marketing, dirty living habits and general sloven-liness" of the Jewish survivors. Simply stated, Jews were "not desirable immi-grants for Canada," as Lieutenant-Colonel Arthur Hicks, who had spent time in a displaced persons camp near Bergen-Belsen, told a Senate committee on immigration in July 1946.

That conclusion would resonate with politicians and bureaucrats in Ottawa and elsewhere for a long time.

Prejudice Exists

The hard-to-believe news of the "war against the Jews" did not diminish Canadian-style antisemitism. In early August 1942, at Crystal Beach on Lake Erie, a Jewish-owned store and hotel were attacked by a small mob who broke windows and destroyed shelving in the store. The incident triggered fighting between the antisemites and Jews. Worse was a full-fledged riot in the Quebec resort town of Plage Laval, on the Mille Îles River opposite Saint-Eustache, a year later. At least seventy-five people took part in a brawl that pitted French-Canadians against Jews, a fight which sent several people to the hospital. In a statement condemning the violence, the CJC described what had happened as "not a mere incident, but part of a planned terror which a band of hooligans are conducting against the Jewish inhabitants of the summer resort." (The thugs included the local police chief's son.) Jewish residents, it was reported, were "living in fear for their lives and property."

That same summer, in what was a more typical Canadian "racial problem," a Winnipeg Jew managed to rent a cottage at upscale Victoria Beach on the southeastern shores of Lake Winnipeg, where there was a widely accepted "gentlemen's agreement" not to sell or rent property to Jews. The restriction had been enforced since at least 1914 by the Victoria Beach Company, which had initially owned most of the lots. Word that an owner had broken the agreement and rented to a Jew set off a storm of protest.

There was a similar incident on the Toronto Islands. In September 1944, the residents' associations on Centre and Ward's Islands were accused by J.B. Salsberg, then a Labour-Progressive member of Ontario's legislative assembly, of banding together to ensure cottages were not rented to Jews. Salsberg had attempted to rent a cottage on three occasions, but was refused each time when he told the owners he was Jewish. The *Globe and Mail* conceded that this case and others showed that even in Ontario "prejudice exists"—an understatement, to be sure. "We have surely learned from the experience of Europe," the *Globe*'s enlightened editors concluded, "that Canada is no place for race or creed baiters. Hitlerism offers a terrifying example of the evils of anti-Semitism."

With George Drew heading a Progressive Conservative minority government in Ontario (following the August 1943 provincial election), Salsberg and the opposition Co-operative Commonwealth Federation had already used their power to convince the premier to introduce pioneering anti-discrimination legislation. Drew was skeptical, arguing that tolerance could not be "created by compulsion." He had a point; nonetheless, the Racial Discrimination Act (RDA) was passed in March 1944. The act did not prevent an employer or property owner from discriminating against Jews or black people; it only prohibited "the publication, broadcasting or display of a sign or other representation indicating an intention to discriminate because of 'race' or 'creed.'" Nor did the legislation have unanimous support from the public or the press; the *Globe and Mail*, for example, which was to so eloquently decry racism in Canada several months later, declared that the proposed bill was an affront to freedom of speech and that "toleration" was "not to be advanced by intolerant laws."

So it was not perfect by any stretch. In September 1944, in the first prosecution undertaken using the RDA, the owner of a lodge on Wilcox Lake, north of Toronto, was caught displaying a "Gentiles Only" sign. But once the owner told the court he would remove the "offensive sign," the Chief Justice, following the recommendation of the Attorney General of Ontario (and supported by Salsberg) did not fine him.

The anti-discrimination act marked the beginning of a decade of landmark human rights legislation which ultimately altered the way Jews and other minorities were treated in Canada, but it hardly eliminated discrimination and it certainly did not eradicate prejudice.

———

In the late 1940s, Ontario school boards had no moral or ethical dilemmas in placing advertisements for teachers with one of the qualifications being that the candidate was "Protestant." Jobs for Jews in banks were non-existent; discrimination in such professions as law and accounting was the norm; and social, sports, and golf clubs still had restricted memberships. At the same time, the impact of twelve tyrannical years of Nazi rule in Germany influenced and inspired more Canadian non-Jews to question this prejudice and discrimination. How, they wondered, could Canadians have fought and died to destroy Nazism and the evil it represented, and yet still tell Jews they were unwelcome at local golf clubs and beaches? In a sign of changing perceptions, antisemitism received prominent and critical attention from two non-Jewish writers: in a novel by Gwethalyn Graham, a young Montreal-based journalist; and in the work of Pierre Berton, who had relocated to Toronto from Vancouver to pen feature articles for *Maclean's* magazine, the start of his prolific career as a writer and popular historian.

Graham, born into a wealthy WASP family in Toronto, vividly captured the ubiquitous character of antisemitism in her 1944 novel, *Earth and High Heaven*. The story, which unfolds in Montreal during the summer of 1942, traces the love affair and complicated relationship between the lovely and determined journalist Erica Drake, of the very Protestant Westmount Drakes, and Marc Reiser, a handsome and smart Jewish lawyer and a junior partner in the Montreal Jewish law firm of Maresch and Aaronson. Her parents, the stuffy Charles and Margaret, are distraught when they learn that Erica is dating Marc. They question his motives and cannot figure out why he doesn't pick a Jewish girl. Charles is especially troubled by the thought that if Erica and Marc get married, his Jewish son-in-law cannot be admitted to his club. All but forgotten today, *Earth and High Heaven* was the first novel published in Canada to reach number one on the *New York Times* bestseller list. It sold 125,000 copies in the U.S, was translated into eighteen languages, and won Graham the Governor General's Award for fiction in Canada.

In the book, upon first meeting, Marc—"the best type of Jew"—it suddenly dawns on Erica that many times she has seen, yet ignored, the "endless" signs on hotels, beaches, golf courses, apartment houses, and "the little restaurants for skiers in the Laurentians" in which Gentiles only were welcome—and no Jews allowed. Erica is as principled and outspoken as Graham was at the time about racism and women's rights. In a clash with her father about Marc, she cuttingly points out that "After all, we Canadians don't really disagree fundamentally with the Nazis about the Jews—we just think they go a bit too far." Reflecting on her own prejudices, she decides, too, that "a Jew describes another Jew simply as a human being; a Gentile describes him first and foremost as a Jew . . . The highest compliment the average Gentile can pay a Jew, apparently, is to say that he doesn't look or behave like one."

In the fall of 1948, several months after writing an article for *Maclean's* about Canada's abysmal treatment of the Japanese in British Columbia, Pierre Berton—having read *Earth and High Heaven*—turned his attention to anti-semitism in Toronto. It was "palpable," he recalled in his memoirs. Following several weeks of research, his worst fears were confirmed: "All the major professions—engineering, the judiciary, higher education, brokerage, banking—were virtually closed to Jews," he wrote. "In all of Canada, there were only eighteen Jewish high school principals and university professors." He also learned, much to his dismay, that *Maclean's* parent company, Maclean Hunter, did not hire Jews either. "It's company policy," he was matter-of-factly informed.

As he chronicled in his eye-opening article "No Jews Need Apply," which was published in the magazine on November 1, 1948, his two female assistants responded to classified ads for office work. The first woman called giving her name as "Miss Grimes," clearly Gentile, and in forty-seven attempts, she received forty-one job interview appointments. The second caller, who told the prospective employer that she had the same qualifications, identified herself to these companies as the Jewish-sounding "Miss Greenberg"; she received only seventeen interviews. In twenty-one cases, "Miss Greenberg" was informed the job was filled, despite calling first. Berton wanted to name the companies in the article, but decided against it since that would have meant tagging his own employer as racist.

He used the same tactic in trying to obtain reservations at ski and summer resorts—for "Mr. Marshall" and "Mr. Rosenberg," and was surprised at how many managers openly told him their establishments were "restricted" or catered to "select clientele" and "discriminating clientele." (The CJC had conducted the same experiment in 1947, with similar results.) Though Berton tried to keep his own opinions out of the article, his indignation was difficult to disguise. Soon after the article was published, he ran into the magazine's former editor, H. Napier Moore ("a silly-ass Englishman," as Berton later called him), who expressed his displeasure. "That article," Moore said to him. "Now we'll have every damn Jew in town applying to us for a job!"

Berton was especially peeved about a 1948 Ontario court ruling dealing with controversial property covenants that seemingly legalized discrimination, and was blatantly contrary to the 1944 anti-discrimination act as well as a prior court ruling.

This issue first had been considered in the 1945 Drummond Wren case. Wren was the general secretary of the Workers' Educational Association of Canada, who had purchased land on a street in East York with the intention of building a house that would be first prize in a raffle. Wren soon discovered that the previous owners of the property had registered a covenant stipulating that the "Land not to be sold to Jews or persons of objectionable nationality." He went to court to ask that the covenant be declared void, though not because of the new anti-discrimination act but because "the restriction was against the public good and therefore . . . contrary to public policy." After several months of deliberation, Justice J. Keiller MacKay (later the Lieutenant Governor of Ontario from 1957 to 1963) agreed with Wren and ruled that the restrictive covenant violated public policy and was illegal. The judge indicated that he was influenced by the founding of the United Nations, which had taken place in San Francisco a week earlier, and quoted from its charter affirming its commitment to human rights.

The leaders of Jewish community in Toronto and elsewhere—the CJC had legal standing in the case—were naturally delighted with MacKay's ruling, and anticipated that similar covenants in Hamilton and Windsor would be quashed as well. That proved true in the summer of 1946, when in another ruling an Ontario judge decided that a clause in a deed to a piece of land near Lake Couchiching, 120 kilometres north of Toronto—which barred

"Hebrews" or members of the "Jewish race" from owning property—was also legally invalid. But precedent or not, this matter was not finished.

In 1933, Annie Noble had purchased a cottage at Beach O' Pines, a summer resort area on the southeastern shores of Lake Huron. As of 1932, the property deed had attached to it a stipulation that "The lands . . . shall never be sold, assigned, transferred, leased, rented . . . to . . . any person of the Jewish, Hebrew, Semitic, Negro or coloured race or blood, it being the intention and purpose to restrict the ownership . . . and enjoyment . . . to persons white or Caucasian races not excluded by this clause." The clause was to expire in August 1962. In 1948, Noble intended to sell her cottage for $6,800 to Bernie Wolf, a Jewish businessman who ran a women's clothing store in London, Ontario. Wolf's young lawyer, Ted Richmond, thought it a good idea to have the objectionable clause taken out of the transaction. Eventually, on Richmond's insistence, the court was asked to invalidate the clause. That, however, made no difference to the Beach O' Pines Protective Association, which represented thirty-five property owners who wanted to keep the covenant in place for another fourteen years and really did not want any Jews or "Negroes" as neighbours. An acrimonious legal battle began.

At the end of June 1948, in what can only be regarded as terrible legal decision (and the decision that raised Berton's ire), Ontario Supreme Court Justice Walter Schroeder, with support from other judges on the court, ruled that the covenant was "legal and enforceable," and that the earlier MacKay decision did not apply in this case. Rabbi Abraham Feinberg of the Holy Blossom Temple called the decision "a blow to the prestige and mature development of Canada." At this point, Noble did not want to pursue the matter and Wolf's wife did not want him to, either. The Canadian Jewish Congress stepped in and assumed the cost of an appeal that eventually landed in the Supreme Court of Canada. More than two years later, the high court, with only one judge dissenting, overturned Schroeder and deemed at long last, as the Globe and Mail reported that "a covenant in a property deed restricting the sale of land to those of 'white or Caucasian races' is invalid."

Though the decision was based less on the sanctity of human rights than legal technicalities—the judges decided that the terms "Hebrews" and

"Negroes" were vague—it was, nonetheless, hailed as a victory for minority rights in Canada. Wolf won court costs and donated the $4,000 to the CJC. He sold the cottage in 1951, because for him the fight had been an issue of fairness and the rule of law. Ontario passed a law in 1950 outlawing such property restrictions, but did not void the ones already in force. In 2001, it was reported that one of the Jewish cottage owners at Beach O' Pines, with a sense of history and irony, had a large sign on his front lawn which read "Shalom."

Confronting anti-Jewish property covenants paled in significance to the tortuous ordeal experienced by twins Leo and Miriam Lowy at the hands of Dr. Josef Mengele, the so-called Angel of Death, when they were the subjects of his horrific medical experiments during their imprisonment at Auschwitz. Leo and Miriam were born in 1928 in Berehovo in Carpathia, which was then part of Czechoslovakia and today is in western Ukraine. Following the German annexation of the Sudetenland in 1938, given to Hitler in the Munich Agreement, Carpathia was in turn ceded by the Nazi leader to Hungary to cement the German-Hungarian alliance. During the war, life for Jews under Hungarian rule was harsh—an estimated 63,000 were killed between 1941 and 1944—but there were no ghettos or mass deportations. That changed in the spring of 1944, after the Hungarian government tried to end its alliance with Germany and the Nazis occupied the country. The Nazis quickly imposed the bureaucratic process of the Holocaust: the abolition of Jewish civil and legal rights, forced segregation in ghettos, and deportations to concentration and death camps, mainly Auschwitz-Birkenau. By the end of the war, of the 825,000 Jews in Hungary, more than 500,000 had been murdered or died from starvation and abuse.

Leo and Miriam, who were sixteen years old in 1944, and the other members of their family were among those deported to Auschwitz. During the dreaded selection, when Mengele and his henchmen determined who would live as slave labourers and who would be marched immediately to the gas chambers to die, Leo and Miriam were identified as twins and sent to a hospital in Birkenau. For the next nine months, the two were subjects in the Nazi doctor's unimaginable medical experiments. They were injected with fluids, and blood samples were taken from them. Their eye colour was analyzed and bone structure was measured regularly. "The doctors never explained what they were doing," Leo recalled many years later. "We were drained physically and emotionally. We lost a lot of weight, not only because of the diet but also because of our fear of what the next step would be." He and a friend, also a twin, had to shine the guards' boots and were regularly beaten; yet, as he said, "I quickly learned not to cry." Being a guinea pig for Mengele kept the twins alive. One day, Leo was accosted by a group of drunken soldiers who likely would have killed him. Yelling the name "Dr. Mengele" saved his life.

During a death march in January 1945, Leo and Miram were separated after Leo had escaped and hid in a basement. Both survived. Leo was soon liberated by soldiers of the Red Army and Miram was freed by American solidiers a few months later. The twins were eventually reunited. Three of their sisters had also survived, though died within months; their parents and the rest of their extended family had all been murdered. Leo's intention was to go to Palestine. That proved difficult, since in the few years before the State of Israel was established in May 1948, the British did not make it easy for Holocaust survivors to emigrate there. Instead, Leo and Miram wound up in a DP camp in Cremona, Italy, where they spent the next eighteen months. While studying to be an electrician, Leo was advised that he and his sister should try to move to Canada. Yet that was easier said than done.

The simple truth was that Canada had enough Jews; most people in the country really did not want any more. That, in short, was the position of the Mackenzie King Liberal government, whose overriding concern—almost an obsession—was that the preservation of the country's racial composition was paramount and the postwar immigration policy was supposed to reflect that. But the world had changed by 1945. Multiple factors—primarily a strong economic demand for workers, but also the lobbying efforts of the CJC and a small (very small) dose of humanitarianism—unlocked the country's doors and enabled approximately 35,000 survivors to start new lives in Canada from 1947 to 1955. Considering how restrictive immigration for Jews had been during the preceding decades, this was a fairly remarkable increase, though it did not happen easily or without survivors like Leo and Miriam Lowy facing a myriad of obstacles. The majority of these traumatized new-comers settled in Montreal and Toronto, as well as Winnipeg, Ottawa, Hamilton, Calgary, and Edmonton. Some also went to Vancouver, where Leo and Miram Lowy ended up as part of the War Orphans Project, which brought 1,123 Jewish children to Canada.

Nearly all of these orphans were between the ages of twelve and eighteen years, mainly because so many younger Jewish children—more than a million in total—had been murdered by the Nazis. The CJC and UNRRA assigned fieldworkers to vet the children in the DP camps, to determine which of them were healthy enough for the journey to North America. That was merely one of many problems involved in the project.

As sympathetic as Jewish Canadians were, it was difficult to find a sufficient number of foster homes for these young men and women. Many potential foster parents felt that they would not be able to supervise a teenage survivor, nor deal with the emotional baggage that the children brought with them. "The community had some compassion," recalled one Jewish Winnipeg social worker, "but didn't really have an understanding of what the kids went through."

Leo and Miriam arrived in Halifax in March 1948 with 113 other orphans. Because they were older than eighteen by two years, they had to fib about their age and alter their birth certificates. No one noticed or questioned them. Members of the small Jewish community in Halifax (about 850 people in 1948) welcomed and fed them and the other orphans. The children were soon dis-patched across the country—about eight hundred or two-thirds of them to Montreal and Toronto, while others wound up in small and isolated communi-ties like Glace Bay, Nova Scotia, and Vegreville, Alberta. Needless to say, it was an enormous adjustment. Susan Garfield, from Budapest, found her time in Vegreville extremely lonely. She missed the theatre, opera, and her friends. She later was able to relocate to Toronto. And it was more of a struggle for children who were Orthodox and forced to live with Jews who were not as religious.

The Lowys were sent on the long train journey to Vancouver, where they were separated and had to live with different foster families. Leo adapted better than Miriam. His foster family eventually assisted him in purchasing a men's clothing business. In time, he married and had three sons. The terrible memory of what he had experienced loomed large for the rest of his life. Though his wife, Jocy, knew what he had gone through, his son Richard says he did not learn about it until he was a teenager. "We knew he was in the war, but he did not directly talk to us about it." Miriam had an even more difficult time and suffered from mental health problems for many years. She married and had two children, yet according to Jocy, she was reclusive. She worked for only a few years before she got married, and always lived in fear, uncertain of who she could trust. Miriam passed away in 1999; Leo lived three years longer and died in late 2002.

The journey of Moses Znaimer, who became a Canadian media guru and entrepreneur, was somewhat different. Even as a child, Znaimer had a media presence: the cover of the *Standard Review* magazine for June 26, 1948 had a large photograph of two young smiling Jewish refugees who had survived the horrors of the Second World War and landed in Halifax with their families to start a new life. The little girl in the photo was Nasha Rosenberg (Norma Kirsh), and the boy with the Red Cross sign tied to his coat was six-year-old Moses Znaimer. They had found each other on the voyage over from Europe aboard the S.S. *Marine Falcon*, a converted U.S. Navy supply ship.

In 1942, Znaimer's parents, Aron and Chaja (or Chaya), had met on a boat fleeing from Nazi-occupied Eastern Europe. Aron was from Kuldīga, Latvia, and Chaja from Łódź, Poland. They made it to Kulyab, Tajikistan (in Central Asia), then part of the Soviet Union. Moses was born soon after they got there. After the war ended, the family, using Chaja's maiden name—Epelszweig— was able to return to Poland when the U.S.S.R. permitted Polish nationals to leave the country. They made it to a displaced persons camp outside the town of Kassel, southwest of Berlin, in a region of Germany controlled by the Americans. One of Moses's most powerful memories of that period was when his mother gave him a piece of fresh warm bread rubbed with garlic. It was so good, he later recalled, that he started to cry.

Their only surviving relatives lived in Montreal, and helped them immigrate to Canada. Since his parents feared that Moses might not pass the health exam required to come to Canada as he would likely test positive for tuberculosis, they shrewdly substituted another boy the same age from the camp—Yosel, the son of their friends—when the family had to meet immigration officials. Yosel easily passed the test and the Znaimers had the health certificate they needed to depart together. Aron Znaimer eventually worked in a shoe store, and Chaja as a waitress in a steak restaurant favoured by Jewish bookies. Though traumatized by the war and the loss of their families, they instilled in Moses and his siblings Libby, a well-known television and radio personality, and Sam, a Vancouver-based venture capitalist, the desire to achieve—but to be careful in doing so.

In Montreal, living on the third floor of a walk-up on St. Urbain Street, Moses learned to be a Canadian. To make extra money, one of his jobs was working as a busboy at Harry Ship's nightclub, Chez Parée, and he revelled in its notoriety. He also attended the Talmud Torah, where one of his teachers was Irving Layton, who was supplementing his writing income by teaching. With his "powerful personality," as Znamier remembers it, he inspired Moses to believe "that words, ideas, art and education matter . . . [and] to believe that thinkers, writers and doers matter."

After obtaining a university education at McGill and then Harvard, Znaimer embarked on a career in television with CBC in Toronto before becoming the hip and cool program director and creative genius behind Citytv. In later years, he worked with CHUM in developing specialty television—and came up with the idea for Speaker's Corner videobooth beside the CHUM building on Queen Street West, so anyone who wanted to could express an opinion—and in 2018, at the age of seventy-six, he steers his latest creation as the founder and head of ZoomerMedia, a company which caters to well-off baby boomers.

Znaimer is a disciple of Marshall McLuhan, the University of Toronto professor who theorized in the early sixties about the tremendous impact of the mass media and anticipated the internet. Znaimer was in many ways more "McLuhanesque" than McLuhan himself and has always been ahead of his time. He grasped the power of television, and its influence, on a much broader canvas than almost anyone else of his generation. He later articulated his mantra like this: "It's my view the battle for hearts and minds will be won by those who recognize that television is not a problem to be managed, but an instrument to be played." And he was a virtuoso.

Postwar Canada also needed workers. At least that's what the cjc's Saul Hayes, as well as garment owners and union leaders, convinced C.D. Howe, the all-powerful Liberal minister of reconstruction and supply who assumed responsibility for immigration after J. Allison Glen, the Minister of Mines and resources in charge of the portfolio, became ill in 1947. Their clever strategy was to lobby the government to permit more European "workers"—rather than "Jews"—and they more or less pulled it off. In truth, the cjc-industry plan was to recruit Holocaust survivors, even those who had the minimum of tailoring skills. All the prospective newcomers had to do was prove that they could sew a few buttons on a coat. And in some cases, even that requirement was quietly waived.

After months of negotiating, the Liberals passed an Order-in-Council in October 1947 approving the admission of 2,136 tailors, 500 furriers, and their families—but no family could bring more than two children with them. That stipulation was a harsh one, since according to ILGWU leader Bernard Shane— who travelled to Europe as part of the selection committee—it "condemned a whole family to the uncertainty of life that DP camps now represent."

Howe was anxious about so many Jews coming at once, so he ruled that only 50 per cent of the tailors or seamstresses could be Jewish, a figure later raised to 60 per cent when an insufficient number of non-Jewish workers applied. The entire exercise was, in fact, a "sham," as Toronto historian Jack Lipinsky puts it. "Industry did not really need labour. The workers and owners of the Jewish-dominated industry saw the proposed labour scheme as a way to bring Jews from Europe."

In search of DP tailors in Europe, Shane and the other members of the Jewish Labour Committee (JLC) selection team—union representatives and garment factory owners—found, as Shane later reported, that "every applicant believed that he or she could be an expert tailor." (The JLC was formed in 1936 and, like the JPRC, fought antisemitism and promoted human rights. The two organizations began working more closely together in 1947.)

The Tailor Project, as it became known, was not "welfare," a fact repeatedly made clear by the manufacturers on the Canadian Overseas Garment Commission (COGC), which sponsored the newcomers. In Canada, the survivors found jobs in garment factories, even if many were overqualified. Some of them were highly educated and were not typical factory workers. "Never before in the history of the garment industry," Philip Weiss, a survivor who came to Winnipeg, liked to say, "were so many coats and gloves sewn by workers educated at the finest schools in Europe." Debts had to be repaid, however. And for as long as it took, the survivors' travel costs of approximately four hundred dollars from Europe to Canada were deducted monthly from their meagre salaries. In the case of Weiss, this amounted to twenty dollars a month off of the total of seventy-two dollars he received. Sixty years later, Weiss, who died in 2008 at the age of eighty-six, laughed and shook his head in dismay at the thought of this bureaucratic inanity.

By the end of 1948, of the 9,636 survivors who had arrived in Canada, 3,332 (about a third) had come via the Tailors' Project. From 1945 to 1956, an estimated 30,000 survivors of the Holocaust came to Canada, compared to about 250,000 who went to Israel and 137,500 who immigrated to the U.S. In the next two years, other skilled (or nearly skilled) workers followed, and among those was Jacob Silberman, his wife Fanny, and their two daughters, both born in DP camps—Rosalie in 1946 and Toni in 1948. Their son Julius, only an infant when the war broke out, was murdered along with his grandmother and uncle at the Treblinka death camp.

Jacob had endured years of abuse as a prisoner in a Nazi labour camp (as had Fanny). He was a lawyer, a profession which was not going to gain him and his family entry to Canada. Somewhat desperate, he was certified by the International Refugee Organization as "a shepherd, second class, with experience in sheep breeding," even though as his daughter Rosalie said in an interview with the *Globe and Mail*, he had never seen a sheep, let alone herded any. That did not help his emigration plans, however.

Finally, in the spring of 1950, with approved qualifications as a tailor, he and his family arrived in Halifax and soon settled in Toronto. Like other survivors, the Silbermans—with no financial resources to speak of—struggled each day, yet persisted. At first, Jacob worked at a garment factory, but in time he was hired as an insurance agent, a job he enjoyed much more. The money he made selling insurance enabled him to purchase a home and move his family from their third-floor apartment in a house near Kensington Market.

Jacob was never able to return to the law, nor was he bitter about it. But his daughter Rosalie followed in his footsteps. She attended the University of Toronto's law school, married historian Irving Abella, and was called to the bar in 1972. Four years later, at the age of twenty-nine (and pregnant with her second child), she was appointed a judge—the first Jewish woman in Canada to be accorded such a distinction. She championed human rights, headed the Royal Commission on Equality in Employment in the early 1980s, and was elevated to the Ontario Court of Appeal. Then, in another first for a Jewish woman, in 2004 Prime Minister Paul Martin appointed her to the Supreme Court of Canada.

Whichever city in Canada the survivors found themselves in, they tended to live in the same neighbourhoods, attend the same synagogues, and socialize with each other. In the early fifties in Toronto, survivors established their own synagogue, Congregation Habonim, where they maintained a Central European–style of Liberal Judaism—part Conservative and part Reform. Most had no immediate family, so they celebrated the holidays with each other. Having lost spouses and children during the war, many remarried and started their lives over again. Many understandably suffered from nightmares, and were wracked by guilt and suffered from depression. Real happiness was elusive.

Jacob Silberman, who died at the age of sixty in 1970, and Fanny, who passed away at ninety-two in 2010, were better able to adapt. They told their daughters about what they had endured, unlike many Holocaust survivors, who did not and could not speak of their wartime experiences—not even to their own children. The survivors' Canadian relatives and friends did not ask them either; nor initially did newspapers like the *Canadian Jewish Chronicle* publish stories about their tragic ordeals (the 1943 Warsaw Ghetto Uprising, a tale of defiance, received more attention). Few Canadians, Jewish or otherwise, could grasp what they and the other survivors had gone through in the camps, fighting as partisans in the forests of Eastern Europe, or hiding for months—even years—to escape death. There is an accepted view in the Jewish community today that the survivors were embraced, yet many remember it quite differently. They felt that they were looked down upon as Yiddish-speaking *greeneh or* "greenhorns," backward newcomers from the *shtetl* and fresh off the boat. Most of the survivors, in fact, had lived in such cities as Kiev, Warsaw, Łódź, and Vilna (Vilnius), as well as smaller towns. Unlike earlier generations of Jewish immigrants, few had resided in villages. One survivor living in Vancouver said she felt like a "leper." Another who was twenty-two when he arrived in Toronto in 1948, recalled that he had a hard time going out on a date because some Jewish mothers "didn't allow their daughters to go out with a D.P."

As a subject of inquiry or discussion, the Holocaust was shunned. Mainstream Jewish schools in Toronto and Vancouver, for instance, at first avoided teaching their students about the Holocaust so as not to "traumatize" them. The socialist-minded Jewish People's School in Montreal was more open about what had transpired in Europe, and hired survivors as teachers. For the most part, however, during the fifties the majority of Canadian Jews did not want to discuss the subject.

Slowly, these attitudes changed. A catalyst was the 1961 trial in Israel of the Nazi Adolf Eichmann, which triggered more serious study and public discussion of the Holocaust. Soon there was an outpouring of academic and popular books, novels, memoirs, children's stories, and films about the Holocaust. Survivors soon felt free to share and write about their harrowing and tragic experiences, and Jewish communities that anointed the Holocaust with sacred status began marking Holocaust memorial days.

Most critically of all, the Holocaust's lessons gradually shaped ideas about tolerance in Canada, impacting further on legal decisions about long-standing discriminatory practices and slowly (very slowly) altering general attitudes about Jews and other minorities.

Devoted Zionists and Loyal Canadians

I f any one event united Jews in Canada in a common cause, it was the establishment of Israel as a Jewish state in 1948. Ideological bickering was all but forgotten—at least temporarily—and emotions ran high. Even in the pages of *Vochenblatt,* Jewish communists from the UJPO, some of whom had questioned the CJC's fervent and absolute commitment to Zionism, now urged Canadian Jews to launch a "mighty struggle against every sign of compromise" on the part of the United Nations (UN). Stalin's arrest of Soviet Jewish leaders and his attack on Jews as "rootless cosmopolitans" became problematic for the Jewish Left, as did Soviet support for the Arab side in its battle with Israel. As historian Alvin Finkel asserts, the UJPO "persistently denied rather conclusive evidence that anti-Semitism was rife in the U.S.S.R." But in 1947 and 1948, the Jewish world rallied around the Zionist cause.

On November 29, 1947, the UN General Assembly voted in favour of ending the British Mandate and partitioning Palestine into two states: one independent state for the Jews—which soon became the State of Israel—and one for the Palestinian Arabs. The Jews accepted the partition, while the Arabs did not; they wanted sovereignty over all of Palestine, and still do. Every major conflict in the area between Israel and the Arab states from that point on would be derived from the Arabs' refusal to accept a small Jewish state. Nonetheless, in November 1947, news of the UN decision was hailed by Jews in Canada and across the world as a modern-day miracle. "It is not in the staid and restrained vocabulary of the editorial column," A.M. Klein wrote in the *Canadian Jewish Chronicle,* "that one can adequately describe the great wave of joy which swept over world Jewry."

A few days earlier, not far from Klein's Montreal office, sixteen-year-old Mordecai Richler witnessed the jubilation on the streets. "Horns were honked," he recalled nearly five decades later. "Photographs of Chaim Weizmann or [David] Ben-Gurion, torn from back issues of *Life* or *Look*, were pasted up in bay windows. Blue-and-white Star of David flags flapped in the wind on some balconies. Many wept as they sang 'Hatikvah,' the Zionist anthem." Across North America, rabbis and American and Canadian Zionist leaders urged synagogues to declare the Sabbath for December 6 as the "Sabbath of Rejoicing".

At the Holy Blossom in Toronto, Rabbi Abraham Feinberg produced a pageant starring his congregants' children, which dramatized "the Jewish race through 2,000 years of pogroms, anti-Semitism and travails," as the *Globe and Mail*'s story on the gathering noted. But Rabbi Feinberg, who was always concerned about the interaction of being a devoted Zionist and a loyal Canadian, asserted that the "dream of a restored Jewish state" did not alter the patriotism of Canadians Jews to Canada. "Palestine has always been the centre of our pristine Jewish culture and faith and the shrine of our sacred memory," he said. "Canada, however, remains the soil on which young Canadian Jewry has been born."

Though few community leaders mentioned it, an ominous cloud hung over the November 29 celebration. The Arab world rejected the partition, and a fair number of Canadians agreed with them—a fact the federal government took notice of. A Gallup poll carried out in February 1948 indicated that 23 per cent of the respondents supported the Arabs, 19 per cent favoured the Jews, and 58 per cent were neutral. In Quebec, 30 per cent of those asked supported the Arabs, and only 15 per cent the Jews.

Throughout the Second World War, officials of the Zionist Organization of Canada (zoc) had been working non-stop to lobby the federal government of Mackenzie King to support a Jewish state in Palestine. It was as tough a battle as Jewish leaders had had with King about immigration and practically every other issue related to the community. In this case, the ever-cautious King adamantly refused to take a stand that was not in line with that of

Britain, which was struggling mightily (and poorly) to manage the growing hostilities between Arabs and Jews in Palestine.

Even before Archie Freiman, the organization's president since 1921, died in June 1944, Samuel Zacks, an affable and successful Toronto stockbroker, had stepped forward to carry the Zionist torch. Born in Kingston, Ontario, in 1904, Zacks attended Queen's University and graduated with a bachelor's degree in 1924. He next studied political economy at Harvard for about a year. By the end of 1925, he had settled in Toronto. Zacks briefly wrote a column on foreign exchange for the *Financial Post* before establishing a brokerage business. His wealth was derived from an astute investment he made in gold mines in the Red Lake area of northwestern Ontario. He also had a keen eye for art and later—with his wife Ayala, who he married in 1947 (during the war, she had fought with the French Resistance)—amassed an impressive and expensive collection, part of which was gifted to the Art Gallery of Ontario. There is also the Samuel J. Zacks Gallery at York University.

Zacks was a proud Jew, and at a relatively young age he became an active supporter and leader of the United Jewish Welfare Fund of Toronto, overseeing fundraising for the city's various Jewish organizations. For two years following Freiman's death, Zacks shared the presidency of the ZOC with Montreal lawyer Samuel Schwisberg and Michael Garber, who was also on the executive committee of the Canadian Jewish Congress. During the crucial years from 1947 to 1949, as the State of Israel's birth was debated, Zacks was the ZOC's sole president. Among other connections, he maintained good relations with Joseph Atkinson, the publisher of the *Toronto Star*, who supported partition, which resulted in many pro-Israel editorials in the *Star* during 1947 and 1948.

Another key individual in the ZOC was Harry Batshaw, who had immigrated to Canada from Russia with his parents as a young boy. A graduate of the McGill Faculty of Law in 1924, two decades later he was a popular Montreal lawyer whose Zionist ties went back to the early thirties, when he had been president of Canadian Young Judaea. In 1944, Batshaw was head of the ZOC's important public relations committee. One of his astute ideas was the establishment of the Canadian Palestine Committee (CPC) under the leadership of Herbert Mowat, an Anglican layman from Toronto who enlisted a high-profile group of non-Jews to support the cause as passionately as he did. The new committee included Lady Flora McCrea Eaton, Senators Salter Hayden and Adrian Knatchbull-Hugessen, poet Frank R. Scott, and Quebec lawyer Aimé Geoffrion.

The various lobbying efforts of the ZOC, its surrogates like the CPC, and the Sam Bronfman/Saul Hayes-led CJC were made more difficult by the violent actions of Jewish extremists in Palestine such as Lehi (also known as the Stern Gang) and Irgun. The assassination of Lord Moyne (Walter Guinness), a former British cabinet minister and at the time of his death in November 1944 the resident minister of state in Cairo, as well as the bombing of the King David Hotel in Jerusalem on July 22, 1946, weakened the case for a Jewish state in the eyes of Mackenzie King as well as the mainstream press.

As events played out in Palestine and at the UN in New York, younger Jewish Canadians embraced Zionism as an adventure. This was mainly through an association with three groups, each with their own ideological bent: Hashomer Hatzair, Habonim, and Young Judaea, the oldest and most middle-of-the-road organization connected to Hadassah. The ultimate, if somewhat unrealistic, goal for a Jewish teenager in the early forties was *aliyah*—to immigrate to Palestine in order to build the Jewish state. To this end, Hashomer Hatzair, more socialist than the other two organizations, promoted itself as a group of *chalutzim* (pioneers who would work the land). At a training camp on a farm near Prescott, Ontario, south of Ottawa, the most ardent and hearty of the bunch prepared themselves for life on a kibbutz or communal agricultural settlement.

Habonim ("the Builders") was closely linked to Labour Zionism, whose main figure in Palestine was David Ben-Gurion, soon to become the first prime minister of Israel. Founded in Britain in 1929, Habonim was perceived at first as a non-political Jewish youth cultural movement not unlike the Boy Scouts. In the late forties and fifties, Hashomer Hatzair and Habonim jointly operated *hachsharah* (training) farms in Sainte-Julie-de-Verchères, northeast of Montreal, and in Smithville, Ontario, east of Hamilton. The latter, according to a 1949 *Montreal Gazette* report, had "6,000 hens, 35 Holstein cattle and several pair of horses as well as ducks, rabbits and bees." But as Ralph Troper from Toronto (the brother of historian Harold Troper), who worked on the Smithville farm for a year—he did not make *aliyah* until many years later—recalls from his home in Rehovot in Israel, "the farming conditions in Canada didn't resemble those in Israel and life on the *hachsharah* farm was nothing like what we found on the kibbutz."

In the U.S. and Canada, all three youth groups organized summer camps to foster Zionist ideals. Sports, (Israeli) dancing, arts and crafts, and drama were all built around imparting a love of Jewish culture and Israel, as well as providing young people with the experience of living as a "kibbutznik."

Young Judaea embarked on a camp development program as early as 1933. Within a decade, the group had opened Camp Hagshama ("Fulfillment") on the shores of Otty Lake near Perth, Ontario; Camp Shalom ("Peace") near Gravenhurst, Ontario; and Camp Kadimah ("Forward") at Port Mouton, on the South Shore of Nova Scotia. The moving force behind Camp Kadimah was thirty-four-year-old Eli Zebberman in Halifax, who met with a lot of resistance from more "traditional" members of the small Atlantic Jewish community (less than 2,500 in 1951). A similar fight between Zionist elders and idealistic Young Judaeans erupted in Winnipeg in 1944 over the alleged "dangerous" Young Judaea program of promoting immigration to Palestine.

Habonim—which in 1982 merged with Dror (meaning "freedom"), a Zionist group organized in Poland in 1915—sponsored a network of summer camps with, as American writer Ben Cohen would put it in 1985, "an atmosphere of Jewish and Hebrew living, a program of self-help and share work and *chavershaft*—camaraderie—that have become models for every other Jewish camping movement." In the summer of 1945, as an example, 1,600 children attended eleven Habonim camps near New York, Chicago, and Detroit, as well as Montreal, Toronto, Ottawa, and Winnipeg. There was a Camp Kvutza in Saint-Faustin, Quebec, in the Laurentians northwest of Montreal; as well as a second one near Lowbanks, Ontario, south of Hamilton, which operated from 1944 to 1965.

The Lowbanks farmland, about forty acres of mainly flat terrain with a sprinkling of trees and an old farmhouse, had been purchased by Labour Zionists. Among the founders was the grandfather of the camp's chronicler,

Tobi "Pidgy" Gordon, who attended the camp during the fifties and early sixties. Her grandfather and the others, she says, "were the new Jews, their spirituality sprung from a passion for Eretz Israel [the land of Israel], not necessarily the Supreme Being." Like other camps, there was not much to the Ontario Camp Kvutza by Lake Erie—a few small cabins and a dining hall—but the bonding between the campers and the memories of a shared Jewish experience was extremely spiritual and powerful. The camp had its own distinct culture with a socialist bent—including the requisite folklore about a "local homicidal maniac, long-dead, never-to-rest (of course) by the name of Anson Miner"—and cemented life-long friendships. "We were," Gordon says, "seduced at an early age by Kvutza, the spectacle and the music."

The camp had a big impact on the life of Teme Kernerman, regarded as the "mother" of Israeli dancing in Toronto. Born in 1932, she was active in Habonim and at the age of fifteen was hired by the camp as an arts and crafts instructor. "Kvutza is the reason I got into Israeli dance," she says. "I did not know much about arts and crafts and less about dance. But I joined the dance group and ended up leading it." She later studied Israeli and modern dancing in Israel and New York, organized dance festivals in Toronto, introduced dancing into the curriculum of the city's Jewish schools, and in the mid-sixties established the popular Nirkoda Israeli Dancers, which for more than two decades was Toronto's lone performing Israeli dance group. Nirkoda folded in the mid-eighties, but was resurrected as an adult group in 2000 by Ronit Eizenman, a former dancer. In 2007, Nirkoda performed at the Karmiel Dance Festival in Israel. As for Kernerman, who turned eighty-five years old in 2017, she has slowed down a little, she says, but still teaches Israeli dancing.

Not every Jewish child who joined Habonim or the other groups or attended the camp was inspired by the cultural and nationalistic connections. Mordecai Richler claimed that while Habonim was his "liberation" from the stifling religious dictates of his Orthodox grandfather, he initially joined because he "longed to meet girls who could stay out after ten o'clock at night." Gossip had it, recalled Richler, that "girls in the movement, especially those who were allowed to sleep over at Camp Kvutza [in the Laurentians], where there was no adult supervision, practiced 'free love.'"

The Habonim camp north of Winnipeg, located at a non-descript spot on Lake Winnipeg between Winnipeg Beach and Sandy Hook, lasted only until 1952. Owing mainly to the efforts of twenty-year-old Soody Kleiman, a devoted member who planned to make *aliyah*, the camp was restarted and renamed Camp Massad in 1953—modelled after two other Camp Massads in Pennsylvania—and was the only Hebrew-speaking summer camp in Western Canada. It has been operating ever since.

B'nai Brith had established summer camps as way to promote Jewish culture and Zionism even earlier than Habonim Camp B'nai Brith of Montreal, located (since 1929) near Lantier in the Laurentians, was founded in 1921. It began as a way for the Mount Royal Lodge to help underprivileged Jewish boys, and expanded into a summer experience in which today more than a thousand children participate. Similar camps were established for Jewish children in Toronto, Ottawa, and Winnipeg. Camp Northland-B'nai Brith, based in Haliburton, about two hundred kilometres northeast of Toronto, grew from a Jewish girls' club which was started in Toronto in 1909, to a summer camp for boys in 1921, and then after several phases to the camp that has been operating in Haliburton since the early forties. Ottawa's Camp B'nai Brith was founded in 1935 at a site near Fitzroy Harbour, west of the city, and just over a decade later had a permanent home near Quyon, Quebec, on the Ottawa River.

In the west, the B'nai Brith camp for Winnipeg youth which had been located in Sandy Hook on Lake Winnipeg (close to Camp Massad) since the mid-1920s found a much more scenic site on Town Island in Lake of the Woods (near Kenora, Ontario) that had been used for the Sea Cadets. Meanwhile, picturesque Camp B'nai Brith at Pine Lake, Alberta, near Red Deer—now called Camp BB Riback after its founder, Calgary Jewish community leader Ted Riback—has been hosting Jewish youth from Calgary, Edmonton, Saskatoon, and Regina since the summer of 1956.

The raison d'être of most of these camps and youth groups was Israel's declaration of independence on May 14, 1948—a singular event whose ramifications have reverberated throughout history ever since. The birth of Israel was, as A.M. Klein poetically put it, "a theme for rhapsody . . . The proclamation of a Jewish State attests to yet another salvation. It attests to the fact that at long last Jewry has regained its voice."

Across Canada, that was certainly true. Jews rejoiced again, openly and proudly. At the Montreal Forum, at least 15,000 of the city's Jews—"a singing cheering flag-waving crowd," as the *Chronicle* reported—celebrated, heard a bevy of community speakers, and sang "Hatikvah." In Winnipeg on May 23, the community held a rally at a downtown movie theatre. The atmosphere was electric. Ideological divisions made no difference on that night, General, Labour, and Religious Zionists in Winnipeg stood side by side in a nationalistic display of solidarity with Jews in Israel and around the globe. Similar gatherings were held in Ottawa, Saint John, Halifax, and Vancouver.

At a boisterous rally at Toronto's Maple Leaf Gardens, a crowd estimated at 20,000 filled every seat. Liberal MP David Croll, who represented the Toronto-Spadina riding, urged Prime Minister King and his colleagues in the federal government to recognize Israel. But that was not to happen for six and half more months (and then not officially until Israel was finally admitted into the UN in May 1949), by which time Louis St. Laurent had succeeded King as prime minister and Liberal Party leader. A number of key factors contributed to the federal government's protracted decision-making. Among them were the ensuing war between the Jews and the Arab nations who refused to accept Israel's existence, then or later; the UN's difficulty in negotiating a ceasefire; and British antagonism toward Israel. At a meeting in early August, St. Laurent told a CJC and ZOC delegation led by Sam Bronfman not to "press their friends too hard."

As five Arab countries—Egypt, Jordan (Transjordan), Syria, Lebanon, and Iraq—launched an attack against the new state, Canadian Jewish leaders urged every community to do its part and donate. Future Israeli prime minister Golda Myerson (later Meir) was dispatched to North America to raise $25 million and she generated pledges for double that amount mainly from U.S. contributions. The Jews of Canada responded with more than half a million dollars of this total, of which close to $400,000—or 80 per cent—was given by Jews in Montreal and Toronto.

Israel also desperately needed soldiers and volunteers, and in the months leading up to May 1948 the ZOC had begun a quiet recruiting campaign for Second World War veterans and other young men "to stand up and be counted." There was no law preventing Canadians from fighting for another country, but that did not stop the RCMP from monitoring the recruitment activities. Assisting local Zionists in their endeavour were Major Ben Adelman from Winnipeg, who had moved to Palestine in the 1930s and fought for the British Army in the Second World War, and Ben Dunkelman, who had distinguished himself serving with the Queen's Own Rifles during the war. Dunkelman soon travelled to Israel, and was one of the few North Americans given command responsibilities.

In all, about 250 Canadians volunteered to serve in what became known as the Machal—from the Hebrew *Mitnadvei Chutz L'Aretz*, which translates as "Volunteers from Abroad." These brave Canadians, Americans, South Africans, and others called themselves "Machalniks." They fought in every corner of the country and in every capacity, and were paid two Palestinian pounds a month, which was about six U.S. dollars in the late forties (there was still no official Israeli currency).

Travelling to the Middle East was easier said than done. As the British Mandate ended, United Nations troops from the U.S., France, Holland, and other countries enforced tight restrictions on Jewish immigration, especially of young men who were of military age. Their clandestine journey was right out of a John le Carré spy novel. In early April 1948, Allan Chapnick from Winnipeg, a wiry eighteen-year-old and a faithful member of Young Judaea, crossed into the United States from Niagara Falls with the fib to the American border guards that he was visiting relatives in New York City. Arriving at Grand Central Station, he was met by Sydney Jacobson, another Winnipegger, and together they located a Zionist contact. They were directed to Room 814 at the Hotel Edison on West 47th Street, where they found thirty-one other anxious Haganah (a paramilitary organization whose name literally meant "The Defence") recruits. The young men were escorted, two at a time, to a cargo ship that took them to the port of Le Havre in northwestern France. From there, another Haganah contact met them—a fourteen-year-old girl—who hid them in the Jewish Quarter before getting them on a train to Marseilles. From Marseilles, a fishing boat took Chapnick and another 150 recruits across the Mediterranean to Palestine, a journey of sixteen days. The whole ordeal took about two months.

Once Israel declared its independence, Chapnick joined the Jewish forces' English-speaking 7th Brigade, led by Ben Dunkelman. Chapnick became attached to an anti-tank platoon and helped liberate the Galil area, north of the city of Haifa. He stayed in Israel for two years. Initially, he contemplated remaining there, but later decided to return to Canada, taking up the Israeli government's offer of a free ticket home for anyone who had served in the Machal.

Unlike Chapnick and his friends, more than half of the Canadians who volunteered were veterans, and close to a hundred served in Israel's nascent air force. Eleven Canadians died fighting in Israel during the country's War of Independence—including twenty-two-year-old Sidney Rubinoff from Toronto, whose experiences as a soldier in Europe and encounter with Holocaust survivors had compelled him to go to Israel in early 1948. After several months in the line of fire, he was wounded in mid-July 1948 in the Battles of Latrun (between Tel-Aviv and Jerusalem), and died on the way to hospital.

Ralph Moster from Vancouver, twenty-four years of age and a former RCAF pilot, also perished. He was killed on December 7, 1948, when his plane crashed into the Sea of Galilee during a training flight. In a letter to his parents of June 12, 1948, he had written, "You must understand one thing: that if anything should ever happen to me I shall not be sorry that I came to Eretz Israel. It is the only good thing I have ever done. I am thankful to you for having brought me into the world at such a time that I have a chance to fight for a free land for the Jews."

Besides men and money, Israel required weapons, tanks, and airplanes. Canadians also played a role in acquiring and illegally smuggling the arms to Israel. With the support of Samuel Zacks and the executive committee, Samuel Schwisberg and Joe Frank had set up the Victory Equipment and Supply Company in a small shop in Old Montreal. It was essentially a "shell company" with one employee—first Walter Loewenson and later Joe Baumholz, a McGill University engineering student—for the sole purpose of using funds provided by legitimate Zionist groups to purchase war surplus equipment, including Harvard trainers, single-engine monoplanes that had been used by the RCAF and later sold to civilian dealers. In the summer of 1948, Baumholz, innovative and a bit brash, obtained two Harvard trainers from an Ontario scrap dealer. The problem of shipping the planes to Israel was solved by a trio of devoted Zionists: Moe Appel, an Ottawa-based journalist who became the ZOC's public relations director; the pro-Zionist Alex "Sandy" Skelton, the recently appointed assistant deputy of the Department of Trade and Commerce (and the eldest son of Oscar D. Skelton, the late deputy minister of Canada's external affairs department) who was a friend of Zacks from their days at Queen's University; and an unidentified Jewish lawyer who helped navigate the legal pitfalls.

During one late-night meeting, Skelton came up with the plan. In the guise of shipping supplies to the non-existent "Tel-Aviv Spring Fair," the planes were taken apart and packed in large crates. Once the crates safely arrived in Israel, the planes were reassembled and used in the war. Baumholz also oversaw a busy operation in which fellow students and young Zionists cleverly disguised shipments of military goods as "wire" and "technical equipment." On shipping documents, flame-throwers were listed as "insecticide sprayers."

Even after a ceasefire was negotiated between February and June 1949, Israelis continued to call on Canadian Jews for help. One day in 1951, Shimon Peres showed up at Sam Bronfman's Seagram's office in Montreal for a meeting arranged by David Croll. One of Israel's greatest politicians and its president from 2007 to 2014, Peres was then a twenty-eight-year-old liaison for the Israeli Ministry of Defence, in New York on a mission to obtain military supplies. Though his English-language skills were rudimentary at best, he had communicated with officials in Ottawa who were prepared to sell Israel several artillery batteries. The problem was, Ottawa wanted $2 million, which Peres and his government definitely did not have. Hence his request for a sit-down with Bronfman. In 1948, "Mr. Sam" was worth (by his son Charles's estimation) $100 million—about $1.1 billion in 2018 Canadian currency.

Waiting with Bronfman for Peres to arrive was Sol Kanee, an astute and genial grain executive, community leader, superb fundraiser, and Winnipeg's key Jewish power broker during the fifties, sixties, and seventies. A Saskatchewan-born lawyer, Kanee had served as an artillery training officer during the war. He also was a board member of the Royal Winnipeg Ballet and Transair (later purchased by Pacific Western Airlines), and epitomized Jewish advancement and acceptance in the larger Canadian society—which was a definite work in progress during the fifties and sixties. Kanee was a close friend and backer of Mitchell Sharp, an influential minister in the Liberal cabinets of Lester Pearson and Pierre Trudeau. In 1966, when Sharp was minister of finance, he appointed Kanee a director of the Bank of Canada, a position he held for seventeen years.

Kanee was active in the CJC as well, and in 1947 he was elected the Congress's western vice president. He worked closely with Bronfman, and also earned Mr. Sam's respect and friendship. Given Kanee's artillery experience during the war, Bronfman figured that it would be wise to have him at the meeting with Peres.

Bronfman asked Peres about the cost of the artillery batteries, and the Israeli told him the hefty price he'd been given, of $2 million. Kanee said that amount was too high. He called Ottawa and made an appointment for the three of them to see C.D. Howe, the formidable Liberal minister. The next day, the three men drove to Ottawa in Bronfman's Cadillac and met Howe for lunch. During the discussion, Kanee managed to convince Howe that he was charging the Israelis too much, especially when they were paying in cash for the weapons. By the time lunch had ended, Howe had agreed to cut the price in half. Now Peres only required a million dollars, still a large sum of money. Back in the car, Bronfman asked Peres if he had enough money for the revised deal. Peres shook his head.

"Where are you going to get it?" asked Bronfman.

"From you," Peres said.

"Why didn't you tell me before?" Sam wanted to know.

"Because then you wouldn't have gone with me."

Immediately, Bronfman had his driver pull the car over at a pay phone.

He called his wife Saidye in Montreal, and instructed her to arrange a dinner party the next evening. A stickler for detail, Bronfman also objected to the white socks Peres was wearing and stopped the car at a store so that Peres could purchase a more appropriate pair of dark-coloured dress socks. On the guest list were fifty of the wealthiest Jews in the Montreal community. From donations made at the fundraiser, Bronfman and Kanee were able to raise enough money for Peres to obtain his artillery.

An Admirable Element of the Community

I f the establishment of the State of Israel was cause for Canadian Jews to rejoice, so too was the legal fight against discrimination. It was a good news/bad news scenario. Enlightened political leaders, who were influenced by the United Nations' (non-binding) Universal Declaration of Human Rights (UDHR) enacted in late 1948, forged ahead with new laws that protected minorities from unjust treatment in the workplace. Anti-semitism was thus tempered, as highlighted by a JPRC report in 1947, but it still continued to be a factor in the lives of many Jews in Canada—and would be at least until the mid-to-late sixties. Such legislation as Ontario's 1951 Fair Employment Practices Act and 1954 Fair Accommodation Practices Act—which prohibited discrimination at the workplace and in public facilities—is today regarded as progress in the fostering of human rights in Canada. These acts and other like-minded legislation were consolidated in 1962 by Premier Leslie Frost's successor, John Robarts, in the landmark Ontario Human Rights Code. But, as in the U.S., they did not alter attitudes or actions overnight.

Frost, the premier of the province from 1949 to 1961, understood more than many of his contemporaries the significance of the UDHR. On the twelfth anniversary of the charter, in December 1960, he reminded the citizens of Ontario of "the duty to defend the rights of others." Yet even he at first had reservations, believing in 1949 that no new laws were needed since Canadians were "democratic people." He did come to accept, however, that defending human rights was necessary, especially in the battle against communism during the Cold War. As Rabbi Abraham Feinberg had told him,

"It is a sham to attempt to defend western democracy against communism if a man or woman is prevented from getting a job because of discrimination against race, religion or colour."

Frost also wisely paid attention to the effective lobbying campaign led by the Joint Public Relations Committee of the cjc and B'nai Brith to protect Jews and other minorities. The group reached out to other supportive organizations, paid for polls that suggested a modest shift in Canadian attitudes, and convinced some newspaper editors to take up the cause. Most importantly, its officials stressed that this was a "human rights" issue, not a Jewish one.

The premier was proud of what he had accomplished. Some of his friends were not as certain. Soon after the bill abolishing discrimination in the sale of property was under discussion in 1950, Ontario judge J.A. McGibbon privately complained in a letter to Frost, his fishing companion, "surely we have not arrived at the stage of life where the Government is going to take it upon itself to dictate to whom I must sell property, and whom I must have as my next door neighbour. I do not want a coon or any Jew squatting beside me, and I know way down in your heart you do not." In response, Frost told the judge that his intolerance was outdated.

A complicated, emotional, and at times wrenching self-examination of values unfolded during the next two and half decades. For every step forward, there were two steps back. Consider that, in 1946, a Jewish war veteran working for a hardware store in Toronto was fired because some customers did not want to be waited on by a Jew. In 1947, as reported by the JPRC, a group of Jewish businessmen who were prepared to purchase a hotel in Sainte-Marguerite, north of Montreal, had to back away from the deal when they were confronted with the antisemitic hostility of locals led by the parish priest. Posters put up around the town declared that "No Jews or communists" were wanted in the Laurentian resort area. And a letter from the newly formed anti-Jewish coalition, Le Comité de la Survivance des Laurentides Canadiennes-Francaises ("The Committee for the Survival of French-Canadians in the Laurentians")—sent to Mackenzie King and published in a French-language newspaper—protested the sale of the hotel to "people who do not share our customs and our conceptions of Christian life."

In 1951, George D. Finlayson, who was embarking on his impressive law career—he was later appointed to the Ontario Court of Appeal—with the firm McCarthy and McCarthy, learned that several of the partners were blatantly antisemitic. Despite having many Jewish clients, one of the partners was so petty and disdainful of Jews that he would not permit an important study on Canadian constitutional law by Bora Laskin (then a University of Toronto law professor) to be shelved in the firm's library. This partner must not have thought much, either of Laskin's appointment to the Ontario Court of Appeal in 1965, his elevation five years later as the first Jew on the Supreme Court of Canada, and in 1973 as the first Jewish Chief Justice.

Laskin knew how the world worked, however. In the mid-fifties, he made a habit of instructing his Jewish law students not to waste their time applying for articling positions in non-Jewish firms in Toronto, because they were definitely not going to be hired. This was a fact of life for most Jewish lawyers in Canada, according to Donald Carr, who graduated from Osgoode Hall in 1951 and has been a stalwart of the Toronto Jewish community for many years. As late as 1962, two Winnipeg law firms offered Jack London, then a University of Manitoba law school student, an articling position—he had red hair and a Gentile-sounding name—only to renege on the offers once both firms learned that he was Jewish.

In this same period, and despite laws to the contrary, many social and sports clubs and university fraternities and sororities still remained off limits to Jews. A *Maclean's* feature article of October 1959 noted that while Jews "are as a people, remarkably law-abiding and rarely in trouble," it was also true that "a citizen of the Jewish faith can't always live where he wants. He can't join a long list of exclusive clubs [and] if employed by a Christian firm, he is apt to find his advancement slower than that of the non-Jew." Given that reality, Jews organized their own clubs, like the Glendale Golf and Country Club in Winnipeg, which opened in 1946 and had no membership restrictions.

There was no particular pattern to this prejudice. In the late forties, Jewish lawyers in Toronto—excluded from the prestigious and snooty Lawyers Club of Toronto—had organized their own social and educational group, the Reading Club. In 1952, in what on paper was an enlightened decision, the

Lawyers Club eliminated its thirty-year-old rule that members had to be "male, white and Christian." But the new policy was more imagined than real, because the exclusion of Jews more or less continued, and certainly any Jews who tried to join the club were made to feel unwelcome. It took another decade for the discrimination to end—at least against Jewish men; Jewish women lawyers were still not admitted—and the clubs to be integrated.

The establishment Rideau Club in Ottawa, which had admitted Jewish MP Sam Jacobs in the twenties—in really nothing more than a token gesture—finally ended its longstanding unwritten "no Jews allowed" rule in 1964, when Louis Rasminsky of the Bank of Canada, Jewish community leader Lawrence Freiman, lawyer Bernard Alexander, and David Golden, then the deputy minister of industry (Golden was a Winnipegger and talented lawyer who at the age of thirty-four in 1954 had become the deputy minister of defence production, the beginning of a long career in the federal civil service) were invited to become members. Journalist Peter C. Newman, then a star in the Ottawa press gallery, had joined in 1960, but he was not a practising Jew and he had not marked his religious affiliation on the application form. The other members of the club paid no attention to this omission.

Officially ending the discrimination in 1964 was a long, drawn-out process managed skilfully by Arnold D.P. Heeney, who (among other high-ranking positions he held) had served as Canada's ambassador to the United States. At one point, Heeney threatened to resign from the club if the membership rules were not altered so that Jews could join. It took another thirty-seven years until Ottawa businessman Michael Baylin became the club's first Jewish president. Private clubs in Winnipeg, Halifax, Toronto, and London (Ontario), among others, went through similar contentious debates about opening their doors to Jews.

The so-called Christmas Carol Controversy of 1950 in Toronto was equally instructive and reflective of Canadian majority attitudes. In early December of that year, Rabbi Abraham Feinberg of the Holy Blossom delivered a sermon in which he suggested that compelling Jewish students attending Ontario public schools to sing Christmas carols and participate in Yuletide festivities violated their minority rights. His remarks were directed against a noticeable expansion of religious instruction that had been implemented by the minority government of Progressive Conservative George Drew in early 1944. While the legislation did permit students to opt out with their parents' permission, it was a reaffirmation that Ontario was a Christian province in a Christian country.

Curiously, the first criticism directed at Feinberg for these remarks came from three Orthodox rabbis, who reminded him that Canada was a "Christian country" whose school officials could include in the curriculum any Christian customs they saw fit. It is safe to assume that the three rabbis had zero patience and little respect for a practitioner of Reform Judaism. Next came a public rebuke from the Christian clergy as well as the press. The most cutting denunciation was courtesy of the *Globe and Mail*. In an editorial of December 5, entitled "A Deplorable Proposal," the newspaper's editors were astounded that someone, in particular a rabbi, would demand to "eliminate Christmas from public schools," ignoring the fact that was not what Feinberg had actually said. From their perspective, the rabbi's suggestion was clearly sacrilegious. "The Jewish people in Canada are on the whole an admirable element of the community," they wrote. "But they are a minority of one to 100. The majority has an absolute right to hold its own beliefs and express them in a manner acceptable to itself . . . Nobody should ask [the majority] to give up their right to be Christians in the full expression of that word, just to avoid hurting the minority's feelings."

Feinberg, needless to say, had not anticipated such a backlash or public shaming of his sermon, and felt compelled to apologize. Yet he could not win: a few Yiddish newspaper editors castigated him for being too humble. The lesson of this mini-controversy for the larger Jewish community was clear: Jews as a minority were welcome to live among the Christian majority, but they should never forget their place in the hierarchical structure.

Irrespective of the ingrained and lingering antisemitism in Canadian society— countered as much as it could be by anti-discrimination legislation—signs of real change were evident. As the personal stories of Harry Batshaw, Samuel Freedman, Louis Rasminsky, Nathan Phillips, Leonard Kitz, and many others show, being Jewish was not always an impediment to professional and political success.

Harry Batshaw's appointment was decidedly less controversial than several of the other individuals, but his achievement attracted far more attention. A well-connected lawyer in Montreal, Batshaw was a staunch Liberal Party supporter and a friend of Douglas Abbott, the Montreal Liberal MP who served as a cabinet minister in the governments of Mackenzie King and Louis St. Laurent. That party loyalty was rewarded in February 1950, when St. Laurent surprised judges and lawyers in Montreal and elsewhere by appointing Batshaw a judge on the bench of the Superior Court of Quebec, making him the second Canadian Jewish judge in the province's history and the first Jew appointed to a superior court in the country.

The news of the appointment was hailed by the CJC as a "notable event in Canadian history." Most other newspaper editors agreed. "Unique Honor Accorded to Jewish Leader," a headline in the *Montreal Daily Star* declared, "Harry Batshaw First of Race Appointed to High Court." At the same time, *Le Devoir* published a lengthy letter which suggested Batshaw, who was "little known" outside the Jewish community, had been appointed simply because he was Jewish.

The criticism aside, the Jewish community rightly revelled in this appointment, as well as that of Samuel Freedman to the Manitoba Court of Queen's Bench in 1952. They were a sign of a more tolerant Canada—at least officially. A year earlier, Freedman also became the first Jewish president of the Manitoba Bar Association. His subsequent appointment as the first Jewish chancellor of the University of Manitoba in 1959 and his elevation to Chief Justice of Manitoba in 1971 were similarly perceived as groundbreaking.

Louis Rasminsky's career path was in many ways even more remarkable, given that it occurred in the stuffy, elitist, and unforgiving Gentile world of the Canadian bureaucracy. His journey to his appointment as the first Jewish Governor of the Bank of Canada in 1961 was not straightforward, nor free of anti-semitism. As Oscar D. Skelton at the external affairs department pointed out to Robert C. Wallace, the principal of Queen's University, in a letter dated April 28, 1938: Rasminsky had "about the most vigorous and clear-cut intellectual equipment I had met as a young man ... [but] the only white man I know who has to struggle against greater prejudice [than a Jew] is the Mormon."

Born in Montreal in 1908, Rasminsky relocated with his family to Toronto in 1913. As a young man, Lou—as he was called—was a committed Zionist and an enthusiastic member of Young Judaea. Rasminsky was not overly religious. But he did attend High Holiday services for much of his life and when his mother died in the mid-fifties he dutifully recited Kaddish for her. A stellar student, after graduating from Harbord Collegiate he continued his education at the University of Toronto. When he did not win a graduate scholarship to Cambridge, one of his professors convinced a wealthy member of the Toronto Jewish community to establish a new scholarship. (The anonymous donor, according to Lou's son Dr. Michael Rasminsky, was Harry Rotenberg, the father of his girlfriend and future wife, Lyla.) Owing to that financial support, Rasminsky was able to study at the London School of Economics, an opportunity that changed his life.

In 1930, when he was only twenty-two years old, Rasminsky beat out three hundred other candidates and was hired by the League of Nations as an economist, based in Geneva, Switzerland. Rasminsky, now married, remained with Lyla in Europe for about a decade. In 1939, in the months before the Second World War began and with the League's future up in the air, he was hired as an economic advisor for the Bank of Canada's Foreign Exchange Control Board, and did double duty until he left the League officially in 1943. The bank's first governor, Graham Towers, was seemingly not troubled by the fact that Rasminsky was Jewish, though this issue was raised several times by opposition MPs such as the bigoted Norman Jaques of the Social Credit Party, who publically derided Rasminsky as "a socialist-trained Jew from the London School of Economics."

Rasminsky's Jewish background may have been a factor in 1949, when he was being considered for the position of deputy governor following Donald Gordon's retirement. His main rival was the Winnipeg-born James Coyne, a Rhodes scholar and accomplished in his own right. At the time, Coyne was Towers's executive assistant. Based on conversations he had with Towers, Rasminsky believed the second-in-command position was his. But, much to his chagrin, Coyne—who was just as deserving of the deputy position—was appointed instead.

Nearly five years later, when Towers stepped down as governor, the same scenario played out, though admittedly Coyne as deputy governor had the upper hand. According to a Bank of England official who visited Canada at the time, "Rasminsky's failure to reach the very top is widely attributed to antisemitism, which is surprisingly strong in Canada and I have no doubt that it has seriously affected Rasminsky." In the opinion of Peter Dempson, the well-connected Ottawa correspondent for the *Toronto Telegram*, the heads of the chartered banks had made it clear to federal officials that they did not want a Jew as governor. Later, Rasminsky was informed by Prime Minister John Diefenbaker that Louis St. Laurent had told him that in 1955 Quebec would not have accepted a Jewish governor of the bank.

In early 1955, Coyne became the governor, Robert Beattie was made his senior deputy, and in a transparent attempt to appease Rasminsky, he and another colleague were appointed deputy governors, two new positions. Within six years, the usually mundane world of Canadian banking was thrown into havoc (at least for bankers) by Coyne's public disagreement and power struggle over bank policy and interest rates with Prime Minister John Diefenbaker and his finance minister, Donald Fleming. The so-called Coyne Affair led to Coyne's resignation and the appointment of Rasminsky as the governor of the bank. Possibly owing to the tumult caused by the affair, the prejudicial reservations the head of the chartered banks and others had expressed earlier now vanished. And the promotion of Rasminsky, who was perceived to be a calming influence, was approved by the wider financial community. In any event, Diefenbaker should be given credit for this enlightened decision.

Rasminsky, who remained governor until 1973 became, in the words of his biographer Bruce Muirhead, the most "humanitarian" central banker Canada has ever known. For members of the larger Jewish community who bestowed several honours on him, Rasminsky—who died in 1998 at the age of ninety— was hailed as a pioneering figure in the fight against discrimination in Canada.

In 1954, while Louis Rasminsky was navigating the inner workings of the Bank of Canada, in Toronto Nathan Phillips, a sixty-two-year-old lawyer and long-time alderman, was preparing for another run to become the city's mayor. Born in Brockville, Ontario, Phillips lived in Cornwall for many years, until in 1914 he became a lawyer in Toronto. His election as an alderman in the 1924 civic election in Ward 4, which encompassed the Jewish immigrant neighbourhoods of St. John's Ward and Spadina, marked the start of his notable three and half decades in civic politics.

As personable and witty a raconteur as Phillips was, becoming Toronto's first Jewish mayor proved challenging. He tried in 1951 and 1952 and was handily defeated in each election, results he believed were due to the fact that stodgy Toronto was not prepared to elect a Jewish mayor—undoubtedly a correct assessment. But he pulled it off in the municipal election of December 1954.

His main rival was the incumbent Leslie Saunders, a proud and defiant member of the Protestant Orange Order. In the previous mayoral elections Phillips had entered, his Jewish background had been subtly hinted at—but not shoved in the voters' faces, forcing them to grapple with their own prejudices. Saunders decided to be more straightforward, a strategy that rubbed a lot of Torontonians the wrong way. During the campaign, he declared himself to be "Leslie Saunders, Protestant" in a listing of civic candidates. Phillips cleverly ignored the taunt and later marketed himself as "mayor of all the people."

Important as well for Phillips was the endorsement of two of the three major daily newspapers, the *Toronto Star* (which had also backed him in 1951 and 1952) and the *Toronto Telegram*. Saunders, meanwhile, was tainted with unproven allegations that he was involved in the misuse of public funds to maintain an expensive room on the seventeenth floor of the Royal York Hotel for secret meetings. When the votes were counted on election night, Phillips had won, becoming Toronto's first Jewish mayor.

A year later, after Phillips won another one-year term, the *Star* rejoiced that the "liberal-minded people of Toronto . . . demonstrated once again that race or creed is not a barrier to public office—that a Jew as well as a Gentile can be elected mayor of the city." This and other self-congratulatory judgements were undoubtedly exaggerations. Yet Phillips's victory was an indication that Canadian attitudes were changing. A slight power shift was taking place, as the so-called ethnic middle class asserted itself politically—both then and in the decade which followed, with the election of city councillor Philip Givens in

1964 as Toronto's second Jewish mayor (Givens had become acting mayor in late 1963 following the death of the incumbent, Donald Summerville). In Halifax, the election in 1955 of lawyer Leonard Kitz as that city's first Jewish mayor was similarly notable.

These electoral accomplishments suggested that, at least in certain individual cases, Canadian majority attitudes were being transformed, though there were mitigating factors, too. Law firms, medical offices, and other professions and businesses started opening their doors to Jews in the late fifties and early sixties, likely more out of self-interest than any great reformation of values. Simply put, in a city such as Toronto where there was a Jewish mayor, "the word on Bay Street," lawyer Arthur Drache, a former Winnipegger, told historian Harold Troper, "was that law firms known to be antisemitic could take a financial hit." From a Jewish standpoint, the trick was, as Troper put it, to "dress British but think Yiddish." Fit into the Anglo world the way Sol Kanee, Louis Rasminsky, and Philip Givens did, for instance, and government and corporate boardrooms would be somewhat more welcoming.

It must be stressed that this process still had a long way to go to reach any kind of true equality. By the early sixties—as sociologist John Porter found in his seminal study *The Vertical Mosaic*, published in 1965—Jews (and he meant Jewish men rather than women), as "the most highly educated group in the country," were achieving exceptional professional and financial success, yet this emphatically did not translate into power and influence. As he made clear, Jews were "scarcely represented at the higher levels of Canada's corporate institutions ... [and they] did not hold directorships in the banks, insurance companies or other dominant corporations . . . The difference between Jewish representation in the economic elite and Jewish representation in the higher occupation levels, particularly the professions, was striking." Porter concluded: "[Jews] were as much over-represented at the professional levels as were the British. They had no such over-representation in the higher levels of the corporate world."

Even if the country's ruling class did not entirely understand or welcome it, this march of economic progress by Jews and other minorities was connected to the expanding diversity of Canada, and no more so than in Toronto.

At some point in the mid-1950s, the city ceased to be a British satellite and reluctantly entered the cosmopolitan age, owing in part to the arrival of more than half a million immigrants who settled in Metropolitan Toronto between 1945 and 1965. While the foreign-born accounted for 31 per cent of the city and suburban population in 1951, a decade later that figure had increased to 42 per cent. To be sure, many established Torontonians, members of the white-Anglo majority, were anxious about this significant demographic change; nevertheless, the city by 1960 was more Hungarian, Ukrainian, Polish, Chinese (once the discriminatory Exclusion Act had been repealed in 1947), Jewish, and Italian than it had been a decade earlier.

The Soviet invasion of Hungary in 1956 brought more than fifteen thousand Hungarians to Toronto. Among the Hungarian Jews settling in Toronto during this period were members of the Reichmann family. By 1958, Paul and Ralph Reichmann (soon joined by their sibling Albert), Orthodox Jews, had established a Toronto branch of their Montreal-based brother Edward's Olympia Trading—a tile importing company. This was the commercial foundation for the family's mammoth property development corporation, Olympia and York, which would impact significantly on Toronto, as well as on New York and London, England.

For the moment, this disparity between economic achievement and exercising real power and influence—except for a select few—was tolerated, since there was little Jews and other minorities could do to alter it as profoundly as they might have desired. Eventually, however, their collective patience with the unequal status quo was to wear out.

Living Together

I n 1959, the Canadian Jewish Congress, led by its venerable president Sam Bronfman, celebrated the two hundredth anniversary of Aaron Hart's arrival in British North America (and thus Jewish settlement in Canada) with pomp and ceremony—including a visit with the newly installed Governor General Georges Vanier at Rideau Hall, his official Ottawa residence. In the minds of Bronfman and his team, the year-long tribute was singularly about promoting Jews as true Canadians and "nation builders," rather than interlopers and "outsiders." Hence their target audience was not the Jewish community, but the mainly white Protestant and Anglo elite, who had more or less shunned Jews for the past two centuries, even if that historical truth was not readily acknowledged. And it worked: Canadian newspapers and magazines paid attention and were effusive in their praise of Jewish contributions and the many years of "peace and co-operation" between Jews and Gentiles, as the *Globe and Mail* described it. Likewise, to the cjc's delight, an October 1959 *Maclean's* feature article extolled: "Our Jewish fellow-citizens are distinguished by keenness of intellect, love of learning, a good sense of humor and few illusions. They are usually energetic, industrious and creative, and place a high value on human freedom. They are Canadians in their hopes, aspirations, love of family, daily life."

This upbeat narrative was the accepted and "official" version used to describe the Jewish experience in Canada, one which stressed the positive contributions and peaceful integration of Jews in shaping the country, despite the intolerance they faced. But there was a second, less well-received narrative that was raw and all too realistic. This was the version that was incorporated into many of Mordecai Richler's novels, most notably *The Apprenticeship of Duddy Kravitz*, published in 1959, his fourth novel and the one that established him as a major force in Canadian literature, at the age of twenty-eight. Early on, Richler made it clear that he eschewed portraying Jews in his fiction as "sympathetic" or "downtrodden." He wanted to depict nakedly the values and idiosyncrasies—good and bad—of Jewish life in Canada.

While the reviews of *Duddy Kravitz* were fairly positive, many members of the Jewish community were troubled, some deeply so, by Richler's negative and even nasty portraits of Jews, Judaism, and Jewish culture. "You are an angry young man," one woman scolded him during a talk he gave at the new Beth Ora synagogue in the Montreal suburb of Saint-Laurent a year later. Another member of the audience objected that his main character was named Duddy Kravitz. "Could you not have called him Tony instead?" he was asked. Yet another audience member was even more direct, suggesting that he should have written about Jews as the Yiddish storyteller Sholem Aleichem had in his many poignant tales of *shtetl* life, rather than all of the "garbage about your people" that Richler had penned.

Richler initially shrugged off the public tongue-lashing. Then, a few months later, he defended himself in an article for *Maclean's* entitled "We Jews are Almost as Bad as the Gentiles." "What I know best is my own background," he wrote, "and so to some I appear to be only critical of Jews." As the negative comments mounted, Richler became angrier. He declared himself, as his biographer Charles Foran writes, "without patience for those who couldn't abide a 'Negro whoremonger, a contented adulterer, or a Jew who cheats on his income tax, buys a Jag with his ill-gotten gains, and is all the happier for it.'"

The passage of time, however, led to a new and more confident perspective. When the film version of *Duddy Kravitz* was released in 1974—with the then twenty-seven-year-old actor Richard Dreyfuss in the starring role as the young hustler trying to make it up the proverbial ladder—Richler's critical portrayal of Montreal Jews was feted and wrapped in an air of bursting nostalgia. It was not only that the filming of the movie at locales along the Main generated the usual Hollywood buzz—so that it was now hip to be part of Richler's Jewish Horatio Alger story—it was also that with the birth of multicultural Canada under Pierre Trudeau and his Liberals, Jews were somewhat more comfortable in their own skins.

Fiction that was more palatable to most Jews was the immigrant world conceived by a contemporary of Richler's, the Winnipeg writer Adele Wiseman, in her 1956 Governor General's Award–winning novel *The Sacrifice*. Born in 1928, she had the typical upbringing in an immigrant family. Her father, Pesach (Paisy), struggled as an overworked and underpaid tailor, while her mother, Chaika, raised Adele and her brother and sister. She grew up in a small house in the North End; one of her neighbours was Manitoba author Margaret Laurence, who became a close friend. In 1949, after Wiseman graduated from the University of Manitoba with a Bachelor of Arts in English, she travelled throughout Europe, worked with the poor in London's East End, and taught at the American Overseas School of Rome.

During this period, she also worked diligently on her first novel, *The Sacrifice*, a story with a biblical theme set in the North End during the thirties. Wiseman skilfully recreated the Yiddish world of her youth—complete with the sweat, tears, humour, generational conflict, and the dark side of immigrant life she had experienced and imagined. The novel received many positive reviews in Canada, the United States, and Britain, yet it was also a case of too much success too soon.

Wiseman was talented, strong-minded, and principled, but she could also be obstinate and sharp. She rebuffed her publisher's firm request for a sequel and instead laboured for several years on a four-hour play, *The Lovebound*, about Jewish refugees from Nazi Germany. She could not find a producer. She accepted a teaching position in Montreal at Macdonald College (McGill University) in the fall of 1963, and wrote a second novel, entitled *Crackpot*, about a woman named Hoda, a Jewish prostitute. It is a depressing and gloomy tale. Over a five-year period, more than twenty publishers rejected it. Finally, in 1974, Jack McClelland of McClelland & Stewart agreed to publish it, though only after Margaret Laurence convinced him to do so.

Reviews were mixed, but Wiseman did not care. Her career stagnated after that. She wrote a memoir about her mother and then started a third novel, but never finished it. Satisfied with what she had accomplished, she "did not regard her incremental loss of literary recognition as fatal," suggests her biographer, Ruth Panofsky. "Her monumental success as a first-time novelist, when she won prestigious awards and honours and reached an international audience, did not impede her vision of the writer as moral witness to her time." Wiseman died in 1992 at the age of sixty-four.

During his prickly talk at the Beth Ora synagogue in 1960, another pointed question Mordecai Richler was asked was why he was "so self-conscious about Jewish people living together." That hit a little too close to home for some members of the audience—primarily because it was true, and to a certain extent still is. As it was in the late nineteenth and early twentieth centuries, so it remained the post-1950 period. Whether it was because they wanted to live within walking distance or a short drive to synagogues, schools, and kosher shops, or whether they were merely drawn to live in neighbourhoods where their relatives and friends resided, most Jews opted to live close to each other. These self-made and self-sustaining urban Jewish ghettos—by 1961, 99 per cent of Jews in Canada lived in cities—endured partly out of strong bonds of ethnicity and religion, and partly owing to self-preservation against the forces of exclusion; or, in Quebec, as a defence against the rising French-Canadian nationalism which continually reminded them that they still did not quite measure up. Collective insecurities, however, dictated that Jews like those challenging Richler did not want this publicly pointed out.

Accusations about clannishness, which had been levelled at Jews for centuries and became a staple of antisemitic propaganda, stung deeply. Dismissing that unpalatable stereotype, Jews perceived their residential connections in a more positive light, as community building and as a necessity based on religious and social imperatives. Beginning in the late forties, as the old immigrant neighbourhoods in Montreal, Toronto, and Winnipeg—as well as in Ottawa, Vancouver and Calgary—were abandoned, Jews relocated en masse to newer, more fashionable middle-class suburbs. This resulted from Jewish educational and business success. The lifelong objective of working-class Jewish parents had been achieved.

By the start of the sixties, more than 58 per cent of Jews in Canada—in 1961 that was close to 150,000 of a total Jewish population of 254,668—had been born in the country. Many of these individuals, as well as those who were born outside of Canada, had a university education. As John Porter's 1965 study determined, there were more Jewish professionals—doctors, lawyers, teachers—and businessmen than peddlers and small shopkeepers. Jewish children accepted this transition as the norm. Pursuing a higher education was now routine among young Jewish men and women.

Across Canada, according to the 1961 census, the average annual income for Jewish men was $7,426, compared to $4,414 for the rest of the male population. With a higher socio-economic status and the gradual lessening of discrimination came a moderation of political views, including a decline in support for socialism and communism, and an attendant demand for middle-class homes and neighbourhoods. Jews succumbed to the 1950s idyllic lifestyle immortalized on the U.S. television show *Leave It to Beaver* no less than any other Canadians of the era.

Jewish women in the fifties and early sixties were supposed to maintain a Jewish home, be a devoted wife and loving mother, and support the Zionist endeavours of Hadassah-WIZO (Women's International Zionist Organization). As journalist Barbara Kay notes, she and many of her friends went to university—like many women in Canada—to "hone" their minds. Nothing, however, was supposed to divert them from their "real vocation as a wife and mother." It took at least another decade before that paternalistic and societal expectation finally changed: by the early 1970s, with few obstacles in their way, young Jewish women were opting for careers as doctors, lawyers, accountants, architects, and even as engineers, though that was rarer.

In Montreal, Jews immigrated west, deserting the Main in droves for the more comfortable confines of Côte Saint-Luc, Côte-des-Neiges, and Snowdon. In 1931, the area around St. Lawrence Boulevard and the Laurier district had a Jewish population of nearly 29,000, which represented about half the Jews (57,997) in the Greater Montreal area. Ten years later this number had declined to 25,767, or 42 per cent of the total; by 1951, it dropped further to 18,658, or 23 per cent; and by 1961 to a mere 1,985, less than 2 per cent of the 102,724 Jews in Montreal. The Main had clearly lost some of its allure, despite the enduring nostalgia about its many charms, real or imagined.

The bagels, pike, and smoked meat notwithstanding, the mass movement away from St. Lawrence Boulevard marked a significant demographic shift in the socio-economic history of Montreal's Jewish population. Côte Saint-Luc, for example, a village that became a city by 1958, had been completely devoid of Jews in 1931. Three decades later, the small city had a Jewish population of 8,300, and 17,460 by 1971. Indicative of this shift was the election of Samuel Moskovitch, a fifty-eight-year-old lawyer who was active in B'nai Brith, as mayor of Côte Saint-Luc in 1963, a position he held until he died thirteen years later. He was the first Jewish mayor of a Montreal-area city and the second in Quebec, after William Hyman, the reeve in Cap-des-Rosiers Township from 1858 to 1882. In time, the area boasted Jewish schools and synagogues. In 1975, Moskovitch visited Israel, where he attended a ceremony twinning Côte Saint-Luc with the Israeli city of Ashkelon.

Outremont, on the other hand, one of the first non-Main areas popular with Jews in the forties and fifties, had 11,566 Jewish residents in 1951. During the next ten to fifteen years, many Jews from the Main and other parts of the city—the small number of ultra-Orthodox Hasidim who had arrived in Montreal after 1940 were the exception—moved to the trendy bedroom community of Dollard-des-Ormeaux, west of Montreal, which had less than twenty Jews in 1961 and 9,150 by 1991. The popular Côte-des-Neiges and Snowdon neighbourhoods grew as well, from 8,300 Jews in 1941 to 31,425 in 1971, which meant that by then, nearly 30 per cent of the Jews in Montreal lived in this suburb. In 1947, following this demographic movement, the Spanish and Portuguese congregation relocated from its third home on Stanley Street to a new synagogue on St. Kevin and Lemieux, in the heart of the Côtes-des-Neiges–Snowdon area.

While wealth and status had long divided the city's "uptown" and "downtown" Jews, nearly all of them could trace their roots back to Western and Eastern Europe and an Ashkenazi tradition. That changed in the fifties with the initial arrival of close to 2,500 French-speaking Sephardic Moroccan Jews, as well as smaller numbers from Iraq and Egypt who had fled to Canada to escape persecution triggered by the end of colonialism and the overwhelming resentment against the establishment of the State of Israel. During the next two decades—and especially following the Six-Day War of June 1967 between Israel and its hostile Arab neighbours—another ten thousand Jews, mainly from Morocco where there were anti-Jewish riots, opted to begin their lives again in Quebec, adding a new (though complicated) community dynamic. According to a study undertaken by Jewish Federations of Canada-UIA, by 2011 the total population of Sephardim in Greater Montreal was 22,225, representing 24.5 per cent of the city's total Jewish population of 90,780.

For this new generation of Sephardim, there were growing pains and adjustment problems. In a repeat of the British-German negative view of the Eastern Europeans in the late nineteenth century, the assimilated Ashkenazi majority tended to look down on the newcomers, and certainly disapproved of an increasing number of intermarriages between Sephardic men and French-Canadian women, in an era where intermarriage rates were still fairly low. "Some Ashkenazim thought we were backward, 1,000 years behind," Maurice Cohen, a Ville Saint-Laurent alderman who emigrated from Morocco in 1964, said in a 1986 interview. "They had the impression we were savages." But the Sephardim persisted, no differently than the Europeans had. They founded their own synagogues and organizations, none more important than the Association Sépharade Francophone (ASF), which in 1976 was renamed the Communauté Sépharade Unifiée du Québec.

Toronto's growing Jewish population, which increased from 49,046 in 1941 to 109,480 in 1971 (see Appendix, Table 2), had local concerns that occupied the attention of its members. After the 1960 Quebec provincial election of Jean Lesage and the Liberals, Toronto Jews—who were just as self-absorbed as the majority of Torontonians—did not fully appreciate the impact of the Quiet Revolution and modern French-Canadian nationalism on Montreal Jews. Nor did Montreal Jews fully understand the challenges posed by Toronto's

WASP and Orange history, its strong British character, and stifling reputation as "Toronto the Good."

Still, the collective experience of Toronto Jews was similar to that of their brethren in Montreal, Winnipeg, and elsewhere. How could it not be? Upwardly mobile Jews gradually began leaving the downtown Spadina–Kensington Market neighbourhood in the early thirties, but it was only a trickle. After the Second World War, that trickle became a mass migration. The vast majority headed north to the upscale village of Forest Hill, and its Jewish population (and that of the adjacent York Township), which centred on and around Bathurst Street, soon exceeded eighteen thousand and kept on rising. In 1951, 40 per cent of the population in the village was Jewish, the "highest proportion in any Canadian municipality."

It took somewhat longer for synagogues and Jewish community institutions to follow the migration north: in 1954, for example, of the forty-eight synagogues in Toronto, only five were located above St. Clair Avenue. In contrast, of the more than 130 synagogues in the GTA today, only a few are south of Dupont Avenue. Contractors could not build houses fast enough, and Bathurst—which up to then had been not much more than a rural road in North York—was transformed into a major artery. Thousands of Toronto Jews were on the move, more than happy to leave immigrant Spadina behind. "By 1958, we were as far north as Finch Avenue [and Bathurst] and by 1964 we're at Steeles [Avenue]," says Toronto historian Frank Bialystok, whose father was a builder. "That is remarkable."

It was the same story in Winnipeg. In 1941, 92 per cent of Winnipeg's 17,027 Jews lived in the heart of the North End, within a three-kilometre radius of Aberdeen Avenue and Salter Street. Nearly all of them—86 per cent—identified Yiddish as their mother tongue. They ran small grocery stores, worked as cutters and pressers in garment factories, did piecework in their homes; they supported their children's education, lived primarily in a Yiddish or Eastern European environment, and bought their kosher meat at shops and prayed at synagogues a half-block from where they resided.

Twenty years later, this close-knit and insular world was dramatically changing. In 1961, Winnipeg's Jewish population had increased to 19,376, but now only 6,693 (34 per cent) lived in the old North End. A number of wealthier and assimilated Jews had moved to the other side of the city, to the charming, tree-lined streets of River Heights in the South End. In 1941, 1,484 Jews lived in the south part of Winnipeg; by 1961, that figure had increased to 5,494. This was one of the reasons the conservative Shaarey Zedek synagogue—led by Rabbi Milton Aron, a young and progressive spiritual leader—had finally abandoned its cramped downtown building, and in 1949–50 constructed a new and modern synagogue at the corner of Academy Road and Wellington Crescent, as close to the homes of Winnipeg's WASP elite as you could get. Within a decade, the synagogue had increased its membership to one thousand families.

Many more Winnipeg Jews opted to move further north up Main Street, into the suburb of West Kildonan, where they could buy medium-size bungalows with room for gardens and backyard swing sets for under $20,000. In the early fifties, the relocation of the old Rosh Pina synagogue from a rundown area of the North End to a new and architecturally beautiful building on the grounds of the recently closed Jewish Orphanage on Matheson Avenue East, a few blocks from the Red River, epitomized the rise of West Kildonan as a focus of Jewish life. By 1961, 30.5 per cent of the 20,077 residents of West Kildonan were Jewish, including a number who had moved into the West Kildonan development of Garden City—a bedroom community that offered large lots and fashionable houses. More Jews would build homes there in the next decade.

In 1961, about 83 per cent of the 254,368 Jews in Canada—210,748—lived in Montreal, Toronto, and Winnipeg (with Montreal and Toronto representing a combined 75 per cent of that total). A decade later, the figures remained about the same, except by then Winnipeg's population had declined slightly. Vancouver's Jewish population had grown from 2,812 in 1941 to 7,301 in 1961, and to 10,085 in 1971 (the 1961 and 1971 figures incorporate Greater Vancouver). Ottawa was next, with a Jewish population of 5,533 in 1961 that increased to 6,385 ten years later; in 1961, Calgary and Edmonton together had approximately the same number as Ottawa, and only a few hundred more (mainly in

Calgary) by 1971; Hamilton had 3,858 in 1961 and 257 more in 1971; and in all of Atlantic Canada there were less than 2,500 Jews in 1961, which gradually declined during the next decade.

In each of these cities, the pattern of residential and institutional development after 1945 was remarkably similar to that in the larger Jewish urban centres. The key difference, however, was that in these smaller communities there were greater financial constraints on synagogues, schools, and kosher shops, as the rise of a larger Jewish middle class coincided with a slow but steady decline in the importance of religion in daily life. Even the Jewish population of Winnipeg eventually faced problems related to money, expensive community infrastructure, and stagnating population growth.

Consider, for example, the postwar histories of the two largest communities after the "big three": Ottawa and Vancouver. By 1971, two-thirds of Ottawa Jews had left Lowertown and Sandy Hill, close to the downtown core, for new neighbourhoods in Alta Vista, Nepean, and Ottawa West. But most of the city's synagogues and institutions stayed in the downtown area for many more years. That included the Jewish Community Centre (JCC) that had been built in the late forties on Chapel Street (as well as Nate's Deli, founded by local philanthropist Dave Smith in 1959). A Talmud Torah was opened in 1949 in the former Rideau Street Public School close to the community centre. Eleven years later, the school relocated into the JCC building, changing its name to the Ottawa Hillel Academy.

The Chapel Street centre "was indeed the heart of the community for decades," as the Jewish Federation of Ottawa's website notes. But the community's institutions ultimately followed the movement of the city's Jewish population. First, in 1965, the Hillel Academy opened a branch in the Alta Vista Public School. And then in 1983 the Jewish Community Campus was established near Broadview and Carling in the West End and the downtown and Alta Vista branches were consolidated. (In 2006 the Hillel Academy merged with the Yitzhak Rabin High School, which had been founded in 1995, into the Ottawa Jewish Community School.) It required longer for the JCC to abandon its downtown home: the new Soloway Jewish Community Centre was opened in September 1998 in a building a block from the school campus.

As in many smaller Jewish centres with declining and aging memberships, many synagogues—beginning in the late fifties and continuing up to the present day—found it financially unfeasible to remain in operation. One answer was amalgamation. In 1956, two of the older Ottawa synagogues—Adath Jeshurun and Agudath Achim—merged to form Congregation Beth Shalom, with a new synagogue adjacent to the JCC on Chapel Street. Beth Shalom would remain in that building for the next six decades.

In 1967, the arrival of British-born Rabbi Reuven Bulka—only twenty-three years old—from New York City, where he had received his rabbinic ordination, was a boost for the community. Bulka became the spiritual leader of the Congregation Machzikei Hadas, which soon departed the Murray Street location in Lowertown where it had been since the late twenties for a new and more modern synagogue in Alta Vista. During the next fifty years, Bulka, a man of many talents—he was a prolific writer, journalist, scholar, television celebrity, and all around maven—emerged as arguably the city's most significant and most visible Jewish religious leader. It was fitting that, when Bulka announced his retirement in 2014—he is now the rabbi emeritus of Machzikei Hadas— he was feted at a gala dinner at the Château Laurier hotel by a who's who of Ottawa, Jews and non-Jews alike (the keynote speaker was Conservative MP Jason Kenney, who described himself as a "goy from Calgary").

Vancouver was more of an outlier in that its community has not been quite as cohesive and geographically centred as other Jewish communities in the country. The more than tripling of Vancouver's Jewish population from the forties to the seventies mainly owed to the migration of Jews from other parts of Canada in search of milder weather; as well as from the arrival of a few hundred Holocaust survivors, refugees from Hungary and other parts of Eastern Europe, and a small number of Sephardic immigrants. By 1972, the community numbered about eleven thousand people (and had contributed a combined $1 million to Israel in 1971), but only 1 per cent of Vancouver's total population. If there was a "Jewish area"—what Vancouver Jews affectionately refer to as the "Borscht Belt"—it was on and around Oak Street, in a newly developed neighbourhood south of Fairview, which had been somewhat of a

Jewish neighbourhood during the period after the First World War, when Jews from working-class Strathcona or the East End had moved there. In 1928, for instance, the city's first Jewish community centre had been built at 11th Avenue and Oak Street, "in the heart of Fairview."

After 1950, the city went through a growth spurt—related to the Canadian Pacific Railway's release of a large tract of land—and families with young children were drawn to the Oakridge area. In 1948, a Talmud Torah day school was opened near 26th Avenue and Oak Street. Then, following the same pattern as in other cities, two older synagogues—Schara Tzedeck, an Orthodox synagogue which had been based downtown since its founding as Benei Yehuda in 1907, and Conservative Beth Israel, which had been in a building near West Broadway since the late twenties—relocated south to newly constructed synagogues down Oak Street, above 19th Avenue. The area was further enhanced in 1962 with a new Jewish Community Centre at Oak and 41st Avenue, and the Louis Brier Home and Hospital for Jewish seniors, which opened six years later. (Brier had made his money mining near Dawson City, Yukon, and had bequeathed $100,000 to the Vancouver Jewish Community Fund for the construction of a Jewish seniors' home.)

The city's active—though relatively small in number—Jewish socialists and Labour Zionists founded the Peretz Shule (today the Peretz Centre) in 1945, which was initially located in the basement of the city's original community centre on Oak Street and 11th Avenue. The school had been established with the objective of fostering left-wing Yiddish culture and providing children "with a non-political, secular Jewish and Progressive education." Ben Chud, who had served in the armed forces in Europe during the Second World War and was a key member of the United Jewish People's Order, was the school's principal. He later co-edited the UJPO's publication, *Outlook*. In 1946, the school moved a few blocks to a house on West Broadway, where it remained until 1961. Typically, it was women who raised funds for the school but men who made the decisions. The women's group known as the *Muter Fareyn* ("Mother's Union") were "permitted" to be represented by two delegates at meetings.

Like elsewhere in Canada, tension between the Vancouver socialists and the rest of the community erupted during the fifties, as the Cold War heated up. In 1951, the CJC's decision to expel the UJPO led to it being blacklisted by the scions of the Vancouver Jewish Administrative Council and to the Peretz Shule losing its ability to raise funds via the United Jewish Appeal for four years. At the time, this was a devastating blow to the school, and the decision generated a lot of bad feelings. Even when funding was permitted again in 1955, the divisiveness remained for many years.

By the early sixties, Canada's Jewish communities were undergoing a transformational change. A large number of Jews still kept kosher, but increasingly (especially beyond Montreal and Toronto), it was out of habit and respect for their more-observant parents. They were keen to send their children to a Hebrew school, but regular attendance at synagogue had dropped off. One writer for Winnipeg's Shaarey Zedek synagogue bulletin in 1948 caustically labelled this affliction "*Moribus Sabbaticus.*" Sufferers of the "disease," it was claimed, were prevented from attending Friday-night and Saturday-morning prayer services, but the affliction did not "interfere with other weekend activities such as football games and movies."

At the same time, the synagogue as an institution was still very much part of life for family celebrations as well as social events. The Orthodox synagogues across Canada—devoid of choirs, English prayers, modern atmospheres, and located in older and declining neighbourhoods—were no longer acceptable to large numbers of Jews. The younger generation desired synagogues that reflected their liberal beliefs and bourgeois status. Reconciling the traditional values of the past with the ever-changing values of the post-1960 modern world—a world which pushed boundaries, battled prejudice, and produced opportunities once considered unreachable—was the challenge confronting Jewish baby boomers and their traditional parents who were frequently confused about modern social and religious trends.

THE
MAKING
OF
TOLERANT
CANADA

21

A Lot of Jews

T he dramatic election of Jean Lesage and the Liberals in the 1960 Quebec provincial election, a year after the death of Premier Maurice Duplessis of the Union Nationale, set in motion what is known in Canadian history as the "Quiet Revolution." It marked the start of a decade (or so) of a (mostly) non-violent movement of social and cultural reform, and the perpetuation of a modern French-Canadian nationalism which promoted the French language and French-Canadian equality within the province and the country. There was no denying its transformative success: by the early 1970s, French Quebecers had become "masters in their own house," as the provincial Liberals' 1962 slogan *Maîtres chez nous* had described it. In Ottawa, federal governments headed by Liberals Lester Pearson and his immediate successor, Pierre Trudeau, attempted to thwart the extreme nationalists of the separatist movement by addressing—or appeasing, depending on your point of view—Quebec's demands for equal treatment for its people, culture, and language. Trudeau, who battled Quebec nationalists more or less throughout his years in power—from 1968 to 1984 (with the exception of part of 1979–80)—was much more antagonistic than Pearson.

In the province's pecking order, Jews were the "third solitude," after the English and French (the phrase derives from Hugh MacLennan's 1945 novel, *Two Solitudes*, about English and French divisions). Though most Montreal Jews could not speak French fluently (in the sixties, at least), they were definitely cognizant of the various ways this restyled nationalism could impact their own community life. Asked to submit a brief for the Royal Commission on Bilingualism and Biculturalism (established by

Pearson in mid-1963), CJC officials hesitated because they were reluctant to push a policy of multiculturalism that might undermine the English and (especially) the French languages and cultures. Instead, Saul Hayes recruited Ruth Wisse, a Yiddishist from Montreal who had been recently hired by McGill University, to write an essay that the commissioners used. She stressed the Jewish desire to fit in and contribute to Canadian society over many generations, and the non-threatening way in which ethnic and religious identities had been perpetuated.

A more revealing example of the Congress's mindset was a 1966 article written with the CJC's past president Sam Bronfman's name on it (according to Harold Troper, he "authorized" the article but did not actually write it). (In order to allow Bronfman to step down gracefully as CJC president in 1962, Sol Kanee and Saul Hayes had created a new Congress body called the board of governors, of which Bronfman was the first chairman.) The article emphasized that Jewish children in Quebec, who wanted to be "part and parcel of the new Quebec," had to learn French. Hayes, who was ever cautious and mindful of French-Canadian sensitivities, preferred that Jews be recognized as a faith, rather than an ethnic group. Thus at the 1967 International and Universal Exposition in Montreal—Expo 67—the CJC sponsored the erection of a small functioning synagogue supported by Orthodox, Conservative, and Reform Jews at the purposely named "Pavilion of Judaism," rather than the "Jewish Pavilion," which would have denoted something more cultural than religious. Arguments ensued over the pavilion's design and themes, and in the end the history of Canadian Jewish institutions, cultural organizations, and significant events of the past (there was a Holocaust memorial) were included in the exhibits.

This religious and cultural mix was also evident in July of that year, during the centennial celebrations held in Ottawa, when the young and enthusiastic Jewish performers of the Chai Dancers—the Winnipeg dance and music group founded by Sarah Sommer in 1964—celebrated Jewish culture and religion in an artistic fashion. Sommer had been student of Winnipeg-born Joyce (Dorfman) Mollov, a dancer and instructor with the Royal Winnipeg Ballet who also worked with Young Judaea. Mollov's interest in Israeli folk dancing had been sparked by New Yorkers Fred Berk and Dvora Lapson, the acknowledged pioneers of Israeli dancing in North America. After Mollov moved to New York and later founded the Jewish Dance Ensemble, Sommer emerged as one of Winnipeg and Canada's leading Israeli dance teachers and proponents.

In its first few years, Chai consisted only of eight female dancers. Then Sommer and her friend Sara Udow, the choir conductor at the Rosh Pina synagogue, added a singing component to the group. Abe Arnold, who was the CJC's western regional director, was an early supporter and found funds so that Chai could perform outside of Winnipeg. Early in 1967, a CBC representative who was assembling performers for a folk-arts gala celebration in Ottawa, in honour of the centennial at which Queen Elizabeth and Prince Philip were to attend, had Chai audition and immediately invited them to join the party. The performance in Ottawa on July 1 was a great success for the expanded group. Tragically, two years later, Sommer died from cancer at the age of thirty-nine, yet her husband Alex and members of the Winnipeg Jewish community kept the group going. In time, under the artistic direction of Jill and Nenad Lhotka, professionally trained European ballet instructors and dancers, Chai was transformed into the Sarah Sommer Chai Folk Ensemble (I was a dancer and singer during the seventies), arguably Canada's finest and most enduring amateur Jewish folk group, which has now performed across North America, in Mexico and Argentina, and in Israel.

Chai's success was made possible in part by the gradual elimination—at least, in the legal sense—of discrimination, the decline of prejudice, and the embracing of multicultural tolerance during the sixties and seventies. It all started with Pierre Trudeau's rise to power as Liberal leader, and his confirmation as prime minister in the federal election of 1968. This was an election in which eight Jewish candidates won seats in the House of Commons—another sign of the progressive times. Among these new Jewish MPs were Robert Kaplan and Barney Danson from Ontario; and, most unusual of all, Jack Marshall—a retired colonel who won as a Progressive Conservative in a Newfoundland riding (Trudeau later appointed him to the Senate, and his son Tom was briefly the Premier of Newfoundland and Labrador in 2014, the first Jewish premier of the province).

Despite Trudeau's youthful dalliance with antisemitic and right-wing ideas in the thirties and early forties, by the time he was elected an MP in 1965—in the riding of Mount Royal in Montreal, a constituency with a high Jewish population he would represent for the rest of his political career—and Liberal leader three years after that, those less-palatable views had been cast aside. As prime minister, Trudeau soon became the most "Jew-friendly" leader in Canadian history. This was not so much that he had suddenly been transformed into the world's greatest philosemite; rather that he appreciated smart and skilled talent, as Allan Gotlieb, a Jewish diplomat who Trudeau appointed Canadian ambassador to the United States in 1981, has suggested. Simply put, many Jews had the credentials and intellect that Trudeau appreciated and required. That such individuals as Bernard Ostry, an academic who served as a federal deputy minister in several departments from 1981 to 1985, were Jewish—as was Ostry's equally talented wife Sylvia, who was the deputy minister of Consumer and Corporate Affairs from 1975 to 1978, and then the head of the Economic Council of Canada—did not necessarily occur to Trudeau.

Some years after he had come to power, he met with a delegation of Jewish leaders. The meeting was supposed to be informal, but one of the guests insisted on making a short speech highlighting all of Trudeau's Jewish political, diplomatic, and judicial appointments. Listening to the speaker read out the names as if he were chanting the Scroll of Esther, Trudeau stopped him. "Yes, that is a lot of Jews, isn't it?" he said dismissively.

Whether he was conscious of it or not, Trudeau's two most notable appointments in the annals of Canadian Jewish history were elevating Windsor MP Herb Gray to the cabinet as a minister without portfolio in 1969, making him the first Jewish cabinet minister at the federal level; and the promotion of Bora Laskin from the Ontario Court of Appeal to the Supreme Court of Canada in 1970 and then making him Chief Justice three years later. While Gray wore a kippah and used a Hebrew Bible for his official swearing-in ceremony, Laskin was somewhat more reticent about playing up the Jewish first designation.

In October 1969, soon after Gray was in the cabinet, Michel Vennat—then a special assistant in the Prime Minister's Office (PMO)—advised Gordon Gibson, Trudeau's executive assistant, that the prime minister should speak to a Jewish audience in the near future to take advantage of the government's "good standing" in the community. Vennat suggested the possibility of Trudeau speaking at the opening of the new CJC building in Montreal, speaking to a B'nai Brith gathering, or delivering a major address in Toronto. Several months later, Trudeau—on the recommendation of both Gibson and Herb Gray—accepted the Anti-Defamation League of B'nai Brith's Canadian Family of Man Award at the Hotel Bonaventure in Montreal.

The *Canadian Jewish News*, the *Jewish Post* and the *Jewish Western Bulletin* all proudly boasted about both appointments. "For the first time in the history of Canada," the editor of the *Canadian Jewish News* declared on October 24, 1969 about Gray's advancement, "a professing Jew has become a federal cabinet minister." Five month later, the newspaper regarded the elevation of Laskin to the Supreme Court as "a new milestone in Canada's progress towards full democracy."

The mainstream press, however—unlike with Harry Batshaw's appointment as the first Jewish judge two decades earlier, which had been generally lauded—ignored the religious affiliations of Gray and Laskin. The *Globe and Mail*, for example, identified Laskin in its March 1970 story about his appointment as a "Russian immigrant's son." That he was also Jewish was seemingly not important or relevant. Again, when he got the nod for Chief Justice, one searches the major Canadian newspapers (and Trudeau's private correspondence) in vain for a reference to Laskin's Jewish background. After Laskin died in March 1984, Montreal lawyer Harold Ashenmil, who spoke with Trudeau on many occasions, asked the prime minister if he intended to replace Laskin with another Jewish appointment to the Supreme Court. Trudeau was annoyed by the query. As Ashenmil recalls: "He replied that he would appoint the best persons to the Supreme Court and, 'If the best people were all Jewish, the Court would have nine Jewish Justices.'"

Following this approach, Trudeau also made significant Jewish judicial appointments across Canada. Samuel Freedman, a Manitoba Court of Appeal judge since 1960, was made the court's Chief Justice in 1971. Nathaniel (Nathan) Nemetz was appointed a Justice of the British Columbia Court of Appeal in 1968, and Trudeau bumped him up to Chief Justice five years later. Alan B. Gold was named Chief Judge of the Court of Quebec in 1970, and Chief Justice of the Superior Court of Quebec in 1983. And Constance Glube was appointed to the Supreme Court of Nova Scotia, the first woman on the court. She became Chief Justice in 1982, the first woman in Canada to be so honoured.

Jewish politicians at the federal and provincial level were everywhere during the 1970s, or so it seemed. This was the result of Jews possessing the education, skills, and backroom connections to get elected, and the fact that Canadian voters, for the most part, did not seem too concerned about whether or not they were casting their ballots for a Jewish candidate. David Lewis—a long-time member of the Co-operative Commonwealth Federation, which in 1961 had joined with the Canadian Labour Congress to form the New Democratic Party or NDP—took over the reins of the federal NDP from Tommy Douglas in 1971. His outspoken and animated son Stephen, who was first elected to the Ontario legislature in 1963 when he was just twenty-six years old, became the leader of the Ontario NDP in 1970 and served as the provincial leader of the opposition from 1975 to 1977.

David Lewis had grown up in a socialist-minded home. Though proud of his roots, religion was not part of his life, nor that of his children. Stephen did not have a bar mitzvah when he turned thirteen, and says today that he did not want one. It was not until much later—when he married Michele Landsberg, a Jewish journalist—that Judaism became a part of Stephen's life.

David was hesitant about succeeding Tommy Douglas as NDP leader because he was Jewish. "He was reluctant and cautious about going after the leadership because he felt that being Jewish might be a negative factor for the party," Stephen says. "He felt that quite strongly. My father wrestled with the idea of [succeeding Douglas] simply and largely on the Jewish question." Nonetheless, when Lewis did become the NDP leader, his Jewish background, while noted in the press, did not impede his work.

Nor did being Jewish ever impact on Stephen's own political career, though that did not mean he was not personally affected by antisemitism. As an Ontario member of Provincial Parliament (MPP) from 1963, Stephen represented Scarborough West, a new suburban Greater Toronto riding. "I'd go to a riding dance and a woman, who ironically enough became a school trustee, would yell from a platform, 'Hey Jew-boy, come over here.'" For a time, Stephen and his family lived close to the riding, where there were very few Jews. In 1975, they were forced to move to Toronto, because their children were experiencing antisemitism at school and in the neighbourhood. He recalls, too, that after he sold their house, there was a big picture on the front page of the *Globe and Mail* with the caption: "Lewis sells house for profit."

"It was all about a socialist making money," he says with a laugh.

It took more than a century, but in 1970 the Liberal Premier of Quebec, Robert Bourassa, appointed the first Jewish cabinet minister in the province's history: Dr. Victor Goldbloom, a pediatrician, who became minister of the environment and minister of municipal affairs. He was defeated in the 1976 provincial election and later served for most of the nineties as Canada's Commissioner of Official Languages.

In Manitoba, with the election in June 1969 of thirty-three-year-old Ed Schreyer as the NDP premier of the province, Jewish politicians Saul Cherniack, Saul Miller, and Sidney Green became provincial cabinet ministers. Lawyer Sidney Spivak, a cabinet minister in the provincial Conservative administrations of Duff Roblin and Walter Weir in the sixties, became the provincial Tory leader in 1971; and Israel (Izzy) Asper, also a lawyer, was elected leader of the Manitoba Liberal Party in 1970, the first Jewish Manitoban to lead a party. The period from 1971 to 1975 was the only time—then or since—that two political parties in the province had Jewish leaders.

Further west, in B.C., being Jewish was not a problem in achieving power. In the provincial election held at the end of August 1972, Dave Barrett, the son of left-wing (and non-observant) Russian Jewish immigrant parents, who had first been elected to provincial assembly for the CCF in 1960, did the unthinkable: he defeated Premier W.A.C. Bennett of the Social Credit Party, who had ruled over B.C. since 1952. With his stunning victory, Barrett became the first Jewish premier in Canada—even if like Laskin he did not draw much, if any, attention to this achievement, and later only made passing reference to it in his memoirs.

In its story about the election, Vancouver's *Jewish Western Bulletin* did point out that in his younger days Barrett had been active in B'nai Brith, and as a social worker had been involved with the Jewish Family Service Agency. Still, the fact was that the local media and the powers that be were much more concerned that socialists had taken over their beloved province than a former Jewish social worker. "I think it's fair to say almost no one realized Dave Barrett was Jewish when he was elected in 1972," says Vancouver-based journalist Rod Mickleburgh, who co-authored a book about the Barrett government. "People only became aware of it when the *Vancouver Sun's* widely read columnist Jack Wasserman, also Jewish, pointed out that Barrett was the province's first Jewish premier." When Barrett passed away in early February 2018, as far as can be determined, there was no mention of his Jewish background in media articles and television stories about his life and career, apart from those by the *Canadian Jewish News*.

As popular as Jewish politicians became, Jew-haters did not suddenly disappear. The dilemma for the Jewish community—one that its members still grapple with to this day—was how to respond to this antisemitism. Was it better to ignore the right-wing extremists and cranks? Or was it essential to draw attention to their demonstrations and vandalism through public denouncements and protest marches?

This was similar to the wrenching internal Jewish debate caused by the rabid antisemitism of 1930s and the rise of Adrien Arcand, when the CJC's leaders had preferred to handle these sensitive matters quietly and diplomatically if possible, while some younger Jews refused to turn the other cheek. Three decades later, as the Congress lobbied federal and provincial governments to strengthen Canada's hate speech laws, Jewish university students—primarily in Toronto, the focal point of the antisemitism—took matters into their own hands, causing some turmoil. For them, with the memory of the Holocaust still fresh, being quiet and docile was not an option.

It was akin to a slap in the face for Canadian Jews—and Jews everywhere—when, in the early sixties, there was a rise in neo-Nazism. This movement of hate spread from Europe and South America to the United States and Canada—with, for example, the establishment of the American Nazi Party under the leadership of George Lincoln Rockwell, a Second World War navy veteran. Two of his disciples in Canada were high-school-aged David Stanley (who eventually recanted his Nazi ties) and William John Beattie, the twenty-three-year-old who founded the Canadian Nazi Party in 1965. Among their followers was Ernst Zündel, a German immigrant who arrived in Toronto in 1958 at the age of nineteen, and who would become one of the country's most notorious Nazi supporters and Holocaust deniers in the early 1980s.

In October 1964, the decision by the producers of the controversial CBC television newsmagazine show, *This Hour Has Seven Days*, to feature an interview with Rockwell—during which he declared that "it's a lie that six million were gassed"—set off a furor not only within the Jewish community but across the country. A few months later, in a follow-up to the Rockwell segment, Larry Zolf—a Jewish Winnipegger and *This Hour*'s most "acerbic and mischievous" journalist (as he was remembered when he passed away in 2011)—conducted an interview with young David Stanley (about a year before his public recantation) as he was distributing antisemitic leaflets in downtown Toronto. The Second World War, Stanley told Zolf, was "useless . . . the six million Jew thing . . . there was no gas chambers." Several people watching the encounter criticized Stanley, who sloughed it off. Most Toronto Jews were not impressed with the CBC's interest in Nazis, even if the interview with Stanley was conducted by someone Jewish.

In light of these and other unsettling developments, the CJC forged ahead somewhat more publicly, and was successful in having the federal justice department study and monitor hate propaganda. CJC officials had also supported Milton Klein, a Jewish Liberal MP from Montreal, who in early 1964 introduced a private member's bill on "respecting Genocide," which would have banned "not only Nazi-type hatred, but all hatred," and would have imposed severe penalties on anyone convicted of distributing hate literature. But the bill died when Lester Pearson, head of a minority government, called an election in 1965. Five years later, amendments to the Criminal Code (sections 318–320), Canada's first hate speech laws, did incorporate many aspects of Klein's proposed act.

As Beattie, Stanley, and their relatively small number of Nazi wannabes continued to distribute anti-Jewish propaganda in early 1965, which found its way into many Jewish mailboxes, a confrontation like that at Christie Pits in 1933 was inevitable. In the spring, news that Beattie planned to hold a rally on May 30 at Allan Gardens, a park just east of downtown, resulted in public censure by the Congress. But it also spurred on a newly created Jewish self-defence group known as "N3"—so named because of Isaac Newton's third law that "for every action, there is an equal and opposite reaction." The group's leader was Mike Berwald, a Hungarian Holocaust survivor who had come to Toronto in 1952 and was president of a local soccer club. Its members were young men who, as one of them put it, "were sick and tired" of the Jewish community "taking a beating." The Congress and N3, along with a few other independent Jewish groups, had spies inside Beattie's organization.

Toronto civic authorities were not happy when Beattie announced his Nazi rally at Allan Gardens, yet they refused to do much about it, despite complaints and pleas from Congress's Ontario members to cancel it. On the afternoon of May 30, a crowd of an estimated five thousand people gathered at the park. The number of anti-Nazi protestors, among them Holocaust survivors and members of N3 as well as other groups—some armed with clubs, sticks, and in the case of forty-two-year-old David Varna of North York, a starter's pistol—far outnumbered Beattie and his supporters. With the police trying in vain to keep the peace, a mini-riot broke out. Eight Jewish participants in the mayhem, none of whom were associated with N3, were arrested (Varna was one of them) and charged with causing a public disturbance; all but one were later acquitted. Beattie was arrested for unlawful assembly, yet also acquitted since he never actually held his rally. It later came to light that several of the people roughed up—members of a motorcycle gang—were bystanders, and were mistakenly assumed to be some of Beattie's thugs.

The next day, rabbis and other members of the community denounced the violence. In a *Globe and Mail* comment article, Rabbi Gunther Plaut pointed out, however, that the presence of Nazis in Toronto, as innocuous as they might have seemed, predictably produced "a high state of anxiety" among survivors who had lived through the Holocaust, and those who cared about their welfare. CJC officials were high and mighty about what had transpired and refused to accept any excuses for the so-called mob violence. For them, the actions of a few Jews repudiated their deliberate, if not always effective, diplomatic approach to dealing with prejudice and discrimination.

Not all that surprisingly, the Congress in turn was harshly criticized for its "precipitancy and dubious wisdom," in the words of the *Canadian Jewish Chronicle*—including by a Holocaust survivor organization for allegedly defending Nazis, a misinterpretation of the CJC's position—though this issue was understandably rife with emotion. Congress leaders, though stung by the negative comments, eventually responded by establishing a more inclusive Community Anti-Nazi Committee, and invited representatives from labour, women's groups, B'nai Brith Youth, and others to join and have their voices heard. Among those who participated was thirty-three-year-old lawyer Alan Borovoy—a "scrappy Jewish kid" who grew up in Hamilton and Toronto, as he described himself—who within three years was to become the counsel for the Canadian Civil Liberties Association, which marked the beginning of his impressive five-decade career as a human rights advocate.

The new Congress committee might have placated the diverse members of the Toronto Jewish community, but it certainly did not halt antisemitic outbursts and vandalism, or stop Holocaust deniers from perpetuating their acts of hate. And while most Jewish community members believed that constant and firm vigilance was required, a unanimous consensus on how to confront these bigots remained elusive.

22

Israel is Everybody's Business

I f there was a difference of opinion among Jews about confronting antisemites, in the spring of 1967 there was much more unity on the need to support Israel in every possible way—financially, emotionally, physically—as it faced its greatest threat since 1948. Fortified by the acquisition of Soviet arms, Egyptian president Gamal Abdel Nasser's rallying of his Arab allies to once and for all "wipe Israel off the map," as President Abdel-Rahman Aref of Iraq put it, alarmed Jews everywhere. American support of Israel in 1967 under President Lyndon B. Johnson was tentative. In the midst of the Cold War and the battle in Vietnam, LBJ feared that another Arab-Israeli war might lead to a confrontation with the Soviet Union, which backed the Arabs. In the weeks before the war broke out on June 5, Johnson did try to negotiate a diplomatic solution, especially after Egyptian president Gamal Nasser mobilized his forces and ordered United Nation Emergency Forces from Sinai, where peacekeepers had been stationed since 1956. This brazen act essentially shut the Straits of Tiran to Israeli shipping. Israeli Prime Minister Levi Eshkol did not want another conflict either. Yet during the next few weeks, the tension increased and negotiating a peaceful resolution became remote.

Israel was a nation of 2.7 million people living in a territory about the size of the state of New Jersey. At its narrowest, it was only fifteen kilometres across (that's less than the distance in Toronto from the corner of Yonge and Bloor to the corner of Yonge and Steeles). It had a standing army of approximately seventy-five thousand, with a thousand tanks and 175 jets. It faced an implacable enemy made up of three major Arab powers—Egypt, Syria, and Jordan—which had financial support and military assistance from another seven countries and a combined army of half a million men, nine hundred combat aircraft, and five thousand tanks.

What happened over the course of six days—from June 5 to 10, 1967—was akin to a story from the Bible. Israel staged one of the greatest military victories of all time, crushing its enemy and expanding its territory to the north, south, and west so it was three and half times its prewar size. This included taking the old city of Jerusalem, which Jordan had controlled and barred Jews from entering since 1948. The scenes televised around the world of Israeli soldiers praying by the Western (or Wailing) Wall of the ancient temple gave a tremendous sense of relief and pride to Jews in Canada and across the globe.

The weeks leading up to the brief but momentous conflict had been tense. At the end of May and for the first few days of June, as Nasser and other Arab leaders ramped up their threats and bravado, Jews in Canada had truly believed that another Holocaust was imminent. "The crisis had triggered something in Jewish minds and hearts," the Holy Blossom Temple's Rabbi Gunther Plaut wrote a few days after a ceasefire had been agreed to. "Jews did not know what would happen [on June 5]; they only knew their fears and their anxieties and their total involvement. I saw many tough men cry on that day." Similarly, Rabbi Wilfred Solomon at Vancouver's Beth Israel synagogue recalled in a 2001 interview that it was "as if we were being held by the throat . . . It was as if someone was about to throw the last Torah in the fire." Even Jews who did not necessarily consider themselves Zionists were caught up in the national Jewish anxiety.

Canadian Jewish support manifested itself in several ways. There were no mass marches of solidarity through the streets of Montreal, Toronto, or other cities; those organized public displays were not to happen for a few more years. Yet even before the fighting erupted, young and idealistic Jewish men and women travelled to Israel to volunteer in any way they could, despite the trepidation of their parents and families.

On May 30, 1967, at Vancouver Airport, surrounded by fifty family members and friends, four young Jewish adults between the ages of twenty and twenty-four left for New York, where they met up with hundreds of other volunteers and proceeded to Israel on an EL AL flight. Their expenses had been paid for by the Vancouver Jewish community. As they said their goodbyes, the large crowd spontaneously burst into a chant of "*Am Yisrael Chai*" ("the Nation of Israel Lives"). This same scene was played out countless times at Canadian airports over the next few weeks.

Among the four from Vancouver was John Maté, today an environmentalist and psychotherapist. Back then, he was twenty-one years old, the son of Hungarian Holocaust survivors who had come to Canada in 1956 in the aftermath of the failed Hungarian Revolution. (His older brother is the well-known physician, Gabor Maté, a recognized expert on drug addiction.) His parents had anglicized his name to John from Janos, a name he reverted to in 2001 after his mother died. As a young teenager in Vancouver, Maté felt like an outsider and was treated like one. He found what he calls a "haven" in the socialist Zionist group Habonim. The group's emphasis on self-realization, he has written, presented him and his friends "with a passionate, empowering, activist philosophy." Its ultimate purpose was *aliyah* or immigration to Israel. To this end, Maté had spent 1966 in Israel, studying and learning Hebrew in Jerusalem as well as working on Kibbutz Urim, located in the Negev or southern part of Israel, twenty-one kilometres from the then-Egyptian-controlled Gaza Strip.

When another war seemed likely, Maté did not hesitate to return, and headed directly to Urim. Everyone there, he recalls, "was anxious." Another Vancouver friend from Habonim (who had spent 1965–66 in Israel)—Peter Maidstone, then twenty—arrived at Urim from Vancouver a day or two before the war started. Janos, Peter, and the others were given "superficial" weapons training (as Maidstone recalls it), using old Czech rifles from the Second World War. The two boys were paired with Israeli university students who had not been placed in combat units, and each night patrolled the kibbutz's perimeter. Once the war broke out, and with Gaza so close, this guard duty became more dangerous. The Canadians were instructed to shoot anyone who approached who did not immediately provide the required password. That situation did not arise, yet it was "nerve-wracking," says Maidstone.

"I experienced a sense of unreality, as if I [were] in a movie," Maté has noted. But like the majority of young volunteers in 1967, he returned to

Canada after about a month. So, too, did Maidstone, who stopped in Montreal to meet his girlfriend and visit Expo 67. "That to me was a real shock, to come from a war and to come back to Canada celebrating its centennial," he says. "Other than [from] Jews, there wasn't much thought to what had happened in Israel."

Neither Maté nor Maidstone—nor most of the Canadian Jewish volunteers in the Six-Day War—considered remaining in Israel. Only one of the friends who was there with them, Harvey Chisick, later did make *aliyah*. During the war, Chisick worked at Kvutzat Yavne, a religious kibbutz, filling sandbags near trenches that had been dug as protection against bombing and strafing. But, as he adds, "they never were [needed]." He returned to Canada when the war ended, studied European history, and in time became a professor at the University of Haifa in Israel.

But Jews like Harvey Chisick were the exception rather than the rule. So content were a majority of Jews in the soon-to-be "multicultural" Canada, where tolerance was to become a national symbol, that making *aliyah*—especially after 1967, when the Palestine Liberation Organization (PLO) and other groups unleashed terrorist attacks on Israelis—became a much less attractive option. As historian Michael Brown has shown in a comparison of *aliyah* rates from the 1950s to the early 1980s between Canada, the United States, Britain, France, Australia and New Zealand, Argentina, and South Africa (and accounting for population differences), Canada consistently ranked near the bottom. From 1968 to 1978, for example, with the total Canadian Jewish population ranging from 270,000 to 286,000, only 552 Canadians (about 0.2 per cent) moved permanently to Israel. Not that the U.S. was much better: in this same ten-year period, the American Jewish population was approximately 5.55 million, and only 6,458 Americans made *aliyah*, an even smaller percentage (about 0.01 per cent). The greatest number of Jewish immigrants to Israel during this decade were from France—16,592 from a Jewish population of about 540,000. Antisemitism was also more blatant in France than in North America as were threats and acts of terrorism.

While Canadian Jews did not rush to live in Israel, they did, as they had always done, open up their wallets—and on the grandest scale to date. The possibility that Israel might be destroyed prompted an avalanche of financial donations that surprised even the most veteran of community fundraisers. The Bronfman family, still the wealthiest Jewish family in the country, usually contributed $2 million to Jewish charities; in 1967, the Bronfmans gave $6 million to Israel (the equivalent of about $43 million in 2018).

"Mr. Sam" made the Israeli cause his own. On June 4, he held a mini-summit of high-rollers at Montreal's Montefiore Club. As the story goes, one of the men in attendance handed him a cheque for $250,000. Bronfman scanned it, and tore it up. "Get serious," he said. He wanted more, and he got it. By the time the meeting was done, he had $13 million in hand. For the larger Canadian Jewish community, Bronfman and other CJC and Zionist leaders at first set their target at $10 million. National delegates at a special meeting in Montreal on June 4 insisted that they could raise more than double that—and they did, reaching $25.4 million, a remarkable amount of money for a community of less than 300,000 people, and more than triple what had been raised in 1956 during the Suez Crisis.

It was a step-up-to-the-plate moment for Jews from Halifax to Vancouver. In Toronto on June 5, two hundred fundraisers convened in a room at the Park Plaza Hotel on Avenue Road, and in ninety minutes they collected $2.1 million in donations. The head of this Emergency Committee for Israel's Survival (as it was dubbed) was former mayor Philip Givens. Meanwhile, to deal with what was billed as an "extraordinary emergency," Vancouver's United Israel Appeal raised $300,000 among the approximately eight thousand Jews in the city. Further east in Regina, a city with a Jewish population of only 750, the community brought in $40,000. Likewise, Hamilton's community of four thousand contributed $180,000 to the United Jewish Appeal (UJA), and Winnipeg's larger Jewish population topped a million dollars for the first time in their fundraising history. Jews who had not had much to do with synagogues or other community institutions for years dug deep—all to save Israel.

Bronfman and his top CJC officials, including Saul Hayes and Sol Kanee, travelled to Ottawa in an attempt to convince the Liberal government of Lester Pearson to back Israel at the United Nations. Though the prime minister and his secretary of external affairs, Mitchell Sharp, promised the group that they would indeed support Israel, this commitment, like Liberal government commitments of the past, was not absolute. With Israel maintaining control of the so-called occupied territories, by the time the next conflict—the Yom Kippur War of October 1973—ended, the Liberals, now under the leadership of Pierre Trudeau, would firmly cling to their traditional position of maintaining a "balanced" or neutral stand in the Middle East, lest any Arab nation be offended.

In 1967, the opposition Conservatives under John Diefenbaker were less wishy-washy when it came to Israel's survival—a party position that would be later echoed under Stephen Harper's leadership. Most Canadians, on the other hand, tended to view the conundrum of the Middle East the same as the Liberals did—or, according to polls conducted by Canadian Institute of Public Opinion in the late sixties and early seventies, their sympathies were with neither side. At the same time, in a December 1975 survey, 25.4 per cent of English Canadians and 20.5 of French respondents agreed with the statement that "Zionism is a form of racism."

In 1967, such contentious disagreements were for arguments yet to come, however. On June 7, Israel's retaking of Jerusalem, close to 1,900 years after the Romans had expelled Jews from the Old City, was a moment no Canadian Jew would ever forget. There were special synagogue services and the *shofar* (ram's horn) was blown, an event that traditionally only happens on Rosh Hashanah and the end of Yom Kippur. But this was not a normal event. "I have never seen anything like it at any synagogue anywhere," commented Rabbi Stuart Rosenberg of Toronto's large Conservative synagogue Beth Tzedec on June 9. "The reaction was visceral—there seemed to be an awareness that this had been the most historic week in modern Jewish history."

Following Israel's victory in 1967, the government of Levi Eshkol offered to return the Sinai Peninsula it had taken from Egypt and the Golan Heights to Syria, in exchange for signed peace treaties. Negotiations for the West Bank and the Gaza Strip were to be held at a later date. But Arab leaders rejected this; it took another decade before Egyptian president Anwar Sadat agreed to peace terms with Israeli prime minister Menachem Begin, a decision which led to Sadat's assassination in 1981 by one of his own army officers.

Events after 1967 and the controversial decision of Israeli governments to permit settlements on the occupied West Bank territory where Palestinians resided led to the demonization of Israel at the United Nations and elsewhere. Zionism was denounced as racism. Charges were made that Israel practised South African–style apartheid in its treatment of the Palestinians. (These charges are still being levelled at Israel today.) Active anti-Zionist movements at Canadian and American university campuses were established. And, more recently, the largely ineffective BDS movement—the "Boycott, Divestment, Sanctions movement [that] works to end international support for Israel's oppression of Palestinians," as the official website explains it—has been waged tirelessly by Israel's dedicated antagonists. For years, too, from the 1972 Munich Olympics massacre of Israeli athletes to suicide attacks on Israeli buses in the eighties and nineties, terrorism against Israel and its citizens has been fairly constant.

The dramatic demographic transformation in the Middle East altered forever Israel's status as a besieged underdog, and changed Canadian Jews' perception of Israel—though not their commitment to its survival. The Jewish state became the number-one focus for most Canadian Jews, more critical for many of them than religious precepts. "Today Israel is everybody's business," wrote Saul Hayes in a 1970 journal article. "Zionism as a creed is being replaced by Israelism as a practical program. It is not that everyone wants to get into the act; it is the act which gets into everyone . . . Large segments of the Jewish people are finding in Israel a real substitute for their former identification. It is a concept or belief." Together with the memory of the Holocaust, which for younger Jews in particular was a powerful unifying force, any perceived threats to Israel had to be confronted and quashed.

Many Canadian Jews felt compelled to assume the role of Israel's ardent defenders, against a barrage of condemnation that continues in the present day. Nothing angers many Jews more than harsh criticism of Israel, particularly if the disapproving comments are made by Jews themselves. During the seventies and eighties, the editors of the *Canadian Jewish News* grappled with the contentious debate about Israel, taking the position, as editor Ralph Hyman explained in June 1977, that "it would be erroneous to equate public opposition to Israel's policies with outright treason." But that's not how a lot of members of the community perceived it, and the paper's editorial board—Toronto *machers* one and all—attempted to clamp down on articles and columns that they felt were too censorious of Israel.

As sure as the sun rises and sets every day, clashes between Israelis and the Palestinians were (and still are) dissected and debated in the letters to the editor sections of major Canadian newspapers, offering condemnation and defence of each side. The letters were frequently passionate, dogmatic, and based on two diametrically opposed views of the history of the troubled Middle East region. Jews were naturally overly sensitive about the condemnation, especially when it came from Arab organizations. "Can one be committed to the survival of Israel and still concern himself with the abject plight of Palestinian refugees whose fortunes sank to new lows as Jewish nationalists drove them from their homes or at very least precipitated their exodus?" asked Evin Elkin in a letter to the *Winnipeg Free Press* of March 8, 1969. Neither side appreciated such a question, then or now.

Not all criticism of Israel was antisemitic, yet that was how it was largely interpreted. On this issue, emotion almost always trumped logic, but for good reason. As the late George Jonas explained in a 2012 *National Post* column, "Some critics of Israel are anti-Semites and some aren't, and no one can tell in advance which one is and which one isn't, although one can often make a shrewd guess." The dust in Sinai had barely settled in June 1967 when the verbal attacks began—and they have never really stopped.

One of the first Canadians to censure Israel publicly and to raise the ire of the CJC, B'nai Brith, and other Jews was Reverend Dr. Alfred C. Forrest, the resolute editor (and later publisher) of the Toronto-based *United Church Observer* from 1955 until his death in late 1978. After a visit to the Middle East in 1968, he determined that Israel was essentially the devil, mistreating Palestinians at every turn. He wrote stinging editorials and articles denouncing Zionism and Israel's "intolerable racist policies." In 1971, Forrest added fuel to the fire with his book, *The Unholy Land*, which excoriated Israel, describing it as "a racist and aggressive state." It took the election in 1972 of

Rev. Dr. Bruce McLeod as moderator of the United Church of Canada, who was somewhat less sympathetic to Forrest's position, for tensions to ease. An interfaith dialogue was started, with positive results—though harsh criticism of Israel did not dissipate.

If anything, the denunciation of Israel merely reinforced the stubborn commitment of Jews to champion it. This powerful attachment resonated for decades within Canadian Jewish communities, leading to substantial financial contributions to Jewish charities and Israel, particularly when the state was at war, as it was again beginning on Yom Kippur, October 6, 1973. The attack on Israel by Egypt and Syria on the Day of Atonement set off a three-week bloody conflict.

Most Canadian Jews found out about the start of the war while they were attending synagogue services, adding to the solemnity of the prayers. No matter what city they were in, or what branch of Judaism they adhered to, each person knew innately what was required of them. Once again, Canadian Jews offered money, emotional support, and young volunteers. George Cohon, the debonair head of McDonald's Canada and the national chair of the Israel Bonds (bonds in which the contributions are utilized by the State of Israel) annual campaign, travelled across the country and raised $50 million. Another $54 million was brought in by the UJA organizations. In a fairly unusual show of public support, at least for the time, huge rallies were held in Montreal, Toronto, and Winnipeg, and passionate chants of "*Am Yisrael Chai*" echoed in synagogues, community centres, and campuses from coast to coast. Immediately, Canadian airports were scenes of moving farewells, as young adults once more boarded unmarked EL AL planes for flights to Israel to help in any way they could.

The Canada-Israel Committee (CIC), a joint operation between the CJC, B'nai Brith, and the Canadian Zionist Federation (the former Zionist Organization of Canada which had changed its name in 1967), had been established in 1970. Disagreements about policy and the oversized egos of its officials initially hampered its work. In 1973, the CIC tried to sway the Liberal government of Pierre Trudeau to side with Israel against the Arab nations, which had attacked the Jewish state. This should have been a no-brainer—but not in

Ottawa, where nothing about Israel ever has been straightforward. Not wish-ing to upset Arab countries rich with oil, Trudeau opted to remain neutral, despite the fact that Canada did not import oil from the Middle East.

These and other setbacks did not lessen the national Jewish devotion to Israel. Indeed, it had the exact opposite effect: throughout the late sixties and seventies, there was an increase in Hebrew school enrolments and a growth of Jewish-Israeli–focused summer camps. In 1979, a survey of Quebec Jews indicated that 60 per cent of the heads of Jewish households had travelled to Israel on at least one occasion.

There was also the birth of pro-Israel groups at several Canadian universi-ties, to counter groups set up by anti-Zionists. But the politics of these Jewish campus organizations, caught up as they were in the rebelliousness of the "make love not war" era, did not always meet with approval from the established Jewish community, whose financial support they required. At Toronto's York University, for example, the Jewish left-wing group Progressive Students for Israel—using money it received from the community—put out its own news-paper, *Masada*. In early January 1970, in its very first issue, it published on the front page an article with the jaw-dropping title "Jewish Students Arise and Unite: Let's Kick the Shit Out of the Jewish Establishment!" The author was nineteen-year-old Gene Colman. He has been a lawyer in Toronto for many years, and today deeply regrets what he calls his "youthful indiscretion." His controversial article nonetheless summed up what many of the Jewish students were feeling at the time, a rejection of the "big, fat, influential Congress–Synagogue–B'nai Brith-type Jews." This sentiment caused a bit of a fuss, until the newspaper's young editors promised to be more circumspect in the future.

On a more positive note, there was also a whole host of Jewish-Israeli cultural endeavours in music, song, and dance, like Toronto's Nirkoda Israeli Dancers, Winnipeg's Chai Folk Ensemble, and Vancouver's Nirkoda Israeli Folk Dancers, which was started by Linda Rubin and operated out of the Jewish Community Centre. Later, in the early seventies, Karen Uretsky Hering organized the Or Chadash Israeli Folkdance Troupe in Vancouver, and when that group folded, the Shalom Dancers group was started, which eventually received financial support from the JCC.

Bolstered by the Trudeau government's support of multiculturalism—as good an excuse as any to come out of the closet and openly declare "I am a Jew and proud of it!"—it followed that when Jews in Winnipeg or Toronto wanted to participate in folk festivals, such as Folklorama in Winnipeg and the International Caravan festival in Toronto, the Jewish communities sponsored pavilions which highlighted Israel.

With the rise of Menachem Begin and the right-wing Likud party in Israel—followed by Israel's invasion of southern Lebanon to stop PLO terrorist attacks in 1982—Canadian Jews were again confronted by charges that Israel had become a militarily aggressive imperialist power. Just mentioning Israel at a dinner party with friends could generate an evening of bitter rancour. It troubled many Jews that the Trudeau Liberals (re-elected in the 1980 federal election) were quick to condemn Israel's incursion into Lebanon but had refused to denounce the Arab attack on Israel in 1973. The CIC was able to convince the government to delay official recognition of the PLO as the Palestinians' principal representative. An academic study of the media coverage of the conflict shows it mostly portrayed Israel as "the aggressor."

On August 3, 1982, a full-page ad ran in the *Globe and Mail* declaring in large block letters, "STOP THE GENOCIDE IN LEBANON." Sponsored by an Ottawa based group calling itself Canadians for Justice in the Middle East (today it is Canadians for Justice and Peace in the Middle East) it was signed by fifty people, a few of whom were (probably) Jewish. The group demanded justice, but not necessarily for Israel. Four days later, eight Jewish academics, led by professors Arnold Ages and Henry Weinberg of Toronto, repudiated the ad in a *Globe and Mail* comment article. "The advertisement," they wrote, "has all the signs of having been composed in accordance with a world-wide campaign orchestrated by centres of propaganda that are exploiting the tragedy in Lebanon for political gains unrelated to the present conflict." Predictably, they were criticized for their pro-Israel bias in subsequent letters to the newspaper's editor.

And so it went: the fiery debate which has never ended.

23

Marching for Refuseniks

T hroughout the Jewish Diaspora, the last two days of the holiday of Sukkot—technically separate but celebrated together—are Shemini Atzeret and Simchat Torah. It is customary for Jews to attend synagogue services on both days. Simchat Torah, the "rejoicing of the Torah," marks the end of the annual reading of the Scriptures that begins anew in the days that follow. During the festivities, there is singing and dancing, and children with flags emblazoned with the Star of David and apples stuck on the top of the flag's stick follow the adults who march with the Torahs through the synagogues. Before safety concerns intervened, burning candles were placed inside the apples. This tradition dates back centuries and is likely connected to the procession of the Jewish tribes with flags and torches during religious festivals in ancient times.

In the late sixties, another Simchat Torah tradition was born to protest the mistreatment of Jews in the Soviet Union. In Moscow in October 1965, on the eve of the holiday, a large crowd had assembled at the Central Synagogue to revel in their lost—even unknown—Jewish heritage, as they had never done before. Out in front of the synagogue, and in defiance of the Soviet authorities, they loudly sang the song "*David Melech Yisrael*" (David, the King of Israel) and chanted "*Am Yisrael Chai*," and danced through the night following the traditional procession of Torahs. On this night, the "Jews of Silence"—as Elie Wiesel, the writer and Holocaust survivor, depicted them in his 1966 book about the Soviet Jewish community—had found their voice. Two years later, twenty thousand Jews would sing and dance at the Moscow synagogue, and Jews in Canada, the United States and the rest of the Diaspora would pay attention.

So it was that on the evening of Saturday October 28, 1967, the day follow-ing Simchat Torah was celebrated that year (and after the Sabbath had ended), several thousand Toronto Jews gathered in Nathan Phillips Square, adjacent to City Hall, to condemn the Soviet Union government's persecu-tion of Jews and its refusal to permit them to immigrate to Israel and other countries including Canada. After that, this protest became an annual event for many years. In October 1969, an estimated three thousand people gath-ered. And the year after that, ten thousand converged on Nathan Phillips Square to protest once again in a public display of solidarity that would never have happened a decade earlier when community members were more reti-cent to draw attention to themselves and their causes. "We shall not rest until all the Jews everywhere are free to live as Jews," visiting Montreal law profes-sor (and future Liberal MP and cabinet minister) Irwin Cotler told the crowd.

Since the Russian Revolution in 1917, Jews had been subject to countless forms of state-sanctioned harassment. Zionism had long been anathema because it perpetuated a false sense of Jewish nationalism and the spirit of the "ghetto." Life for Jews had been bad under Vladimir Lenin and terrible under Joseph Stalin, when anyone labelled a Zionist was subject to arbi-trary arrest, secret trial, and imprisonment in a Siberian labour camp or worse. Even with Stalin's death in 1953 and the rise of his successor Nikita Khrushchev, who soon denounced Stalin's repression and purges, Jews still suffered. They were a second-class minority, with the label *Evrey* (Jew) stamped on their internal passports, and were branded as aliens, Zionists, cosmopolitans, and traitors. Synagogues were closed, Torahs were confis-cated, and circumcisions were banned, as was the baking of matzah on Passover. Israel was denounced in the Soviet press as an imperialistic aggressor and as "hell on earth."

The Jews were trapped in what Moshe Decter, the director of research of the American Jewish Congress, described in a 1961 article on Soviet anti-semitism in the journal *Foreign Affairs* as "an inextricable vice." For his part, Khrushchev denied that antisemitism existed in the Soviet Union, but still targeted Jews who were accused of committing "economic crimes" against the state—a Jewish bookkeeper was charged with "profiteering," and a fruit seller with "speculation in fruit."

Inspired by the speeches of Israeli prime minister David Ben-Gurion and Leon Uris's 1958 novel about the birth of Israel, *Exodus*, which had been smuggled into the country and translated into Russian, the Soviet Jews became more emboldened—as they so courageously demonstrated in October 1965 at the Simchat Torah celebrations at the Moscow synagogue. The Soviet government was not about to be dictated to by Jews, however. From the end of Stalin's rule to the Six-Day War of June 1967, only six thousand or so Jews had been granted the required permission to leave the country. Many more had been refused. They suffered the consequences of losing their jobs and hence being blacklisted as a *parazit* ("parasite"). Eventually some were permitted to leave—between 1967 and 1993, close to 640,000 went to Israel and another 280,000 immigrated to the United States—yet, especially before 1972, others were denied exit visas on the grounds that as a result of their employment they were privy to state secrets and therefore posed a "security risk." These "refuseniks," as they became known, were trapped, harassed by the KGB, desperate, and alone.

By 1965–66, CJC leaders were moved, like many Canadian Jews, by the repression of Jews by the Soviets—the Cold War enemy, the supplier of weapons to the Arabs, and the regime that had also repressed their grandparents and relatives. The CJC gradually organized a coherent campaign to lobby for Soviet Jews, though it would take until late 1972 before the Congress— together with B'nai Brith and the Canadian Zionist Federation—established the Canadian Committee for Soviet Jewry. The annual Simchat Torah rallies and soon-to-be frequent protests in front of the Soviet embassy in Ottawa added to the feeling that their messages on behalf of their Soviet brethren were making a dent in the Soviet armour. That was a fallacy, but by 1969–70, the new Trudeau administration was at least aware of what was going on.

The situation became more desperate in June 1970, when eleven refuseniks— ten men and one woman (twenty-six-year-old Sylva Zalmanson)—were arrested at Leningrad Airport with the half-baked plan to hijack a small plane and fly it to Sweden so that they could eventually reach Israel. They carried with them one small gun and a few truncheons. Yet they never got close to the plane. Of those apprehended, nine were Jewish. Following a show trial, two of the Jewish men were sentenced to death, while the others received prison and labour-camp terms of between five and twelve years.

When news of the harsh verdict reached the West, it generated a wave of anger and protest. On October 30, five thousand members of the Toronto Jewish community, accompanied by Ontario politicians and church leaders, marched in the city's downtown. In Ottawa, hundreds stood in the bitter cold outside the Soviet embassy. Similar marches of support were held in Montreal and Winnipeg. This time, the worldwide outcry had an effect: on December 31, the Soviet Supreme Court, noting that the alleged hijacking never took place, commuted the two death sentences to fifteen-year prison terms, and reduced the prison sentences of the other defendants.

A second and larger protest was held in Ottawa on January 3, 1971, with about six thousand people, many of whom had been bused in from Montreal and Toronto. As the police tried to maintain calm, a group of young men heaved a coffin onto the embassy grounds. It was plastered with such slogans as "Soviet Anti-Semitism Equals Murder." In Vancouver, the community dispatched one thousand aerogram letters—messages of support for the condemned men and woman. A week later, a few hundred demonstrators chanted outside Toronto's Massey Hall, where the Moscow Chamber Orchestra was performing.

Pierre Trudeau's foreign policy was primarily about chartering a separate course from the Cold War–obsessed United States. Though very much cognizant of the harshness of the Soviet regime—including its treatment of Jews— he also believed diplomacy and increased trade was preferable to bluster and war mongering. Prior to a trip to the Soviet Union in mid-May 1971, Trudeau nonetheless informed Saul Hayes that he was prepared to raise the issue of Soviet Jews, especially concerning reuniting family members in Canada. True to his word, he did this during his talks with Premier Alexei Kosygin, the Soviet Union's second-most important leader after Communist Party chairman Leonid Brezhnev, who had replaced Khrushchev in 1964. Kosygin was not happy about it, asserting that Soviet Jews were an internal government matter and insisting that Jewish emigration had increased.

Not satisfied, the community geared up for Kosygin's visit to Canada in mid-October. The Trudeau government hardly desired that their foreign visitor, whether he represented a dictatorial state or not, should be greeted with protests wherever he went—but that is precisely what occurred. Emotions naturally ran high. The Jewish establishment worried about the planned marches turning violent and about the unpredictable activities of the New York–based Jewish Defence League (JDL) led by the extremist Rabbi Meir Kahane, who had shown up in Montreal to rally his followers in Canada.

Even before Premier Kosygin's plane had landed, a group of fifty rabbis from nearly every city and town in Canada had already arrived in Ottawa for what must be the most unique protest in Canadian Jewish history. The next day, as the rabbis proceeded toward the Soviet embassy, they were stopped about a kilometre away by federal and provincial police who steered them into a nearby park. Undeterred, their leader Rabbi Gunther Plaut read a letter the rabbis had composed for Kosygin, demanding "religious and cultural freedom" for Soviet Jews. The following day, there was a much larger demonstration, as close to five thousand Jews from Ottawa, Montreal, Toronto, Hamilton, and Cornwall marched on the embassy. Again, due to the blockades and heavy police presence, they were forced to gather in the same park. And once more, Rabbi Plaut demanded action.

The two Ottawa protests set the tone for the rest of Kosygin's travels. When he visited Vancouver and Edmonton, he was greeted by peaceful Jewish crowds holding signs and chanting for justice for Soviet Jews. As part of a worldwide movement for Soviet Jews, the Canadian protests were effective. The Soviets allowed more and more Jews to leave, but not as many as wanted to: between 1970 and 1976, of the 284,827 first-time Jewish emigration applicants, 114,312—less than half—were granted permission. Twenty-eight-year-old Anatoly (now Natan) Sharansky, a gifted mathematics student, was not one of the lucky ones. He had tried to leave for Israel in 1974 with his wife Avital. She was permitted to depart, he was not. Three years later, he was arrested by the KGB, charged falsely with espionage, sentenced to thirteen years in prison, and was not freed until 1986 when he was part of a prisoner exchange with the United States. Throughout his ordeal, he endured physical and psychological tortures, but the Soviets could not break his remarkable spirit.

Among those in Canada who devoted themselves to freeing Sharansky was Wendy Eisen, a young wife and the mother of four daughters. She was born in Toronto and educated at McGill in Montreal, where she was then living. In 1974, she attended a meeting about Soviet Jews at the home of Andrea Cohen, a dedicated Jewish philanthropist. At the time, Andrea was married to clothing manufacturer David Cohen, the grandson of Lyon Cohen and first cousin of musician and poet Leonard Cohen. (In 1982, in what was a second marriage for both, she wed Seagram magnate Charles Bronfman. She died in January 2006 at the age of sixty, when she was accidentally struck by a car while crossing a street in New York City.) At that 1974 gathering, the Montreal women dedicated themselves to the cause of Soviet Jews. They called themselves "The 35s," after a similar group established in London, England, in June 1971, which had adopted the name because it was the age of the female Jewish refusenik they were fighting for. Eventually, there were also 35s in Ottawa, Toronto, and Winnipeg.

Eisen, who was eventually nominated chair of the Montreal 35s, did not want to be accused of not doing enough, as Jews had in the thirties and forties. Hence, for the next decade, she and her friends—who all had young children—fought on behalf of Sharansky and other refuseniks. The women participated in marches on the Soviet embassy in Ottawa, and stood for hours outside the Soviet consulate in Montreal, where on occasion they wrapped themselves in bloody bandages holding signs that read "Visas, not beatings." Eisen organized more meetings than she can remember, and made several visits to the Soviet Union. In September 1987, nineteen months after Sharansky was released, Eisen proudly introduced him at Massey Hall in Toronto, where he finally received the honorary law doctorate York University had bestowed upon him five years earlier in absentia.

The various aspects of these protests, events, and personality conflicts were covered by a handful of Canadian Jewish newspapers—some of which, like the *Chronicle* and the *Jewish Standard* in Toronto, had been operating for many years. By the early seventies, if Jews in Canada subscribed to a Jewish community newspaper, the odds were good that it was an English-language one rather than a Yiddish paper. Whereas in 1951, when 50 per cent of Canadian Jews had still identified Yiddish as their mother tongue, by 1971 it was a mere 16.6 per cent. That statistical change signalled the end of the line for the Yiddish press.

The matriarch of these newspapers, Montreal's *Keneder Adler*, went from a daily to a weekly in 1963, and then offered articles in English, French, and Hebrew in addition to Yiddish in the seventies. But this tinkering still did not improve the paper's bottom line. It finally had to shut down in 1988. Likewise, *Der Yiddisher Zhurnal* in Toronto gradually faded away in the late sixties and seventies, as did *Dos Yiddishe Vort* in Winnipeg, which folded in 1981. The Winnipeg paper lost more than $7,000 in 1972 and $3,500 in 1973.

While they were read more frequently, the English-language newspapers were struggling financially as well. Boosting circulation and attracting reliable advertisers was a difficult task, and not for the faint of heart. By the early sixties, even the once-durable *Canadian Jewish Chronicle* was in serious financial trouble. Its demise had started after A.M. Klein left the paper in 1954 due to health issues; he would die in 1972 having not written again. Even still, while Klein the poet was revered, Klein the journalist was criticized for sometimes being indifferent to his readers' tastes and views. By the early sixties, more than a decade after founder Harry Wolofsky had died and his two sons, Daniel and Max, took over the *Chronicle*, advertising revenues were in steep decline.

In 1963, the Wolofsky brothers sold the Montreal-based newspaper to a group of businessmen, yet it had only nine hundred subscribers in a city with a Jewish population of 100,000. The new owner, architect and developer Stanley Shankman and the editor he hired, Max Melamet, formerly an executive with the Zionist Organization of Canada, repackaged the *Chronicle* as a tabloid. They also bought out their main English-language, Toronto-based competitor, the *Canadian Jewish Review*, creating the *Canadian Jewish Chronicle Review* (CJCR). Though advertising revenue increased, as did circulation, the editors—like most other editors of Jewish newspapers throughout time—rubbed their readers the wrong way. In the CJCR's case, many subscribers objected to the editors' criticism of holding gambling fundraisers at synagogues.

Jews in Canada had long preferred that their community newspapers— which they mistakenly viewed (and still do) as the mouthpieces of Jewish communities, rather than as private businesses which operate independently—to toe the party line. Over the years, editors and writers who tried to practise critical journalism often found themselves under attack for holding contrary opinions to that of the establishment.

In a last gasp effort, the *Canadian Jewish Chronicle Review* was transformed once more in 1970 into a ten-issues-per-year magazine—now called simply the *Chronicle Review*—with Arnold Ages, then a professor of French literature at the University of Waterloo, as editor. Yet even with his talents, Ages was not able to stop the bleeding, especially with the rise of the *Canadian Jewish News* (CJN) in Toronto as the sole Jewish publication backed by the financial power of the city's United Jewish Welfare Fund, which was purchasing CJN subscriptions for its donors. The writing was on the wall: in the fall of 1974, in a consolidation move, the CJN purchased the *Chronicle Review*, announcing at first that it would continue to be published as an independent magazine. That experiment lasted only two years, and the venerable *Chronicle* ended its six decades of operation with a $65,000 deficit.

The original brain behind the *Canadian Jewish News*, somewhat ironically given its long-time reputation as the "establishment newspaper," was Meyer Nurenberger, an Orthodox and right-wing Zionist who was a friend and staunch supporter of Menachem Begin. Remembered at the time of his death in 2001 at the age of ninety as a "raconteur and an inspired conversationalist," Nurenberger was a bit of a ringer for David Ben-Gurion: a "short, burly, leonine-looking man," according to Toronto journalist Lewis Levendel. He had been born in Kraków, Poland, grew up in France, and started his career as a journalist writing for a Yiddish newspaper in Belgium. He left Europe for New York City seven months before the Second World War started. There, he was ordained as a rabbi and worked as a writer for the Yiddish daily, the *Morgen Journal* ("Jewish Morning Journal"). As a war correspondent, he covered the

Nuremberg trials of Nazi war criminals, and purposely sat close to the defendants' box wearing a kippah and holding a Yiddish newspaper high enough so it could be seen by all.

By 1957, heeding a suggestion from Begin, he accepted a job in Toronto as editor of *Der Yiddisher Zhurnal*, which had been bought by a group of Revisionist Zionists and Begin supporters. When the *Zhurnal* was sold in 1959, Nurenberger and his wife, Dorothy Cohn Nurenberger, came up with the idea for the English-language weekly *Canadian Jewish News*. The Nurenbergers obtained funding for the enterprise from a few investors, including John Bassett, part-owner of the *Toronto Telegram*. However, when the *Telegram* ran a few articles about the impending launch of the CJN, Meyer and Dorothy received antisemitic death threats and their garage door was vandalized. That negative experience actually increased the CJN's visibility and its subscribers. With Dorothy running the business side of things, and Meyer the editorials and some of the articles, the first edition of the CJN came out on January 1, 1960, with a declaration from a partisan editor that his paper would be "strictly non-partisan and will endeavour to become the spokesman of our Jewish community."

And for a brief time it was, but financial concerns compelled Nurenberger to sell the newspaper to two businessmen, Meyer Gasner and J. Irving Oelbaum. The sale, negotiated in 1962, included Nurenberger remaining as editor for a modest salary. Looking to enhance the paper's resources, Oelbaum quickly made a deal with representatives of Toronto's United Jewish Appeal, Welfare Fund, and Zionist Organization of Canada to purchase subscriptions for their donors—which amounted to a total of about $18,000—making it truly "the official spokesman for Organized Jewry," as the CJN now billed itself.

A disgruntled Nurenberger later referred to himself as a mere "bottle-washer." Unhappy with the new arrangement, he figured out a way to buy back the newspaper. He expanded its weekly circulation, though the paper still only had three thousand paid subscribers in a city with a Jewish population of about ninety thousand. Eschewing past editorial policy, he was soon boldly publishing editorials and columns that rubbed the establishment the wrong way (these included articles supporting the extremist Rabbi Meir Kahane and the JDL).

If an organization did something Nurenberger objected to, he was not shy about saying so. "In North America, the problem of a Jewish newspaper in the English language in any Jewish community is manifold," he wrote in an editorial of January 1967. "Primarily it must deal with an establishment not always attuned to the fact that a publication for a Jewish community can be effective only when independent of the organizations and the so-called organized community. Though not always right—for there is no absolute truth— nonetheless it must pursue the cause of community survival with dedication and loyalty, not to men or organizations but to the supreme ideal of the particular group it professes to serve."

After Dorothy died from cancer in 1970 at the age of fifty-three, Nurenberger sold the newspaper—he owed the bank $50,000—to a group of Toronto Jewish leaders that included Ray Wolfe, the fifty-three-year-old head of the Oshawa Group, Murray Koffler of Shoppers Drug Mart, and Albert Latner, a wealthy property developer and entrepreneur. This new partnership had made arrangements for the UJA to purchase sixteen thousand subscriptions for its donors at $3.50 per subscription, a total of $56,000 annually. Later, Toronto Israel Bonds, the Jewish National Fund, and the United Israel Appeal did the same, enhancing the CJN's account books but in the process turning it into a community organ. Because with all that money came expectations about the newspaper's content and coverage. (Interestingly, many donors to these organizations questioned whether subsidizing a newspaper was proper.)

Maurice Lucow, who became editor in 1980, insisted that the CJN had its own voice and that the UJA and other organizations were merely buying a service. But questions lingered. The problem for the CJN as well as other newspapers, like Winnipeg's *Jewish Post*, was that they were beholden to an elite group of wealthy patrons who philosophically believed in freedom of the press—except when it came to sensitive matters which concerned their particular Jewish organizations.

In Winnipeg, the *Jewish Post* and *Western Jewish News* battled for advertisers and readers for about six decades, and the fight only ended when the *Post* bought out the *News* in 1986 (becoming the *Jewish Post & News*). From its earliest days, the *Post* had seen itself as the official recorder of Manitoba Jewish life. At the same time, as a community paper dependent on the goodwill of local businesspeople and organizations, it had to be careful not to offend. The lifeblood of the paper for decades was the society pages—births, weddings, and teas—and the classifieds. They could make the *Post* seem like a glorified bulletin board, but its financial survival depended on them. "Getting your picture" in the *Post* (except in the weekly obituary section, that is) or the CJN was a big deal for many people—and it still is.

The bottom line, however, was that the financial realities of running a Jewish community paper were to remain a perpetual problem in the years ahead. Dwindling subscribers, decline of interest in the machinations of Jewish communal affairs, and the birth of online news were all to play a part in making life difficult for the publishers and editors of many Canadian ethnic newspapers.

24

Nationalistic Impulses

On November 15, 1976, the election of René Lévesque and the Parti Québécois (PQ) "brutally shocked" many members of Montreal's large Jewish community, according to Michael Yarosky, director general of the Jewish Community Research Institute in Montreal, despite the new government's promise to hold a referendum before any decision on sovereignty-association—the separation of Quebec from Canada—was made. "No other event in the recent history of the Jewish community of Quebec," Yarosky wrote in 1979, "has been able to generate such ongoing anxieties and tensions within this community."

The scions of the Canadian Jewish Congress advised community members to remain calm and not to panic. But Monroe Abbey, a former CJC president, was so paranoid that he admonished the *Canadian Jewish News* over a Passover supplement published after the PQ victory, which had two unrelated articles on the same page: one touted Quebec as a holiday destination, and the other depicted the story of Moses leading the Jews out of Ancient Egypt. The supposed implication was that a second Jewish exodus was about to occur in Quebec.

Charles Bronfman, the owner of the Montreal Expos baseball team—and who by 1976, following the death of his father Sam five years earlier, was running Seagram together with his older brother Edgar—had aggravated Congress officials. The day before the election, unaware that there was a journalist present, Bronfman delivered what he now considers an "ill-advised" speech in front of a well-heeled audience, in which he threatened to move his business empire out of the province if the PQ won. "I also accused the separatists of being anti-Semitic," he recalled in his memoirs. Within days of the PQ victory, he backed down, urging "all my friends in the business community of Canada [to] preserve and enhance our beloved country." His initial comments were definitely not appreciated, he says, and his sister Phyllis, who was sympathetic to the PQ, still fumes about his remarks to this day.

Despite the CJC's pleas for Montreal's Jewish community to take a wait-and-see approach, a second exodus—albeit not quite as large as the one reluctantly sanctioned by Egyptian Pharaoh Ramesses II—soon began. Understandably, the unstable political environment in Quebec made lots of people anxious, Jews and non-Jews alike. And like Moses in the Sinai desert, Montreal's pre-eminent law firm Stikeman Elliott led the way. In late 1976, the company relocated its head office to Toronto, where it already had a satellite office. It was followed by the Royal Bank of Canada, the Bank of Montreal in 1977, Sun Life Assurance Company of Canada a year after that, and several hundred other companies between 1977 and 1980. Many of the city's Anglos and Jews followed.

It was not by coincidence that, between 1971 and 1981, Metro Toronto's population surpassed Metro Montreal, making Metro Toronto the largest urban centre in Canada—with 2.99 million people in 1981, compared to 2.82 million in Montreal. Within twenty years that disparity was to widen further, with the GTA reaching a population of 4.68 million and Montreal rising to 3.42 million. By 1984, there were an estimated eighty thousand former Montrealers living in Greater Toronto, and many of them were Jewish.

So many Jews left that, in November 1978, the *New York Times* could report that Toronto had emerged as "Canada's major Jewish center." Of the fifty-five thousand Quebecers who left the province within two years of the 1976 election, approximately fifteen thousand were Jewish. A popular joke told at the time went as follows:

Question: How does a smart Montreal Jew talk to a dumb Montreal Jew?
Answer: Long distance.

This was funny because it was true. Rabbi Wilfred Shuchat of the Shaar Hashomayim synagogue attributed the merger in 1980 of two Reform

congregations—Temple Emanu-El and Beth Sholom—as a direct consequence of the post-election migration of young Montreal Jews from the suburbs. Toronto's Jewish population of 103,730 in 1971 had ranked second to
Montreal's 109,480. Within two years of the Quebec election, Toronto had
surpassed Montreal with a Jewish population of 125,000, and it was growing
fast. In later years, immigration of Jews from the former Soviet Union, South
Africa, and Israel—by 2011, Greater Toronto was home to an estimated thirty
thousand Israelis (more than half were Israelis who had been born in
Russia)—was to boost Toronto's Jewish population still higher. Before 1980,
however, most of the increase was due to Montreal Jews packing up their
belongings and trekking west along the Highway 401. "Your mood each day
depended on what you last heard on the news," one young Jewish lawyer from
Montreal who moved to Toronto told the New York Times. "It was clear that
my career future was limited because I wasn't a French-Canadian."

Lawyers Kenneth and Sharon Prehogan, who were starting out their
lives together, were among those who decided to depart Montreal. Ken,
who was twenty-five years old in 1976, initially did not want to leave. He
had grown up in the Montreal "Jewish" suburb of Saint-Laurent (north of
Côte Saint-Luc) where he attended Gardenview Elementary School, which
he estimates had a student population that was about 90 per cent Jewish.
"On the High Holidays the school stayed open, but there were only three
kids in my class who showed up," he says. His father had helped found the
Beth Ora synagogue, close to the family home. Ken was a die-hard Montreal
Canadiens and Expos fan. He truly wanted to stay in the city where his
parents remained. But his life changed on November 15, 1976. He and
Sharon reasoned that there would be an air of uncertainty hanging over
them, especially after they had children. "If you wanted to have more stabil-
ity, buy a house, and raise a family," he explains, "this idea of separatism in
Quebec was always going to be a destabilizing factor." By 1978, he and
Sharon had both found positions in Toronto law firms. They left Montreal,
and have lived in Toronto ever since.

Thus, among many (though certainly not all) Montreal Jews, an "attitude
of hopelessness set in," as Montrealer Joe Baumholz suggested. Indeed, a 1978

survey among Montreal Jews indicated that 80 per cent would leave the city if Quebec ever separated. This demographic shift was cause for concern. From 1971 to 1981, there was an 11.8 per cent decrease in Quebec's Jewish population, and it has not increased since then. Other than tiny communities in Sainte-Agathe, north of Montreal, and Quebec City, organized Jewish congregations have vanished outside of Greater Montreal. Meanwhile, as of 2013, the number of Jews in Toronto had reached approximately 200,000, while Montreal's had declined to about 90,000. Even with the failed referendum in 1980 that rejected pursing sovereignty-association, followed by the return of the Liberals to power in Quebec in late 1985, the threat of separatism still left many Jews uneasy—as did provincial legislation which further strengthened French as the primary language of work, business, and education. In all, an estimated thirty to forty thousand Jews are believed to have left Quebec since that fateful night in November 1976.

Those loyal Montrealers who refused to migrate to Toronto or Calgary or Vancouver tried to remain positive, as they had been ever since the Quiet Revolution had started. A decade before the PQ's electoral victory, Montreal journalist Peter Desbarats had written that there were two types of Jews in Quebec: "The optimists who teach their children French and the pessimists who teach them Hebrew." Teaching Jewish children to speak French became paramount.

When it came down to it, most of those who stayed merely did not want to abandon the lives, family members, and friends that they cherished in Montreal—or give up the bagels and smoked meat. Because no matter how hard bakery and deli owners in Toronto (and elsewhere) tried, they could not duplicate those delicacies—and still can't.

As support for separatism seemingly declined after the second failed Quebec referendum in 1995, Montreal Jews had even more reason to be optimistic. They could not however ignore the outburst by PQ premier Jacques Parizeau once it was announced that—as in 1980—the pro-sovereignty forces had lost again, even if this time it was by a whisker. What infuriated Parizeau, who was clearly frustrated as he stood before his loyal followers, was that while the overall vote was 50.58 to 49.42 per cent against pursuing sovereignty, 60 per cent of Francophones had in fact voted yes. Despondent, he lashed out at "money and ethnic votes" for costing nationalists their triumphant win.

There was no hiding Parizeau's meaning—that the province's Jews, Italians, and other ethnic groups had ruined the PQ's victory party. "Defeat is a test of character which Parizeau has failed this evening," Rabbi Reuben Poupko, the then-president of the Rabbinical Council of Montreal, commented on the night of the referendum. "It was a speech replete with racism and crass demagoguery." Nearly every other representative of the Jewish community, as well as leaders of Quebec's other ethnic groups, agreed with that assessment.

The truth was that Quebecois nationalists had always made Jews a bit nervous. "On the one hand, Jews understand, even sympathize with the aspirations for self-renewal on the part of French-Canadians," Ruth Wisse and Irwin Cotler had written in 1977. "At the same time, Jews fear the inevitable fallout of these nationalistic impulses and oppose their repressive dimensions."

Six years earlier, René Lévesque had tried but failed to soothe a Toronto Jewish audience he was addressing. "I know that eighty to ninety percent of the Jews of Quebec are nervous about the effects of separatism," he said. "I know that history shows that a rise of nationalism means Jews get it in the neck. But what can I do about it? I can't change your history. But I also know that anti-Semitism is not a significant French-Canadian characteristic."

Though Lévesque and the always entertaining Mordecai Richler had a begrudging mutual respect for each other, as well as a shared affinity for cigarettes and whisky, they came from different worlds. Lévesque made his life's work the elevation of French-Canadian nationalism and the separation of Quebec from the rest of Canada. Richler, despite living away from Montreal for many years, never shed the St. Urbain Street–Jewish persona of his most famous fictional characters, rife as he was with nervous energy. Moreover, he had a perpetual chip on his shoulder and he was not shy about publicizing his views, which many in the French intelligentsia found uncomfortable and aggravating.

For a while, during 1991 and 1992, no one in Montreal or elsewhere in the province seemed to be talking or writing about anything else except *L'affaire*

Richler. Day after day, the articles and commentary—pro and con, sympathetic and angry—flowed non-stop, hyper-analyzing Richler's sharp dissection of Quebec nationalism, French-language laws, and the history of Quebec's Jewish minority (laced with sarcasm, wit, and humour, as was his unique style).

Richler and the PQ had been sniping at each other for years, though from a respectful distance. Richler blamed Anglo Quebecers for the PQ's controversial Charter of the French Language passed in 1977, which had restricted access to English instruction in the province, because so many of them had refused to learn French (in 1974, the Quebec Liberal government of Robert Bourassa had made French the province's official language). Richler was nonetheless quick to portray most nationalists—if not all of them—as anti-semitic. "I am fearful that what we are really seeing is not the coming of justice," he wrote in late December 1977, in a *Globe and Mail* op-ed article about the new PQ government's language charter, "but rather one form of intolerance displacing another."

A decade later, in June 1988, Richler and other Montreal Jews were hardly shocked when a nasty public spat erupted between the growing Hasidic minority in Outremont—which then numbered about three thousand people in the suburb's total population of approximately twenty-four thousand—and the Outremont city council. The fight was over the council's rejection of a zoning bylaw that would have permitted the construction of a new synagogue, the ninth in the area. For many of the predominately French-Canadian inhabitants of Outremont, it was one thing to live among Jews who integrated into the larger community, but it was quite another to reside among an isolated sect for which assimilation was not an option and never would be.

The opposition to the synagogue was led by Gérard Pelletier, who had been defeated in a recent mayoral election (he is not to be confused with Gérard Pelletier, the Liberal MP and cabinet minister). He and his supporters feared that if the synagogue was built, then even more ultra-Orthodox Jews would come to Outremont. Insisting that he was not racist, Pelletier told a *Montreal Gazette* reporter that "we do not want a neighborhood of Outremont to become a ghetto." Despite an appeal by the Hasidic community, the city council held firm in its position against the synagogue.

The main French-language newspaper in Montreal, *La Presse*, then exacerbated the situation. A feature article published on September 13, 1988 (which happened to be the second day of Rosh Hashanah) about the conflict was entitled "*Outremont se découvre un 'probléme Juif*" or "Outremont discovers a 'Jewish problem,'" and portrayed the Hasidim as a "bizarre minority, with its men in 'pigtails,' all in black like bogeymen, its women and children dressed like onions." The *La Presse* article warned that the Hasidim liked to have lots of children, "and with their families of often 10 or more ... [they] will keep taking up more space."

Predictably, cjc officials were incensed by *La Presse's* tactless writing, and denounced the article—as did the B'nai Brith's League for Human Rights as "the most serious example of hostility against the Jewish community" in years. Letters poured in to the newspaper, many of which favoured the council's position, but there were also some—like the one from Claude Ryan, the former editor of *Le Devoir* who was then a Liberal member of the Quebec assembly and education minister—which supported the Hasidim.

La Presse issued a partial apology (that was coincidentally published on Yom Kippur) in which its editors denied any antisemitic intent and instead explained the tension in Outremont in the context of French versus English. The Hasidim, however, were not then, nor ever had been, your typical ethnic English group. Meanwhile, the Outremont council refused to reconsider the matter, and three years later the site for the proposed synagogue remained empty. In the years that followed, there were more inevitable clashes over the Hasidim's attempts to extend their minority rights in a way that impeded the rights of the French-Canadian majority (as it was perceived).

One positive sign in the Outremont neighbourhood occurred in November 2013 with the election of twenty-five-year-old Mindy Pollak, who "made history," as Janice Arnold of the *Canadian Jewish News* put it, when she won a seat on the Outremont borough council, becoming the first Hasidic woman elected to public office in Quebec. Pollak was supported in what was a rather unusual endeavour for an ultra-Orthodox Jewish woman by the Friends of Hutchison Street, a group that "promotes harmonious relations between Hasidim and other residents."

———

The treatment of the Hasidim in Outremont was fodder for Richler when in 1991 he was commissioned by *The New Yorker* magazine to write a feature article on Quebec's language laws. Those laws, especially the provision that all outdoor signs had to be in French, resulted in bureaucratic nationalistic pettiness. Francophone zealots reported alleged "violations" of outdoor commercial English sign postings to the Office de la Langue Francais, which then sent its inspectors to crack down on the offenders. The government forced Eaton's to drop the apostrophe on its signs, and went after greasy-spoon diners in predominately English-speaking communities who dared post their menus in English. In December 1988, the Supreme Court of Canada determined that the sections of the Charter of the French Language enforcing the sole use of French on outdoor commercial signs were unconstitutional under Canada's Charter of Rights and Freedoms. Soon after, Quebec's premier Robert Bourassa, head of a Liberal provincial government which supported the language laws, used the Charter of Rights' notwithstanding clause to override the ruling—thus allowing the sign law to be legally implemented—causing an uproar across the country. This controversial decision was taken in the midst of a heated debate about the (failed) Meech Lake Accord, which if passed would have constitutionally recognized Quebec as a "distinct society."

After several months of procrastination, Richler finally submitted his lengthy article, "Inside/Outside," which was published in the September 23, 1991 issue of the magazine. It was dynamite. In a piece of more than twenty thousand words—for which he was paid the *New Yorker*'s rate of two dollars a word—he catalogued, criticized, and lampooned the province's language regulations, as well as French Canada's complicated relationship with Jews. Much of the material on Quebec's French-Jewish history was taken from Esther Delisle's contentious doctoral dissertation for Laval University, which was later the basis of her just-as-contentious 1993 book, *The Traitor and the Jew*.

To say that the *New Yorker* article generated a furor is putting it mildly. In New York and throughout the United States, Richler had humiliated Quebec and its nationalist elite; it was unforgiveable. French and English journalists and academics pounced on his errors and manipulation of facts; his harsh condemnation of such nationalistic icons as the newspaper *Le Devoir* and the revered cleric and historian Lionel Groulx; his sweeping generalizations; and his failure to point out that antisemitism existed in the rest of Canada as well. He was dismissed as a Quebec-hater.

But Richler was not done yet. Less than a year later, he expanded the article into a short book, with the catchy title *Oh Canada! Oh Quebec!: Requiem for a Divided Country*, published by Alfred A. Knopf. The book set off another round of apoplectic media commentary, much of it nasty and negative. *Le Devoir*'s editor Lise Bissonnette condemned what she regarded as Richler's attacks against Quebec, though as the *Gazette* columnist William Johnson pointed out, it took some time for Bissonnette to acknowledge the anti-Jewish tone of *Le Devoir* in the thirties. In the House of Commons, independent Quebec MP Gilles Duceppe and Progressive Conservative Pierrette Venne—the following year both would be officially affiliated with the Bloc Québécois—denounced Richler as a purveyor of "hate propaganda." Venne rather hysterically demanded that the book be banned. That wasn't about to happen: *Oh Canada! Oh Quebec!* sold forty thousand copies in its first few weeks in bookstores, and was reprinted three times in the next six months.

Appearing on CBC's *The Journal* in March 1992, Richler stood his ground in an interview with Barbara Frum. Why, he asked, was he still identified as a "Jewish writer" when Michael Tremblay was not identified as a "Catholic writer" or Alice Munro called a "Protestant." That was an excellent point, and touched on something many Jews in Canada also had experienced. "Richler is a writer who happens to be Jewish," B'nai Brith officials said in a statement published in the *Montreal Gazette* and *La Presse*. "That imposes no special obligation on the Jewish community to evaluate every word, whether it be fact, fiction or opinion. We cannot recall American congressmen calling upon that country's Jewish organizations to comment on Saul Bellow, Philip Roth or Woody Allen." But other community leaders felt that Richler had needlessly antagonized French Canadians with his acerbic remarks.

The notion that Canadian Jews spoke with one voice always had been false, and particularly so by the 1990s—a reality Richler readily acknowledged. "The truth is," he wrote some months later, "I don't speak for the

Jewish community, but neither does the Canadian Jewish Congress ... There is no such thing as a monolithic Jewish community."

He was right, even if the CJC leaders did not quite see it that way. A growing disaffection with the Congress—from B'nai Brith, who had long advocated a more aggressive and public display of anger when it came to antisemitism; as well as from younger Jews, who regarded the organization as unrepresenta-tive and elitist—was brewing. This feud would ultimately result in a signifi-cant reorganization of Jewish community governance.

25

Confronting the Deniers and Israel-Haters

No matter how much the Quebec intelligentsia rebuffed the accusation that Quebecers had been, and continued to be, more anti-semitic than the rest of the country, surveys and opinion polls more or less confirmed the charge. A survey B'nai Brith conducted from 1983 to 1985, for instance, showed that an average of 22 per cent of Montreal residents felt that Jews had "too much power," compared to 16 per cent in Toronto and 5 per cent in Vancouver. A similar poll undertaken by Montreal sociologist Morton Weinfeld in the early 1990s indicated that 64 per cent of Francophones versus 37 per cent of Anglophones in Quebec believed that "Jews had too much power in business" in the province.

Other academic studies, however, suggested that although antisemitism did exist in Quebec—as it did throughout Canada—it was "quite modest," as a 1991 *Canadian Journal of Sociology* article concluded. It was a matter of perception. In yet another survey, conducted in 1987 by York University, it was found that nearly 40 per cent of all Canadians who responded believed that "most Jews are pushy" (84 per cent of Francophones agreed with this statement), and 28 per cent of Canadians (42 per cent of Francophones) thought that "Jews are more willing than others to use shady practices to get ahead."

Such negative attitudes about Jews—and Israel—have on occasion been taken to more extreme levels. In 2002, B'nai Brith Canada reported that there had been 459 antisemitic incidents in the country in 2002, a number which increased to 584 in 2003. About 30 per cent of those involved vandalism, and approximately 66 per cent were harassment—individuals were bothered or mugged on the way to and from synagogue. One of the worst acts of antisemitism occurred in April 2004, when Montreal's United Talmud Torah School's library was firebombed. The perpetrator was a nineteen-year-old supporter of the Palestinian extremist group Hamas.

Very different, though still revealing, was the overwhelming objection to Liberal Quebec premier Jean Charest's 2005 proposal to increase public funding to Jewish private schools. A tremendous outcry denounced the influence of "the Jewish lobby . . . rich, powerful and organized," as a columnist in *La Presse* put it. Charest caved into the pressure and cancelled the plan.

The two most infamous cases of antisemitism in Canada during the 1980s and 1990s were not, however, in Quebec. They occurred in Ontario and Alberta and revolved around the repugnant actions and attitudes of Ernst Zündel and Jim Keegstra. The two were classic Holocaust deniers, whose far-fetched antisemitic writings and teachings landed them in court. Both argued that their right to freedom of expression had been curtailed, and both were represented by Doug Christie, an outspoken lawyer from Victoria and "the perennial legal defender of Canadian antisemites," in the words of Manuel Prutschi, a former CJC executive.

With his outlandish antics, perennial hard hat, and right-wing supporters, Zündel—who would be deported from Canada in 2005 after a Federal Court judge ruled he was a risk to national security, and was incarcerated in Germany for a few years—was perceived to be the greater threat. Yet in many ways, it was the non-violent Keegstra, a "fringe right antisemite" (as opposed to Zündel, a "radical right Jew-hater"), who was more dangerous.

Keegstra was a high school teacher in the small town of Eckville, Alberta (west of Red Deer), and he certainly left a lasting impact on his brainwashed students. He taught them that Jews had perpetrated a variety of evil deeds throughout history—he insisted that Abraham Lincoln's assassin, John Wilkes Booth, was Jewish, and that a Jewish conspiracy had plotted the French Revolution, Vietnam War, and the Watergate scandal. Keegstra regularly described Jews as "treacherous," "subversive," "sadistic," "money-loving," "power hungry," and "child killers."

"If you wrote on the Jewish conspiracy . . . then you passed," one former student later recalled. "If you wrote against it, then your mark wasn't the best.

Everyone knew it." Worst of all, Keegstra convinced his many students that the Holocaust was a myth. Some students were troubled by the constant anti-semitic barrage. "Why should I go out into the world and hate a Jew?" a student interviewed by the CBC in 1991 asked. "I don't even know a Jew. I've never met a Jew but was supposed to hate Jews. That's what he teaches us in school."

The Zündel and Keegstra cases—as well as a third one involving Holocaust denier Malcolm Ross, a Moncton schoolteacher who in 1991 was transferred out of the classroom (though he did not teach the objectionable material directly to his students)—crystallized the importance of Holocaust educa-tion. There were already Holocaust remembrance committees, which orga-nized annual memorials—the Holocaust Memorial Day Act was passed by Parliament in November 2003—and an ambitious oral history project had started in 1976 with the aim of recording survivor testimonies in Montreal, Toronto, Winnipeg, and Ottawa. As the project expanded with financial sup-port from the CJC, video interviews of the survivors were also completed. In 1989, TVO, Ontario's educational network, broadcast *Voices of Survival*, a doc-umentary featuring seven of the survivors who had been interviewed.

Each major Jewish community also worked diligently to overcome the usual bickering that was a feature of most large community projects, in order to establish Holocaust memorial centres and museums. The idea for the Montreal Holocaust Memorial Centre was born in the early seventies, and the museum opened in 1979. One of its chief organizers was Steven Cummings, who—unlike the museum founders in other cities—was not a survivor. He was in his mid-twenties, and a member of one of Montreal's most prominent Jewish families. His grandfather Maxwell Cummings, a suc-cessful real estate broker and developer and wealthy philanthropist, had largely financed the construction of the city's Jewish federation building in 1973. Philanthropy was thus in Steven's bloodline. He was motivated to com-memorate the Holocaust following a visit to Yad Vashem, the Holocaust memorial in Jerusalem. Working with a group of dedicated survivors, he and his friends raised the more than $200,000 necessary to construct the centre in Montreal.

In Toronto, an impressive Holocaust remembrance and educational centre—now the recently renovated Sarah and Chaim Neuberger Holocaust Education Centre—was opened in 1985 with half a million dollars raised privately by survivor Gerda Steinitz-Freiberg and her team, along with public donations from the Ontario government and the government in West Germany. Around the same time, plans for the Vancouver Holocaust Education Centre (VHEC) were being discussed, the initiative of a group of survivors led by University of British Columbia professor of psychiatry Dr. Robert Krell, a child survivor who was only five years old when the Second World War ended. As an infant, he had been hidden by a non-Jewish family in Holland, and then, as he has put it, "returned to my parents who had also miraculously survived." Since its official opening in 1994, the VHEC has been recognized for its creative work, as a teaching museum that engages with twenty-five thousand students and educators each year.

When the new Asper Jewish Community Campus, as ambitious a project as the Jewish community of Winnipeg had ever undertaken, was opened in September 1997, a Holocaust Education Centre (HEC)—now the Freeman Family Holocaust Education Centre—was an integral part of it. The HEC's annual Holocaust Symposium at the University of Winnipeg attracts hundreds of mainly non-Jewish students, who listen to talks from local survivors. The HEC, in conjunction with the Jewish Heritage Centre of Western Canada (under which the HEC operates) oversaw the Asper Foundation's Human Rights and Holocaust Studies program. Since its inception in 1997, over fourteen thousand students and chaperones in 204 communities across Canada have participated in this initiative. (More than a thousand of these program students were First Nations, Métis, and Inuit.) The program culminates with a trip to the United States Holocaust Memorial Museum in Washington, D.C. It was this program that initially sparked the idea for the Canadian Museum for Human Rights, the most enduring accomplishment of the late media mogul Izzy Asper and his family's foundation.

The participation of the dwindling number of survivors (there were only ten thousand worldwide in 2016) in the March of the Living program has been integral to its success, even if it took a few years to involve them.

Launched in 1988, the march combines a week in Poland, in which students visit Holocaust sites, followed by a week in Israel. As of 2016, more than 220,000 participants from fifty-two countries had marched the three kilometres from Auschwitz to Birkenau on Holocaust Remembrance Day. By all accounts it is an emotional and life-affirming experience. It also links arguably the two most significant components of Jewish identity for young people: the Holocaust and Israel. "Most of the students are sincere, passionate and committed," says Eli Rubenstein, who organized the inaugural March in Canada in 1988–89 with financial help from United Israel Appeal (UIA) and the Jewish federations, and has overseen it ever since. "They have a very positive, very uplifting experience in terms of their Jewish identity . . . [but] it is a sobering experience in terms of their understanding of the Holocaust as well as human rights issues." In more recent years, Polish Christians have also participated, an excellent "bridge-building" exercise, as Rubenstein calls it. The presence of survivors on the trip adds to the poignancy, especially on the visits to the former death camps.

Survivors of the Holocaust are continuing their work—no matter how physically and mentally exhausting the exercise of baring their souls to a classroom of teenage students may be. Almost until the day he passed away in September 2008, Philip Weiss of Winnipeg continued to give presentations about his experiences during the war. He titled his 2007 book of memoirs and essays *Humanity in Doubt*. Yet he wrote that he had seen, even in the darkest of times, "unfathomable spiritual faith, courage, resiliency, sacrifice and inspiring acts of love." In 1993, when the movie *Schindler's List* was released, which depicted the horrors of the Plaszów concentration camp that Weiss had endured, he sponsored screenings for thousands of students. It took Philip Riteman of Halifax forty years to stand in front of a group of people and relate his wartime experience as a prisoner in Auschwitz. Once he started, he did not stop, and in 2010 he published his memoirs. Likewise, Max Eisen of Toronto—who was a teenager during the time he survived Auschwitz—published his memoirs, *By Chance Alone*, at the age of eighty-seven in 2016, after many years of speaking to student groups. The process of remembering so many details "was a nightmarish experience," he says, but as the lone survivor of his immediate and extended family, he felt he owed to them.

A second consequence of the Holocaust-denier trials was that it convinced the new Conservative government of Brian Mulroney, elected in a landslide in 1984, to establish an official inquiry headed by Quebec judge Jules Deschênes, in order to investigate how many war criminals were in Canada. It was long believed that more than two thousand Nazi war criminals—the actual number is disputed—fled to Canada after 1945. Many entered the country due to poor or inefficient immigration screening procedures; a small number were assisted by Western intelligence agencies which regarded some former Nazis as valuable in fighting the Soviets during the Cold War. Once in Canada, many assumed new identities. Others, like Imre Finta, who was later tried but acquitted for his role in rounding up Hungarian Jews for deportation to Auschwitz, lived openly in Canada.

Starting in 1949, the cjc had regularly sent names of suspected Nazis to justice officials in Ottawa—such as Antanas Kenstavicius, a Lithuanian police chief and ss collaborator who came to Canada in 1948 and settled in Hope, B.C. But nothing was done with this information. It took until 1997 for Canadian authorities to begin deportation proceedings against Kenstavicius, then ninety years old; and he died the day the hearings into his wartime activity began.

In the aftermath of the war and following the trials at Nuremberg, the British had quietly decided in 1948 that to continue pursuing ex-Nazis was counterproductive to establishing positive relations with West Germany. Successive Canadian federal governments adhered to that line of thinking. Jewish community leaders, however, had no knowledge of this directive and would not until it was referenced in the Deschênes report more than three decades later.

Into the sixties and seventies, the cjc was preoccupied with lobbying the federal government to support Israel and rescue Soviet Jews, and the issue of war criminals was not given priority. Even when presented with names of Nazis or Eastern European collaborators, Pierre Trudeau, for example, did not want to stir up bad feelings in ethnic communities whose votes he wanted. In 1982, the publication of Irving Abella and Harold Troper's book *None Is Too Many*—which for the first time fully documented the intransigence and antisemitism in Canada's immigration department and the federal Liberal government's refusal to permit German Jewish refugees into the country— spurred the Mulroney government on to action. No politician wanted to be accused of deliberately pursuing such a discriminatory policy ever again. The book—and phrase "None is too many"—became, as Abella observed thirty years later, "an ethical yardstick against which contemporaneous government policies are gauged."

In the early 1980s, the Liberals were still slow to move forward on war criminals, but five months after the Mulroney Conservatives came to power, they announced the Deschênes inquiry, much to the delight and surprise of the CJC. Following about two years of hearings, Justice Deschênes delivered his report in late 1986, which was partly released the following March. It was not particularly encouraging reading. The report detailed the wilful blindness of federal politicians, who ignored the fact that likely Nazi war criminals had lived comfortably in Canada and were continuing to do so. It later became known that Deschênes had identified 883 alleged war criminals. At least eighty-six had died in Canada, four could not be located, and there was insuf- ficient evidence about 154 of those listed. The report made non-Jewish Eastern European politicians and leaders nervous, given that Ukrainians, Lithuanians, Poles, and others were among the potential war criminals and Nazi collaborators noted. Disagreements about the report's findings set off a war of words between Jews and Ukrainians, who were most sensitive about these accusations.

In any case, it was all a little too late. Any alleged war criminals were old men: a twenty-five-year-old Nazi or collaborator who had murdered Jews or herded them into ghettos and cattle cars in 1942–44 was at least seventy years old in 1987. In an attempt to appease the various constituencies with a stake in this controversial issue, the Conservatives, who had been praised for taking the initiative when past governments would not, now refused to create a special investigation unit within the Department of Justice, similar

to the Office of Special Investigations in the United States—the sole function of which was to identify and prosecute war criminals. The result was
that from 1987 to 1992, only twenty cases were investigated and examined
by Canadian justice officials, and only four were proceeded with though
none resulted in a guilty verdict.

There was no disputing the antisemitism of the Ernest Zündels and Jim
Keegstras of the world, but what about the loud and dogmatic critics of Israel
and the country's alleged "occupation" of land taken in the Six-Day War of
June 1967?

In September 2002, Benjamin Netanyahu, who had been Prime Minister
of Israel from 1996 to 1999 (in November 2002, Israeli prime minister Ariel
Sharon appointed him the foreign minister, and he became prime minister
again following the 2009 Israeli election) had been invited to give a speech at
Montreal's Concordia University. Yet after a full-fledged riot broke out led by
students supporting a "Free Palestine," the speech was cancelled. Windows
were smashed, chairs were hurled, and the hundred police officers present
had difficulty containing the large angry crowd. In the ensuing melee,
Montreal Rabbi Howard Joseph and his wife Norma, a Concordia religion
professor, who were there to listen to the lecture, were physically assaulted.
(Four years later, Netanyahu still expressed disappointment at what had
transpired.) One of the rioters, outspoken activist Jaggi Singh, attempted to
justify the protest as the only recourse open to pro-Palestinian supporters
against "a former right-wing Israeli prime minister who has built a reputation
on keeping the Palestinians 'in their place.'"

Singh and his comrades did not regard themselves as antisemitic, but
merely as anti-Zionists, standing up for the oppressed Palestinians. Was he
being honest or disingenuous? Is it, in fact, possible to articulate a decidedly
anti-Zionist position and not be automatically dismissed as antisemitic? It's
a conundrum that has confounded Jews and non-Jews alike, produced hundreds of thousands of words of media commentary and debate, and invaded
campuses across the country (and the U.S.) with ill-conceived and mis-
named "Israeli Apartheid Weeks," held each March (scholar Ruth Wisse

has called this a form of "March Madness," though very different from the popular college national basketball championship tournament). More recently, the all-out fight from the anti-Israeli BDS movement, especially at universities, has left Jewish students feeling unsafe and caused bitter arguments among members of the Canadian Jewish community. In the spring of 2013, a mural of a Palestinian demonstrator holding a rock was displayed in the York University Student Centre. Immediately, it caused the usual back-and-forth sniping about its appropriateness and anti-Jewish/anti-Israeli depiction.

For the past fifty years, no subject has been more sensitive to Jews in Canada than Israel. At any gathering, big or small, the topic can generate the entire gamut of human emotions and reactions: anger, disbelief, obstinacy, narrow-mindedness, fervour, and devout commitment—and that's to name only a few. For many Canadian Jews, Zionism is their religion. As journalist and magazine editor Jonathan Kay has suggested: "It is not an exaggeration to say that Zionism is not just the dominant factor in Jews' political lives—but also in their spiritual lives." This was also the reason why so many Jews in Canada hailed Conservative prime minister Stephen Harper's total support of Israel on the world stage. Some critics in the media yelped about how tragic it was that Canada had lost its middle-power broker status—nurtured during the years when Lester Pearson was secretary of state for external affairs (1948-1957) and then prime minister (1963-1968)—which was more imagined than real in any event. But the country's Jews cheered and voted for a political leader who in their view understood what was moral and right.

This much is clear: it is possible to criticize, even condemn, Israel's treatment of the Palestinians and its construction of settlements in the West Bank—its political and military policies have been, and are currently, far from perfect—without being a Jew-hater. Yet demonizing Israel, questioning its legitimacy, and singling it out as a pariah state—as many of its detractors are apt to do—is another thing entirely. Back in 1981, the always-wise Arnold Ages explained the issue like this:

There is a point at which opposition to the Jewish state goes beyond simple political disapprobation and becomes identical to traditional antisemitism. In recent years, it has become fashionable for mischievous men to make their hostility towards Jews with the guise of anti-Zionism. Drawing a distinction between the "bad" Zionists and the "good" Jews, they make all criticism of Israel and Zionism legitimate. This sort of anti-Zionism is merely recycled antisemitism and a particularly subtle form of attack upon the integrity of the Jewish people.

There is, moreover, a blinkered single-minded narrowness about the anti-Zionist (or anti-Jewish, because for all intents and purposes they are one and the same, though passionate anti-Zionist or anti-Israel advocates would no doubt disagree) view of the world that permeates such events as Israeli Apartheid Week, which made its inaugural debut on the campus calendar at the University of Toronto in 2005. Proponents of Apartheid Week couch their lectures in academic pretensions, though this cannot disguise their deceptive approach, or the overtly biased aspect of their anti-Israel propaganda masquerading as legitimate and fair comment. As Barbara Kay pointed out in a *National Post* column in February 2016, the McGill University BDS Action Network, for example, is supported by an array of groups: the Black Students' Network of McGill, McGill Students for Feminism, the McGill Syrian Students' Association, the environmental activist group Divest McGill, and the Union for Gender Empowerment. The fact, she noted, that Israel leads the world in water conservation research or that it is the only country in the Middle East which treats gay people tolerantly should be relevant to these groups, but is not. She wondered, moreover, why the Syrian Students' Association did not publicly condemn the thousands of Syrians who had died in that country's civil war. "Welcome to the topsy-turvy world of Western progressivism," Kay added, "where hatred of Israel is so fierce it can derail activists from attending to the causes they allegedly represent."

The same anger has greeted perceived bias at the CBC of the tense Middle East situation. In 2002, after putting the CBC reporting under a microscope, the Canada-Israel Committee charged that the reports on Israel were "unbalanced" and that there was "an unwillingness to use the words 'terrorist' and 'terrorism' in regard to attacks on Israelis." Not surprisingly, CBC news executive Tony Burman rejected the accusation.

The CBC's Middle East correspondent from 1998 to 2003, Neil MacDonald, was the subject of much anger and scrutiny—in particular from HonestReporting Canada, the "independent grass-roots organization" established in 2000 to monitor "fairness and accuracy in Canadian media coverage of Israel and the Middle East." In one report, for example, MacDonald referred to "the ferocious appetite of Jewish settlers for Arab land," and in another, as HonestReporting's executive director in 2004 noted, "He asked rhetorically whether the terror group Hezbollah is 'a national liberation movement or, as Israel and its supporters maintain, a murderous global menace?'" Izzy Asper, whose media company Canwest Global had in a mammoth deal with Conrad Black and Hollinger Inc. purchased fourteen major newspapers, repeatedly accused MacDonald of using loaded language to portray Israel in as poor a light as possible. (The Aspers also caused a stir in newsrooms across the country with the accusation—which the family disputes—that directives from head office stipulated that editorials about Israel had to be pro-Israel.) Never one to back down from a fight, MacDonald defended himself as much as his critics attacked him. "All good reporters use some form of editorializing," he told the *Ryerson Review* in a 2005 interview. "There are people who tell you that you shouldn't judge other cultures— which I have no problem at all doing. That's what you're there for." More than a decade later, HonestReporting continues on regular basis to go after the CBC for example, and other media outlets for its perceived bias against Israel. This is part of the longest-running political debate in Jewish history: Israel's past, present and future.

26

The Hadassah Ladies Rise Up

B y the early to mid-2000s, women in most spheres of Canadian society had achieved professional success once not thought possible. Jewish women were now doctors, lawyers, journalists, accountants, teachers, nurses, business executives, and community leaders at the highest levels. In 2000, educator and community activist Myra Freeman was appointed the lieutenant governor of Nova Scotia, the first Jew and the first woman in any province to hold this office. Volunteerism among Jewish women remained high—in 2004, Hadassah-wizo had a membership of fifteen thousand women in thirty-four cities—yet women had come a long way since the days when Ida Siegel and Lillian Freiman had to fight to be recognized as legitimate leaders among the male *machers* who controlled the agenda of every Jewish community in the country.

This shift of influence and power had started in the late seventies, when women in Montreal, Toronto, and Winnipeg became for the first time high-ranking Jewish community officials. In Toronto, the determined and dedicated Rose Wolfe, a mentor to a generation of Jewish women, became the first woman chair of the cjc's Ontario region in 1978. That was merely one of many achievements in a lengthy and outstanding professional career. Born in 1916, her Romanian immigrant parents, Clara and Morris Senderowitz, operated a bakery in Kensington Market. Wolfe became a social worker and worked for the Jewish and Child Family Service for many years. During the thirties, she had attended the University of Toronto (as had her three sisters), and she was associated with the university for the rest of her life. She served on the university's governing council in the seventies, and in 1991 was appointed chancellor, the first Jew to hold that position. She enjoyed pointing out that during her six-year term, she "graduated" sixty thousand students at ninety convocations. In later years, she and her husband Ray—an entrepreneur who was one of the founders of Toronto's United Jewish Welfare Fund and the president of the *Canadian Jewish News*—established the Chancellor Rose and Ray Wolfe Chair in Holocaust Studies. When she died four months after her hundredth birthday, in late December 2017, she was hailed by U of T's former president, Robert Prichard, as a "powerful force for good."

Wolfe was followed as the CJC's Ontario chair by Mira Koschitzky. She was a "hidden child" during the Second World War, and came to Canada after being reunited with her parents in 1947 when she was twelve years old. She worked tirelessly for Zionist causes and also became the CJC's national chair in 1989.

In Montreal in 1983, Dorothy Heppner (she was given the nickname "Dodo" when she was two years old and it stuck) was elected president of the Allied Jewish Community Services (AJCS), which became the Federation CJA in 1997. A volunteer in the community for much of her adult life, Heppner—who is still a force of nature at the age of ninety-one—joined the board of the Herzl Health Centre (which later merged with the Jewish General Hospital) in 1960. "I have a vivid memory of the first Herzl board meeting I attended," she says with a laugh. "There was a levitation when I walked into the room. All the men rose out of their seats." Five years later, at her first meeting after she became the organization's first female president in 1965, an elder of the community tapped her on the shoulder. "Okay, little girl," she recalls him saying to her, "let's see what you can do." She was a thirty-eight-year-old woman at the time. She and her husband, Lyone (who passed away in November 2006 at the age of ninety) were active in the AJCS, and at one point during the seventies they were both officers of the board. However, before they were confirmed, there was a great debate over whether it was appropriate for a husband and wife to be concurrent officers. She did not aspire to become the president in 1983; it merely was offered and she accepted the appointment. Yet the fact that a woman had been elected the president of the AJCS was "talked about a lot," she remembers. At the first board meeting she chaired, she made her position clear in typical Dodo style: "I'm here to work. I know I'm the first woman, but that's the end of that discussion," she declared. And it was.

In Winnipeg, six years after the creation of the Winnipeg Jewish Community Council (WJCC)—which had followed lengthy negotiations between the Jewish Welfare Fund, the western region of the CJC, and the Winnipeg Congress Council that were only slightly less complicated than the peace talks in Paris after the First World War—Marjorie Blankstein was elected the WJCC's president in 1981. Following in the footsteps of her mother, Rose Rady (Sam Bronfman's sister), Blankstein was a volunteer from a young age. It was, she says, "ingrained" in her. A social worker, her elevation as head of the WJCC was a natural progression for a professional volunteer who had been involved on the WJCC executive for several years. She served as the president of the National Council of Jewish Women and secretary of the Canadian Jewish Congress, among many other organizations. She was honoured with the Order of Canada in 1982. She later served a second term as WJCC president in 1986–87 and was one of several key players in making the Asper Jewish Community Campus a reality in 1997.

But the most notable achievement of Jewish women during the eighties was possibly that of Dorothy Reitman from Montreal, who in 1986 at the age of fifty-three was elected the first female national president of the CJC. It had only taken sixty-seven years for a woman to break that barrier. Born Dorothy Salomon in 1932, she attended McGill University and in 1952 married Cyril Reitman, whose family had owned a women's clothing store on St. Lawrence Boulevard that expanded into one of the largest retailers in Canada.

An avid volunteer, Reitman was involved in assisting battered women and individuals with drug addictions. She was also the president of the National Council of Jewish Women from 1975 to 1977, and two decades later was named a member of the Order of Canada. She also had experience as a journal editor and talk show host. The National Council had conducted a survey of the involvement of women as volunteers among other Jewish organizations, and found that there were few at the highest levels. Reitman, as she recalls, became the "guinea pig" to challenge the CJC's male domination.

At the CJC's annual meeting in May 1986 she was challenged by lawyer Moshe Ronen, then twenty-seven years old, for the organization's presidency—and defeated him by a sizable majority vote. (Ronen later was the CJC's president from 1998 to 2001.) Reitman made it clear that she had no intention of "feminizing" the CJC, but stated that "when we talk about women and decision-making, we are talking about women being involved in making all important decisions—decisions that affect everybody." Nonetheless, several male members of the CJC board were unhappy with a female president. "Some of the men were nervous and there was 'attitude,'" she says. "I wasn't shocked, but more annoyed. Some of the men wanted to give me a hard time. They were anxious to derail me and plotted to upset me. They wanted desperately to make me cry. But I never did."

Reitman served a three-year term, and in that time dealt effectively with a myriad of issues. She lobbied the federal government to improve the deficiencies of its refugee policy, spoke out on behalf of Soviet Jews, and pushed and prodded the government to support Israel.

It was not until 1995 that Goldie Hershon, a community activist also from Montreal, became the second female CJC president in the organization's history (she would also be the last). Hershon, a teacher who had served as national vice chairman of the Congress, had to win what is recalled as a "bitter" contest with Thomas Hecht, a Holocaust survivor and the founder of a pharmaceutical products company. She was the "establishment" candidate, while he was an outspoken "outsider"—and supporter of Likud, the right-wing Israeli political party—who had suggested during the Israel–Lebanon War of 1982 that Jews in Canada "should keep their criticism of Israel to themselves." Hecht was accused of "buying votes" by paying the Congress membership fees of supporters so that they could cast their ballots for him. In the end, Hershon won by sixteen votes. The election procedures were later investigated by Justice Herbert Marx of the Quebec Superior Court, who recommended changes to the way delegates were registered, to avoid such conflict in the future.

That same year, social worker Sandra Brown, who was born and grew up in Saint John and had behind her decades of community service, became the first woman to head the Jewish Federation of Greater Toronto. She says that she did not "look at things gender-wise" and was not on the receiving end of any sexist comments. But she does admit that, in retrospect, becoming head of the federation and working on a variety of community projects, some of which involved contentious issues and difficult personalities, was "quite unusual at the time."

Since Brown's time, Jewish women have no longer been denied their rightful place in community boardrooms or in executive positions. As of early 2017, women were CEOs or executive directors of no less than seven of the twelve Jewish federations in Canada—in Atlantic Canada, Montreal, Ottawa, Hamilton, London, Winnipeg, and Edmonton. And that tally does not include one of the more influential Jewish women in the country, Linda Kislowicz, a former Montrealer who moved to Toronto in 2006 to become the president and CEO of Jewish Federations of Canada-UIA, which oversees the operations of the local federations and organizes national programs. By then, Kislowicz—who describes herself as a "Jewish communal lifer"—was fifty-four and had been active in community organizations for more than three decades. She had been the executive director of Montreal's YM-YWHA Jewish Community Centre for several years, and before that was the executive director of the city's Jewish Family Services.

In Toronto, Kislowicz took over from Maxyne Finkelstein, the first woman to head Jewish Federations of Canada-UIA (from 1999 to 2006). A decade on, Kislowicz says that while there is a "particular set of challenges" in being a woman and head of a large community institution, she has not experienced any male bias. She was, in fact, recruited to succeed Finkelstein, and thus for close to two decades the top executive at the Jewish Federations national office has been a woman.

Outside the community boardrooms, Jewish women continue to leave their mark across a broad spectrum of professional pursuits. Three among the numerous success stories are scholar and community leader Dr. Anne Golden; her sister, journalist Barbara Kay; and executive and philanthropist Gail Asper. Golden, born in 1941, is the eldest of the group; and Asper, born in 1960, the youngest. They have had different career paths and life experiences, yet share one thing in common: an overwhelming drive to achieve and to contribute to society in a meaningful way.

"Anne Golden can more or less simultaneously tell a long and funny ethnic joke, pour you a cup of tea, show off pictures of her grandchildren, and explain the sector-by-sector funding patterns of social services in the Greater Toronto Area," wrote the *Globe and Mail*'s Margaret Wente in a November 1996 column. "She blends in perfect harmony the soul of a warm Jewish *bubbe* and the brain of a seriously smart policy strategist." That's as accurate a description as there is of Golden, who is personable, witty, and clever. She was born in Toronto in May 1941, the eldest of three daughters of Theodore (Ted) and Florence Richmond. He was the son of poor Jewish immigrants and grew up in the Ward. A hard worker, he established a furniture-manufacturing business, and designed and produced an innovative vending machine, which was bought and distributed by a big American firm. Ted Richmond, who died in 1985 at the age of sixty-seven, was also a philanthropist and *macher* in the Toronto Jewish community, appropriately recognized in 1981 at the Jewish National Fund's annual Negev Dinner where he was honoured for outstanding contributions to Jewish life and concerns. Golden won the same award fourteen years later. Her mother, Florence, who was raised in Detroit, taught her about fighting racism and injustice.

Ted Richmond's business success enabled Golden and her sisters— Barbara Kay and Nancy Kumer—to grow up in Forest Hill, which in the forties and fifties was the most desirable Toronto neighbourhood for well-off Jews. Her family was thoroughly modern Jewish, as Barbara Kay recalls: "We kept kosher at home, but we ate non-kosher in restaurants. We sat down unfailingly to beautiful Sabbath dinners, but we drove cars and used electricity on the Sabbath. Synagogue attendance was mandatory on Jewish holidays, but not on Sabbath. We were welcome to engage in friendships with any girls we liked, but dating non-Jewish boys was strictly forbidden." Life events were important, and when Anne was twelve years old, she had one of the first bat mitzvahs at the downtown Goel Tzedec synagogue.

She obtained a Bachelor of Arts degree from the University of Toronto in 1963, but initially followed quite a traditional route for women of this era. In 1960, at the age of nineteen, she married her high school sweetheart Ron

Golden, who was studying to be a dentist. They would eventually have two daughters. After completing her undergraduate studies at the University of Toronto, Anne found herself in New York, where Ron had decided to special- ize as a periodontist. She enrolled in graduate school at Columbia University, and by 1964 had obtained a Master of Arts in American history. She then continued with a doctorate degree at the University of Toronto, with a dis- sertation about the U.S. press and the Cold War.

In 1972, two years after she had successfully defended her thesis, she was up for a tenure-track job in the University of Toronto's history department. Her competition for the position was two male candidates. By her account, she was the best of the three candidates, but did not get the position. She says she lost out more because she was a woman than a Jew. "The chair of the department said to me that they were going to hire [one of the men]," she recalls. "His words were, 'Your husband is a dentist and you don't need the job.'" The thing was, as she admits now, "His reasoning made sense to me at the time."

By this time, she was a mother and a part-time lecturer at the University of Toronto's Etobicoke campus and at York University. The same year she was turned down by the history department, she became involved in urban poli- tics. One night, she heard mayoral candidate and urban activist David Crombie, who was inspired by Jane Jacobs (and later won the election) speak, and was hooked. She offered to help his campaign and soon became his oper- ations coordinator. This led her into a career as a public policy analyst with the City of Toronto, and then several years as director of research with the Ontario Liberal Party.

In 1987, she changed the direction of her career by applying to become the president and CEO of United Way of Greater Toronto. As a Jewish woman, she concedes she was not the "predictable candidate" for an organization that was WASP in orientation. During her fourteen years with the United Way, she doubled campaign donations from approximately $35 million to $70 million in 2000. Then, in 2001, she made another unpredictable move by applying for the top position at the staid Conference Board of Canada, the think tank based in Ottawa. "It was another WASP organization," she says, "which had only ever hired a few Jews. All of the senior team was male and non-Jewish.

There was not a Jew on its board of directors. And yet, I was surprisingly chosen." She remained in that position until June 2012.

During her postings at the United Way and the Conference Board, she was also appointed to lead several high-profile task forces and received much media attention. In the spring of 1995, Ontario NDP premier Bob Rae—three months before his crushing defeat by Mike Harris and the Progressive Conservatives in the 1995 provincial election—established the Greater Toronto Area Task Force and put Golden in charge. Her assignment was to solve the eternal conundrum of how to reform the governance of the GTA. She and the four other commissioners spent months studying this complex issue and received more than three hundred submissions. She delivered her 270-page report to the Harris government in January 1996. Among other recommendations, the task force urged that the Metro Toronto government be dissolved and replaced by an appointed GTA regional council that would have responsibility for coordinating certain services in the current Metro area, and beyond into the outlying regions. Separate municipal governments like Toronto's city council would continue, with revised powers. The report also suggested revamping the property tax system to make it more equitable. But Harris ignored the report and went ahead with a full-scale amalgamation of the GTA. In 1998, the first mayor of the amalgamated city, Mel Lastman (who was also Jewish) appointed Golden to study the problem of homelessness.

Four years earlier, *Chatelaine* magazine had included Golden in its list of the fifty most influential women in Canada, one of only four Jewish women recognized for exceptional achievement (the others were entrepreneur Heather Reisman of Indigo Books; Chaviva Hošek, then the director of the Liberal Party of Canada's caucus research bureau; and Toronto fiction editor Ellen Seligman). After she left the Conference Board of Canada, Golden became a board member of Metrolinx, the public agency that oversees transportation issues in the Greater Toronto and Hamilton region, and in 2012 was appointed a distinguished visiting scholar and special advisor at Ryerson University.

Barbara Kay, born in November 1942, is eighteen months younger than Golden. Just as bright and insightful, Kay also possesses a sharp and witty sense of

humour like her older sister. Having reinvented herself as an editorial columnist for the *National Post* at the age of sixty, Kay is not shy, nor does she mince
her words, especially when it comes to issues close to her heart: Judaism, Israel,
and the future of Quebec, where she has lived for much of her adult life. She
even stood her ground in a fierce, though friendly, April 2016 debate at
Toronto's Holy Blossom Temple about Jews and Israel, when her opponent
was her eldest child, journalist Jonathan Kay, former editor of the *Walrus* magazine as well as the former comment editor of the *National Post*. She chided him
throughout the exchange for what she regarded as his flawed "progressive" view
of Israel, which in her opinion was anti-Zionism in disguise.

Growing up in the forties and fifties in Toronto, she acknowledges that
apart from the influence of her parents, two factors have made her what she
is today: "I am female and I am a Jew," she has written. She does not, however, subscribe to the usual view that being a Jewish woman in the post–
Second World War years has impeded her career or life. A good student
who enjoyed learning, she followed Anne to the University of Toronto in
1960—and hung out with other Jewish students at University College,
where they were welcome. She admits that obtaining a humanities degree
did not "divert me from my real vocation as a wife and mother." She received
a Woodrow Wilson Fellowship in 1963, which offered her the opportunity
to attend graduate school, and also met her future husband, Ronny Kay, a
nice Jewish boy from Montreal who had already obtained an engineering
degree and was heading to McGill for an MBA. In short order, the two were
married, and she followed Ronny to McGill and Montreal, where they have
remained ever since.

For several years, she taught part-time, reviewed books, and became active
in the Jewish Public Library (JPL). She figured out immediately that many
Montreal Jews were somewhat different from the Jews she had grown up
with in Toronto. "When I was invited to join the board of the [JPL] . . . I was
shocked at my first meeting when half the discussion was carried on in
Yiddish—with no translation," she later recalled. "I was the only person (and
only Torontonian) there who did not speak or at least fully understand
Yiddish, even though I was by no means the only person there in my thirties."

Her life changed in the late nineties, after Jonathan Kay left his career in law and transformed himself into a journalist and a member of the *National Post* editorial board. Like any Jewish mother, she regularly suggested articles and ideas the newspaper should address. One day, Jonathan told her that if she felt "so strongly" about certain issues, she should write about them. He offered to pass them on to the then comment editor, Natasha Hassan (now with the *Globe and Mail*). "The rest, as they say, is my history," she remembers. "I wrote an op-ed about Quebec. To my amazement it was published. It was a thrilling moment. I continued to send unsolicited op-eds in for the next three years. An encouraging proportion of them were published." In June 2003, Hassan offered her a weekly column.

Kay concedes that she has "always been something of a ham," and was eager to share her many opinions in a newspaper column. She has taken on a myriad of hot-button issues: the language laws of Quebec, the security of Israel, feminism, gay rights, the restrictive nature of Hasidic life, the obnoxiousness of Jewish haters of Israel—you name it, she has tackled it. "She bravely resists the turn of the moment, and the preoccupations of the politically correct," her fellow *Post* columnist Rex Murphy has pointed out. "Ms. Kay is not a provocateur. That is to say she does not harass or vex for the sake of vexation and harassment. Indeed, one notable feature of her writing is her tactfulness . . . She fights, but is not fanatic."

Nothing, however, matched the furor she confronted in early August 2006 after wrote what she thought was a fairly routine column about a pro-Lebanon/Hezbollah march in Montreal. With a few strokes of her laptop keys and a provocative headline she had no part in composing—"The rise of Quebecistan"—the so-called Barbara Kay controversy, as it is attributed on Wikipedia, was born. (Kay says she does not care how biased the Wikipedia entry is, and refuses to edit or correct it.)

In July 2006, Israel and Hezbollah had faced off once more after Hezbollah fired Iranian-supplied rockets into northern Israel and attacked one of its military patrols. Israel countered with a ground invasion into southern Lebanon that resulted in Hezbollah casualties as well as civilian deaths. The fighting lasted until the UN negotiated a ceasefire in mid-August. About a

week earlier, fifteen thousand Quebecers—mostly Lebanese-Canadians—
had marched through the streets of Montreal, ostensibly for "justice and
peace." Yet, as Kay argued in her column, the march was, in fact, "a virulently
anti-Israel rally." What really angered her was the participation in the demonstration of four Quebec politicians, who she says "should've known better":
Bloc Québécois leader Gilles Duceppe, Liberal MP Denis Coderre (who was
the mayor of Montreal from 2013 to 2017); André Boisclair, who was then the
leader of the Parti Québécois; and Amir Khadir, of the far-left and sovereign-
tist provincial party Québec Solidaire, which had been established in
February of that year (he was elected to the Quebec assembly in the provincial election of 2008). "All four politicians had signed a statement by the organizers the day before the march," Kay wrote, "in which Israel is lambasted for
its depredations in Lebanon, Gaza and the West Bank—but the word 'terrorism' is never mentioned, nor Hezbollah assigned any blame for the war."
The "kicker" was at the end of the column, when she suggested that if Quebec
were ever to become an independent state, the odds were good, "that
Hezbollah would be off the official terrorism list by Day two of the Republic
of Quebec's existence. By Day three, word would go out to the Islamosphere
that Quebec was the new 'Londonistan,' to cite the title of a riveting new
book by British journalist Melanie Phillips, chronicling the rise of militant
Islam in her country."

Kay submitted the column and did not think much about it. But as
L'affaire Richler had shown more than a decade earlier, nothing sets off
Quebec nationalists more than being accused of intolerance or antisemitism. She arrived home on the day the piece was published to find a media
throng waiting for her. Her inbox was soon filled with six hundred mostly
nasty, angry, and hateful emails about her allegedly insulting comments.
"Many of the emails were written in French," she says. "One suggested
'I know you can't read this because you can't read French.' But I can and
replied to that one in better French than was written to me." She was
denounced in letters to the editor and in the French-language Quebec
media; even Quebec premier Jean Charest weighed in, remarking that the
term "Quebecistan" was *une grossièreté* (very crude).

In a strongly worded rejoinder published a week later in the *National Post*, André Pratte, editor of *La Presse*, castigated Kay for falsely painting a "prejudiced view of Quebec ... by associating it with the devil." In his view—and Pratte identifies himself as a Quebec federalist—Kay entirely missed the fact that "Quebec is a vibrant, diverse, tolerant and deeply democratic society." French-Canadian columnist Brigitte Pellerin, who at the time wrote regularly for the *Ottawa Citizen*, offered a more nuanced view, suggesting Quebecers were being disingenuous on the subject of Israel and Jews; while *La Presse* columnist Yves Boisvert, in an article published in English in the *Toronto Star*, censured Kay for her "helium-inflated accusations [of] hate propaganda ... [and] lies on the subject of Quebec."

Kay was not bothered by the journalistic criticism; it all comes with being an opinion writer in a national newspaper. But she was troubled when the Société Saint-Jean-Baptiste (ssjb) filed a complaint with the Quebec Press Council against her, declaring that she had "defamed all Quebecers." The ssjb's leaders drew attention to the fact that, way back in the 1830s, the Lower Canadian assembly had passed legislation emancipating Jews. "There has unfortunately been anti-Semitism in Quebec at various times, as throughout the rest of the western world," the ssjb's complaint conceded, but they maintained that Kay had failed "in her journalistic duties" for not adding that "the intellectual nationalist elites of Quebec have often been at the forefront of the struggle for freedom and equality of the Jews."

The Press Council's mandate is to monitor the media in the province. But it is a watchdog, nothing more, and its rulings are not legally binding—a fact that Kay's editor, her son, pointed out to his initially distraught mother after she received a subpoena-like document from the council in the mail. Somewhat predictably, after six months of deliberation the council upheld the complaint against Kay for portraying "francophone Quebecers, especially sovereigntists, as soft on terrorism and anti-Semitic." The council ruled that Kay's column (as well as a follow-up on August 17 entitled "Quebecers in denial") lacked "balance, rigour, level-headedness, and ... respect for certain social groups."

Reflecting on the entire affair, Kay wrote that she felt as if she had become a character in a Franz Kafka novel, yet stood by what she had written. "Judging

from their see-no-evil behaviour before and during a 'peace' march fairly
humming with anti-Semitism, I predicted a soft-on-Islamism political culture in a putatively independent Quebec," she noted. "Edgy, but business as
usual in the lively comment section of my newspaper." She also added that
while the council had criticized her for "altering" the facts, they did not offer
any hard evidence on which facts she had allegedly altered. A decade after this
classic Quebec hullabaloo, she continues to write about the important issues
that matter to her with award-winning and always readable columns, while
also being the best grandmother she can be.

Every year, the *Winnipeg Free Press* compile a list of the thirty most powerful
Manitobans. Not all that surprisingly, there are always a lot of Jewish names,
and some are usually among the top ten. The list in 2007 was especially
remarkable: the second-most powerful person in the province was deemed to
be a Jewish woman, Gail Asper, the head of the Asper Foundation who spent
more than a decade deflecting political, bureaucratic, and media naysayers in
making the Canadian Museum for Human Rights (CMHR)—which opened
in 2014—a reality. Spirited and independent, she is at heart persistent.
"Everything is doable," her father, the media-empire builder Izzy Asper once
said. "If you are tenacious enough, you can do whatever you set out to do.
Because all you need is more determination than the guys who are trying to
stop you." That, in a nutshell, is Gail's raison d'être.

Asper, who was born in Winnipeg in 1960, had been preparing for the CMHR
project her whole life. She followed her father's footsteps and became a lawyer,
obtaining her BA and LLB from the University of Manitoba in 1981 and 1984
respectively. From her mother, Ruth—or "Babs," as she was known—she inherited her genuine kindness and love of the arts. After receiving her call to the
Nova Scotia bar in 1985—she was living in the province at the time with her
husband Michael Paterson—Asper practised corporate and commercial law in
Halifax, before joining Canwest Global Communications in 1989 as corporate
secretary and legal counsel. She was a member of Canwest's board of directors
from 1991 to 2010, and from 1998 to 2008 was a member of the board of Great-
West Lifeco and its subsidiaries. She serves and has served on the boards of

numerous not-for-profit groups, and has avidly supported the arts in Manitoba and Canada for many years. In 2005, she was recipient of the Ramon John Hnatyshyn Award for Voluntarism in the Performing Arts. Two years later, she was awarded the Order of Manitoba, and a year after that she was made an Officer of the Order of Canada. In 2014, she received an honorary doctorate from the Hebrew University in Jerusalem, one of many Jewish institutions she has championed.

By the time Izzy Asper died on October 7, 2003 at the age of seventy-one, the master plan for the CMHR and proposed government funding was more or less in place. Raising the required $60 million in private donations—an amount that was to triple during the next decade—had been next on the media mogul's list of things to do. Impatient to the end, if you had told him in the fall of 2003 that it was to take another eleven years before the museum was opened, he would have been appalled.

The CMHR could have died the day Izzy Asper did, but his family, colleagues, and friends refused to let that happen. Despite their enormous grief at his loss, Babs, Gail, and her two brothers David and Leonard—along with Moe Levy, the executive director of the Asper Foundation, and the foundation's lawyer Richard Leipsic—vowed on the day of his funeral that the museum project would be completed. It was a near-impossible task, requiring intense dedication and effort—especially from Gail and Moe Levy—that bordered on crazy. Every possible roadblock was put in their way, not the least of which were the Ottawa bureaucrats who were dead set against establishing a national museum outside of the capital, and a variety of political leaders who were lukewarm about the project.

In the end, Gail and her family and Levy's absolute refusal to surrender—along with the generosity of private and corporate donors and, most significantly (as of the 2006 federal election), the full support of Conservative prime minister Stephen Harper—enabled the CMHR, with a final price of $351 million, to rise at the historic junction of the Red and Assiniboine rivers in downtown Winnipeg. At the gala held at the museum in mid-September 2014 to celebrate its completion, Gail Asper said that it "pained" her that her parents had not lived to see this day (Babs Asper died in 2011). Yet, saluting the glitzy crowd, she added that she "was privileged with the adventure of a lifetime." As a *Winnipeg Free Press* editorial put it the next day, "Izzy may have been the brilliant visionary, while [Gail] Asper was the delightful pitbull who wouldn't take No for an answer."

In June 2015, the Jewish Federation of Winnipeg was left without a CEO when Adam Bronstone, who had been appointed earlier that year, abruptly resigned. Elaine Goldstine, who had first volunteered and then worked for the Winnipeg federation for more than two decades—and who had also been a candidate for the top job when Bronstone was selected—was asked to fill in as interim CEO. Born and raised in Winnipeg, Goldstine had worked for the University of Manitoba and served as the president of the National Council of Jewish Women before joining the federation. Within six months, she was appointed the permanent CEO. The fact that she is a woman was not the reason the federation's board chose Bronstone over her in 2014, nor was it a factor in selecting her to replace Bronstone after he left. She was simply the best person for the job. For a Jewish community run by men for close to 140 years, that is indeed progress.

27

Checks and Balances

B y the 1990s, operating the fairly extensive infrastructure of Jewish communities—synagogues, schools, sports facilities, summer camps, and services for children and the elderly—required a full-time bureaucracy, thousands of volunteer fundraisers, and lots and lots of generous donors. At the top of this Jewish pyramid is (as noted) the national Jewish Federations of Canada-UIA (JFC-UIA), as it is known today, the result of the 1998 union of Jewish Federations Canada (established in 1967) and the United Israel Appeal. The merger took place with the chief objective of working collaboratively with local welfare funds, councils, and federations in every major city, as well as in smaller communities. Over the years, the federations provided the money, and such organizations as the Canadian Jewish Congress and the Canadian Zionist Federation fought antisemitism, promoted human rights and social justice, and advocated on behalf of Jews everywhere (along with an independent B'nai Brith). In Montreal, Toronto, Winnipeg, Ottawa, Vancouver, and other locales, the same individuals who were usually involved in the federations were also the leaders of the CJC, B'nai Brith, and the Zionist groups. But at some point in the late seventies and early eighties, that began to change. The fear of rising anti-Zionism on campuses, and concern over Israel's survival in general, led in the early 2000s to a dramatic restructuring of the national Jewish communal governance—as controversial a development as there had been in the entire Jewish history of Canada.

When Sam Bronfman was in charge of the CJC, he called the shots with the help of Saul Hayes, Sol Kanee, and others. The organization had representation from across the country, and Bronfman never interfered in the human rights agenda of the Congress's Joint Public Relations Committee. Still, the CJC was not a democratic organization in the true sense of the term; a small elite controlled its agenda, while the federations oversaw its budget.

In those days, money was not an issue for the Congress, and nor did Bronfman have to worry about what the community welfare funds provided, because if there were shortfalls Mr. Sam personally added to the CJC's coffers to make up any difference required. Arguments were kept to a minimum— at least for a Jewish organization. But when the Bronfman era ended in the sixties and funds continued to flow to the Congress questions were raised. Why did the CJC automatically speak to the media on behalf of Canadian Jews and direct key policy decisions, when it was the federations that had the funds that subsidized the CJC's operations?

As early as 1972, Toronto's Rabbi Stuart Rosenberg had wondered in the survey of Jewish Canada he prepared for the *American Jewish Year Book*: "Could Congress still retain its role in a larger, better educated, more ideo-logically diverse, and thus more complex Jewish community? Indeed, in an age of so-called participatory democracy, could, or should, any single group purport to speak for 'all' Jews? Even in Canada?"

Congress officials acknowledged that the old generation's "lingering adhe-sion of ghetto life" had been "shed" and "replaced by a new, vigorous, and healthy diaspora Jewish posture and meaning," as they observed in a bulletin of October 1970. They understood, too, at least intellectually, that young people were becoming increasingly "apathetic" about community institutions. But in the years that followed, little changed—though the CJC did finally relocate its head office from Montreal to Ottawa in 1999—and the grumbling about the dictatorial power structure and the Congress's greater concern for human rights than for Israel grew louder.

The impetus for radical change was the anti-Israel protests at Canadian campuses between 2000 and 2002, culminating with the "shocking and appalling" (in the words of Maxyne Finkelstein, then the executive vice pres-ident of JFC-UIA) melee that erupted when Benjamin Netanyahu was invited to speak at Concordia University in September 2002. Many of the wealthiest donors to the federations' finances, steadfast Zionists one and all—like the husband and wife duo of Gerald Schwartz, the head of Onex Corporation, and Indigo CEO Heather Reisman—decided after some reflection that the Congress, the organization that their money funded, was not doing enough to advocate for Israel. In their view, the CJC was not adequately responding to the very real anti-Zionist/antisemitic threat, and nor were its leaders addressing in a public way the soft support of Israel offered by the federal Liberal government of Jean Chrétien—ironically a government many of them had supported. They were determined to shake things up; and shake things up they did. A more effective advocacy agenda was required.

Schwartz and Reisman helped convene a private "Israel emergency cabinet," as it was dubbed. Its members were a who's who of Jewish corporate power in Canada. Apart from Schwartz and Reisman, the elite group included heavyweights Larry Tanenbaum, chairman of Maple Leaf Sports and Entertainment; real estate tycoon Steven Cummings of Montreal; media mogul Izzy Asper of Canwest Global Communications, who was to pass away soon after the cabinet's first meeting in October 2003; Stephen Reitman, executive vice president of Reitmans Canada; Senator Leo Kolber of Montreal, who was linked to the Bronfman family; Toronto financier Brent Belzberg; and philanthropist Julia Koschitzky, also of Toronto, who had been a Jewish Federations Canada leader for many years.

They spoke with a number of individuals, including policy consultant Hershell Ezrin, the chairman and CEO of GPC International (which in 2006 merged with FleishmanHillard). Ezrin had served as former Liberal premier of Ontario David Peterson's principal secretary. To confirm what they already knew or suspected about anti-Israel attitudes, a comprehensive poll was carried out, financed by funds mainly supplied by Schwartz. Once the poll revealed the negative sentiments about Israel among many Canadians, further meetings and discussions of the emergency cabinet followed, and a new lobby group was born: the Canadian Council for Israel and Jewish Advocacy or CIJA 1.0 (as it is now referred to in order to differentiate it from the current CIJA 2.0).

This first version of CIJA was created with little—if any—consultation with CJC leaders or staff. Thus the idea has persisted that this elite group of wealthy community members surreptitiously hijacked the Canadian Jewish agenda. "It's a convenient myth," argues Shimon Fogel, the former CEO of the Canada-Israel Committee and current CEO of CIJA 2.0. "What this small group of philanthropists did was to say that they were prepared to double the amount of resources that go toward advocacy, if we [made some changes] and got it right. We needed to re-examine the organizational structure." But, he insists, "they didn't dictate what was going to be; they did not presume to play that role and did not want to take that leadership position. They were simply saying that they understood that the advocacy enterprise was undersourced and they were prepared to take the lead providing the additional resources to do the job. Yet at the same time, they needed to have a degree of confidence that we were going to look at CIJA's [operational] structure and tweak it."

By the end of 2003, CIJA 1.0—re-examined and fine-tuned—was transformed, says Fogel, into an "umbrella" group to function as "the conductor and facilitator" atop the Jewish community pyramid. Under this initial restructuring, the CJC and the CIC were maintained as separate entities. Yet, as of December 2004, both organizations became subservient to CIJA's financial and political dictates, which worked in unison with the Jewish Federations of Canada-UIA. Promises were made that the budgets of the two would be increased, though officials from both organizations were definitely uneasy with what transpired. Having no recourse, since their operating funds were allocated by the federations and CIJA, CJC, and CIA officials had no choice but to acquiesce to CIJA's revised format amidst a lot of grumbling.

In an interview with the *Toronto Star* in early October 2003, JFC-UIA spokesperson Maxyne Finkelstein had denied that CIJA 1.0 would "put control of Jewish lobbying efforts in Canada into the hands of few wealthy and powerful individuals." That may have been true, as Fogel maintains today, but he admits that even as CIJA 1.0 was conceived, it was "doomed to fail." It did not eliminate the intense competition for resources, nor the community's relationships with politicians and representation in the media. And no matter how JFC-UIA and CIJA officials spun it, the creation of CIJA 1.0 and the centralization of power in the hands of its executives and board was indeed a vote of no confidence in the CJC and the CIC. (In part because the CIC's budget was only slightly reduced, Fogel and other members of the CIC were much more at ease about this than their counterparts at the CJC.) Within eight years, both would be history.

Hershell Ezrin was hired in January 2004 as the CEO of CIJA 1.0 and was a believer. "I'm doing it for the really simple reason," he told the *Canadian Jewish News* at the time, "that when you grow up with the name 'Hershell' and you don't change it, it's easy to understand what's going on around you." Cummings and Belzberg were the first co-chairs of the new CIJA board, with Schwartz and Resiman as members, along with another eighteen individuals chosen from across Canada. Most had been involved with the CJC or their local federations—such as lawyer Bernard Pinsky of Vancouver and businessman Mel Lazareck of Winnipeg. In the mix, too, were Anne Golden; Joseph Gabay, a leader of Montreal's Sephardi community; and Barbara Bank, a stalwart of the Toronto federation and a supporter of March of the Living.

During the next five years with Ezrin at the helm, CIJA was busy leading missions to Israel, successfully lobbying the new Liberal prime minister Paul Martin to be more supportive of Israel at the UN (Schwartz, a friend of Martin's, clearly had some influence), and addressing the perceived anti-Israeli sentiments at Canadian universities with the establishment of the Canadian Federation of Jewish Students, which linked more than thirty Jewish student associations. The results were noticed. Commenting on the shift in Canada's Middle East policy under Martin, John Ibbitson of the *Globe and Mail* wrote in mid-October 2004: "Senior government officials are increasingly angry—that most undiplomatic of emotions—about what they claim is a major but surreptitious shift in this nation's foreign policy. Canada, they say, is moving away from a balanced approach toward the Middle East in favour of explicit and virtually unqualified support for Israel."

But as effective as CIJA 1.0 might have been, by 2010 it was clear that were still too many organizations trying to call the shots. Specifically, why did CIJA and JFC-UIA continue to have to fund the CJC and CIC, when a single centralized body could theoretically look after human rights and social justice issues as well as Israel? Behind closed doors, intense meetings began. Bernie Farber, a lively, principled, and opinionated Jewish community leader who had been involved with the CJC since 1984 and its CEO since 2005, says he saw "the writing on the wall." In the spring of 2010, he announced his departure—he insists that any suggestion that he was fired is incorrect—and that he was going to run as a Liberal in the Ontario provincial election of October 2011. (He lost in the Jewish-dominated riding of Thornhill to Progressive Conservative Peter Shurman—who is also Jewish.) Around the same time, Ezrin announced he was leaving CIJA to return to his private consulting business.

At the end of November 2010, a story appeared in the *Canadian Jewish News* that CIJA and JFC-UIA had decided that another restructuring was required. There was to be "a single Jewish public affairs organization encompassing the national and regional level." Funding of the CJC and the CIC was to cease, which meant the two organizations would have to halt all operations. It was eventually announced that Shimon Fogel, then fifty years old, was to replace Ezrin as head of what became known as CIJA 2.0. The twist was the name change from the Canadian Council for Israel and Jewish Advocacy to the Centre for Israel and Jewish Affairs.

Supporters of the Congress were beside themselves. Historian Frank Bialystok, who at the time was the chair of the CJC's Ontario region, recalls that there were two unpleasant telephone conference calls with Steven Cummings, who was in charge of the restructuring. "He promised two things," says Bialystok. "That the new organization [called Newco during the planning stages] would be a human rights organization, and that whichever Congress employees wanted to stay would be able to." In the end, several CJC officials were handed their walking papers, and the focus of CIJA 2.0 has arguably been more Israel advocacy than human rights and domestic issues. Farber was also consulted about the dramatic change and not surprisingly offered a contrary view. "Congress had more cachet outside of the Jewish community than inside, which is one of the reasons it finally folded," he says. "It was a historical gem. I thought it was a huge error in judgement and told them so." He suggested CIJA at least keep the CJC name, given it was a recognizable brand. "[CIJA's officials] said they'd think about it, yet they did not." To this, Fogel counters that the "offer was on the table but they rejected it."

News that the ninety-two-year-old Canadian Jewish Congress was to be relegated to the history books was met with loud and angry criticism that took a while to subside—if it ever has. "The Congress isn't just about Jews," journalist Andrew Cohen argued in a commentary in the *Ottawa Citizen*. "It has championed human rights and social justice . . . It has fought anti-Semitism everywhere with a nuance unknown to the blustering B'nai Brith, which lacks credibility. Does every Canadian Jew agree with the Canadian Jewish Congress? Of course not. At root, though, it is an instrument of good in Canada. Only fools and amnesiacs would dissolve it." There were numerous letters to the CJN from readers, one of who found what was going on "profoundly disturbing."

Sally Zerker, a York University professor emeritus, argued then and since that the process used to abolish the CJC was "totally undemocratic," as she explained in a lengthy and passionately argued CJN article. But Fogel stood his ground, forcefully defending the change—and still does. The child of Holocaust survivors, he grew up in Montreal and graduated from Clark University's Department of Government and International Relations in Massachusetts. He also holds two rabbinic ordinations. "We had an opportunity to integrate and consolidate all the thematic agendas—campus, antisemitism, Israel relations, social policy agenda at the local community level—all of those things could be brought into one holistic institution," he said in a June 2011 interview. In a follow-up with the *National Post* two months later, he addressed the conspiracy theorists and naysayers: "For some, a mythology has emerged that somehow this was a small, rogue group of monied individuals who pulled the community in a particular direction. However, this entire process involved the widest possible level of consultation. Every community across the country . . . had the opportunity to weigh in." (Bialystok, for one, disputes that there was much consultation before the changes were implemented.)

Six years later, Fogel is as adamant in his resolve that the new structure is more effective. He also dismisses the charge made by Zerker and others that the decision was made undemocratically. "How someone can suggest it was undemocratic is a puzzle to me," he says. "Democracy has nothing to do with it. It wasn't a choice between a democratic election and dictatorship. The question is not 'Was it democratic?' but 'Was it representative?' The structure of the re-organization committee reflected amazing representation from across the country. Not just at the elite level, but at community level, too." And he firmly points out: "It wasn't a casual exercise. It went on for eighteen months. It was an intense process."

The second complaint about CIJA is that its preoccupation with Israel has come at the expense of issues that were in the Congress's mandate, such as social justice, social policy, antisemitism beyond Israel, and outreach programs. These, supposedly, have been forgotten. "I can accept that a concern was expressed about whether those elements of the advocacy agenda were fully attended to back in 2010 and 2011," says Fogel. "But I won't accept that that same question has been relevant since 2012, and certainly in 2017. When you look at the record of what CIJA has engaged in beyond Israel, it is staggering. It represents a total eclipse of the engagement of the Jewish community pre-CIJA in these issues."

He points, for example, to CIJA's important work in supporting South Sudan, helping the Yazidis (a persecuted Iraqi ethnic and religious minority), addressing problems of poverty in Canadian Jewish communities, building partnerships with First Nations, and confronting gender and transgender discrimination. "I am not just proud of our commitment to the 'domestic agenda,' I'm outraged that anyone would suggest we are giving it short shrift or that it has suffered an iota since CIJA's establishment," he says, his voice rising. "If anything, on the local and national levels, Jewish advocacy has been given a booster shot that puts us in a different category. And it is why so many groups in Canada are asking for our partnerships and our expertise to advance their own issues."

Beyond all the drama of the community boardrooms, the national federation and its local affiliates also had to address numerous financial and demographic issues—none more pressing than saving Jewish community schools from extinction. Aside from synagogues—many of which have their own financial problems, owing to aging members and buildings in need of costly upkeep—Jewish schools have been the most integral part of ensuring he community's long-term survival. But they are not inexpensive to operate.

This is particularly the case in Ontario, where tuition is high owing to a pre-Confederation law entrenched in the British North America Act of 1867 that stipulated the only denominational schools eligible for full government funding were those operated by Roman Catholics. Jewish as well as Islamic and non-Catholic Christian schools have been left wanting. In the fall of 2014, for example, the average per-student tuition at a Toronto-area Jewish elementary school was approximately $14,000. Jewish parents in Montreal, on the other hand, paid about $5,300, while in Winnipeg it was $9,900, and Calgary, $9,400. Only Vancouver's Talmud Torah, with a tuition of $13,600, was comparable to what Torontonians forked over. Sending a child to Toronto's Jewish high school like the Anne and Max Tanenbaum Community Hebrew Academy of Toronto (or TanenbaumCHAT) was even higher: $24,900, only about $6,000 less than the cost at the prestigious Upper Canada College. In short, parents in Toronto with two children who wanted to have them both attend a Jewish day school from kindergarten to grade twelve were looking at a total expenditure of more than $400,000.

At various times, Jewish lobby groups in Toronto have pushed and prodded the provincial government to correct this perceived injustice, but to no avail. In November 1996, the Ontario Jewish Association for Equality in Education—working with the Ontario Alliance of Christian Schools—took their case all the way to the Supreme Court of Canada, arguing that the non-funding of Jewish schools was unconstitutional under the Charter of Rights and Freedoms. Yet the judges ruled against them. A decade later, John Tory, then the provincial Conservative Party leader (since December 2014 he has been the mayor of Toronto), went out on a limb during that year's election campaign, declaring that he would extend public funding to all faith-based schools. This pledge, however, backfired, as the reigning Liberals led by Premier Dalton McGuinty charged that Tory's plans would take millions of dollars out of the public education system. The outcry forced Tory to reverse his position—he promised a free vote on the issue—and it contributed to his loss in the election.

Because a Jewish education was and still is regarded as so paramount, Jewish parents, even those in Toronto, have made great economic sacrifices.

Most Jewish schools offer reduced tuition based on income, but it is a protracted and intrusive process. In 1998, there were thirty-five Jewish day schools in Toronto and nineteen in Montreal, which included Sephardi/Francophone and Ashkenazi/Anglophone schools. Jewish education is a "big business," as Morton Weinfeld has called it. In 1998, educating Jewish students in Montreal cost a total of $42 million, with about $17 million from tuition, $18 million derived from government funding, $2 million from Jewish community grants and the balance from donors. Yet the burden in markets like Toronto with high housing costs has made Jewish education difficult to sustain. By 2012, 10,600 children were enrolled at Jewish day schools in Toronto, or 31 per cent of the total Jewish student population. Of that total, nearly nine thousand attended schools affiliated with the Toronto Jewish Federation, and the tuition of 25 per cent of the students was subsidized.

The high tuition is a financial hardship for many families to bear, says Claire Sumerlus, the head of Toronto's Robbins Hebrew Academy, an egalitarian Jewish school with 380 students from junior kindergarten to grade eight. As of 2018 the tuition fees average just under $17,000. There are, she adds, two factors that Jewish schools must consider. "The first is the cost and the second has to do with priorities," she says. "It is easy to be Jewish in Toronto, and easy, too, for many Jewish parents to introduce their children to Jewish events, holidays, and camps without the financial sacrifice involved in sending their children to private schools." Sumerlus agrees as well that there are too many schools in the GTA and that closures and mergers are likely in the future. But that, she notes, will involve the challenge of dealing with firm philosophical and religious differences that presently exist between the various schools.

Jewish high schools in Toronto and elsewhere have had the most challenging time, partly because of the excessive fees, but also because by the time children reach grade nine many Jewish parents feel that their children have had a sufficient Jewish education. Not surprisingly, enrolment at TanenbaumCHAT declined from a high of 1,530 in 2008 to 1,038 in 2015, a 32 per cent reduction. In 2006, 79 per cent of students graduating from Toronto Jewish elementary day schools continued on to the high school; in 2015, that had dropped to 52 per cent. In the spring of 2017, declining enrolment forced

CHAT to close its northern campus in Vaughan, moving all the students to the Wallenberg Campus on Wilmington Avenue, west of Bathurst Street and south of Finch Avenue. Two donations totalling $14 million reduced CHAT's tuition to $18,500 for 2018, and it will remain at less than $19,000 until 2023.

The organization Grassroots for Affordable Jewish Education (GAJE) was founded by a highbrow group which included the former editor of the CJN, Mordechai Ben-Dat; Israeli-Canadian Sara Dobner, a senior policy advisor with the Ontario government; and Rabbi Jay Kelman, the founding director of Torah in Motion who teaches Jewish law and rabbinics at CHAT. GAJE's mission is "to make Jewish education in our community affordable for every family that wishes to send its children to a Jewish day school."

The personal stories on GAJE's website of parents who want to send their children to a Jewish day school yet cannot afford to do so are just plain sad. One mother writes of the humiliating experience of essentially begging for a subsidy. A father—who with his wife has a combined gross income of less than $120,000—relates how they are forced to scrimp and save each and every day using food coupons and avoiding buying red meat, all so they can afford a subsidized tuition for their children.

As sincere and dedicated as the founding members of GAJE are, the price of tuition keeps going up and parents will continue to be faced with hard choices in the foreseeable future. A survey of Toronto Jewish parents in 2016, for example, found that for 75 per cent with children in a Jewish day school, the number-one consideration as to whether to continue their children in the system past grade eight was money.

Outside of Toronto and Montreal, demographics are another big factor in schools attempting to sustain themselves. After the 2015 school year, the Ottawa Jewish Community School's board of directors was forced to close the city's only Jewish high school. At the time there were only twenty-four students enrolled, which meant—as the *Ottawa Jewish Bulletin* pointed out— that of the "estimated 900 high school–aged Jewish students in Ottawa only about two percent of Jewish families in the city are choosing Jewish day high school for their children." The board, which announced the decision early in

2015, had intended to phase out the school over a two-year period, but that was not financially feasible.

Even with the slight increase in the Jewish population of Winnipeg since the mid-nineties, with the arrival of Argentinian Jews and Russian Israelis—who were seeking a less difficult economic life and preferred that their children did not serve in the Israeli army—the Gray Academy's high school, Joseph Wolinsky Collegiate, has seen its student numbers decline. Overall, the number of students at Gray Academy—which had a total grades-one-to-twelve population of about 650 in 2004—has dropped to under 500 in recent years. Unlike other Jewish schools in Canada, the Gray Academy has to compete with the popular Hebrew-bilingual program at Brock Corydon, a nearby River Heights public elementary school, which was introduced in 1981. It is the only such program in North America that is publicly funded. The Jewish students in the program—as of the 2016–17 school year there were an estimated two hundred—learn Hebrew and are introduced to Jewish holidays, culture, and history.

In Vancouver, despite the high cost of living and the Toronto-like tuition fees, the city's Jewish schools—the main ones are Talmud Torah, the Richmond Jewish Day School, the (Orthodox) Vancouver Hebrew Academy, and King David High School—are holding their own. In 2015, King David had 190 students enrolled, an increase of fifty from the year before. The community of twenty-six thousand keeps on growing, a result no doubt of Vancouver's modest climate for a Canadian city and the arrival of immigrants from South America, Eastern Europe, and Russians from Israel. "The success of the Vancouver Talmud Torah has been born out of its long history and shared growth with the broader community," says its current board president, Dr. Jonathon Leipsic, yet another transplanted Winnipegger and the head of radiology for B.C.'s Providence Health Care. "As it heads into its one-hundredth year, [Talmud Torah] is very much the cradle of community, having supported and fostered its growth. Its importance . . . cannot be overstated, particularly as [the city's Jewish population] has been forced to spread out more widely with increasing housing costs . . . it brings the community together in a way that few other institutions can."

———

The absolute dedication to sustaining community schools is further evidence that Jews have always taken care of the young, old, and poor. It has defined the community for generations. All the major cities have Jewish foundations with millions of dollars in assets to continually raise funds and ensure the survival of the communities in the future.

Yet the affluence of the foundations as well as other fundraising endeavours by no means supports the widely held view that "all Jews are well off." Yes, many who are high-paid physicians, lawyers, accountants, or other professionals and business owners are indeed wealthy. By the mid-nineties, close to 50 per cent of all Canadian Jews aged seventeen or higher were either enrolled in a university or had completed a bachelor's degree or higher. (In 1994, 16 per cent of Jews had obtained master's degrees or doctorates, compared to only 4 per cent of the Canadian population as a whole.)

Thus, the image of the poor Jewish immigrant from the early twentieth century has faded. "Canadian Jews are better off economically than are Canadians as a whole, with fewer Jews falling into the lowest income levels," a report in the 1995 *American Jewish Year Book* noted. "For example, two out of three Canadians (65.2 percent) aged 15 and over in 1991 earned less than $25,000, compared to 52.6 percent of Jews. Differences in income between Jews and Canadians generally are most noticeable at the upper levels. The proportion of Jews earning over $75,000 in 1991 was close to four times that in the Canadian population as a whole (10.2 percent vs. 2.6 percent)." These percentages have remained fairly consistent since then; Jewish wealth in Canada is a fact.

But it is also undeniable that Jewish poverty does exist. According to the Jewish Federations of Canada's 2011 study, 57,195 Jews—or 14.6 per cent of the total Jewish population at the time—were living below the poverty line in Canada. Many of these were elderly Jewish women. In late 2014, Nancy Singer, executive director of the Kehilla Residential Programme, a non-profit housing agency in Toronto, told the CJN that for the first time in two decades, "Jewish poverty in Toronto is on the rise." Two years later, the non-profit Jewish Free Loan Toronto reported that demand for loans in the Toronto Jewish community had increased. In 2011, 147 loans were given out; by 2015 that number had risen to 238. The total amount of money loaned that year was about $1.2 million, the highest amount given in the agency's ninety-two year history. In Montreal, which the JFC-UIA study added "has consistently had the highest incidence of poverty of any major Jewish community in the country," two organizations—Agence Ometz, the social services agency of Federation CJA, and Hessed, the charity arm of the Communauté Sépharade Unifiée du Québec—work together to address the problem.

Likewise, a network of Jewish child and family services and senior homes—all sustained by community and partial government support, and managed by a large and devoted staff of social workers and caregivers—provide much-needed assistance to thousands of individuals and families. No one in the community is compelled to use a Jewish agency, and many of these agencies are Jewish in name only. But ethnic and religious bonds are strong, and for more than three centuries, when Jews in Canada have been in distress, the odds are they have sought out help from other Jews. It is just the way it is.

The Never-Dying Canadians

In an October 1959 *Maclean's* feature article entitled "The Jew in Canada," Phyllis Lee Peterson, a Montreal-based writer, posed the question, "Where does he stand today?" Her answer was that, two centuries after the first Jew had settled permanently in Canada, "he" was not doing too badly. True, some Jews were still not permitted to join exclusive clubs or be included in "intimate [Gentile] gatherings," she wrote, but Jews had "made contributions out of all proportion to their numbers to Canadian business and trade, art, literature, music, entertainment, medicine, law, science, research and university life. By standard measures of citizenship they rank very high."

Despite the paternalistic tone of the piece, Peterson's list of enterprises operated by Jews and individual achievements was indeed impressive. The businesses she highlighted were Tip Top Tailors, People's Jewellers, Handy Andy (automotive), Steinberg's supermarket stores, and the Bronfman family's distillery corporation. And among the stellar cast of Jewish professionals and characters were Toronto mayor Nathan Phillips; David Golden, deputy defence minister; Samuel Berger, former president of the Canadian Football League's Ottawa Rough Riders; John Hirsch of the Winnipeg Little Theatre; Louis Applebaum, a Stratford musical director; Anne Kahane, a sculptress; writers and poets Mordecai Richler, Irving Layton, Miriam Waddington, and Adele Weisman; actors Lorne Greene and William Shatner; and the comedy duo of Johnny Wayne and Frank Shuster. Wayne and Shuster might not have been able to become members of the posh Granite Club, but within a few years they were the highest-paid performers in Canada.

In 1959—and for at least two, even three decades after—it was important to point out the Jewish background of each high achiever and the significant contribution they had made to Canadian society. But does it matter in 2018? Would it not be a real sign of the country's famed multicultural tolerance that when someone Jewish succeeds, the religious and ethnic identifier is not mentioned at all? The answer to this query is open to debate, though when you ask a rabbi or two about it, a convincing case can be made to maintain the status quo.

"I do think it is important to note a person's Jewish background," argues Rabbi Daniel Korobkin of Toronto's Beth Avraham Yoseph congregation, otherwise known as the BAYT, one of the largest Orthodox synagogues (modern and traditional) in North America. He adds:

> I think we should take credit for the success of Jews and attribute that success, even if it is a very small part, to one's Jewish upbringing. There is something about a Jewish upbringing that motivates one to excel and succeed. Not all the time. But there is a tendency—culturally, educationally, religiously—that emphasizes a sense of conscience, a sense of caring for others in society as whole and trying to make the world a better place. It's not a coincidence that twenty-two per cent of Nobel Prize winners [of all individual recipients worldwide between 1901 and 2016] have been Jewish, even though we are less than one per cent of the world's population. It should be celebrated.

His colleague on the other side of the religious spectrum, Rabbi Yael Splansky of the Reform Holy Blossom Temple, concurs. "There's a difference between Jewishness and Judaism," she explains. "Judaism is about beliefs, values, and actions. And if there's a person who is living a life according to Jewish values in a way that is having an influence or impact on the world, then I think Judaism should get some credit for that."

But whether Jews are identified or not may be beside the point. In September 1998, historian Irving Abella stressed in a lecture at Toronto's York University that in comparing Canadian and American Jewish communities,

the situation was better for Canadian Jews, who are "arguably the most affluent, integrated community in the country." And he was right. By then, the
immigrant generation of the early twentieth century that defined so much of
Canadian Jewish life—in addition to the Holocaust survivors who had
arrived in the late forties and early fifties—had given way to their Canadian-
born children, "worshipping very different household gods from those ... of
their fathers and grandfathers," as CJC officials had observed nearly three
decades earlier. This new generation was university educated, more comfortable, and arguably more indifferent about Jewish institutions. In the years
ahead, those among this generation who did participate in community governance would have to confront this reality and adapt accordingly.

Like with most complex issues, there's good and bad news. Any success, of
course, must be tempered with a healthy dose of skepticism about the future.
After all, that's the Jewish thing to do. Among positive modern developments
was the steady increase of the Jewish population of Canada from 286,500 in
1971 to nearly 392,000 by 2011. This growth partly owed to the arrival of Jews
from the Soviet Union and then Russia after 1991, as well as former Soviet
Jews who had emigrated to Israel and then decided to relocate to Canada (as
well as the United States and Western Europe). The majority of these newcomers—and most came via Israel—followed the historic trend and settled
in Toronto, where by 2016 there were an estimated fifty to seventy thousand
Russian-speaking Jews, and Montreal where about twenty thousand now live.
In Montreal, for instance, the Jewish Russian Community Centre was opened
in 2012 to accommodate a Jewish group who tend to stick to themselves.
About two thousand also landed in Winnipeg—at the Asper Jewish
Community Campus one hears Russian as well the as Spanish spoken by
Argentinean Jewish immigrants as frequently as English—and a few hundred
opted for Halifax, like Olga and Gregory Shepshelevich.

In 2013, Olga and Gregory, who were both in their early thirties, were seeking a less complicated life. They had met in Israel. He was born in Dnipro (then
Dnipropetrovsk) in central Ukraine, and arrived in Israel with his parents in
1991; she was born in western Ukraine and came to Israel as a student six years

later. Olga was Russian with a Jewish grandfather; when she had been told about her family's roots at the age of twelve, she was drawn to learn more. Once she moved to Israel and fell in love with Gregory, she converted to Judaism.

After conducting research and speaking to a few friends, Olga and Gregory decided that Nova Scotia was the place for their family. They have two sons, both born in Israel. Canadian Jewish officials do not like to admit that they recruit Jews to leave Israel; that is counter to all Jewish thinking and Zionist ideology. But if Israelis such as the Russians want to depart, they are happy to accommodate them. Once in Canada, it is definitely a transition for many of them, which may explain why so many seek out other Russian émigrés. "In Ukraine we were called Jewish, in Israel we were called Russian, and here we are Russian Jews," Olga said in a 2014 interview, "but I'm fine with that." Olga and Gregory are somewhat unique for Russian-Israeli immigrants. They are members of Halifax's Beth Israel congregation and are raising their children in a Jewish home. Many of the Russian-Israelis, unlike Jewish immigrants of other eras, are not as intent on joining synagogues, sending their children to Jewish schools, and integrating into the larger Jewish communities.

The Russians' experiences, like the plethora of activities offered in local communities, received extensive coverage in the weekly *Canadian Jewish News*, the most important Jewish publication in the country. (The *Jewish Post & News* in Winnipeg, a bi-weekly, is a smaller operation headed by owner and editor Bernie Bellan; he took over the paper from his brother Matt, who passed away in 2009. Apart from Israeli news, its main focus is the machinations of Winnipeg's lively community.) The CJN reaches more than thirty thousand readers in Toronto and Montreal, and connects with Jews across the country via its website. Nonetheless, in the spring of 2013, the CJN was in serious financial trouble and an announcement was made that it was closing after fifty-three years of serving Canada's two largest communities. Almost immediately, a rescue plan was organized by community leaders who believed the newspaper was essential to perpetuating the Jewish story in Canada. By the end of the year, thirty-three-year-old Yoni Goldstein had been hired to become the CJN's new editor.

Many of his subscribers, however, who perceive the paper as representative of community opinions, have become upset when he has published articles or columns—most notably those which are critical of Israel—that they don't agree with. In this regard, not much has changed since the seventies and eighties, when the newspaper was also castigated for occasionally including negative commentary of Israel. Goldstein handles this criticism carefully and judiciously. "Our role, as we see it," he has written, "is to strike a balance and invite Canadian Jews to debate and discuss our most pressing dilemmas and concerns. Certainly, you won't agree with everything we publish—quite the opposite. But I urge you to join us in the job of community-building. From our point of view, nothing could be more valuable."

Since Goldstein's reign as editor started, there are (apart from Israel) probably few issues of the cjn published without a mention of antisemitism in some manifestation—even in 2018. Its form has clearly changed: Canadian Jews who are less than about forty-five years of age almost certainly have never been rejected for a job, denied service, or refused a club membership because they are Jewish. But there is no denying that antisemitism still exists in Canada, as B'nai Brith's annual audit of antisemitic incidents indicates (from 2014 to 2016, 84 to 90 per cent of the incidents reported in the audits involved verbal harassment). The bds movement at Canadian (and American) university campuses, illogical and ineffective as it is, also rages on—as do other inane college anti-Israel or anti-Zionist protests.

Jews are still targeted in hate crimes—the most targeted victims in Canada in 2016, according to the Statistics Canada document "Police-Reported Hate Crime"—and there is vandalism and online antisemitism as well. In November 2016, two synagogues and a rabbi's home in Ottawa were vandalized with antisemitic graffiti; the culprit turned out to be a troubled teenage boy. And in Winnipeg at the beginning of 2017, a Jewish woman married to a non-Jewish man came home to find a large rock sitting on her front steps painted with an offensive message. The words "Die Jew Bitch" were printed on one side, and on the other was a red swastika and the word "Einsatzgruppen," a reference to the mobile Nazi killing squads that murdered Jews during the Second World War. In comparison to past violent incidents, none of these incidents were terribly serious, but they are disturbing and the Jewish community's grave concern is justified.

It is not, however, rabid antisemitism that Jews in Canada have to worry about anymore, but much thornier issues like the decline of religion, the financial difficulties experienced by some synagogues—mostly outside Toronto and Montreal—intermarriage, and assimilation. Ironically enough, Jews are now being "killed by kindness," as the well-known American Jewish lawyer Alan Dershowitz describes it. Back in 1986, in one of his last speeches as the president of the Canadian Jewish Congress, Milton Harris—an American-born businessman—arrived at this conclusion as well. He cautioned that "the real threat" to Jewish survival was an "open society," which was free of discrimination. "We can no longer rely on external hostility to us to maintain our Jewish identity and communal cohesiveness," he told the CJC delegates in Ottawa. But no Jewish leader in their right mind would argue for a return to the antisemitism of the past as way to keep Jews united. So the trick is figuring out how to maintain Jewish religion and culture in a more welcoming non-Jewish society in which barriers to total assimilation have vanished.

It is a given that Orthodox synagogues in Canada, whose congregations are more devout than those in Conservative and Reform synagogues, have had less problems retaining and growing their memberships. And between Conservative and Reform, the former has probably had the most difficult time, a point conceded by Rabbi Baruch Frydman-Kohl of Toronto's Beth Tzedec congregation. "The Conservative movement over the last years," he says, "has been nibbled away at by more aggressive Orthodoxy and a more traditional Reform. Each of those nibbles at the edges. Being a passionate centrist is not easy."

During the past thirty years, many synagogues have shut their doors or merged with other congregations. In Calgary in 1986, the Shaarey Tzedec and Beth Israel congregations agreed to merge to create a new Conservative synagogue, the Beth Tzedec, which opened the following year. In 2002, after two years of intense negotiations, three synagogues in Winnipeg—the Conservative Rosh Pina and Beth Israel and the Modern Orthodox B'nai Abraham (the Rosh Pina dated back to 1893 and the B'nai Abraham to

1955)—joined together as the new Etz Chayim congregation, with its home
in the Rosh Pina's building. The merger, along with the near disappearance
of kosher butchers symbolized the decline of religion (or religious priorities)
in the lives of many Jews in Winnipeg.

Similarly, in Ottawa, in the spring of 2016 financial realities led to
Congregation Beth Shalom—itself a 1956 merger of the Adath Jeshurun and
Agudath Achim—to amalgamate with the Agudath Israel congregation,
established in 1932, to form the Kehillat Beth Israel. The new synagogue,
located in a building in the west end of the city, describes itself as a "modern,
egalitarian Conservative congregation" of more than eight hundred families.
Even in Toronto, synagogues have had problems: in June 2016, after forty-
four years of operation, the Shaar Shalom synagogue in Thornhill was forced
to close.

Unlike Orthodox and Reform synagogues, Conservative ones have more
members who only show up three times a year during the High Holidays, and
for bar and bat mitzvahs and weddings. These "Jell-O Jews," as Frydman-
Kohl calls them—because like a Jell-O mould they may or may not hold
together—pay their membership dues more out of habit than a desire to
participate in prayer services and synagogue-sponsored events like their parents and grandparents did. Rabbis are frustrated by this lack of interest, but
there is only so much they can do to counter it.

Winnipeg's Conservative Shaarey Zedek, the city's oldest and what would
be considered its "establishment" synagogue, is typical of this trend. It is an
egalitarian institution in which women fully participate, a shift in religious
ritual that dates back to 1977 (the decision to integrate women into the service and count them as part of a *minyan* took five years of deliberations). Its
total membership is approximately three thousand congregants, enough that
two services are still required on the High Holidays. Most Saturdays, if there
is no bar or bat mitzvah, the morning service attracts a crowd of approximately 150 people. That's a dramatic increase from the fifty or so congregants
who used to show up; a rise in numbers which is mainly due to recent changes
that shortened the service to ninety minutes and incorporated a new prayer
book and the use of musical instruments.

The addition of music was central to a revamping of the High Holiday services as well. In 2016, Rabbi Alan Green (who is retiring in 2018)—a kind soul with a strong interest in Kabbalah mysticism—and the synagogue board decided after protracted discussions to overhaul the High Holiday prayers. The size of the choir was significantly reduced and replaced with a jazzier smaller group, now accompanied by an electric piano and other musical instruments. A two-and-half-hour time limit was set on the modified prayer services, which are still mostly Conservative in nature—men wear kippot and tallit (prayer shawls) and will for the foreseeable future—yet there is a touch of Reform.

"Let's put it this way," said the synagogue's cantor, Rabbi Anibal Mass, "it's the service of the twenty-first century." According to Ian Staniloff, the synagogue's executive director, the feedback on the new format was "overwhelmingly positive," yet he also adds that some of the older and more traditional members were less enthusiastic. It remains to be seen whether it will have the overall impact synagogue officials anticipate.

Just like churches have, Shaarey Zedek and every other synagogue in Canada has had to manage other twenty-first century realities as well: the equality rights of women in a religion with an ancient male hierarchy; same-sex marriage; and intermarriage, the most controversial and potentially detrimental issue affecting Western Jews today. Naturally, rabbis and their congregants do not always see eye to eye on these frequently contentious social issues. Though Orthodox synagogues continue to segregate men and women, Conservative congregations have embraced mixed seating for many years, and Reform synagogues did from the beginning. At Conservative Beth Tzedec in Toronto, for instance, women have been honoured with Torah readings since 1995, though they have only been counted as part of *minyan* since 2011.

Same-sex marriage has proved more challenging. In April 2005, in what was called an "unprecedented move," Orthodox Jewish leaders declared their opposition to the House of Commons vote that altered the Civil Marriage Act and made same-sex marriage legal. Not surprisingly, Reform synagogues were the first to officiate same-sex marriages, even before the federal legislation was enacted—though at Holy Blossom in Toronto, for example, the couple getting married both have to be Jewish. Winnipeg's Shaarey Zedek was the first Conservative synagogue in Canada to offer LGBT Jews full membership rights, including family membership, burial rights, and the performance of marriages. But like every Conservative synagogue in Canada, it draws the line at intermarriages.

Reform congregations have mostly married and welcomed intermarried couples, though it is not universal across the country. Temple Shalom in Winnipeg was an early advocate, with intermarriages first being conducted in 1999, a decision which was highly criticized at the time by Orthodox and Conservative rabbis in the city. The first intermarriage at Temple Israel, Ottawa's only Reform synagogue, took place in April 2013. Montreal's Reform Temple Emanu-El-Beth Sholom has a slight twist. The synagogue marries interfaith couples and welcomes them as members, provided their committed to establishing a Jewish home and raising their children according to Jewish tradition—as variously as that can be interpreted. And at Vancouver's Temple Sholom, Rabbi Dan Moskovitz does not officiate at interfaith ceremonies but he will do interfaith premarital counselling. "If the couple agree to have a Jewish home and raise any children exclusively in the Jewish faith," he explains, "I will also do a blessing for them after their wedding on the *bima* [pulpit] in our sanctuary, during a Shabbat service."

The steadily rising intermarriage rate is indeed a cause for concern. As Alan Dershowitz has wryly noted, "Everyone wants to marry a Jew, except Jews themselves." That's a bit of an exaggeration, but not by much. To anyone worried about Jewish survival, the statistics are distressing. In the first half of the twentieth century, the intermarriage rate for Canadian Jews did not rise above 10 per cent. By 1991, it had reached 17 per cent; by 2001, 20.5 per cent; and by 2011, 26 per cent. From 1991 to 2011, the number of intermarried households rose by a big margin to 59 per cent. Victoria at 73.5 per cent and Vancouver at 43.5 per cent were the cities with the highest intermarriage rates, followed by Kingston (65 per cent), Regina (55 per cent), and Halifax (53 per cent). According to the 2011 Jewish population study, there were 184,705 couples in Canada in which at least one spouse was Jewish; and of those, 48,515 "involve a marriage to a non-Jew." For Jews under the age of thirty-nine, the odds were about one in four that they would have married a non-Jew. As of 2011, 29 per cent of Jewish children in the country lived in an intermarried home, and of those, 73 per cent were not identified as Jews.

In a community like Halifax, with about 1,500 Jews, intermarriage can have a significant impact. "By the time Jewish children are twenty-one years old, fifty per cent are gone," says Jon Goldberg, the former executive director of the Atlantic Jewish Council, who retired in 2016 after more than two decades of service. "They intermarry, have children who are not Jewish, and are gone from the community. I have friends who belonged to Young Judaea and went to Zionist camps with me many years ago. But they married non-Jews, had children who are not Jewish, and I never see them. They ceased to be part of the community."

The wide acceptance of Jews in Canada has meant that intermarriages are no longer taboo. Once, Jewish parents mourned or disowned their child—as Tevye the Dairyman does in the Broadway musical *Fiddler on the Roof*—when their son or daughter married someone not Jewish, but not anymore. It is still a concern, however. Reform synagogues may open their doors to intermarried couples, but as Rabbi Frydman-Kohl asks, "How can you keep your Jewish character when fifty per cent of your constituents are not Jewish?" It is a good question with no magical solution or answer.

Rabbis, sages, philosophers, and writers have been predicting the end of Jews for a long time. Between intermarriage and low birth rates, the future looks bleak. (On the other hand, antisemitism, while still prevalent, has declined.) In early 1996, the World Jewish Congress declared that Jews were an "endangered species." Nearly five decades earlier, with the memory of the Holocaust still raw the Polish-born American Jewish philosopher Simon Rawidowicz had called Jews the world's "ever-dying people." Yet unlike a lot of commentators, he argued that there are no people "better equipped to resist disaster" than Jews, a truth borne out in the pages of this book.

From the beginning of Jewish settlement in the land that would become Canada, Jews have employed creative adaptive powers which have sustained them through turbulence and tragedy. Despite the many obstacles and realities of the internet age, there is no reason to believe that they will not be successful. Or, as Rabbi Stuart Rosenberg suggested in a June 1967 feature article on Jews in the *Globe and Mail*: "The fact that we always worry about vanishing is the best guarantee that we won't." Amen to that.

When all is said and done, being Jewish in Canada comes down to family, and the desire of parents to pass down to their children the traditions of the past.

It is a Friday evening in early June 2017 in Toronto and I am visiting the Annex neighbourhood home of Ryla Braemer and Yacov Fruchter. They are part of a resurgence of young Jewish couples drawn to the area, close to the intersection of Bathurst and Bloor Streets, where detached and semi-detached homes— the same ones in which Jews resided during the interwar years—are somewhat affordable in Toronto's expensive housing market. The busy and devoted couple are in the process of herding their two exuberant and cute-as-a-button daughters, Sheelo, five, and Lev, two, to the Shabbat dinner table. (Ryla and Yacov had a son, Sela, in March 2018.) Apart from me, they have invited another Jewish couple—both born and bred in Toronto—and their two young girls, who live a few streets over.

The Braemer-Fruchter family typifies Canadian Jewish modern life: Ryla (the daughter of close friends, who I have known since the day she was born) is a thirty-six-year-old Winnipegger who moved to Toronto in 2003; Yacov is thirty-four and was born and raised in Montreal. They met, fittingly, while both were employed by Hillel, the organization that promotes Jewish education and Israel among university students. Married in 2009, they have opted to live in Toronto, where they can pursue careers in Jewish life.

Ryla is currently the director of Israel Engagement for the UJA Federation of Greater Toronto, and is the first non-Israeli to hold this position aimed at connecting Israelis and Canadians in a meaningful way. Yacov, meanwhile, was the spiritual leader of the popular and pluralistic Annex Shul for six years before accepting the position of the director of community building and spiritual engagement at Beth Tzedec. Among his other responsibilities at the congregation, he says, is "finding ways for as many people as possible to feel that they can have an active role in the synagogue and the community."

Their full-time engagement in the Jewish community stems directly from their own upbringings. Ryla's grandparents were all born in Canada; while Yacov's were Holocaust survivors. She grew up in a home in which Zionism, Israel, and Holocaust education were stressed. In Montreal, Yacov and his family lived in Jewish neighbourhoods in Snowdon and then Côte Saint-Luc. His parents were both immigrants; his mother, who was born in Romania after the Second World War, immigrated to Israel when she was a young girl and later met his father there. They moved to Quebec in the early sixties, despite neither speaking English or French very well. The family is Modern Orthodox, and Yacov attended a Modern Orthodox Montreal school. Ryla, who is fluent in Hebrew, learned the language and received a Jewish education at Winnipeg's Talmud Torah and Joseph Wolinsky Collegiate, now part of the Gray Academy. It was for this reason that in late 2016 they decided to move Sheelo from a public school kindergarten in the Annex to a similar program at a Jewish day school, with the attendant high tuition costs.

"Our life lists are a little bit different about what is significant [from a Jewish perspective]," explains Ryla. "For me, it was important that Sheelo speaks Hebrew and learns about Israel and social justice, and Yacov wanted a level of Jewish literacy and connection to the [biblical] texts." After only three months, they noticed a difference, and are planning to keep Sheelo in the school and have Lev join her when she is old enough. For now, both girls accompany Yacov to synagogue on Saturday mornings. The family keeps kosher, keeps the Sabbath, and celebrates all of the holidays.

The scene during my visit is a mix between tradition and modern; between the customs of the *shtetl* and the customs of 2017 Canada. Since, officially, the Sabbath on a Friday night in June does not begin until late in the evening, Yacov can barbecue chicken burgers, along with hotdogs and vegetables. Inside, Ryla leads her two daughters and her friends' daughters in an early lighting and blessing of the Shabbat candles and a round of lively Shabbat songs. On cue, Yakov emerges from the backyard to recite the Kiddush over the wine and everyone recites the blessing for the Shabbat challah. The mood is casual and geared toward the children's needs—hence the early Shabbat prayers—but Canadian Jewish all the same.

Ever respectful, Ryla and Yacov believe firmly in individual choice and do not judge their friends or anyone else who does not practise Judaism as rigorously. But in choosing to live their lives as they do, they have ensured that their daughters will fully embrace Jewish life in Canada, and pass the religious and cultural traditions on to the next generation. That is the essence of the Jewish experience in Canada—as it has been for the past three centuries.

TABLE I: JEWISH POPULATION OF CANADA

CENSUS YEAR	NUMBER	PERCENTAGE OF TOTAL POPULATION
2011	391,665	1.2
2001	374,060	1.3
1991	359,110	1.3
1981	313,865	1.2
1971	286,550	1.3
1961	254,368	1.4
1951	204,836	1.5
1941	168,585	1.5
1931	155,766	1.5
1921	125,445	1.42
1911	74,760	1.03
1901	16,493	0.31
1891	6,501	0.13
1881	2,443	0.06
1871	1,331	0.03
1861	1,186	0.04
1851	451	0.02
1841	154	0.01
1831	107	0.01

Sources: Charles Shahar, 2011 *National Household Survey Analysis: The Jewish Population of Canada*, (Toronto: Jewish Federations of Canada-UIA, 2014) www.jewishdatabank.org /Studies/downloadFile.cfm?FileID=3131. See esp. "Part 1: Basic Demographics," and "Part 2: Jewish Populations in Geographic Areas."; Gerald Tulchinsky, *Branching Out: The Transformation of the Canadian Jewish Community* (Toronto: Stoddart, 1998), 356.

TABLE 2:

JEWISH POPULATION OF SELECTED CANADIAN CITIES

CITY	1891	1901	1911	1921	1931	1941	1951	1961	1971	1981	1991	2001	2011
Montreal	2,473	6,941	28,807	45,802	57,997	63,721	90,829	102,724	109,840	101,385	96,155	88,765	90,780
Toronto	1,425	3,090	18,300	34,770	46,751	49,046	66,773	88,648	103,730	123,725	150,100	164,510	188,710
Winnipeg	645	1,158	9,023	14,837	17,660	17,027	18,514	19,376	18,351	15,350	13,160	12,760	13,690
Ottawa	46	398	1,781	3,041	3,842	3,809	4,558	5,553	6,385	8,470	9,665	11,325	14,010
Vancouver	85	205	982	1,399	2,458	2,812	5,467	7,301	10,085	12,865	14,160	17,270	26,255
Calgary	6	1	604	1,247	1,622	1,794	2,110	2,881	3,275	5,580	5,335	6,530	8,335
Edmonton	1	0	171	821	1,057	1,449	1,753	2,495	2,475	4,250	3,930	3,980	5,550
Regina	9	1	130	860	1,010	944	740	817	759	710	490	700	900
Halifax	18	102	254	585	582	758	1,012	1,188	1,315	1,220	1,140	1,575	2,120

From 1891 to 1991, the figures are by religion; 2001–2011 are based on the "Jewish Standard Definition," a combination of religion and ethnicity. For 1961 to 2011, the figures are for census metropolitan area.

Sources: Louis Rosenberg, "The Jewish Population of Canada: A Statistical Summary from 1850 to 1943," AJYB 48 (1946–47): 35–36; Gerald Tulchinsky, *Canada's Jews: A People's Journey* (Toronto: University of Toronto Press, 2008), 499; Charles Shahar, *2011 National Household Survey Analysis: The Jewish Population of Canada,* (Toronto: Jewish Federations of Canada-UIA, 2014). See esp. "Part 1: Basic Demographics," and "Part 2: Jewish Populations in Geographic Areas."; Shahar, "Part 1" and "Part 2" in *2011 National Household Survey Analysis.*

Works and sources frequently cited have been identified by the following abbreviations:

AI	Author's interview
AJYB	*American Jewish Year Book*
CIJA	Centre for Israel and Jewish Affairs
CJC	Canadian Jewish Congress
CJCH	*Canadian Jewish Chronicle* (Montreal)
CJN	*Canadian Jewish News* (Toronto)
CJS	*Canadian Jewish Studies*
CJR	*Canadian Jewish Review* (Toronto)
CJHS	*Canadian Jewish Historical Society Journal*
CR	*Chronicle Review* (Montreal)
CVWM	Canadian Virtual War Memorial
DCB	*Dictionary of Canadian Biography*
GL	*Globe* (Toronto, 1844–1936)
GM	*Globe and Mail* (Toronto, 1936–present)
IP	*Israelite Press* (Winnipeg)
JHS	Jewish Historical Society of Western Canada (Winnipeg)
JHSSA	*Journal of the Jewish Historical Society of Southern Alberta*
JMABC	Jewish Museum and Archives of British Columbia
JP	*Jewish Post* (Winnipeg)
JPL	Jewish Public Library (Montreal)
JPN	*Jewish Post & News* (Winnipeg)
JTA	Jewish Telegraphic Agency
LAC	Library and Archives Canada
MFP	*Manitoba Free Press* (Winnipeg)
MG	*Montreal Gazette*
MJM	Museum of Jewish Montreal

NP	*National Post* (Toronto)
OJA	Ontario Jewish Archives
TS	*Toronto Star*
VHEC	Vancouver Holocaust Education Centre
WLMK	William Lyon Mackenzie King
WFP	*Winnipeg Free Press*

Introduction: *The Quintessence of a Minority*

1   *One evening, early in:* CJN, February 12, 1970; Harold Troper, *The Defining Decade: Identity, Politics, and the Canadian Jewish Community in the 1960s* (Toronto: University of Toronto Press, 2010), 289–90.

1   *But, not all that surprisingly:* LAC, 26-07, Rt. Hon. Pierre Trudeau Fonds, vol. 121 Code 313.05–Gibson, "Itinerary Meetings," SD 69/61 "Family of Man Award."

2   *Accepting the award:* Ibid.

2   *In 2011, the Jewish population:* See Appendix, Table 1.

3   *Toronto, in particular:* There are approximately 134 synagogues in the Greater Toronto Area. I am relying on figures provided to me from the following sources: Rabbi Asher Vale, Director Beis Din, Vaad Harabonim of Toronto to author February 20, 2018; Rabbi Jennifer Gorman, MERCAZ-Canada, to author, February 22, 2018; Sandy Levy, Coordinator Programming and Administration, Canadian Council for Reform Judaism (Toronto) to author, February 21, 2018. See also, Canadian Council Of Conservative Synagogues https://jewishtoronto.com/directory/tag/17. The total of 134 breaks down as 105 Orthodox Synagogues, 14 Conservative Synagogues, and 15 Reform Synagogues.

3   *From pricy private:* CJN, January 29, 2009; May 13, 2015; Morton Weinfeld, *Like Everyone Else . . . But Different: The Paradoxical Success of Canadian Jews* (Toronto: McClelland & Stewart, 2001), 120–25.

3   *As Rabbi Yael Splansky:* AI with Rabbi Yael Splansky.

4   *There is in the vicinity:* Etan Diamond, *And I Will Dwell in Their Midst: Orthodox Jews in Suburbia* (Chapel Hill: University of North Carolina Press, 2000), 5–6.

4   *Jews in Canada represent:* See Appendix, Table 1; Elliot Olshansky, "Jewish Fighter Goes to Cage," *Forward*, August 18, 2012, http://forward.com/schmooze/161348/jewish-fighter-goes-to-cage/.

4   *More than a century ago:* A.M. Klein, "Autobiographical," in *Complete Poems: Part 2, Original Poems, 1937–1955 and Poetry Translations*, ed. Zailig Pollock (Toronto: University of Toronto Press, 1990), 564–66.

4   *"There are only two"* Gwethalyn Graham, *Earth and High Heaven* (New York: J.P. Lippincott and Company, 1944), 84.

4   (footnote) *Throughout this book*: Emil Fackenheim, "Post-Holocaust Anti-Jewishness, Jewish identity, and the Centrality of Israel," *World Jewry and the State of Israel*, ed. Moshe Davis (New York: Arno Press, 1977), 11, n.2. See also Ira Robinson, *A History of Antisemitism in Canada* (Waterloo: Wilfrid Laurier University Press, 2015), 5–6; John P. Marschall, *Jews in Nevada: A History* (Reno, N.V.: University of Nevada Press, 2008), 329, n.1; and B'nai Brith Canada, *Annual Audit of Antisemitic Incidents 2015*, 6.

5   *In tabulating Jewish population*: Shahar, *2011 National Household Survey Analysis*, 99.

5   *As Kurt Lewin*: Kurt Lewin, *Resolving Social Conflicts* (New York: Harper and Brothers, 1948), 180.

6   *"I can be with a person"*: AI with Barbara Kay.

7   *"To my parents' generation"*: Barbara Kay, *Acknowledgments: A Cultural Memoir and Other Essays* (St. Catharines, ON: Freedom Press Canada, 2013), 2.

7   *Bernie Farber, who worked*: AI with Bernie Farber.

10   *For the most part*: Harold Waller, "Power in the Jewish Community," in *The Canadian Jewish Mosaic*, ed. Morton Weinfeld, William Shaffir, and Irwin Cotler (Toronto: John Wiley & Sons, 1981), 152.

10   *As the late Toronto rabbi*: Troper, *Defining Decade*, 23.

10   *Gerald Tulchinsky, the dean*: CJN, September 29, 2005, B7.

11   *At least two generations*: Mordecai Richler, "Their Canada and Mine," *Commentary* 32:2 (August 1961), 139.

11   *In 1919, when discussion*: AI with Bernie Farber.

11   *"In Canada, the Jews are"*: Samuel Bronfman, "Canadian Jewry Today," *World Jewry* 9:1 (January–February 1966), cited in Troper, *Defining Decade*, 3718. The article likely had been penned by someone on the CJC executive.

12   *And yet as Rabbi Baruch Frydman-Kohl*: AI with Rabbi Baruch Frydman-Kohl.

12   *They came seeking*: Klein, "Autobiographical."

Chapter One: They Came First

15   *As early as the 1560s*: Robin McGrath, *Salt Fish and Shmattes* (St. John's, NL: Creative Book Publishing, 2006), 3–4; "Descendants of Portuguese Jewish Family Revive Claim for Possession of Labrador," JTA, July 7, 1950, www.jta.org/1950/07/07/archive/descendants-of-portuguese-jewish-family-revive-claim-for-possession-of-labrador#ixzz3LknQ36Oe.

15   *Another version has it*: Sheldon J. Godfrey and Judith C. Godfrey, *Search Out the Land: The Jews and the Growth of Equality in British Colonial America 1740–1867* (Montreal: McGill-Queen's University Press, 1995), 40.

16   *Two hundred and thirty years*: MG, March 10, 1927; *The Dutch Intersection: The Jews and the Netherlands in Modern History*, ed. Yosef Kaplan (Leiden, Netherlands: Brill, 2008), 200–01.

16   *The case stalled*: "Descendants of Portuguese Jewish Family Revive Claim for Possession of Labrador," JTA, July 1, 1950; *Milwaukee Sentinel*, September 9, 1951; *Times Daily* (Florence AL), January 25, 1984; McGrath, *Salt Fish and Shmattes*, 4–5.

16   *Catholic and autocratic*: James Pritchard, *In Search of Empire: The French in the Americas, 1670–1730* (Cambridge: Cambridge University Press, 2004), 27.

16   *This order was given* "Code Noir," Liberty, Equality, Fraternity: Exploring the French Revolution, https://chnm.gmu.edu/revolution/d/335/; Irving Abella, *A Coat of Many Colours: Two Centuries of Jewish Life in Canada* (Toronto: Lester & Orpen Dennys, 1990), 3.

16   *The most well-known*: Gaston Tisdel, "Esther Brandeau," DCB, vol. 2, www.biographi.ca/en/bio/brandeau_esther_2E.html; Abella, *Coat of Many Colours*, 1-3.

17   *It is not known*: Tisdel, "Brandeau," 1–3; Godfreys, *Search Out the Land*, 35.

17   *"She is so flighty"*: Tisdel, "Brandeau," 1–3.

17   *By the fall of 1739*: Abella, *Coat of Many Colours*, 2.

18   *During the late fifteenth and sixteenth*: Allan Levine, *Scattered Among the Peoples: The Jewish Diaspora in Twelve Portraits* (New York: The Overlook Press, 2003), 118.

18   *No law was passed*: Levine, *Scattered Among the People*, 138; Todd Endelman, *The Jews of Britain, 1656–2000* (Berkeley, CA: University of California Press, 2002), 15–26, 32–8.

18   *Jews in Britain*: Endelman, *The Jews of Britain*, 36.

18·   *This did not remove*: Godfreys, *Search Out the Land*, 10.

19   *Apart from Jacobs*: Ibid.,73–8.

19   *So desperate was*: Godfreys, *Search Out the Land*, 75–6; C. Bruce Fergusson, "Jewish Communities in Nova Scotia," *Nova Scotia Journal of Education* 11 (1961), 45–8.

20   *Nonetheless, the change*: Godfreys, *Search Out the Land*, 75–6.

20   *He received a land grant*: Denis Vaugeois, "Samuel Jacobs," DCB, vol. 4, www.biographi.ca/en/bio/jacobs_samuel_4E.html.

21   *To make this honour*: Godfreys, *Search Out the Land*, 98–100.

21   *His account books*: Vaugeois, "Samuel Jacobs."

21   *While many of his neighbours* Godfreys, *Search Out the Land*, 109–10; Assorted Correspondence with Samuel Jacobs, 1775–1779, Benedict Arnold Collection, R2945–0-1–E, LAC.

21   *Two of his daughters*: Jacob Rader Marcus, "Jews and the American Revolution: A Bicentennial Documentary." *American Jewish Archives* 27:2 (November, 1975), 176. http://americanjewisharchives.org/publications/journal/PDF/1975_27_02_00.pdf.

21   *In 1786, only months before*: Jacob Rader Marcus, ed., *American Jewry: Documents—Eighteenth Century* (Cincinnati: Hebrew Union College Press, 1959), 34–7.

22   *In December 1781*: Reid to Jacobs, December 3, 1781, in Marcus, *American Jewry*, 25–6.

22   *According to merchant*: Grant to Jacobs, December 3, 1781, in Marcus, *American Jewry*, 26.

22   *Disheartened, Jacobs asked*: Jacobs to Grant, February 15, 1782, in Marcus, ed., *American Jewry*, 27; Samuel Jacobs Jr. to Jacobs, October 30, 1785, in Marcus, *American Jewry*, 29–30.

22   *"I was disputing all"*: Marcus, "Jews and the American Revolution," 176.

Chapter Two: La Famille Hart

23   *The Harts' motto*: Abraham Rhinewine, *Looking Back a Century on the Centennial of Jewish Political Equality in Canada* (Toronto: Kraft Press, 1932), 83; Denis Vaugeois, *The Extraordinary Story of the Hart Family, 1760–1860* (Montreal: Baraka Books, 2012), 70.

23   *The choice came down*: Vaugeois, *The Extraordinary Story of the Hart Family*, 49.

23   *Since Hart was short*: Vaugeois, *The Extraordinary Story of the Hart Family*, 50–1; Godfreys, *Search Out the Land*, 98.

23   *Another significant appointment*: Sheldon J. Godfrey, "Jacob (John) Franks," DCB, vol. 7, www.biographi.ca/en/bio/franks_jacob_7E.html.

24   *This was, as Sheldon Godfrey*: Ibid.

24   *Back in Trois-Rivières*: Denis Vaugeois, "Aaron Hart," DCB, vol. 4, www.biographi.ca/en/bio/hart_aaron_4E.html.

24   *This consortium consisted*: Walter S. Dunn Jr., "Lucius Levy Solomons," DCB, vol. 4, www.biographi.ca/en/bio/solomons_lucius_levy_4E.html; Godfreys, *Search Out the Land*, 83, 90.

24   *Caught in the midst*: Dunn Jr., "Lucius Levy Solomons"; David E. Heineman, "The Startling Experience of a Jewish Trader during Pontiac's Siege of Detroit in 1763," *American Jewish Historical Society Publications* 23 (1915), 31–5; John Heckewelder, *History, Manners, and Customs of the Indian Nations Who Once Inhabited Pennsylvania and the Neighboring States* (Philadelphia: Publication Fund of the Historical Society of Pennsylvania, 1881), 257–58. https://archive.org/stream/histmannerscustooheckrich/histmannerscustooheckrich_djvu.txt

25   *"Tied to the stake"*: Heckewelder, *History, Manners, and Customs of the Indian Nations*, 258.

25   *As early as 1858, this*: Gerald Tulchinsky, *Taking Root: The Origins of the Canadian Jewish Community* (Toronto: Lester, 1992), 30.

25   *He also had slaves*: Vaugeois, *The Hart Family*, 113.

25   *More than a decade earlier*: Vaugeois, "Aaron Hart."

26   *The Hart family house*: Vaugeois, *The Hart Family*, 105–06.

26　*In 1790, Hart wrote*: Aaron Hart to Moses Hart, March 28, 1790, in Marcus, *American Jewry*, 50; Vaugeois, *The Hart Family*, 80–1.

26　*Despite his adherence*: Vaugeois, *The Hart Family*, 13; Esther I. Blaustein, Rachel A. Esar, and Evelyn Miller, "Spanish and Portuguese Synagogue (Shearith Israel) Montreal, 1768–1968," *Transactions & Miscellanies* (Jewish Historical Society of England) 23 (1969–1970), 123.

26　*He left his wife*: Denis Vaugeois, "Moses Hart," DCB, vol. 8, www.biographi.ca/en /bio/hart_moses_8E.html; Vaugeois, *The Hart Family*, 110.

27　*"Moses was born"*: Cited in Vaugeois, "Moses Hart."

27　*When he was in his early twenties*: Ibid.

27　*"What I do not like"*: Vaugeois, "Moses Hart."

27　*In 1798, when he applied*: Godfreys, *Search Out the Land*, 158–60.

28　*He ran in another*: Vaugeois, "Moses Hart."

28　*During one civil court proceeding*: Vaugeois, *The Hart Family*, 116–70.

28　*As Sarah summed up*: Cited in Ibid., 166.

28　*Increasingly eccentric*: Ibid., 177–79.

29　*After attending school*: Denis Vaugeois, "Ezekiel Hart," DCB, vol. 7, www.biographi.ca /en/bio/hart_ezekiel_7E.html; Denis Vaugeois, "Aaron Ezekiel Hart," DCB, vol. 8, www.biographi.ca/en/bio/hart_aaron_ezekiel_8E.html.

29　*Anti-Jewish feelings*: Richard Menkis, "Antisemitism and Anti-Judaism in Pre-Confederation Canada," *Antisemitism in Canada: History and Interpretation*, Alan T. Davies, ed. (Waterloo: Wilfrid Laurier University Press 1992), 15. For a more traditional interpretation of these events, see A.J. Arnold, "Ezekiel Hart and the Oath Problem in the Assembly of Lower Canada," CJHS 3:1 (1979), 10–26.

30　*In 1806 they had formed*: Assemblée Nationale Quebec, "Pierre-Stanislas Bédard," www.assnat.qc.ca/en/deputes/bedard-pierre-stanislas-1939/biographie.html; Charles Blattberg, *Shall We Dance? A Patriotic Politics for Canada* (Montreal: McGill-Queen's University Press, 2003), 141.

31　*Pointing out in an*: Le Canadien, April 18, 1807, cited in Arnold, "Ezekiel Hart and the Oath Problem," 14.

31　*He could have eliminated*: Godfreys, *Search Out the Land*, 158–60, 145–47; D.A. Sutherland, "Samuel Hart," DCB, vol. 5, www.biographi.ca/en/bio/hart_samuel _5E.html.

31　*Or, as the motion*: February 17, 1808, *Journal of the House of Assembly of Lower-Canada from the 29th January to the 14th April, 1808* (Quebec: John Neilson, 1808), 122. http://eco.canadiana.ca/view/oocihm.9_00938_17/124?r=0&s=1; Rhinewine, *Jewish Political Equality in Canada*, 35–6.

32　*Their endgame was*: Godfreys, *Search Out the Land*, 176–77.

32　*"I profess the religion"*: February 17, 1808, *Journal of the House of Assembly of Lower-Canada*, 122; Vaugeois, *The Hart Family*, 131.

32   *The majority of the*: Rhinewine, *Jewish Political Equality in Canada*, 38–9.

32   *In one last attempt*: Vaugeois, *The Hart Family*, 134–45.

32   *In the interim*: Godfreys, *Search Out the Land*, 179.

33   *Now they argued*: Arnold, "Ezekiel Hart and the Oath Problem," 19–21.

33   *"With regard to the"*: Godfreys, *Search Out the Land*, 181.

34   *The attitude of Bédard*: Menkis, "Antisemitism and Anti-Judaism," 15.

34   *As a loyal Lower Canadian*: Vaugeois, "Ezekiel Hart."

34   *The first Jew known*: Stephen A. Speisman, *The Jews of Toronto: A History to 1937* (Toronto: McClelland & Stewart, 1979), 11–12.

35   *He also had a good*: Vaugeois, *The Hart Family*, 156.

35   *First, in 1828*: Godfreys, *Search Out the Land*, 187-88; Rhinewine, *Jewish Political Equality in Canada*, 78–9.

35   *Next was a petition*: Rhinewine, *Jewish Political Equity in Canada*, 74-7; David Rome, *Samuel Becancour Hart and 1832* (Montreal: National Archives, Canadian Jewish Congress, 1982), 22–33.

36   *As historian Irving Abella*: Abella, *Coat of Many Colours*, 30.

36   *Even after 1832*: Godfreys, *Search Out the Land*, 189.

36   *Instead he maneuvered*: Ibid., 203.

37   *The Harts and other Jews*: Carman Miller, "Benjamin Hart," DCB, vol. 8, www.biographi.ca/en/bio/hart_benjamin_8E.html.

37   *Perhaps for that reason*: Tulchinsky, *Taking Root*, 37.

38   *The illusion that the members*: Michael Brown, *Jew or Juif? Jews, French Canadians, and Anglo-Canadians, 1759–1914* (Philadelphia: Jewish Publication Society, 1987), 64–5.

38   *The German and Polish*: Tulchinsky, *Taking Root*, 34–7.

38   *By 1859, the English, German, and Polish*: Wilfred Shuchat, *The Gate of Heaven: The Story of Congregation Shaar Hashomayim of Montreal 1846–1996* (Montreal and Kingston: McGill-Queen's University Press, 2000), 17–19, 39–40.

Chapter Three: A British Subject (and Israelite) I Was Born

39   *This group included*: Godfreys, *Search Out the Land*, 116.

39   *Among them was*: Godfreys, *Search out the Land*, 115–16; "Canada," *Jewish Encyclopedia* (1906), www.jewishencyclopedia.com/articles/14692–victoria; Bill Gladstone, "Fur Trader's Family Reunion," JTA, July 20, 2003, www.jta.org /2003/07/20/life-religion/features/fur-traders-family-reunion.

40   *Lazarus had acquired*: Elinor Kyte Senior in collaboration with James H. Lambert, "David David," DCB, vol. 6, http://www.biographi.ca/en/bio/david _david_6E.html; Blaustein, "Spanish and Portuguese Synagogue," 114; *The Continuing History of the Spanish & Portuguese Congregation of Montreal 1768– 1993: 25 Years of Renaissance* (Montreal: Robert Davies Publishing, 1996), 11.

40   *Disrupting meetings*: Ira Robinson, ed., *Canada's Jews: In Time, Space, and Spirit* (Boston: Academic Studies Press, 2013), 31.

41   *With the "bearing"*: Brown, *Jew or Juif*, 190; George Maclean Rose, ed., *A Cyclopaedia of Canadian Biography*, Volume II (Toronto: Rose Publishing 1886), 96–100, https://archive.org/details/cyclopaediaofcano2roseuoft.

41   *David Aaron de Sola was*: Kenneth Wyman, "Abraham de Sola and His Intellectual World" (master's thesis, University of Toronto, 2002), 2–3.

42   *It was a thriving city*: Paul-André Linteau, *The History of Montréal: The Story of a Great North American City* (Montreal: Baraka Books, 2013), 72; Louis Rosenberg, *Canada's Jews: A Social and Economic Study of Jews in Canada* (Montreal: Bureau of Social and Economic Research, cjc, 1939), 10.

42   *"The English language"*: Linteau, *The History of Montréal*, 73.

42   *His motto was*: Levine, *Scattered Among the Peoples*, 194.

42   *"I too am a reformer"*: De Sola to Leeser, November 24, 1887, Gershwind-Bennett Isaac Leeser Digitization Project, Penn Libraries, http://leeser.library.upenn.edu/documentDisplay.php?id=LSDCBx1FF4_18.

43   *Within five years*: Carman Miller, "Alexander Abraham de Sola," DCB, vol. 11, www.biographi.ca/en/bio/de_sola_alexander_abraham_11E.html.

43   *According to educator*: Susan Landau-Chark, "The Montreal Rebbetzin: Portraits in Time," cjs 16-17 (2008–09), 185.

43   *The Spanish and Portuguese free school*: Shuchat, *The Gate of Heaven*, 14.

44   *He wrote articles*: Miller, "Alexander Abraham de Sola"; cjn, December 8, 2005; Tulchinsky, *Taking Root*, 43–8.

44   *Dawson "has a claim on Jews"*: Cited in Tulchinsky, *Taking Root*, 44.

44   *In 1858, McGill*: Miller, "Alexander Abraham de Sola."

44   *He was not the first*: Brown, *Jew or Juif*, 96.

45   *He participated in*: Tulchinsky, *Taking Root*, 42.

45   *Still, he was a Sephardi*: B.G. Sack, *History of the Jews in Canada* (Montreal: Harvest House, 1965), 139–41; Shuchat, *The Gate of Heaven*, 21.

45   *He had similar attitudes*: Abraham de Sola, *The Sanatory Institutions of the Hebrews* (Montreal: J. Lovell, 1861), 34, https://archive.org/stream/cihm_64730/cihm_64730_djvu.txt.

45   *As his reputation*: Miller, "Alexander Abraham de Sola"; Brown, *Jew or Juif*, 46.

45   *In an 1886 feature*: Lucien Wolf, "Old Anglo-Jewish Families," in *Essays in Jewish History* (London: Jewish Historical Society of England, 1934), 223–24; Brown, *Jew or Juif*, 30.

46   *His eldest son*: Blaustein, "Spanish and Portuguese Synagogue," 118.

46   *Underneath that veneer*: Brown, *Jew or Juif*, 54; Shuchat, *The Gate of Heaven*, 79-80.

46   *In 1888, he even*: Brown, *Jew or Juif*, 202.

46   *At the dedication: Montreal Herald*, September 1, 1890; Blaustein, "Spanish and Portuguese Synagogue," 123.

47   *Owing to Clarence's:* Gerald Tulchinsky, "Clarence de Sola," DCB, vol. 14, www.biographi.ca/en/bio/de_sola_clarence_isaac_14E.html.

Chapter Four: Synagogue Politics

48   *In 1855, the brothers:* Mike Filey, *More Toronto Sketches: The Way We Were* (Toronto: Dundurn Press, 1993), 109.

48   *When it opened:* Speisman, *Jews of Toronto*, 14.

49   *Dissatisfied with their future:* GL, November 15, December 6, 1862; S.J. Birnbaum, "Pioneers of Toronto's Jewish Community," *Jewish Times*, 1912, as reprinted in the *Jewish Standard*, 1934, www.billgladstone.ca/?p=7071.

49   *Lewis Samuel, an Orthodox:* Sigmund Samuel, *In Return: The Autobiography of Sigmund Samuel* (Toronto: University of Toronto Press, 1963), 6–11; Stephen Speisman, "Lewis Samuel," DCB, vol. 11, www.biographi.ca/en/bio/samuel_lewis _11E.html.

49   *In early September 1856:* Samuel, *In Return*, 11; Irving Abella, "A Brief History of Holy Blossom Temple's First 150 Years," www.holyblossom.org/wp-content /uploads/2012/12/A-Brief-History-of-Holy-Blossom-Temple%E2%80%99s-First -150-Years.pdf; *City of Toronto Directory, 1867–68* (Toronto: W.C. Chewett and Company, 1867).

49   *The Toronto Hebrew congregation:* Speisman, *Jews of Toronto*, 31.

50   *Samuel, then the synagogue:* GL, January 21, 1876.

50   *Reverend Meldola de Sola:* Ibid.

50   *An early, though not lasting:* Sheldon J. Godfrey, "Newman Leopold Steiner," DCB, vol. 13, www.biographi.ca/en/bio/steiner_newman_leopold_13E.html; Bill Gladstone, "Jews in Canadian Politics," CJN, June 29, 2017, 24.

51   *But the fact that Elzas:* Brown, *Jew or Juif*, 54.

51   *In Hamilton, he had:* "The History of Temple Anshe Sholom," www.anshesholom.ca /index.php?option=com_content&view=article&id=55&Itemid=262; "Obituary of Edmund Scheuer," July 3, 1943, www.billgladstone.ca/?p=6897.

51   *As a member of the:* Speisman, *Jews of Toronto*, 47; "Obituary of Edmund Scheuer."

51   *He tried to appease:* Speisman, *Jews of Toronto*, 47.

52   *A year later:* Speisman, *Jews of Toronto*, 47; "About Beth Tzedec," Beth Tzedec Congregation, www.beth-tzedec.org/page/about-beth-tzedec; Kevin Plummer, "Historicist: Torn Between the Synagogue and the Concert Hall," *Torontoist*, December 13, 2014, http://torontoist.com/2014/12/historicist-torn-between-the -synagogue-and-concert-hall/; GL, May 14, 1906; February 4, 1907; Arthur D.

Hart, ed., *The Jew in Canada* (Toronto and Montreal: Jewish Publications Limited, 1926), 131–32;. Bill Gladstone to author, February 14, 2018.

52   *Likewise, a group*: Sara Ferdman Tauben, *Traces of the Past: Montreal's Early Synagogues* (Montreal: Véhicule Press, 2011), 26-9.

52   *Their first services*: Bill Gladstone, "McCaul Synagogue Golden Anniversary (1938)," December 20, 2011, http://www.billgladstone.ca/?p=5266.

53   *Though the two*: Speisman, *Jews of Toronto*, 102.

53   *By 1914, there were close*: Ibid., 101.

53   *In 1890, a group of*: CJN, November 11, 2010.

54   *The sordid details*: *Mail and Empire*, April 14, 1906; GL, April 14, 1906.

54   *There was no hiding*: Speisman, *Jews of Toronto*, 103.

54   *Ottawa's tiny Jewish*: "Ottawa's Jewish History," Jewish Federation of Ottawa, http://jewishottawa.com/ottawa-jewish-archives/faq.

54   *The Orthodox Russian Jews*: *Canadian Israelite* (Winnipeg), May 30, 1912; Levine, *Coming of Age*, 63–4.

54   *The English and German settlers*: Goldie Gelmon Weatherhead, *Congregation Shaarey Zedek: One Hundred Years* (Winnipeg: Shaarey Zedek Synagogue, 1990), 20.

55   *One of Rosh Pina's members*: Michael Marrus, *Mr. Sam: The Life and Times of Samuel Bronfman* (Toronto: Viking, 1991), 21–32.

55   *On one occasion*: Levine, *Coming of Age*, 66.

56   *That same year*: MFP, October 15, 18, 1895; Mildred Gutkin, "Early Jewish Theatre in Winnipeg," (Paper, Jewish-Mennonite-Ukrainian Conference, August 28–30, 1995), 1.

Chapter Five: From Coast to Coast

57   *As the story goes*: M.M. Lazar and Sheva Medjuck, "In the Beginning: A Brief History of Jews in Atlantic Canada," CJHS 5:2 (Fall 1981), 93; Sheva Medjuck, *The Jews of Atlantic Canada* (St John's, NL: Breakwater Press 1986), 23.

57   *Green was born*: Katherine N.E. Biggs-Craft, "Nathan Green," DCB, vol. 15, www.biographi.ca/en/bio/green_nathan_15E.html.

57   *In 1882, Green's eldest*: Ibid.

58   *Their son Soloman Hart Green*: Levine, *Coming of Age*, 122.

58   *As of 2013*: "Saint John," Atlantic Jewish Council, https://theajc.ns.ca/history /the-jewish-community-of-saint-john/.

58   *Since Confederation*: Rosenberg, *Canada's Jews*, 20; Medjuck, *The Jews of Atlantic Canada*, 24, 30–31, 75; "Beth Israel Synagogue in Halifax, Nova Scotia," http://thebethisrael.com/about/history/.

59   *By 1862, the newly*: Christine B. Wiesenthal, "Insiders and Outsiders: Two Waves of Jewish Settlement in British Columbia, 1958–1914," MA thesis, University of British Columbia, 1987, 14–20, 47.

59   *The next year*: Cyril E. Leonoff, "Pioneer Jewish Merchants of Vancouver Island and British Columbia," *cjhs* 8:1 (Spring 1984), 13; "Congregation Eman-El's History," Temple Emanu-El History Summary, 1–10, www.congregationemanuel.ca /uploads/1/8/6/0/18606224/temple-emanu-historical-report_sept2011.pdf; *British Colonist*, November 26, 1862.

60   *In the* British Colonist's *coverage*: *British Colonist*, June 3, 1863.

60   *In the years that followed*: Cyril E. Leonoff, *Pioneers, Pedlars, and Prayer Shawls: The Jewish Communities in British Columbia and the Yukon* (Victoria: Sono Nis Press, 1978), 31–33, 45–50.

60   *The Franklin brothers*: Dorothy Blakey Smith, "Lumley Franklin," *dcb*, vol. 10, www.biographi.ca/en/bio/franklin_lumley_10E.html; Leonoff, "Pioneer Jewish Merchants," 28–9.

60   *The Franklins wisely*: *British Colonist*, May 19, June 9, 1857; Godfreys, *Search Out the Land*, 220.

60   *Selim's wealth did not go*: David Rome, *The First Two Years: A Record of the Jewish Pioneers on Canada's Pacific Coast, 1858–1860* (Montreal: H.M. Caiserman, 1942), 53; *British Colonist*, March 10, May 19, 1860.

61   *Moreover, Governor Douglas*: Abella, *Coat of Many Colours*, 70.

61   *"It is utterly absurd"*: *Victoria Gazette*, March 5, 1860, cited in Godfreys, *Search Out the Land*, 224.

61   *In reply, Franklin wrote*: Victoria *Gazette*, November 9, 11, 21, 1865; Blakey Smith, "Lumley Franklin."

61   *In 1856, George Benjamin*: Sheldon J. Godfrey and Judith C. Godfrey, *Burn This Gossip: The True Story of George Benjamin of Belleville, Canada's First Jewish Member of Parliament* (Toronto: Duke and George Press, 1991), 85.

61   *Born in London*: Daily Colonist, August 27, September 23, 1870.

62   *In Ottawa, the thirty-year-old*: *Daily Colonist*, May 28, 1873; Abella, *Coat of Many Colours*, 71.

62   *In search of new business*: Peter Liddell and Patricia E. Roy, "David Oppenheimer," *dcb*, vol. 12, www.biographi.ca/en/bio/oppenheimer_david_12E.html.

62   *They smartly followed*: Ibid. One hundred and fifty years later, the oldest company in British Columbia, the Oppenheimer Group—or Oppy as it was rebranded in 2012—is a multimillion-dollar, Vancouver-based produce enterprise that imports more than a hundred varieties of fresh fruit and vegetables from more than twenty-five countries worldwide. In the 1950s and 1960s, Oppy was the first fruit supplier to import New Zealand Granny Smith apples and kiwi to retailers in North America. See "Company History," *Oppy*, https://oppy.com/who-we-are /company-history; "With Waterproof leds, B.C.'s Oldest Company Saves $9,400 a Year," B.C. Hydro News, August 8, 2015, www.bchydro.com/news/conservation /2015/oppenheimer-group.html; Dee Hon, "Entrepreneur of the Year 2015: Food

and Beverage finalists," B.C. Business, September 25, 2015, www.bcbusiness.ca /careers/entrepreneur-of-the-year-2015–food-and-beverage-finalists.

63   *Late on February 1, 1861:* Daily Colonist, February 25, 1861; David Rome, "Notes on Some of the First Jews West of Ontario," cjhs 2:1 (Spring 1978), 71–2; Leonoff, "Pioneer Jewish Merchants," 26.

63   *With the CPR's decision:* Liddell and Roy, "David Oppenheimer."

63   *Though not without:* Ibid.

63   *When he died:* Ibid.

64   *Twenty years after:* Western Call (Vancouver), December 15, 1911.

64   *At some point:* Levine, Coming of Age, 34.

64   *The eldest brother:* Levine, Coming of Age, 34–6; MFP, January 16, 1922; Arthur Chiel, The Jews in Manitoba: A Social History (Toronto: University of Toronto Press, 1961), 15.

65   *George Frankfurter, who:* Levine, Coming of Age, 39–40.

Chapter Six: In Search of the Golden Land

67   *Only one young:* Zvi Gitelman, A Century of Ambivalence: The Jews of Russia and the Soviet Union, 1881 to the Present (New York: Schocken Books, 1988), 2–5; Levine, Scattered Among the Peoples, 220–21.

67   *For instance, in mid-June 1881:* GL, June 16, 1881; February 9, May 12, 15, 1882.

68   *By the 1850s:* Joel Perlmann, "The Local Geographic Origins of Russian-Jewish Immigrants, Circa 1900," Levy Economics Institute of Bard College Working Paper No. 465 (August 2006), 5.

68   *Canada was a clear:* John Powell, Encyclopedia of North American Immigration, (New York: Infobase Publishing, 2009), 165.

69   *"The emigrants must be":* Cited in Irving Howe, World of Our Fathers (New York: Harcourt Brace Jovanovich, 1976), 30.

69   *Meanwhile, established Jews:* Cited in Stanley Feldstein, The Land That I Show You: Three Centuries of Jewish Life in America (New York: Anchor Press, 1978), 157.

69   *Worse, by association:* Cited in Henry Trachentenberg, "Opportunism, Humanitarianism, and Revulsion: 'The Old Clo Move' Comes to Manitoba, 1882-83," Canadian Ethnic Studies 22:2 (1990), 9.

69   *In Montreal in January:* Rebecca Margolis, Jewish Roots, Canadian Soil: Yiddish Culture in Montreal, 1905–1945 (Montreal: McGill-Queen's University Press, 2011), 111–12.

69   *On February 1, 1882:* Jewish Chronicle (London), February 3, March 24, 1882; Ronald Sanders, Shores of Refuge: A Hundred Years of Jewish Emigration (New York: Henry Holt & Company, 1988), 94.

70   *Alexander Galt, astute:* Donald Creighton, John A. Macdonald: The Old Chieftain, vol. 2 (Toronto: Macmillan, 1965), 14.

70   *In his opinion*: Alexander Galt to John. A. Macdonald, January 25, 1882, John A. Macdonald Papers, vol. 219, LAC 26–A, 93316; Galt to Macdonald, January 28, 1882, John A. Macdonald Papers, vol. 219, 93323–24.

70   *But he agreed with Galt*: John A. Macdonald to Alexander Galt, February 28, 1882, Letterbook 21, 680. See also John A. Macdonald Papers, vol. 82, De Winton to Macdonald, February 18, 1882, 31996–97.

70   *According to the* Gazette: MG, May 16, 1882; Margolis, *Jewish Roots*, 112.

71   *A warehouse near*: Margolis, *Jewish Roots*, 112–13.

71   *However, the optimistic*: Levine, *Coming of Age*, 49.

71   *About seventy of the newly arrived*: GL, May 27, June 17, 1882.

71   *With hardware merchant*: Dirk Hoerder, *Creating Societies: Immigrant Lives in Canada* (Montreal: McGill-Queens University Press, 1999), 124; Levine, *Coming of Age*, 53.

72   *"The Jewish immigrants"*: *Winnipeg Daily Times*, June 3, 1882; MFP, June 5, 1882.

72   *W. L. Bruce*: *Winnipeg Daily Times*, September 8, 1882.

72   *But then they*: Moses Finkelstein, "Personal Reminiscences of an Early Jewish Settler in Western Canada," in *Reform Advocate*, Jews of Winnipeg Edition (Chicago, 1914), 4.

72   *In early July*: MFP July 4, 1882.

73   *But the most notorious*: MFP August 4, 1882; Levine, *Coming of Age*, 55.

73   *"The complainant is"*: Cited in Arthur Chiel, *Jewish Experiences in Early Manitoba* (Winnipeg: Manitoba Jewish Publications, 1955), 20; Levine, *Coming of Age*, 55.

74   *In the view of Yosef Bernstein*: Cited in Robinson, *A History of Antisemitism in Canada*, 41–2.

74   *Historian Gerald Tulchinsky*: Tulchinsky, *Taking Root*, 231; Gerald Tulchinsky, "Goldwin Smith: Victorian Canadian Antisemite," *The Canadian Jewish Studies Reader*, ed. Richard Menkis and Norman Ravvin, eds. (Calgary: Red Deer Press, 2004), 43–5.

74   *Decades later, when*: February 20, 1946, William Lyon Mackenzie King Diaries, R10383–0-6–E, 26 J13, LAC.

74   *Before coming to Canada*: Ramsay Cook, "Goldwin Smith," DCB, vol. 13, www.biographi.ca/en/bio/smith_goldwin_13E.html; Allan Levine, *Toronto: Biography of a City* (Toronto: Douglas & McIntyre, 2014), 104.

75   *In Smith's view*: Tulchinsky, *Taking Root*, 231–34; Levine, *Coming of Age*, 55–6. See also, Goldwin Smith, "Can Jews Be Patriots?" *Nineteenth Century* 3, May 1878, 877; MFP, January 24, 1891; Chiel, *Jews in Manitoba*, 49–50.

75   *An editorial in the*: GL, July 11, 1882.

75   *Was there a "more helpless"*: *Winnipeg Daily Times*, August 9, 1882; *Edmonton Bulletin*, June 10, 1882; Trachtenberg, "Opportunism, Humanitarianism, and Revulsion, 6.

76   *The Manitoba Free Press was*: MFP, August 11, 1882.

76   *By January 1883*: MFP January 12, 1883; Henry Trachtenberg, "Opportunism, Humanitarianism, and Revulsion," 8.

76   *At the official opening*: Speisman, *Jews of Toronto*, 48–50.

77   *Yet it was also*: Ibid., n.2, 127.

77   *He was president*: Valérie Beauchemin and David Gilbert, "Louis Rubenstein Residence," MJM, http://imjm.ca/location/1095.

77   *In the 1880s*: "Louis Rubenstein," *Canadian Encyclopedia*, www.thecanadianencyclopedia.ca/en/article/louis-rubenstein/.

77   *Politicians from all*: MG, January 6, 1931; *Montreal Star*, January 6, 1931.

78   *Hence, their requirement*: Speisman, *Jews of Toronto*, 71.

78   *This was a point*: Ibid., 189.

78   *Even when confronting*: Tulchinsky, *Taking Root*, 151.

78   *Similarly, in Toronto*: Speisman, *Jews of Toronto*, 63.

79   *In October 1882*: MFP October 10, 1882.

79   *Slightly more than*: Ibid., October 19, 1882.

Chapter Seven: It's a Living

84   *He found that Jews*: WLMK, "Foreigners Who Live in Toronto," *Mail and Empire* (Toronto), September 25, 1897.

84   *Owning a pushcart*: Deena Nathanson, "A Peddler and His Cart: The Ward's Rag Trade," *The Ward: The Life and Loss of Toronto's First Immigrant Neighbourhood*, John Lorinc, Michael McClelland, Ellen Scheinberg, and Tatum Taylor, eds. (Toronto: Coach House Books, 2015), 198.

85   *The Manitoba Free Press claimed*: MFP, August 25, 1893; Henry Trachtenberg, "Peddling, Politics and Winnipeg Jews 1891–1895: The Political Acculturation of an Urban Immigrant Community," *Social History* 29:57 (May 1996), 175.

85   *Gentile mothers invoked*: Cited in William Kurelek and Abraham J. Arnold, *Jewish Life in Canada* (Edmonton: Hurtig Publishers, 1976), 52.

85   *A newspaper in rural*: Abella, *Coat of Many Colours*, 99.

85   *Even the revered novelist*: Lucy Maud Montgomery, *Anne of Green Gables*, Chapter 27, "Vanity and Vexation of the Spirit," (1908), www.gutenberg.org/files/45/45-h/45-h.htm#link2HCH0027.

85   *This was so much so*: Trachtenberg, "Peddling, Politics and Winnipeg Jews," 177; *Winnipeg Tribune*, May 11, 1894.

85   *"Any rags, any rubbers"*: Laura Sapper Rackow, "I Remember Winnipeg: Childhood," in JHS, *Jewish Life and Times: A Collection of Essays*, vol. IV (Winnipeg: Jewish Historical Society of Western Canada, 1985), 61.

85   *Stories of Jewish*: See, for example, *Daily Nor'Wester* (Winnipeg), May 11, 1894; Henry Trachtenberg, "Ethnic Politics on the Urban Frontier: 'Fighting Joe' Martin and the Jews of Winnipeg, 1893–96," *Manitoba History* 35 (Spring/Summer 1998), 7; Levine, *Coming of Age*, 70-1.

85   *In Montreal, for a*: Tulchinsky, *Taking Root*, 146; Stephanie Tara Schwartz, "Young Men's Hebrew Benevolent Society," MJM, http://imjm.ca/location/1395.

86   *"There were flies"*: Alton Goldbloom, *Small Patients: The Autobiography of a Children's Doctor* (Philadelphia and New York: Lippincott, 1959), 17.

86   *Goldbloom remembered*: Ibid., 22–2.

86   *More stable and upwardly*: Nathanson, "A Peddler and his Cart," 29–33.

87   *Jewish garment-factory*: Steven Lapidus, "Solomon Levinson," DCB, vol. 16, www.biographi.ca/en/bio/levinson_solomon_16E.html.

87   *"Many families"*: Sherry Olson and Patricia Thornton, *Peopling the North American City: Montreal, 1840–1900* (Montreal and Kingston: McGill-Queen's University Press, 2011), 277.

88   *Testifying in 1889*: Evidence, Quebec, Part I, *Report of the Royal Commission on the Relations of Labor and Capital in Canada* (Ottawa: A. Senecal, 1889), 557–59.

88   *He was escorted*: King Diary, September 18, 1897. See also, "Report Upon the Sweating System in Canada," *Sessional Papers* 61 (Ottawa: King's Printer, 1896), http://epe.lac-bac.gc.ca/100/200/301/pco-bcp/commissions-ef/wright1896–eng/wright1896–eng.pdf.

88   *The immigrants he*: WLMK, "Toronto and the Sweating System," *Mail and Empire*, October 9, 1897.

89   *For Jews, working*: Yossi Katz and John C. Lehr, "Jewish and Mormon Agricultural Settlement in Western Canada: A Comparative Analysis," *Canadian Geographer* 35:2 (1991), 134.

89   *His objective, as he*: Erna Paris, *Jews: An Account of their Experience in Canada* (Toronto: Macmillan, 1980), 234.

89   *The wealthy German*: "Baron Maurice de Hirsch," Jewish Virtual Library, www.jewishvirtuallibrary.org/baron-maurice-de-hirsch.

89   *"A false impression"*: Louis Rosenberg, "There are Jewish Farmers in Canada," *Jewish Standard*, March 30, 1934, cited in Paris, *Jews*, 211. For a contrary view about Jews as farmers, see John McAree, "The Jews in Canada," *Maclean's* 24:1 (May 1912), 22.

90   *But though there were*: Galt to A.M. Burgess, January 30, 1888, Dominion Lands Bureau File 73568, vol. 87, LAC; A.J. Arnold, "The New Jerusalem: Jewish Pioneers on the Prairies," *The Beaver Magazine* 74:4 (August–September, 1994), 38–9.

90   *Wapella's "spiritual" leader*: Cyril E. Leonoff, *Wapella Farm Settlement: The First Successful Jewish Farm Settlement in Western Canada, Pictorial History* (Winnipeg: Historical and Scientific Society of Manitoba and JHS, 1972), 17; A.J. Arnold, "New Jerusalem: Religious Settlement on the Prairies," *Visions of the New Jerusalem: Religious Settlement on the Prairies*, ed. Benjamin G. Smillie (Edmonton: NeWest Press, 1983), 100.

90   *To supplement his*: Marrus, *Mr. Sam*, 35–6.

91   "*God help the*": Cited in Cyril E. Leonoff, *The Jewish Farmers of Western Canada*
      (Vancouver: The Jewish Historical Society of British Columbia and the Western
      States Jewish History Association, 1984), 29.

91   *Rabbi Marcus Berner*: Paris, *Jews*, 233.

91   *Israel and Clara*: Clara Hoffer and F.H. Kahan, *Land of Hope* (Saskatoon:
      Modern Press, 1960), 21.

91   *Exasperated that there*: Ibid., 29.

92   *Among the new arrivals*: Levine, *Coming of Age*, 84–6.

92   *By the time*: "Hall of Fame," *Report on Business Magazine, Globe and Mail*, 20:5
      (November, 2003), 43.

92   *A JCA agent*: Cited in Paris, *Jews*, 247.

92   *Representative of the traditionalists*: Norman Rosenberg, ed., *Edenbridge: A History*
      (Melfort, S.K.: Phillips Publishers, 1980), 108; Gerry Posner, "The Vickars,"
      Shaarey Zedek Shofar (March 2003).

93   *Their first few months*: Paris, *Jews*, 244; Leonoff, *The Jewish Farmers of Western
      Canada*, 50; Rosenberg, *Edenbridge*, 107–13; Levine, *Coming of Age*, 88.

93   *The other two*: Levine, *Coming of Age*, 89.

93   *The traditionalists were challenged*: Ibid., 89–90.

93   *Once the Usiskins*: Michael Usiskin, *Uncle Mike's Edenbridge: Memoirs of a Jewish
      Pioneer Farmer* (Winnipeg: Peguis Publishers, 1983), 141.

94   "*The spirit and attitudes*": Cited in Paris, *Jews*, 260.

94   *The agricultural settlements*: Levine, *Coming of Age*, 99.

94   *As the late braham Arnold*: A.J. Arnold, "The Contribution of Jews to the Opening
      and Development of the West," in JHS, *Jewish Life and Times: A Collection of Essays*,
      vol. III (Winnipeg: Jewish Historical Society of Western Canada, 1983), 29.

95   "*Experience has shown*": Louis Rosenberg, "Jewish Agriculture in Canada," YIVO
      Annual of Jewish Social Sciences 5 (1950), 214.

Chapter Eight: Out of Ghetto Streets

96   *Soon after they*: Usher Caplan, *Like One That Dreamed: A Portrait of A.M. Klein*
      (Toronto: McGraw-Hill Ryerson, 1982), 17–18, 29.

96   *In Montreal, the Kleins*: Margolis, *Jewish Roots*, 23. Thanks to Professors Pierre
      Anctil and Jean-Claude Marsan for educating me on St. Lawrence Boulevard's
      history. Anctil to author, August 15, 2017; Marsan to author, August 16, 2017.

97   *In Abraham's opinion*: Ben Kravitz, a "shameless self-promoter," according to Eiran
      Harris, archivist emeritus at Montreal's Jewish Public Library, claimed that he
      opened the first official deli in Montreal in 1908, 1909, or 1910— the date changed
      each time he told the story—and was responsible for introducing the highly cele-
      brated Montreal smoked meat to the city. Ben cured and smoked the meat

according to a family recipe his grandfather and mother had perfected in Lithuania. After the shop was relocated in 1929 from St. Lawrence to De Maisonneuve Boulevard, his smoked meat sandwiches were in even higher demand at his popular delicatessen, Bens (there was no apostrophe), until it closed in 2006. But Kravitz's pioneering claim is a "pile of baloney," Harris has said. According to his research, smoked meat was first available in Montreal as early as 1884 from Aaron Sanft, a Jewish immigrant from Romania who owned a butcher shop on Craig Street. The first butcher who sold smoked meats on St. Lawrence Boulevard was probably A. Jacobson in 1909; while the first actual delicatessen-style restaurant was not Ben Kravitz's, but that of Hyman Rees (or Herman Rees Roth) who opened the British-American Delicatessen on St. Lawrence near Ontario Street. Bens, says Harris, made its debut as a deli more than likely in 1912. See "Montreal Smoked Meat: An interview with Eiran Harris conducted by Lara Rabinovitch, with the cooperation of the Jewish Public Library Archives of Montreal," *Cuizine* 1:2 (2009), www.erudit.org/en/journals/cuizine/2009–vi–n2–cuizine3336/037859ar/. See also David Sax, *Save the Deli: In Search of Perfect Pastrami, Crusty Rye, and the Heart of Jewish Delicatessen* (Toronto: McClelland & Stewart, 2009), 195; Joe King, *From the Ghetto to the Main: The Story of the Jews of Montreal* (Montreal: Montreal Jewish Publication Society, 2001), 127–31.

97 *As Klein portrayed*: A.M. Klein, "Autobiographical."

98 *The soulful Leonard Cohen*: Ira Bruce Nadel, *Various Positions: A Life of Leonard Cohen* (Toronto: Random House of Canada, 1996), 20; Shuchat, *The Gate of Heaven*, 192.

98 *He had little time*: Caplan, *Like One That Dreamed*, 22–3.

98 *Among the latter group*: Cameron Smith, *Unfinished Journey: The Lewis Family* (Toronto: Summerhill Press, 1989), 1–15.

99 *He found a job*: Ibid., 14.

99 *In 1901, Jacob Pinsler*: Brown, *Jew or Juif*, 241; David Fraser, *Honorary Protestants: The Jewish School Question in Montreal, 1867–1997* (Toronto: University of Toronto Press, 2015), 141–47; Pinsler v. Protestant Board of School Commissioners, cited in Hirsch v. Protestant Board of School Commissioners, Supreme Court of Canada, SCR 246 (1926), https://scc-csc.lexum.com/scc-csc/scc-csc/en/item/9145/index.do#_ftnref3.

99 *By 1914, Jewish students*: Brown, *Jew or Juit*, 241–42.

99 *To this end*: Troper, *Defining Decade*, 64–6; Fraser, *Honorary Protestants*, 163–64.

100 *Jews were in control*: Caplan, *Like One That Dreamed*, 32–5.

100 *During the first two*: Rosenberg, *Canada's Jews*, 136.

100 *Still, whether they*: Ibid., 308–21.

100 *In mid-1899*: McGrath, *Salt Fish and Shmattes*, 44.

101 *Yet the journey*: Israel Medres, *Montreal of Yesterday: Jewish Life in Montreal 1900–1920* (Montreal: Véhicule Press, 2000), 59.

101   *Whether they lived*: Rosenberg, *Canada's Jews*, 136.

101   *The Globe's editors*: GL, March 21, 1922; Speisman, *Jews of Toronto*, 320–21.

101   *"An influx of Jews"*: Toronto Telegram, September 22, 1924; Speisman, *Jews of Toronto*, 321.

102   *It was the conventional*: See Charles J. Hastings, "Medical Inspection of Public Schools," *Canadian Journal of Medicine and Surgery* 21 (1907), 73.

102   *There was some truth*: See Richard Dennis, "Property and Propriety: Jewish Landlords in Early Twentieth-Century Toronto," *Transactions of the Institute of British Geographers* 22:3 (1997), 384–86. One exception to this poverty in Toronto was Jacob Singer, a Jewish immigrant from Austria. He acquired nearly a hundred houses, many of them in the Ward, and left an estate of nearly $350,000 when he died in 1912.

102   *In 1906, a group*: Cited in Levine, *Coming of Age*, 105–06.

102   *In Montreal in 1908*: Tulchinsky, *Taking Root*, 172.

102   *The long list of Jewish*: Howard Moscoe, "My Grandmother the Bootlegger," in Lorinc, *The Ward*, 36–8; Ellen Scheinberg, "Strange Brew: The Underground Economy of 'Blind Pigs,'" in Lorinc, *The Ward*, 95–7; Zachary Leader, *The Life of Saul Bellow: To Fame and Fortune, 1915–1964* (New York: Penguin Random House, 2015), 1–2.

103   *Offering some relief*: See King, *From the Ghetto to the Main*, 93; Valérie Beauchemin, trans. Helge Dascher, "Taube Kaplan ("Greene Rebbetzin")— Hebrew Maternity Hospital," MJM, http://imjm.ca/location/2152; Photo Gallery, Jewish General Hospital Archives, http://jgh.ca/en /archivesphotogallery3#/photos/75/resized_PF7_9_2_2a.JPG; "Memoirs of Dorothy Goldstick Dworkin," *Jewish Standard*, August 15, 1960; *Growing up Jewish: Canadians Tell Their Own Stories*, Rosalie Sharp, Irving Abella, and Edwin Goodman, eds. (Toronto: McClelland & Stewart, 1997), 56; Michael Brown, "Ida Siegel 1885–1982," *Jewish Women: A Comprehensive Historical Encyclopedia*, http://jwa.org/encyclopedia/article/siegel-ida; "Our History," Mount Sinai Hospital, www.mountsinai.on.ca/about_us/who-we-are/history; Linda Frum, "How Jewish Women Shaped Our Nation," CJN Special Canada 150 issue, June 29, 2017; Dee Dee Rizzo, *Mount Carmel Clinic: A History, 1926–1986* (Winnipeg: Mount Carmel Clinic, 1986), 5–7.

103   *Siegel was from Pittsburgh*: Speisman, *Jews of Toronto*, 150–52; Gail Labovitz, "Multiple Loyalties: A Great-Granddaughter's reflection on the Life of Ida Lewis Siegel," *Canadian Woman Studies* 16:4 (Fall 1996), 95–98; CJN, November 25, 2016.

103   *Lillian Freiman and her husband*: Bernard Figler, *Lillian and Archie Freiman: Biographies* (Montreal: Northern Printing and Lithographing Company, 1962); Michael Brown, "Lillian Freiman," Jewish Women's Archive, http://jwa.org/ency-clopedia/article/freiman-lillian.

104 *In a 1909 interview*: Cited in King, *From the Ghetto to the Main*, 94.

104 *On the other hand*: Brown, *Jew or Juif*, 223–24.

104 *Expressing a widely shared*: GL, March 4, 1904.

104 *French-Canadian nationalists*: Olivar Asselin, "The Jews in Montreal," *The Canadian Century* 4:11 (September 16, 1911), 10–11, cited in Brown, *Jew or Juif*, 223–24.

105 *In J.S. Woodsworth's book*: See J.S. Woodsworth, *Strangers Within Our Gates* (Toronto: University of Toronto Press, 1972), 155, 158–60.

105 *This meant teaching*: Marianne Valverde, *The Age of Light, Soap, and Water: Moral Reform in English Canada, 1885–1925* (Toronto: McClelland & Stewart, 1991), 19; Robert Harney and Harold Troper, *Immigrants: A Portrait of the Urban Experience, 1890–1930* (Toronto: Van Nostrand Reinhold, 1975), 110; Harney and Troper, *Immigrants*, 110; Levine, *Toronto*, 125. See also George F. Chipman, "The Melting Pot," *Canadian Magazine* 33:5 (1909), 410–11.

105 *"Better by far"*: *Winnipeg Telegram*, May 13, 1901.

106 *Jews—it was argued*: Canada, Parliament, *House of Commons Debates*, April 5, 1906, 1011, 1014; Robinson, *A History of Antisemitism*, 53; Brown, *Jew or Juif*, 244–45. See also Sheldon Indig, "Canadian Jewry and their Struggle for an Exemption in the Federal Lord's Day Act of 1906," part I, *CJHS* 3:1, 27–56; and "Canadian Jewry and their Struggle for an Exemption in the Federal Lord's Day Act of 1906," part II, *CJHS*, 3:2, 61–114.

106 *Plamondon modelled himself*: Sylvio Normand, "Jacques-Édouard Plamondon," DCB, vol. 15, www.biographi.ca/en/bio/plamondon_jacques_edouard_15E.html.

106 *An instant bestseller*: Stephen Wilson, *Ideology and Experience: Antisemitism in France at the Time of the Dreyfus Affair* (East Brunswick, NJ: Associated University Press, 1982), 171.

106 *Using Drumont's writings*: Normand, "Jacques-Édouard Plamondon."

106 *Two prominent members*: Ibid.

106 *One of the lawyers*: Bernard Figler, *Sam Jacobs: Member of Parliament* (Montreal: n.p., 1970), 23–9.

107 *The trial took place*: Medres, *Montreal of Yesterday*, 127–28; Robinson, *A History of Antisemitism in Canada*, 55.

107 *The Quebec Superior Court*: Normand, "Jacques-Édouard Plamondon."

107 *In late 1914, Plamondon*: Normand, "Jacques-Édouard Plamondon."; GL, December 29, 1914.

107 *In 1919, Queen's University*: Cited in Tulchinsky, *Taking Root*, 240.

107 *In 1904, thirty-two-year-old*: Finkelstein, "Personal Reminiscences" in *Reform Advocate*, Jews of Winnipeg edition; Levine, *Coming of Age*, 121; Pearl Silverstone, "Reminiscences," unpublished manuscript (courtesy of Paul Silverstone).

108 *Ten years later*: Phyllis M. Senese, "Samuel Davies Schultz," DCB, vol. 14, www.biographi.ca/en/bio/schultz_samuel_davies_14E.html.

108 *And in 1918*: David M. Rayside, *Small Town in Modern Times: Alexandria, Ontario* (Montreal and Kingston: McGill-Queen's University Press, 2014), 245–6.

Chapter Nine: Intellectuals and Radicals

109 *The Ahavith Achim*: Craig Chouinard, "A Tale of Two Synagogues: Culture, Conflict and Consolidation in the Jewish Community of Saint John, 1906–1919," CJS 2 (1994), 1–3.

109 *Bitter disagreements erupted*: Ibid., 5.

110 *Teenagers from the Hazen Avenue*: Ibid., 11.

110 *Sustaining two synagogues*: "Saint John," Atlantic Jewish Council.

110 *Born in a town*: Kimmy Caplan, "There is No Interest in Precious Stones in a Vegetable Market: The Life and Sermons of Rabbi Jacob Gordon of Toronto," *Jewish History* 23 (2009), 151–53.

110 *Gordon was very much*: Caplan, "There is No Interest in Precious Stones," 153–55; Speisman, *Jews of Toronto*, 278.

111 *Rabbi Kahanovitch, who*: Sophie Helman, "The Rabbi at Home and in Western Canada," *Western Jewish News*, Centennial Edition, 1970, 15; Levine, *Coming of Age*, 135–36.

111 *But he was also*: Reuben Slonim, *Grand to be an Orphan* (Toronto: Clarke, Irwin & Company, 1983), 29–30.

111 *In Toronto, the Simcoe Street*: Speisman, *Jews of Toronto*, 171–74, 310.

111 *In Winnipeg, with*: Levine, *Coming of Age*, 141; MFP, July 29, 1912; Chiel, *Jews in Manitoba*, 99–100.

112 *According to the 1921 census*: Rosenberg, *Canada's Jews*, 257.

112 *Nowhere was that*: Margolis, *Jewish Roots*, 26.

113 *By the 1930s*: Margolis, *Jewish Roots*, 125; Levine, *Coming of Age*, 152.

113 *But these popular secular*: Speisman, *Jews of Toronto*, 176; Chiel, *Jews in Manitoba*, 103.

113 *In Montreal, for example*: Margolis, *Jewish Roots*, 135.

113 *In Toronto, there was also*: Margolis, *Jewish Roots*, 124; Levine, *Coming of Age*, 152–54.

113 *"We felt, but did not"*: Yaacov Zipper, ed., *Leyzer tsuker gedenk bukh* (Montreal: Komitet fun haverim, 1968), 23, cited in Margolis, *Jewish Roots*, 133–34.

114 *This same folk spirit*: Benjamin Kayfetz and Stephen A. Speisman, *Only Yesterday: Collected Pieces on the Jews of Toronto* (Toronto: Now & Then Books, 2013), 186.

114 *Montreal journalist*: Medres, *Montreal of Yesterday*, 95.

115 *The Adler was the*: "Hirsch Wolofsky," Jewish Virtual Library, www.jewishvirtuallibrary.org/wolofsky-hirsch; Lewis Levendel, *A Century of the Canadian Jewish Press: 1880s–1980s* (Ottawa: Borealis Press, 1989), 17–18.

115 *More than once*: Hirsch Wolofsky, *Journey of My Life* (Montreal: Eagle Publishing Company, 1945), 52–4.

115 *While the Adler was*: Margolis, *Jewish Roots*, 54.

115 *This was probably*: Margolis, *Jewish Roots*, 54; Medres, *Montreal of Yesterday*, 144–45.

115 *In 1914, Wolofsky*: Levendel, *A Century of the Canadian Jewish Press*, 8, 57–6; Linda Kay, "Ida Seigler," JPL Presents, http://www.jpl-presents.org/exhibits /show/seigler/seiglerbio.

115 *In 2005, fifty-six years*: Richard Kreitner, "Hirsch Wolofsky and the Keneder Adler—Eagle Publishing Co.," MJM, http://imjm.ca/location/2102.

115 *Above all, the Adler's*: Margolis, *Jewish Roots*, 53, 77, 89–91; Medres, *Montreal of Yesterday*, 58; Excerpt from Margolis, *Jewish Roots*, "History," JPL, www.jewishpubliclibrary.org/en/aboutus/history/.

116 *As David Rome*: Margolis, Margolis, *Jewish Roots*, 98.

116 *Among those who*: Margolis, *Jewish Roots*, 48–53; JTA, September 25, 1963.

116 *An intense and soulful*: Margolis, *Jewish Roots*, 48; Medres, *Montreal of Yesterday*, 66, 144–45; Excerpt from Margolis, *Jewish Roots*, "History," JPL, www.jewishpubliclibrary .org/en/aboutus/history/.

116 *One of his successors*: Shmuel Mayer Shapiro, *The Rise of the Toronto Jewish Community* (Toronto: Now & Then Books, 2010), 45.

Chapter Ten: Class Struggle

117 *In a 1912*: John McAree, "The Jews in Canada," 58.

118 *"At a machine"*: John McAree, "The Jews in Canada," part II, *Maclean's*, Vol. [TK], August 1912, 58.

118 *Their labour was plentiful*: Robert McIntosh, "Sweated Labour: Female Needle-workers in Industrializing Canada," *Labour/Le Travail* 32 (Fall 1993), 105–38.

118 *Tellingly, one of the*: Medres, *Montreal of Yesterday*, 27.

118 *"God gave me this plant"*: "TimeLinks: Vulcan Iron Works," Manitoba Historical Society, www.mhs.mb.ca/docs/features/timelinks/reference/db0131.shtml.

118 *Hence, strikes over*: Tulchinsky, *Taking Root*, 207.

118 *Another of the affected*: Hart, *The Jew in Canada*, 348.

118 *In Montreal, the*: Sarah Woolf, "Clothing Manufacturers' Association of Montreal—Freedman Company," MJM, http://imjm.ca/location/1323.

119 *In his lifetime*: CJCH, May 4, 1928.

119 *He famously welcomed*: MJM, "Lyon Cohen and the Jewish Times," http://imjm.ca /location/1070.

119 *Fed up by*: Cited in Medres, *Montreal of Yesterday*, 141.

119 *One of the leaders*: Margolis, *Jewish Roots*, 108–09; Valérie Hénault, "H.M. Caiserman—Residence," MJM, http://imjm.ca/location/1799.

119 *He was born*: Hart, *The Jew in Canada*, 38; "Peter Bercovitch," Assemblée Nationale Quebec, www.assnat.qc.ca/en/deputes/bercovitch-peter-2007/biographie.html.

119   *A graduate of McGill*: Tulchinsky, *Taking Root*, 211.

119   *Throughout his political*: CJCH, February 12, 1924, January 10, 1930; MG, January 6, 1930, August 10, 1936; Tulchinsky, *Taking Root*, 211.

120   *The garment factory*: MG, June 11, 13, 1912; *Montreal Star*, June 13, 1912; Tulchinsky, *Taking Root*, 209–12.

120   *The head of the company*: Ruth A. Frager, "Sewing Solidarity: The Eaton's Strike of 1912," *A Nation of Immigrants: Women, Workers, and Communities in Canadian History, 1840s–1960s*, Franca Iacovetta, Paula Draper, and Robert Ventresca, eds. (Toronto: University of Toronto Press, 1998), 316.

120   *The men said no*: Ruth A. Frager, "Class, Ethnicity, and Gender in the Eaton Strikes of 1912 and 1934," Ibid., 193.

120   *The Jewish community*: Frager, "Class, Ethnicity, and Gender," 195; Susan Gelman, "Anatomy of a Failed Strike: The T. Eaton Co. Lockout of Cloakmakers, 1912," CJHS 9:2 (Fall 1985), 103.

121   *The key problem*: *Lance*, March 9, 1912, cited in Gelman, "Anatomy of a Failed Strike," 105.

121   *Many of them*: Frager, "Class, Ethnicity, and Gender," 196; Gelman, "Anatomy of a Failed Strike," 106; Levine, *Toronto*, 132–33.

121   *In 1914, an internal*: Tulchinsky, *Taking Root*, 215–16; Gil Ribak, *Gentile New York: The Images of Non-Jews among Jewish Immigrants* (New Brunswick, NJ: Rutgers University Press, 2012), 122–23.

122   *It was the association's*: General Proceedings of the Third Biennial Convention of the Amalgamated Clothing Workers of America (Baltimore), May 13–19, 1919, 91, https://ia802702.us.archive.org/34/items/generalexecuti1919amaluoft /generalexecuti1919amaluoft.pdf.

122   *As further accusations*: General Proceedings of the Third Biennial Convention, 90, 223; Craig Heron, *The Workers' Revolt in Canada, 1917–1925* (Toronto: University of Toronto Press, 1998), 99.

122   *By mid-February 1917*: Tulchinsky, *Taking Root*, 217–18.

122   *So unpopular was*: Ferdman Tauben, *Traces of the Past*, 50; Wolofsky, *Journey of My Life*, 80.

122   *During one court proceeding*: General Proceedings of the Third Biennial Convention, 90.

122   *Following a protest*: *Le Devoir*, February 22, 1917, cited in Tulchinsky, *Taking Root*, 223.

123   *Most, too, regarded*: Tulchinsky, *Taking Root*, 226.

123   *Three months later*: General Proceedings of the Third Biennial Convention, 103–04.

Chapter Eleven: For King and Country

124   *Others took steps*: "Samuel Waskey," CVWM, www.veterans.gc.ca/eng/remembrance /memorials/canadian-virtual-war-memorial/detail/1577061.

124   *Others, according to*: Rosenberg, *Canada's Jews*, 249.

124   *By the end of the war*: Gerald Tulchinsky, *Canada's Jews*, 174; Alan Simons, "A Tribute to Our Jewish War Veterans of Canada," CIJA, www.cija.ca/jewish-war-veterans-canada/; Zachariah Kay, "A Note on Canada and the Formation of the Jewish Legion," *Jewish Social Studies* 3:29 (July 1967), 177; Louis Rosenberg, "Two Centuries of Jewish Life in Canada 1760–1960," AJYB 63 (1962), 49.

124   *At least seventy-five*: Rosenberg, *Canada's Jews*, 250; CJCH, December 22, 1939.

124   *Most of the men*: Joe Spier, "Samuel Hackman (1890–1916): Calgary's First Jewish Fatal Casualty of World War I," JHSSA (Winter 2012), 4–6.

125   *His family called him*: "Seidelman Family Introduction," JMABC, http://archives.jewishmuseum.ca/seidelman-family.

125   *The Seidelmans owned*: Joseph Seidelman to Rachel Seidelman, June 27, 1917, Seidelman Family Fonds, Private Seidelman's Letters, file 12, June 1917, A. 2009.003, JMABC.

125   *Nearly six decades*: Naomi Katz, "Interview with Rachel Morris and Harry Seidelman," June 6, 1972, JMABC, http://archives.jewishmuseum.ca/rachel-morris.

125   *Early in 1917*: University of British Columbia Archives, "Western Universities Battalion, 'D' Company, 196th Battalion Collection" (2010), Finding Aid, www.library.ubc.ca/archives/u_arch/wub.pdf.

125   *In the first week*: Joseph Seidelman to Rachel Seidelman, April 7, 1917, Private Seidelman's Letters, file 10, JMABC.

126   *The victory was*: Jewish Historical Society of Southern Alberta, "Simon Zuidema," http://jhssa.org/profile/single-profile/?id=497.

126   *At the end of the month*: Joseph Seidelman to Rachel Seidelman, May 7, 22, 30, 1917, Private Seidelman's Letters, file 11, JMABC.

126   *Seidelman returned*: Joseph Seidelman to Rachel Seidelman, June 10, 1917, Private Seidelman's Letters, file 12, JMABC; "Obituary for Private Edward Joseph Seidelman," *Vancouver Daily Province*, undated clipping, 1917, JMABC, http://archives.jewishmuseum.ca/obituary-for-private-edward-joseph-seidelman.

126   *Then, on October 10*: Private Seidelman's Letters, file 16, Joseph Seidelman to Rachel Seidelman, October 10, 1917.

126   *Young Joseph Seidelman*: JMABC, "Joseph Seidelman Death Certificate," http://archives.jewishmuseum.ca/death-certificate. See also Canadian Great War Project, "Private Edward Joseph Seidelman," www.canadiangreatwarproject.com/searches/soldierDetAIl.asp?ID=59066. Rachel Seidelman became a teacher and was active in Vancouver's Jewish community as a member of B'nai Brith and the National Council of Jewish Women. In 1925, she married William Morris, one of Vancouver's first Jewish doctors, and lived a long life, passing away in 1985 at the age of eighty-seven.

127   *A member of the famed:* CJCH, December 22, 1939; Edward Andrew Collard, "St. Andrew and St. Paul," MG, September 8, 1973; John Kalbfleish, "Lieutenant MacCohen's Memorial," MG, November 2, 2013; King, *From the Ghetto to the Main*, 113; "Lieutenant Myer Tutzer Cohen," Canadian Great War Project, www.canadiangreatwarproject.com/searches/soldierDetAIl.asp?ID=30711.

127   *The idea had been:* Medres, *Montreal of Yesterday*, 152.

127   *And so Sam Hughes:* Medres, *Montreal of Yesterday*, 152; "Captain Isidore Freedman," Canadian Great War Project, www.canadiangreatwarproject.com /searches/soldierDetail.asp?ID=140041.

127   *Soon there were:* King, *From the Ghetto to the Main*, 112.

127   *The patriotic appeal:* King, *From the Ghetto to the Main*, 112; CJCH, July 21, 1916; Hart, *The Jew in Canada*, 209, 506.

128   *Thereafter, Jews and Bolshevism:* Robinson, *A History of Antisemitism*, 87; Martin Robin, *Shades of Right: Nativist and Fascist Politics in Canada 1920–1940* (Toronto: University of Toronto Press, 1992), 186; Speisman, *Jews of Toronto*, 319, 330.

128   *In one incident:* MFP, May 27, 1918; Morris Mott, "The 'Foreign Peril': Nativism in Winnipeg, 1916–1923," (MA thesis, University of Manitoba, 1970) 23–25.

128   *A report sent to:* Cited in Henry Trachtenberg, "The Winnipeg Jewish Community and Politics: The Inter-War Years, 1919-1939." Manitoba Historical Society Transactions 3:35 (1978-79), 121.

128   *The most prominent Jewish:* Harry Gutkin and Mildred Gutkin, *Profiles in Dissent: The Shaping of Radical Thought in the Canadian West* (Edmonton: NeWest Press, 1997), 165–65; Levine, *Coming of Age*, 164–65.

Chapter Twelve: Dreaming of Zion

130   *As in Russia:* Theodor Herzl, *Der Judenstaat* [The Jewish State], trans. Sylvie D'Avigdor (1896; reprint: New York: American Zionist Emergency Council, 1946), 7, www.mideastweb.org /jewishstate.pdf.

131   *For the vast majority:* Brown, *Jew or Juif*, 228; Joseph B. Glass, "Isolation and Alienation: Factors in the Growth of Zionism in the Canadian Prairies, 1917–1939," CJS 9 (2001), 92.

131   *By November 1899:* Tulchinsky, *Taking Root*, 182–83, 196; Glass, "Isolation and Alienation," 100.

131   *When Sokolow came:* Speisman, *Jews of Toronto*, 125.

131   *An observant Jew:* Tulchinsky, "Clarence de Sola," DCB.

131   *He was also a generous:* Stephen Speisman, "Moses Bilsky," DCB, vol. 15, www.biographi .ca/en/bio/bilsky_moses_15E.html; Anna Bilsky, *A Common Thread*, 2–7.

131   *He was indeed a devoted:* Tulchinsky, *Taking Root*, 185, 201.

132   *Among the founders:* "Hadassah-WIZO," www.ontariojewisharchives.org/Explore

/Themed-Topics/Hadassah-WIZO, OJA; "The Holy Blossom Sisterhood at 90," Holy Blossom Temple, http://holyblossom.org/2011/06/sisterhood-at-90/.

132   *Together with Labour Zionism's*: Tulchinsky, *Taking Root*, 198.

132   *Archie, who was born*: Anna Bilsky, ed., *A Common Thread: A History of the Jews of Ottawa* (Renfrew, ON: General Store Publishing House, 2009), 26–7.

133   *At the end of the First*: Figler, *Lillian and Archie Freiman*, 18–19, 33–44; Michael Brown, "Lillian Freiman," Jewish Women's Archive, http://jwa.org/encyclopedia /article/freiman-lillian. Prime Minister Mackenzie King was not overly fond of Jews, nor did he approve of them buying property near his estate in Gatineau, Quebec, but he did enjoy the company of the Freimans, loyal Liberals, who had a summer home near Meech Lake. See Allan Levine, *King: William Lyon Mackenzie King: A Life Guided by the Hand of Destiny* (Vancouver: Douglas & McIntyre, 2011), 286–89. On his friendship with the Freimans, see King Diary, October 26, 1927, February 14, 1930, June 28, 1933, August 13, 1936, February 15, 1940.

133   *They were "frantically active"*: Cited in Tulchinsky, *Branching Out*, 150.

133   *As one Labour Zionist*: Tulchinsky, *Branching Out*, 152; Levine, *Coming of Age*, 186–87.

133   *"A Canadian Zionist"*: Aaron Horowitz, *Striking Roots: Reflections on Five Decades of Jewish Life* (Oakville, ON: Mosaic Press, 1979), 60–1, 65.

134   *In the midst*: Jonathan Schneer, *The Balfour Declaration: The Origins of the Arab-Israeli Conflict* (Toronto: Doubleday Canada, 2010), 343, 366.

134   *Months later, de Sola*: See *Manchester Guardian*, November 9, 1917, 5; *New York Times*, November 9, 1917, 3; *Globe*, November 10, 1917, 12.

134   *The wording, which had been*: A detailed discussion and analysis of the arduous negotiations around the Balfour Declaration can be found in Schneer, *The Balfour Declaration*. See, in particular, 333–46.

134   *In truth, as historian*: Ibid., 369–76.

134   *For years after*: Schneer, *The Balfour Declaration*, 348; JTA, November 5, 1928; *Heritage and History: The Saskatoon Jewish Community*, (Saskatoon: Congregation Agudas Israel, 1998), 39; Glass, "Isolation and Alienation," 101.

135   *In 1919, at a Zionist*: Medres, *Montreal of Yesterday*, 160–61.

135   *In 1910, the precocious*: Tulchinsky, *Branching Out*, 199; "History," Canadian Young Judaea, https://youngjudaea.ca/history/.

135   *The majority of those*: MG, February 2, 1921.

135   *During the 1948*: Liel Leibovitz, "Israel's Mister Austerity," *Tablet*, January 4, 2013, http://www.tabletmag.com/jewish-life-and-religion/120697/israels-mister-austerity; King, *From the Ghetto to the Main*, 252.

136   *Reuben Brainin, who was*: Abella, *Coat of Many Colours*, 158; Speisman, *Jews of Toronto*, 270.

136   *In the hundreds*: CJCH, February 14, 1919.

136   *This show of democracy*: Tulchinsky, *Taking Root*, 269.

137   *This included the Congress's:* Jack Lipinsky, *Imposing Their Will: An Organizational History of Jewish Toronto, 1933–1948* (Montreal and Kingston: McGill-Queen's University Press, 2011), 30.

137   *There was a tremendous:* CJCH, March 14, 1919; "Minutes of Meeting, First Canadian Jewish Congress, March 1919," Canadian Jewish Archives, Fond CJC0001, File ZA-1919–10-5, www.cjhn.ca/wpp-images/CJCCCNA/docs/CJC -ZA-1919–10-5–FirstCJCMinutesExcerpt.pdf.

137   *Then Lyon Cohen's:* CJCH, March 21, 1919.

137   *But though they debated:* Harry Gutkin, *Journey into our Heritage: The Story of the Jewish People in the Canadian West* (Toronto: Lester & Orpen Dennys, 1980), 198.

138   *For decades after:* David Bercuson, *Canada and the Birth of Israel: A Study in Canadian Foreign Policy* (Toronto: University of Toronto Press, 1985), 20.

138   *Still, after his victory:* Figler, *Sam Jacobs*, 61.

138   *Summing up that:* CJCH, March 21, 1919.

Chapter Thirteen: Gentiles Only

139   *She recruited to:* Figler, *Lillian and Archie Freiman*, 52; CJCH, November 26, December 10, 1920.

139   *In the meantime:* Cited in Tulchinsky, *Branching Out*, 42.

139   *By the spring of 1921:* CJCH, April 29, 1921; Tulchinsky, *Branching Out*, 44; Figler, *Lillian and Archie Freiman*, 60.

140   *During the twenties:* Irving Abella, "Anti-Semitism in Canada in the Interwar Years" *The Jews of North America*, ed. Moses Rischin, (Detroit: Wayne State University Press, 1987), 244.

140   *According to Louis:* Rosenberg, *Canada's Jews*, 131.

140   *Antisemitism became an:* See, for example, *Toronto Telegram*, September 22, 1924; *Canadian Jewish Times*, October 3, 1924; CJCH, November 21, 28, 1924; TS, October 3, 1924; Speisman, *Jews of Toronto*, 322.

140   *Summer resorts, beaches:* According to a few testimonies, the sign "No Dogs or Jews Allowed" was also posted at Palm Beach, a public beach on the Ottawa River, and in front of the Blue Haven Motel in Amherstburg, south of Windsor, among other locales. However, this may be an example of the inaccuracies of historical memory and of stories told and retold so many times that it is unclear what the truth actually is. The Blue Haven Motel, for example, was owned by Sol Goldman, a wealthy property magnate and burlesque operator with links to Detroit mobsters, who was Jewish. It's highly doubtful that he would have erected such a sign. As far as can be determined, there are no known archival or newspaper photographs of such signs,

and their existence has been rightly called into question. See Bilsky, *A Common Thread*, 99; Kayfetz and Speisman, *Only Yesterday*, 115; Robinson, *A History of Antisemitism*, 67–8; Levine, *Toronto*, 166–67; Jonathan V. Plaut, *The Jews of Windsor, 1790–1990: A Historical Chronicle* (Toronto: Dundurn Press, 2007), 130; Marty Gervais, *My Town: Faces of Windsor* (Windsor, Ontario: Biblioasis, 2016), 80; Cyrill Levitt and William Shaffir, "The Swastika as Dramatic Symbol: A Case-Study of Ethnic Violence in Canada," *The Jews in Canada*, Robert J. Brym, William Shaffir, and Morton Weinfeld, eds., (Toronto: Oxford University Press, 1993), 80. See also Ron Csillag, "Perspectives: 'No Dogs, No Jews'—No Evidence," *CJN*, April 8, 2015, http://www.cjnews.com/news/perspectives-no-dogs-no-jews-no-evidence. Csillag believes the signs may well have existed, but he questions the lack of archival evidence, as does Ira Robinson: Csillag to author, June 26, July 5, 2017; Robinson to author, June 26, 2017. As Saara Mortensen, an archivist at the Ottawa Jewish Archives, told Csillag about the reference in Bilsky's book about the sign at Palm Beach on the Ottawa River, "The Archives does not have any photographs of this sign in the collection, only a handful of (unsupported) references to such a sign in recorded interviews with members of the community."

140 *St. Andrews Golf Club*: Tulchinsky, *Branching Out*, 194; *TS*, January 30, 2010; Levine, *Toronto*, 167.

141 *In 1923, Westdale*: Craig Heron, *Lunch-Bucket Lives: Remaking the Workers' City* (Toronto: Between the Lines, 2015), 53.

141 *If Jews were indeed*: CJCH, November 12, 1920.

141 *"Jews are expected"*: CJR, August 27, 1926.

141 *Jewish doctors and medical*: Kayfetz and Speisman, *Only Yesterday*, 136; Stephen Speisman, "Antisemitism in Ontario: The Twentieth Century," *Antisemitism in Canada*, ed. Davies, 116–17; Robinson, *A History of Antisemitism*, 68; Sophia Sperdakos, "'A Forum for Discussion' and a Place of Respite: Jewish Lawyers and Toronto's Reading Law Club," *The Windsor Yearbook of Access to Justice* 30:2 (2012), 169–70, http://ojs.uwindsor.ca/ojs/leddy/index.php/WYAJ/article/view/4374/3451; Monda Halpern, *Alice in Shandehland: Scandal and Scorn in the Edelson/Horwitz Murder Case* (Montreal and Kingston: McGill-Queen's University Press, 2015), 46.

142 *As Winnipeg's Jewish Post*: JP, January 13, 1928.

142 *Starting in 1926*: Robinson, *A History of Antisemitism*, 71; Paul Axelrod, *Making a Middle Class: Student Life in English Canada During the Thirties* (Montreal and Kingston: McGill-Queen's University Press, 1990), 32–33.

142 *Ira Mackay, McGill's dean*: Mackay to Currie, April 23, 1926, cited in Axelrod, *Making a Middle Class*, 33.

143 *Officials griped about*: Elson I. Rexford, *Our Educational Problem: The Jewish Population and the Protestant Schools* (Montreal, 1924), 26, https://archive.org

/stream/oureducationalproorexfuoft/oureducationalproorexfuoft_djvu.txt; Tulchinsky, *Branching Out*, 65–6.

143   *The issue split*: Tulchinsky, *Branching Out*, 68–9.

143   *Still, it was not much*: Pierre Anctil, "Interlude of Hostility: Judeo-Christian Relations in Quebec in the Interwar Period, 1919–39" in Davies, *Antisemitism in Canada*, 153.

143   *As the editors*: *Le Soleil*, February 3, 1926, cited in Tulchinsky, *Branching Out*, 82. For a more nuanced view, see Anctil, "Interlude of Hostility," 135–61.

143   *"We owe nothing to Jews"*: *Le Soleil*, February 3, 1926, cited in Tulchinsky, *Branching Out*, 82.

144   *More extreme in their*: Abella, "Anti-Semitism in Canada in the Interwar Years," 237–41.

144   *Typical was the anti-Jewish*: E-V. Lavergne, "Haine aux Juifs," *L'Action Catholique*, September 21, 1921, in Richard Jones, *L'idéologie de l'Action catholique 1917–1939* (Québec: Les Presses de l'Université Laval, 1974), 71–2. See also, E-V. Lavernge, "Le péril juif," *L'Action Catholique*, June 1, 1922, cited in Jones, 71–2; CJCH, December 4, 1931.

144   *One solution to Quebec's*: Abella, "Anti-Semitism in Canada in the Interwar Years," 238; Ronald Rudin, *In Whose Interest?: Quebec's Caisses Populaires, 1900–1945* (Montreal and Kingston: McGill-Queens University Press, 1990), 5; David Rome, *Clouds in the Thirties: On Antisemitism in Canada, 1929–1939*, section 2 (Montreal: Canadian Jewish Archives, 1977), 12–18.

144   *"If we do not buy"*: Abella, "Anti-Semitism in Canada in the Interwar Years," 238–39; Robinson, *A History of Antisemitism*, 79–80.

144   *In a lucid moment*: Tulchinsky, *Branching Out*, 173–75, 185–86; Esther Delisle, *The Traitor and the Jew* (Montreal-Toronto: Robert Davies Publishing, 1993), 55–73. See also Ross Gordon, "The Historiographical Debate on the Charges of Anti-Semitism Made Against Lionel Groulx," (MA thesis, University of Ottawa, 1996).

145   *And it was true*: Bill Gladstone, *A History of the Jewish Community of London Ontario: From the 1850s to the Present Day* (Toronto: Now and Then Books, 2011), 112–13.

145   *He lived his life*: Marrus, *Mr. Sam*, 17.

145   *Gossip over the years*: Ibid., 59.

145   *Sam later estimated*: Ibid., 69.

146   *That meant that the Bronfmans*: Ibid., 147–48.

146   *Late on the night*: Marrus, *Mr. Sam*, 103–05; Doug Gent, "Biography of Paul Matoff", https://www.gent-family.com/Bienfait/paulmatoffbio.html; GL, October 5, 1922; *Quebec City Chronicle*, March 21, 1923.

146   *It was not illegal*: Marrus, *Mr. Sam*, 77.

147   *He transformed himself*: Edgar M. Bronfman, *Why Be Jewish?: A Testament*. (Toronto: Signal, 2016), 77.

147   *For years, all Sam*: Marrus, *Mr. Sam*, 406–11. Bronfman's chief rival for the Senate seat was Zionist leader Archie Freiman, who also lobbied for the appointment (which never happened). According to Mackenzie King's version of a conversation

he had with Freiman—his friend and political supporter—in February 1940, Freiman somewhat uncharacteristically used his influence with the prime minister to speak against Bronfman. "[Freiman] talked of Bronffman [sic] of Montreal," King noted in his diary. "I agreed with his statement that he would be a discredit to any representation of the Jews in Parliament." See King Diary, February 15, 1940.

147   *"Despite their immense"*: Bronfman, *Why Be Jewish*, 78.

148   *In 1918, when the* YMCA: Speisman, *Jews of Toronto*, 313; "Sports," OJA, www.ontariojewisharchives.org/Explore/Sports. OJA, "The History of the Y.M.H.A.," http://www.ontariojewisharchives.org/exhibits/ymha/index.html.

148   *It was during the*: David Lewis, *The Good Fight: Political Memoirs 1909–1958* (Toronto: Macmillan of Canada, 1981), 19; Caplan, *Like One That Dreamed*, 33–9.

148   *Lewis also introduced*: "Irving Layton Biography," http://www.irvinglayton.ca /Biography/index.html; Caplan, *Like One That Dreamed*, 99; Smith, *Unfinished Journey*, 149.

149   *In a 1961 essay*: Mordecai Richer, "Their Canada and Mine," 137.

149   *St. John's High*: Levine, *Coming of Age*, 199–200.

149   *Toronto's Harbord Collegiate*: Eddie Goodman, *Life of the Party* (Toronto: Key Porter Books, 1988), 12; Jim Coyle, "The Heroes of Harbord," TS, April 27, 2012; Rosemary Bergeron, "Wayne and Shuster at the National Archives of Canada: The Frank Shuster Fonds," *The Archivist* 119, www.collectionscanada.gc.ca /publications/archivist-magazine/015002-2132–e.html.

150   *At Harbord, there was*: Christina Burr and Carol A. Reader, "Fanny 'Bobbie' Rosenfeld: A 'Modern Woman' of Sport and Journalism in Twentieth-Century Canada," *Sport History Review* 44:2 (November 2013), 122; GM, June 15, 1987.

150   *Rosenfeld was invited*: M. Ann Hall, *The Girl and the Game: A History of Women's Sport in Canada* (Toronto Broadview Press, 1999), 45–9.

150   *A woman with a mind*: Hall, *The Girl and the Game*, 49; Bobbie Rosenfeld, "Feminine Sports Reel," GM, January 6, 1940, 16.

150   *In 1925, Bobbie*: GL, September 21, 1925.

150   *Her most celebrated*: Burr and Reader, "Fanny 'Bobbie' Rosenfeld," 125–26; GL, August 4, 1928.

150   *A Globe sports*: GL, Ibid.

151   *In communities such as*: Rosenberg, *Canada's Jews*, 308.

151   *Not that arguing*: Bilsky, *A Common Thread*, 72–7.

151   *In his history*: Chiel, *Jews in Manitoba*, 58.

152   *In the case of Sam Kliman*: Levine, *Coming of Age*, 230–32; AI with Mayer Rabkin and Lou Kliman. See also "Sarah Kliman Interview," JHS, tape 261, June 21, 1982 (conducted by the author).

152   *Sam Kliman had married*: "Sarah Kliman interview," JHS, tape 261, June 21, 1982 (conducted by the author).

153 *On the executive committee:* "Minutes of the Federation of Philanthropies of Montreal, March 26, 1917, JPL Archives, www.jewishpubliclibrary.org/blog/wp-content/uploads /2010/06/1917–Minutes_Federation-of-Jewish-Philanthropies.pdf; "UJA Federation of Greater Toronto," OJA, www.ontariojewisharchives.org/Explore/Themed-Topics /UJA-Federation-of-Greater-Toronto; Lipinsky, *Imposing Their Will*, 25–6; Gail Labovitz, "Multiple Loyalties: A Great-Granddaughter's Reflection on the Life of Ida Lewis Siegel," *Canadian Woman Studies* 16:4 (Fall 1996), 95–98.

154 *In Montreal, there was:* Ira Robinson, "The Kosher Meat War and the Jewish Community Council of Montreal, 1922–1925," *Canadian Ethnic Studies* 22:2 (1990), 43–7.

154 *Matters took a turn:* Speisman, *Jews of Toronto*, 288, 301, n.17.

155 *Uncertain how to:* TS, July 19, 1926; Speisman, *Jews of Toronto*, 291.

155 *In their ruling:* Speisman, *Jews of Toronto*, 289–99; Rabbi Shlomo Jacobovits, "Beth Jacob: Its First Century," www.bethjacobtoronto.org/pdf/History-Beth %20Jacob%20Synagogue-Jacobovits.pdf.

155 *As the editors:* CJR, July 30, 1926.

Chapter Fourteen: The Jewish Problem

157 *Bennett, who declared:* Cited in Pierre Berton, *The Great Depression: 1929-1939* (Toronto: McClelland & Stewart, 1990), 177.

157 *Factor won by 564:* GL, July 29, 1930.

157 *Factor had come to Toronto:* GM, August 22, 1962; GL, July 29, 1930.

158 *Thirty-year-old David Croll:* CJCH, July 13, 1934.

158 *"The Star regards":* Border Cities Star (Windsor), December 6, 1930.

158 *In late 1932:* Border Cities Star (Windsor), December 6, 1932; Plaut, *The Jews of Windsor*, 94; Ottawa Citizen, November 11, 1971.

159 *Neither Mackenzie King:* King Diary, August 23, 1945.

159 *Quotas, resort and club:* Kelly McParland, *The Lives of Conn Smythe: From the Battlefield to Maple Leaf Gardens* (Toronto: McClelland & Stewart, 2011), 42.

160 *In March 1935:* Ottawa Journal, March 21, 1935; Ottawa Citizen, March 8, 1935; Lita-Rose Betcherman, *The Swastika and the Maple Leaf: Fascist Movements in Canada in the Thirties* (Toronto: Fitzhenry and Whiteside, 1975), 42.

160 *Though their total numbers:* Jean-François Nadeau, *The Canadian Führer: The Life of Adrien Arcand* (Toronto: James Lorimer & Co., 2011), 173.

160 *In 1931, there were:* Anctil, "Interlude of Hostility," 140–41.

160 *Universities did not:* Michael Brown, "On Campus in the Thirties: Antipathy, Support, and Indifference," *Nazi Germany, Canadian Responses: Confronting Antisemitism in the Shadow of War*, ed. Ruth Klein, (Montreal and Kingston: McGill-Queen's University Press, 2012), 157-61; Robinson, *A History of Antisemitism*, 71.

160   *A token number*: Martin L. Friedland, *The University of Toronto: A History* (Toronto: University of Toronto Press, 2000), 307–08; Public Service Labour Relations Board, "Jacob Finkelman, 1907–2003," http://pslreb-crtefp.gc.ca /resources/finkelmanbio_e.asp.

161   *One of Finkelman's*: Philip Girard, *Bora Laskin: Bringing Law to Life* (Toronto: University of Toronto Press, 2005), 10–24.

161   *As a Jewish articling*: Ibid., 60–4.

161   *Yet when he returned*: Ibid., 105.

161   *"Unfortunately, he is"*: Cited in Ibid., 106.

161   *When Laskin's wife*: Ibid., 324.

162   *Leiff was appointed*: GM, February14, 2007.

162   *Asked in 1938*: Brown, "On Campus in the Thirties," 159; Delisle, *The Traitor and the Jew*, 37.

162   *Dean Simpson might have*: Claude Bélanger, "Chronology of the Notre-Dame Hospital Internes' Strike, 1934," Marianopolis College, http://faculty.marianopolis .edu/c.belanger/quebechistory/chronos/strike.htm.

162   *Demanding that the hospital*: Olivar Asselin, "The Internes' Strike," *L'Ordre*, June 22–23 1934 in *Pensée française, Pages choisies*, (Montreal, Edition Canadienne-française, 1937), 185–196, reproduced at Marianopolis College, Ibid., http://faculty.marianopolis.edu /c.belanger/quebechistory/docs/jews/strike/21.htm.

162   *While the interns did*: Abella, "Anti-Semitism in Canada in the Interwar Years," 235; MG, June 18, 1934. See also CJCH, June 22, 1934.

163   *Apologists for the students*: Anctil, "Interlude of Hostility," 148.

163   *After interviewing several*: Asselin, "The Internes' Strike."

163   *Unwilling to be responsible*: Peter Wilton, "Historical Notes: Days of Shame, Montreal, 1934," CMAJ 169:12 (December 9, 2003), www.cmaj.ca/con-tent/169/12/1329.full.

163   *The interns' abysmal*: "History," Jewish General Hospital, http://jgh.ca/en/1930?mid =ctl00_LeftMenu_ctl00_TheMenu-menuItem008; Leo Kolber and Ian Macdonald, *Leo: A Life* (Montreal and Kingston: McGill-Queen's University Press, 2003), 211.

163   *On the seventieth anniversary*: Wilton, "Historical Notes: Days of Shame"; CJN, November 25, 2010.

163   *In February 1934*: Regina Leader-Post, February 28, March 3, 1934.

164   *On the defensive*: "Minutes of Board of Governors, Regina General Hospital," March 13, 27, 1934, Executive Directors' Office, 1921–1969, Regina Qu'Appelle Health Region Archives, 1999.1—Regina General Hospital. Thanks to Dan Davies, Records and Information Archivist at the RQHR Archives, for locating this information for me.

164   *While there was no quota*: Friedland, *The University of Toronto*, 352; Brown, "On Campus in the Thirties," 160. The high number of medical students at the

University of Toronto did not go unnoticed. In 1934, Claris Silcox, an Ontario-born clergyman then working at the Institute of Social and Religious Research in New York published a research study entitled "Canadian Universities and the Jews." He expressed grave concern about the "high number percentage of [Jews in the University of Toronto's] entering class in medicine," which he argued was detrimental "to the province, to the medical profession, to the Jewish students ... [and] to the university." Cited in Brown, *On Campus in the Thirties*, 160–61. On Wilcox's career, see Haim Genizi, *Holocaust, Israel, and Canadian Protestant Churches* (Montreal and Kingston: McGill-Queen's University Press, 2002), 52–3.

164   *Admittance to the*: Terence Moore, "Crumbling Foundation: The Medical School and the Depression," *Manitoba Medicine* 58:4 (1988–89), 140. In the booklet published by the University of Manitoba's Faculty of Medicine to commemorate its centennial in 1983, the story of the quota system is alluded to in the most delicate prose imaginable, as a way to manage the number of students that could be accepted into the program. "The process of selecting medical students had worked well for years," the authors write, "but the restrictive nature and implied biases of the selection process were becoming vocalized." See John Gemmell, ed., *The Faculty of Medicine, The University of Manitoba: Centennial Program* (Winnipeg: University of Manitoba, 1983), 53.

164   *Starting that* year: Percy Barsky, "How 'Numerus Clausus' was Ended in the Manitoba Medical School," JHS, *Jewish Life and Times: A Collection of Essays*, vol. III (1983), 123–24; Levine, *Coming of Age*, 260-62.

164   *Mindel Cherniak, the daughter*: Jewish Virtual Library, "Mindel Cherniack Sheps," www.jewishvirtuallibrary.org/mindel-cherniack-sheps; JPN, September 14, 2016.

165   *In 1933, Mathers told*: JPN, November 23, 2016.

165   *In any event*: Barsky, "How 'Numerus Clausus' was Ended," 123.

165   *Each applicant had*: Ibid., 123–24. It was possible for Jewish students to succeed, as Rueben Cherniack (no relation to Mindel Cherniack) did. He graduated from the faculty in 1948 and embarked on a brilliant medical career in pulmonary physiology in Winnipeg and then Denver. See "Reuben M. Cherniack," National Jewish Medical and Research Centre, University of Colorado, http://atopicderm.org/faculty/cherniack.html; "Obituary," WFP, July 14, 2006.

165   *As far as can be*: "Dr. Mathers, Dean of the Faculty of Medicine, Declares at Hearing, That Hospitals Are Prejudiced Against Interns of Certain Nationalities," IP, March 17, 1944, 1; Jonathan Fine, "Anti-Semitism in Manitoba in the 1930s and 40s," *Manitoba History* 32 (Autumn 1996), 28; Levine, *Coming of Age*, 261.

165   *Significantly, this occurred*: JPN, July 18, 1990.

166   *In 1943, after learning*: Barsky, "How 'Numerus Clausus' was Ended," 125.

166   *The minister denied*: Ibid. 125.

166   *Five months later*: Ibid., 126–27.

167   *This was the result*: Nadeau, *The Canadian Führer*, 66.

167   *Catholic and nationalist journals*: Delisle, *The Traitor and the Jew*, 134–35; Michael
      Oliver, *The Passionate Debate: The Social and Political Ideas of Quebec Nationalism
      1920–1945* (Montreal: Vehicule Press, 1991), 185–86.

167   *Jews—wrote the*: Cited in Delisle, *The Traitor and the Jew*, 134.

167   *According to Delisle's content analysis*: Ibid., 43. See specifically articles she cites on
      pp. 47, 124–25, 129, 168–69.

167   *Needless to say*: Georges Pelletier, "À chacun ses Juifs" ["To each its Jews"], *Le
      Devoir* December 3, 1938, cited in Delisle, *The Traitor and the Jew*, 138.

167   *Among them was*: Tulchinsky, *Branching Out*, 186–88; Max and Monique Nemni,
      Young Trudeau: Son of Quebec, Father of Canada, 1919–1944 (Toronto:
      McClelland & Stewart/Douglas Gibson Books, 2006), 58–9, 187–89, 194–95;
      Jacques Langlais and David Rome, *Jews and French Quebecers: Two Hundred Years
      of Shared History* (Waterloo: Wilfrid Laurier Press, 1991), 102–03.

168   *He had as his*: Nadeau, *The Canadian Führer*, 13–14. See also Ira Robinson,
      "Reflections on Antisemitism French Canada," *cjs* 21 (2013), 104–05.

168   *But it all started*: Nadeau, *The Canadian Führer*, 64; Abella, "Anti-Semitism in
      Canada in the Interwar Years," 241.

168   *Promoting himself*: Nadeau, *The Canadian Führer*, 17–71.

168   *In Ottawa and Winnipeg*: Betcherman, *The Swastika and the Maple Leaf*, 43–4;
      Figler, *Lillian and Archie Freiman*, 262–63; "A.J. Freiman vs. J. Tissot," Today in
      Ottawa's History, August 21, 2014, https://todayinottawashistory.wordpress.com
      /2014/08/21/a-j-freiman-versus-j-tissot/. See also *Ottawa Citizen*, October 9,
      1935; Figler, ibid., 263. On Whittaker, see GL, October 27, 1938; Betcherman, *The
      Swastika and the Maple Leaf*, 65; *Winnipeg Tribune*, March 2, 1934.

168   *Yet for a variety*: James Walker, "Claiming Equality for Canadian Jewry: The
      Struggle for Inclusion, 1930–1945" *Nazi Germany, Canadian Responses*, Ruth Klein,
      ed., 221–22; Speisman, "Antisemitism in Ontario," 122–23; GM, November 9, 1937.

169   *The first such law*: JP, February 22, 1934, 3; Chiel, *Jews in Manitoba*, 180;
      Trachtenberg, "The Winnipeg Jewish Community and Politics," 132; Henry
      Trachtenberg, "Marcus Hyman," DCB, vol. 16, http://www.biographi.ca/en/bio
      /hyman_marcus_16E.html.

169   *Soon after the act*: Gutkin, *Journey into our Heritage*, 212; Levine, *Coming of Age*,
      257–58.

169   *Utilizing the new law*: Gutkin, *Journey into our Heritage*, 212; Betcherman, *The
      Swastika and the Maple Leaf*, 74; Trachtenberg, "The Winnipeg Jewish
      Community and Politics," 132; Levine, *Coming of Age*, 257.

169   *On the day of the march*: Fred Narvey, "Personal Perspective on Theatre," *Jewish
      Radicalism in Winnipeg, 1905–1960*, ed. Daniel Stone (Winnipeg: Jewish
      Heritage Centre of Western Canada, 2002), 84; WFP, June 6, 1934; Brian

McKillop, "A Communist in City Hall," *Canadian Dimension* (April, 1974), 49-50; Levine, *Coming of Age*, 259.

170   *During July and August*: Cyril Levitt and William Shaffir, *The Riot at Christie Pits* (Toronto: Lester & Orpen Dennys, 1987), 81–2. This section on the riot at Christie Pits is based on the author's account, in Levine, *Toronto*, 167–69.

170   *That year, these unwanted*: Levitt and Shaffir, *The Riot at Christie Pits*, 78–9; Speisman, *Jews of Toronto*, 332–33.

170   *The police—who were known*: Speisman, *Jews of Toronto*, 333; Levitt and Shaffir, *The Riot at Christie Pits*, 38–9, 82–5.

170   *The simmering animosity*: TS, August 15, 1933; Levitt and Shaffir, *The Riot at Christie Pits*, 152–53.

171   *This set the scene*: Levitt and Shaffir, *The Riot at Christie Pits*, 155–73.

171   *The riot at Christie Pits*: TS, August 17, 1033; *Toronto Telegram*, August 17, 18, 1933; *Mail and Empire* (Toronto), August 17, 1933; GL, August 18, 1933; Levitt and Shaffir, *The Riot at Christie Pits*, 166–75.

171   *The Jewish community's*: Der Yiddisher Zhurnal, August 22, 1933; Levitt and Shaffir, *The Riot at Christie Pits*, 174.

172   *Most recently, on the eightieth*: GM, August 10, 2013; NP, August 10, 2013.

172   *That hardly dissuaded*: Howard Palmer, "Politics, Religion and Antisemitism in Alberta, 1880–1950," *Antisemitism in Canada*, ed. Davies, 174–75; Janine Stingel, *Social Discredit: Anti-Semitism, Social Credit, and the Jewish Response* (Montreal and Kingston: McGill-Queen's University Press, 2000), 4.

172   *At the height of his career*: John Irving, *The Social Credit Movement in Alberta* (Toronto: University of Toronto Press, 1959), 31–2; Allan Levine, *The Devil in Babylon: Fear of Progress and the Birth of Modern Life* (Toronto: McClelland & Stewart, 2005), 252–54.

173   *While Aberhart, who*: Stingel, *Social Discredit*, 4, 17–19.

173   *In September 1938*: Stingel, *Social Discredit*, 21–2; Palmer, "Politics, Religion and Antisemitism in Alberta," 176.

173   *Even if this publicity*: CJCH, July 22, 1938; Max Beer, "The Montreal Jewish Community and the Holocaust," *Current Psychology* 26:3 (2007), 195.

173   *"The most frightening"*: Hananiah Caiserman, "Anti-Semitism in Canada, 1938–39," cited in Stingel, *Social Discredit*, 27.

174   *At a convention*: Marrus, *Mr. Sam*, 260–61.

174   *But old divisions*: Lipinsky, *Imposing Their Will*, 110–11; Irving Abella and Harold Troper, *None is Too Many: Canada and the Jews of Europe, 1933–1948* (Toronto: Lester & Orpen Dennys, 1982), 10–11.

174   *That poorly disguised*: Richard Menkis and Harold Troper, *More Than Just Games: Canada and the 1936 Olympics* (Toronto: University of Toronto Press, 2015), 66; Lipinsky, *Imposing Their Will*, 141.

174 *His father was*: Sammy Luftspring, *Call Me Sammy* (Scarborough: Prentice-Hall of Canada, 1975), 7–8; Kevin Plummer, "Historicist: Hometown Rivals," *Torontoist*, July 11, 2015, http://torontoist.com/2015/07/historicist-hometown-rivals/.

174 *He learned to*: "The History of the Y.M.H.A.," OJA.

175 *He also revelled*: Lipinsky, *Imposing Their Will*, 142.

175 *At first, Luftspring*: GL, June 16, 1935.

175 *Otto Roger of the CJC*: Menkis and Troper, *More Than Just Games*, 163–64.

175 *Finally, on July 7*: GL, July 7, 1936; Lipinsky, *Imposing Their Will*, 142.

175 *The only Canadian Jewish*: Menkis and Troper, *More Than Just Games*, 126; Plaut, *The Jews of Windsor*, 251; GM, October 13, 2009.

176 *Classically, as Abella and*: Abella and Troper, *None is Too Many*, 8.

176 *Jewish groups and an assortment*: Abella and Troper, *None is Too Many*, 64; Lita-Rose Betcherman, *Ernest Lapointe: Mackenzie King's Great Quebec Lieutenant* (Toronto: University of Toronto Press, 2000), 41

176 *As Blair told Oscar D. Skelton*: Abella and Troper, *None is Too Many*, 64. See also Skelton to WLMK, June 8, 1939, WLMK Papers, Primary Series Correspondence, vol. 280, C-3750, 237087–89, LAC; Skelton to WLMK, June 9, 1939, 237095–96, LAC.

176 *Samuel Jacobs, who had*: King Diary, March 5, 1925; Herman Abramowitz, "Samuel William Jacobs," AJYB 41 (1939–1940), 107. In most sources, it is noted that the Rideau Club did not admit a Jewish member until 1964, but Jacobs was, in fact, a member as of 1925. See, for example, Bilsky, *A Common Thread*, 162; Bruce Muirhead, *Against the Odds: The Public Life and Times of Louis Rasminsky* (Toronto: University of Toronto Press, 1999), 221; Troper, *Defining Decade*, 249.

177 *Likewise, in 1940*: King Diary, July 2, 1940.

177 *In 1937, Jacobs was keen*: King Diary, January 14, 1937; Betcherman, *Ernest Lapointe*, 231.

177 *Well aware of the hostility*: Betcherman, *Ernest Lapointe*, 241.

177 *King frequently expressed*: Levine, *King*, 289.

177 *A guarantee made*: Abella and Troper, *None is Too Many*, 25; Betcherman, *Ernest Lapointe*, 243.

178 *"The sorrows which the"*: King Diary, November 12, 1938.

178 *Neither a series*: Abella and Troper, *None is Too Many*, 40–1; Levine, *King*, 290.

178 *At a cabinet meeting*: King Diary, November 24, 1938. See also King Diary, December 1, 13, 1938; Levine, *King*, 291–92.

178 *"We don't want to"*: Abella and Troper, *None is Too Many*, 46–50. In 1983, soon after *None is Too Many* was published, A.E. Ritchie, the former undersecretary of state for external affairs and Canadian ambassador to the United States from 1966 to 1970, wrote a letter to *Quest* magazine in Toronto, in response to an editorial about the book in which Norman Robertson's statement had been quoted. Ritchie

stated that he had visited the national archives and researched the memorandum in which Robertson was alleged to have made this comment. He suggested that the evidence was lacking. In reply, Irving Abella wrote that the statement was taken from a brief entitled "Canada and the Refugee Problem," dated November 29, 1938, and that Robertson's initials were on the title page. Abella concluded that the memorandum was "presumably written by Norman Robertson." He added that, "without a doubt, Robertson genuinely sympathized with the plight of European Jewry . . . [But] Robertson was a loyal public servant. If it was government policy to keep Jewish refugees out of Canada . . . then Robertson followed orders. Thus he rationalized to an American diplomat in 1939 that allowing Jewish refugees into Canada would 'set the country on fire,' warned his government in 1943 that opening Canada's doors would mean the entry of 'Eastern European Jews of not a high standard of education and skill' and, in the same year, opposed the holding of a conference in Ottawa to consider the rescue of European Jews, since it would 'lead to awkward questions in Parliament.'" See "Editor's Page," *Quest*, April 1983, 5; "Letters," *Quest*, September 1983, 8. Thanks to Irving Abella for bringing this to my attention and to *Quest*'s former editor Michael Enright for sending me copies of the editorial and letters.

178   *Like U.S. president Franklin*: Levine, *King*, 291–92.

179   *The consequence of*: Abella and Troper, *None is Too Many*, x; Levine, *King*, 292. In an article in the 2016 issue of *Canadian Jewish Studies*, Justin Comartin, who obtained a MA from the University of Ottawa, argues that Abella and Troper's figure of 5,000 Jewish refugees was too low. His research shows that 8,787 Jews arrived in Canada from 1933 to 1945, a number which increases to 11,127 when interned refugees are included in the tally. To this, Harold Troper counters that "the Jewish internees were brought to Canada not as refugees or immigrants but as enemy aliens and at first put into prisoner of war camps alongside German POWs. There was no intent on the part of government that they would be allowed to remain in Canada." He and Abella also did not count "the Jews who knowingly and successfully misrepresented themselves as non-Jews in order to get into Canada." Moreover, he concludes, "five thousand or nine thousand, by any measure of humanity, Canada's record was still abysmal." Troper to author, January 16, 2017; See Justin Comartin, "Opening Closed Doors: Revisiting the Canadian Immigration Record (1933–1945)," CJS 4 (2016), 79–102.

179   *In 1938, the* Toronto Telegram: Cited in GM, October 14, 1967.

Chapter Fifteen: We Demand Work

180   *At the age of eleven*: Sharp, *Growing up Jewish*, 120–21.

180   *Max Bregman and two partners*: Ibid., 151–55.

180   *Following Max's death*: "Business Booms for the Bagel King," GM, January 14, 1961.

180 *In Montreal in 1931*: Charles Foran, *Mordecai: The Life and Times* (Toronto: Alfred A. Knopf Canada, 2010), 4–15.

181 *People ate subsistence*: Foran, *Mordecai*, 17; Irving Layton, *Waiting for the Messiah: A Memoir* (Don Mills, ON: Totem Press 1985), 143.

181 *"Misery and heartbreak"*: Layton, *Waiting for the Messiah*, 143.

181 *The* Keneder Adler: Israel Medres, *Between the Wars: Canadian Jews in Transition* (Montreal: Véhicule Press, 2003), 59; CJCH, January 2, 1931.

181 *In 1931, the People's Kitchen*: Tulchinsky, *Branching Out*, 98.

181 *Miss A. Schwartz*: CJCH, January 23, 1931.

181 *An ad was placed*: Joe Zuken, "The Impact of the Depression on the Jewish Community," *Jewish Life and Times: A Collection of Essays*, vol. III, 130, JHS.

181 *Author Adele Wiseman*: Harry Gutkin with Mildred Gutkin, *The Worst of Times, The Best of Times* (Toronto: Fitzhenry & Whiteside, 1987), 22.

182 *By 1931, Jews*: Ruth A. Frager, *Sweatshop Strife: Class, Ethnicity and Gender in the Jewish Labour Movement of Toronto 1900–1939* (Toronto: University of Toronto Press, 1992), 17, 233 (n. 25); Tulchinsky, *Branching Out*, 384, n.38; Rosenberg, *Canada's Jews*, 175–78.

182 *"How's business"*: Cited in Tulchinsky, *Branching Out*, 100.

182 *In the major*: James Gray, *The Winter Years* (Toronto: Macmillan of Canada, 1966), 71.

182 *As was revealed*: No. I, v. 60-65, *Royal Commission on Price Spreads, Minutes of Proceedings and Evidence* (Ottawa: King's Printer, 1935), 5163, https://babel.hathitrust.org/cgi/pt?id=mdp.39015043005464;view=1up;seq=3; JHS, *Jewish Life and Times: Women's Voices: Personal Recollections*, vol. VII (Winnipeg: Jewish Historical Society of Western Canada, 1998), 26; Frager, "Class, Ethnicity, and Gender in the Eaton Strikes of 1912 and 1934," 206.

183 *Perceiving themselves as*: Frager, *Sweatshop Strife*, 211–12; JHS, *Women's Voices*, 27.

183 *An effective tactic*: Frager, *Sweatshop Strife*, 84–92.

183 *In 1933, for instance*: Ibid., 85–6.

183 *Jewish owners, too*: Ibid., 89–90. See also Ibid., 70–4; Tulchinsky, *Branching Out*, 105.

183 *Back in 1925*: GL, February 3, 1925; TS, February 4, 1925; Frager, *Sweatshop Strife*, 72–3; Jodi Giesbrecht, "Accommodating Resistance: Unionization, Gender, and Ethnicity in Winnipeg's Garment Industry, 1929–1945," *Urban History Review* 39:1 (Fall 2010), 6.

184 *One such move*: CJCH, March 9, 1934.

184 *"Are there not many"*: CJR, January 1, 1937.

184 *During the height*: Michiel Horn, ed., *The Dirty Thirties: Canadians in the Great Depression* (Toronto: Copp Clark Company, 1972), 122–23.

184 *During the 1932*: Evelyn Katz, "Lessons My Father Taught Me: A Personal Perspective on Radical Education in the 1930s and 1940s," in Stone, *Jewish Radicalism in Winnipeg*, 35.

185   *Many of the workers*: Sarah Woolf, "Rose Pesotta, Bernard Shane, and Les Midinettes," MJM, http://imjm.ca/location/1250; Tulchinksy, *Canada's Jews*, 259; TS, August 22, 24, 1934; Paris, *Jews*, 140–41.

185   *He had immigrated*: Irving Abella, "Portrait of a Jewish Professional Revolutionary: The Recollections of Joshua Gershman," *Labour* 2 (1977), 189–99.

185   *He later recalled that*: Ibid., 195.

186   *Later, he became*: Sharp, *Growing up Jewish*, 48; Levendel, *Century of the Canadian Jewish Press*, 130–35.

186   *During the 1934 strike*: MG August 23, 1934; Dumas, *The Bitter Thirties in Québec*, 48.

186   *Gershman remembered*: Abella, "Portrait of a Jewish Professional Revolutionary," 201.

187   *Neither was ever*: Dumas, *The Bitter Thirties in Québec*, 65–7.

188   *During one altercation*: *Toronto Telegram*, July 21, 1934; Levine, *Toronto*, 163.

188   *A young agitator*: WFP, September 13, 1933.

188   *Her fellow workers*: WFP, September 13, 1933; Giesbrecht, "Accommodating Resistance," 10.

188   *Following a brief trial*: WFP, April 8, 1935. See also, "Rex v. Richards and Woolridge," [1934] 3 D. L. R. 332 *University of Toronto Law Journal* 1:1 (1935), 187–89.

189   *Coodin may have*: WFP, April 8, 1935, Levine, *Coming of Age*, 270.

189   *On her headstone*: Joan Sangster, "Making a Fur Coat: Women, the Labouring Body and Working-Class History," *International Review of Social History* 52: 2 (August 2007), 260; Shaarey Zedek Synagogue Cemetery files, JHS.

189   *Herbst then negotiated*: Winnipeg Cloakmakers' Union, *Twentieth Anniversary Book* (Winnipeg, 1955), 4; Levine, *Coming of Age*, 271–74.

190   *Other bitter strikes*: Winnipeg Cloakmakers' Union, 5; Levine, *Coming of Age*, 274–75.

190   *Such Montreal nightclubs*: Suzanne Morton, *At Odds: Gambling and Canadians, 1919–1969* (Toronto: University of Toronto Press, 2003), 118.

190   *This notorious Jewish*: Albert Fried, *The Rise and Fall of the Jewish Gangster in America* (New York: Holt, Rinehart, and Winston, 1980), 125; "Lepke," *Life Magazine*, February 28, 1944, 86; *New York Times*, August 31, 2012.

190   *But though there may not*: Stephen Schneider, *Iced: The Story of Organized Crime in Canada* (Toronto: John Wiley & Sons Canada, 2009), 161–71.

190   *He grew up dirt poor*: Morton, *At Odds*, 85; Schneider, *Iced*, 164.

191   *The Royal Canadian Mounted Police*: Schneider, *Iced*, 164.

191   *By the time the Depression*: Ibid., 167.

191   *One of Feigenbaum's*: MG, July 5, 1992.

191   *He also made money*: Schneider, *Iced*, 167; MG, July 5, 1992.

191   *He had intimate*: GL, September 29, 1934.

191   *In a brief trial*: MG, Ibid.

191   *Late in the afternoon*: GL, September 29, 1934; D'Arcy O'Connor, *Montreal's Irish Mafia* (Toronto: John Wiley & Sons, 2011), 35.

192   *The murder was famous*: MG, July 5, 1992.

192   *True, the murder*: Keneder Adler, August 23, 1934, cited in Morton, *At Odds*, 119.

192   *A month later*: GL, September 29, 1934; O'Connor, *Montreal's Irish Mafia*, 35–6.

192   *With the death of*: O'Connor, *Montreal's Irish Mafia*, 34.

192   *In the spring of 1946*: Ibid., 36–7.

193   *At his trial three months later*: GM, January 29, 1958.

193   *The funeral of Harry Davis*: GM, July 29, 1946.

193   *The Adler was once*: Keneder Adler, July 30, 1946, cited in Morton, *At Odds*, 119.

193   *With the death of Davis*: O'Connor, *Montreal's Irish Mafia*, 37–8.

193   *He was also later celebrated*: Morton, *At Odds*, 118; Foran, *Mordecai*, 67; Valérie
       Beauchemin and David Gilbert, "Harry Ship—Chez Parée," MJM, http://imjm.ca
       /location/2078.

194   *Besides operating the popular*: William Weintraub, *City Unique: Montreal Days and
       Nights in the 1940s and '50s* (Toronto: McClelland & Stewart, 1996), 74–5; MG,
       June 21, 1998.

194   *Evidence presented by Plante*: GM, January 14, 1948.

194   *The case wound its way*: GM, February 10, 1948, March 1, 1949.

194   *Once out of prison*: MG, December 23, 1998.

Chapter Sixteen: A Duty to the Jewish People the World Over

197   *When Canada officially*: Wayne Ralph, *Aces, Warriors and Wingmen*
       (Mississauga, ON: John Wiley & Sons, 2005), 153.

197   *After a three-hour*: Ibid.

197   *Like the other nearly*: Tulchinsky, *Branching Out*, 209–10. On Canadian Jewish women
       in the war, see Saundra Lipton, "She Also Served: Bringing to Light the Contributions
       of the Canadian Jewish Women Who Served in World War II," CJS 25 (2017), 92–115.

198   *"I knew that Hitler"*: Ralph, *Aces, Warriors and Wingmen*, 153.

198   *This and other successes*: Ibid.

198   *"I ran into very"*: Ibid., 156.

198   *On one occasion*: Ibid., 155–56.

198   *Another time, flying*: King, *From the Ghetto to the Main*, 218.

199   *His work with rockets*: Ibid.

199   *He played a key role*: GM, February 3, 2007.

199   *Among Canadian Jewish servicemen*: Ellin Bessner, *Double Threat: Canadian Jews,
       the Military, and World War II* (Toronto: New Jewish Press, 2018), [xvi]; Peter J.
       Usher, "Jews in the Royal Canadian Air Force, 1940–1945," CJS 20 (2012) 97–7; Eli
       Gottesman, *Canadian Jewish Reference Book and Directory 1965* (Montreal: Jewish
       Institute of Higher Research, 1965), III.

199   *"One of the best"*: Usher, "Jews in the Royal Canadian Air Force," 98–9.

199   *George Meltz of Toronto*: CJN, June 2, 2014, August 11, 2011; GM, August 19, 1944.

200   *Tall, dark, and charming*: Levine, *Coming of Age*, 278–79.

200   *"Being the padre"*: David Rome, *Canadian Jews in World War II*, vol. 1 (Montreal: Canadian Jewish Congress, 1947), 68.

200   *Margolis had operated*: Jock Switzer, "Paul Belkin's Last Mission," *JHSSA Newsletter* November, 2006, 6–7.

200   *Rose Goodman was born*: "Jewish Airwoman Dies in 1943 Alberta Air Crash," *JHSSA*, June 2004, 3; "Rose Jette Goodman," CVWM, www.veterans.gc.ca/eng /remembrance/memorials/canadian-virtual-war-memorial/detail/2687659; Lipton, "She Also Served," 101.

200   *Other Jewish women*: Lipton, "She Also Served," 101–04

201   *Though Syd Shulemson*: On Ziona Levin, see JHS, *Women's Voices*, 91; Lipton, "She Also Served," 100.

201   *"I know he can't"*: Cited in Usher, "Jews in the Royal Canadian Air Force," 95.

202   *Joe "was Jewish"*: Peter J. Usher, "Removing the Stain: a Jewish Volunteer's Perspective in World War Two," CJS 23 (2015), 41, 46–7.

202   *He even detested*: Ibid., 46.

202   *His father, who was not*: MG, August 6, 1943; Usher, "Removing the Stain," 59; CVWM, www.veterans.gc.ca/eng/remembrance/memorials/canadian-virtual-war -memorial/detail/2648189?Joseph%20Alfred%20Jacobson.

202   *About 49 per cent*: Tulchinsky, *Branching Out*, 210.

202   *"What is the Jews' favourite"*: Walker, "Claiming Equality for Canadian Jewry," 237; Usher, "Removing the Stain," 45.

202   *"It was 'a lie'"*: WFP, September 6, 1940.

203   *Sam Bronfman, who*: Marrus, *Mr. Sam*, 270–71.

203   *He had a lot*: Ibid. 278; Lipinsky, *Imposing Their Will*, 180–85.

203   *The committee opened*: Marrus, *Mr. Sam*, 281; Tulchinsky, *Branching Out*, 205, 208, 213–14; CJCH, October 9, 12, 1942; MG, October 12, 1942; Beer, "The Montreal Jewish Community and the Holocaust," 11.

203   *Canada's military was*: David J. Bercuson, "Canadian Jews in the Second World War: A Few Thoughts," (Unpublished paper, Association for Canadian Jewish Studies Conference, May 2016) 5. Thanks to David Bercuson for sending me this paper.

203   *Ben Dunkelman, the son*: Ben Dunkelman, *Dual Allegiance* (Toronto: Macmillan of Canada, 1976), 7–8, 11–12.

203   *Ben and his brother*: GM, July 8, 1997.

204   *In the fall of 1939*: Dunkelman, *Dual Allegiance*, 46–7; Levine, *Toronto*, 182.

204   *According to Toronto*: Ellin Bessner to author, February 17, 2018. Thanks to both Ellin Bessner and Jack Granatstein for their assistance on the issue of Canadian Jews in the Royal Canadian Navy in the Second World War.

204 *When Ernest Sirluck first*: Ernest Sirluck, *First Generation: An Autobiography* (Toronto: University of Toronto Press, 1996), 83.

204 *Toronto lawyer Eddie Goodman*: Tulchinsky, *Branching Out*, 215; Goodman, *Life of the Party*, 18.

204 *For the most part*: Bercuson, "Canadian Jews in the Second World War," 7. See also Janice Arnold, "Jewish Vets Reminisce, Say No Anti-Semitism in Canadian Army," CJN, June 13, 2017.

204 *In the* RCAF: Usher, "Jews in the Royal Canadian Air Force," 106–07.

205 *They also enthusiastically*: Gottesman, *Canadian Jewish Reference Book*, 128.

205 *Levi's appointment had been:* Rabbi S. Gershon Levi, *Breaking New Ground: The Struggle for a Jewish Chaplaincy in Canada* (Montreal: Canadian Jewish Congress, 1994), 4–21; Shuchat, *The Gate of Heaven*, 132–34.

205 *Levi had to define*: Levi, Breaking New Ground, 40–1, 45–6

205 *After D-Day*, Levi, Ibid., 65.

205 *Many Canadian Jews*: Federation-CJA (Montreal), "1937–1946," http://www.federationcja.org/100/decades/1937–1946/.

205 *Captain Maurice Victor*: Rome, *Canadian Jews in World War II*, vol. 1, 85; Levine, *Coming of Age*, 281.

206 *In November 1944*: Rome, *Canadian Jews in World War II*, vol. 1, 85.

206 *In an interview*: Gutkins, *The Worst of Times*, 75–6.

206 *Early in the conflict*: Rebecca Margolis, "A Review of the Yiddish Media: Responses of the Immigrant Jewish Community in Canada," in *Nazi Germany, Canadian Responses*, Ruth Klein, ed., 122–23.

206 *These news articles*: Margolis, "A Review of the Yiddish Media," 122.

207 *"I saw with my"*: Cited in Abella and Troper, *None is Too Many*, 188–89.

207 *By September 1943*: *New York Times*, December 18, 1942; *Manchester Guardian* December 18, 1942. Cited in À *chacun ses Juifs: 60 éditoriaux pour comprendre la position du Devoir à l'égard des Juifs (1910–1947)*, Pierre Anctil, ed. (Sillery, QC: Septentrion, 2014), 237.

207 *Across the country in Alberta*: Stingel, *Social Discredit*, 88–9.

207 *It was not only members*: Friedland, *The University of Toronto*, 349–50.

207 *Of the major Canadian*: Ulrich Frisse, "The 'Bystanders' Perspective': *The Toronto Daily Star* and its Coverage of the Persecution of the Jews and the Holocaust 1933–1954," *Yad Vashem Studies* 39:1 (2011), 215, 224, 230–31; TS, April 1, 1942. See also, David Goutor, "The Canadian Media and the 'Discovery' of the Holocaust, 1944-1945," CJS 4-5 (1996-97), 88-119.

207 *Throughout the rest*: TS, June 1, December 24, 1942; Frisse, "The Bystanders' Perspective," 231–38.

208 *On June 24, 1943*: *Winnipeg Tribune*, June 24, 1943.

208 *Five months later*: *New York Times*, November 29, 1943.

208   *The following year*: Anna Louise Strong, "Mass Murder," *Maclean's*, September 1, 1944, 11, 39–41; GM, September 22, 1944; Goutor, "The Canadian Media and the 'Discovery' of the Holocaust, 1944–1945," 90–97, 106; Ralph Parker, "Murder for Profit," *Liberty*, October 28, 1944, 20, 21, 65, 66.

208   *By then, the federal*: Norman Erwin, "The Holocaust, Canadian Jews, and Canada's 'Good War' against Nazism," CJS 24 (2016), 109–11.

208   *"The reports were so"*: Cited in Franklin Bialystok, *Delayed Impact: The Holocaust and the Canadian Jewish Community* (Montreal and Kingston: McGill-Queen's University Press, 2000), 24.

208   *Nonetheless, in mid-October 1942*: CJCH, July 24, 1942, 15; WFP, October 12, 1942; GM, October 13, 1942; Erwin, "The Holocaust, Canadian Jews, and Canada's 'Good War' against Nazism," 116.

209   *Prime Minister Mackenzie King*: Abella and Troper, *None is Too Many*, 150–51.

209   *One of the internees*: NP, February 7, 2014.

209   *This modest achievement*: Paula Jean Draper, "The Accidental Immigrants: Canada and the Interned Refugees, Part II," CJHS 2:2 (Fall 1978), 86–7.

209   *"Where is the thunderbolt"*: CJCH, July 17, 1942.

209   *Three years later*: JP, May 24, 1945.

210   *He had worked for the Adler*: Levendel, *A Century of the Canadian Jewish Press*, 134–35.

210   *During the thirties*: Paris, *Jews*, 145–46; Matthew B. Hoffman and Henry F. Srebrnik, *Vanished Ideology: Essays on the Jewish Communist Movement in the English-Speaking World in the Twentieth Century* (Albany, NY: SUNY Press, 2016), 111.

210   *Conceived as an independent*: Alvin Finkel, "The Decline of Jewish Radicalism in Winnipeg, 1945–1965," *Jewish Radicalism in Winnipeg*, Stone, 1991; Ester Reiter and Roz Usiskin, "Jewish Dissent in Canada: The United Jewish People's Order," (Paper, Forum on Jewish Dissent, a conference of the Association of Canadian Jewish Studies in Winnipeg, May 30, 2004); Ester Reiter, *A Future Without Hate or Need: The Promise of the Jewish Left in Canada* (Toronto: Between the Lines, 2016), 41.

210   *Many of its members*: Reiter, *A Future Without Hate or Need*, 42–3;

211   *"In the Cold War atmosphere"*: Reiter and Usiskin, "Jewish Dissent in Canada"; Reiter, *A Future Without Hate or Need*, 123, 135-37.

211   *Roz Usiskin lamented*: CJN, June 15, 22, 2016.

211   *Sam Lipshitz would become*: Gerald Tulchinsky, *Joe Salsberg: A Life of Commitment* (Toronto: University of Toronto Press, 2013), 103–19; Bialystok, *Delayed Impact*, 31; Reiter, *A Future Without Hate or Need*, 42–3.

211   *"The impression was shattering"*: Cited in Bialystok, *Delayed Impact*, 32–3.

212   *That amount only translated*: Lipinsky, *Imposing Their Will*, 218–19.

212   *As the prolific and caustic*: CJCH, April 5, 1946.

212   *King was moved*: King Diary, February 7, 1947; Abella and Troper, *None is Too Many*, 224.

212   *In a major speech*: House of Commons, *Debates*, May 1, 1947, 2644–46.

213   *Nonetheless, in the late forties*: "Memorandum: Re: Immigration," September 5, 1945, cited in Abella and Troper, *None is Too Many*, 199.

213   *In October 1946*: Nancy Tienhaara, *Canadian Views on Immigration and Population: An Analysis of Post-war Gallup Polls* (Ottawa: Manpower and Immigration, 1974), 59. See also Jean M. Gerber, "Immigration and Integration in Post-War Canada: A Case Study of Holocaust Survivors in Vancouver 1947–1970," (masters thesis, University of British Columbia, 1989) 26–7.

213   *One official who visited*: Cited in Tulchinsky, *Branching Out*, 264.

213   *Simply stated, Jews were*: Cited in Abella and Troper, *None is Too Many*, 231.

Chapter Seventeen: Prejudice Exists

214   *In early August 1942*: "Anti-Semites Riot in Canadian Resort Town; Vandals Invade Jewish Shops," JTA, Aug 6, 1942.

214   *In a statement*: "Son of Canadian Chief of Police Sought in Connection with Anti-Jewish Riots," JTA, Aug 6, 1943; MG, July 30, 1943.

214   *That same summer*: The *Victoria Beach Herald* editorial was reprinted in the WFP, August 17, 1943.

214   *In September 1944*: GM, September 27, 1944; Tulchinsky, *Joe Salsberg*, 68–9.

215   *The Globe and Mail*: GM, September 28, 1944.

215   *Drew was skeptical*: Tulchinsky, *Joe Salsberg*, 74; Walker, "Claiming Equality for Canadian Jewry," 246; "The Racial Discrimination Act Adopted in Ontario," Canadian Human Rights Commission, www.chrc-ccdp.ca/historicalperspective/en/timePortals/milestones/45mile.asp.

215   *Nor did the legislation*: GM, March 10, 1944.

215   *In September 1944*: GM, September 26, 1944.

215   *The anti-discrimination act*: See Allan Levine, "Slow Road to Tolerance," *Canada's History Magazine*, April–May 2016, 40–7.

216   *In the late 1940s*: GM, July 28, 1945, 17; Robinson, *A History of Antisemitism*, 113.

216   *Jobs for Jews*: Saul Hayes, "Report on Anti-Semitism in Canada," March 26, 1949, cited in Bialystok, *Delayed Impact*, 70; Robinson, *A History of Antisemitism*, 113.

216   *Graham, born into*: Rachel Gordan, "The Precursor to 'Gentleman's Agreement,'" *Moment Magazine* November 11, 2014, www.momentmag.com/precursor-gentlemans-agreement/; Gwethalyn Graham, *Earth and High Heaven*, 11.

216   *Her parents, the stuffy*: Graham, *Earth and High Heaven*, 105–06, 119. Graham's novel was released three years before the more well-known American novel (also about antisemitism), *Gentleman's Agreement*, by New York Jewish author Laura

Hobson (she was born Laura Zametkin), which became the basis in 1947 for the Hollywood film of the same name starring Gregory Peck and Dorothy McGuire. Ironically, Hobson was inspired to write her book after reading Graham's novel, and Peck had initially signed on with movie mogul Samuel Goldwyn to star with Joan Fontaine in a film adaptation of *Earth and High Heaven* before that project was abruptly cancelled after news that Twentieth Century Fox had obtained film rights to *Gentleman's Agreement*. Had Goldwyn gone ahead with his plans there would, in fact, have been three films in 1947 about antisemitism, as it was also front and centre in *Crossfire*, a murder mystery starring Robert Mitchum. *Crossfire* and *Gentleman's Agreement* were nominated for several Academy Awards, including Best Picture, which *Gentleman's Agreement* won. The antisemitic theme of *Crossfire*, however, was a Hollywood adaptation. The movie was based loosely on the 1945 novel *The Brick Foxhole*, by screenwriter Richard Brooks, which had explored homophobia. But anything to do with that topic was really taboo in 1947, so antisemitism was used instead. See, *New York Times*, October 12, 1946; Gordan, "The Precursor to 'Gentleman's Agreement'"; James Naremore, *More than Night: Film Noir in Its Contexts* (Berkeley and Los Angeles: University of California Press, 2008), 115–20.

216   *All but forgotten:* Gordan, "The Precursor to 'Gentleman's Agreement.'"

216   *In the book, upon:* Graham, *Earth and High Heaven*, 31–33.

217   *In a clash with her:* Ibid., 51.

217   *Reflecting on her own:* Ibid., 81.

217   *In the fall of 1948:* Pierre Berton, *My Times: Living with History 1947–1995* (Toronto: McClelland & Stewart, 1995), 23.

217   *It was "palpable":* Ibid., 23–4.

217   *The first woman called:* Berton, *My Times*, 24; Pierre Berton, "No Jews Need Apply," *Maclean's*, November 1, 1948, 7, 53, 55-57.

217   *He used the same:* Berton, "No Jews Need Apply," 56.

218   *Soon after the article:* Berton, *My Times*, 25.

218   *Wren was the:* "Ontario Supreme Court, Drummond Wren, October 31, 1945," http://oppenheimer.mcgill.ca/IMG/pdf/Re_Drummond_Wren.pdf; GM, November 1, 1945.

218   *That proved true:* GM, July 18, 1946.

219   *In 1933, Annie Noble:* GM, May 24, 1948; George D. Finlayson, *John J. Robinette: Peerless Mentor: An Appreciation* (Toronto: Dundurn Press, 2003), 40–1.

219   *At the end of June 1948:* GM, June 12, 1948.

219   *Rabbi Abraham Feinberg:* Ibid., June 19, 1948.

219   *More than two years later:* GM, November 21, 1950; Noble et al. v. Alley, Supreme Court of Canada, November 20, 1950, https://scc-csc.lexum.com/scc-csc/scc-csc/en/item/3691/index.do.

219   *Though the decision:* GM, November 21, 22, 1950; TS, March 3, 2001.

220　*In 2001, it was:* TS, March 3, 2001.

220　*Leo and Miriam Lowy:* VHEC, "Leo Lowy," testimony, Open Hearts, Closed Doors: The War Orphans Project, http://www.virtualmuseum.ca/sgc-cms/expositions-exhibitions/orphelins-orphans/english/biographies/lowy/chapter1.html.

221　*During a death march:* "Leopold and Miriam Lowy," Candles Holocaust Museum and Education Centre (Terre Haute, Indiana) https://candlesholocaustmuseum.org/file_download/inline/a3c4f7f4-5242-4f83-b6f3-3a277baf833b.

221　*Multiple factors:* Adara Goldberg, *Holocaust Survivors in Canada: Exclusions, Inclusion, Transformation, 1947–1955* (Winnipeg: University of Manitoba Press, 2015), 2, 46–7; Lipinsky, *Imposing Their Will*, 220.

222　*"The community had":* Cited in Sybil Shack and Sharon Chisvin, *Making A Difference: Celebrating Winnipeg's Jewish Child and Family Service* (Winnipeg: Jewish Child and Family Service, 2004), 45.

222　*The children were soon:* Goldberg, *Holocaust Survivors in Canada*, 86.

222　*Susan Garfield, from Budapest:* Ibid., 90–1, 95.

222　*The Lowys were sent:* AI with Richard Lowy and Jocy Lowy.

223　*Even as a child, Znaimer:* Levine, *Toronto*, 268.

223　*In 1942, Znaimer's parents:* Westwood Creative Artists and The Dominion Institute, *Passages: Welcome Home to Canada* (Toronto: Doubleday Canada, 2002), 182–84.

223　*One of Moses's most:* Ibid. 185.

223　*Since his parents:* Ibid., 187–88.

224　*With his "powerful personality":* Ibid., 195.

224　*After obtaining a university:* Levine, *Toronto*, 269–70; Etan Vlessing, "Moses Znaimer, Television: TV Guru Revolutionized Small Screen," *Playback: Canada's Broadcast and Production Journal*, June 25, 2007, 36.

224　*He later articulated:* Cited in Vlessing, "Moses Znaimer," 36; Levine, *Toronto*, 269.

225　*Their clever strategy:* Goldberg, *Holocaust Survivors in Canada*, 47; Abella and Troper, *None is Too Many*, 265–67.

225　*After months of negotiating:* Lipinsky, *Imposing Their Will*, 237; Bialystok, *Delayed Impact*, 50–1.

225　*That stipulation was:* CJCH, March 5, 1948; Lipinsky, *Imposing Their Will*, 242.

225　*Howe was anxious:* Abella and Troper, *None Is Too Many*, 263-64.

225　*The entire exercise:* Lipinsky, *Imposing Their Will*, 238.

225　*In search of "DP Tailors":* CJCH, February 20, 27, March 5, 1948.

226　*The Tailors Project:* Goldberg, *Holocaust Survivors in Canada*, 47–8.

226　*"Never before in the":* AI with Philip Weiss; Levine, *Coming of Age*, 296.

226　*By the end of 1948:* Goldberg, *Holocaust Survivors in Canada*, 50.

226　*From 1945 to 1956:* Bialystok, *Delayed Impact*, 73.

226　*Jacob had endured:* GM, July 30, 2016; Donna Baily Nurse, "'Just' Rosie," *University of Toronto Magazine* (Winter 2006), http://magazine.utoronto.ca/winter-2006/rosalie-abella-supreme-court-of-canada-women-judges/.

226   *He was a lawyer:* Nurse, "'Just' Rosie,"

227   *In the early fifties:* AI with Eli Rubenstein; "Our History," Congregation Habonim, www.congregationhabonim.org/our-history.

227   *Real happiness:* Paula Jean Draper, "Canadian Holocaust Survivors: From Liberation to Rebirth," CJS 4–5 (1996–97), 56; Lisa Appignanesi, *Losing the Dead* (Toronto: McArthur & Company, 1999), 4.

227   *Jacob Silberman, who died:* GM, July 30, 2016; TS, February 18, 2010.

227   *There is an accepted:* Bialystok, *Delayed Impact*, 78.

228   *They felt that:* Ibid., 80–1.

228   *One survivor living in:* Gerber, "Immigration and Integration in Post-War Canada," 81–2.

228   *Mainstream Jewish schools:* Bialystok, *Delayed Impact*, 92, 70.

228   *Survivors soon felt:* Bialystok, *Delayed Impact*, 72; AI with Philip Weiss.

Chapter Eighteen: Devoted Zionists and Loyal Canadians

229   *Even in the pages:* Vochenblatt, April 29, 1948, cited in Tulchinsky, *Branching Out*, 130. See also, Reiter, *A Future Without Hate or Need*, 188.

229   *As historian:* Alvin Finkel, "The Decline of Jewish Radicalism in Winnipeg," 199.

229   *On November 29:* Michael B. Oren, *Six Days of War: June 1967 and the Making of the Modern Middle East* (New York: Oxford University Press, 2002), 4–5.

229   *The Jews accepted:* New York Times, September 30, 1947.

229   *"It is not in the staid":* CJCH, December 5, 1947.

230   *"Horns were honked":* Mordecai Richler, *This Year in Jerusalem* (Toronto: Alfred A. Knopf Canada, 1994), 33.

230   *Across North America:* GM, December 6, 1947; *New Herald Tribune*, December 5, 1947; *New York Times*, December 6, 1947.

230   *At the Holy Blossom:* GM, December 6, 1947.

230   *A Gallup poll:* Zachariah Kay, *Canada and Palestine: The Politics of Noncommitment* (Jerusalem: Israel Universities Press, 1978), 106–07; David Bercuson, *Canada and the Birth of Israel: A Study in Canadian Foreign Policy* (Toronto: University of Toronto Press, 1985), 137.

230   *In this case:* Bercuson, *Canada and the Birth of Israel*, 22–7.

231   *Born in Kingston:* GM, April 27, 1970; Zacks Gallery, "History," www.zacksgallery.ca /history.html.

231   *For two years following:* David J. Azrieli, *Rekindling the Torch: The Story of Canadian Zionism* (Toronto: Key Porter Books, 2008), 92.

231   *Among other connections:* Zachariah Kay, "The Canadian Press and Palestine: A Survey, 1939–48," *International Journal* 18:3 (1963), 364.

231   *Another key individual:* Bercuson, *Canada and the Birth of Israel*, 20.

231 One of his astute ideas: Bercuson, Canada and the Birth of Israel, 24–5; Azrieli, Rekindling the Torch, 84.

232 The assassination of Lord Moyne: Bercuson, Canada and the Birth of Israel, 27–9, 42–4; Kay, "The Canadian Press and Palestine," 364.

232 At a training camp: CJR, August 24, 1945.

232 In the late forties: Cited in "Hachshara Farms," JPL, www.cjhn.ca/en/permalink /cjhn17235.

232–33 But as Ralph Troper: Ralph Troper to author, November 30, 2016.

233 Young Judaea embarked: "History," Canadian Young Judaea.

233 The moving force: "Mission and History," Camp Kadimah. www.campkadimah.com /about-our-camp/mission/.

233 A similar fight: Tulchinsky, Branching Out, 249–51.

233 Habonim—which in: J.J. Goldberg and Elliot King, ed., Builders and Dreamers: Habonim Labour Zionist Youth in North America (New York: Herzl Press, 1993), 18, 268.

233 The Lowbanks farmland: Tobi "Pidgy" Gordon, Remembering Camp Kvutza (Toronto: Invisible Books 2013), 34–7, 68; CJN, July 30, 2008.

234 The camp had a big: AI with Teme Kernerman; Ruth P. Schoenberg and Ruth R. Goodman, "Israeli Folk Dance Pioneers in North America," Jewish Women's Archive, https://jwa.org/encyclopedia/article/israeli-folk-dance-pioneers-in-north-america; CJN, July 30, 2008; "Choreographer Teme Kernerman," Israeli Dances, http://israelidances.com/choreographer.asp?name=temekernerman.

234 Nirkoda folded in: Ronit Eizenman to author, March 23, 2017.

234 Mordecai Richler claimed: Richler, This Year in Jerusalem, 21, 31.

235 The Habonim camp north: Levine, Coming of Age, 335–39. See also WFP, July 26, 1969, Leisure Magazine, 5.

235 Camp B'nai Brith of Montreal: "History," Camp B'nai Brith of Montreal, http:// cbbmtl.org/our-camp/history/; MG, July 16, 1988.

235 Camp Northland-B'nai Brith: "History," Camp Northland, http://campnbb.com/ about-us/history/.

235 Ottawa's Camp B'nai Brith: "Our Story," Camp B'nai Brith of Ottawa, www.cbbottawa.com/all-about-cbb.aspx.

235 In the west, the B'nai Brith: Levine, Coming of Age, 333–35; "Town of Kenora Accepts BB Camp's Offer to Purchase 30 Acres of Town Island," Winnipeg Jewish Review, July 3, 2014, www.winnipegjewishreview.com/article_detail.cfm?id=4292.

235 Meanwhile, picturesque Camp B'nai Brith: Maxine Fischbein, "Camp BB-Riback: Memories Midor L'Dor," Heritage, 16:3 (Summer 2014), 6–9, http://dw1juh2mqzlmq.cloudfront.net/wp-content/uploads/2015/12 /JAHSENA-Camp-BB-Article-11.pdf.

235 The birth of Israel: CJCH, May 14, 1948.

236 *Across Canada, that was:* Ibid., May 19, 1948.

236 *At a boisterous rally:* GM, May 17, 1948.

236 *At a meeting in early August:* Bercuson, *Canada and the Birth of Israel,* 196–98, 221–22.

236 *Future Israeli prime minister:* "Golda Meir," Jewish Women's Archive, https://jwa.org/thisweek/jan/21/1948/golda-meir; "Golda Meir: An Outline of a Unique Life," Golda Meir Center for Political Leadership, Metropolitan State University of Denver, https://msudenver.edu/golda/goldameir/chronologyofgoldameir/; Azrieli, *Rekindling the Torch,* 106.

237 *Israel also desperately:* David Bercuson, "They Fought for the Nascent Jewish state," CJN, February 21, 2008, B18.

237 *There was no law:* Azrieli, *Rekindling the Torch,* 106; Bercuson, "They Fought for the Nascent Jewish state," B18–B22.

237 *Assisting local Zionists:* Bercuson, "They Fought for the Nascent Jewish state," B18–B22; CJN, June 19, 1997; Azrieli, *Rekindling the Torch,* 107.

237 *In all, about 250:* David Bercuson, *The Secret Army* (Toronto: Lester & Orpen Dennys, 1983), xiii; Aliyah Bet & Machal Virtual Museum, "North American Volunteers In Israel's War of Independence," http://israelvets.com/pictorialhist_AIrding_ground_forces.html.

237 *Their clandestine journey:* AI with Allan Chapnick; JPN, August 2, 1989; Levine, *Coming of Age,* 301–02,

238 *Eleven Canadians died:* CJN, October 22, 2009.

238 *Ralph Moster from:* Jewish Western Bulletin, April 27, 1973; CJN, February 28, 2008; Calgary Herald, May 4, 2003.

238 *In a letter to his parents:* Jewish Western Bulletin, ibid.

238 *With the support of:* Bercuson, *The Secret Army,* 45–7; Azrieli, *Rekindling the Torch,* 102; Richard Kreitner, "Victory Equipment and Supply company," MJM, http://imjm.ca/location/1443; Canadian Warplane Heritage Museum, www.warplane.com/AIrcraft/AIrcraft-history.aspx?AIrcraftId=31.

239 *In the summer of 1948:* Bercuson, *The Secret Army,* 47–8.

239 *One day in 1951:* Marrus, *Mr. Sam,* 428–29; Charles Bronfman with Howard Green, *Distilled: A Memoir of Family, Seagram, Baseball, and Philanthropy* (Toronto: HarperCollins, 2016), 4.

240 *A Saskatchewan-born lawyer:* Levine, *Coming of Age,* 285–89, 357–62; Troper, *Defining Decade,* 86–7; "Sol Kanee Biography," Sol Kanee Lecture Series on Peace and Justice, University of Manitoba, https://umanitoba.ca/colleges/st_pauls/mauro_centre/media/Sol_Kanee_Biography.pdf.

240 *Bronfman asked Peres about:* Marrus, *Mr. Sam,* 429–30.

241 *A stickler for detail:* Bronfman, *Distilled,* 163–64.

Chapter Nineteen: An Admirable Element of the Community

242 *Antisemitism was thus*: "Summary of Activities of the National Joint Public Relations Committee of the Canadian Jewish Congress and the B'nai Brith (1947)," (hereafter, JPRC Report, 1947) Berman Jewish Policy Archive, Stanford University, 8.

242 *On the twelfth anniversary*: GM, December 6, 1960.

242 *As Rabbi Abraham Feinberg had*: Cited in Carmela Patrias and Ruth A. Frager, "'This Is Our Country, These Are Our Rights': Minorities and the Origins of Ontario's Human Rights Campaigns," *Canadian Historical Review* 82:1 (March 2001), 15.

243 *Soon after the bill abolishing*: McGibbon to Frost, February 17, 1950, and Frost to McGibbon, February 21, 1950, cited in Roger Graham, *Old Man Ontario: Leslie M. Frost* (Toronto: University of Toronto Press, 1990), 262–65.

243 *Consider that, in 1946*: AJYB, 48, (1946–1947), 279.

243 *In 1947, as the reported*: JPRC Report, 1947, 19.

243 *And a letter*: Ibid., 19.

244 *In 1951, George D. Finlayson*: Finlayson, *John J. Robinette: Peerless Mentor*, 4.

244 *This was a fact*: AI with Donald Carr.

244 *As late as 1962*: AI with Jack London; Levine, *Coming of Age*, 256.

244 *A Maclean's feature*: Phyllis Lee Peterson, "The Jew in Canada: Where Does He Stand Today?" *Maclean's*, October 24, 1959, 22.

244 *Given that reality*: Levine, *Coming of Age*, 267; Gladstone, *A History of the Jewish community of London Ontario*, 182–83.

244 *In the late forties*: AI with Donald Carr; Sperdakos, "'A Forum for Discussion' and a Place of Respite," 166–67.

245 *The establishment Rideau Club*: Charles Lynch, *Up from the Ashes : The Rideau Club Story* (Ottawa: University of Ottawa Press, 1990), 102; Bilsky, *A Common Thread*, 162; Muirhead, *Against the Odds*, 221; "David Golden," University of Manitoba, http://umanitoba.ca/admin/governance/senate/hdr/1092.html.

245 *Journalist Peter C. Newman*: Christopher McCreery, *Savoir Faire, Savoir Vivre: Rideau Club 1865–2015* (Toronto: Dundurn Press, 2014), 43; Peter C. Newman, *Here Be Dragons: Telling Tales of People, Passion and Power* (Toronto: McClelland & Stewart, 2011), 133.

245 *Officially ending the*: McCreery, ibid., 43–47.

245 *Private clubs in*: Gladstone, *A History of the Jewish community of London Ontario*, 184; *London Free Press*, April 19, 1968; Levine, *Coming of Age*, 254–55; Judith Fingard, Janet Guildford, and David Sutherland, *Halifax: The First 250 Years* (Halifax: Formac Publishing Company, 1999), 175; NP, October 16, 2010; Troper, *Defining Decade*, 248–49, 253–62.

245 *In early December*: GM, December 2, 1950; Martin Sable, "George Drew and the Rabbis: Religious Education in Ontario's Public Schools," CJS 6 (1998), 26–7, 32–3.

246 *Curiously, the first*: GM, December 4, 1950; Sable, "George Drew and the Rabbis," 32–3.

246 *Next came a public*: GM, December 5, 1950.

246 *The most cutting*: GM, December 5, 1950; Sable, "George Drew and the Rabbis," 37.

246 *The lesson of this*: Sable, "George Drew and the Rabbis," 42.

247 *Harry Batshaw's appointment*: King, *From the Ghetto to the Main*, 285.

247 *That party loyalty*: King, *From the Ghetto to the Main*, 285; Pascale Greenfield, "Lord Reading Law Society—Montefiore Club," MJM, http://imjm.ca/location/1688. See also Phyllis M. Senese, "Samuel Davies Schultz," DCB, vol. 14, www.biographi.ca/en /bio/schultz_samuel_davies_14E.html.

247 *The news of the*: "Correspondence 1950–1970," *Congress Bulletin*, June 1950, 17, Harry Batshaw Papers, vol. 1, LAC, 31 E33; David Rome to David Croll, March 17, 21, 1950; Harry Batshaw Papers, vol. 2, clipping files; *Montreal Daily Star*, February 15, 1950; *La Presse*, February 15, 1950; *Relations*, March 1950; *Toronto Star*, February 22, 1950; CJCH, April 28, 1950.

247 *A year earlier, Freedman*: Levine, *Coming of Age*, 353–57.

247 *As Oscar D. Skelton*: Cited in Terry Crowley, *Marriage of Minds: Isabel and Oscar Skelton Reinventing Canada* (University of Toronto Press, 2000), 202.

248 *Rasminsky was not*: Michael Rasminsky to author, January 29, 2018.

248 *The anonymous donor*: Michael Rasminsky to author, December 2, 2015.

248 *The bank's first governor*: Ibid., 108, 148; Standing Committee on Banking and Commerce, *Proceedings and Evidence*, December 11–13, 1945 (Ottawa: King's Printer), 130.

248 *Rasminsky's Jewish background*: Muirhead, *Against the Odds*, 147–48.

249 *Nearly five years later*: Ibid.

249 *In the opinion of Peter Dempson*: Peter Dempson, "Found Room at the Top Despite Faith or Name," *Toronto Telegram*, July 25, 1961; Muirhead, *Against the Odds*, 176.

249 *Later, Rasminsky was informed*: Muirhead, *Against the Odds*, 77. This was according to Dr. Michael Rasminsky.

249 *Possibly owing to*: Robert Moon, "Canada's Banker Takes Over," *Christian Science Monitor*, August 16 1961, 11; Bruce Phillips, CBC news commentary, July 25, 1961 cited in Muirhead, *Against the Odds*, 179.

249 *Rasminsky, who remained*: Muirhead, *Against the Odds*, x.

249 *For members of the larger*: CJN, June 4, 1981.

250 *Born in Brockville, Ontario*: Levine, *Toronto*, 134; Jamie Bradburn, "Meet a Toronto Mayor: Nathan Phillips," Torontoist, (September 16, 2014), https://torontoist.com /2014/09/meet-a-toronto-mayor-nathan-phillips/.

250 *He tried in 1951*: Nathan Phillips, *Mayor of All the People* (Toronto: McClelland & Stewart, 1967), 90–1.

250 *During the campaign*: Ibid., 98–9.

250 *Important as well*: Phillips, *Mayor of All the People*, 96–7; Maggie Siggins, *Bassett: John Bassett's Forty Years in Politics, Publishing, Business and Sports* (Toronto: James Lorimer & Company, 1979), 124; Levine, *Toronto*, 208.

250 *Saunders, meanwhile, was tainted*: Levine, *Toronto*, 208.

250 *A year later, after Phillips*: TS, December 6, 1955.

250 *A slight power shift*: Troper, *Defining Decade*, 90; Myer Siemiatycki, Tim Rees, Roxana Ng, and Khan Rahi, "Integrating Community Diversity in Toronto," in *The World in a City*, Paul Anisef and Michael Lanphier, eds., (Toronto: University of Toronto Press, 2003), 384; Levine, *Toronto*, 208–09.

251 *In Halifax, the election*: Fingard, *Halifax: The First 250 Years*, 175; AI with Alan Kitz and John Kitz; *Chronicle-Herald* (Halifax), May 30, 1997; GM, February 4, 2006; Election Returns, April 28, 1955, Halifax Municipal Archives, 254–55, http://legacycontent.halifax.ca/archives/HalifaxCityMinutes/documents/102 -1a-1955-03-16to05-05p213-270.pdf; Election Returns, April 27, 1956, 309–10 http://legacycontent.halifax.ca/archives/HalifaxCityMinutes/documents /102-1a-1956-04-19to05-17p283-389.pdf.

251 *Simply put, in a city*: Troper, *Defining Decade*, 93.

251 *From a Jewish standpoint*: Ibid., 86.

251 *By the early sixties*: John Porter, *The Vertical Mosaic: An Analysis of Social Class and Power in Canada* (Toronto: University of Toronto Press, 2015), 86–8, 286. Interestingly, in the *Globe and Mail*'s *Report on Business* magazine's 2017 ranking of the fifty most powerful and influential Canadians, only one Jew made the list, at number 26: Aubrey Drake Graham, otherwise known as the musician and rapper Drake. His mother Sandi is Jewish. Writing in the CJN, Toronto journalist Michael Fraiman makes the case that Drake is "the most influential Canadian Jew alive." See "The Power 50," *Report on Business Magazine* 33:9 (May 2017), 24–35; see also, Michael Fraiman, "Drake: 'The Most Influential Canadian Jew Alive'" CJN, July 20, 2017, 16.

252 *At some point in the mid-1950s*: Levine, *Toronto*, 193.

252 *The Soviet invasion of Hungary*: TS, January 13, 2010.

252 *By 1958, Paul and Ralph Reichmann*: Anthony Bianco, *The Reichmanns: Family, Faith, Fortune, and the Empire of Olympia and York* (Toronto: Random House of Canada, 1997), 231–40; Levine, *Toronto*, 194.

Chapter Twenty: Living Together

253 *In 1959, the Canadian*: Troper, *Defining Decade*, 4; GM, October 14, 1959.

253 *In the minds of Bronfman*: Troper, *Defining Decade*, 8.

253 *And it worked*: GM, October 14, 1959.

253 *Likewise to the CJC*: Peterson, "The Jew in Canada," 22–3, 62–5.

254   *Early on, Richler*: Foran, *Mordecai*, 220–21.

254   *"You are an angry"*: Ibid., 261–62, 334.

254   *"What I know best"*: Mordecai Richler, "We Jews are Almost as Bad as the Gentiles," *Maclean's*, October 22, 1960, 10, 78–9.

254   *He declared himself*: Foran, *Mordecai*, 263.

254   *When the film*: Ibid., 432–33.

255   *Born in 1928*: Levine, *Coming of Age*, 341; *Ottawa Citizen*, June 6, 1992.

255   *During this period*: Ruth Panofsky, *The Force of Vocation: The Literary Career of Adele Wiseman* (Winnipeg: University of Manitoba Press, 2006), 11–12. See also Gutkins, *Worst of Times*, 205–06; Levine, *Coming of Age*, 341–42.

255   *The novel received*: *New York Times*, September 14, 1956; *New York Herald Tribune*, September 16, 1956; *Chicago Daily Tribune*, September 6, 1956; GM, May 4, 1957; *Queen's Quarterly* 63:4 (January 1, 1956), 62; *Manchester Guardian*, November 20, 1956. One of the lone critical reviews came from writer Algene Ballif, who argued that Wiseman's novel had been "overpraised." See Algene Ballif, "The Sacrifice," *Commentary* 24 (January 1957), 381.

255   *Wiseman was talented*: Levine, *Coming of Age*, 342.

255   *She rebuffed her publisher's*: Gutkins, *Worst of Times*, 205–06.

255   *Over a five-year period*: Panofsky, *The Force of Vocation*, 32, 84–6; Levine, *Coming of Age*, 342.

256   *Satisfied with what*: Panofsky, *The Force of Vocation.*, 133–34; Levine, *Coming of Age*.

256   *During his prickly talk*: Foran, *Mordecai*, 262.

256   *These self-made*: Troper, *Defining Decade*, 42–3; Porter, *The Vertical Mosaic*, 75.

256   *The lifelong objective*: CJCH, August 25, 1967.

257   *By the start of the*: Ibid.

257   *Across Canada, according to*: Tulchinsky, *Canada's Jews*, 421.

257   *Pursuing a higher education*: See Kay, *Acknowledgments*, 12.

257   *Jewish women in the fifties*: Tulchinsky, *Branching Out*, 280–81.

257   *As journalist Barbara Kay*: Kay, *Acknowledgments*, 12.

257   *In Montreal, Jews*: King, *From the Ghetto to the Main*, 278; Richler, "Their Canada and Mine," 136.

258   *Three decades later*: King, *From the Ghetto to the Main*, 279; "Samuel Moskovitch Dead at 71," JTA, May 26, 1976; AI with Monna (Moskovitch) Malkinson.

258   *In 1975, Moskovitch*: King, *From the Ghetto to the Main*, 277; "Ashkelon and Côte Saint-Luc: Twin Cities," City of Côte Saint-Luc, http://www.cotesaintluc.org/ashkelon.

258   *Outremont, on the other*: King, *From the Ghetto to the Main*, 277-78.

258   *During the next ten*: King, *From the Ghetto to the Main*, 278; Weinfeld, *The Canadian Jewish Mosaic*, 278–79; Shuchat, *The Gate of Heaven*, 167.

258   *In 1947, following this*: "About," The Spanish and Portugeuse Synagogue, http://thespanish.org/about/; Shuchat, *The Gate of Heaven*, 168–69.

258 *That changed in the fifties*: King, *From the Ghetto to the Main*, 256; Troper, *Defining Decade*, 44.

259 *According to a study*: Federation-CJA, "2011 National Household Survey Analysis: The Jewish Community of Montreal," http://www.federationcja.org/en/jewish _montreal/demographics/.

259 *In a repeat of the British-German*: Troper, *Defining Decade*, 44–5.

259 *"Some Ashkenazim thought"*: MG, July 16, 1986.

259 *But the Sephardim persisted*: Langlais and Rome, *Jews and French Quebecers*, 134; Weinfeld, *The Canadian Jewish Mosaic*, 232–35; Marian Pinsky, "Jean-Claude Lasry—Association sépharade francophone," MJM, http://imjm.ca/location/2561; École Maïmonide, "History of the School," www.ecoleMAImonide.org/histoire; Weinfeld, *Canadian Jewish Mosaic*, 233–35, n.33, 469.

260 *Upwardly mobile Jews*: Levine, *Toronto*, 206; Richard Harris, *Creeping Conformity: How Canada Became Suburban, 1900–1960* (Toronto: University of Toronto Press, 2004), 89–90.

260 *In 1951, 40 per cent*: Timothy J. Colton, *Big Daddy: Frederick G. Gardiner and the Building of Metropolitan Toronto* (Toronto: University of Toronto Press, 1980), 43; Diamond, *And I Will Dwell in Their Midst*, 30–33, 40.

260 *It took somewhat longer*: Levine, *Toronto*, 206.

260 *"By 1958, we were"*: AI with Frank Bialystok. See also Diamond, *And I Will Dwell in Their Midst*, 29. Erna Paris and her nouveau riche parents (as she describes them) had migrated to Forest Hill from their home in the Annex when she was a young girl, long before she became a successful journalist and writer. Forest Hill, she recalled, was a world unto itself. "Our lives in the Forties and Fifties were insular and 'unreal'—unconnected to the WASP reality of Toronto, unconnected to the rural reality of Canada," she wrote in a 1972 memoir. "We knew almost nothing beyond the Village, the downtown department stores where we'd sometimes wander on Saturday afternoon and charge clothes to our fathers' accounts, and the bits of northern Ontario where we summered and wondered at the people who stayed there after Labor Day." See Erna Paris, "Ghetto of the Mind: Forest Hill in the Fifties," *Toronto Live*, November 1972, cited in William Kilbourn, ed., *The Toronto Book* (Toronto: Macmillan of Canada, 1976), 101–02, 104.

260 *In 1941, 92 per cent*: Louis Rosenberg, *The Jewish Community of Winnipeg* (Montreal: Canadian Jewish Congress, 1946), 24.

260 *In 1961, Winnipeg's Jewish*: Louis Rosenberg, *A Study of the Growth and Changes in the Distribution of the Jewish Population of Winnipeg, 1961* (Montreal: Canadian Jewish Congress, 1961), 7.

261 *This was one of the reasons*: Levine, *Coming of Age*, 313–14.

261 *By 1961, 30.5 per cent*: Rosenberg, *Winnipeg, 1961*, 7; Levine, *Coming of Age*, 312.

261   *In 1961, 83 per cent:* See Tulchinsky, *Branching Out*, 358.

261   *Vancouver's Jewish population:* Charles Shahar and Jean Gerber, "The Jewish
      Community of Greater Vancouver," 2001 Census Analysis Series, Part II,
      (Vancouver: Jewish Federation of Greater Vancouver, 2004), 10.

261   *Ottawa was next:* Tulchinsky, *Branching Out*, 358 and Appendix, Table 1.

262   *By 1971, two-thirds:* Bilsky, *A Common Thread*, 190.

262   *That included the Jewish:* Laurie Dougherty, "History of the Jewish Federation of
      Ottawa," (2009), https://jewishottawa.com/history-of-the-jewish-federation
      -of-ottawa.

262   *A Talmud Torah was opened:* "Ottawa Talmud Torah Board fonds," Ottawa
      Jewish Archives, www.archeion.ca/ottawa-talmud-torah-board-fonds.

262   *The Chapel Street centre:* "About Ottawa's Jewish History," Jewish Federation of
      Ottawa, https://jewishottawa.com/ottawa-jewish-archives/faq

262   *First, in 1965:* "Ottawa Talmud Torah Board fonds."

263   *During the next fifty years:* CIJA, "Rabbi Dr. Reuven P. Bulka," www.cija.ca/theexchange
      /rabbi-dr-reuven-p-bulka/; *Ottawa Citizen*, March 18, 2002, June 9, 2006.

263   *It was fitting that:* *Ottawa Citizen*, June 16, 2014.

263   *Vancouver was more:* Troper, *Defining Decade*, 28; Michael Schwartz, Coordinator
      of Programs and Development, JMABC, to author, November 22, 2016.

263   *By 1972, the community:* Ann Rivkin, "The Jews of Vancouver," CR, June 1972, 17, 20.

263   *If there was a "Jewish area":* Rivkin, "The Jews of Vancouver," 17; JMABC,
      "Oakridge," http://jewishmuseum.ca/exhibit/oakridge/.

264   *In 1928, for instance:* "Oakridge," JMABC.

264   *After 1950, the city:* Rivkin, "The Jews of Vancouver," 17, 20; Michael Schwartz to
      author, November 22, 2016.

264   *The school had been:* "Our History," Peretz Centre, http://peretz-centre.org/our
      -history/; Faith Jones, "Between Suspicion and Censure: Attitudes towards the
      Jewish Left in Postwar Vancouver," CJS 6 (1998), 3–4.

264   *Typically, it was women:* Jones, "Between Suspicion and Censure," 3–6.

265   *In 1951, the CJC's decision:* Ibid., 9–18.

265   *One writer for Winnipeg's:* Weatherhead, *Congregation Shaarey Zedek*, 38.

Chapter Twenty-One: A Lot of Jews

269   *In the province's pecking:* Troper, *Defining Decade*, 41–2; Gerald Tulchinsky, "The
      Third Solitude: A.M. Klein's Jewish Montreal, 1910-1950," *Journal of Canadian
      Studies* 19:2 (Summer 1984), 96-112.

270   *She stressed the:* Ruth R. Wisse, "Jewish Participation in Canadian Culture," in *Royal
      Commission on Bilingualism and Biculturalism: The Cultural Contribution of the Other
      Ethnic Groups* (Ottawa: Queen's Printer, 1970), 98; Troper, *Defining Decade*, 74.

270 *A more revealing*: Bronfman, "Canadian Jewry Today," 37–8; Troper, *Defining Decade*, 66–7.

270 *Thus at the 1967*: Troper, *Defining Decade*, 77–8; Wilfred Shuchat, "The Jewish History of Montreal's Expo 67 You Probably Didn't Know," cjn, May 11, 2017, www.cjnews.com/perspectives/jewish-history-montreals-expo-67.

270 *This religious and cultural*: Levine, *Coming of Age*, 342–45.

270 *Sommer had been a student*: Ruth P. Schoenberg and Ruth R. Goodman, "Israeli Folk Dance Pioneers in North America."

271 *This was an election*: Troper, *Defining Decade*, 215-16.

272 *As prime minister*: Ibid., 205–06.

272 *Some years after*: Cited in Ibid., 220.

272 *While Gray wore*: jpn, December 8, 1993; Canadian Press, April 21, 2014; "Gray, Hon. Herbert," Greenberg to Trudeau, November 6, 1969, Trudeau Fonds, vol. 112, Code 312, File 12.

273 *In October 1969*: File Vennat to Gibson, October 28, 1969, "Personal and Confidential, 25 September 1969–May 1971," Trudeau Fonds, vol. 112 Code 313.05; "Itinerary Meetings," "Family of Man Award," Trudeau Fonds, vol. 112 Code 313.05–Gibson, SD 69/61.

273 *The* Canadian Jewish News: See, for example, cjn, October 24, 1969; March 27, 1970; *Jewish Western Bulletin*, October 24, 1969.

273 *"For the first time"*: cjn, Ibid., 4.

273 *Five months later*: Ibid., March 27, 1970, 4.

273 *The* Globe and Mail: gm, March 21, 1970. See also Trudeau Fonds, vol. 303, Code 343, 1969–1974.

273 *After Laskin died*: Harold Ashenmil to author, December 13, 2016.

274 *Though proud of his*: ai with Stephen Lewis.

274 *Stephen did not have*: Ibid.

274 *David was hesitant*: Ibid.

275 *Nor did being Jewish*: Ibid.

275 *He recalls, too*: Ibid.; gm, April 3, 1975.

275 *It took more than*: mg, February 16, 2016.

276 *With his stunning*: Dave Barrett and William Miller, *Barrett: A Passionate Political Life* (Vancouver: Douglas & McIntyre, 1995), 3–14.

276 *In its story*: Jewish Western Bulletin, September 8, 1972.

276 *"I think it's fair"*: Rod Mickleburgh to author, December 11, 2016; Rod Mickleburgh, "1975: B.C.'s Nastiest Election Campaign," December 30, 2015, https://mickleblog.wordpress.com/2015/12/30/b-c-s-nastiest-election -campaign/. See also, Geoff Meggs and Rod Mickleburgh, *The Art of the Impossible: Dave Barrett and the* ndp *in Power 1972–1975* (Vancouver: Harbour Publishing, 2012), 286–87.

276   *When Barrett passed*: See, *Vancouver Sun*, *Times Colonist* (Victoria), GM, WFP, February 3, 2018; CBC, Global TV, CTV, February 2, 2018 broadcasts; CJN, February 7 2018.

277   *This movement of hate*: Frederick J. Simonelli, *American Fuehrer: George Lincoln Rockwell and the American Nazi Party* (Chicago: University of Illinois Press, 1999), 2–3. See also GM, August 23, 1965; Benjamin Kayfetz, "Neo-Nazis in Canada," *Patterns of Prejudice* 13:1 (1979), 29–32; Bernie Farber, "Nazi Nobody," *Toronto Now*, September 11, 2014, https://nowtoronto.com/news/nazi-nobody/.

277   *Among their followers*: Manuel Prutschi, "The Zündel Affair" *Antisemitism in Canada*, Davies ed., 249–57.

277   *In October 1964*: GM, October 26, 28, 1964, March 13, 1972; Bialystok, *Delayed Impact*, 113–14.

277   *The Second World War*: Bialystok, *Delayed Impact*, 113–14; CJN, January 15, 1965; CJCH, January 17, 1965.

277   *CJC officials had also*: MG, January 6, 2008; Ben Kayfetz, "Canada's New Anti-Hate Law," *Patterns of Prejudice* 4 (1970), 5–8; Philip Rosen, "Hate Propaganda," Library of Parliament of Canada, https://lop.parl.ca/content/lop/researchpublications/856-e.htm.

278   *But it also spurred*: Troper, *Defining Decade*, 108.

278   *The group's leader*: Bialystok, *Delayed Impact*, 126.

278   *The Congress and N3*: GM, September 17, 1966; Bialystok, ibid., 127–28.

278   *On the afternoon*: GM, May 31, June 2, 1965, Bialystok, ibid., 132–33; Troper, *Defining Decade*, 110.

279   *In a Globe and Mail comment*: GM, June 5, 9, 1965.

279   *Among those who participated*: Canadian Civil Liberties Association, "Our Mission and History," https://ccla.org/our-mission-and-history/; Bialystok, *Delayed Impact*, 142.

Chapter Twenty-Two: Israel is Everybody's Business

280   *Fortified by the*: Cited in *The Guardian* (London), September 4, 2007; Michael B. Oren, *Six Days of War: June 1967 and the Making of the Modern Middle East* (New York: Ballantine Books, 2003), 164.

280   *American support of Israel*: "The 1967 Arab-Israeli War," Office of the Historian, U.S. Department of State, https://history.state.gov/milestones/1961–1968/arab-israeli-war-1967.

280   *In the weeks before*: An excellent account of the events leading up to the Six Day War can be found in Oren, *Siex Days of War*, 61-127.

280   *It had a standing army*: Oren, *Six Days of War*, 164.

281   *What happened over*: Ibid., 305–12.

281 *"The crisis had triggered"*: GM, June 13, 1967.

281 *Similarly, Rabbi Wilfred Solomon*: Cited in Troper, *Defining Decade*, 128–29.

281 *On May 30, 1967*: *Western Jewish News*, June 2, 1967; Harvey Chisick to author, December 25, 2016.

282 *As a young teenager*: AI with Janos Maté; Janos Maté, "Families 1956," Pier 21, http://www.pier21.ca/culture-trunks/hungary/stories/janos-mat%C3%A9; Janos Maté, "The Making of a Greenpeace Activist," *Believer*, July 13, 2013, https://logger.believermag.com/post/2013/07/13/the-making-of-a-greenpeace-activist-by-janos-mate.

282 *Everyone there, he recalls*: AI with Janos Maté.

282 *Janos, Peter, and the*: AI with Peter Maidstone.

282 *The two boys were paired*: AI with Janos Maté; AI with Peter Maidstone.

282 *"I experienced a sense"*: Maté, "The Making of a Greenpeace Activist."

283 *Only one of the friends*: Harvey Chisick to Author, December 25, 2016.

283 *As historian Michael Brown*: Michael Brown, "The Push and Pull Factors of Aliyah and the Anomalous Case of Canada: 1967–1982," *Jewish Social Studies* 48:2 (Spring 1986), 147–49, 153–55; "France," Jewish Virtual Library, www.jewishvirtuallibrary.org/jsource/vjw/France.html#f.

284 *The Bronfman family*: Azrieli, *Rekindling the Torch*, 157.

284 *On June 4, he held*: Marrus, *Mr. Sam*, 447–48.

284 *National delegates at*: CJN, June 2, 1967; Marrus, *Mr. Sam*, 448; David Taras, "From Passivity to Politics: Canada's Jewish Community and Political Support for Israel," in *The Domestic Battleground: Canada and the Arab-Israeli Conflict*, David Taras and David H. Goldberg, eds. (Montreal and Kingston: McGill-Queen's University Press, 1989), 48.

284 *In Toronto on June 5*: GM, June 6, 1967.

284 *Meanwhile, to deal with what*: GM, June 10, 1967; *Western Jewish News*, June 2, 1967.

284 *Further east in*: Troper, *Defining Decade*, 141–51.

284 *Bronfman and his top*: Marrus, *Mr. Sam*, 448–49.

285 *In 1967, the opposition Conservatives*: Canada, Parliament, *House of Commons Debates*, June 8, 1967, 1298.

285 *Most Canadians*: Werner Cohen, "English and French Canadian Public Opinion on Jews and Israel: Some Poll Data," *Canadian Ethnic Studies* 11:2 (January 1979), 38–9; Tulchinsky, *Branching Out*, 294–96.

285 *"I have never seen"*: GM, June 10, 1967.

286 *And, more recently*: BDS, https://bdsmovement.net/

286 *"Today Israel is"*: Saul Hayes, "The Changing Nature of the Jewish Community," *Viewpoints* 5:3 (Fall 1970), 26–7. See also Harold Waller, "The Impact of the Six-Day War on the Organizational Life of Canadian Jewry" in *The Six Day War and World Jewry*, Eli Lederhendler, ed. (Potomac, M.D.: University Press of Maryland, 2000), 96.

286 *During the seventies and eighties:* CJN, June 24, 1977; Levendel, *A Century of the Canadian Jewish Press*, 356–58.

287 *Jews were naturally overly:* See, for example, letters in GM, December 13, 21, 1973, November 21, 1975, May 30, 1986.

287 *"Can one be committed":* WFP, March 8, 1969.

287 *As the late George Jonas:* NP, November 3, 2012. See also Cohen, "English and French Canadian Public Opinion on Jews and Israel," 34.

287 *After a visit: Watertown Daily Times* (Watertown, New York), May 31, 1969, http://www.billgladstone.ca/?p=8081; AJYB 75 (1974–75), 347–47; David Taras, "A Church Divided: A.C. Forrest and the United Church's Middle East Policy" in *The Domestic Battleground*, Taras and Goldberg eds., 90.

287 *In 1971, Forrest added:* A.C. Forrest, *The Unholy Land* (Toronto: McClelland & Stewart, 1971), 151; Taras, "A Church Divided," 91; Azrieli, *Rekindling the Torch*, 165; W. Gunther Plaut, *Unfinished Business: An Autobiography* (Toronto: Lester & Orpen Dennys, 1981), 253.

288 *George Cohon:* Azrieli, *Rekindling the Torch*, 165; Taras, "From Passivity to Politics," 55–6.

288 *The Canada-Israel Committee:* Azrieli, *Rekindling the Torch*, 156-59.

288 *In 1973, the CIC:* Ibid., 159

288 *This should have been:* Taras, "From Passivity to Politics," 56; Janice Gross Stein, "Canadian Foreign Policy in the Middle East after the October War," *Social Praxis* 4:3–4 (1976–1977), 280–84.

289 *These and other setbacks:* Brown, "The Push and Pull Factors of Aliyah," 143.

289 *In early January 1970:* Gene Colman, "Jewish Students Arise and Unite: Let's Kick the Shit Out of the Jewish Establishment!" *Masada*, January 6, 1970; AI with Gene Colman, December 1, 2016; Troper, *Defining Decade*, 201–02.

289 *On a more positive note:* Trudy Harowitz to author, December 23, 2016; Troper, *Defining Decade*, 171–78, 200–01.

290 *Bolstered by the Trudeau government's:* GM, March 2, 1979. In Toronto's case, B'nai Brith, which was hosting the pavilion in 1979, decided to name it "Jerusalem," in line with how other pavilions were identified. "Tel-Aviv" might have been a less problematic choice. The organizers of the Caravan Festival approved the "Jerusalem" moniker provided that B'nai Brith agreed that the pavilion portray only the "cultural co-operation between Jewish, Arab and Christian populations of Jerusalem." B'nai Brith fully complied, yet that did not satisfy the leaders of the Arab Palestine Association who called the decision "very biased, bigoted and undemocratic" and proceeded to take the matter to court. That ploy failed when a provincial court judge denied the Arab Community Centre's request for an injunction to stop Caravan from permitting B'nai Brith use the name "Jerusalem" for its pavilion. See GM March 2, 3, 15, 1979.

290   *It troubled many:* Taras, "From Passivity to Politics," 58; David Dewitt and John
       Kirton, "Foreign Policy Making Towards the Middle East: Parliament, the Media,
       and the 1982 Lebanon War," in *The Domestic Battleground*, Taras and Goldberg
       eds., 168–69.

290   *An academic study:* Dewitt and Kirton, "Foreign Policy Making Towards the
       Middle East," 176–80. See also David Dewitt and John Kirton, "Canadian and
       Mideast Realities," *International Perspectives* (January/February 1984), 21–22.

290   *Sponsored by an Ottawa:* GM, August 3, 1982.

290   *"The advertisement":* Ibid., August 7, 1982.

290   *Predictably, they were:* Ibid., August 12, 1982.

Chapter Twenty-Three: Marching for Refuseniks

291   *In Moscow in October 1965:* Sylvia Rothchild, *A Special Legacy: An Oral History of
       Soviet Jewish Emigrés in the United States* (New York: Simon and Schuster, 1985),
       10–20; Levine, *Scattered Among the Peoples*, 378–81.

291   *On this night:* Elie Wiesel, "The Rejoicing of the Law," in *The Unredeemed: Anti-
       Semitism in the Soviet Union*, Ronald I. Rubin, ed., (Chicago: Quadrangle Books,
       1968), 243–4.

291   *Two years later:* New York Times, October 29, 1967.

292   *So it was:* TS, October 27, 1967; GM, October 6, 1969, October 26, 1970; Troper,
       Defining Decade, 269; Bilsky, *A Common Thread*, 204.

292   *They were a second-class:* Levine, *Scattered Among the Peoples*, 376–77; Martin
       Gilbert, *The Jews of Hope* (London: Macmillan, 1984), 56.

292   *The Jews were trapped:* Moshe Decter, "The Status of the Jews in the Soviet
       Union," *Foreign Affairs* 41:2 (January 1963), 430. See also TS, April 11, 1961; Stuart
       E. Rosenberg, *The Real Jewish World: A Rabbi's Second Thoughts* (Toronto:
       Clarke Irwin, 1984), 296–97.

293   *From the end of Stalin's rule:* Levine, *Scattered Among the Peoples*, 384; Nora Levin,
       The Jews in the Soviet Union Since 1917: Paradox of Survival, vol. II (New York:
       New York University Press, 1988), 684; Yaacov Ro'i, *The Struggle for Soviet Jewish
       Emigration 1948–1967* (Cambridge: Cambridge University Press, 1991), 327–28;
       "Immigration to Israel: Total Immigration, from Former Soviet Union," Jewish
       Virtual Library, http://www.jewishvirtuallibrary.org/total-immigration-to-israel
       -from-former-soviet-union; AJYB 94 (1994), 3.

293   *The CJC gradually:* Wendy Eisen, *Count Us In: The Struggle to Free Soviet Jews:
       A Canadian Perspective* (Toronto: Burgher Books, 1995), 53.

293   *The situation became:* Levin, *The Jews in the Soviet Union Since 1917*, vol. II, 672–
       78; Leonard Schroeter, *The Last Exodus* (New York: Universe Books, 1974), 141–
       46, 175; Levine, *Scattered Among the Peoples*, 389–90.

294   *On October 30:* GM, October 31, 1970; Troper, *Defining Decade*, 237.

294   *This time, the worldwide:* New York Times, January 1971.

294   *A second and larger:* GM, January 4, 11, 1971.

294   *Prior to a trip:* GM, May 18, 1971; Eisen, *Count Us In*, 39–40. See also J.L. Granatstein, "Gouzenko to Gorbachev: Canada's Cold War," *Canadian Military Journal* 12:1, www.journal.forces.gc.ca/vol12/no1/41–granatstein-eng.asp; John English, *Just Watch Me: The Life of Pierre Elliott Trudeau, 1968–2000* (Toronto: Vintage Canada, 2010), 165–66, 273.

294   *True to his word:* New York Times, May 24, 1971; *Washington Post*, May 24, 1971.

295   *The Jewish establishment:* GM October 19, 20, November 23, 1971; Troper, *Defining Decade*, 273; Eisen, *Count Us In*, 41–2.

295   *The next day, as the rabbis:* GM, October 19, 1971.

295   *And once more, Rabbi Plaut:* GM, October 20, 25, 1971.

295   *The Soviets allowed:* Levin, *The Jews in the Soviet Union Since 1917*, vol. 11, 715.

295   *He had tried to leave:* See Natan Sharansky, *Fear No Evil* (New York: Random House, 1988).

296   *In 1974, she attended:* AI with Wendy Eisen.

296   *At that 1974 gathering:* AI with Wendy Eisen; Eisen, *Count Us In*, 64–5; Wendy R. Eisen, "Canadian Soviet Jewry Movement," Speech to the UJA Federation of Greater Toronto, May 2015, https://jewishtoronto.com/wendyspeech.

296   *The women participated:* Eisen, *Count Us In*, 65–7.

296   *In September 1987:* Ibid., 241, 268; AI with Wendy Eisen.

297   *Whereas in 1951:* Louis Rosenberg, "Jewish Population Characteristics," Montreal, *Congress Bulletin*, September 1956, 3; Joseph A. Norland, "Canada's Jewish Population: Selected Demographic Characteristics," *Canadian Studies in Population* 1 (1974), 85.

297   *It finally had:* Levendel, *A Century of the Canadian Jewish Press*, 22, 27–8, 34–6.

297   *By the early sixties:* Ibid., 63–4; Elizabeth A. Popham, *Abraham Moses Klein: The Letters* (Toronto: University of Toronto Press, 2011), vii.

297   *In 1963, the Wolofsky brothers:* Levendel, *A Century of the Canadian Jewish Press*, 67.

298   *In a last gasp effort:* Ibid., 70–3.

298   *Remembered at the time:* CJN, August 23, 2001; Levendel, *A Century of the Canadian Jewish Press*, 319.

298   *As a war correspondent:* CJN, August 23, 2001; TS, August 23, 2001.

299   *When the Zhurnal was:* Levendel, *A Century of the Canadian Jewish Press*, 329–30.

299   *However, when the Telegram:* CJN, August 23, 2001, January 1, 1960.

299   *The sale, negotiated:* Levendel, *A Century of the Canadian Jewish Press*, 322–24.

299   *Looking to enhance:* Ibid., 322-23.

299   *A disgruntled Nurenberger:* Ibid., 323

300   *"In North America,":* CJN, January 6, 1967.

300   *After Dorothy died:* Levendel, *A Century of the Canadian Jewish Press*, 329, 342–43.

300   *Interestingly, many donors:* Ibid., 342-43.

300   *In Winnipeg:* Levine, *Coming of Age,* 215–16. It was the *Israelite Press* that began
the unique Winnipeg custom—which persists to the present day in the *Jewish
Post & News*—of selling lucrative memoriam ads with photographs of the
deceased in the newspaper each year on the anniversary of the person's *yarzheit*
(date of death) according to the Hebrew calendar. Writing in the *Canadian Jewish
Chronicle* in 1942, A.M. Klein lampooned the tradition. "Now we ask what macabre
morbidity is it that prompts editors to accept these unearthed cadavers, to display
them . . . upon the weekly galleys. We mean no disrespect to the dead; some of
our best friends are corpses of long-standing—if that is a word. But why should
it not be enough merely to mention the fact of the anniversary? . . . Why the
touching photograph dressed in the latest style of 1909—of a man or woman who
has departed this life and all its vanities, full many a year agone?" See, A.M. Klein,
"Your Picture in the Paper," CJCH, June 13, 1942.

Chapter Twenty-Four: Nationalistic Impulses

302   *On November 15:* Michael Yarosky, "The Jewish Community of Quebec Province:
Bridging the Past and the Present," *Journal of Jewish Communal Service* 56:1
(September 1979), 19. See also Ruth R. Wisse and Irwin Cotler, "Quebec Jews
Caught in the Middle," *Commentary* 64:3 (September 1977), 57–9.

302   *"No other event":* Yarosky, "The Jewish Community of Quebec Province," 19.

302   *But Monroe Abbey:* Levendel, *A Century of the Canadian Jewish Press,* 376; AJYB
77 (1977), 277.

302   *The day before:* GM, November 17, 1976; Bronfman, *Distilled,* 44.

302   *"I also accused":* Bronfman, *Distilled,* 44.

302   *Within days of:* GM November 19, 1976; Bronfman, *Distilled,* 44.

303   *And like Moses:* Richard Pound, *Stikeman Elliott: The First Fifty Years* (Montreal
and Kingston: McGill-Queens, 2002), 97; Monty Berger, *Lament for a Province:
The Tragic Costs of Quebec's Flirtation with Separatism* (Toronto: Lugus Publications
1995), 7, 92–102; Morton Weinfeld, "The Jews of Quebec: Perceived Antisemitism,
Segregation, and Emigration," *Jewish Journal of Sociology* 22 (1980), 17.

303   *It was not by coincidence:* Demographia, "Canada: 20 Top Census Metropolitan
Areas: Population from 1931," http://demographia.com/db-cancma.htm.

303   *By 1984, there were:* GM, September 25, 1984.

303   *So many Jews:* New York Times, November 12, 1978.

303   *A popular joke:* Cited in Wisse and Cotler, "Quebec Jews Caught in the Middle," 58.

303   *Rabbi Wilfred Shuchat:* Shuchat, *The Gate of Heaven,* 168.

304   *Within two years:* Charles Shahar, *The Jewish Community of Toronto 2011,* Part 8,
Immigration and Language (Toronto: Jewish Federations of Canada-UIA,
Toronto, 2015), 4.

304   *"Your mood each":* New York Times, November 12, 1978.

304 *Lawyers Kenneth and Sharon*: AI with Kenneth Prehogan; Fran Grundman to author, December 16, 2016.

304 *Thus, among many*: Joseph Baumholz, "Quebec Jewry's Future," *Viewpoints* 12 (May 1983), 7; Brown, "The Push and Pull Factors of Aliyah," 147; Wisse and Cotler, "Quebec Jews Caught in the Middle," 59.

305 *From 1971 to 1981*: Brown, "The Push and Pull Factors of Aliyah," 147. See also, Shahar, Part I Basic Demographics, *2011 National Household Survey Analysis: The Jewish Population of Canada*, 30.

305 *Other than tiny communities*: Michael Benazon, "Ostropol on the St. Francis: The Jewish community of Sherbrooke, Quebec—a 120-year presence," *Journal of Eastern Townships Studies* 12 (Spring 1998), 21; GM, April 30, 1984; Ira Robinson, "No Litvaks Need Apply: Judaism in Quebec City," working paper, https://www.concordia.ca/content/dam/artsci/jewish-studies/docs/working -papers/Workingpapers3IraRobinson.pdf; Canadian Jewish Congress Charities Committee National Synagogue Directory, Quebec, 2011–12; www.cjarchives.ca /media/9529/cjccc-synagogue-directory-5772–quebec.pdf.

305 *Meanwhile, as of 2013*: CIJA, "Basic Demographics of the Canadian Jewish Community," www.cija.ca/resource/canadian-jewry/basic-demographics-of-the-canadian-jewish-community/; CIJA, "Toronto," www.cija.ca/near-you/toronto/.

305 *In all, an estimated*: Ron Csillag, "Will Rising Nationalism Renew Montreal Jewish Exodus?" JTA, October 8, 2013.

305 *A decade before*: AJYB 75, (1974–75), 320.

305 *When it came down*: See Jonathan Kay, "Guilty Memories from an Anglo Montreal Childhood," *The Walrus*, December 15, 2016, https://thewalrus.ca /guilty-memories-from-an-anglo-montreal-childhood/.

306 *Despondent, he lashed out*: GM, October 31, 1995; TS, December 9, 1995; NP, June 28, 2012.

306 *"Defeat is a test"*: MG, October 31, 1995; Mordecai Richler, *Belling the Cat: Essays, Reports & Opinions* (Toronto: Alfred A. Knopf Canada, 1998), 327.

306 *"On the one hand, Jews"*: Wisse and Cotler, "Quebec Jews Caught in the Middle," 55.

306 *"I know that eighty"*: AJYB 73 (1972), 409.

307 *Richler blamed Anglo*: Foran, *Mordecai*, 474–75, 504–05, 560–61; GM, December 30, 1977. For a review of Quebec language legislation see, CBC News, "Looking Back at 40 Years of French as Quebec's Official Language," July 31, 2014, www.cbc.ca/news/canada/montreal/looking-back-at-40-years-of-french-as -quebec-s-official-language-1.2724050

307 *"I am fearful"*: GM, ibid.

307 *A decade later, in June 1988*: MG, June 12, 1988.

307 *The opposition to the synagogue*: Ibid.

307 *Insisting that he was not*: Ibid.

308   *The main French-language*: Ibid., September 17, 1988.

308   *Predictably, CJC officials*: Ibid., September 17, 22, 1988.

308   *Letters poured into*: Mordecai Richler, "A Reporter at Large: Inside/Outside," *New Yorker* (September 23, 1991), 71; Robinson, *A History of Antisemitism*, 119–20.

308   *La Presse issued a*: William Shaffir, "Boundaries and Self-Preservation among the Hasidim: A Study in Identity Maintenance" in *New World Hasidim: Ethnographic Studies of Hasidic Jews in America*, Janet S. Belcove-Shalin, ed., (Albany, NY: State University of New York Press, 1995), 55.

308   *Meanwhile, the Outremont*: GM, November 22, 1991.

308   *In the years that followed*: See, for example, "Synagogue's Complaints Prompt Gym to Tint Windows, Angering Athletes," CBC News, November 7, 2006, www.cbc.ca/news/canada/montreal/synagogue-s-complaints-prompt-gym-to-tint-windows-angering-athletes-1.578075; GM, March 20, 2007.

308   *One positive sign*: CJN, February 3, 2014.

309   *Francophone zealots reported*: Raquel Fletcher, "French Language Police Take Issue with 'Grilled Cheese' in Restaurant Name," *Global News*, January 15, 2016.

309   *In December 1988*: See, Peter Russell, "The Notwithstanding Clause: The Charter's Homage to Parliamentary Democracy," *Policy Options*, February 1, 2007, http://policyoptions.irpp.org/magazines/the-charter-25/the-notwithstanding-clause-the-charters-homage-to-parliamentary-democracy/.

309   *After several months*: Richler, "A Reporter at Large: Inside/Outside," 70–1; Foran, *Mordecai*, 570–71.

309   *Much of the material*: Delisle, *The Traitor and the Jew*, 17–33; Charles Foran, "That Book of Esther's," *Saturday Night* 108: 8 (Oct 1993), 30–34.

309   *Richler had humiliated*: See MG, October 2, 1991; TS, April 14, 1992; GM, July 7, 2001; Foran, *Mordecai*, 571–73.

310   *He was dismissed*: See Mordecai Richler, "My Life as a Racist," GM, February 16, 1993, A17.

310   *The book set off*: TS, March 21, 1992.

310   *Le Devoir's editor*: MG, March 18, 20, 25, 1992; GM, March 19, 1992; Foran, *Mordecai*, 579–82.

310   *Appearing on CBC's*: "The Last Word: Mordecai Richler with Barbara Frum," CBC, *The Journal*, March 10, 1992, www.cbc.ca/archives/entry/the-last-word-mordecai-richler-with-barbara-frum; "Mordecai Richler Writes the Literary Scandal of the Season," CBC, March 30, 1992, www.cbc.ca/archives/entry/mordecai-richler-writes-the-literary-scandal-of-the-season.

310   *"Richler is a writer"*: Cited in Richler, "My Life as a Racist."

310   *But other community leaders*: MG, March 12, 1992; Foran, *Mordecai*, 579–80; CJN, July 12, 2001.

310   *"The truth is"*: Richler, "My Life as a Racist."

Chapter Twenty-Five: Confronting the Deniers and Israel-Haters

312   *A survey B'nai Brith*: "Anti-Semitic Sentiments are Rife in the Province of Quebec," JTA, November 4, 1986, www.jta.org/1986/11/04/archive/anti-semitic -sentiments-are-rife-in-the-province-of-quebec.

312   *A similar poll undertaken*: Morton Weinfeld, "The Jews of Quebec," in Brym, *The Jews in Canada*, 187.

312   *Other academic studies*: Robert J. Brym and Rhonda L. Lenton. "The Distribution of Anti-Semitism in Canada in 1984," *The Canadian Journal of Sociology* 16:4 (Autumn 1991), 416; MG February 20, 1989. See also, Paul M. Sniderman, David A. Northrup, Joseph F. Fletcher, Peter H. Russell, and Philip E. Tetlock, "Psychological and Cultural Foundations of Prejudice: The Case of Anti-Semitism in Quebec," *The Canadian Review of Sociology and Anthropology* 30.2 (May 1993), 242-70.

312   *In yet another survey*: MG, February 20, 1989.

312   *In 2002, B'nai Brith*: AJYB 104 (2004), 246–47.

312–313 *One of the worst acts*: "Man Admits to Firebombing Montreal Jewish School," CBC News, December 16, 2004, www.cbc.ca/news/canada/man-admits-to -firebombing-montreal-jewish-school-1.490700.

313   *A tremendous outcry*: NP, January 21, 2005.

313   *Both argued that their right*: Prutschi, "The Zündel Affair," 250–51.

313   *Yet in many ways*: Stanley Barrett, *Is God a Racist?: The Right Wing in Canada* (Toronto: University of Toronto Press, 1987), 8–12, 215. See also *R. v. Zundel*, August 27, 1992, Supreme Court of Canada, https://scc-csc.lexum.com/scc-csc/scc-csc/en /item/904/index.do; Alan Davies, "The Keegstra Affair," in *Antisemitism in Canada*, 228–43; GM, June 13, 2014; "Canada's Anti-Hate Law: The Keegstra Case," CBC News in Review, February 1991; "The Young Must Learn the Lessons of Auschwitz," CBC, May 26, 1983, www.cbc.ca/archives/entry/auschwitz-the-young-must-learn.

313   *He taught them*: Peter Bowal, "What Ever Happened to . . . Jim Keegstra," *Law Now*, July 1, 2012, www.lawnow.org/what-ever-happened-to-jim-keegstra.

313   *"If you wrote on the Jewish"*: Cited in GM, June 13, 2014.

314   *"Why should I go out"*: "Canada's Anti-Hate Law: The Keegstra Case," CBC News in Review, February 1991.

314   *The Zündel and Keegstra*: Bialystok, *Delayed Impact*, 239.

314   *There were already Holocaust*: Ibid., 181–83.

314   *One of its chief organizers*: Ibid., 190–91.

314   *He was motivated*: "Steven Cummings," Jewish General Hospital, www.jgh.ca/en /BioCummings; "Mission and Organisation," Montreal Holocaust Memorial Museum, www.mhmc.ca/en/pages/history.

315   *In Toronto, an impressive*: Bialystok, *Delayed Impact*, 213.

315   *As an infant*: Robert Krell, "My Journey as a Child Holocaust Survivor," The Holocaust and the United Nations Outreach Program, Discussion Paper no. 9,

2012, www.un.org/en/holocaustremembrance/docs/paper18.shtml; Vancouver Holocaust Education Centre, www.vhec.org/about.html; *Vancouver Sun*, November 3, 2000.

315   *Since its inception*: The Asper Foundation, http://asperfoundation.com /hrhs-program/.

316   *As of 2016*: "Thousands Join March of the Living in Poland," Behind the News, https://behindthenewsisrael.wordpress.com/2016/05/05/thousands-join-march -of-the-living-in-poland/.

316   *"Most of the students"*: AI with Eli Rubenstein. See also Eli Rubenstein, *Witness: Passing the Torch of Holocaust Memory to New Generations* (Toronto: Second Story Press, 2015), 92; See also "Robbie Waisman," VHEC, Survivor Testimonies, www.vhec.org/robbie1.html.

316   *Almost until the day*: Philip Weiss, *Humanity in Doubt: Reflections and Essays* (Winnipeg, 2007); Allan Levine, "Philip Weiss," GM, December 22, 2008. .

316   *It took Philip Riteman*: "Holocaust Survivor Philip Riteman Speaks About Auschwitz," CBC, January 27, 2015, www.cbc.ca/news/canada/nova-scotia /holocaust-survivor-philip-riteman-speaks-about-auschwitz-1.2934018.

316   *Likewise, Max Eisen*: GM, April 16, 2016; Max Eisen, *By Chance Alone: A Remarkable True Story of Courage and Survival at Auschwitz* (Toronto: HarperCollins, 2016).

317   *It was long believed*: David Matas, "The Case of Imre Finta," *University of New Brunswick Law Journal* 43 (1994), 281; NP, June 22, 2014; Howard Margolian, *Unauthorized Entry: The Truth About Nazi War Criminals in Canada, 1946–1956* (Toronto: University of Toronto Press, 2000), 3–4.

317   *Many entered the*: Margolian, *Unauthorized Entry*, 201–06.

317   *Starting in 1949*: NP, June 22, 2014.

317   *In the aftermath*: Commission of Inquiry on War Criminals, Report, Part I, (Ottawa 1986), 26–27, 33.

317   *Even when presented*: Ibid., 225.

318   *The book—and phrase*: GM, February 26, 2013. In 1979, the two authors had sent an academic journal article based on their research for the book to Ron Atkey, the immigration minister in the newly elected government of Joe Clark. It came with a cautionary note: "We hope Canada will not be found wanting in this refugee crisis the way it was in the last." At the time, Atkey was trying to figure out a proper response to the emergency precipitated by the Vietnamese "boat people" fleeing from North Vietnamese Communist rule. Canada had taken in only about 6,000 of an estimated 130,000 refugees. Atkey's deputy minister, John Manion, read Abella and Troper's article about Mackenzie King's closed-door policy and passed it on to the minister with a warning: "This should not be you." Atkey spoke to Clark about it, who agreed to a dramatic shift in the government's position. Working with a large network of volunteers, the Conservatives opened Canada's doors wide enough for more than 50,000 refugees to come to the

country. Ron Csillag, "Politician Opened Door to Boat People," GM, May 24, 2017; Abella to author, May 25, 2017.

318 *The report detailed*: Grant Purves, "War Criminals: The Deschênes Commission," Political and Social Affairs Division, Government of Canada, Ottawa, October 16, 1998, http://publications.gc.ca/collections/Collection-R/LoPBdP/CIR/873–e.htm; NP, June 22, 2014.

318 *The report detailed*: Ron Vastokas and Lubomyr Luciuk, "The Deschenes Report: A Time for Healing," *Whig-Standard*, March 16, 1987; Gerald Tulchinsky, "Deschenes Inquiry," *Whig-Standard Magazine*, May 30, 1987; Harold Troper and Morton Weinfeld, *Old Wounds: Jews, Ukrainians and the Hunt for Nazi War Criminals in Canada* (Toronto: Penguin, 1989).

318 *In an attempt to appease*: Irving Abella, "Where Time is the Enemy," TS, May 23, 1987.

319 *The result was*: Purves, "War Criminals: The Deschênes Commission"; Irwin Cotler, ed., *Nuremberg Forty Years Later: The Struggle Against Injustice in Our Time: International Human Rights Conference, November 1987, Papers and Proceedings and Retrospective 1993* (Montreal and Kingston: McGill-Queen's University Press, 1995), 212-13.

319 *Yet after a full-fledged*: GM, September 10, 2002.

319 *Four years later*: AI with Benjamin Netanyahu, Jerusalem, December 26, 2006.

319 *One of the rioters*: GM, September 13, 2002.

320 *In the spring of 2013*: NP, April 18, 2016; CJN, May 17, 2016.

320 *"It is not an exaggeration"*: Jonathan Kay, "Understanding the Zionist Religion," *The Walrus*, April 22, 2016, https://thewalrus.ca/understanding-the-zionist-religion/.

320 *Some critics in the media*: "Harper's Historic Speech to Knesset," GM, January 20, 2014, www.theglobeandmail.com/news/politics/read-the-full-text-of-harpers-historic-speech-to-israels-knesset/article16406371/; "Jew v. Jew v. Jew v. Jew v. Jew," *The Walrus*, September 1, 2015, https://thewalrus.ca/jew-v-jew-v-jew-v-jew-v-jew-v-jew/; John Ibbitson, "With Harper in His Corner, Netanyahu Gets Warm Canadian Welcome" GM, May 30, 2010; Jeffrey Simpson, "With Friends like Harper, Bibi Can Do No Wrong," GM March 2, 2012; Weinfeld, *Like Everyone Else . . . But Different*, 272–73.

320 *Back in 1981*: Weinfeld, *The Canadian Jewish Mosaic*, 391. See also CJN, February 4, 2010.

321 *As Barbara Kay*: NP, February 16, 2016.

321 *In 2002, after putting*: AJYB 104 (2004), 239–40. See also AJYB 103, (2003), 307–08; GM, September 11, 2001; *Windsor Star*, October 13, 2001; NP, March 22, 2003; Norman Spector, *Chronicle of a War Foretold: How Mideast Peace Became America's Fight* (Vancouver: Douglas & McIntyre, 2003).

322 *In one report*: Dov Smith, "Neil Macdonald Must Go," NP, December 22, 2004, A22. See also Vivianne Spiegelman, "'Drop' TV Reporter for Anti-Israel Bias, CBC

Urged," *Jewish Tribune* (Toronto), December 16, 2004; Peter C. Newman, *The Passionate Life and Turbulent Times of Izzy Asper, Canada's Media Mogul* (Toronto: HarperCollins, 2008), 254.

322   *Izzy Asper, whose:* Newman, *The Passionate Life and Turbulent Times of Izzy Asper*, 255–58.

322   *"All good reporters":* Cited in Keren Ritchie, "Rough, Tough, and Ready to Rumble," *Ryerson Review*, June 1, 2005, http://rrj.ca/rough-tough-and-ready-to -rumble/.

322   *More than a decade:* Barbara Kay, "When Pointing to CBC's Anti-Israel Bias, There Are Plenty of Examples," NP, April 25, 2017.

Chapter Twenty-Six: The Hadassah Ladies Rise Up

323   *By the early to mid-2000s:* CJN, September 29, 2005; June 30, 2017.

323   *In Toronto, the determined:* GM, March 15, 1978; Lauren Kramer, "The Power Couple That Led the Community in Business and Social Causes," CJN, June 29, 2017, 30.

324   *She enjoyed pointing:* TS, June 23, 1996.

324   *In later years:* NP, January 2, 2017; AI with Sandra Brown.

324   *She was a "hidden child":* CJN, August 14, 1997.

324   *"I have a vivid memory":* AI with Dodo Heppner.

325   *A social worker, her elevation:* Levine, *Coming of Age*, 372-3, 399–403.

325   *But the most notable:* In June 1958, Dorothy and Cyril were involved in a terrify-ing incident that fortunately ended well. Their two-and-half-year-old son Joel— now a financier who has served on CIJA's executive—was kidnapped by Gerda Goede, a forty-six-year-old German nanny the family had recently hired. For a few days, the story captured national and international headlines. At first, it was believed the nanny had been taken along with the boy, though eventually the police determined that Goede was the perpetrator. The unknown kidnapper had asked for a $10,000 ransom, which the Reitmans left at the Montreal bus station. Meanwhile Goede took Joel by bus to Ottawa and eventually left him in the care of a taxi driver's wife she encountered. The police found Joel at the tax driver's home and the boy was reunited with his distraught parents. Goede was soon apprehended and a month later convicted of the kidnapping and sentenced to seven years. The judge at her trial speculated that the woman was "insane." See, GM, June 18, 19, July 9, 1958; *Washington Post*, June 18, 1958.

325   *An avid volunteer:* AI with Dorothy Reitman; Michael Brown, "Dorothy Reitman," Jewish Women's Archive, https://jwa.org/encyclopedia/article/reitman-dorothy; MG, May 26, 1986.

326   *At the CJC's annual:* AI with Dorothy Reitman; GM, May 12, 1986; AJYB 88 (1988), 252–54.

326 *Reitman made it clear:* MG, May 26, 1986; CJN, November 13, 1986.

326 *Nonetheless, several male:* AI with Dorothy Reitman.

326 *Reitman served a three-year term:* Ottawa Citizen, April 6, 1987; MG, October 3, 1987; TS, March 31, 1989; Bernie Farber, "The Powerhouse Women of Canadian Jewish Congress," CJN, Feb 2, 2017.

326 *It was not until 1995:* AJYB, 96 (1996), 203-04.

326 *She was the "establishment":* MG, April 19, May 12, 15, 22, 1995; Farber, "The Powerhouse Women of Canadian Jewish Congress.

326 *The election procedures:* AJYB 97 (1997), 247.

326 *That same year, social worker:* CJN, June 15, 1995; Michael Brown, "Sandra Brown," Jewish Women's Archive, https://jwa.org/encyclopedia/article/brown-sandra; AI with Sandra Brown.

327 *By then, Kislowicz:* CJN, May 18, 2006; AI with Linda Kislowicz.

327 *A decade on:* AI with Linda Kislowicz.

328 *"Anne Golden can more"* GM, November 23, 1996.

328 *Ted Richmond, who died:* GM, October 16, 1985; CJN, November 25, 1999; AI with Anne Golden.

328 *Her family was thoroughly:* Kay, Acknowledgments, 8.

329 *"The chair of the department":* AI with Anne Golden; AI with Natalie Zemon Davis.

329 *This led her into:* AI with Anne Golden; "City Woman: Anne Golden and her Plan," Toronto Life 30:2 (February 1996), 40–43.

329 *As a Jewish woman:* AI with Anne Golden; TS, November 6, 1987; Canada News Wire, January 25, 2001.

329 *"It was another WASP":* AI with Anne Golden.

330 *She delivered her 270-page report:* "Report of the GTA Task Force," January 1996, 13–14, www.scribd.com/doc/99998119/English; GM, January 15, 1996; TS, January 17, 1996; Levine, Toronto, 316–17.

330 *In 1998, the first mayor:* John Lorinc, "The Next Mayor," Toronto Life 36:16 (October 2002), 80.

330 *Four years earlier:* Patricia Best, "50 Influentials," Chatelaine, 67:9 (September 1994), 55–62.

331 *She even stood her:* "Kay vs. Kay," CJN, April 8, 2016.

331 *Growing up in the forties:* Kay, Acknowledgments, 1–2.

331 *She admits that:* Ibid. 12.

331 *In short order, the two were:* Ibid., 16–17.

331 *"When I was invited":* "Jew v. Jew v. Jew v. Jew v. Jew," The Walrus.

332 *One day, Jonathan:* Kay, Acknowledgments, 36–7; AI with Barbara Kay.

332 *Kay concedes that:* Kay, Acknowledgments, 13; AI with Barbara Kay.

332 *"She bravely resists":* Rex Murphy, "Foreword," in Kay, Acknowledgments, iii.

332   *With a few strokes of her laptop:* "Barbara Kay Controversy," https://en.wikipedia.org /wiki/Barbara_Kay_controversy.

332–333 *About a week earlier:* Cited in Barbara Kay, "The Rise of 'Quebecistan,'" NP, August 9, 2006.

333   *Yet, as Kay argued:* Ibid.

333   *She arrived home:* AI with Barbara Kay.

333   *She was denounced:* Ottawa Citizen, August 24, 2006.

334   *In a strongly worded:* André Pratte, "The Myth of 'Quebecistan'" NP, August 16, 2006.

334   *French-Canadian columnist:* Ottawa Citizen, August 24, 2006; TS, August 20, 2006.

334   *"There has unfortunately":* Quebec Press Council, Decision D2006–08–009, February 2, 2007, http://conseildepresse.qc.ca/decisions/d2006–08–009/.

334   *But it is a watchdog:* AI with Barbara Kay.

334   *Somewhat predictably:* Quebec Press Council, Decision D2006–08–009.

334   *Reflecting on the entire:* NP, May 31, 2007.

335   *The list in 2007:* WFP, October 28, 2007.

335   *"Everything is doable":* Allan Levine, *From Winnipeg to the World: The Canwest Global Story* (Winnipeg: Canwest Global Corp., 2002), 2.

335   *Asper, who was born:* Peter C. Newman and Allan Levine, *Miracle at the Forks: The Museum That Dares Make a Difference* (Vancouver: Figure 1 Publishing, 2014), 29–30.

336   *By the time Izzy Asper:* Ibid., 33.

336   *The CMHR could have:* See ibid., 55–104.

336   *At the gala:* WFP, September 20, 2014.

337   *As a* Winnipeg Free Press: Ibid.

337   *In June 2015:* AI with Elaine Goldstine.

Chapter Twenty-Four: Checks and Balances

338   *The merger took place:* Harold M. Waller, "The Canadian Jewish Polity," CJN, September 29, 2005, B18–22.

339   *Why did the CJC2:* Waller, "The Canadian Jewish Polity," B18–22; Tulchinsky, *Branching Out*, 306.

339   *As early as 1972:* AJYB 73 (1972), 397–98.

339   *Congress officials acknowledged:* Cited in AJYB 73 (1972), 397-98.

339   *But in the years:* Waller, "The Canadian Jewish Polity."

340   *In their view, the CJC:* Ottawa Citizen, November 7, 2000; CJN, December 11, 2003.

340   *Schwartz and Reisman helped:* TS, October 4, 2003; CJN, October 9, 2003; David Noble, "The New Israel Lobby in Action Canadian," *Canadian Dimension* 39:6

(November/December 2005), 30–35; AI with Bernie Farber and Frank Bialystok; Michael Brown, "Julia Koschitzky," Jewish Women's Archive, https://jwa.org /encyclopedia/article/koschitzky-julia.

340 *To confirm what they:* AI with Shimon Fogel.

340 *This first version:* Franklin Bialystok to author, October 24, 2017.

341 *"It's a convenient myth":* AI with Shimon Fogel.

341 *By the end of 2003:* Ibid.

341 *Promises were made:* TS, October 9, 2003; CJN, December 4, 2003; AI with Bernie Farber.

341 *Having no recourse:* TS, October 9, 2003; CJN, December 4, 2003.

341 *In an interview:* TS, October 9, 2003.

341 *That may have been:* AI with Shimon Fogel.

342 *"I'm doing it":* CJN, January 22, 2004. Hershell Ezrin is reticent to speak about his involvement in CIJA. He indicated to me that he would consider talking about it only after a sufficient number of years have passed—sometime in the mid-2020s. Author telephone conversation with Hershell Ezrin, January 9, 2017.

342 *Commenting on the shift:* GM, October 15, 2004.

342–343 *Bernie Farber, a lively:* AI with Bernie Farber.

343 *At the end of November:* CJN, November 25, 2010.

343 *Historian Frank Bialystok:* AI with Frank Bialystok.

343 *"Congress had more":* AI with Bernie Farber.

344 *"The Congress isn't":* Ottawa Citizen, November 29, 2010; CJN, December 9, 2010.

344 *Sally Zerker, a York University:* CJN, August 25, 2011; CJN, March 27, 2013.

344 *"We had an opportunity":* CJN, June 30, 2011.

344 *In a follow-up:* NP, August 31, 2011.

344 *Bialystok, for one:* Bialystok to author, October 24, 2017.

344 *"How someone can":* AI with Shimon Fogel.

345 *"I can accept that":* Ibid.

346 *In the fall of 2014:* CJN, September 2, 2014.

346 *Yet the judges:* Adler v. Ontario, Supreme Court of Canada, November 21, 1996, https://scc-csc.lexum.com/scc-csc/scc-csc/en/item/1446/index.do; GM, November 22, 1996.

346 *In November 1996:* AJYB, 98 (1998), 204.

346 *A decade later:* GM, September 13, October 11, 2007.

347 *Jewish education is:* Weinfeld, Like Everyone Else . . . But Different, 231.

347 *In 1998, educating Jewish:* Ibid., 231, 421, n.13.

347 *Yet the burden:* CJN, August 23, 2013.

347 *The high tuition is:* AI with Claire Sumerlus.

347 *Jewish high schools:* CJN, December 9, 2016.

347 *In the spring:* Ibid., March 15, 27, 2017.

348   *The organization*: Grassroots for Affordable Jewish Education (GAJE), https://gaje.ca/.

348   *The personal stories*: "Parents tell their stories," GAJE, https://gaje.ca/parents-tell
-their-stories/parents-tell-their-stories-1/; https://gaje.ca/parents-tell-their
-stories/parents-tell-their-stories-2/.

348   *A survey of Toronto*: CJN, May 25, 2016.

348   *After the 2015 school year*: CJN, February 13, 2015; Michael Regenstrief, editor at
Ottawa Jewish Bulletin, to author, January 4, 2017.

349   *Even with the slight*: CJN, March 25, 2015; JPN, October 29, 2014.

349   *It is the only such*: "Hebrew Bilingual Program," See Brock Corydon School,
www.winnipegsd.ca/schools/BrockCorydon/AcademicsAndClasses/hebrew
-program/Pages/Default.aspx.

349   *In 2015, King David*: CJN, March 25, 2015, January 5, 2016.

349   *"The success of the Vancouver"*: Jonathan Leipsic to author, January 20, 2017.

350   *By the mid-nineties*: Jim L. Torczyner and Shari L. Brotman, "The Jews of
Canada: A Profile from the Census," AJYB 95 (1995), 235–36.

350   *"Canadian Jews are better"*: Ibid., 235.

350   *According to the Jewish Federations*: Charles Shahar, "Part 3: Jewish Seniors," and
"Part 4: The Jewish Poor," in *2011 National Household Survey Analysis: The Jewish
Population of Canada* (Toronto: Jewish Federations of Canada-UIA, 2014), iv.

350   *In late 2014*: CJN, October 13, 2014.

350   *Two years later*: CJN, June 8, 2016.

351   *In Montreal*: Charles Shahar, "Part 3: Jewish Seniors," and "Part 4: The Jewish Poor,"
in *2011 National Household Survey Analysis: The Jewish Population of Canada*
(Toronto: Jewish Federations of Canada-UIA, 2014), iv; CJN, March 30, 2016.

351   *But ethnic and religious bonds*: Weinfeld, *Like Everyone Else . . . But Different*, 178–81.

Conclusion: The Never-Dying Canadians

352   *Her answer was that*: Peterson, "The Jew in Canada," 22–3, 62–5.

352   *The businesses she highlighted*: Ibid., 62–3.

352   *Wayne and Shuster might*: Marc Glassman, "Wayne and Shuster: Duo were
Canada's Comedy Ambassadors," *Playback*, May 26, 2008.

353   *"I do think it is"*: AI with Rabbi Daniel Korobkin.

353   *"There's a difference between"*: AI with Rabbi Yael Splansky.

353   *In September 1998*: AJYB 99 (1999), 224.

354   *By then, the immigrant*: AJYB 73 (1972), 397.

354   *The majority of these newcomers*: CJN, November 9, 2016; Yoni Goldstein,
"Montreal's Jews Aren't Going Anywhere," *Haaretz* (Tel-Aviv), October 26, 2007.

354   *In 2013, Olga and Gregory*: Philip Moscovitch, "Leaving Israel, Russian Jews Find a
New Home in Halifax," *Tablet*, July 8, 2014, www.tabletmag.com/jewish-life-and

-religion/177177/russian-jews-in-halifax; Olga Shepshelevich to author, January 20, 2017.

355   *Many of the Russian-Israelis:* CJN, November 10, 2016; JPN, December 7, 2016; Uriel Heilman, "Seeking Newcomers Overseas, Winnipeg Jews Don't Get What They Expected," JTA, March 25, 2014; Olga Shepshelevich to author; AI with Max Kretskiy.

355   *Nonetheless, in the spring:* CJN, May 9, 2013; Bernie Farber, "Why We Must Rescue the Canadian Jewish News," *Huffington Post Canada*, May 1, 2013, www.huffingtonpost.ca /bernie-farber/why-we-must-rescue-the-ca_b_3187754.html.

355   *By the end of the year:* AI with Yoni Goldstein. Born in Toronto, Goldstein grew up in an Orthodox family. After completing high school, he attended a Yeshiva in Israel, but opted not to become a rabbi. Returning to Canada, he studied English literature at York University where he received bachelor's and master's degrees. From there, he moved into journalism as an intern with the *Jerusalem Report* magazine, before landing an editorial job at the *National Post*, where he says he learned much from the *Post*'s comment editor at the time, Jonathan Kay. After he left the *Post*, he worked briefly for *Maclean*'s and edited a fashion magazine. Then the CJN board, with the idea of injecting some youth into the publication, came calling. His first day on the job was in early January 2014 and he is still going strong, having improved the paper with crisper writing, opinionated columnists, and enhanced professionalism.

356   *Many of his subscribers:* See, for example, Mira Sucharov, "Canada 150 and 50 Years of Israel's Occupation Need Sober Reflection," CJN, May 3, 2017; Yoni Goldstein, "From Yoni's Desk," CJN, May 5, 2017.

356   *But there is no denying:* See *Annual Audit of Antisemitic Incidents 2016*, League for Human Rights B'nai Brith Canada, (Toronto, 2017), 11, www.bnaibrith.ca /2016_a_record_setting_year_for_antisemitism_in_canada.

356   *The BDS movement:* In November 2016, the *McGill Daily*, the university student newspaper, was accused in a complaint of being antisemitic. The paper's editorial board was taken aback by this charge. As it subsequently explained, the editors take "allegations of anti-Semitism seriously, as we recognize that anti-Semitism is a persistent and pervasive reality of our society." Further investigation revealed that the whole thing was apparently a mistake: What was taken for antisemitism was, in fact, they explained, anti-Zionism. That led to this bit of contorted logic: "The *Daily* maintains an editorial line of not publishing pieces which promote a Zionist worldview, or any other ideology which we consider to be oppressive. While we recognize that, for some, Zionism represents an important freedom project, we also recognize that it functions as a settler-colonial ideology that perpetuates the displacement and the oppression of the Palestinian people." In other words, as American journalist Chloé Valdary commented, "This blunt statement is a reminder that hatred of the Jewish state is rapidly becoming the default position on many college campuses."

See, *McGill Daily*, November 7, 2016, www.mcgilldaily.com/2016/11/in-response-to
-a-ssmu-equity-complaint-about-anti-semitism-mentioning-the-daily/.

356 *Jews are still targeted*: CJN, November 29, 2017; March 21, 2016; "Police-Reported
Hate Crime, 2016," Statistics Canada, www.statcan.gc.ca/daily-quotidien/171128
/dq171128d-eng.htm.

356 *And in Winnipeg*: "Winnipeg Police Investigating Hate Crime after Anti-Semitic
incident," CTV News, January 5, 2017, http://www.ctvnews.ca/canada/winnipeg
-police-investigating-hate-crime-after-anti-semitic-incident-1.3228978.

357 *Ironically enough, Jews*: Alan M. Dershowitz, *The Vanishing American Jew*
(Boston: Little, Brown and Company, 1997), 1.

357 *Back in 1986*: *Ottawa Citizen*, May 12, 1986.

357 *"The Conservative movement"*: AI with Rabbi Baruch Frydman-Kohl.

357 *In Calgary in 1986*: Gordon Legge, "Synagogue a Tribute to Faith," *Calgary Herald*,
May 19, 1990.

357 *In 2002, after two years*: Levine, *Coming of Age*, 427–29.

358 *Similarly, in Ottawa*: Louise Rachlis, "Agudath Israel and Beth Shalom to
Become Kehillat Beth Israel," *Ottawa Jewish Bulletin*, March 29, 2016,
www.ottawajewishbulletin.com/2016/03/agudath-israel-and-beth-shalom-to
-become-kehillat-beth-israel/; Kehillat Beth Israel, "Our History,"
http://kehillatbethisrael.com/about-kbi/history/.

358 *Even in Toronto*: CJN, March 14, 2016.

358 *These "Jell-O Jews"*: AI with Rabbi Baruch Frydman-Kohl.

358 *Most Saturdays*: AI with Ian Staniloff.

359 *"Let's put it this way"*: WFP, September 24, 2016; AI with Ian Staniloff.

359 *At Conservative Beth Tzedec in Toronto*: Rabbi Baruch Frydman-Kohl to author,
January 14, 2017. See also CJN, December 5, 2002.

359 *In April 2005*: Canada Newswire, April 14, 2005.

359 *Not surprisingly, Reform*: AI with Rabbi Yael Splansky; GM, May 17, 2014; "Life
Cycle Occasions at Holy Blossom," Holy Blossom Temple, http://holyblossom.org
/jewish-life-events/wedding/.

360 *Winnipeg's Shaarey Zedek*: "Congregation Shaarey Zedek Announces Opening of
Shaarey Shamayim Jewish Interfatih," Congregation Shaarey Zedek,
Cemetery," www.szwinnipeg.ca/funeral_and_cemetery/shaareyshamayim.htm.

360 *Temple Shalom in Winnipeg*: Levine, *Coming of Age*, 422–23.

360 *The first intermarriage*: CJN, August 23, 2013.

360 *Montreal's Reform Temple*: CJN, March 2, 2012; Rabbi Lisa Grushcow, Temple
Emanu-El-Beth Sholom, to author, February 25, 2018; https://www.templemontreal
.ca/life-cycle/weddings/.

360 *"If the couple agree"*: Rabbi Dan Moskovitz to author, January 21, 2017.

360 *As Alan Dershowitz*: Dershowitz, *The Vanishing American Jew*, 1–2.

360 *By 1991, it had reached*: The Jewish Population of Canada 2015 (Montreal: The Jewish Community Foundation of Montreal, 2015), 9–10; Charles Shahar, "Part 6: Intermarriage," in 2011 National Household Survey Analysis: The Jewish Population of Canada, iv, 30–3.

360 *According to the 2011*: Shahar, ibid., 10; CJN, July 27, 2016.

361 *"By the time Jewish"*: AI with Jon Goldberg.

361 *Reform synagogues may*: AI with Rabbi Baruch Frydman-Kohl.

361 *In early 1996*: MG, January 30, 1996.

361 *Nearly five decades earlier*: Simon Rawidowicz, "Israel: The Ever-Dying People," in The Ever-Dying People and Other Essays (Cranbury, NJ: Associated University Presses, 1986), 53–61. Rawidowicz, who died in 1957 at the age of sixty, wrote this essay in Hebrew in 1948. It was published in English in the journal Judaism in 1967. See, Judaism 16:4 (Fall 1967), 423-33.

362 *Or, as Rabbi Stuart Rosenberg*: Oliver Clausen, "The Jews: A New Elite?" GM, October 14, 1967.

362 *The Braemer-Fruchter family*: AI with Ryla Braemer and Yacov Fruchter.

Abella, Irving. *A Coat of Many Colours: Two Centuries of Jewish Life in Canada.* Toronto: Lester & Orpen Dennys, 1990.

Abella, Irving. "Portrait of a Jewish Professional Revolutionary: The Recollections of Joshua Gershman." *Labour* 2 (1977): 185–213.

Abella, Irving and Harold Troper. *None is Too Many: Canada and the Jews of Europe 1933–1948.* Toronto: Lester & Orpen Dennys, 1982.

Abramson, Henry. "'Just Different': The Last Jewish Family of Ansonville, Ontario." *Canadian Jewish Studies* 9 (2001): 155–69.

Abramson, Zelda. "From Rags to Comfort: Women Holocaust Survivors Rebuilding Lives in Montreal, 1947–1958." *Canadian Jewish Studies* 23 (2015): 92–117.

Anctil, Pierre, ed. À *chacun ses Juifs: 60 éditoriaux pour comprendre la position du Devoir à l'égard des Juifs (1910–1947).* Sillery, QC: Septentrion, 2014.

Anctil, Pierre. *Jacob Isaac Segal 1896–1954: Un poéte Yiddish de Montréal et son milieu.* Quebec: Presses de l'Université Laval, 2012.

Anisef, Paul and Michael Lanphier, eds. *The World in a City.* Toronto: University of Toronto Press, 2003.

Arnold, A.J. "The Contribution of the Jews to the Opening and Development of the West." *Manitoba Historical Society Transactions* 3:25 (1968–69): 23–37.

Arnold, A.J. "The Earliest Jews in Winnipeg 1874–1882." *The Beaver* 54:2 (Autumn, 1974): 4–11.

Arnold, A.J. "Ezekiel Hart and the Oath Problem in the Assembly of Lower Canada." *Canadian Jewish Historical Society Journal* 3:1 (1979): 10–26.

Arnold, A.J. "Jewish Immigration to Western Canada in the 1880s." *Canadian Jewish Historical Society Journal* 1:2 (October 1977): 82–96.

Arnold, A.J. "The New Jerusalem: Jewish Pioneers on the Prairies." *The Beaver* 74:4 (August–September, 1994), 37–42.

Aronson, Michael. *Troubled Waters: The Origins of the 1881 Anti-Jewish Pogroms in Russia.* Pittsburgh: University of Pittsburgh Press, 1990.

Axelrod, Paul. *Making a Middle Class: Student Life in English Canada During the Thirties.* Montreal and Kingston: McGill-Queen's University Press, 1990.

Azrieli, David J. *Rekindling the Torch: The Story of Canadian Zionism.* Toronto: Key Porter Books, 2008.

Babcock, Robert H. "A Jewish Immigrant in the Maritimes: The Memoirs of Max Vanger." *Acadiensis* 16:1 (Autumn 1986): 136–148.

Barrett, Dave and William Miller. *Barrett: A Passionate Political Life.* Vancouver: Douglas & McIntyre, 1995.

Barrett, Stanley. *Is God a Racist?: The Right Wing in Canada.* Toronto: University of Toronto Press, 1987.

Beer, Max. "The Montreal Jewish Community and the Holocaust." *Current Psychology* 26:3 (2007): 191–205.

Belcove-Shalin, Janet S., ed. *New World Hasidim: Ethnographic Studies of Hasidic Jews in America.* Albany, NY: State University of New York Press, 1995.

Benbassa, Esther. *The Jews of France: A History from Antiquity to the Present.* Princeton, N.J.: Princeton University Press, 2001.

Bercuson, David J. *Canada and the Birth of Israel: A Study in Canadian Foreign Policy.* Toronto: University of Toronto Press, 1985.

Bercuson, David J. "Canadian Jews in the Second World War: A Few Thoughts." Paper presented at the Association for Canadian Jewish Studies Conference, Calgary, May 2016.

Bercuson, David J. *The Secret Army.* Toronto: Lester & Orpen Dennys, 1983.

Bercuson, David J., and Douglas Wertheimer. *A Trust Betrayed: The Keegstra Affair.* Toronto: Doubleday, 1985.

Berger, Monty. *Lament for a Province: The Tragic Costs of Québec's Flirtation with Separatism.* Toronto: Lugus, 1995.

Berk, Stephen M. *Year of Crisis, Year of Hope: Russian Jewry and the Pogroms of 1881–1882.* Westport, CT: Greenwood Press, 1985.

Berton, Pierre. *The Great Depression 1929–1939.* Toronto: McClelland & Stewart, 1990.

Berton, Pierre. *My Times: Living with History 1947–1995.* Toronto: McClelland & Stewart, 1995.

Bessner, Ellin. *Double Threat: Canadian Jews, the Military, and World War II.* Toronto: New Jewish Press, 2018.

Betcherman, Lita-Rose. *The Swastika and the Maple Leaf: Fascist Movements in Canada in the Thirties.* Toronto: Fitzhenry and Whiteside, 1975.

Betcherman, Lita-Rose. *Ernest Lapointe: Mackenzie King's Great Quebec Lieutenant.* Toronto: University of Toronto Press, 2000.

Bialystok, Franklin. *Delayed Impact: The Holocaust and the Canadian Jewish Community.* Montreal and Kingston: McGill-Queen's University Press, 2000.

Bilsky, Anna, ed. *A Common Thread: A History of the Jews of Ottawa.* Renfrew, ON. General Store Publishing House, 2009.

Blaustein, Esther I., Rachel A. Esar, and Evelyn Miller, "Spanish and Portuguese Synagogue (Shearith Israel) Montreal, 1768–1968." *Transactions & Miscellanies* (Jewish Historical Society of England) 23 (1969–1970): 111–42.

Borovoy, A. Alan. *At the Barricades: A Memoir.* Toronto: Irwin Law, 2014.

Briansky Kalter, Bella. "A Jewish Community That Was: Ansonville, Ontario, Canada." *American Jewish Archives Journal* 30:2 (November 1978): 107–25.

Bronfman, Charles, with Howard Green. *Distilled: A Memoir of Family, Seagram, Baseball, and Philanthropy.* Toronto: HarperCollins, 2016.

Bronfman, Edgar M. *Why Be Jewish? A Testament.* Toronto: Signal/McClelland & Stewart, 2016.

Brown, Michael. *Jew or Juif? Jews, French Canadians, and Anglo-Canadians, 1759–1914.* Philadelphia: Jewish Publication Society, 1987.

Brown, Michael. "Divergent Paths: Early Zionism in Canada and the United States." *Jewish Social Studies* 44:2 (Spring 1982): 149–68.

Brown, Michael. "The Push and Pull Factors of Aliyah and the Anomalous Case of Canada: 1967–1982." *Jewish Social Studies* 48:2 (Spring 1986): 141–62.

Brown, Michael, ed. *Approaches to Antisemitism: Context and Curriculum.* New York: American Jewish Committee, 1994.

Brym, Robert J., William Shaffir, and Morton Weinfeld, editors. *The Jews in Canada.* Toronto: Oxford University Press, 1993.

Brym, Robert J., and Rhonda L. Lenton. "The Distribution of Anti-Semitism in Canada in 1984." *The Canadian Journal of Sociology* 16:4 (Autumn 1991): 411–18.

Burr, Christina and Carol A. Reader. "Fanny 'Bobbie' Rosenfeld: A 'Modern Woman' of Sport and Journalism in Twentieth-Century Canada." *Sport History Review* 44:2 (November 2013): 120–43.

Caplan, Usher. *Like One That Dreamed: A Portrait of A.M. Klein.* Toronto: McGraw-Hill Ryerson, 1982.

Chiel, Arthur. "Manitoba Jewish History—Early Times." *Manitoba Historical Society Transactions* 3:10 (1953–54) www.mhs.mb.ca/docs/transactions/3/jewishhistory.shtml.

Chiel, Arthur. *Jewish Experiences in Early Manitoba.* Winnipeg: Manitoba Jewish Publications, 1955.

Chiel, Arthur. *The Jews in Manitoba: A Social History.* Toronto: University of Toronto Press, 1961.

Chouinard, Craig. "A Tale of Two Synagogues: Culture, Conflict and Consolidation in the Jewish Community of Saint John, 1906–1919." *Canadian Jewish Studies* 2 (1994): 1–19.

Cohen, Rich. *Tough Jews: Fathers, Sons, and Gangster Dreams in Jewish America.* New York: Simon and Schuster, 1998.

Cohen, Werner. "English and French Canadian Public Opinion on Jews and Israel: Some Poll Data." *Canadian Ethnic Studies* 11:2 (January 1979): 31–48.

Cole, Stephen J. "Commissioning Consent: An Investigation of the Royal Commission on the Relations of Labour and Capital, 1886–1889." PhD thesis, Queen's University, 2007.

Comartin, Justin. "Opening Closed Doors: Revisiting the Canadian Immigration Record (1933–1945)." *Canadian Jewish Studies* 24 (2016): 79–102.

Craig, Terrence. *Racial Attitudes in English-Canadian Fiction, 1905–1980.* Waterloo, ON: Wilfrid Laurier Press, 1987.

Davies, Alan T., ed. *Antisemitism in Canada: History and Interpretation*. Waterloo, ON: Wilfrid Laurier University Press 1992.

Delisle, Esther. *The Traitor and the Jew*. Montreal-Toronto: Robert Davies Publishing, 1993.

Dennis, Richard. "Property and Propriety: Jewish Landlords in Early Twentieth-Century Toronto." *Transactions of the Institute of British Geographers* 22:3 (1997): 377–97.

Dershowitz, Alan M. *The Vanishing American Jew*. Boston: Little, Brown and Company, 1997.

Diamond, Etan. *And I Will Dwell in Their Midst: Orthodox Jews in Suburbia*. Chapel Hill: University of North Carolina Press, 2000.

Diner, Hasia R. *Roads Taken: The Great Jewish Migrations to the New World and the Peddlers Who Forged the Way*. New Haven, CT: Yale University Press, 2015.

Douville, Raymond. *Aaron Hart: récit historique*. Trois-Riviere: Editions du bien public, 1938.

Draper, Paula Jean. "The Accidental Immigrants: Canada and the Interned Refugees, Part I." *Canadian Jewish Historical Society Journal* 2:1 (Spring 1978): 1–38.

Draper, Paula Jean. "The Accidental Immigrants: Canada and the Interned Refugees, Part II." *Canadian Jewish Historical Society Journal* 2:2 (Fall 1978): 80–112.

Draper, Paula Jean. "Canadian Holocaust Survivors: From Liberation to Rebirth." *Canadian Jewish Studies* 4–5 (1996–97): 39–62.

Dumas, Evelyn. *The Bitter Thirties in Québec*. Montreal: Black Rose Books, 1975.

Dunkelman, Ben. *Dual Allegiance*. Toronto: Macmillan of Canada, 1976.

Eban, Abba. *Heritage: Civilization and the Jews*. New York: Summit Books, 1984.

Eisen, Wendy. *Count Us In: The Struggle to Free Soviet Jews: A Canadian Perspective*. Toronto: Burgher Books, 1995.

Endelman, Todd. *The Jews of Britain, 1656 to 2000*. Berkeley, CA: University of California Press. 2002.

Endicott, Stephen Lyon. *Raising the Workers' Flag: The Workers' Unity League of Canada, 1930–1936*. Toronto: University of Toronto Press, 2012.

Erwin, Norman. "The Holocaust, Canadian Jews, and Canada's 'Good War' Against Nazism." *Canadian Jewish Studies* 24 (2016): 103–123.

Eyman, Scott. *Lion of Hollywood: The Life and Legend of Louis B. Mayer*. New York: Simon and Schuster, 2005.

Figes, Orlando. *A People's Tragedy: The Russian Revolution 1891–1924*. London: Jonathan Cape, 1996.

Figler, Bernard. *Lillian and Archie Freiman: Biographies*. Montreal: Northern Printing and Lithographing Company, 1962.

Figler, Bernard. *Sam Jacobs: Member of Parliament*. Montreal: n.p., 1970.

Fine, Jonathan. "Anti-Semitism in Manitoba in the 1930s and 40s." *Manitoba History* 32 (Autumn 1996): 26–33.

Ferdman Tauben, Sara. *Traces of the Past: Montreal's Early Synagogues*. Montreal: Véhicule Press, 2011.

Foran, Charles. *Mordecai: The Life and Times*. Toronto: Alfred A. Knopf Canada, 2010.

Frager, Ruth. A. *Sweatshop Strife: Class, Ethnicity, and Gender in the Jewish Labour Movement of Toronto 1900–1939*. Toronto: University of Toronto Press, 1992.

Frager, Ruth. A. "Class, Ethnicity, and Gender in the Eaton Strikes of 1912 and 1934." In *Gender Conflicts: New Essays in Women's History*. Edited by Franca Iacovetta and Mariana Valverde. Toronto: University of Toronto Press, 1992: 189–228.

Fraser, David. *Honorary Protestants: The Jewish School Question in Montreal, 1867–1997*. Toronto: University of Toronto Press, 2015.

Fried, Albert. *The Rise and Fall of the Jewish Gangster in America*. New York: Holt, Rinehart, and Winston, 1980.

Friedland, Martin L. *The University of Toronto: A History*. Toronto: University of Toronto Press, 2000.

Frisse, Ulrich. "The 'Bystanders' Perspective': *The Toronto Daily Star* and its Coverage of Persecution of the Jews and the Holocaust 1933–1954." *Yad Vashem Studies* 39:1 (2011): 213–43.

Gabler, Neal. *An Empire of Their Own: How the Jews Invented Hollywood*. New York: Crown Publishers, 1988.

Gerber, Jane S. *The Jews of Spain: A History of the Sephardic Experience*. New York: Free Press, 1992.

Gerber, Jean. "Opening the Door: Immigration and Integration of Holocaust Survivors in Vancouver, 1947–1970." *Canadian Jewish Studies* 4–5 (1996–1997): 63–87.

Gelman, Susan. "Anatomy of a Failed Strike: The T. Eaton Co. Lockout of Cloakmakers, 1912." *Canadian Jewish Historical Society Journal* 9:2 (Fall 1985): 93–119.

Giesbrecht, Jodi. "Accommodating Resistance: Unionization, Gender, and Ethnicity in Winnipeg's Garment Industry, 1929–1945." *Urban History Review* 39:1 (Fall 2010): 5–19.

Girard, Philip. *Bora Laskin: Bringing Law to Life*. Toronto: University of Toronto Press, 2005.

Gladstone, Bill. *A History of the Jewish Community of London Ontario: From the 1850s to the Present Day*. Toronto: Now and Then Books, 2011.

Glass, Joseph B. "Isolation and Alienation: Factors in the Growth of Zionism in the Canadian Prairies, 1917–1939." *Canadian Jewish Studies* 9 (2001): 85–123.

Godfrey, Sheldon J. and Judith C. Godfrey. *Search Out the Land: The Jews and the Growth of Equality in British Colonial America 1740–1867*. Montreal and Kingston: McGill-Queen's University Press, 1995.

Godfrey, Sheldon J. and Judith C. Godfrey. *Burn This Gossip: The True Story of George Benjamin of Belleville, Canada's First Jewish Member of Parliament*. Toronto: Duke and George Press, 1991.

Goldberg, Adara. *Holocaust Survivors in Canada: Exclusions, Inclusion, Transformation, 1947–1955*. Winnipeg: University of Manitoba Press, 2015.

Goldberg, J.J., and Elliot King, eds. *Builders and Dreamers: Habonim Labour Zionist Youth in North America*. New York: Herzl Press, 1993.

Goldbloom, Alton. *Small Patients: The Autobiography of a Children's Doctor*. Philadelphia and New York: Lippincott, 1959.

Gottesman, Eli. *Canadian Jewish Reference Book and Directory: 1965*. Montreal: Jewish Institute of Higher Research, 1965.

Goutor, David. "The Canadian Media and the 'Discovery' of the Holocaust, 1944–1945." *Canadian Jewish Studies* 4–5 (1996–1997): 88–119.

Graham, Gwethalyn. *Earth and High Heaven*. New York: J.P. Lippincott and Company, 1944.

Gray, Charlotte. *Sisters in the Wilderness: The Lives of Susanna Moodie and Catharine Parr Traill*. Toronto: Viking, 1999.

Gray, James. *The Winter Years*. Toronto: MacMillan of Canada, 1966.

Greenstein, Michael. *Third Solitudes: Tradition and Discontinuity in Jewish-Canadian Literature*. Montreal and Kingston: McGill-Queen's University Press, 1989.

Gross Stein, Janice. "Canadian Foreign Policy in the Middle East after the October War." *Social Praxis* 4 (1976–1977): 271–97.

Gutkin, Harry. *Journey into Our Heritage: The Story of the Jewish People in the Canadian West*. Toronto: Lester & Orpen Dennys, 1980.

Gutkin, Harry, with Mildred Gutkin. *The Worst of Times, The Best of Times*. Toronto: Fitzhenry & Whiteside, 1987.

Gutkin, Harry, and Mildred Gutkin. *Profiles in Dissent: The Shaping of Radical Thought in the Canadian West*. Edmonton: NeWest Publishers, 1997.

Halpern, Monda. *Alice in Shandehland: Scandal and Scorn in the Edelson/Horwitz Murder Case*. Montreal and Kingston: McGill-Queen's University Press, 2015.

Harney, Robert, and Harold Troper. *Immigrants: A Portrait of the Urban Experience, 1890–1930*. Toronto: Van Nostrand Reinhold, 1975.

Hart, Arthur D., ed. *The Jew in Canada*. Toronto and Montreal: Jewish Publications Limited, 1926.

Hayes, Saul. "The Changing Nature of the Jewish Community." *Viewpoints* 5:3 (Fall 1970): 24–28.

Heckewelder, John. *History, Manners, and Customs of the Indian Nations Who Once Inhabited Pennsylvania and the Neighboring States*. Philadelphia: Publication Fund of the Historical Society of Pennsylvania, 1881. https://archive.org/stream/histmannerscustooheckrich/histmannerscustooheckrich_djvu.txt.

Heineman, David E. "The Startling Experience of a Jewish Trader during Pontiac's Siege of Detroit in 1763." *American Jewish Historical Society Publications* 23 (1915): 31–35.

Heritage and History: The Saskatoon Jewish Community. Saskatoon: Congregation Agudas Israel, 1998.

Heron, Craig. *Lunch-Bucket Lives: Remaking the Workers' City*. Toronto: Between the Lines, 2015.

Hiebert, Daniel J. "Jewish Immigrants and the Garment Industry of Toronto, 1901–1931: A Study of Ethnic and Class Relations." *Annals of the Association of American Geographers* 83:2 (June 1993): 243–71.

Hoffer, Clara, and F.H. Kahan. *Land of Hope*. Saskatoon: Modern Press, 1960.

Horowitz, Aaron. *Striking Roots: Reflections on Five Decades of Jewish Life*. Oakville, ON: Mosaic Press, 1979.

Iacovetta, Franca, Paula Draper, and Robert Ventresca, eds. *A Nation of Immigrants: Women, Workers, and Communities in Canadian History, 1840s–1960s*. Toronto: University of Toronto Press, 1998.

Iacovetta, Franca, and Mariana Valverde. *Gender Conflicts: New Essays in Women's History*. Toronto: University of Toronto Press, 1992.

Indig, Sheldon. "Canadian Jewry and their Struggle for an Exemption in the Federal Lord's Day Act of 1906, Part I." *Canadian Jewish Historical Society Journal* 3:1, 27–56.

Indig, Sheldon. "Canadian Jewry and their Struggle for an Exemption in the Federal Lord's Day Act of 1906, Part II." *Canadian Jewish Historical Society Journal* 3:2, 61–114.

Jewish Historical Society of Southern Alberta. *Land of Promise: The Jewish Experience in Southern Alberta*. Calgary: Jewish Historical Society of Alberta, 1996. (http://www.ourroots.ca/e/toc.aspx?id=1314.)

Hoerder, Dirk. *Creating Societies: Immigrant Lives in Canada*. Montreal and Kingston: McGill-Queens University Press, 1999.

Hoffman, Matthew B., and Henry F. Srebrnik. *A Vanished Ideology: Essays on the Jewish Communist Movement in the English-Speaking World in the Twentieth Century*. Albany, NY: SUNY Press, 2016.

Howe, Irving. *World of Our Fathers*. New York: Harcourt Brace Jovanovich, 1976.

Jewish Historical Society of Western Canada. *A Selection of Papers Presented in 1969–1970*, vols. I (1970) and II (1972). Winnipeg: Jewish Historical Society of Western Canada.

Jewish Historical Society of Western Canada. *Jewish Life and Times: A Collection of Essays*, vols. III (1983), IV (1985), and V (1988). Winnipeg: Jewish Historical Society of Western Canada.

Jewish Historical Society of Western Canada. *Jewish Life and Times: Personal Recollections: The Jewish Pioneers on the Prairies*, vol. VI. Winnipeg: Jewish Historical Society of Western Canada, 1993.

Jewish Historical Society of Western Canada. *Jewish Life and Times: Women's Voices: Personal Recollections*, vol. VII. Winnipeg: Jewish Historical Society of Western Canada, 1998.

Jones, Faith. "Between Suspicion and Censure: Attitudes towards the Jewish Left in Postwar Vancouver." *Canadian Jewish Studies* 6 (1998): 1–25.

Jones, Richard. *L'idéologie de L'Action catholique 1917–1939*. Québec: Les Presses de l'Université Laval, 1974.

Kallen, Evelyn. *Spanning the Generations: A Study in Jewish Identity*. Toronto: Longman Canada, 1977.

Katz, Yossi, and John C. Lehr. "Jewish and Mormon Agricultural Settlement in Western Canada: A Comparative Analysis." *Canadian Geographer* 35:2 (1991): 128–42.

Kay, Barbara. *Acknowledgments: A Cultural Memoir and Other Essays*. St. Catharines, ON: Freedom Press Canada, 2013.

Kay, Zachariah. *Canada and Palestine: The Politics of Noncommitment*. Jerusalem: Israel Universities Press, 1978.

Kay, Zachariah. "A Note on Canada and the Formation of the Jewish Legion." *Jewish Social Studies* 3:29 (July 1967): 171–77.

Kay, Zachariah. "The Canadian Press and Palestine: A Survey, 1939–48." *International Journal* 18:3 (Summer 1963): 361–73.

Kayfetz, Benjamin. "Canada's New Anti-Hate Law." *Patterns of Prejudice* 4:3 (1970): 5–8.

Kayfetz, Benjamin. "Neo-Nazis in Canada." *Patterns of Prejudice* 13:1 (1979): 29–32.

Kayfetz, Benjamin, and Stephen A. Speisman. *Only Yesterday: Collected Pieces on the Jews of Toronto*. Toronto: Now and Then Books, 2013.

King, Joe. *Fabled City: The Jews of Montreal*. Montreal: Price-Patterson, Ltd., 2009.

King, Joe. *From the Ghetto to the Main: The Story of the Jews of Montreal*. Montreal: Montreal Jewish Publication Society, 2001.

Klein, A.M. *Complete Poems Part 2, Original Poems, 1937-1955*. Edited by Zailig Pollock Toronto: University of Toronto Press, 1990.

Klein, Ruth, ed. *Nazi Germany, Canadian Responses: Confronting Antisemitism in the Shadow of War*. Montreal and Kingston: McGill-Queen's University Press, 2012.

Klein, Ruth, and Frank Diamant, eds. *From Immigration to Integration: The Canadian Jewish Experience: A Millennium Edition*. Toronto: Malcom Lester and B'nai Brith, 2001.

Kurelek, William, and Abraham Arnold. *Jewish Life in Canada*. Edmonton: Hurtig Publishers, 1976.

Kurman, Louis A. "The Hamilton Jewish Community." *Wentworth Bygones* 8 (1969): 8–12.

Labovitz, Gail. "Multiple Loyalties: A Great-Granddaughter's Reflection on the Life of Ida Lewis Siegel." *Canadian Woman Studies* 16:4 (Fall 1996): 95–98.

Landau-Chark, Susan. "The Montreal Rebbetzin: Portraits in Time." *Canadian Jewish Studies* 16–17 (2008–09): 185–206.

Langlais, Jacques, and David Rome. *Jews and French Quebecers: Two Hundred Years of Shared History*. Waterloo, ON: Wilfrid Laurier Press, 1991.

Lapidus, Steven. "The Forgotten Hasidim: Rabbis and Rebbes in Prewar Canada." *Canadian Jewish Studies* 12 (2004): 1–30.

Layton, Irving. *Waiting for the Messiah: A Memoir*. Don Mills, ON: Totem Press 1985.

Lazar, M.M., and Sheva Medjuck. "In the Beginning: A Brief History of the Jews in Atlantic Canada." *Canadian Jewish Historical Society Journal* 5:2 (October 1981): 91–107.

Leonoff, Cyril E. *Pioneers, Pedlars, and Prayer Shawls: The Jewish Communities in British Columbia and the Yukon*. Victoria: Sono Nis Press, 1978.

Leonoff, Cyril E. "Pioneer Jewish Merchants of Vancouver Island and British Columbia." *Canadian Jewish Historical Society Journal* 8:1 (Spring 1984): 12–43.

Leonoff, Cyril E. *The Jewish Farmers of Western Canada*. Vancouver: The Jewish Historical Society of British Columbia and the Western States Jewish History Association, 1984.

Leonoff, Cyril E. *Wapella Farm Settlement: A Pictorial History*. Winnipeg: Historical and Scientific Society of Manitoba and Jewish Historical Society of Western Canada, 1972.

Levendel, Lewis. *A Century of the Canadian Jewish Press: 1880s–1980s*. Ottawa: Borealis Press, 1989.

Levi, Rabbi S. Gershon. *Breaking New Ground: The Struggle for a Jewish Chaplaincy in Canada*. Montreal: Canadian Jewish Congress, 1994.

Levine, Allan. *From Winnipeg to the World: The Canwest Global Story*. Winnipeg: Canwest Global Communications Corp., 2002.

Levine, Allan. *Scattered Among the Peoples: The Jewish Diaspora in Twelve Portraits*. New York: Overlook Press, 2003.

Levine, Allan. *The Devil in Babylon: Fear of Progress and the Birth of Modern Life*. Toronto: McClelland & Stewart, 2005.

Levine, Allan. *Coming of Age: A History of the Jewish People of Manitoba*. Winnipeg: Heartland/Jewish Heritage Centre of Western Canada, 2009.

Levine, Allan. *King: William Lyon Mackenzie King: A Life Guided by the Hand of Destiny*. Vancouver: Douglas & McIntyre, 2011.

Levine, Allan. *Toronto: Biography of a City*. Vancouver: Douglas & McIntyre, 2014.

Levine, Allan. "Slow Road to Tolerance." *Canada's History Magazine*, April–May 2016, 40–7.

Levitt, Cyril, and William Shaffir. *The Riot at Christie Pits*. Toronto: Lester & Orpen Dennys, 1987.

Lewis, David. *The Good Fight: Political Memoirs 1909–1958*. Toronto: Macmillan of Canada, 1981.

Linteau, Paul-André. *The History of Montréal: The Story of a Great North American City*. Montreal: Baraka Books, 2013.

Lipinsky, Jack. *Imposing Their Will: An Organizational History of Jewish Toronto, 1933–1948*. Montreal and Kingston: McGill-Queen's University Press, 2011.

Lipton, Saundra. "She Also Served: Bringing to Light the Contributions of the Canadian Jewish Women Who Served in World War II." *Canadian Jewish Studies* 25 (2017): 92–115.

Lorinc, John, Michael McClelland, Ellen Scheinberg, and Tatum Taylor, eds. *The Ward: The Life and Loss of Toronto's First Immigrant Neighbourhood*. Toronto: Coach House Books, 2015.

Marcus, Jacob Rader, ed. *American Jewry: Documents: Eighteenth Century*. Cincinnati: Hebrew Union College Press, 1959.

Marcus, Jacob Rader, ed. "Jews and the American Revolution: A Bicentennial Documentary." *American Jewish Archives* 27:2 (November, 1975): 103–258. http://americanjewisharchives .org/publications/journal/PDF/1975_27_02_00.pdf.

Margolis, Rebecca. "Culture in Motion: Yiddish in Canadian Jewish Life." *Journal of Religion and Popular Culture* 21:4 (Fall 2009): 1–51.

Margolis, Rebecca. *Jewish Roots, Canadian Soil: Yiddish Culture in Montreal, 1905–1945.* Montreal and Kingston: McGill-Queen's University Press, 2011.

Margolis, Rebecca. "The Yiddish Press in Montreal, 1905–1950." *Canadian Jewish Studies* 16–17 (2008–2009): 3–26.

Margolian, Howard. *Unauthorized Entry: The Truth About Nazi War Criminals in Canada, 1946–1956.* Toronto: University of Toronto Press, 2000.

Marrus, Michael R. *Mr. Sam: The Life and Times of Samuel Bronfman.* Toronto, Viking, 1991.

Matas, David. "The Case of Imre Finta." *University of New Brunswick Law Journal* 43 (1994): 281–97.

Maynard, Fredelle Bruser. *Raisins and Almonds.* Toronto: Penguin Books Canada, 1985.

McCreery, Christopher. *Savoir Faire, Savior Vivre: Rideau Club 1865–2015.* Toronto: Dundurn Press, 2014.

McGrath, Robin. *Salt Fish and Shmattes: A History of Jews in Newfoundland and Labrador from 1770.* St. John's, NL: Creative Book Publishing, 2006.

Mcintosh, Robert. "Sweated Labour: Female Needleworkers in Industrializing Canada." *Labour/Le Travail* 32 (Fall 1993): 105–38.

Medjuck, Sheva, *The Jews of Atlantic Canada.* Saint John, NB: Breakwater Press, 1986.

Medres, Israel. *Between the Wars: Canadian Jews in Transition.* Montreal: Véhicule Press, 2003. Originally published as *Tsvishn tsvey velt milkhomes* in 1964.

Medres, Israel. *Montreal of Yesterday: Jewish Life in Montreal 1900–1920.* Montreal: Véhicule Press, 2000. Originally published as *Montreal fun Nekhtn* in 1947.

Meggs, Geoff, and Rod Mickleburgh. *The Art of the Impossible: Dave Barrett and the NDP in Power 1972–1975.* Vancouver: Harbour Publishing, 2012.

Menkis, Richard. "Historiography, Myth and Group Relations: Jewish and Non-Jewish Québécois on Jews and New France." *Canadian Ethnic Studies* 23:2 (1991): 24–38.

Menkis, Richard. "Both Peripheral and Central: Toward a History of Reform Judaism in Canada." *CCAR Journal: A Reform Jewish Quarterly* 51 (Fall 2004): 43–56.

Menkis, Richard, and Norman Ravvin, eds. *The Canadian Jewish Studies Reader.* Calgary: Red Deer Press, 2004.

Menkis, Richard, and Harold Troper, *More Than Just Games: Canada and the 1936 Olympics.* Toronto: University of Toronto Press, 2015.

Meyer, Marion E. *The Jews of Kingston.* Kingston: The Limestone Press, 1983.

Milner, Elizabeth Hearn. "Bishop's Medical Faculty 1871–1905: Its Jewish Dean, Aaron Hart David, and its Jewish Students." *Canadian Jewish Historical Society Journal* 6:2 (Fall 1982): 73–86.

Morton, Suzanne. *At Odds: Gambling and Canadians, 1919–1969.* Toronto: University of Toronto Press, 2003.

Muirhead, Bruce. *Against the Odds: The Public Life and Times of Louis Rasminsky.* Toronto: University of Toronto Press, 1999.

Nadeau, Jean-François. *The Canadian Führer: The Life of Adrien Arcand.* Toronto: James Lorimer & Company, 2011.

Nadel, Ira Bruce. *Various Positions: A Life of Leonard Cohen.* Toronto: Random House of Canada, 1996.

Nathanson, Deena. "A Social Profile of Peddlers in the Jewish Community of Toronto, 1891–1930." *Canadian Jewish Studies* 1 (1993): 27–40.

Newman, Peter C. *Izzy: The Passionate Life and Turbulent Times of Izzy Asper, Canada's Media Mogul.* Toronto: HarperCollins, 2008.

Newman, Peter C., and Allan Levine. *Miracle at the Forks: The Museum That Dares Make a Difference.* Vancouver: Figure 1 Publishing, 2014.

Obe, Don. "The Dissident Rabbi." *Toronto Life* (August 1982): 29–36.

O'Connor, D'Arcy. *Montreal's Irish Mafia: The True Story of the Infamous West End Gang.* Toronto: John Wiley and Sons Canada, 2011.

Oliver, Michael. *The Passionate Debate: The Social and Political Ideas of Quebec Nationalism 1920–1945.* Montreal: Véhicule Press, 1991.

Olson, Sherry, and Patricia Thornton. *Peopling the North American City: Montreal, 1840–1900.* Montreal and Kingston: McGill-Queen's University Press, 2011.

Oren, Michael B. *Six Days of War: June 1967 and the Making of the Modern Middle East.* New York: Oxford University Press, 2002.

Panofsky, Ruth. *The Force of Vocation: The Literary Career of Adele Wiseman.* Winnipeg: University of Manitoba Press, 2006.

Paris, Erna. *Jews: An Account of Their Experience in Canada.* Toronto: Macmillan of Canada, 1980.

Patrias, Carmela, and Ruth A. Frager. "'This Is Our Country, These Are Our Rights': Minorities and the Origins of Ontario's Human Rights Campaigns." *Canadian Historical Review* 82:1 (March 2001): 1–19.

Perlmann, Joel. "The Local Geographic Origins of Russian-Jewish Immigrants, Circa 1900." Working Paper No. 465. The Levy Economics Institute of Bard College, August 2006.

Phillips, Nathan. *Mayor of all the People.* Toronto: McClelland & Stewart, 1967.

Plaut, Jonathan V. *The Jews of Windsor, 1790–1990: A Historical Chronicle.* Toronto: Dundurn Press, 2007.

Plaut, W. Gunther. *Unfinished Business: An Autobiography.* Toronto: Lester & Orpen Dennys, 1981.

Popham, Elizabeth A. *Abraham Moses Klein: The Letters.* Toronto: University of Toronto Press, 2011.

Porter, John. *The Vertical Mosaic: An Analysis of Social Class and Power in Canada,* 50th Anniversary Edition. Toronto: University of Toronto Press, 2015.

Powell, John. *Encyclopedia of North American Immigration*. New York: Infobase Publishing, 2009.

Pritchard, James. *In Search of Empire: The French in the Americas, 1670–1730*. Cambridge: Cambridge University Press, 2004.

Ralph, Wayne. *Aces, Warriors and Wingmen*. Mississauga, ON: John Wiley and Sons Canada, 2005.

Reiter, Ester. *A Future Without Hate or Need: The Promise of the Jewish Left in Canada*. Toronto: Between the Lines, 2016.

Rhinewine, Abraham. *Looking Back a Century on the Centennial of Jewish Political Equality in Canada*. Toronto: Kraft Press, 1932.

Ribak, Gil. *Gentile New York: The Images of Non-Jews among Jewish Immigrants*. New Brunswick, NJ: Rutgers University Press, 2012.

Richler, Mordecai. "A Reporter at Large: Inside/Outside." *New Yorker* (September 23, 1991).

Richler, Mordecai. *Oh Canada! Oh Quebec!: Requiem for a Divided Country*. Alfred A. Knopf Canada, 1992.

Richler, Mordecai. *The Street*. Toronto: McClelland & Stewart, 1969.

Richler, Mordecai. *This Year in Jerusalem*. Toronto: Alfred A. Knopf Canada, 1994.

Rischin, Moses, ed. *The Jews of North America*. Detroit: Wayne State University Press, 1987.

Robinson, Ira. *A History of Antisemitism in Canada*. Waterloo, O.N.: Wilfrid Laurier University Press, 2014.

Robinson, Ira., ed. *Canada's Jews: In Time, Space, and Spirit*. Boston: Academic Studies Press, 2013.

Robinson, Ira. "The Canadian Years of Yehuda Kaufman (Even Shmuel): Educator, Journalist, and Intellectual." *Canadian Jewish Studies* 15 (2007): 129–42.

Robinson, Ira. "The Kosher Meat War and the Jewish Community Council of Montreal, 1922–1925." *Canadian Ethnic Studies* 22:2 (1990): 41–53.

Robinson, Ira. "Ninety-Nine Meetings: The Jewish Public Library of Montreal in its First Century." *Canadian Jewish Studies* 22 (2014): 16–31.

Robinson, Ira. "Reflections on Antisemitism in French Canada." *Canadian Jewish Studies* 23 (2015): 90–122.

Robinson, Ira, and Mervin Butovsky, eds. *Renewing Our Days: Montreal Jews in the Twentieth Century*. Montreal: Véhicule Press, 1995.

Rogger, Hans. *Jewish Policies and Right-Wing Politics in Imperial Russia*. Berkeley: University of California Press, 1986.

Rome, David. *Clouds in the Thirties: On Antisemitism in Canada, 1929–1939*, sections 1–2. Montreal: Canadian Jewish Archives, 1977.

Rome, David. "Early British Columbia Jewry: A Reconstructed 'Census.'" *Canadian Ethnic Studies* 3:1 (June, 1971): 57–60.

Rome, David. *The Early Jewish Presence in Canada*. Montreal: Jewish Public Library, 1971.

Rome, David. *The First Two Years: A Record of the Jewish Pioneers on Canada's Pacific Coast, 1858–1860.* Montreal: H.M. Caiserman, 1942.

Rome, David. "Notes on Some of the First Jews West of Ontario." *Canadian Jewish Historical Society Journal* 2:1 (Spring 1978): 70–75.

Rome, David. *Samuel Becancour Hart and 1832.* Montreal: National Archives, Canadian Jewish Congress, 1982.

Rosenberg, Danny. "Athletics in the Ward and Beyond: Neighborhoods, Jews, and Sport in Toronto, 1900-1939." In *Sporting Dystopias: The Making and Meaning of Urban Sport Cultures,* edited by Ralph C. Wilcox, David L. Andrews, Robert Pitter, and Richard L. Irwin. Albany: State University of New York Press, 2003: 137–51.

Rosenberg, Louis. *Canada's Jews: A Social and Economic Study of Jews in Canada.* Montreal: Bureau of Social and Economic Research, Canadian Jewish Congress, 1939.

Rosenberg, Louis. *Chronology of Canadian Jewish History.* Montreal: Canadian Jewish Congress, 1959.

Rosenberg, Louis. "Jewish Agriculture in Canada." *YIVO Annual of Jewish Social Sciences* 5 (1950): 205–215.

Rosenberg, Louis. *The Jewish Community of Winnipeg.* Montreal: Canadian Jewish Congress, 1946.

Rosenberg, Louis. *The Jewish Population of Canada.* Philadelphia: American Jewish Committee and Jewish Publication Society, 1947.

Rosenberg, Louis. *A Study of the Growth and Changes in the Distribution of the Jewish Population of Winnipeg, 1961.* Montreal: Canadian Jewish Congress, 1961.

Rosenberg, Stuart E. *The Jewish Community in Canada: A History,* vol. 1. Toronto: McClelland & Stewart, 1970.

Rosenberg, Stuart E. *The Real Jewish World: A Rabbi's Second Thoughts.* Toronto: Clarke Irwin, 1984.

Rubenstein, Eli. *Witness: Passing the Torch of Holocaust Memory to New Generations.* Toronto: Second Story Press, 2015.

Sable, Martin. "George Drew and the Rabbis: Religious Education in Ontario's Public Schools." *Canadian Jewish Studies* 6 (1998): 26–54.

Sachar, Howard M. *A History of the Jews in America.* New York: Alfred A. Knopf, 1992.

Sack, B.G. *Canadian Jews: Early in this Century.* Montreal: Canadian Jewish Congress Archives, 1975.

Sack, B.G. *History of the Jews in Canada.* Montreal: Harvest House, 1965.

Samuel, Sigmund. *In Return: The Autobiography of Sigmund Samuel.* Toronto: University of Toronto Press, 1963.

Sanders, Ronald. *Shores of Refuge: A Hundred Years of Jewish Emigration.* New York: Henry Holt and Company, 1988.

Sax, David. *Save the Deli: In Search of Perfect Pastrami, Crusty Rye, and the Heart of Jewish Delicatessen.* Toronto: McClelland & Stewart, 2009.

Schlappner, Carrie. "Unapologetically Jewish: Unapologetically Canadian." *B.C. Historical News* 32.1 (Winter 1998/1999): 18–23.

Schneer, Jonathan. *The Balfour Declaration: The Origins of the Arab-Israeli Conflict.* Toronto: Doubleday Canada, 2010.

Schneider, Stephen. *Iced: The Story of Organized Crime in Canada.* Toronto: John Wiley & Sons Canada, 2009.

Segal, Agnes Romer. "Dancing into History: A Glimpse into the Jewish Community of Calgary, 1912–13." *Canadian Jewish Studies* 15 (2015): 123–30.

Seidel, Judith. "The Development and Social Adjustment of the Jewish Community in Montreal." Master's thesis, McGill University, 1939.

Shahar, Charles. *2011 National Household Survey Analysis: The Jewish Population of Canada.* Toronto: Jewish Federations of Canada-UIA, 2014.

Shahar, Charles. *2001 Census Analysis Series: The Jewish Community of Canada.* Toronto: Jewish Federations of Canada-UIA, 2004.

Shapiro, Shmuel Mayer. *The Rise of the Toronto Jewish Community.* Toronto: Now and Then Books, 2010.

Sharp, Rosalie Wise. *Rifke: An Improbable Life.* Toronto: ECW Press, 2007.

Sharp, Rosalie, Irving Abella, and Edwin Goodman, eds. *Growing up Jewish: Canadians Tell Their Own Stories.* Toronto: McClelland & Stewart, 1997.

Shuchat, Wilfred. *The Gate of Heaven: The Story of Congregation Shaar Hashomayim of Montreal 1846–1996.* Montreal and Kingston: McGill-Queen's University Press, 2000.

Slan, Jon. "The Holy War between Beth Tzedec and Rabbi Rosenberg." *Toronto Life* (April 1976): 36–45.

Slonim, Reuben. *Grand to Be an Orphan.* Toronto: Clarke, Irwin & Company, 1983.

Smith, Cameron. *Unfinished Journey: The Lewis Family.* Toronto: Summerhill Press, 1989.

Smith, Doug. *Joe Zuken: Citizen and Socialist.* Toronto: James Lorimer & Company, 1990.

Sniderman, Paul M., David A. Northrup, Joseph F. Fletcher, Peter H. Russell, and Philip E. Tetlock. "Psychological and Cultural Foundations of Prejudice: The Case of Anti-Semitism in Quebec." *The Canadian Review of Sociology and Anthropology* 30:2 (May 1993): 242–70.

Speisman, Stephen A. *The Jews of Toronto: A History to 1937.* Toronto: McClelland & Stewart, 1979.

Spector, Norman. *Chronicle of a War Foretold: How Mideast Peace Became America's Fight.* Vancouver: Douglas & McIntyre, 2003.

Stingel, Janine. *Social Discredit: Anti-Semitism, Social Credit, and the Jewish Response.* Montreal and Kingston: McGill-Queen's University Press, 2000.

Stone, Daniel, ed. *Jewish Radicalism in Winnipeg, 1905–1960.* Vol. VIII of *Jewish Life and Times.* Winnipeg: Jewish Heritage Centre of Western Canada, 2002.

Sturman, Gladys, ed. *Pioneer Jews of British Columbia*. Vancouver: Jewish Historical Society of British Columbia, 2005.

Taras, David, and David H. Goldberg, eds. *The Domestic Battleground: Canada and the Arab-Israeli Conflict*. Montreal and Kingston: McGill-Queen's University Press, 1989.

Trachtenberg, Henry. "Ethnic Politics on the Urban Frontier: 'Fighting Joe' Martin and the Jews of Winnipeg, 1893–96." *Manitoba History* 35 (Spring/Summer 1998): 2–13.

Trachtenberg, Henry. "Opportunism, Humanitarianism, and Revulsion: 'The Old Clo' Move Comes to Manitoba, 1882–83." *Canadian Ethnic Studies* 22: 2 (1990): 1–15.

Trachtenberg, Henry. "Peddling, Politics, and Winnipeg Jews, 1891–1895: The Political Acculturation of an Urban Immigrant Community." *Social History* 29:57 (May 1996): 161–86.

Trachtenberg, Henry. "The Winnipeg Jewish Community and Politics: The Inter-War Years, 1919–1939." *Manitoba Historical Society Transactions* 3:35 (1978–79): 115–53.

The Continuing History of the Spanish & Portuguese Congregation of Montreal 1768–1993: 25 Years of Renaissance. Montreal: Robert Davies Publishing, 1996.

Troper, Harold. *The Defining Decade: Identity, Politics, and the Canadian Jewish Community in the 1960s*. Toronto: University of Toronto Press, 2010.

Troper, Harold. *The Rescuer: The Amazing True Story of How One Woman Helped Save the Jews of Syria*. Toronto: LMB Editions, 2007. Originally published in 1999 as *The Ransomed of God: The Remarkable Story of One Woman's Role in the Rescue of Syrian Jews*.

Troper, Harold, and Morton Weinfeld. *Old Wounds: Jews, Ukrainians and the Hunt for Nazi War Criminals in Canada*. Toronto: Penguin, 1989.

Troper, Harold, and Morton Weinfeld, eds. *Ethnicity, Politics, and Public Policy: Case Studies in Canadian Diversity*. Toronto: University of Toronto Press, 2000.

Tulchinsky, Gerald. *Branching Out: The Transformation of the Canadian Jewish Community*. Toronto: Stoddart, 1998.

Tulchinsky, Gerald. *Canada's Jews: A People's Journey*. Toronto: University of Toronto Press, 2008.

Tulchinsky, Gerald. *Joe Salsberg: A Life of Commitment*. Toronto: University of Toronto Press, 2013.

Tulchinsky, Gerald. *Taking Root: The Origins of the Canadian Jewish Community*. Toronto: Stoddart, 1992.

Usher, Peter J. "Jews in the Royal Canadian Air Force, 1940–1945." *Canadian Jewish Studies* 20 (2012): 93–114.

Usher, Peter J. "Removing the Stain: A Jewish Volunteer's Perspective in World War Two." *Canadian Jewish Studies* 23 (2015): 37–67.

Usiskin, Michael. *Uncle Mike's Edenbridge: Memoirs of a Jewish Pioneer Farmer*. Winnipeg: Peguis Publishers, 1983.

Usiskin, Roz Wolodarsky, ed. *A Lifetime of Letters: The Wolodarsky Family*. Winnipeg: n.p., 1995.

Valverde, Marianne. *The Age of Light, Soap, and Water: Moral Reform in English Canada, 1885–1925*. Toronto: McClelland & Stewart, 1991.

Vanger, Max. "Memoirs of a Russian Immigrant." *American Jewish Historical Quarterly* 63:1 (September 1973): 57–88.

Vaugeois, Denis. *The Extraordinary Story of the Hart Family, 1760-1860*. Montreal: Baraka Books, 2012.

Vipond, Robert. *Making a Global City: How One Toronto School Embraced Diversity*. Toronto: University of Toronto Press, 2017.

Weimann, Gabriel, and Conrad Winn. *Hate on Trial: The Zundel Affair, the Media, and Public Opinion in Canada*. Oakville, ON: Mosaic Press, 1986.

Weimann, Gabriel, and Conrad Winn. "The Misperception of Public Opinion: The Canadian Nazi Trials and Their Implications." *PS: Political Science & Politics* 19:3 (July 1986): 641–45.

Weinfeld, Morton. "The Jews of Quebec: Perceived Antisemitism, Segregation, and Emigration." *Jewish Journal of Sociology* 22 (1980): 5–20.

Weinfeld, Morton. *Like Everyone Else . . . But Different: The Paradoxical Success of Canadian Jews*. Toronto: McClelland & Stewart, 2001.

Weinfeld, Morton, W. Shaffir, and I. Cotler, editors. *The Canadian Jewish Mosaic*. Toronto: John Wiley & Sons, 1981.

Weintraub, William. *City Unique: Montreal Days and Nights in the 1940s and '50s*. Toronto: McClelland & Stewart, 1996.

Westwood Creative Artists and the Dominion Institute. *Passages: Welcome Home to Canada*. Toronto: Doubleday Canada, 2002.

Wiesenthal, Christine B. "Insiders and Outsiders: Two Waves of Jewish Settlement in British Columbia, 1958–1914." Master's thesis, University of British Columbia, 1987.

Wisse, Ruth R., and Irwin Cotler. "Quebec Jews Caught in the Middle." *Commentary* 64:3 (September 1977): 55–59.

Wolofsky, Hirsch. *Journey of My Life*. Montreal: Eagle Publishing Company, 1945.

Woodsworth, J.S. *Strangers Within Our Gates*. 1909; Toronto: University of Toronto Press, 1972.

Woodsworth, J.S. *My Neighbour*. 1911; Toronto: University of Toronto Press, 1972.

Wyman, Kenneth. "Abraham de Sola and His Intellectual World." Master's thesis, University of Toronto, 2002.

Yarosky, Michael. "The Jewish Community of Quebec Province: Bridging the Past and the Present." *Journal of Jewish Communal Service* 56:1 (September 1979): 19–27.

Zolf, Larry. *Zolf*. Toronto: Exile Editions, 1999.

Interviews conducted by the author 2016–17, in person and via telephone and email:

Interviews conducted by the author 2008–13:

Irving Abella

Frank Bialystok

Ryla Braemer

Sandra Brown

Donald Carr

Harvey Chisick

Gene Colman

Natalie Davis

Wendy Eisen

Ronit Eizenman

Bernie Farber

Shimon Fogel

Yacov Fruchter

Rabbi Baruch Frydman-
 Kohl

Trudy Harowtiz

Jon Goldberg

Anne Golden

Yoni Goldstein

Elaine Goldstine

Fran Grundman

Dorothy Heppner

Barbara Kay

Teme Kernerman

Linda Kislowicz

Rabbi Daniel Korobkin

Max Kretskiy

Stephen Lewis

Jocy Lowy

Richard Lowy

Peter Maidstone

Kenneth Prehogan

Dorothy Reitman

Eli Rubenstein

Olga Shepshelevich

Rabbi Yael Splansky

Claire Sumerlus

Harold Troper

Ralph Troper

Ken Wolch

Gail Asper

Allan Chapnick

Kinneret Chiel

Yude Henteleff

Lou Kliman

Moe Levy

Jack London

Abby Morris

William Neville

Meyer Rabkin

Philip Weiss

Numbers refer to plates in the photo insert.

Alex Dworkin/Canadian Jewish Archives: 6, 25, 37

Bibliothèque et Archives nationales du Québec: 1

The Canadian Press/Ryan Remiorz: 29

City of Toronto Archives: 23, 32

Courtesy of Justive Rosalie Abella: 33

Courtesy of Ryla Braemer: 39

Courtesy of Mel Kliman: 14

Courtesy of Leo Lowy and family: 34

Courtesy of Dr. Michael Rasminsky: 32

Federation Canadian Jewish Archives, Montreal: 38

Jewish Heritage Centre of Western Canada: 2, 3, 4, 10, 11, 12, 13

The Jewish Museum and Archives of British Columbia: 7. Image JMABC L.13156.

Jewish Public Library Archives of Montreal: 8, 27

Library and Archives Canada: 5, 15, 16, 17, 18, 19, 28, 30

McCord Museum, Montreal: 9

Ontario Jewish Archives: 20. "Gentiles only" sign at Forest Hill Lodge at Burleigh Falls, 28 January 1940. Ontario Jewish Archives, Blankenstein Family Heritage Centre, fonds 17, series 5-3, file 64, item 1; 21. Ida Siegel with Edmund Scheuer at the Canadian Jewish Farm School, Georgetown, [ca. 1927]. Ontario Jewish Archives, Blankenstein Family Heritage Centre, fonds 15, file 37, item 24; 22. Sammy Luftspring, Toronto, 1930. Ontario Jewish Archives, Blankenstein Family Heritage Centre, item 2516; 31. 1943 Provincial Election Campaign, 1943. Ontario Jewish Archives, Blankenstein Family Heritage Centre, fonds 92, series 3, file 12, item 1; 36. Hadassah-WIZO Toronto Chapter meeting [ca. 1950s]. Ontario Jewish Archives, fonds 71, item 1.

Winnipeg Tribune Photo Collection, University of Manitoba Archives & Special Collections: 26

A

Abbey, Monroe, 302
Abbott, Douglas, 247
Abbott, John C., 90
Abella, Irving, 36, 144, 176,
227, 318, 353
Aberhart, William, 172–73
Abraham, Chapman, 24, 25, 39
Abramovitch, Sholem, 112
Abramowitz, Rabbi Herman,
107
Abramson, Mark, 199
Adath Israel congregation, 209
Adath Jeshurun congregation,
54, 122, 132, 133, 263, 358
Adelman, Ben, 237
Adler. See Keneder Adler
Adler, Jacob, 114
Agence Ometz, 351
Ages, Arnold, 290, 298,
320–21
Agudath Achim synagogue,
263, 358
Agudath Israel synagogue, 358
Ahavith Achim synagogue,
109, 110
Aitken, J.W. Max, 199
Aitken, Max, Lord
Beaverbrook, 199
Alberta. *See also* Calgary;
Edmonton
antisemitism in, 172–73
Albert Edward, Prince of
Wales, 48
Aleichem, Sholem, 6, 68, 112,
254
Alexander, Bernard, 245
Alexander II, Czar, 67

Alexander III, Czar, 67
All-Canadian Congress of
Labour, 183
Alliance Israélite Universelle,
69
Allied Jewish Community
Services (AJCS), 324
Almi, A., 116
Amalgamated Clothing
Workers of America, 183
American Hebrew, 69
American Jewish Congress,
136, 292
American Jewish Joint
Distribution
Committee, 211
American Revolutionary War,
21, 30, 39
Am Olam, 71
Anglo-Jewish Association of
Montreal, 69
Anne and Max Tannenbaum
Community Hebrew
Academy of Toronto,
346
Anne of Green Gables
(Montgomery), 85
Annex Shul, 362
Anshay Roosia congregation,
54
Anti-Defamation League of
B'nai B'rith, 1, 202–3, 273
Anti-Fascist League of
Winnipeg, 169
antisemitism. *See also* attacks/
violence against Jews
advice about dealing with,
141

and anti-Zionism, 319–20
attacks against
Nurenberger, 298
attempts to counter, 202–3
Berton research on, 217–18
in Canada, 7–8, 74, 106–7,
140–42, 148, 159–61,
214–16, 249, 356
in Canadian military, 198,
202, 204–5
changing attitudes in
Canada, 216, 246–47,
250–51
and clannish nature, 256
coining of term, 29
and criticism of Israel, 287
early case of, 29–32
in early Winnipeg, 72–73
in Europe, 7, 130, 141
fear of as barrier to enlisting, 204
in France, 283
in Germany, 173
during Great Depression,
141
in immigration depart-
ment, 318
incidents of, 312–13
Jews' attitude to, 159
Keegstra case, 313–14
laws against, 168–69, 215
in medicine, 162–66
in newspapers, 167–68
in property purchases,
218–20
in Quebec, 104, 143–44,
166–68, 312–13
of Quebec nationalists, 307

responding to, 151, 173–75,
276–79, 338
in small towns, 152
of Smith, 74–75
in social and sports clubs,
244–45
in Soviet Union, 292–93
tempering of, 242
in Toronto, 101–2, 243–44
and unions, 183
in universities, 160
in Winnipeg, 75–76
Zündel case, 313
Appel, Moe, 239
*The Apprenticeship of Duddy
Kravitz* (Richler), 194,
254
Arabs
refusal to accept Israel's
existence, 236
rejection of partition of
Palestine, 230
and Six-Day War, 259
Arbeiter Ring, 181
Arbiter Ring School, 113
Arcand, Adrien, 160, 167, 168,
172, 276
Aref, Abdel-Rahman, 280
Arnold, Abraham, 94–95,
271
Arnold, Benedict, 21
Arnold, Janice, 308
Aron, Rabbi Milton, 261
Aronson, Michael, 68
Art Gallery of Ontario, 231
Ascher, Albert, 50
Ascher, Gottschalk, 49–50
Ashenmil, Harold, 273
Ashkenazi Jews, 18, 34, 38,
258, 259
Asper, David, 336
Asper, Gail, 327, 335–37

Asper, Israel (Izzy), 275, 315,
322, 335, 336, 337, 340
Asper, Leonard, 336
Asper, Ruth, 335, 336
Asper Foundation, 335, 336
Asper Jewish Community
Campus, 315, 325, 354
Asselin, Olivar, 104, 162, 163
assimilation
and being outsider, 12
controlled, 11
of Jews in Montreal, 78–79
of Jews in Toronto, 76–77,
78
in the New World, 19
of Sephardi Jews in
England (1650s), 18
Atkinson, Joseph, 231
Atlantic Jewish Council, 361
attacks/violence against Jews.
See also antisemitism
British response to, 69–70
in Crystal Beach, 214
in Manitoba, 72–73
in Montreal, 106, 154
in Quebec, 214
in Russia, 67–68
in Toronto, 154–55
in Ukraine, 67
in Winnipeg, 128
Auschwitz-Birkenau, 178,
208, 211, 220–21, 316, 317
"Autobiographical" (Klein), 4,
12, 97–98
Avukah Zionist Society, 165,
166
Aylmer, Lord, 36

B
Baker, Eddie "Kid," 191, 192
Balfour, Arthur, 134
Balfour Declaration, 134

Balmy Beach Swastika Club,
170
Bank, Barbara, 342
Bank of Montreal, 303
Baron Byng High School,
100, 148, 149, 197
Baron de Hirsch Hebrew
Benevolent Society syn-
agogue, 58
Baron de Hirsch Institute, 85,
105–6
Barrett, Dave, 275–76
Barrett, L.R., 118
Barsky, Kieva, 73
Basman, Marcia Usiskin, 94
Bassett, John, 298
Batshaw, Harry, 231, 246, 247,
273
Battle for Vimy Ridge, 126
Battle of Quebec (1775), 21
Battle of the Plains of
Abraham, 20
Baumholz, Joe, 239, 304
Baylin, Michael, 245
Beattie, Robert, 249
Beattie, William John, 277,
278–79
Bédard, Pierre-Stanislas, 30,
32, 34
Begbie, Justice Matthew, 63
Begin, Menachem, 285, 290,
298
Bellan, Bernie, 355
Bellan, Matt, 355
Bellow, Abraham, 102–3
Bellow, Saul, 102–3
Belzberg, Brent, 340, 342
Ben Adam (Mitchell),
Shlomo, 166
Ben-Dat, Mordechai, 348
Benderly, Samson, 111
Benei Yehuda, 263

ben Eliezer, Rabbi Yisrael, 154
Ben-Gurion, David, 131, 232, 293, 298
Benjamin, Abraham, 65, 66
Benjamin, Alfred, 78
Benjamin, George, 61
Bennett, Archie, 212
Bennett, R.B., 157
Bennett, W.A.C., 276
Bercovitch, Louis, 192–93
Bercovitch, Peter, 119, 122, 168
Bercuson, David, 204
Berk, Fred, 271
Berner, Rabbi Marcus, 91
Bernstein, Yosef, 74
Berton, Pierre, 216, 217–18, 219
Berwald, Mike, 278
Bessner, Ellin, 204
Betcherman, Lita-Rose, 177
Beth Avraham Yoseph congregation, 353
Beth David congregation, 52
Beth Hamidrash Hagadol Chevra Tehillim congregation, 52–53
Beth Israel Anshei Minsk congregation, 53
Beth Israel congregation (Calgary), 357
Beth Israel congregation (Halifax), 355
Beth Israel congregation (Winnipeg), 55, 357
Beth Israel synagogue (Halifax), 58
Beth Israel synagogue (Vancouver), 263, 281
Beth Jacob synagogue, 101, 110
Beth Ora synagogue, 254, 256, 304
Beth Sholom congregation, 304

Beth Tzedec synagogue, 12, 52, 53, 285, 357, 359, 362
Beth Yehuda congregation, 52
Bevis Marks synagogue, 19, 39, 41
Bialystok, Frank, 260, 343, 344
Bilsky, Moses, 132
Bissonnette, Lise, 310
Black, Conrad, 322
Black, Joe, 172
Blair, Frederick, 176, 178, 208, 209
Blankstein, Marjorie, 325
Blumenberg, Sam, 128
B'nai Brith
    advocacy for Jews, 338
    antisemitism audit, 312–13, 356
    and Barrett, 276
    and Canada-Israel Committee, 288
    and CJC, 311
    and La Presse article, 308
    lobbying campaign for human rights, 243
    as recipient of Trudeau speech, 273
    and Soviet Jews, 293
    summer camps, 235
    survey on attitudes to Jews, 312
    and University of Manitoba quota system, 166
B'nai Jacog congregation, 52
Boisclair, André, 333
Boisvert, Yves, 334
Bond, William Bennett, 69
Booth, John Wilkes, 313
Borah, William E., 161
Borden, Laura, 139

Borden, Sir Robert, 139
Borovoy, Alan, 279
Boulton, Harriet (Dixon), 74–75
Boulton, William Henry, 74
Bourassa, Henri, 167
Bourassa, Robert, 275, 307, 309
Bowen, Justice Edward, 32–33
Boycotts, Divestment and Sanctions (BDS), 144, 286, 320, 356
Braemer, Ryla, 362, 363–64
Braham, Alfred, 35
Brainin, Reuben, 116, 127, 136
Brandeau, Esther, 16–17
Brandon. See also Manitoba
    Jewish population in, 101
Brecher, Pincus "Pinky," 191, 192
Bregman, Louis, 180
Bregman, Max, 180
Brezhnev, Leonid, 294
Brickner, Rabbi Barnett, 132
Brickner, Rebecca, 132
British Columbia. See also Vancouver
    Jewish politicians in, 275–76
Brock Corydon, 349
Bronfman, Charles, 147, 239, 296, 302–3
Bronfman, Edgar, 147, 302
Bronfman, Ekiel, 55, 89, 90
Bronfman, Harry, 90, 145
Bronfman, Phyllis, 303
Bronfman, Saidye, 147, 241
Bronfman, Samuel, 11, 55, 90, 145, 147–48, 174, 203, 208, 232, 236, 239–41, 270, 302, 325, 338, 339
Bronstone, Adam, 337
Brotman, Edel, 90

Brown, Michael, 46, 283
Brown, Sandra, 326–27
Brown (Braun), Philip, 64, 65
Bruce, W.L., 72
Buchalter, Louis "Lepke," 190
Buck, Tim, 185
Bulka, Rabbi Reuven, 263
Burman, Tony, 322
Burns, Charlie, 145
business ventures and occu-
    pations
    bootlegging, 102–3, 144–45
    cultural enterprises, 115–16
    difficulty of entering pro-
        fessions, 141–42
    drug trade, 190, 191
    in education, 160–61, 162,
        257
    farming, 93–94, 95
    in finance, 247–49
    fur business, 108
    gambling operations,
        190–94
    garment industry, 98, 99,
        101, 117–19, 120–23
    during Great Depression,
        180
    and income levels, 350
    law, 108
    in law, 119, 160–62, 247,
        257, 272–74
    liquor trade, 145–46, 147
    medical, 162–65, 257
    peddling, 101
    in politics (See political
        activity)
    publishing, 115
    retail, 152
    shopkeeping, 108
    undertaken by Jews, 352
    wholesale, 152
    by women, 323, 327–28

Buttar, William, 20
By Chance Alone (Eisen), 316
Byng, Baron, 148
Bystander, 75

C
Caiserman, Hananiah Meir,
    119, 137, 173, 174, 203,
    210, 211
Calgary
    Jewish population in, 262
    merging of synagogues, 357
    tuition at Jewish schools,
        346
Camp BB Riback, 235
Camp B'nai Brith, 235
Camp Hagshama, 233
Camp Kadimah, 233
Camp Kvutza, 233–34
Camp Massad, 235
Camp Northland-B'nai Brith,
    235
Camp Shalom, 233
Canada
    acceptance of Jews, 361
    antisemitism in, 7–8, 159–
        61, 221–22, 356
    attitude to Israel, 340
    attitude to refugees, 74
    average income (1961), 257
    changes in Jewish commu-
        nities, 265
    desired immigrants, 83
    early political system, 30
    first Jewish premier in, 276
    first Jews in, 15–18, 16–17
    hate crimes in, 356–57
    Jewish communities in
        compared to U.S.,
        353–54
    Jewish life in pre-Confed-
        eration, 37

Jewish population in, 2–3,
    4, 5, 34, 100, 101, 140,
    151, 256–57, 261–62, 283,
    354
Jews in compared to U.S.,
    10–11
Jews' role in centennial cel-
    ebrations, 270–71
living conditions for immi-
    grants, 102
makeup of, 101
Middle East policy, 342
modern challenges facing
    Jews in, 357
northwest as destination
    for refugees, 71
postwar need for workers,
    225
rates of intermarriages,
    360–61
recognition of Jewish con-
    tributions, 253
recognizes Israel, 236
stand on Middle East, 285,
    289
support for multicultural-
    ism, 290
unemployment in
    Depression, 180
wariness about Jews, 5
Zionist support in, 130–32
Canada East. See Quebec
Canada-Israel Committee
    (CIC), 288, 290, 321–22,
    341–42, 343
Canada West. See Ontario
Canadian Broadcasting
    Corporation, 321–22
Canadian Civil Liberties
    Association, 279
Canadian Committee for
    Soviet Jewry, 293

INDEX · 465

Canadian Council for Israel and Jewish Advocacy (CIJA 1.0), 340–42, 341–43
Canadian Family of Man award, 1–2
Canadian Federation of Jewish Students, 342
Canadian Hadassah. See Hadassah
Canadian Jewish Alliance, 136
Canadian Jewish Chronicle, 100, 115, 137, 138, 141, 143, 181, 209, 212, 227, 229, 279, 296, 297
Canadian Jewish Chronicle Review, 297, 298
Canadian Jewish Congress (CJC)
　abolishing, 7, 343–44
　on anti-Jew violence, 214
　and antisemitism, 173, 174, 176, 202
　antisemitism research of, 218
　associated with UJPO, 210–11
　becomes dormant, 138
　and bilingualism and biculturalism, 270
　and Caiserman, 119, 173, 174
　and Canada-Israel Committee, 288
　candidates for, 136–37
　celebrates anniversary of Hart's arrival, 253
　changes in, 339–42
　choice of name, 11
　control of, 339
　creation of, 11, 136
　and election of Parti Québécois, 302, 303
　Expo 67 pavilion, 270

female presidents, 325–26
first plenary session, 137
funding of, 342, 343
goals of, 136
lobbying efforts, 209, 210, 232, 293
money raising efforts for war survivors, 211–12
and postwar orphans, 222
projects of, 338
and property rights, 219–20
questioning of role, 339–40
reaction to war news from Europe, 208–9
and Regina General Hospital, 164
reluctance to speak out, 166
response to antisemitism, 276–79
Richler on, 311
and synagogue construction conflict, 308
and war criminals, 317–19
Canadian Jewish News, 273, 276, 286, 298, 302, 308, 324, 343, 355–56
Canadian Jewish Review, 141, 155, 184, 297
Canadian Jewish Times, 115
Canadian Labour Congress, 274
Canadian Museum for Human Rights, 315, 335, 336
Canadian Nazi Party, 277
Canadian Olympic Committee, 174
Canadian Overseas Garment Commission (COGC), 226

Canadian Palestine Committee (CPC), 231–32
Canadians for Justice in the Middle East, 290
Canadian Zionist Federation, 288, 293, 338
Canadian Zionist Society, 46
Canwest Global Communications, 322, 335
Capone, Al, 145, 146
Carleton, Guy, 24
Carr, Donald, 244
Casgrain, Pierre-François, 177
Casper, Samuel, 35
Castlereagh, Lord, 33
Catherine the Great, 68
Cecil, Robert, 134
cemeteries
　burials of non-Jewish individuals, 40
　in early settlements, 8, 20
　funds for, 40
　right to hold title, 35
Centre for Israel and Jewish Affairs (CIJA 2.0), 6, 343–45
Chai Dancers, 270, 271
Chai Folk Ensemble, 289
Chancellor Rose and Ray Wolfe Chair in Holocaust Studies, 324
Chapnik, Allan, 237–38
Charest, Jean, 313, 333
Chatelaine, 330
Cherniack, Joseph Alter, 164
Cherniak, Mindel, 164–65
Cherniak, Saul, 275
Chevra Kadisha congregation, 52
Chiel, Rabbi Arthur, 151
Chisick, Harvey, 283

Chouinard, Craig, 109–10
Chrétien, Jean, 340
Christie, Doug, 313
Christmas Carol Controversy, 245–46
Chronicle Review, 298
Chud, Ben, 264
Church, Tommy, 157, 158
circumcision
    of A. Hart's sons, 40–41
    in early settlements, 20, 26
Citizens' Committee Jewish Relief Fund, 69
civil rights
    in Britain, 36
    fight for in Quebec, 35–36
    of Jews in British North America, 18–19, 20
    of Jews in England, 18
Coblentz, Aachel, 64
Coblentz, Adolphe, 64, 65
Coblentz, Edmond, 64
Coblentz, Gabriella, 65
Coblentz, Sarah, 64, 65
Coblentz, William, 64
Code Noir, 16
Coderre, Denis, 333
Cohen, Andrea, 296
Cohen, Andrew, 344
Cohen, Ben, 233
Cohen, David, 296
Cohen, Jacob (butcher), 154
Cohen, Jacob (first Jewish magistrate), 121
Cohen, Jacob Raphael, 40–41
Cohen, Joseph Raphael, 26
Cohen, Leonard, 98, 296
Cohen, Lyon, 78, 118, 119, 122, 137, 138, 296
Cohen, Maurice, 259
Cohen, Myer Tutzer, 127
Cohen, Phyllis, 200

Cohen, Rabbi Zui Hirsch, 154
Cohon, George, 288
Colman, Gene, 289
Combined Jewish Appeal, 104
Communauté Sépharade Unifiée du Québec, 259
Communist Party, 182, 184, 185, 189, 210, 211
Community Anti-Nazi Committee, 279
community institutions
    challenges of creating in small towns, 151–52
    conflict about, 154–55
    in urban centres, 153–55
concentration camps, 206, 207, 208, 211. *See also* Auschwitz-Birkenau
Concordia University, 319, 339
Conference Board of Canada, 329–30
Congregation Adath Israel, 53
Congregation Beth Shalom, 358
Congregation Emanu-El, 59
Congregation Machzikei Hadas, 263
Congregation Mikveh Israel, 43
Congregation Beth Shalom, 263
Constitutional Act (1791), 27, 30, 32, 33
Coodin, Freda, 188–89
Co-operative Commonwealth Federation, 215, 274
Cornwall, Duke and Duchess of, 47
Cornwallis, Edward, 19–20
Cotler, Irwin, 292, 306

Coyne, James, 248, 249
Crackpot (Wiseman), 255
Craig, James, 30, 32, 33
Cramahé, Hector, 23
Crerar, Thomas, 178
Croll, David, 147, 158–59, 236, 239
Crombie, David, 329
cultural undertakings
    dance, 270–71, 289
    of Jews in Canada, 352
    literature, 254–56
Cumberland, Frederick Barlow, 104
Cummings, Maxwell, 314
Cummings, Steven, 314, 340, 342
Currie, Arthur, 126, 142

D
Danson, Barney, 271
David, David, 40
David, Lazarus, 40
Davidson, W.C., 161
Davies, Raymond, 207
Davis, Harry (Chaskel Lazarovitch), 190–91, 192–93
Davis, Henriettte, 139
Davis, Sir Mortimer, 127, 139
Dawson, William, 44
Decter, Moshe, 292
de Hirsch, Baron Maurice, 85, 89, 91
Delisle, Esther, 167, 309
Dempson, Peter, 249
Dershowitz, Alan, 357, 360
Der Yiddisher Zhurnal, 297, 298
Der Zeitgeist, 69
Desbarats, Peter, 305
Deschênes, Justice Jules, 317

Deschênes inquiry, 318
De Sola, Aaron, 41
De Sola, Abraham, 41–46
De Sola, Clarence, 43, 47, 131, 133–35
De Sola, David, 41
De Sola, David Aaron, 41
De Sola, Katie, 51
De Sola, Meldola, 43, 46–47, 50
Diamond, Etan, 4
Diefenbaker, John, 249, 285
dietary customs. *See also* kosher food
    ritual slaughterhouse in early settlements, 8
    two kitchens, 26
Dillege, Lee, 146
discrimination
    benefits of elimination, 271
    Christmas Carol Controversy, 245–46
    in education, 99
    laws against, 242
    in social and sports clubs, 244–45
Dobner, Sara, 348
donations. *See also* fundraising
    by Bronfman family, 284
    and Six-Day War, 283–84
    to support Israel, 9
    to support national organizations, 9
Dos Yiddish Vort, 297
Douglas, Clifford H., 172, 173
Douglas, James, 60, 61
Douglas, Tommy, 164, 274
Douville, Raymond, 27
Drache, Arthur, 251
Draper, Paula, 209
Drew, George, 215

Dreyfus, Alfred, 130
Dreyfuss, Richard, 254
Drumont, Édouard, 106
Dubinsky, David, 189
Dubois, Louise, 39
Duceppe, Gilles, 310, 333
Dunkelman, Ben, 203–4, 237, 238
Dunkelman, David, 203
Dunkelman, Joe, 203
Dunkelman, Rose, 132, 203
Duplessis, Maurice, 187, 269
Dylex, 188
Dysart, Justice A.K., 166

E
Eagle Life Assurance Company of London, 34
Earth and High Heaven (Graham), 4, 216–17
Eastern European Jews
    aid to, 139
    effect of, 136–37
    enclaves of, 83
    in the Maritimes, 58
    as peddlers, 84
    traditions of, 52, 78, 109
Eaton, John Craig, 120
Eaton, Lady Flora McCrea, 232
Eaton, Timothy, 77
Eaton's, 184, 187, 309
Edmonton. *See also* Alberta
    Jewish population in, 100, 262
education
    about Holocaust, 228
    antisemitism in universities, 142, 160–61, 162
    of Bronfman sons, 147
    Canadianizing process, 148

    closing of schools, 347–49
    decline in school enrolment, 349
    dissension over, 113
    enrolment in Toronto, 347
    first Jewish private day/boarding school, 43
    Hebrew classes, 111
    higher, of Jews, 257
    Jewish community schools, 345–50
    of Jewish women, 257
    of Jews in Canada, 354
    of Jews in early settlements, 21–22, 26
    left-wing secularist, 112–13
    levels of Jews, 350
    in Montreal, 43, 99–100, 142–43
    in Ottawa, 262
    proposed increased funding in Quebec, 313
    in Quebec, 99, 148–49, 167
    schools in early communities, 9
    school survival in Vancouver, 349
    in small towns, 153
    Supreme Court and school funding, 346
    in Toronto, 149–50
    tuition at Jewish schools, 346, 347, 348
    university, 107
    in Winnipeg, 149
    of women, 323
Eichmann, Adolf, 228
Eisen, Max, 316–17
Eisen, Wendy, 296
Eizenman, Ronit, 234
Elitzer, Moishe, 55
Eliyahu, Rabbi, 154

Elizabeth II, Queen of England, 271
Elkin, Evin, 287
Elkin, Jacob, 119
Ellis, Sir John Whitaker, 69
Elmsley, John, 28
Elzas, Barnett, 51
Endelman, Todd, 18
English, German, and Polish Congregation, 38
Eshkol, Levi, 280, 285
Etz Chayim congregation, 358
Exodus (Uris), 293
Expo 67, 270, 283
Ezrin, Hershell, 340, 342, 343

F

Factor, Samuel, 157–58, 159, 176, 177
Falconer, Robert, 176
Farber, Bernie, 7–8, 342–43
Federation CJA, 324
Federation of Jewish Philanthropies, 104, 153
Federation of Zionist Societies of Canada, 131
Federman, Max, 186
Feigenbaum, "Fat" Charlie, 191–92, 193
Feigenbaum, Jackie, 191
Feinberg, Annie, 65–66
Feinberg, Rabbi Abraham, 219, 242–43, 245, 246
Fiddler on the Roof, 68, 361
Finkel, Alvin, 229
Finkelman, Jacob, 160–61
Finkelstein, Maxyne, 327, 339, 341
Finkelstein, Moses, 108
Finlayson, George D., 244

Finta, Imre, 317
First World War
    Canadian Jews enlisted in, 124–27
    and charitable works, 103–4
    effect on garment industry, 121
    ending of, 128
    immigration after, 140
    neutrality towards, 127–28
Fish, Justice Morris, 149
Fleming, Donald, 249
Fogel, Shimon, 341, 342, 343, 344–45
Folklorama, 290
Foran, Charles, 254
Ford, Henry, 173
Forkin, Joe, 189
Forrest, Rev. Dr. Alfred C., 287, 288
Foss, Roy, 201
Frager, Ruth, 183
Frank, Joe, 238
Frank, Rabbi Solomon, 165
Frankfurter, Edgar, 65
Frankfurter, George, 65
Frankfurter (Saunders), Fanny, 65
Franklin, Lumley, 59, 60, 61
Franklin, Selim, 59, 60, 61
Franks, John, 23–24
Freedman, Isidore, 127
Freedman, Samuel, 161, 246, 247, 274
Freeman, Myra, 323
Freeman Family Holocaust Education Centre, 315
Freidman, Dr. J., 163–64
Freiman, Archie, 103, 132, 133, 135, 231
Freiman, Lawrence, 245

Freiman, Lillian, 10, 103–4, 132, 133, 139, 140, 323
French and Indian War (1754), 20
Friedman, Noah, 119
Frisse, Ulrich, 207
Frost, Leslie, 242, 243
Fruchter, Yacov, 362–64
Frum, Barbara, 310
Frydman-Kohl, Rabbi Baruch, 12, 357, 358, 361
fundraising. *See also* donations
    for Canadian Museum for Human Rights, 336–37
    for community survival, 350
    by de Sola, 133
    by Hadassah, 133
    for Holocaust memorials, 314, 315
    for Israeli war equipment, 240–41
    for orphaned children, 139–40
    for schools, 264
    and Six-Day War, 284
    through United Jewish Welfare Fund, 231
    and Yom Kippur War, 288
fur trade, 24–25

G

Gabay, Joseph, 342
Galt, Alexander T., 70, 90
Garber, Michael, 231
Garfield, Susan, 222
garment industry
    ease of setting up factory, 117–18
    and First World War, 121
    language in, 112
    occupations in, 86–89, 98

postwar need for workers,
225–26
strikes in, 115, 117, 118, 119,
120–23, 186–90
unions in, 118–19, 120–23
in Winnipeg, 189–90
working conditions and
wages, 87–89, 101, 112,
117, 118, 120, 189
Gasner, Meyer, 298
Gatward, Ken, 198
Gelfman, Gesia, 67
Gelman, Gertrude, 93
Gelman, Sophie, 93
Geoffrion, Aimé, 232
George III, King of England,
31
Germany
antisemitism in, 173
as First World War enemy,
128
Jewish refugees from, 176
Kristallnacht, 178, 201
Nazism in, 173
Nuremberg Laws, 174
Olympics in, 174–75
Gershman, Joshua "Joe," 185–
86, 210
Gershon Levy and Company,
24
G. Frankfurter & Sons, 65
ghettos
in Canada, 104
in Russia, 68
urban, 256
Gibson, Gordon, 273
Giller Prize, 149
Girdler, Charles, 149
Givens, Philip, 149, 251, 284
Glasgow, Al, 198
Glass, John J., 168, 169
Glen, J. Allison, 225

Glendale Golf and Country
Club, 244
Globe and Mail, 92, 151, 168,
193, 215, 219, 246, 273,
275, 279, 290
Glube, Constance, 274
Godfrey, Judith, 19, 61
Godfrey, Sheldon, 19, 24, 61
Goel Tzedec congregation, 52,
110
Goel Tzedec synagogue, 328
Gold, Alan B., 274
Gold, Isaac, 88
Goldberg, Jon, 361
Goldbloom, Alton, 86
Goldbloom, Dr. Victor, 275
Goldbloom, Samuel, 86
Golden, David, 245
Golden, Ron, 328–29
Golden (Richmond), Dr.
Anne, 327, 328–30, 331,
342
Goldenberg, Gael, 188
Goldfarb, Martin, 149
Goldstein, Maxwell, 104
Goldstein, Yoni, 355–56
Goldstick, Barry, 137
Goldstine, Elaine, 6, 337
Gooderham and Worts, 147
Goodman, Eddie, 204
Goodman, Rose, 200–201
Goodman, Sol, 200
Gordin, Jacob, 114
Gordon, Donald, 248
Gordon, Rabbi Jacob, 110, 111,
154, 155
Gordon, Tobi "Pidgy," 234
Gotleib, Allan, 272
Graham, Gwethalyn, 4, 216,
217
Grant, Charles, 22
Grant, Ulysses, 44

Grassroots for Affordable
Jewish Education, 348
Graubart, Rabbi Yehuda
Leib, 154, 155
Gray, Herb, 272–73
Gray, Morris, 166
Gray Academy, 349, 363
Great Britain
expelling of Jews (1290), 18
Jewish pride in being
British subjects, 47
policy shift toward Jews,
134
as source of potential
Jewish emigrants, 19–20
Great Depression
antisemitism during, 141
and Canadians' view on
race, 159
charitable aid, 181
and creation of Social
Credit Party, 172
diets during, 181
effect on families, 180, 197
and garment industry,
182–84
unemployment and immi-
gration, 179
wages during, 184
working conditions, 182
Greater Toronto Area Task
Force, 330
Great-West Lifeco, 335
Green, Louis, 57–58
Green, Nathan, 57
Green, Rabbi Alan, 359
Green, Sidney, 275
Green, Solomon Hart, 58
Greisman, Henry, 86–87
Greisman, Joseph, 86
Grondin, Abbé Philibert,
144

Groulx, Abbé Lionel, 144, 167, 310
Gurofsky, Benjamin, 88

H
Habonim, 232, 234, 235, 282
Habonim Camp B'nai Brith, 235
Hackman, Samuel, 124–25
Hadassah, 10, 103, 104, 132, 133
Hadassah-WIZO, 257, 323
Haganah, 237–38
Haig, Douglas, 126
Haldimand, Frederick, 23
Halifax, 354–55
Hamas, 313
Hamilton, 51, 262
Harbord Collegiate, 148, 149–50
Harper, Stephen, 285, 320, 336
Harris, Mike, 330
Harris, Milton, 357
Hart, Aaron, 17–18, 21, 23, 24, 25–26, 27, 30, 34, 38, 40, 43, 253
Hart, Aaron Ezekiel, 29, 35
Hart, Aaron Philip, 36
Hart, Alan J., 118
Hart, Alexander, 28, 41
Hart, Alice, 57
Hart, Arthur Wellington, 34–35
Hart, Benjamin, 29, 34, 35, 36, 38, 40–41
Hart, Elizabeth, 57–58
Hart, Ezekiel, 26, 27, 29–32, 30–34, 119
Hart, Harriot, 34
Hart, Jane, 57
Hart, Moses, 26, 27–29

Hart, Samuel, 31
Hart, Samuel Becancour, 35–36
Hart, Solomon, 57
Hashomer Hatzair, 232
Hasidim, 42, 46, 154, 258, 307–8, 309
Hassan, Natasha, 332
Hay, John, 21
Hayden, Salter, 232
Hayes, Moses Judah, 36
Hayes, Saul, 203, 208, 209, 210, 225, 232, 270, 284, 286, 294, 338
Hays, Moses, 45
Heaps, Abraham, 128–29, 176
Hebrew Immigrant Aid Society, 69
Hebrew Maternity Hospital, 103
Hebrew Philanthropic Society, 45
Hebrew Religious School, 111
Hecht, Thomas, 326
Heckewelder, John, 25
Heeney, Arnold D.P., 245
Hepburn, Mitch, 158–59, 168
Heppner, Dorothy, 324–25
Heppner, Lyone, 324
Herbst, Sam, 189
Hering, Karen Uretsky, 289
Heritage Minute, 35
Heron, Craig, 141
Hershman, Hersh (Harry), 116
Hershon, Goldie, 326
Herzl, Theodor, 46, 130
Herzl Dispensary, 103
Herzl Health Centre, 324
Hezbollah, 322, 332–33
Hickman, Justice Alex, 16
Hicks, Arthur, 213

Hillel, 362
Hiram Walker, 147
Hirsch, Hershl, 116
Hirsch, Rabbi Samson Raphael, 42
Historica Canada, 35
Hitler, Adolf, 159, 167, 168, 206, 220
Hocken, Horatio, 131
Hocquart, Gilles, 17
Hoffer, Clara, 91
Hoffer, Israel, 91
Hoffer, Moshe, 91
Holocaust
   and Canada's postwar refugee policy, 209–10
   CJC support for survivors, 225–26
   comprehension of, 212
   deniers, 277, 278–79, 313–14
   education about, 314–17
   fear of another, 281
   process of, 220
   reports of, 206, 207, 208
   survival rate, 211
   survivors' willingness to talk about, 227, 228
   as unifying force, 286
Holocaust Education Centre, 315
Holocaust Memorial Day Act, 314
Holocaust Remembrance Day, 316
Holy Blossom synagogue, 49–50, 51–52, 71, 76, 121, 219, 230, 245, 331, 353, 359–60
HonestReporting Canada, 322
Horowitz, Aron, 134

Hošek, Chaviva, 330
Houde, Camille, 77
Howe, C.D., 225, 240
Hudson's Bay Company, 147
Hughes, Sam, 127
Humanity in Doubt (Weiss), 316
Hunters' Lodges, 37
Hurtig, Abraham, 188
Hyman, Marcus, 169
Hyman, Ralph, 286–87
Hyman, William, 258

I
Ibbitson, John, 342
I.L. Peretz Schools, 112–13
immigrants
    aid to, 103–4, 119, 137
    Canadianizing, 105
    children as, 222–23
    Jewish, to Canada, 140
    jobs undertaken by, 84–85
    number of refugees admit-
        ted, 179
    success stories, 108
immigration
    after First World War, 140
    aliyah, 135, 233, 235, 282, 283
    antisemitism in depart-
        ment, 318
    backlash against, 104–5
    to Canada, 68, 101
    challenges for newcomers,
        83
    from Eastern Europe, 4, 52
    farming by newcomers,
        89–92
    to Great Britain, 70
    to Israel, 226
    Jewish attitude to, 37–38
    and Jewish refugees, 176–
        79, 203

negative view of, 102
and postwar need for
    workers, 225–26
postwar policy, 212, 221–22
from Russia, 4, 68
before and during Second
    World War, 203
to United States, 68, 226
Industrial Union of Needle
    Trades Workers of
    Canada, 182, 183
Industrial Union of Needle
    Trade Workers, 185, 186,
    189
intermarriages
    ceremonies offered, 360
    desirability of, 37
    fear of, 153
    in Montreal, 39
    rising rate of, 360–61
    status of children, 5
International Caravan, 290
International Fur Workers'
    Union, 183
International Ladies'
    Garment Workers'
    Union, 183–84, 185, 187,
    188, 189
International Red Cross, 139
International Refugee
    Organization, 226
Israel
    army size, 280
    assistance for, 9
    campus groups supporting,
        289
    Canadian position on, 285
    Canadians' attitude to, 340
    celebration of indepen-
        dence, 235–36
    criticism of, 5, 286–88,
        290, 319, 356

devotion to, 289
donations to support,
    283–84
establishment of as a uni-
    fying force, 229
fundraising for, 236
and Hezbollah, 332–33
need for soldiers, 237
need for war equipment,
    238–39
negotiations with Arab
    leaders, 285
and occupied territories,
    285, 286
and partitioning of
    Palestine, 229
response to creation of,
    230
retaking of Jerusalem, 285
as sensitive topic, 320
Six-Day War, 259, 281–83,
    319
size of, 280, 281
support for, 280, 281–82,
    320, 340
terrorist attacks on, 283,
    286, 290
travel to, 289
treatment of Palestinians,
    286
U.S. relations with, 280
violence in leadup to parti-
    tion, 232
War of Independence, 238
and West Bank settle-
    ments, 286, 320
Yom Kippur War, 285, 288
Israel Bonds, 288
Israel Engagement, 362
Israeli Apartheid Weeks,
    319–20, 321
Israeli dancing, 234, 271

IUNTW, 182, 185, 186

J

Jacob and Crowley, 189
Jacobs, Jane, 329
Jacobs, Marie-Geneviève, 21
Jacobs, Rabbi Solomon, 121
Jacobs, Samuel, 17–18, 19,
    20–22, 24, 78, 106, 122,
    137, 174, 176, 177, 245
Jacobs, Samuel Jr., 21–22
Jacobson, Joe, 201–2
Jacobson, Percy, 201–2
Jacobson, Sydney, 237–38
Jaques, Norman, 248
Jeune-Canada, 168
Jewish and Child Family
    Service, 323
Jewish Colonization
    Association (JCA), 71,
    89–90, 91, 92, 94
Jewish Community Centres,
    3
Jewish Community Research
    Institute, 302
Jewish Dance Ensemble, 271
Jewish Defence League
    (JDL), 295, 298
Jewish Disabilities Bill, 60
Jewish Dispensary, 103
Jewish Emigration Society
    (JEAS), 69, 71
Jewish Federation of Greater
    Toronto, 327
Jewish Federation of
    Philanthropies, 181
Jewish Federation of
    Winnipeg, 6, 337
Jewish Federations Canada,
    338, 340

Jewish Federations of
    Canada-UIA (United
    Israel Appeal), 9, 259,
    327, 338, 341, 343, 350
Jewish Folk School, 113
Jewish Folks' Shule, 113
Jewish Free Loan Toronto,
    350
Jewish General Hospital, 163,
    324
Jewish Immigrant Aid
    Society (JIAS), 137, 139
Jewish Labour Committee,
    225
Jewish Legion, 135
Jewish National Fund, 300
Jewish Orphanage, 261
Jewish People's School, 113,
    228
Jewish Post, 142, 181, 209, 273,
    300–301
Jewish Post & News, 300, 355
Jewish Public Library, 331–32
Jewish Russian Community
    Centre, 354
Jewish Standard, 296
Jewish Standard Definition, 5
Jewish Welfare Fund, 325
Jewish Western Bulletin, 273,
    276
The Jews in Manitoba (Chiel),
    151
Johnson, Lyndon B., 280
Johnson, William, 310
Joint Public Relations
    Committee, 202–3, 242,
    243
Jonas, George, 287
Joseph, Bernard, 135
Joseph, Esther, 43

Joseph, Henry, 34
Joseph, Henry (Harry), 43
Joseph, Judah, 34
Joseph, Norma, 319
Joseph, Rabbi Howard, 319
Joseph Wolinsky Collegiate,
    349, 363
The Journal, 310
Judah, Dorothea, 25–27
Judah, Samuel, 25
Judah, Sarah, 28
Judah, Uriah, 25, 28

K

Kahane, Rabbi Meir, 295, 298
Kahanovitch, Rabbi Israel
    Isaac, 110, 111
Kanee, Sol, 240, 251, 270, 284,
    338
Kaplan, Rabbi Jacob, 103
Kaplan, Robert, 271
Kaplan, Taube, 103
Kay, Barbara, 6, 7, 257, 321,
    327, 328, 330–35
Kay, Jimmy, 187
Kay, Jonathan, 320, 331, 332
Kay, Ronny, 331
Kayfetz, Ben, 186
Keegstra, Jim, 313–14
Kehilla Residential
    Programme, 350
Kehillat Beth Israel, 358
Keller, Harris, 119
Kelman, Rabbi Jay, 348
Keneder Adler, 114–16, 122,
    123, 127, 136, 138, 181, 192,
    193, 207, 210, 297
Kennedy, W.P.M., 161, 162
Kenney, Jason, 263
Kenstavicius, Antanas, 317

Kernerman, Teme, 234
Khadir, Amir, 333
Khrushchev, Nikita, 211, 292
"Kiever" synagogue, 53
King, Joe, 199
King, William Lyon
    Mackenzie, 74, 84, 88,
    157, 159, 176, 177–79,
    203, 208, 209, 212, 221,
    230–31, 232, 236, 247
King David High School, 349
King Suspender & Neckwear
    Company, 87
Kirshner, Max, 152
Kislowicz, Linda, 327
Kitz, Leonard, 246, 251
Kives, Edith, 92
Kives, Kiva, 92
Kives, Laya, 92
Kives, Moses, 92
Kives, Philip, 92
Kleiman, Soody, 235
Klein, A.M., 1, 4, 12, 96–98,
    99, 100, 112, 148, 149,
    209, 229, 235–36, 297
Klein, Kalman, 96, 98
Klein, Milton, 277, 278
Klein, Yetta, 96
Kliman, Meyer, 152
Kliman, Sam, 152
Knatchbull-Hugessen,
    Adrian, 232
Koffler, Murray, 300
Kolber, Leo, 340
Korobkin, Rabbi Daniel, 353
Koschitzky, Julia, 340
Koschitzky, Mira, 324
kosher food
    available in early
        Winnipeg, 66

changing attitudes to, 155–
    56, 265
conflict about, 153–54
decline in, 358
in early settlements, 20, 26
for refugees, 78
regulations about, 155
in small towns, 153
Kosygin, Alexei, 294, 295
Kozlov, Bessie, 148
Kraisman, Sam, 188
Krell, Dr. Robert, 315
Kristallnacht, 178, 201
Kumer, Nancy, 328

L
Labour-Progressive Party, 210
Labour Zionism, 232, 233–34
Labrador, 16
Lacoste, Jimmy, 146
Ladies' Hebrew Benevolent
    Society, 45
La Fargue, Jacques, 16–17
L'affaire Hart, 29–32
La France juive, 106
La Libre Parole, 106
land acquisition
    by A. Hart, 25
    antisemitism in, 218–20
    attempts by M. Hart,
        27–28
    for farm settlements,
        89–90
    by L. David in Montreal,
        40
    by Oppenheimers, 63
    for schools, 111
    for synagogues, 50
    in Toronto, 48, 86–87
    in Victoria, 59

of worthless property, 72
Landau, Herman, 89
Landau-Chark, Dr. Susan, 43
Landsberg, Michele, 274
languages
    English, 42, 54, 72, 74, 76
    French, 269, 270, 305, 307,
        309, 332
    Hebrew, 111, 112, 135
    newspapers in English,
        297, 299, 300
    Yiddish, 98, 110, 112
Lansky, Meyer, 146, 190
La Penha, Daniel de, 16
La Penha, Isaac de, 16
La Penha, Joseph de, 15–16
Lapointe, Ernest, 177, 178
Lapointe, Marie-Josette
    Audet dit, 19, 21
La Presse, 308, 310, 334
Lapson, Dvora, 271
Laskin, Bora, 161, 207, 244,
    272–73
Laskin, Peggy, 161
Lastman, Mel, 330
Latner, Albert, 300
Laurence, Margaret, 255
Laurendau, André, 167–68
Laurier, Wilfrid, 83
Lavergne, Abbé Édouard-
    Valmore, 144
Lawrence, William, 208
Lawyers Club of Toronto,
    244–45
Layton, Irving, 98, 148–49,
    181, 224
Lazareck, Mel, 342
Lazarovitz, Louis, 106, 107
Lazarus, Abraham, 76
Lazarus, Frances, 29

League for the Defense of
    Jewish Rights, 170
League of Nations, 139
Le Canadien, 30, 31
Le Devoir, 310
Leduc, René, 106, 107
Leeser, Isaac, 43, 44, 45
Leiderman, J.M., 183
Leipsic, Dr. Jonathon, 349
Leipsic, Richard, 336
Lenin, Vladimir, 292
Lesage, Jean, 259, 269
Levendel, Lewis, 298
Lévesque, René, 36, 302, 306
Levi, Rabbi Gershon, 205
Levine, Samuel "Red," 190
Levinsky, John, 59
Levinsky, Louis, 59
Levinsky, Mark, 59
Levinson, Solomon, 87, 118
Levitt, Cyril, 172
Levy, Alexander, 44
Levy, Eleazar, 21
Levy, Gershon, 24–25
Levy, Isaac, 20
Levy, Moe, 336
Lewin, Kurt, 5–6
Lewis, Charlie, 98
Lewis, David, 98, 148, 274–75
Lewis, Doris, 98
Lewis, Samuel, 103
Lewis, Stephen, 274–75
Lewis, Trudy, 199
Lewis (Losz), Moishe, 98, 99
Lewis (Losz), Rose, 98
Lhotka, Jill, 271
Lhotka, Nenad, 271
Liberal Party: ties to Jewish
    community, 138
Liberty, 208
libraries, 116
Lieff, Abraham "Abe," 160–61

Linteau, Paul-André, 42
Lipinksky, Jack, 225
Lipshitz, Manya, 211
Lipshitz, Sam, 210, 211
Lipton, Saundra, 197, 201
Liptzin, Keni, 114
Lloyd George, David, 134
Loewe, Dr. Louis, 41–42
Loewenson, Walter, 239
Logan, Alexander, 71
London, Jack, 244
Lord's Day Act (1906), 105–6
Louis Brier Home and
    Hospital, 263
Louis XIV, King of France, 16
Love, Neil, 49
The Lovebound (Wiseman),
    255
Lower Canada. See Quebec
Lowy, Jocy, 223
Lowy, Leo, 220–21, 222–23
Lowy, Miriam, 220–21, 222,
    223
Lowy, Richard, 223
Lubelsky, Sigmund, 121
Lucow, Maurice, 300
Luftspring, Sammy, 102,
    174–75
Lyon, Benjamin, 24, 39

M
MacDonald, Neil, 322
Macdonald, Sir John A., 47,
    62, 70, 71, 87, 91
Machal, 237, 238
Machray, Robert, 71
Machzikei Hadath, 54
Mackay, Ira, 142, 165
MacKay, Justice J. Keiller, 218,
    219
Mackenzie, Alexander, 20, 24
Maclean Hunter, 217

Maclean's, 208, 216, 217, 244,
    254, 352
MacLennan, Hugh, 269
Maidstone, Peter, 282, 283
Manitoba. See also Winnipeg
    first Jew elected to legisla-
       ture, 58
    Jewish politicians, 275
Manitoba Defamation Act,
    169
March of the Living, 315–16
Margolis, Albert "Sherry," 200
Margolis, Rebecca, 96, 115, 206
Maritimes/Atlantic Canada
    difficulty of establishing
       structure in, 9
    Eastern European Jews in,
       58
    first Jewish wedding in,
       57–58
    Jewish population in, 34,
       58, 262
Marr, Wilhelm, 29
Marsh, Lou, 175
Marshall, Jack, 271
Marshall, Tom, 271
Martin, Paul, 227, 342
Marx, Justice Herbert, 326
Mashaal, Danielle
    Benchimol, 41
Mass, Rabbi Anibal, 359
Maté, Gabor, 282
Maté, John (Janos), 282–83
Mathers, Dr. Alvin T., 164,
    165, 166
Matoff, Paul, 146
McAree, John, 117, 118
McBride, Richard, 64
McClelland, Jack, 255
McGibbon, Justice J.A., 243
McGill Faculty of Medicine,
    162

McGill University, 44, 142

McGuinty, Dalton, 346

McLeod, Rev. Dr. Bruce, 288

McLuhan, Marshall, 224

McNab, Mary, 183–84

medicine
  antisemitism in, 162–66
  strike at hospital, 162–63

Medres, Israel, 114

Meighen, Arthur, 139

Meighen, Isabel, 139

Meiklejohn, H.G., 200

Melamet, Max, 297

Meldola, Dr. Raphael, 41

Meltz, George, 199–200

Meltz, Nathan, 199

Meltz, Rachel, 199

men
  in Canadian Jewish
    Congress, 137
  as decision makers, 10
  in Orthodox synagogues, 46
  segregation from women,
    359
  on synagogues' executives,
    41

Mengele, Dr. Josef, 220–21

Menkis, Richard, 34

Merchant of Venice
  (Shakespeare), 8

Mercury, 30

Meretsky, Irving "Toots," 175

Metrolinx, 330

Mickelson, Mollie, 201

Mickleburgh, Rod, 276

Milchige synagogue, 54

Miller, Hyman, 65, 69

Miller, Saul, 275

Modern Orthodox B'nai
  Abraham, 357

Mollov (Dorfman), Joyce,
  270–71

Molson, Percival T., 213

Montefiore, Sir Moses, 45

Montgomery, Lucy Maud, 85

Montreal
  antisemitism in, 160,
    162–63
  areas settled by Jews, 83
  as British city, 42
  changing population pat-
    terns in, 257–58
  compared to Toronto, 331
  cost of Jewish education
    in, 347
  employment and busi-
    nesses, 87
  exodus after PQ win,
    303–5
  gambling in, 190–94
  garment trade in, 88
  Jewish population in, 3, 34,
    45, 101, 262, 304, 305
  living conditions in, 84, 86,
    87–88
  the Main, 96–97
  makeup of in 1847, 42
  maturing of, 42
  population of, 42, 303
  roots of Jews in, 258–59
  strikes in, 185–87
  synagogues in, 52
  tuition at Jewish schools,
    346

Montreal Clothing
  Manufacturers'
  Association, 118, 122

Montreal Gazette, 310

Montreal Holocaust
  Memorial Centre, 314

Moore, H. Napier, 218

Morgen Journal, 298

Moscoe, Howard, 102

Moskovitch, Rabbi Dan, 360

Moskovitch, Samuel, 258

Mosley, Oswald, 168

Moster, Ralph, 238

Mount Carmel Clinic, 103

Mount Royal Lodge, 235

Mount Sinai Hospital, 103

Mowat, Herbert, 231–32

Moyne, Lord (Walter
  Guinness), 232

Muirhead, Bruce, 249

Mulroney, Brian, 317, 318

multiculturalism, 1, 7, 255,
  270, 271, 283, 290, 353

Munro, Alice, 310

Murphy, Rex, 332

Murray, James, 21, 24

Museum of Jewish Montreal,
  97

Mussolini, Benito, 167, 168

Myers, Haym, 40

Myerson (Meir), Golda, 236

N

N3, 278

Nadeau, Jean-François, 168

Nasser, Gamal Abdel, 280,
  281

Nathan, Henry Jr., 59, 61–62,
  138

Nathan, Henry Sr., 61

Nathans, Nathan, 20

National Clothing Workers
  of Canada, 183, 187

National Council of Jewish
  Women of Canada, 78,
  325, 337

National Post, 331, 332, 334

Nemetz, Nathaniel (Nathan),
  274

neo-Nazism, 277, 278–79

Netanyahu, Benjamin, 319,
  339

Netter, Charles, 69

New Brunswick. *See also* Maritimes

New Democratic Party, 274

Newfoundland: early Jewish navigators, 15

New France, 16–17, 19. *See also* Canada

Newman, Alex, 180

Newman, Peter C., 245

newspapers, 114–15, 296–301, 355–56

The New Yorker, 309

New York Times, 208

Nirkoda Israeli Dancers, 234, 289

Nirkoda Israeli Folk Dancers, 289

N.L. Steiner Marble Works, 50

Noble, Annie, 219

None Is Too Many (Abella and Troper), 176, 318

Notre-Dame Hospital, 162–63

Nova Scotia. *See also* Maritimes; Maritimes/ Atlantic Canada

Jewish immigrants to, 19, 354–55

need for population growth, 19–20

Nurenberger, Dorothy Cohn, 298, 300

Nurenberger, Meyer, 298– 300

O

Oakdale Golf Club, 141

Oaths Act, 61

oath-taking issues, 18, 24, 31–33, 36, 60–61

Occident, 44

Oelbaum, J. Irving, 298

Office de la Langue Francais, 309

Offstein, Ruth, 201

Oh Canada! Oh Quebec! (Richler), 310

Olson, Sherry, 87

Olymics, Winter and Summer (1936), 174–75

Olympia and York, 252

Olympia Trading, 252

Ontario. *See also* Hamilton; Ottawa; Toronto

civil and political rights in, 36

education system in, 346

Ontario Alliance of Christian Schools, 346

Ontario Boys' Wear, 183

Ontario Human Rights Code, 242

Ontario Jewish Association for Equality in Education, 346

Oppenheimer, Charles, 62

Oppenheimer, David, 59, 62–64

Oppenheimer, Isaac, 62, 63

Oppenheimer Brothers, 63

Or Chadash Israeli Folkdance Troupe, 289

Ortenberg, Benjamin, 106, 107

Orthodox Jews

amalgamating with Reform Jews, 110

conflict with Reform Jews, 60

decreases in, 265

dedication to tradition, 109–10

De Sola's views on prac- tice, 43

feud with Reform Jews, 51–52

growth of synagogues, 357

and kosher rules, 154

opinion of theatre, 114

refugees as, 78

and same-sex marriage, 359

stand on intermarriage, 5

support for, 46

support for Conservative branch, 42

synagogues of, 52

transition to Reform, 50

Ostry, Bernard, 272

Ostry, Sylvia, 272

Ottawa

closing of Jewish schools, 348–49

education in, 262

Jewish community in, 54

Jewish population in, 101, 262

merging of synagogues, 358

synagogues in, 263

Ottawa Hillel Academy, 262

Ottawa Jewish Community School, 348

Oungre, Dr. Louis, 92

Outlook: Canada's Progressive Jewish Magazine, 211

Oxen un Motoren (Usiskin), 94

P

Palestine

Arab response to partition, 229

as home for Jews, 134, 135, 136
partitioning of, 229
supporters of, 319
support for Jewish state in, 230
violence in leadup to partition, 232
Palestine Liberation Organization (PLO), 283, 290
Panofsky, Ruth, 256
Papineau, Louis-Joseph, 35–36, 37
Parizeau, Jacques, 305–6
Paterson, Michael, 335
Pearson, Lester, 162, 240, 269, 277, 284, 320
Pellerin, Brigitte, 334
Pelletier, Georges, 167
Pelletier, Gérard, 307
People's Olympiad, 175
Peres, Shimon, 239–41
Peretz, Isaac Leib, 112
Peretz Centre, 263
Peretz Shule, 264, 265
Pesotta, Rose, 186
Peterson, Phyllis Lee, 352
Philip, Prince, 271
Phillips, Melanie, 333
Phillips, Nathan, 158, 246, 249–51
Pinksy, Bernard, 342
Pinsler, Jacob, 99
Pioneer Women, 10, 133
Plamondon, Jacques-Édouard, 106, 107
Plantation Act, 1740, 18, 19, 20, 33
Plante, Pacifique "Pax," 194
Plaut, Rabbi Gunther, 10, 279, 281, 295

Poland
concentration camps in, 206, 208
Jews' survival rate in Holocaust, 211
Poles allowed to return to homeland, 223
political activity
acceptance of Jews in, 274–76
of Bercovitch, 119, 168
of Croll, 147, 158–59
of D. Lewis, 274–75
of D. Oppenheimer, 63
of E. Hart, 29–33
of Factor, 157, 158, 177
of Finkelstein, 108
first Jewish mayor of Canadian city, 61
first Jewish MP, 61
forbidden to Jews in Britain, 32
of Givens, 251
of Goldbloom, 275
of Gray, 166
of Heaps, 129
of Jews in Toronto, 157
of Kitz, 251
of L. Franklin, 61
Liberal Party and Jewish community, 138
Marxist and socialist, 98–99
of M. Hart, 27, 28
of Nathan Jr., 61–62
of N. Phillips, 249–51
of Phillips, 158
of Rubenstein, 77
of S. Franklin, 60–61
of Simon, 108
of S. Jacobs, 78, 106–7, 137–38, 177
of S. Lewis, 274–75

of S. Moskovitch, 258
in Toronto, 50
Trudeau's Jewish appointments, 272–74
weakened interest in socialism, 257
political rights, 18–19, 35–36
Pollak, Mindy, 308
Pontiac, 24
Porter, John, 251, 257
Portigal, Isaac, 55
Posluns, Abraham, 187
Posluns, Louis, 187
Posluns, Sam, 187, 188
Posluns, Wilfred, 187
Poupko, Rabbi Reuben, 306
poverty, 350–51
Pratte, André, 334
Prehogan, Kenneth, 304
Prehogan, Sharon, 304
Price, Benjamin, 21
Price, Morris, 63
Prichard, Robert, 324
Prince Edward Island. See Maritimes
Progressive Students for Israel, 289
Prohibition, 145–46
Prutschi, Manuel, 313

Q
Quebec. See also New France
antisemitism in, 166–68, 312–13
early settlers in, 20–21
education in, 167
effect of nationalism on Jews, 306
election of Parti Québécois, 302
fight for civil and political rights, 35–36

first Jew born in, 40
first Jewish cabinet minis-
    ter, 275
growing nationalism in,
    259, 269
Jewish immigrants to, 19
Jewish population in, 305
Jewish support for British
    in, 37, 39
Jews as "third solitude," 269
language laws, 307, 309, 332
march against Israel-
    Hezbollah fighting,
    332–34
Quiet Revolution, 259,
    269, 305
referendums in, 302, 305–6
Richler *New Yorker* article,
    309–11
school system, 43
Quebec Press Council, 334

R
rabbinical councils, 153–54
rabbis, in early settlements, 8
Raber, Esther, 201
Rabinovich, Samuel, 162, 163
Rabinovich, Solomon, 112
Rabinovitch, Jack, 149
Rabkin, Jacob, 152
Rabkin, Max, 152
Racial Discrimination Act, 215
Rady, Rose, 325
Rae, Bob, 330
Rasminsky, Dr. Michael, 248
Rasminsky, Louis, 149, 245,
    246, 247–48, 249, 251
Rasminsky (Rotenberg),
    Lyla, 248
Rawcliffe, Colin, 146

Rawidowicz, Simon, 361
Reading Club, 244
Reform Jews
    amalgamating with
        Orthodox Jews, 110
    Canada's first synagogue
        for, 51
    conflict with Orthodox
        Jews, 60
    controversy about, 51
    feud with Orthodox Jews,
        51–52
    growing movement for, 42
    in Holy Blossom, 76
    and intermarriage, 360
    opposition to, 46
    and same-sex marriages,
        359
    splits with Orthodox Jews,
        109–10
    stand on intermarriages, 5
    support for, 51
    transition from Orthodox,
        50
refugees
    assistance to, 69, 71–72, 78,
        174
    attitude to, 74
    to Canada, 69, 70
    Canada's postwar policy,
        210
    displaced persons, 212
    Jews as, 69, 70
    King's refusal to accept, 212
    lobbying for admittance,
        208–9
    work taken on by, 72
Regina: antisemitism in, 164
Regina General Hospital,
    163–64

Reichmann, Albert, 252
Reichmann, Edward, 252
Reichmann, Paul, 252
Reichmann, Ralph, 252
Reid, Dr. John, 22
Reinberg, Rabbi Abraham,
    230
Reisman, Heather, 330, 340,
    342
Reiter, Ester, 210, 211
Reitman, Cyril, 325
Reitman, Stephen, 340
Reitman (Salomon),
    Dorothy, 325–26
Riback, Ted, 235
Richler, Avrum, 180
Richler, Lily, 180
Richler, Mordecai, 1, 98, 149,
    180, 194, 230, 234, 254,
    256, 306–7, 309–11
Richler, Moses, 180
Richmond, Florence, 327
Richmond, Ted, 219, 327
Rideau Club, 245
The Riot at Christie Pits
    (Levitt and Shaffir), 172
Ripstein, David, 65–66, 79
Ripstein, Isaac, 65
Ripstein, Simon, 65
Riteman, Philip, 316
Robarts, John, 242
Robbins Hebrew Academy,
    347
Robertson, Norman, 178
Robillard, Louis, 207
Robinowitz, Max, 180
Roblin, Duff, 275
Rockwell, George Lincoln, 277
Roger, Otto, 175
Rome, David, 116

Ronen, Moshe, 326
Roosevelt, Franklin, 178
Rose, Fred, 210
Rosen, Harry, 149
Rosen, Jacob, 88
Rosen, Sarah, 152
Rosenberg, Louis, 89–90, 94, 95, 124, 140
Rosenberg, Nasha (Norma Kirsh), 223
Rosenberg, Rabbi Stuart, 285, 339, 362
Rosenberg, Rabbi Yudel, 154
Rosenfeld, Fanny "Bobbie," 150–51
Rosenthal, Hiram, 65
Rosh Pina synagogue, 55, 261, 271, 357, 358
Ross, Malcolm, 314
Rossin, Marcus, 48–49
Rossin, Samuel, 48–49
Rossin House Hotel, 48–49
Rotenberg, Harry, 248
Rothschild, Walter, 134
Rothstein, Arnold, 146
Royal Bank of Canada, 303
Royal Canadian Air Force, 197, 198, 199, 200, 201, 204–5
Royal Canadian Army Medical Corps, 205–6
Royal Canadian Artillery, 199, 200
Royal Canadian Navy, 204
Royal Commission on Bilingualism and Biculturalism, 269–70
Royal Commission on Price Spreads, 182, 187
Royal Winnipeg Ballet, 240, 270

Rubenstein, Eli, 316
Rubenstein, Louis, 77, 150
Rubin, Linda, 289
Rubinoff, Sidney, 238
Russian Jews, 53. See also refugees
  aid to, 139
  attitude to, 74
  concerns about, 135–36
  emigration to Canada, 70–71
  farming by, 90
  interest in socialism, 93
  in Winnipeg, 54
Ryan, Claude, 308
Ryerson University, 330

S
The Sacrifice (Wiseman), 255
Sadat, Anwar, 285
Safer, Morley, 149
Saint John
  Jewish community in, 57
  Jewish population in, 58, 100
Salsberg, Joseph B., 211, 214–15
Samuel, Lewis, 49, 50
Samuel, Mark, 49
Samuel, Sigmund, 49
Samuel J. Zacks Gallery, 231
Samuels, Annie, 51
Sandwell, B.K., 176
Sarah and Chaim Neuberger Holocaust Education Centre, 315
Sarah Sommer Chai Folk Ensemble, 271
Saskatoon: Jewish population in, 100, 101

Saunders, Leslie, 250
Schara Tzedeck synagogue, 263
Scheuer, Edmund, 51
Schild, Erwin, 209
Schindler's List, 316
Schneer, Jonathan, 134
Schreyer, Ed, 275
Schroeder, Justice Walter, 219
Schultz, Samuel, 108
Schwartz, Gerald, 340, 342
Schwartz, Reuben, 97
Schwisberg, Samuel, 231, 238
Scott, Frank R, 232
Scott, Frederick G., 107
Seckelman, Kate, 49
Second World War. See also Auschwitz-Birkenau; concentration camps; Holocaust
  awards and medals, 198, 199, 205
  Canadian Jewish deaths in, 199–201, 202
  enlisting of Jews in, 197, 201, 202, 204
  treatment of Jews during, 206–7
Segal, J.I., 116
Seidelman, Edward Joseph, 125–27
Seidelman, Rachel, 125, 126
Seidelman, William, 125
Seidelman (Pearlman), Esther, 125
Seigler, Ida, 115
Selick, Anna, 132
Seligman, Ellen, 330
Selim Franklin & Company, Auctioneers and Land Agents, 60

Senderowitz, Clara, 323
Senderowitz, Morris, 323
Sephardic Jews
    as early immigrants to
        Canada, 16–18
    in Holland, 18
    migrate to England
        (1650s), 18
    in Montreal, 259
    in Shearith Israel congre-
        gation, 38
Seven Years' War, 19, 20, 23
Sewell, Jonathan, 32
Shaarei Tzedec synagogue, 53
Shaarei Zedek synagogue, 58,
    110
Shaarey Zedek Cemetery, 189
Shaarey Zedek synagogue,
    54, 55, 165, 261, 265, 357,
    358, 359, 360
Shaar Hashomayim syna-
    gogue, 38, 107, 123, 205,
    303
Shaar Shalom synagogue, 58,
    358
Shaffir, William, 172
Shallit, Rabbi Max, 93
Shalom Dancers, 289
Shane, Bernard, 185, 186–87,
    225
Shankman, Stanley, 297
Shapiro, Mary, 66
Sharansky, Anatoly (Natan),
    295–96
Sharon, Ariel, 319
Sharp, Mitchell, 240, 284
Shatner, William, 149
Shaw, John, 77
Shearith Israel synagogue, 26,
    38, 39, 40–41, 43, 46, 52
Sheps, Ben, 200
Sheps, Roberta, 200

Sheps, Sam, 200
Shepshelevich, Gregory,
    354–55
Shepshelevich, Olga, 354–55
Shinbane, Mark, 134
Ship, Harry, 190, 193–94, 224
Sholem Aleichem Club, 148
Shomrai Shabbos Anshei
    Estreich Minhag Sefard
    congregation, 53–54
Shomrai Shabbos-Chevrah
    Mishnayos congrega-
    tion, 53
Shopsowitz, Sam, 149
Shtall Shulach synagogue, 54
Shuchat, Rabbi Wilfred, 303
Shulemson, Syd, 197, 198–99,
    201, 203
Shumacher, Getel, 102
Shumacher, Shmuel, 102
Shurman, Peter, 343
Shuster, Frank, 149–50
Siegel, Benjamin "Bugsy," 190
Siegel, Ida, 10, 103, 104, 153,
    323
Sifton, Clifford, 83
Silberman, Fanny, 226, 227
Silberman, Jacob, 226–27
Silberman, Julius, 226
Silberman, Toni, 226
Silberman (Abella), Rosalie,
    226, 227
Silverstone, Paul, 108
Simchat Torah, 291, 293
Simon, George, 108
Simpson, Dr. J.C., 162
Singer, Nancy, 350
Singh, Jaggi, 319
Sirluck, Ernest, 204
Six-Day War, 259, 281–83,
    319
Skelton, Alex "Sandy," 239

Skelton, Oscar D., 176, 239,
    247
slavery, 25
Smith, Dave, 262
Smith, Goldwin, 74–75, 77
Smith, Sidney, 161
Smythe, Conn, 159
Sniderman, Harry, 175
Sniderman, Sam, 149
Social Credit Party, 172, 173,
    207, 248
Société Saint-Jean-Baptiste
    (SSJB), 334
Sokolov, Hy, 209
Sokolow, Dr. Nahum, 131
Solomon, Elias, 22
Solomon, Rabbi Wilfred, 281
Solomons, Ezekiel, 24, 39–40
Solomons, Levy, 24, 39, 41, 43
Sommer, Alex, 271
Sommer, Sarah, 270
Soviet Union
    demonstrations against,
        293
    denial of exit visas, 293
    granting of exit visas, 295
    Jewish demonstrations in,
        293
    Jews allowed to leave, 293
    Jews from in Canada, 354
    protests against, 292, 294,
        295
    "refuseniks" in, 293–94
    treatment of Jews in, 291,
        292
Spanish and Portuguese syn-
    agogue, 16, 39, 41, 46,
    49, 118, 123, 201, 258. See
    also Shearith Israel syn-
    agogue
Speisman, Stephen, 78
Spivak, Sidney, 275

Splansky, Rabbi Yael, 3, 353
sports, 77, 150
Stalin, Joseph, 211, 229, 292
St. Andrews Golf Club, 140
Staniloff, Ian, 359
Stanley, David, 277, 278
Steiner, Newman Leopold, 50–51
Steinitz-Frieberg, Gerda, 315
Steinschneider, Moritz, 29
Stern, Rabbi Harry, 184
Stikeman Elliott, 303
Stingel, Janine, 207
St. John's Technical High School, 148, 149
St. Laurent, Louis, 159, 236, 247, 249
Strangers Within Our Gates (Woodsworth), 105
Strauss, Stephen, 201
Streicher, Julius, 168
strikes
    in garment industry, 118–21, 122–23, 182–83, 184–85, 186–90
    and Great Depression, 186
    hospital, 162–63
    in Montreal, 186–87
    victory in, 187
    in Winnipeg, 188–90
Sumerlus, Claire, 347
Summerville, Donald, 251
Sun Life Assurance Company of Canada, 303
Superior Cloak Company, 187–88
synagogues. See also individual synagogues and congregations
    attendance at, 358
    Canada's first, 26
    Canada's first Reform, 51
    challenge of finding officials for, 51
    changes in, 358–59
    conflicts between Orthodox and Reform, 60
    conflicts over customs and rituals, 52–53
    controversy over construction, 307–8
    decline in and merging of, 357–58
    decreasing attendance, 265
    demand for Orthodox, 78
    disputes and dissension in, 41, 45, 53–54, 55
    early, in Montreal, 38
    early, in Toronto, 49
    establishment of, 8
    financial pressures on, 263
    lack of in early Winnipeg, 66
    as location for celebrations, 265
    modern challenges facing, 359–60
    in Ottawa, 263
    Sephardi, as model, 39
    in Toronto, 49–50, 52–53
    in Vancouver, 264
    in Winnipeg, 54–56
    woman as president of, 41
Syrian Students' Association, 321
Szold, Henrietta, 132

T
The Tailor Project, 226
Talmud Torahs, 111, 148, 151, 175, 224, 262, 264, 346, 349, 363
Tanenbaum, Larry, 340
TanenbaumCHAT, 346, 347–48
Taylor, Louis, 64
Taylor, R. Bruce, 107
T. Eaton Company, 120–21
Teitelbaum, Dr. M.D., 163–64
Temple Anshe Sholom, 51
Temple Emanu-El, 59–60, 184, 304
Temple Emanu-El-Beth Sholom, 360
Temple Israel, 360
Temple Shalom, 360
Temple Sholom, 360
35s, 296
This Hour Has Seven Days, 277
Thornton, Patricia, 87
Tissot, Jean, 168
Tobias, William "Billy," 169
Torah in Motion, 348
Toronto
    antisemitism in, 160–61, 164, 170–72
    areas settled by Jews, 83
    attitude to Jews, 76–77
    changing population patterns in, 260
    closing of synagogues, 358
    compared to Montreal, 331
    enrolment at Jewish schools, 347
    first Jew to settle in, 34
    garment trade in, 88
    increasing diversity of, 251–52
    Jewish population in, 3–4, 34, 48, 50, 101, 157, 259, 262, 304, 305
    land purchases, 48
    living conditions in, 84

population of, 303
strikes in, 185, 187–88
synagogues in, 49, 52–53
tuition at Jewish schools,
346, 347, 348
Toronto General Hospital,
164
Toronto Israel Bonds, 300
Toronto Star, 207, 208, 231, 250
Toronto Telegram, 249, 250,
298
Tory, John, 346
Towers, Graham, 248, 249
The Traitor and the Jew
(Delisle), 167, 309
Treaty of Paris (1763), 20
Tremblay, Michael, 310
Trépanier, Raoul, 187
Troper, Harold, 176, 233, 251,
270, 318
Troper, Ralph, 232
Trudeau, Pierre, 1–2, 162, 168,
240, 255, 269, 271–72,
273–74, 285, 288–89,
290, 294, 317–18
Tulchinsky, Gerald, 10, 74, 132
Two Solitudes (MacLennan),
269

U
Udow, Sara, 271
Uncle Mike's Edenbridge
(Usiskin), 94
Ungerman, Irving, 180
The Unholy Land (Forrest),
287
unions, 118, 119, 120, 121, 122–
23, 182–83, 187
United Church Observer, 287
United Hebrew Relief, 181
United Israel Appeal, 284,
300, 316, 338

United Jewish Appeal, 284,
288, 298, 300
United Jewish People's Order
(UJPO), 210–11, 229,
264, 265
United Jewish Relief
Agencies of Canada, 211
United Jewish Welfare Fund
of Toronto, 231, 298, 324
United Nations Relief and
Rehabilitation
Admininstration
(UNRRA), 211, 212, 222
United States
immigration to, 68
integration of Jews in, 10
Jews in compared to
Canada, 10–11
patriotism of Jews, 10
population of Jews in, 283
Prohibition, 145–46
United Talmud Torah
School, 313
United Way of Greater
Toronto, 329, 330
Unity and Goodwill
Association, 174
Universal Declaration of
Human Rights, 242
University of Manitoba, 161,
164, 200, 244, 247, 255,
335, 337
University of Manitoba
Faculty of Medicine,
164–65
University of Toronto, 74,
160, 161, 164, 176, 204,
207, 224, 227, 244, 248,
321, 323, 328, 329, 331
University of Toronto Faculty
of Medicine, 164
Upper Canada. *See* Ontario

Uris, Leon, 293
Usher, Peter J., 202
Usiskin, David, 93–94
Usiskin, Mike, 93–94
Usiskin, Roz, 210, 211

V
Vaad Ha'ir, 115
Vancouver
education in, 264, 349
Jewish population in, 262,
263
makeup of Jews in, 263
political leanings of Jews
in, 263–64
synagogues in, 264
tuition at Jewish schools,
346
Vancouver Board of Trade, 63
Vancouver Holocaust
Education Centre, 315
Vanier, Anatole, 167
Vanier, Georges, 253
Varna, David, 278
Vaugeois, Denis, 27, 28
Venat, Michael, 273
Venne, Pierrette, 310
The Vertical Mosaic (Porter),
251
Vickar, David, 92, 93
Vickar, Louis, 92, 93
Vickar, Sam, 92, 93
Victor, Dr. Ben, 205
Victor, Maurice, 205–6
Victoria, 58–59
Victoria, Queen, 48
Victoria Hebrew Benevolent
Society, 59
Victorson, Victor, 71
Victory Equipment and
Supply Company,
238–39

Vigneau, Stanislas, 21
Vineberg, Harris, 119
Voices of Survival, 314
volunteerism
    political, 329
    by women, 323, 324–25
    in Zionist movement, 132,
        133

W
Wallace, Robert C., 247
Waller, Harold, 10
Walrus, 331
war criminals, 317–19
War Efforts Committee, 203
War of 1812, 34
War of Independence (1948),
    199
War Orphans Project, 222
Waskey, Samuel, 124
Wasserman, Jack, 276
Wayne, Johnny (Louis
    Weingarten), 149–50
Weinberg, Henry, 290
Weinfeld, Morton, 312, 347
Weinreb, Rabbi Joseph, 154, 155
Weir, Walter, 275
Weiss, Philip, 226, 316
Weizmann, Chaim, 134
Wente, Margaret, 328
Western Jewish News, 300
Wetheim, Louis, 65
Whittaker, William, 168, 169,
    170, 172
Wicks, Charles, 73
Wiesel, Elie, 291
Wilhelmina, Queen of The
    Netherlands, 206
William III, King of England,
    15–16
William of Orange, 15
Willowvale Swastika Club, 171

Winnipeg. *See also* Manitoba
    antisemitism in, 164–66,
        173–74
    areas settled by Jews, 83–84
    attendance at synagogues,
        358
    attitude to Jews, 75–76
    businesses in early, 64, 65
    Canadian Jewish Congress
        in, 173–74
    changing population pat-
        terns in, 260–61
    combating racism in, 173–74
    decline in school enrol-
        ment, 349
    as destination for Russian
        refugees, 71
    establishment of Jewish
        community, 64
    fascist and anti-fascist
        clash, 169–70
    Jewish community in,
        54–56
    Jewish population in, 262
    kosher food in, 66
    lack of synagogues in early,
        66
    living conditions in, 84
    merging of synagogues,
        357–58
    newspapers in, 300–301
    Sabbath services in, 72
    strikes in, 128–29, 185,
        188–90
    theatrical culture in, 56
    tuition at Jewish schools,
        346
Winnipeg Congress Council,
    325
Winnipeg Free Press, 335
Winnipeg Hebrew Free
    School, 111

Winnipeg Jewish Charities
    Endorsation Bureau, 153
Winnipeg Jewish
    Community Council
    (WJCC), 325
Winters, Robert, 162
Wiseman, Adele, 181, 255–56
Wiseman, Chaika, 255
Wiseman, Pesach (Paisy), 255
Wisse, Ruth, 270, 306,
    319–20
Wolf, Bernie, 219, 220
Wolfe, Ray, 300, 324
Wolfe, Rose, 323–24
Wolofsky, Daniel, 297
Wolofsky, Harry, 297
Wolofsky, Hirsch, 115, 116, 122
Wolofsky, Max, 297
women
    in Canadian Jewish
        Congress, 137
    Canadian Jews in Second
        World War, 200–201
    careers of, 323
    discrimination against in
        medicine, 164–65
    education, 323
    as fund raisers, 264
    Jewish, in 50s and 60s, 257
    lack of power, 10
    and male-dominated fed-
        erations, 153
    Order of Canada recipi-
        ents, 325, 336
    in Orthodox synagogues, 46
    pay for, 182
    as presidents of syna-
        gogues, 41
    in professions, 327–28
    in Second World War,
        197–98
    segregation from men, 359

serving in Jewish federa-
tions, 327
treatment by socialist men,
113
volunteering by, 323, 324–25
Wood, Edmund Burke, 73, 74
Woodsworth, J.S., 105, 129
Workers' Unity League, 182
World Jewish Congress, 361
Wren, Drummond, 218
Wright, Cecil "Caesar," 161, 162
Wright, Justice William H., 155
Wrong, George, 176

Y
Yack, Norman "Baby," 175
Yad Vashem, 314
Yarosky, Michael, 302
Yom Kippur War, 285, 288
York University, 289, 296, 312,
320, 329
Yoseph, Dov, 135
Young, Scott, 208
Young Hebrew Social
Assembly Club, 56
Young Judaea club, 135, 231,
232, 233, 237, 248, 270

Young Judaea National
League of Canada, 135
Young Men's Hebrew
Association, 9, 56, 77, 148
Young Men's Hebrew
Benevolent Society,
45, 85

Z
Zacks, Ayala, 231
Zacks, Samuel, 231, 238
Zalmanson, Sylva, 293
Zebberman, Eli, 233
Zerker, Sally, 344
Zionism
and Canadian patriotism,
230
CJC's commitment to, 229
denunciation of, 286, 287
as divisive factor, 5
Hayes on, 286
importance of, 320
interest in by young
Canadian Jews, 232
opponents of, 321
provision of funds for war
equipment, 239

summer camps support-
ing, 233–35
support for, 46, 100, 130–31
Zionist movement
accusations of hypocrisy,
133–34
and Balfour Declaration, 134
conflict within, 134–35
factions in, 131
role of Hadassah, 132, 133
as uniting force in Canada,
135
Zionist Organization of
Canada (ZOC), 230–
32, 237, 297, 298
Zlotnick, Joe, 188
Znaimer, Aron, 223, 224
Znaimer, Chaja, 223, 224
Znaimer, Libby, 224
Znaimer, Moses, 223–25
Znaimer, Sam, 224
Zolf, Larry, 277
ZoomerMedia, 224
Zuker, Esther, 113–14
Zukerman, William, 173
Zündel, Ernst, 277, 313